**th edition**

PURCHASING
Principles and Applications

Stuart Heinritz

Paul V. Farrell, C.P.M.
Contributing Editor, *Purchasing World*

Larry C. Giunipero, Ph.D., C.P.M.
College of Business
Florida State University

Michael G. Kolchin, D.B.A., C.P.M.
College of Business and Economics
Lehigh University

PRENTICE HALL, Englewood Cliffs, New Jersey 07632

Library of Congress Cataloging-in Publication Data

Purchasing : principles and applications / STUART HEINRITZ . . . [et al.].—8th ed.
   p. cm.
  Rev. ed. of Purchasing / Stuart F. Heinritz, ©1981.
  Includes bibliographical references and index.
  ISBN 0-13-742081-1
  1. Purchasing. I. Heinritz, Stuart F. II. Heinritz, Stuart F. Purchasing.
HF5437.H4   1991
658.7'2—dc20   90-43515

Editorial/production supervision: *Edith Riker / Bea Marcks*
Cover design: *Mike Fender Design*
Prepress buyer: *Trudy Pisciotti*
Manufacturing buyer: *Robert Anderson*

 © 1991, 1986, 1981, 1971, 1965, 1959, 1951, 1947 by Prentice-Hall, Inc.
A Paramount Communications Company
Englewood Cliffs, New Jersey 07632

Printed in the United States of America

10 9 8

ISBN   0-13-742081-1

Prentice-Hall International (UK) Limited, *London*
Prentice-Hall of Australia Pty. Limited, *Sydney*
Prentice-Hall Canada Inc., *Toronto*
Prentice-Hall Hispanoamericana, S.A., *Mexico*
Prentice-Hall of India Private Limited, *New Delhi*
Prentice-Hall of Japan, Inc., *Tokyo*
Simon & Schuster Asia Pte. Ltd., *Singapore*
Editora Prentice-Hall do Brasil, Ltda., *Rio de Janeiro*

Contents

3   **ETHICAL STANDARDS IN PURCHASING**   40

SECTION II
PURCHASING STRATEGIES, ORGANIZATION, AND SYSTEMS

4   **PURCHASING STRATEGY AND POLICIES**   57

5   **THE BASIC PURCHASING PROCESS**   72

6   INFORMATION TECHNOLOGY IN PURCHASING   86

7   ORGANIZING AND STAFFING A PURCHASING DEPARTMENT   104

SECTION III
MANAGING BASIC PURCHASING DECISIONS

8   PURCHASING'S RESPONSIBILITY FOR QUALITY   127

20 VALUE ANALYSIS/STANDARDIZATION

21 PURCHASING SERVICES

22 PURCHASING'S ROLE IN CAPITAL EXPENDITURES

23 MEASURING PURCHASING PERFORMANCE

Preface

The purchasing function should reach new heights of respect, professionalism, and organizational recognition in the 1990s. During the mid-1970s top management finally realized that purchasing did something besides place orders. Its ability to keep operations running through the acquisition of key material during a material shortage era was vital. The computer focused attention on inventory and materials management became a buzzword.

During the 1980s the purchasing function's major challenge was keeping the firm profitable in an increasingly competitive environment where prices and sales would not automatically rise unless a product quality rose. Thus, the 1980s will be known as a decade of increased quality, supplier base reductions, international sourcing, and just-in-time inventories.

The 1990s will bring purchasing even greater responsibilities and challenges in several areas.

1. Purchasing will become more involved and have more input into strategic planning, while making sound business decisions which meet ethical and environmental concerns.
2. Competitive pressures and technological changes will continue to require selective, long term partnerships. This is vital to keep product quality high and stay current with technology. In many cases supplier selection will be based on technology transfer.
3. Product cost competitiveness will require achievement of high quality without higher material costs and delivery systems.
4. Worldwide economic changes in the communist bloc and Far East will result in increased world trade and more worldwide sourcing opportunities and requirements.
5. Electronic/computer ordering will replace the traditional purchase order as the means of transferring information between buyers and sellers.
6. Limited funding, taxpayer resistance, and cost containment will characterize the non-profit sector, all levels of government buying, and hospital/institutional buying.

This revised edition updates and relates basic principles and procedures that enable purchasing and materials managers and their staffs to meet the challenges and responsibilities of the new decade. To accomplish these goals, the eighth edition has expanded coverage on

- purchasing strategy and planning
- ethical practices in purchasing
- supplier selection, development, and evaluation
- materials management principles and practices
- retail purchasing
- public sector and institutional purchasing
- technology management

The book is designed as a text that business students at all levels can use, whether they have a particular interest in purchasing as a career, or require knowledge of the function as a part of their overall education. It will serve equally well in training programs for practicing purchasing personnel.

For practitioners it will prove quite useful as a guide to studying for the Certified Purchasing Manager's Examination. It also can continue to serve as a current general reference on purchasing and materials management operations. The text is written to be used in a variety of academic settings, including: community college level, four-year institutions, and Masters programs in either Business, Public Administration, or Retailing departments.

Textbook authors must necessarily be somewhat arbitrary in the presentation of their material. Users, on the other hand, may have varying ideas on the order in which different phases of the subject should be considered. Some instructors, for example, believe that students of purchasing should be introduced early to some of the more dramatic aspects of purchasing, such as negotiation and value analysis; others think that a grounding in fundamental principles and systems should come first. To aid those teachers and students who prefer a flexible approach to the study of purchasing concepts, we have grouped the twenty-six chapters of the book under six major section headings that deal, respectively, with: (1) the purchasing department's overall position and responsibility; (2) the strategies of organizations and systems in purchasing; (3) basic purchasing decisions; (4) managing material flows; (5) specialized purchasing techniques; and (6) retail, institutional, and government purchasing.

The last section, section six, develops purchasing practices in the nonmanufacturing sector and was completely rewritten or in the case of retail purchasing, specifically added for the eighth edition in response to the increasing attention being paid to purchasing in these important sectors of our economy. The work included in chapters 24, 25, and 26 is part of a larger study conducted by one of the authors for the Center for Advanced Purchasing Studies in Tempe, Arizona.

Case studies are grouped together in the appendix rather than placed singly at the end of individual chapters. This has been done to make it easier for instructors to make maximum use of those cases that involve principles covered in more than one chapter.

We have been helped enormously, both directly and indirectly, by a large number of purchasing professionals, educators, and journalists. We are grateful for their generous assistance. We want to thank particularly the reviewers for their suggestions for improving this edition. We wish to thank our families their support and endurance.

Paul V. Farrell
Larry C. Giunipero
Michael G. Kolchin

1

Purchasing's Role and Objectives

PURCHASING ARRIVES AS A DYNAMIC BUSINESS FUNCTION

With many manufacturing firms spending up to 65 percent of their sales revenues on purchased goods and services, the role of the purchasing function is becoming an increasingly important one. This transition can be clearly seen in the evolution of purchasing from its roots as a purely clerical function in the early part of this century, to its more traditional role of expense control through most of the century, and now to its role as manager of outside manufacturing. As the nature of the function has changed, so have the requirements for purchasing professionals.

Why the change? That is, why the greater recognition of the importance of the purchasing function and of the need for more professionally trained purchasing personnel? Perhaps the reason can be seen by tracing the development of the purchasing function over the past century.

Evolution of the Purchasing Function

Although good buying has always been an important part of any successful business—"a product well bought is half sold"[1]—purchasing is most likely to come to management's attention during periods of raw-material scarcity. A good example was the time just after the Second World War when many purchasing departments were able to demonstrate their value to their companies. Pent-up demand by war-weary Americans, caused by years of emphasis on war production, put a serious strain on the ability of many companies to produce sufficient consumer goods. Every manufacturer needed raw materials, presenting an opportunity for purchasing departments to serve their corporations by finding these scarce items. Successfully responding to this challenge enabled alert purchasing departments to gain recognition.

The oil crises of the 1970s presented another challenge for proactive purchasing departments. Petroleum products and their derivatives became very scarce during this period. Not only were fuel oil and gasoline difficult to come by, but so were various types of plastics and petrochemicals. Again, innovative and proactive purchasing was required. Successful purchasing departments responded and allowed their companies to compete successfully in a very tight market.

The high inflationary periods of the 1970s and early 1980s also brought recognition to the importance of having a good purchasing department. Sharply rising price levels caused the costs of raw materials to skyrocket, forcing many companies to search for less expensive substitutes. Once again, proactive purchasing departments were given an opportunity to demonstrate their value.

The government's actions to restrain inflation's effects further exacerbated the materials situation. The price controls imposed by the government not only failed to solve the problem of inflation but actually made it worse. Now products were expensive and also difficult to obtain, as domestic firms turned offshore

[1]H.N. Broom and J. G. Longenecker, *Small Business Management* (Cincinnati, Ohio: Southwestern Publishing Co., 1961) p. 555.

to escape price controls. One of the best examples of this situation was the case of the paper industry: Domestic mills could obtain up to four times as much for their products in foreign markets. During this period finding sources of supply for paper products for U.S. firms was a purchasing challenge that successful purchasing departments were able to meet. These departments were rewarded with increased respect.

The inflationary spiral of this period created still another problem for modern purchasing departments. Rapidly increasing raw-materials costs meant soaring inventory costs as well. Reducing inventory costs became a major purchasing challenge in the late 1970s and early 1980s, and the best purchasing departments were able to develop more effective purchasing procedures that resulted in reduced raw-materials inventories.

These examples illustrate the increasing role purchasing plays in making today's companies more profitable. While it has been recognized for some time that net purchasing savings result in a direct contribution to the bottom line, the examples show that not all purchasing savings come from reduced prices of purchased goods and services. The benefits companies derived from effective purchasing in the situations described above came about as a result of purchasing efforts in areas other than price reductions. They resulted from finding new sources of supply, finding substitute products, making recommendations for specification changes that allowed for the use of less costly and scarce materials, and making changes in ordering and delivery patterns that resulted in lower levels of inventory. All of these actions allowed purchasing to fulfill their role as the expense controller for the corporation and increased regard for the purchasing department as a contributor to profits.

Purchasing in Nonprofit Organizations and Government

These concerns relate as well to purchasing in nonprofit organizations, such as governmental agencies and various types of institutions. Pressed by shortages of funds and rising costs, these organizations are also trying to operate at maximum efficiency and at minimum cost. Good purchasing is a critical element in these efforts.

The same principles apply to purchasing in fields other than manufacturing. In a public-utility company for example, the first point would be to support the service, operating, and construction schedule rather than the manufacturing schedule; in purchasing for a municipal government, it would be to support the various services, such as police and fire protection; maintenance of streets, parks, and public buildings; garbage collection and disposal; and all other activities essential to a complete civic administration. In buying for a hospital, a university, or a governmental unit, where the profit motive and competitive factors are absent, getting maximum value for the expenditure of a fixed budget appropriation for materials is a prime goal. Taking a word from the slogan of one eminently successful municipal purchasing department, good government purchasing means getting additional "mileage" out of the tax dollar.

In government units and institutions purchases for a particular department or account are usually strictly limited by the annual budget or the unexpended portion thereof. Specialized procedures and policies employed in buying for government and for nonprofit institutions are discussed in Chapters 25 and 26.

Purchasing is done to implement other phases of a company's, a government agency's, or an institution's operations. It starts in every case with a need that is established due to operating requirements.

Finally, organizations of all sizes need effective purchasing. One of the authors of this book conducted a study of small businesses (in the Lehigh Valley, Pennsylvania) and found a very strong correlation between purchasing effectiveness and financial performance.[2] Additionally, statistics show the majority of members of the National Association of Purchasing Management come from firms with purchasing departments containing ten or fewer members.

IMPORTANCE OF PURCHASING

Purchasing's Share of the Sales Dollar

Recent Bureau of Census data indicate that on the average, more than half of every dollar taken in as income from sales of manufactured products is spent for the purchase of materials, supplies, and equipment needed to produce those goods. Perhaps the most significant indicators of the scope and importance of purchasing in relation to sales, however, are corporations' annual reports (see Figure 1-1).

Following are the percentages of sales spent on purchased goods and services in a representative group of companies

- Apple Computer, 65 percent
- Bethlehem Steel, 55 percent
- Ford Motor Company, 60 percent
- General Electric, 46 percent
- Texas Instruments, 50 percent[3]

In the majority of manufacturing companies, materials costs are found to be reasonably close to the average, from 40 to 60 percent of total product cost. But in special cases purchases may range widely beyond these limits, according to the type of business and the kinds of materials used. Purchase expenditures in nonprofit organizations generally represent a lower percentage of income.

In the basic processing of a single raw material that makes up the bulk of the finished product, the purchase cost of material is generally a high proportion of finished product cost—up to 85 percent or more. Examples are found in those industries producing fabrics, shoes, food, and similar products. A high degree of mechanization, which reduces labor cost per unit of product, also tends to make

[2]M. J. Dollinger and M. G. Kolchin, "Purchasing and the Small Firm," *American Journal of Small Business*, Winter 1986, pp. 33–45.
[3]"Top 100 1989," *Purchasing*, November 23, 1989, pp. 51–72.

Sales to Industries   Where the Sales Dollar Went

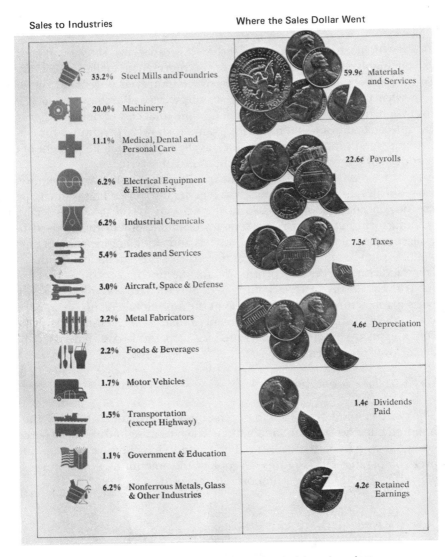

Sales to Industries	Where the Sales Dollar Went
33.2% Steel Mills and Foundries	59.9¢ Materials and Services
20.0% Machinery	22.6¢ Payrolls
11.1% Medical, Dental and Personal Care	7.3¢ Taxes
6.2% Electrical Equipment & Electronics	4.6¢ Depreciation
6.2% Industrial Chemicals	1.4¢ Dividends Paid
5.4% Trades and Services	4.2¢ Retained Earnings
3.0% Aircraft, Space & Defense	
2.2% Metal Fabricators	
2.2% Foods & Beverages	
1.7% Motor Vehicles	
1.5% Transportation (except Highway)	
1.1% Government & Education	
6.2% Nonferrous Metals, Glass & Other Industries	

Figure 1-1 Air Reduction Company's purchases of materials and services accounted for almost 60 percent of the sales dollar as shown in an Airco annual report.

materials cost a higher percentage of the total, even though the materials themselves may be relatively low in terms of unit cost. Most mass-production industries are in this category. The same thing is true of assembly operations, in which product components are purchased in more highly fabricated form and have thus acquired additional costs in the earlier stages of fabrication, prior to purchase.

On the other hand, in extractive industries, such as mining or oil production, in which the product is manufactured from purchased materials but comes from natural deposits, the purchase ratio is relatively low. Purchased materials and services in such industries generally account for about 25 percent of the sales dollar.

In more labor-intensive industries, especially those requiring highly skilled, highly paid workers, purchases also represent a smaller percentage of total costs. Similarly, in some established service industries purchased supplies are a somewhat minor means of backing up the service. Purchases in such cases are likely to be relatively low in proportion to the total cost of doing business. A typical railroad operating statement, for example, shows expenditures for equipment, materials, and supplies, including fuel, as slightly less than 25 percent of the total cost of providing and maintaining the railroad service.

In some manufacturing industries, despite rising wages, the ratio of purchased materials to total product cost is generally rising. This is due in part to increasing mechanization and also to the growing trend toward specialization in manufacturing. Automobile makers, for example, buy many car parts from specialized producers: tires, batteries, wheels and axles; engine components and assemblies; and so on. Thus the prices they pay for these items include the suppliers' labor, indirect charges, and profits. Yet for the auto makers these prices represent the true cost of the materials purchased. Several decades ago, when more of the parts manufacturing was being done in the automobile plants, average materials cost in the industry was about 52 percent of total product cost. Today, when many components are procured in fabricated form, materials costs have risen to an average of over 60 percent.[4]

Large Dollar Expenditures

The dollar amounts involved in purchasing are substantial. In 1989 the top one hundred purchasers spent $500 billion, which represented about 10 percent of all economic activity in the country. The trend in expenditures was up 20 percent over comparable 1987 figures.[5] A look at the amount of expenditures indicates why effective purchasing is important to profitability.

- General Motors $62 billion
- Ford $54 billion
- Chrysler $22 billion
- IBM $19 billion
- General Electric $18 billion

Efficiency in purchasing affords opportunities for making important savings and avoiding serious waste and loss. The effect on product cost is such that it may easily spell the difference between leadership in an industry and an untenable competitive position. Management properly gives close and continuous attention to labor costs, production efficiency, and costs of distribution. The materials item is sometimes taken for granted, as if it were a fixed cost and nothing could be done about it. Yet in terms of the value received in return for purchase expenditures,

[4]Ibid.
[5]Ibid.

this factor also reflects good and poor management and performance. It is, in fact, of equal importance with other functions of industrial activity and the other elements of product cost in attaining successful, profitable company operation.

Profit Impact

Purchasing savings affect bottom-line profits dramatically. Each dollar saved adds an extra dollar to corporate profits. Thus a buyer who produces a $10,000 net savings for his or her company has contributed $10,000 to company profits. Meanwhile a salesperson who sells an extra $10,000 of goods contributes only a portion of the $10,000 to profits, depending on the company's relative profitability. This concept is termed the purchasing multiplier and is shown in Table 1-1.

Using a more complex example, we can see that there is as much profit in a 1.5 percent purchasing saving in an average manufacturing company as there is in a 10 percent sales increase.

Assume a sales volume of $60 million in the XYZ Company, of which 53.7 percent, or $32.2 million, went for purchased materials, supplies, and services. The average profit margin in the industry is 8.2 percent before taxes. Therefore, it would have taken $6 million in additional sales—a 10 percent increase—to make an additional $492,000 profit. But a reduction of only 1.5 percent in purchasing costs would mean close to $492,000 that could be added to profit.

A prominent management consultant has suggested another way to estimate purchasing's potential economic impact. He recommended that management set a reasonable improvement goal for each broad parameter of company profitability (e.g., sales volume, gross profit margins, labor costs) and then set one for purchasing—a reduction of 5 percent in materials cost, for example. A profit-sensitivity analysis, such as that shown in Figure 1-2, may reveal that the profit potential in improved purchasing easily outstrips the potential for gains in those other areas that normally are more closely scrutinized by top management. It should be noted that the effect of purchasing in nonprofit organizations must be judged by other standards.

Table 1-1   Purchasing Multiplier

Purchasing Savings	Purchasing Profit Contribution	Sales	Profit on Sales	Profit
$1	$1	$20	.05	$1
$1	$1	$10	.10	$1

Formula: $\dfrac{\$1 \text{ Purchasing Savings}}{\text{Average Profit on Sales}}$ = Purchasing Multiplier

$$\frac{\$1}{.05} = \$20$$

$20 sales = $1 purchase savings

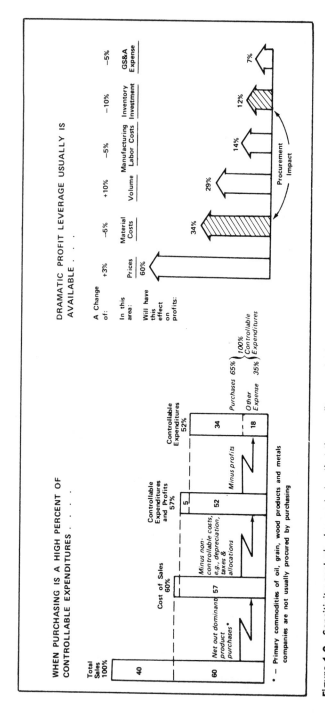

Figure 1-2 Sensitivity analysis demonstrates that the profit potential in improved purchasing may outstrip potential gains in other areas. Courtesy of *Journal of Purchasing and Materials Management.*

Effect of Purchasing on Other Costs

Direct expenditure for materials and components is not the only way in which purchasing affects end-product costs. The effect of *delays* due to lack of materials has already been noted. Shutdowns and waiting time at machines may be charged to production costs, but the end result is the same. The situation is worse when purchased materials are on hand as needed but are not uniform in quality or dimension or are otherwise of inferior workability. *Improper materials* impair manufacturing efficiency and add to the so-called hidden costs of production. In addition, they may involve extra costs for closer inspection and result in greater waste and rejections. That sacrifices not only the spoiled material itself but also the time and labor expended on it.

Such cases obviously reflect poor purchasing performance. That could be avoided by giving better attention to the buying function. But there are other cases in which purchasing may be done strictly in accordance with stated requirements, on time, and at a favorable price, yet the end cost may be unnecessarily high. This occurs, for example, when the *specifications* for a material or component are so rigid that the purchasing department cannot exercise its special talents in buying the item. There may be a limited number of suppliers for the product— possibly only one. The specifications might automatically exclude commercially standard items or otherwise acceptable substitutes. Factors such as these are inherent in the economics of purchasing decisions. An organization can expect to get the most advantageous end costs only when purchasing factors are balanced against factors of utility and usage, when materials cost is considered in its relation to other costs.

Sound purchasing frequently discloses cases in which it eventually costs less to buy more expensive materials or supplies, when the additional cost will be offset by manufacturing economies. The reverse may be true in other cases. It may be economical to incur some additional manufacturing cost to take advantage of substantially cheaper materials that are adequate for the purpose. Or it may be found more economical to switch from making parts in the plant to buying them on the outside from a lower-cost producer.

Impact on Economic Trends

Since purchasers control such large amounts of purchase-dollar expenditures, their collective action can have significant impacts on economic trends. Research by Dr. John Hoagland has indicated that concerted activities by purchasing managers has affected economic trends.[6] The major causes of great changes in buying behavior are threats to supply. These threats to supply can occur in all major countries when they are experiencing growth, political upheaval, war, strikes or threats

[6]Dr. John Hoagland has written many articles and delivered numerous presentations concerning the purchasing functions impact on economic trends. For further discussion see John H. Hoagland "Keys to Business Forecasting" 12th Annual *American Production and Inventory Control* Society November 6, 1969 and Aljain's Purchasing Handbook, Forecasting, Forward Buying and Hedging (Chapter 13) 4th Edition pp. 13-1, 13-10; McGraw-Hill New York 1982.

of strike. When such events occur, buying behavior changes, and the change can affect economic activities. Hoagland's research has shown that steel contract negotiations of the 1950s and 1960s affected the economy. Purchasers had loaded up on steel prior to strike threats, creating a business cycle expansion. Then a short recession followed after contract settlement, as producers used up their inventories. The recent trend toward more labor-management cooperation and a decline in the number of manufacturing jobs under union members has lessened the impact of strikes. However, alert purchasing managers follow their labor contract expiration dates and avoid threats to supply. Further, the 1980s were not characterized by the supply shocks that occurred during the 1973–1974 period when such key commodities as steel, copper, and oil were in short supply.

The close monitoring of the "NAPM Report on Business" by leading economists and government policy makers demonstrates purchasers' influence on the economy. This survey of 250 purchasing executives is published monthly in the *Wall Street Journal,* giving the financial community a picture of economic activity prior to the release of official government data. The report is sent monthly to the chairman of the Federal Reserve Board. It will be discussed further in Chapter 19.

OBJECTIVES OF PURCHASING

The purchasing objective is sometimes defined as buying materials of the *right quality,* in the *right quantity,* at the *right time,* at the *right price,* from the *right source.* This is a broad generalization, indicating the scope of the purchasing function, that involves policy decisions and analyses of various alternative possibilities prior to the act of purchase. The significance of the definition depends, of course, on the interpretation of what is "right" and requires the consideration of many factors that are discussed in detail in later chapters. At this point, we are more concerned with the objectives to be attained.

The fundamental objectives of a purchasing department for a manufacturing firm may be summarized as follows:

1. To maintain standards of quality in materials, based on suitability for use
2. To procure materials at the lowest cost consistent with the quality and service required
3. To maintain continuity of supply to support the manufacturing schedule
4. To do so with the minimum investment in materials inventory, consistent with safety and economic advantage
5. To avoid duplication, waste, and obsolescence with respect to materials
6. To maintain the company's competitive position in its industry and to conserve its profits, insofar as materials are concerned
7. To analyze and report on long-range availability and costs of major purchased items
8. To search the market continually for new and alternative ideas, products, and materials whose adoption might improve company efficiency and profitability

THE BASIS OF PURCHASING'S AUTHORITY

The purchaser is an agent for his or her company and is given authority by the principal (owner or management) of the firm. Thus, in most organizations the buyer is the only person legally authorized to commit company funds.

In both the governmental and the private sector there is a monetary limit to the amount that may be spent for any single purchase without securing specific approval of the expenditure from general management. These monetary limitations vary from several thousand dollars to several hundred thousand dollars.

In addition to legal authority to commit funds, management also delegates purchasers authority to carry out functional duties. The general management principle involved here is that authority should be comparable with responsibility and the ability to meet responsibility. The first criterion is more important. If the person charged with responsibility does not have the required abilities, management will find a purchaser who has, even if it means training someone.

The scope of authority corresponds to the functional responsibilities assigned by management. For example, we say that it is outside the province of purchasing to decide what to buy for a particular purpose but that purchasing does have the authority to select the source from which it buys. The distinction is not one of privilege but of two different responsibilities—for suitability and for value.

The purchasing manager has authority to buy. But there must first be evidence of a need: a requisition from another department, a reorder quantity established by inventory policy, a bill of materials for a factory work order, or some other means of authorization.

The design or using departments make the final decision as to the type and quality of materials to be purchased. But the selection of a source is a prerogative of purchasing. Requisitioners may recommend a source or a brand, and purchasing should consider these preferences as long as no sacrifice in price, quality, or service is involved. When required products are identified by a manufacturer's brand name or number, the qualifying statement "or equal" should be added to give the buyer greater choice. It is then up to purchasing to show that alternative products are equally suitable for the purpose.

Traditionally, purchasing departments established two or more sources for all items in regular use. The purpose was to increase the assurance of supply and maintain competition. Recently, however, many companies have been negotiating long-term contracts with single suppliers of given parts or materials. In either case, production and other using departments should test alternative materials and supplies from various sources and give their opinions of those they consider satisfactory for inclusion on an "approved list" or designation as a sole supplier. When the approved-list approach is used, purchasing chooses the supplier with the assurance that the using department agrees. If a single source is used, it is purchasing's responsibility to monitor all aspects of the supplier's performance—quality, delivery, price, and service—and renegotiate the contract at the appropriate time.

THE SCOPE OF PURCHASING'S AUTHORITY

Four prerogatives of the purchasing department should be emphasized.

First, selection of the supply source is wholly a matter of purchasing authority. The need to buy originates in other departments, and required quality is defined. So long as these measures of *what* to buy are satisfied, the decision on *where* or *from whom* to buy is the responsibility of the purchasing manager.

Second, all contacts with vendors and their representatives should be made through the purchasing department, from the first sales interview, through the process of negotiation and ordering, follow-up for delivery, and correspondence relating to materials and purchases, to approval of the vendor's invoice or any adjustments that may be necessary. Legitimate contacts with technical and plant personnel should be arranged only with the knowledge of the purchasing department and are not to be conducted or construed as in any way prejudicing the purchasing department's freedom of negotiation or its latitude of choice in selecting the supplier. Some exceptions may arise in centralized purchasing for branch plant requirements (see Chapter 6).

Third, it is the duty of the purchasing managers and buyers to check purchase requests against the need. It is their privilege to suggest modifications of the requested quality for more economical or more expeditious procurement and to revise quantities on a particular order so long as the total quantity is procured in time to meet the need.

Fourth, the commercial aspects of the purchase are wholly within the jurisdiction of the purchasing department. These include the manner of purchase, the price, the terms and conditions of the order or contract, packing and shipping instructions, and the like.

It will be recalled that the purchasing responsibility is defined as buying materials of the right quality, in the right quantity, at the right time, at the right price, from the right source. Quality is definable in the specifications; the other factors are matters of judgment and decision. In their constant search for the most advantageous purchases, these prerogatives must be reserved to the buyers as the means of making their judgment and decisions effective.

RESPONSIBILITY FOR ANALYZING REQUIREMENTS

In making requests to purchase, using departments are responsible for providing complete and accurate information on what is required. The purchasing department has the *duty* of buying to fulfill any legitimate, properly authorized requisition. It has the *privilege* of questioning any requisition as to the material or quantity specified for purchase, if in its judgment the request is out of line with current usage or best buying policy. This is in no sense a challenge to the authority of other departments. It is simply a prudent precaution, consistent with purchasing's position as a watchdog over purchase expenditures, wasteful duplication, possible errors in description or estimating, or occasional misuses of requisitioning privileges. Usually purchasing also has the privilege of revising quantities on a requisition for purposes of buying most advantageously, provided the total requirement is procured in time to meet the need. Examples are the adjustment of quantities to conform with economical lot sizes, quantity discount brackets or standard packaging and shipping units, and the deferring or anticipating of purchases to take advantage of expected market fluctuations.

Where possible, product specifications should be so clear and specific that when they are met, there is no question as to the acceptability of the purchased item. The purchasing department should have a voice in the preparation of such specifications to avoid special details that would restrict the sources from which materials might be procured or that would entail extra costs for unnecessary deviations from commercial standards and tolerances.

In ways such as these, flexibility and competition are made possible in purchasing for company benefit without prejudice to the interest of the plant personnel who have to use the material.

The scope of responsibility suggested here is very broad. But even the simple delegated authority to buy may be limited *qualitatively* by stated exceptions to the general rule or *quantitatively* by a monetary limit on commitments made by the purchasing department. Limitations on authority may reflect basic management policy and philosophy. They may also be based on management doubts in the ability of the department to handle more than a certain degree of responsibility. In the latter case the purchasing managers with initiative and ability, seeing ways to improve purchasing service and performance by broadening the scope of his or her activity, may persuade management to rewrite its definition of his or her authority. Or in the absence of formal authorization, the purchasing manager may assume added responsibility, acting beyond the scope of his or her stated function, assuming that the manager does not infringe upon the authority of other departments.

RESPONSIBILITY FOR SPECIFYING

Ultimate responsibility for the type and quality of materials to be bought must rest with those who use them and are responsible for results. In this sense, the using departments are "customers" of the purchasing department, and they must be satisfied. But this does not place the responsibility or authority for selection in the using department. Rather, theirs is a responsibility for accurate definition or specification of the product, in terms of formula or analysis, accepted commercial standards, blueprints or dimensional tolerances, or the intended purpose of the material. Most industrial materials, supplies, and equipment can be bought in competitive markets and from a variety of sources, and it is the function of purchasing to select the particular material and source most advantageous to the company, patronizing two or more alternative sources if it is desirable to stimulate competition or assure continuity of supply, always bearing in mind that the essential requirement, as defined, must be met.

In addition to quality, the request for materials involves a statement of the quantity desired and the date or time at which they will be needed. It is the responsibility of purchasing managers to check these factors against the actual need, from their knowledge of the operating program or from their records of past purchases and use, and to question any apparent deviation from normal requirements, even though the authorization of a request may otherwise be in good order. This kind of scrutiny is a part of the purchasing manager's duty to avoid duplication, excessive stocks, and unnecessary rush orders that would disrupt the procurement program and incur extra transportation and other costs.

When the quantity and delivery requirements have been established, it is the responsibility of purchasing and inventory control to decide whether the goods shall be bought in a single lot, or in a series of smaller transactions over a period of time from one or more suppliers, or on a single long-term contract with delivery schedules to be specified according to the need. All these considerations, weighed in conjunction with quantity discounts, carrying charges, market conditions, and the like, have a bearing on the ultimate cost of the material, so that there is a considerable range of opportunity or advantage open to purchasing judgment, even within the strict specification of quantity and delivery requirements.

Commercial aspects of the transaction—negotiations as to price, delivery, guarantees, terms, and conditions of the contract and adjustments as to over- and undershipments or deficiencies in quality—are wholly purchasing responsibilities.

The extent to which the purchasing department is responsible beyond the point of issuing the order varies in different companies. Instances can be found in which this act marks the end of purchasing jurisdiction, but they are not typical; the test of purchasing performance lies in satisfactory deliveries against the order. In some companies, the purchasing function is interpreted to include the follow-up for delivery, reconciling receipts and vendors' invoices with the purchase order, and passing invoices for payment.[7] In well over half the cases, it includes the responsibility of storekeeping and complete accountability for materials until they are issued to the using departments. Inspection and quality testing of deliveries for acceptance are sometimes included in the purchasing function.

NEED FOR MANAGEMENT UNDERSTANDING

Top management has an obligation to see the total organization and profit picture and to see each part in proper perspective. It has an obligation to demand not only that each function adequately within its own area of responsibility but also that it

---

[7]Some purchasing and sales managers dislike the connotation of the term "vendor" and prefer to use "supplier" instead. Usage varies widely, however, in purchasing organizations. The *Purchasing Handbook*, 4th edition (McGraw-Hill), defines *vendor* as "an outside supplier of raw materials, supplies and equipment or services needed in the operation of an organization." The terms are used interchangeably in this text.

make the greatest possible contribution toward the total operating and profit objectives. This entails defining the areas of functional responsibility and authority and correlating them in the larger scheme so that each will have scope to realize its full potential.

Purchasing is inescapably a part of that picture. Therefore, the manager must be at least "literate" in respect to the objectives, opportunities, and methods of modern purchasing.

Without this understanding of purchasing principles, management lacks the means of even a rudimentary appraisal of purchasing performance. It is not enough to delegate the act of buying and to charge the buyer to procure needed materials at lowest cost. That approach to purchasing quite literally authorizes the purchasing agent to become a "price buyer," the qualification for which is little more than the ability to recognize that a price of $99 for an item is lower than a price of $100. But the moment that we go beyond the concept of price buying, as we must, the matter becomes more complex. The questions for management become, How much can we expect of the purchasing department? Where does it fit into our management and operating policies?

There is no single, universal answer to these questions, as will be shown. But the answers in any given case may be surprising, for the developments in purchasing science and the experience of progressive purchasing departments reveal a potent profit tool that management can ill afford to ignore. The sharpness of that tool and the way it is used are matters that management, first, then the purchasing manager must determine. Viewed in this light, purchasing is more than just another job to be done; it is an integral part of successful management.

WHAT MANAGEMENT EXPECTS OF PURCHASING

Having established purchasing as a separate department with specific authority, management expects, first, the *competent performance* of purchasing duties and the accomplishment of the basic purchasing objectives. It expects a department that understands and accepts the responsibilities of its function in the overall organization. It expects a department that is *efficiently administered* and that develops appropriate policies and procedures that will result in economical cost of procurement as well as economical cost of materials. It expects a well-informed department that can serve as an *information center* for the entire company on the commercial and market aspects of materials—availability, costs, supply and demand trends—and so can aid in the formulation of broad business policies. See Figure 1-3 for an example of the stated goals of Xerox in this regard.

Management expects its purchasing people as well to put company interests and objectives ahead of departmental interests. It wants a department that *can get along* with other departments and work with them toward the attainment of company objectives without compromising sound purchasing principles.

Management expects the purchasing department, in its contacts and dealings with supplier companies and their representatives, to act with *fairness, courtesy, and dignity* and to maintain high standards of business relationships. This

---

Xerox Procurement Philosophy

Objectives
The primary goal of the Xerox Corporate Procurement function is to insure the sound location, selection, development, administration and motivation of suppliers to Xerox for purchased components, materials, equipment, supplies and services, in order that a dynamic blend of the following technical, business and financial objectives may be achieved:

Balanced Value
Optimum Quality • Continuity of Supply
Minimum Final Cost • Supplier Know-How
Supplier Service • Good Xerox/Supplier Relations

Profit Contribution
Tight Economic Control • Constant Search for Value

Creative Business Leadership
Innovative Procurement Techniques • Highly Qualified
and Creative People • Flexible Organization

Figure 1-3 Goals and responsibilities of a corporate procurement department as listed in a booklet distributed within the company and to suppliers. Courtesy of Xerox Corporation.

public relations aspect of purchasing is now recognized as one of the most important opportunities and responsibilities of the purchasing department.

With the development of purchasing science and the broadening concept of the scope of purchasing activity, the occasional plaint of progressive purchasing managers is that management expects too little, rather than too much, of the purchasing department. It is well, therefore, at this point to note also what purchasing expects of management. It expects buying authority commensurate with its responsibilities. It expects a clear-cut definition of its activities and authority, particularly when they impinge upon the activities of other departments. It expects the backing of management in the enforcement of approved purchasing policies and procedures throughout the company. It expects management to provide the physical and technical facilities for efficient purchasing work.

Beyond this, purchasing expects management to understand the larger aims of progressive purchasing practice, so that the legitimate scope of activities may not be unduly circumscribed; to grant purchasing a voice in policy-making councils and decisions; to listen with an open mind to purchasing proposals affecting materials usage in other departments and company investment in materials; and to permit the department to extend its activities and influence when benefit to the company can be demonstrated.

The purchasing department should regularly make available to management and to all interested departments its special knowledge and appraisal of *economic and market conditions*. Purchasing is in a unique position to acquire valuable information. Through its study of markets and its day-to-day contact with a variety of supplier industries, it can obtain insight into ideas and plans of suppliers (as well as those of suppliers' other customers). New products and processes and new applications of old materials typically come first to the attention of the purchasing department. Labor relations in supplier industries and other factors affecting present and future supply can be significant indicators in the formulation of sound business policies. Purchasing department reports can be a valuable service to management, supplementing other research.

PURCHASING VIS-A-VIS OTHER DEPARTMENTS

The independence of purchasing as a major function of business should be merited only on the basis of the service and cooperation that it gives to other departments (see Figure 1-4). It would be fatal to the department and injurious to the company if purchasing were to concentrate on its own "prerogatives" and procedures as ends in themselves, unrelated to the needs of the rest of the company. The nature of the purchasing function dictates that it service other departments. One major corporation specifically refers to the functions that interface with purchasing as its "internal customers." Much information flows both into and out of the purchasing department. Better service and management of these information flows dictate purchasing moves toward closer relations with its internal customers. Operating in rapidly changing environments characterized by short product life cycles lower inventories and flexible manufacturing systems create an environment that requires joint cooperation.

Relationship with Production

Insistence on the separation of purchasing from direct control by the production department does not imply any basic divergence of interest. It is still a primary function of purchasing to serve the production program, and the latter must be

Figure 1-4 Purchasing/materials interfaces.

satisfied. The relationship between the two departments should be considered rather from the viewpoint of their common objective, which is to contribute most effectively to the company's overall advantage. From this viewpoint, there is excellent reason why neither should dominate the other. At the same time, there is compelling reason for the closest possible cooperation.

Support for this approach is found in official U.S. Air Force instructions for evaluating the procurement efficiency of defense contractors:

> The analysis of the contractor's organization should develop a clear understanding of the functional relationships of purchasing to manufacturing, quality control, engineering, etc. It shall be ascertained whether the organizational level of the purchasing department allows it to operate at maximum effectiveness. For example, unclear lines of responsibility or placing of the purchasing function subordinate to another management function may impair the capability to make objective purchasing decisions.[8]

Production or operating departments should advise purchasing promptly, and as far in advance as possible, concerning the program to be carried on. This includes contemplated work schedules, special projects or contract jobs to be undertaken, new products to be produced, changes in design that will affect items to be purchased, and any significant changes in rate of production. In the absence of specific information, the routine guide of the buyer is the record of past consumption. This record would be a misleading criterion in the event of a change of schedule, leading to possible shortages if requirements were increased without notice. It would also create excessive inventories and losses through obsolescence if certain parts were discontinued or their use curtailed. The aim at all times should be to permit a planned program of procurement for systematic purchasing. "Lead time" in buying not only involves the supplier's manufacturing cycle and a normal period for delivery but should also include a reasonable time for finding the best source and negotiating an advantageous purchase.

Data furnished to purchasing should also include a realistic statement as to when materials will actually have to be on hand for use. The safety factors of timing, anticipation of requirements, forward coverage, and delivery schedules are matters of purchase policy and planning. A realistic statement of need fixes purchasing responsibility, whereas unwarranted requests for delivery in advance of the actual need tend to reduce the flexibility of the purchasing program and generally to increase the risk of wasteful buying.

Purchasing, in turn, has the responsibility to keep using departments informed as to the status of their request for material. A copy of the purchase order is usually routed to the requisitioner to show that the need has been provided for. If the vendor's delivery promise does not meet the time specified on the requisition, or if later delays make it necessary to revise delivery schedules, using departments should be advised so that schedules can be adjusted.

[8]U.S. Air Force, *Air Force Systems Command Manual*, AFSCM 70–3, "Contractor Procurement Review Manual," p. S1-7.

Purchasing and Engineering

Cooperation between purchasing and engineering departments is chiefly concerned with matters of product design and specification preliminary to the actual production requirements.

The purchasing manager and the engineer traditionally differ in their approach to the materials problem. The engineer tends to specify wide margins of quality, safety, and performance, whereas the purchasing manager tends to narrow such margins and work to minimum requirements. The engineer, by temperament and training, seeks the ideal material or design or equipment, frequently with insufficient regard for cost. The purchasing manager seeks materials and equipment adequate for the intended purpose, at the lowest *ultimate* cost—that is, the best price after quality, delivery, and service have been assured. The two viewpoints have been brought closer together in recent years as number of technically educated people have entered purchasing work in industry. In many companies purchasing engineers have been assigned or attached to purchasing department staffs, or buyers have been assigned to service and buy just for engineering. Whether or not a technical person is actually included in the purchasing department organization, it behooves the buyer to take advantage of the knowledge and advice of the engineering staff on any and all points where they can aid toward more effective selection of materials.

In some procurement organizations, arrangements for purchasing-engineering liaison are quite well established. Prior to the introduction of a new subcompact car, Chrysler established a technical-planning unit to work closely with production planning, body engineering, general manufacturing, product-cost planning, and design. IBM San Jose formed a "procurement engineering" group within the procurement department to provide all the technical support required to assure that supplier fabricate purchases to specification and schedule, at the proper price (see Figure 1-5). Both these developments are treated at greater length in Chapter 6.

Engineering specifications may call for excessively close dimensional tolerances. These may add to product quality and uniformity, but they often place the requirement outside the scope of commercial standards, restrict the number of potential suppliers, raise costs, and increase the percentage of rejections, without any significant increase in utility. Cooperation with the purchasing department will frequently result in arriving at a more practicable and economical standard. Today purchasers frequently involve suppliers earlier in the design process. This early supplier involvement (ESI) assures that engineers will consider the commercial aspects of a design as opposed to designing a part or product that cannot be procured or produced.

Standardization of materials and dimensions in product design is a field in which purchasing and engineering cooperation can yield very beneficial results. Such a program is logically initiated by the purchasing manager because of its possibilities in the direction of reducing the number of stock items, permitting the consolidation of requirements, increasing purchase quantities, and reducing in-

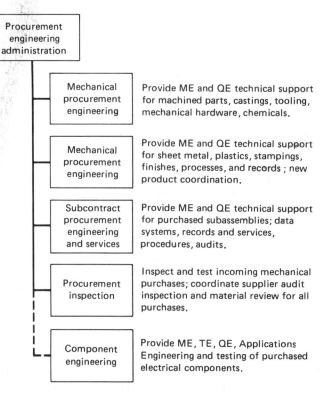

Figure 1-5 Procurement Engineering Group responsibilities in relation to other departments. ME, TE, and QE refer to mechanical, tooling, and quality engineering, respectively. Courtesy of *Journal of Purchasing and Materials Management.*

ventory investment. The final decision is within the province of the engineer, whose judgment is invaluable in determining where, how, and to what extent the principle can be applied without jeopardizing product quality.

As in the case of the purchasing-production relationship, cooperation between purchasing and engineering is most effective if it starts at the planning stage, when designs and specifications are still formative and flexible.

Purchasing and Marketing

Sales departments should keep purchasing informed of sales quotas and expectations as a guide to probable quantity requirements of materials. Purchasing should also be advised when special contracts or new products are contemplated, so that the necessary preliminaries of the purchasing program may be undertaken well in advance of the actual need.

Modern selling organizations are also developing closer relationships with their customers; consequently, sales can keep purchasing up to date on the customer's needs. This closer communication between a firm and its customers allows for a more accurate schedule of production, making the purchase of goods a much smoother process.

One of the functions of the purchasing department is to prepare estimates of the cost of materials for use in sales quotations and in the planning of product lines within a stated price range or cost limitation. The purchasing department can be of great assistance in determining how much quality or quantity can be built into a product or item within such limitations. It can also suggest means of cost reduction or quality improvement to enhance the salability of the product. In this way it contributes to the competitive position of the company as compared with the rest of the industry.

The purchasing department files and daily mail provide a wealth of first-hand information on the sales policies, promotional methods, and similar activities of other manufacturers and examples of how other companies handle special situations. This accumulation of material is particularly valuable because it has been objectively received and appraised by the purchasing staff, and that it makes available a practical basis for determining what policies, what sales approach, and what type of sales material are most effective.

A leading manufacturer of electronic business machines provides an interesting example of purchasing-marketing cooperation. The marketing department is responsible for selection and sale of peripheral equipment and supplies (bought from outside suppliers). It is marketing's function to seek out such new products using conventional purchasing techniques, including vendor contacts. The purchasing department is responsible for negotiating terms with suppliers, coordinating all contacts and transactions, and issuing the contract. Marketing is therefore expected to notify purchasing immediately of its requirements and to seek purchasing's assistance in its vendor contacts. Meanwhile, purchasing is expected to conduct simultaneous surveys of its own and keep marketing informed of all potential suppliers, substitutes, or equivalents.

Purchasing and Stores

The relationship between purchasing and stores departments is inherently so close and so basic that the two are combined in more than half of industrial organizations. The percentage is even higher in institutions, such as hospitals and universities. Functionally, the effect is to extend the responsibility for materials from the point of acquisition to the point of issue and use. The activities between these two end points are chiefly of a custodial nature, including the receipt and care of purchased items and accountability for material stocks, both physically and in accurate record form. This is the continuation of a single process. Except for the verification of quantities actually received against purchase orders, there is no purpose of "checks and balances" to be served by separating the two functions. The administration of stores may be a job of considerable magnitude in itself, but widespread experience shows that it can be handled effectively within the general framework of the purchasing department.

There are cogent reasons for combining the purchasing and stores functions. Inventory stores are implemented wholly by purchasing action. A large part of the purchasing program is usually initiated by requisitions from stores departments, to replenish stocks. Duplication of records can be minimized. Stores records are essential to the buyer, not only as to receipts and quantities on hand but also as to disbursements and rates of use. This information is vital to the formulation of a sound purchasing policy and program, for inventories and stock turnover are among the measures of purchasing performance and efficiency. The determination of maximum and minimum stock quantities is not primarily a control over purchasing, merely a guide; it is purchasing's means of controlling inventory investment, of maintaining balance, and of assuring the adequacy of supplies in relation to the need. As a mere quantitative measurement, such figures have little meaning. As a matter of fact, they are effective only to the extent that they are adjustable—and adjusted—to the use requirements and purchasing policy they implement.

To fulfill purchasing objectives, it is necessary also to know that materials are definitely correlated to the purchase order when received and that they are issued and applied to the purposes for which they are bought. Special attention should be given to inactive and slow-moving items, to avoid losses from depreciation and obsolescence and the accumulation of excessive carrying costs over a long period of time. All are properly chargeable to the materials account and add to the cost of materials up to the time of use or disposal and thereby come within the scope of purchasing responsibility. The accountability for materials cannot be divided without sacrificing efficiency and control.

In any event, there must be a daily, detailed flow of information between the buying and the stores divisions. Purchasing must advise stores regarding orders placed and deliveries expected in sufficient detail so that orders received may be readily identified, promptly placed at the service of using departments, and accurately accounted for. Stores, in turn, must keep purchasing advised regarding the fulfillment of orders and the status of inventories, as noted above.

Purchasing and Inventory Control

Inventory control involves the determination of quantities, coverage, and balance among items carried in stock. It is usually set apart from purchasing as a special, independent function. Recent trends toward combining some of the routine buying functions with inventory control have emerged in the buyer-planner concept. In this concept one person is responsible for ordering and controlling the inventory levels.

Where the functions are not integrated buyers and planners need to be in constant communication concerning supplier delays, production schedule changes, lead-time change, and quality problems. For inventory control is undeniably a major consideration in management policy, with significant effect upon the costs of operation. Determination of optimum ordering and inventory quantities is a part of modern purchasing (see Chapters 16 and 17). In a purchasing department that understands the full import of its responsibilities, inventory-control factors are weighed against commercial aspects of the transaction as a standard procedure in making buying decisions.

Purchasing and Traffic

Purchased materials have to be brought from the supplier's plant or warehouse to the point of use, and transportation charges make up a distinct and sometimes substantial part of ultimate delivered cost. The purchasing department is therefore concerned with incoming traffic costs. Purchasing usually takes cognizance of this by giving preference to nearby sources or to those that are strategically located in relation to good transportation facilities, as one means of minimizing this cost factor.

In addition to cost, just-in-time systems dictate selection of reliable carriers who ship within a tight time frame. Thus the carrier selection problem is complex. The availability of a variety of alternative transport methods, proper freight classification, consolidated shipments, and the like, offer additional means of savings. Further, the development of new services, such as fast freight, truck-rail combinations, and air express, have materially extended the economical purchasing radius and are to be considered in buying policies and decisions. The purchasing department can therefore make good use of expert traffic knowledge. Meanwhile, purchasing can help traffic by assisting in negotiations with carriers.

Most purchase orders include shipping instructions for the vendor. A well-informed traffic department determines what is the "best way" for various types of shipments from various source locations, and this information is incorporated in the purchasing department's vendor file for quick reference and application when orders are issued. Other traffic services to purchasing include the tracing of shipments, expediting in transit, and the handling of claims on shipments damaged in transit.

Deregulation of the transportation industry has accelerated a trend toward placing the traffic responsibility in the purchasing or materials-management department. The basis for such a move is the realization that transportation services can now be purchased and contracted for just as materials and supplies are. In other words, freight rates on both incoming and outgoing shipments can be negotiated with carriers rather than imposed by a government agency as previously. This change and other facets of the transportation function are discussed in Chapter 17.

Purchasing and Quality Assurance

Quality assurance needs to be involved in audits of the supplier's quality capabilities prior to purchase of materials, goods and services. This involves checking suppliers' incoming, in-process, and outgoing quality as well as management's involvement in providing high quality products. Modern purchasing departments seek a proactive relationship with quality assurance which seeks to prevent poor quality as opposed to inspecting for poor quality.

The majority of the work is done before suppliers ship material. The end result is certification of suppliers who meet quality audit parameters. Shipments from certified suppliers are not checked by incoming inspection.

Thus progressive purchasers have interest in the general field of quality control as practiced by suppliers. It helps in the analysis and selection of vendors and can substantially reduce the necessity and expense of acceptance testing at the buyer's plant. To get maximum benefit from this buying technique, audits should be correlated with the quality-control practices and standards in the buyer's own company.

A primary purchasing responsibility with respect to quality control is to procure materials and products that conform to the specification. The quality-control department usually handles acceptance testing of purchased materials. In that case it should be made clear to purchasing, and through purchasing to the vendor, what test methods are to be applied and what are the criteria of acceptability. Such advance information minimizes the chances of misunderstanding and controversy and, in the long view, aids substantially in the procurement of consistently acceptable materials.

In the case of rejections, it is important to observe the principle previously stated—that complaints and adjustments be handled through the purchasing department and not directly between quality control and the vendor. Only in this way can satisfactory vendor relationships be maintained. It is also important from the standpoint of keeping purchase records accurate, for a rejected shipment means that the need has not been satisfied and the purchasing responsibility has not ended.

Acceptance testing should be done promptly upon the receipt of a shipment and the results reported to purchasing, rather than waiting until goods are issued from stores to production departments. Vendors' warranties are generally limited in time. Each day of delay makes adjustment more difficult or even impossible if the warranty period has expired. Meanwhile, shortcomings in quality may multiply owing to the vendor's assumption, in the absence of prompt corrective action, that previous shipments have been satisfactory to the buyer.

Purchasing and Finance

Every purchase made represents an expenditure or commitment of company funds. It sets in motion a series of accounting operations, such as charging the expense to the proper contract or department account, the verification and approval of the invoice, payment of the charge, and final audit. In the case of extraordinarily large or unforeseen expenditures, it may require special financial arrangements or credit considerations. Under some forms of government contracts there are further requirements that must be met to secure prompt reimbursement for the expenditure. The relationship between the purchasing and finance departments is therefore a vital one.

Purchasing and financial managers must work closely on investment in inventory, since the high cost of carrying goods (see Chapter 17) may outweigh the advantages of volume buying.

The finance department should be consulted and in many cases should be included in negotiating sessions when major purchases are to be made. This is particularly important in negotiations for long-term contracts or for capital-equipment purchases. Both often involve such finance-related terms and conditions as partial payments, progress payments, and penalties and incentive payments.

For proper cash-flow planning, the finance department needs regular reports from the purchasing department on its outstanding commitments. Both departments should also cooperate on cash-discount policy. Depending on current interest rates, it may be more advantageous to the company to take the maximum time to pay suppliers' invoices than to take cash discounts offered for early payment.

An important phase of purchasing-finance cooperation is the setting of standard costs. These are the costs per unit of production developed in advance and used as a standard for a given accounting period. When standard costs are based on the costs of purchased materials, they are in effect a purchase materials budget. (Standard costs and their relation to purchasing are discussed at greater length in Chapter 23.)

In some companies certain accounting operations are usually handled by invoice clerks in the purchasing department. These operations would include verification of prices and terms and in most cases verification of extensions and totals as well. In other companies invoices go directly to accounting to be matched with the accounting purchase order and receiving report copies. Any discrepancies noted are then referred to the appropriate buyer in the purchasing department for resolution.

POINTS FOR REVIEW

1. Justify the claim made by purchasing departments that they should have authority to question purchasing decisions made by operating departments.
2. Explain the significance of the phrase "or equal" as it applies to purchasing requisitions.
3. Name the major departments with which purchasing should maintain close communication and coordination, and explain why.
4. Cite the basic prerogatives of purchasing discussed in the text.
5. Contrast the concerns of purchasing departments of years ago—for example, in the period prior to World War II—with those of a modern department.
6. Compare management's expectations of purchasing and purchasing's expectations of management.
7. Explain the role of purchasing in modern industry and the importance of effective purchasing to the profitability and competitive position of a company.
8. Name the fundamental objectives of a purchasing department.
9. Identify at least six activities normally and regularly carried on by a purchasing department.
10. Enumerate the reasons purchasing responsibility and authority should be delegated to specific persons in a separate, specialized department.
11. Discuss the special demands that are put on the purchasing function in periods of severe economic change, with reference to current or recent abnormal conditions.
12. List the major adverse consequences of ineffective purchasing.

Purchasing in a Dynamic Worldwide Economy

In Chapter 1 we posed rhetorical questions for management: How much can we expect of purchasing? Where does it fit into our operating and management policies?

Management has not had to think too long or too hard to come up with a reply. The questions have, in effect, been answered for them by the profound transformation of the economy that began in the 1970s and promises to continue into the next century. Management, itself battered by changes in those turbulent years, has had to raise its expectations of purchasing. As a result, the function is changing in its nature, organization, and responsibilities.

These are some of the developments that are reshaping industry, and with it, the procurement function for the 1990's and beyond:

- The United States no longer dominates the international business and industrial scene. Foreign nations, particularly Japan, showing remarkable manufacturing and marketing skills, have outsold American producers in their own backyard—and in the rest of the world as well. The quality of their products and their competitive prices have proved irresistible to customers everywhere—one need look no further than the local main street or municipal parking lot to see the evidence. Japanese quality and inventory-control techniques are being widely studied and to some degree imitated.
- Almost all businesses are having to learn to operate in a one-world market. Breakthroughs in transportation and communications bring foreign suppliers practically as close as domestic ones. Overseas plant visits and negotiating sessions have become almost routine for many U.S. industrial purchasing executives and buyers.
- Management, aroused by the fuel crisis and supply shortages of the mid-1970s, now sees long-range materials availability as crucial to survival. Just knowing that the various raw materials are on or below ground is not enough. There are many questions that must be answered: Are there enough of our critical materials to go around? Will developing nations be aggressively competing with us for scarce materials? Will the quality of the product be maintained? Are our suppliers financially stable? Are they in business for the long haul? What effect are local and international politics likely to have on supply and prices? What about near-term and long-term price trends?
- New developments in worldwide competition and concern over availability of materials are affecting corporate planning and strategy. The generally accepted idea has been that strategy is made at the top and is carried out at the bottom.[1] But that is changing. Industry is learning that the production function can make a significant contribution when brought in to participate in strategic planning and decision making. That kind of participation makes two things clearer: (1) all major corporate functions are interdependent, and (2) the various functions must cooperate and synchronize their policies and operations.
- Rapid advances in technology have redirected certain aspects of business and technical education and have created demand for new types of specialists in procurement.

---

[1]The authors are indebted to George W. Harris, former vice-president, material, TRW, Inc., for his helpful comments on strategic planning. *Production function* is a collective term that includes manufacturing and industrial engineering, quality control, material planning and control, and purchasing.

- Computerization has opened the door to the information age. Information, data, facts—however we describe specifics—are being generated, collected, disseminated, and analyzed at speeds only dreamed of a generation ago. That in turn has been leading to a division of labor. On one side are those who collect and transmit data; on the other side are those who are supposed to make decisions based on their interpretation of the data. In the past, functional specialists who considered themselves managers often tried to handle what is basically a clerical job—moving data around. Now these specialists have no choice. Management wants clerks to handle clerical tasks, managers to handle analysis and decision making.
- The relationship between the buyer and the seller appears to be in transition. Taylor noted these trends in the international market several years ago: company mergers and acquisitions reduce competition; standardization of products industrywide forces buyers to purchase what is available rather than forcing suppliers to sell what buyers require; rising costs of research and development have driven many smaller suppliers out of business; the emergence of cartels of resource-rich nations (e.g., OPEC) has changed the balance of economic power; and the rising tide of protectionism is a hazard to the free exchange of goods and services.[2] Add to the list the growing use of long-range buyer-seller contracts, extending ten to twenty years in some cases. American businesses, especially, have drifted away from the tradition of "at least three suppliers for every critical item."

Singly and in combination these changes have profound implications for the purchasing function. Purchasing managers and their staffs are being called on to play an active role in managing change. It is no exaggeration to say that how well they help their companies adjust to the powerful trends in the world economy will have a serious effect on the companies' profitability and even survival.

These changes were the focus of discussion by an ad hoc committee of the National Association of Purchasing Management (NAPM) formed in late 1987. The deliberations of this committee resulted in a report on the major trends that will affect all aspects of the purchasing professions during the 1990s and beyond, including the function and process of procurement, the organization of the function, and the people who fulfill the procurement function in many of the country's larger corporations. These trends are reported below.[3] Figure 2-1 highlights these trends.

TRENDS INVOLVING PURCHASING FUNCTION AND PROCESS

1. Increasing utilization of *information technology*. The burgeoning use of specialized applications of information technology will continue to impact most purchasing operations, with particular emphasis on the larger, more complex types of organizations. The more common specific applications include: (1) Informa-

[2]A. M. Taylor, "The Great Transition," *Journal of Purchasing and Materials Management,* Winter 1978, p. 13.

[3]The following is the preliminary report of the future-trends subcommittee of the National Association of Purchasing Management, December 1987. (Committee members: Donald Dobler, Harold Fearon, Michael Kolchin, Robert Monczka, and Harry Page.)

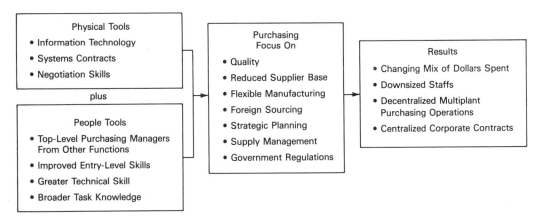

Figure 2-1 Summary of Important 1990s Purchasing Trends.

tion systems development and networking that can integrate individual materials functions, and also tie the purchasing operation more closely to other major operating departments in the firm; (2) Analytic applications that permit much more precise and thorough analysis of operating data in the purchasing decision-making process (the development of computer-based buyer work stations will likely become a trend); (3) More extensive use of bar coding for purposes of material identification and management; (4) The use of electronic data interchange (EDI) in various forms will become commonplace in certain types of purchasing operations; (5) The increasing use of computer-aided design and computer-aided manufacturing (CAD/CAM) will continue to impact certain types of purchasing operations.

2. The increasing emphasis on *quality.* The accelerating drive for improved product and operations quality in most organizations today is requiring the purchasing function to assume "ownership" for the quality of supplier performance in all areas. Purchasing personnel are required to develop a more comprehensive understanding of quality techniques. Additionally, they must be able to communicate and interface effectively in the quality area with users inside their own organization, as well as with suppliers with whom they deal.

3. Reduction of the *supplier base.* In large manufacturing organizations a clear trend is emerging to develop a relatively small number of strategic suppliers. Effective utilization of this approach requires the development of quasi-partnership relationship with the suppliers, in which each firm shares with the other a wide range of operating and planning data.

4. Increased use of *negotiation;* reduced use of competitive bidding. In a growing number of large industrial firms, negotiation will be used more heavily, and competitive bidding less extensively, in pricing and contracting activities. In firms subscribing to the supplier-base reduction concept, this is a logical implementation strategy. Completely apart from this factor, however, is the fact that in many specialty product markets the composition of the market makes competitive bidding less effective than in the traditional standard product markets.

5. Increasing emphasis on *competitive analysis.* In larger manufacturing and retailing organizations the drives for cost reduction and quality improvement are leading to much more complete and precise analysis of competing alternatives and the cost/quality data associated with them. Make-buy analysis is assuming a significant role in many sourcing investigations. Similarly, analysis involving end product *vs.* component *vs.* part purchases from given suppliers is also becoming a

routine part of many sourcing investigations. In addition, though sometimes related to these activities, cost analysis, value analysis, and related types of investigations are receiving increasing emphasis in a growing number of firms.

6. The increasing development and emergence of *flexible manufacturing systems*. The manner in which the buying plan for production materials in large manufacturing organizations is developed is being affected increasingly by the development of "flexible" manufacturing systems—both in the buyer's organization and in supplier's organizations. These capabilities in the manufacturing area lead to the design of "fragmented production," which improves the firm's ability to respond to customer needs. The results clearly impact contracting, timing, and inventory decisions in buying and selling organizations alike.

7. Increasing purchasing involvement in *technology transfer*. Large industrial and governmental purchasing units increasingly are becoming more heavily involved in the establishment of a specific technology base and the subsequent technology transfer from that base. These large organizations, in many cases, are buying technology rather than products. Such purchases represent a small percentage of the firm's buying activity, but often are major volume purchases involving significant long-term commitments.

8. Development of more *selective foreign sourcing*. This trend stems from careful attention to three separate but related factors:
   • A sharpened focus on the "best value" by considering worldwide sourcing possibilities.
   • The increasing competitiveness of many U.S. suppliers in certain materials markets.
   • The continued volatility of the value of the U.S. dollar in international trade (i.e., fluctuating foreign exchange rates).
   The interaction of these three factors is leading to more careful analysis in sourcing and timing decisions on the part of most large buyers. Expectations generally held are that the absolute volume of foreign buying will probably decline during the 1990's. In addition, the potential for counter trade activities is expected to increase, particularly as Pacific Rim and other Third World countries become competitive in world markets.

9. Variability in the *strategic planning* for materials. The emphasis on strategic planning for materials appears to be driven primarily by pragmatic considerations tied to the stability of the markets for given basic materials. When markets are unstable, major buying organizations assess the environment more carefully and develop longer range plans that assure the availability and affordability of the materials in question. As markets become more stable, the need for such planning becomes less imperative, and less strategic planning is done. As firms move into the 1990's, the generally held view is that most major markets will be relatively stable, and that less strategic planning for materials will be done by major manufacturing organizations.

10. The *changing mix of purchasing dollars* expended. In many firms, the percentage of purchasing expenditures for services will continue to increase, while the percentage of expenditures for production and operations materials will decline. This appears to be a phenomenon observed most clearly in larger organizations that elect or are required to increase expenditures for such service items as health care, information systems services, security services, food services, selected personnel services, and custodial services.

11. The increasing use of *systems contracting*. There is nothing new about this trend. However, the continued cost/quality drive across the board throughout most buying organizations will promote the continued, if not increasing, emphasis on systems contracting for commonly used MRO items.

12. The potential for *increasing governmental regulation* and/or influence. The past decade has witnessed a significant growth in the impact of governmental influ-

ence on virtually all types of business and governmental organizations. Although the trend may taper off a bit, it is reasonable to expect that it will continue into the 90's. Certainly the potential for this development exists—and probably will be conditioned by emerging political forces during this period.

TRENDS PRODUCED BY ORGANIZATIONAL DYNAMICS

13. Increasing emphasis on *downsizing* the *purchasing staff*. The tremendous pressure on operating costs in most private-sector organizations during the past five years has produced a strong incentive, if not a mandate, to reduce the size of both line and staff departments. Although the "biggest hit" may already have been taken, the trend toward staff reduction and increased operating efficiency in purchasing will likely continue into the 1990's. In these organizations this move typically results in a combining of buying responsibilities, or buying and expediting responsibilities, and in expansion of the individual buyer's job. Although these consolidations may be facilitated by the increased use of more sophisticated information systems and analytical techniques, the potential for a conflict with effective purchasing planning and practice does exist.

14. A broadening of the purchasing function, emphasizing *supply management*. Most industrial and Federal Government buying organizations are acquiring a broader set of responsibilities that tends to focus on the management of supply activities. Results of this movement vary from one organization to another, but typically tend to include some or all of the following elements: (1) A continued and refined integration of the materials management functions in the organization; (2) A combining of the responsibilities traditionally found in the buyer's and the materials planner's jobs to produce a more integrated buyer-planner job; (3) A pro-active orientation in the development of more thorough and more sophisticated materials buying plans, for a year or more in duration; and (4) An expanded pro-active service orientation that tends informally to involve purchasing personnel more closely with their operating customers.

15. The increasing *decentralization* of buying decisions in *multi-site operations*. This trend is evident largely in large-scale manufacturing operations. It appears to be driven by two factors—first, the cost reduction imperative, and second by the desire of management to move buying decisions closer to the responsible using manager. (The matter of delegating to site managers operating authority that is commensurate with their operating responsibilities.) Depending on a number of variables in each particular case, the results of such decentralization can have both positive and negative effects on professional, cost-effective purchasing activity.

16. Increasing *centralization* of corporate *"contract buying"*. This is simply a continuation of a trend which has been evident in well-managed purchasing operations for several decades. The primary motivation for this continuing effort appears to be cost driven. This trend is evident in virtually all purchasing organizations, with the exception of the small single site operation.

TRENDS FOCUSING ON PEOPLE

17. A tendency to draw *top-level* purchasing management *personnel* from *other departments*. Large manufacturing organizations that have moved toward implementation of the supply management concept in recent years have tended to fill the top

purchasing management job with a broadly experienced individual who comes from another administrative area. The expanded scope of the job, coupled with the fact that staff reductions in other areas have freed up a number of competent managers provide a sound rationale for such decisions. Although this trend affects a relatively small number of firms, it appears to be one that will continue into the future.

18. Changing characteristics of *entry-level* purchasing personnel. During the past half dozen years or so the characteristics of entry level personnel have changed markedly. Key changes have been: (1) An increasing number of women entering the profession; (2) A sharp increase in the number of college graduates entering the profession; (3) The job and career expectations brought to the work place by the newcomers typically are significantly higher than those of their predecessors; (4) Most newcomers focus more heavily on long-term personal objectives; (5) Most newcomers are less likely to develop a strong loyalty to a given organization in the short to intermediate term. One product stemming from these inputs is an increasing percentage of entry-level personnel do not necessarily see purchasing as a long term career for themselves. In combination, these key factors clearly produce a different type of management challenge for senior-level purchasing managers. This trend appears primarily to impact the larger industrial and governmental organizations, and clearly is expected to continue into the future.

19. The requirement for *greater technical* and *operating* competencies among buyers. The larger governmental and industrial buying organizations the increasing levels of operating sophistication simply require more task knowledge than was true in past years. If the sophistication of the purchasing operation is to keep pace with the increasing level of sophistication throughout the organization, it is imperative in these types of operations that buyers become more knowledgeable and more actively involved in a hands-on manner in user activities and materials applications.

20. The requirement for *broader, non-purchasing* task knowledge among buyers. In the most highly developed, sophisticated organizations, typically found in the larger governmental, retail, and industrial units, buyers are expected by experienced people in other departments to exhibit a management perspective, to a certain extent. To interface effectively with these individuals a buyer must have at least a rudimentary understanding of the managerial aspects of financial activities, cost accounting, transportation, personnel activities, potential legal issues, as well as a general understanding of the organization's operating activities.

While not all purchasing organizations will be affected equally by these trends, most large organizations will need to deal with these trends if they are to compete in a global economy. If American firms are to compete with their foreign competitors, then they must offer more perceived value. These trends are indications of how purchasing can help in providing better value.

MEETING COMPETITION WITH BETTER VALUE

It is widely admitted that Japan—up until recently, at least—has beaten American industry at its own game. It is also agreed that it would be pointless for us, mainly because of cultural differences, to try to win back our economic leadership by slavishly imitating everything the Japanese have done. Few would deny, however, that we can learn something from their successes with quality control and high inventory turnover.

Japanese firms require certified quality in their purchased goods and on-time, just-in-time delivery from suppliers, and their purchasing departments are the "enforcers."[4] It is not surprising, then, that American purchasing departments are learning to do the same thing. They were, in fact, urged to do just that by W. Edwards Deming, the quality guru of Japan. Speaking at the annual conference of the National Association of Purchasing Management in 1981, Deming said:

> It is up to purchasing personnel to discard the old philosophy that accepts common defects in purchased items. Get rid of the disease of saying it's only necessary that the vendor meet the specifications. Reduce the number of vendors you buy from. Find one who can supply the same item day after day and submit evidence of what he's doing. Don't talk about having two or more vendors until you can find one who can meet this requirement.

A study of five diverse companies shows purchasing playing a pivotal role in bringing suppliers into line on tough quality standards.[5]

General Electric Company's corporate sourcing department, for example, describes its pressure for better quality as a "way of business life—not a program with a beginning and an end." To bring supplier expertise into the quality picture early, GE buyers revamped and refined specifications on a wide range of products and services. The buyers work with suppliers to reconcile GE specifications with their manufacturing capabilities before contracts are negotiated. GE purchasing, engineering, and quality-control personnel hold quarterly meetings with major suppliers to document and discuss problems with parts quality.

Polaroid Corporation's camera division rewards high-quality performance by certifying suppliers; that is, it identifies them as meeting or beating Polaroid's quality requirements. That, of course, assumes that the other purchasing standards of cost, delivery, and service are also met. The basic requirement is that they supply parts with documented 100 percent fitness for use. Certified suppliers actually improve their own operations in their efforts to meet Polaroid standards. Even more rewarding is the larger share of business they receive.

Ford Motor Company made supplier quality improvement a critical part of a major cost-cutting effort. Ford's goal was a 45 percent reduction in the manufacturing cost differential between U.S. and Japanese cars. Better supplier performance is expected to account for half of those savings. Ford's approach is to train suppliers—particularly their managements—in the techniques of process control. Conventional quality measurement consists of inspecting purchased parts after they are received. Process control is a method of measuring quality during production at the supplier's plant. It involves taking samples of a part in batches during various stages of production. If the sample shows variations outside estab-

---

[4]Both these concepts are discussed in greater detail in later chapters, as are overseas purchasing, strategic planning, computerization, and buyer-seller relationships.
[5]Special report, "Purchasing Plays Pivot in the Quality Game," *Purchasing World*, December 1983, p. 40.

lished limits of variation, the process is shut down until the cause is diagnosed and corrected.

Pressing for better supplier quality is purchasing's major responsibility in Tennant Company's "zero-defects" campaign. Purchasing and quality engineering classify suppliers on the basis of quality performance against specified goals: qualified, conditionally qualified, and unqualified. Qualified suppliers are in two categories: A and B. On shipments from A suppliers, the only receiving inspection performed is a visual check. Shipments from B suppliers are those held up because they lack the documentation that they meet zero-defect goals.

General Electric Corporation's Major Appliance Business Group in Louisville realized quality improvement and lower cost by changing their sourcing practices.

In 1980, D.J. Inc. of Louisville, Kentucky was one of GE Appliance's 100 suppliers of plastic parts. Today D.J. is GE Appliance's single source of molded plastic parts requiring up to 250 tons press size. The company produces 40 million parts a year for its various customers. GE Appliance has not rejected one lot of D.J.'s parts since 1978. When asked how customers have helped D.J. achieve this quality record, Ray Pelle, president, laughed and replied, "In 1983, GE Appliance taught us everything we ever wanted to know about SPC. We learned the theory behind what we were already doing."[6]

There now is an open pipeline between D.J. engineers and its customers' engineers. Recently, a company asked D.J. to comment on the design of a part that had rectangular slots on its sides. By recommending an increase in the angle of the side from 0° to 7°, D.J.'s engineers simplified the required tooling. Consequently, its cost decreased by 5% to 7%, and its likely life increased by 15%. The customer gained two all-in-cost benefits: lower unit prices and less likelihood of future quality problems since the revised tooling is more durable.[7]

UNDERTAKING INTERNATIONAL SOURCING

American manufacturers' interest in international sources of supply surged during the 1970s. Many raw materials had, of course, been imported before that time—in some cases for over a century. What was new in international trade was the volume and variety of products, parts, assemblies, and machines being purchased abroad. The foreign buying binge accelerated in the 1980s as the value of the dollar rose steadily vis-à-vis foreign currencies. Managements realized that it simply made economic sense to buy from low-cost suppliers (assuming all other purchasing criteria were met) wherever they were located. The 1990's should see a continuation of the trend to buy at the lowest cost worldwide.

Coping with this apparently irreversible trend posed a challenge to purchasing executives. Evaluation and selection of suppliers, a major purchasing responsibility, requires careful analysis. The process can be exacting with domestic

[6]David N. Burt, "Managing Suppliers Up to Speed" *Harvard Business Review.* July-August 1989, p. 132.
[7]Ibid, p. 132.

suppliers. It is definitely more so with foreign sources. Problems facing U.S. buyers moving into overseas markets were summarized by two experts in the field:

> Greater distances and leadtimes; national differences as to customs, currencies, financial methods and business practices; difficulties in communicating directly and promptly; problems of interpretation or understanding; governmental and trade regulations of both the importing and exporting nation; special requirements and provisions for insurance, shipping, customs, inspection and legal contingencies.[8]

Problems notwithstanding, purchasing executives have moved vigorously into the new markets. During the latter part of the 1980s there was a move to better organize and focus international sourcing efforts. For a 1987 report on trends, manufacturing firms found that firms viewed global sourcing as a competitive weapon.[9]

In June 1989, Texas Instruments Corporation (TI) established its first International Purchasing Office (IPO) in Hong Kong. The mission of the IPO was to assist all TI sites in achieving the lowest total procurement cost consistent with TI's global procurement strategy as well as quality and service requirements.[10] Three other major trends dictate a more global sourcing orientation in the 1990's. They are: 1) the European Common Market of 1992 which will allow free flow of goods, services, people and capital between country borders, 2) the thawing of relations with the Soviet Union resulting in new buying and selling opportunities in the Soviet Union and Eastern Europe, and 3) improved trade relations with Communist China and the Chinese regaining control over Hong Kong in 1992.

Many organizations are now handling this new phase of the procurement job with a variety of tactics and techniques. These are discussed in Chapter 11.

PURCHASING JOINS IN STRATEGIC PLANNING

As we have seen, purchasing is reacting positively to change in the world market. Purchasing departments have sharpened their basic buying techniques to improve their companies' competitive positions. Purchasing's concerns (and management's), however, should go beyond short-term profit and focus as well on long-term corporate survival. But that has not always been the case. First, relatively few companies engaged in serious strategic planning until forced into it by the crises of the 1970s. Second, those that did usually took the attitude described earlier in this chapter: top management makes the plans (strategy) and the various functions, such as purchasing, simply carry them out (tactics).

[8]C.L. Scott and Eddie S. W. Hong, "An Operational Approach to International Purchasing," in *Guide to Purchasing* (New York: National Association of Purchasing Management, Inc. 1975), pp. 1-31.

[9]J.G. Miller, A Report on Manufacturing Trends, Boston University, Boston, 1987.

[10]Alan Ng and Gary Appenfelder, "IPO Established in Hong Kong" *Procurement Highlights*, Vol. 6, No. 3, September, 1989, p. 1.

American managers have been learning a lesson from competitors in Japan and elsewhere in the world. They have come to accept the concept that strategic planning is essential—and that there is real value in involving production functions in that planning.

Many purchasing departments are responding to these changes as indicated in a quote by John Kappler in a recent article written for NAPM's *Insights* magazine.

> In a general sense, the purchasing department is finding new and better ways of demonstrating to management that it contributes to improving the company's competitive position. As proactive procurement gains momentum, department staff prove dynamic working efficiency through:
>
> 1.) Taking a profit contribution approach to a company's purchasing goals, objectives, and day-to-day administrative activities, meaning that all actions taken by members of the purchasing function reduce total costs and increase performance by their ability to negotiate and commit on behalf of the corporation;
>
> 2.) Recognizing that value lies not in the processing of paperwork and expediting tasks, but in the role of project management to support their company's operations and administrative functions; and
>
> 3.) Showing that they, too, can respond and change their role in relation to the increasingly complex and changing demands that occur internally and externally as the global economy solidifies, material and labor shortages intensify, and competition increases.[11]

The need for bottoms-up raw-materials strategic planning—and for purchasing's input to that planning—is especially urgent. The United States, with 5 percent of the world's population, has been consuming close to one-third of the world's production of raw materials. The country's dependence on imports of key nonfuel minerals and metals has accelerated in the past decade. Meanwhile, competition for supply of materials has grown, and the end is not in sight. The demands for raw materials by other industrial countries and by the developing nations have been rising steadily. Corporate planners will need all the help they can get to protect and improve their companies' positions in materials. That help will consist of such information as evaluations of alternative materials and supply sources; estimates of long-range supply and price trends; analysis of future transportation costs and methods; inventory recommendations; effects of political disruptions on supply; and overall evaluations of suppliers' capabilities, finances, and long-term strength.

THE SUPPLIER-BUYER TIE

Despite its age and constant use, a venerable purchasing axiom is still valid: "Suppliers are an extension of our manufacturing capability." As such, they are having

---

[11]John E. Kappler, "Purchasing Strategies," *NAPM Insights,* January, 1990, Vol. 1, No. 1, pp. 21-22.

to react to the pressures of a new, dynamic economy. And they are doing it, necessarily, in concert with their counterparts in purchasing.

There has been a dramatic change from the adversarial buyer-seller relationship that existed twenty years ago, as the purchasing vice-president of a large company observed recently. What was predominant then was what he called, ironically, the "power of purchasing"; "I have the money in hand, you have something to sell, and you had better do what I say." Today's purchasing executives, he said, realize that they cannot do business that way anymore; there has to be more of a partnership arrangement.

Partnerships are successful, however, only when the partners pull together and share the work—as well as the profits. Purchasing departments have taken the lead in pressing suppliers for better quality and for greater help in maintaining a just-in-time inventory system. But there are rewards for suppliers who meet those expectations: a greater share of the business and long-term contracts. The contracts they get for superior performance on a continuing basis are not for one order or a year's orders. They range from three to five years, and in some cases as much as five times those figures. Thus selected suppliers become, in a real sense, part of a customer's strategic plan.

John Pughe, the materials executive quoted earlier on buyer participation in strategic planning, had this to say on the supplier's role in that activity:

> We are looking at several alternatives to develop a continuing marriage, a wholesome relationship with suppliers, so that they understand our marketplace and where we want to be. We take suppliers right into our forecasting module so that they can read what the requirements are; what the first six months are; what the tentative next six months are; and what our whole planning is for the next two or three years. We want to rely on them to do their jobs, to make that component for us, keep us competitive, and put components right into the assembly line without incoming or receiving inspection labor—all of which add to the cost of the product.

A NEW BREED OF BUYERS

As can be seen by the changes we have detailed, purchasing is no longer a simple function of sending out for three bids and selecting the lowest-price vendor. Today's purchasing manager must become more intimately involved with his or her company's vendor base. Purchasing managers must possess the technical skills necessary to evaluate the capabilities of a company's suppliers. They must have the capability to evaluate the quality of vendors' products and the capabilities of vendors' production processes. More important, with a shrinking vendor base, today's purchasing managers must be able to evaluate their suppliers' design capabilities and insure that they are keeping their companies competitive not only in terms of price but in technology as well. Without the use of the competitive bidding process to insure market competitiveness, today's purchasing professional must substitute product knowledge to insure that the vendor base is not becoming complacent and, hence, noncompetitive. Cost analysis and negotiation become increasingly important in purchasing decisions. Additionally, today's purchasing professional must become more knowledgeable in the other functions involved in the manufacture of the company's products. These functions include such areas as design, production planning and control, manufacturing, inventory control, accounting, finance, marketing and, most important, quality assurance. In short, today's purchasing manger must be better educated and better equipped to act as the company's manager of outside manufacturing.

This expanding role of the purchasing function suggests the need for a new breed of buyers, and major firms are now recognizing this need. Consider, for instance, that in 1981 purchasing rated a scant sixteen lines in a college recruiting brochure distributed by Air Products & Chemicals, Inc. Two years later the new edition of that brochure contained a significant change: purchasing received a two-page, four-color billing, right along with marketing, engineering, and finance. Today many major firms such as NCR, Westinghouse, Hewlett Packard, Harris Corporation and others give purchasing the space equivalent to other functions in their recruiting literature.

The change indicates how major American companies are upgrading the quality of the purchasing staffs to meet new economic realities. In the case of Air Products, management was still edgy over the energy and supply crunch of the mid-1970s. It resolved, among other things, to strengthen the materials function as a matter of strategic policy. Among the guidelines for reorganization set down by the chairman and chief executive officer was one calling for development of staff resources.

How well purchasing met that requirement of developing staff resources is evident from these figures: the number of professional procurement staff members holding one degree jumped from five 10 years earlier to thirty-eight; those with two degrees rose to seven from two; with triple degrees from zero to three.

The challenge to purchasing, particularly to purchasing personnel, in a fast-changing, dynamic economy is succinctly summarized by John Kappler in the following quote:

> Contributing to the bottomline begins with developing a long-term strategy using proactive procurement to govern the purchasing department's direction and mission. The strategy is not limited to changing certain tasks. The list below summarizes some concepts inherent in the development of a proactive procurement approach to the purchasing function.
>
> 1.) A company's internal structure dealing with suppliers must continue to be organized to support the numerous industry bases with which it transacts business.
>
> 2.) Purchasing performance must be linked to business cycles, transaction timeliness, quality control, and total line-item cost instead of the older performance measurements such as purchase orders processed.
>
> 3.) An increase in the coordination of purchasing personnel with other company personnel to include the development of special groups, such as cross-functional teams, to bring more expertise to the buying process is required.
>
> 4.) Companies will demand higher technical skill levels and managerial ability in purchasing positions. Departments need to plan training and educational

needs as well as develop specific hiring and compensation packages that will assure well-educated, technical people will be there to fill positions.

5.) An increased abililiy to perform the many types of analysis is required today to support purchasing decisions and strategy.[12]

POINTS FOR REVIEW

1. Name the most important forces in the economy that are reshaping the role of the purchasing function.
2. Point out the purchasing and material-management policies that have significantly helped Japanese industry achieve leadership in the world market.
3. Describe what some purchasing departments in the United States are doing to improve the quality of their companies' products.
4. Specify what the purchasing department can contribute to corporate long-range planning.
5. Explain how the supplier-buyer relationship is changing in the new economic environment.
6. Describe changing management attitudes toward the purchasing function.

[12]Ibid., p. 22.

Ethical Standards in Purchasing

Webster defines *ethics* as the study of standards of conduct and moral judgment and *ethical* as conforming to the standards of conduct of a given profession. In discussing ethics it is easy to become embroiled in personal moral philosophies or values, especially those applied to personal conduct. In business ethics we are all concerned with a set of moral principles and values and norms that guide business behavior. From a general business viewpoint, every company develops a code of conduct, sometimes written, often unwritten. Operating within this code, the purchasing department develops an ethical code of its own. Ethics in society covers a large spectrum and includes honesty, treatment of others, religious values, and the like (Figure 3-1). Meanwhile, businesses have a set of values as they deal with their constituencies. These constituencies are stockholders, employees, and customers, and actions that appease or satisfy one group may harm another group. A decision to spray trees with a potentially carcinogenic spray might result in quicker profits and a nicer-appearing product (fruit) but may harm the consumer and ultimately the community. In such a case is it the responsibility of the firm to tell the public about the potential dangers? On another note, a recent probe by federal government prosecutors found an inside information ring (known as the clique) was collecting classified information about the Defense Department's long-range spending plans.[1] This espionage effort involved executives of major companies, highly sensitive Pentagon data, and billions of dollars in weapons contracts. With its inside information, the companies gained an unfair advantage over competitors and even over the Pentagon officials with whom they negotiated.[2] These actions certainly are outside normal ethical practices. They raise questions about ethical conduct that will be discussed from the purchaser's perspective. Beyond ethics, social changes and forces also change and shape business behavior, and they will also be discussed later in the chapter.

[1] Andy Pasztor and Rick Wartzman, "How a Spy for Boeing and his Pals Gleaned Data on Defense Plans," *Wall Street Journal*, January 15, 1990, p. 1.
[2] Ibid.

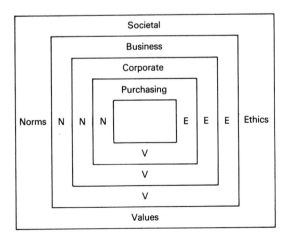

Figure 3-1 Simplified Illustration of the Ethics Process.

PURCHASING STANDARDS

Although purchasing has developed certain methods, rules, and formulas, its decisions remain largely a matter of personal judgment and it is necessarily carried on, to a great extent, through personal contacts and relationships. The purchasing manager is the custodian of company funds, responsible for their conservation and wise expenditure. Moreover, through his or her contacts and dealings with vendors, the purchasing manager is a custodian of the company's reputation for courtesy and fair dealing. The ultimate act of selecting a vendor and awarding the order is essentially a matter of patronage. For all these reasons, a high ethical standard of conduct is essential. The purchasing manager not only must act ethically but should be above the suspicion of unethical behavior. Just as standard principles and patterns of procedure have evolved in the development of this function, so a code of conduct has also been formulated. The best statement of this code is embodied in the "Principles and Standards of Purchasing Practice" advocated by the National Association of Purchasing Management:

1. To consider, first, the interests of his company in all transactions and to carry out and believe in its established policies
2. To be receptive to competent counsel from his colleagues and to be guided by such counsel without impairing the dignity and responsibility to his office
3. To buy without prejudice, seeking to obtain the maximum ultimate value for each dollar of expenditure
4. To strive consistently for knowledge of the materials and processes of manufacture and to establish practical methods for the conduct of his office
5. To subscribe to and work for honesty and truth in buying and selling and to denounce all forms and manifestations of commercial bribery
6. To accord a prompt and courteous reception, so far as conditions will permit, to all who call on a legitimate business mission
7. To respect his obligations and to require that obligations to him and to his concern be respected, consistent with good business practice
8. To avoid sharp practice
9. To counsel and assist fellow purchasing agents in the performance of their duties, whenever occasion permits
10. To cooperate with all organizations and individuals engaged in activities designed to enhance the development and standing of purchasing

While these standards of ethical behavior were first established by the National Association of Purchasing Management in 1929, they still offer guidance for the behavior of purchasing professionals in today's world. However, much has changed since 1929, and the association, recognizing this fact, has recently undertaken a review of these standards and intends to publish a revised code in the near future.

Several specific issues that will be dealt with in the revised standards include: more specific guidelines on the acceptance of gifts; an admonition to refrain from all forms of reciprocity; a recommendation to discourage all forms of personal purchase; and a challenge to encourage the purchasing profession to aid in the development, socially and economically, of disadvantaged businesses.

The key in the revised code, as it was in the original, will be the emphasis on the need for purchasers to be perceived as fair and ethical in all of their dealings with suppliers and others; while effectively performing their responsibilities.

ETHICAL OBLIGATIONS

The above code is necessarily of a general nature and requires some further elaboration or interpretation as to its application to specific circumstances. As a generalization, it is an exceedingly practical code, like a great deal of our folk wisdom on the theme that "honesty is the best policy." Hardheaded business moralizing is not predicated on the principle that virtue is its own reward; it recognizes much more tangible dividends. It is certainly true in purchasing that courtesy and fair dealing beget confidence and cooperation on the part of the supplier—assets that frequently spell the difference between a merely adequate purchasing performance and a major contribution to operating efficiency and sound profits. Without them, ordinary purchasing problems can readily become serious supply emergencies, particularly in times of economic change or stress. There are opportunists and "sharp-shooters" in purchasing as in every other field, but they are rarely successful over any extended period of time. Any going concern that expects to be in business a year or ten years hence will do well to insist upon and to support high ethical standards in its procurement policies and practices.

OBLIGATIONS TO THE COMPANY

The purchasing manager's obligations to his or her own company, covered by the first four points of the code and in part by the seventh, essentially consist of the responsibility for doing a complete and conscientious job in the function to which he or she has been assigned. Such terms as "the interests of his company" and "maximum ultimate value" are basic and self-explanatory; they summarize, in effect, the objectives of this entire study and discussion of the procurement function. "Knowledge of materials" and "practical methods for the conduct of his office" are the means of implementing these aims.

The code wisely goes beyond this, however, in emphasizing the obligation to buy without prejudice. That implies the obligation to maintain an open mind on purchasing matters. Prejudice is usually interpreted as discrimination against particular suppliers, their representatives, or their product, usually on personal or irrelevant grounds. Basically, however, prejudice concerns an attitude of mind on the purchasing manager's part that has implications far beyond this relatively simple and elementary example. Prejudice is not altogether a negative concept. A good part of all sales effort consists of the attempt to prejudice a buyer in favor of a product or supplier. There is nothing remotely unethical about this. Often it succeeds only too well. There are probably more orders placed because of the inertia that comes from habit, reinforced by relatively trouble-free experience with an established source of supply, than are withheld because of annoyance with a salesperson's mannerisms or dislike for his or her taste in shoes.

Freedom from prejudice implies a thoroughly objective approach to the purchasing problem. It means that propositions are not to be prejudged nor decisions predetermined, because the purchasing manager has closed his or her mind to facts and considerations that might modify or change previously held opinions. It means that irrelevant and superficial details, including personalities, should not be permitted to influence the just evaluation of a product or source. It means that prejudices on the part of technical or operating personnel are to be combated just as consistently as those of vendors with the same objective of maximum ultimate value.

An open mind, receptive to new ideas and capable of clear and objective judgment, is one of the outstanding characteristics of the successful buyer. Frequently it represents the difference between a merely competent job of buying and truly constructive and profitable procurement.

The purchasing manager has an ethical responsibility to the company not to be put under special obligation to any supplier by the acceptance of excessive entertainment or by permitting sales representatives consistently to buy his or her lunches, even though this may be done in the spirit of ordinary business courtesy. Such relationships should be kept on a thoroughly equitable basis. For this reason, progressive companies provide their purchasing executives and buyers with expense accounts.

THE PROBLEM OF GIFTS

A special case arises in the case of Christmas remembrances. It is a fairly common practice for a company to distribute some sort of gift to its customers at Christmas time. It is natural for sales representatives to direct some of these gifts to the purchasing department. In the great majority of cases, such gifts are relatively inexpensive and represent a genuine expression of appreciation and goodwill.

Many purchasing departments, however, have established a definite policy against the acceptance of such favors: first, because of the possible suggestion of commercial bribery; and second, because the cost of such gifts is a "sales expense" that eventually must be reflected in the price of the goods sold and purchased. Some weeks before the holiday season, suppliers are notified of this policy by letter. Any gifts received contrary to the policy are returned with an explanation or donated to a charity. Items of small value, usually of an advertising nature, may be exceptions to such a rule. But there is danger in the haphazard interpretation that "two cigars are acceptable, but a box of cigars must be returned."

The Effects of Example

There are many cases in which careful observation of the rule may verge on the ridiculous. One of the authors once observed the purchasing director of a large corporation examine a box containing a dozen popular candy bars that a supplier had left for him. After several minutes of discussion with his secretary, he decided not to return it but to send it to a local hospital. But it is one of the penalties of the purchasing function that standards cannot be relaxed. The distribution of gifts can extend down the line. That is why the head of the department must not only establish a strong policy but set a good example.

Department heads concerned with prestige and efficiency in the buying operation will avoid placing themselves under any obligation to a supplier, as a matter of ordinary business sense. Buyers can be similarly motivated if they are convinced that the company policy is firm and is enforced and observed at every level of the company, starting at the top. Various forms of commercial bribery have taken place in many company departments, even in top management—more than most people realize. One large company was quite aware of the possibility when it included the following in its statement of corporate policy on the ethics of buying:

> Every sort of influence, inducement and sales strategy is brought to bear at one time or another on those of us involved in buying for the company.
>
> You're a new-product engineer, specifying certain components purchased on the outside. Maybe you have a choice of sources, maybe you don't—but you know which supplier's devices are acceptable when you write your specifications. You're involved.
>
> You're a quality assurance engineer continually surveying present and potential suppliers for quality control practices and procedures that meet our requirements. Your survey report can result in a supplier being approved or disapproved. You're involved.
>
> You're a lawyer and you need some highly specialized advice; you know just the man. Your work has to do with advertising, sales promotion, maybe public relations—and hardly a day goes by that you don't farm out work to artists, photographers, printers you select. You're in product distribution, picking freight carriers and riggers and staying on top of them every working hour. Involvement.
>
> You manage a data center and you want the extra capability offered by company A's disc drives even though B's are lower priced. Purchasing signs the purchase orders—but you know they're going to be strongly influenced by what you say.
>
> You're a branch manager who helps the real estate department find you better space. Again, influence.
>
> In these and dozens of similar situations our people outside the purchasing department help the system work. For better or worse.

Following a review of potential ethical problems, the company laid down strict regulations about acceptance of gifts, gratuities, and entertainment—by anyone in the company.

CONFLICTS OF INTEREST

The company's policy on another area of ethical conduct—conflicts of interest—is equally clear and blunt:

> There can be no conflict of interest between your personal affairs and those you conduct for this company. Specifically, you may not have a significant financial

A·B·DICK®   PURCHASING MANUAL

SUBJECT	NO.
CONFLICT OF INTEREST	C-4

I N S T R U C T I O N

I.   PURPOSE

This instruction acknowledges the right of Company employees to engage in activities other than Company employment which are private in nature, are conducted outside the normal working hours for the employee and do not conflict with or reflect unfavorably upon other employees or the Company.

II.   DEFINITION

A conflict of interest is any action taken in private or under auspicious of Company assigned responsibility by an employee which can be construed as causing doubt about the employee's ability to make decisions in the best interest of the Company and/or restrict or inhibit the rights of other Company employees to perform their responsibilities in such a manner that serve the best interest of the Company.

III.   CRITERIA

This instruction is issued as a supplement to standing Company policy described in Supervisors' Policy Manual, Section F, titled "General Personnel Administration", Page 22A dated June 12, 1962 and/or revisions and amendments thereto that may be made from time to time.

Employees should avoid any action, position or situation which could be considered, in fact or by implication, to involve a conflict between their personal interest and the Company's interest. Employees should not use their position of trust and confidence within the Company to further their private interest.

Employees shall be especially mindful of this policy if their position with the Company is such that they may influence decisions concerning firms or individuals with whom the Company may have business relationships. For example, Company employees or members of their families should not own a significant interest in a supplier or any other business entity if the employee is in a position to influence orders placed or other decisions involving A. B. Dick Company's interest.

ISSUED BY:	DATE ISSUED	SUPERSEDES ISSUE DATED
Clifton L. Smith	11/7/74	
MANAGER · PROCUREMENT		PAGE 1 OF 4

Figure 3-2 First page of section on conflict of interest from a company purchasing manual. Courtesy of A.B. Dick Company.

interest in any company with which you do business as part of your work for [this company].

A significant interest means anything substantial enough to color your judgment, to interfere with your concern for the best interests of this company. Ten shares of General Electric won't cause a problem—or would they? What's at issue here is not one or ten shares or a hundred. It's you.

It's also your immediate family—your wife or husband, children, or any relative. Any significant financial interest in their name is a conflict under yours.

Conflict of interest can occur in other ways as well, or seem to. You may have a family or personal relationship with a supplier, or with his salesman or someone on his staff. In such cases you should talk to your manager about it as soon as you become aware of it.

Many companies spell out their policies on conflicts of interest in policy manuals. One example of such a statement is shown in Figure 3-2.

SUPPLIER RELATIONS

All department heads, but particularly purchasing managers, have an ethical responsibility to see that their companies enjoy a reputation for scrupulously fair dealing. As the point of contact in dealing with suppliers, they have a special responsibility in this respect. Their actions and conduct are critically judged, and this judgment is quickly and widely disseminated among salespeople at large. Frequently, these impressions are inaccurate. They may be colored by disappointment and pique on the part of salespeople who have lost business. But whether or not the criticism is justified, purchasing managers cannot afford to ignore it.

It should be clear that purchasing managers are under no moral obligation to see every salesperson. Sales interviews are but one of the many activities that occupy them. This does not contradict the policy of receptiveness and openness mentioned earlier. Some matters are not appropriate to the company's needs; others are not timely at the moment the salesperson chooses to call. Some salespersons are inconsiderate in making frequent calls when they have nothing new to contribute. Purchasing managers and not sales representatives are the proper judges of when calls become too frequent. But this does not relieve buyers of the obligation of courtesy—a prompt acknowledgment of the call and a reason for not granting an interview. Every salesperson should be seen on the first call and be given an opportunity to tell his or her story; subsequent policy will depend on the particular circumstances. There is no justification for keeping any caller waiting for a protracted period if the interview is to be denied. And in any event, waiting time should be kept at a minimum.

That may be primarily a matter of organizing the reception procedure. Callers should be announced to the buyer on arrival. If there is an immediate answer, it can be given at that time. If there is to be any appreciable delay before the interview can be granted, for any reason, the sales representative should be apprised of the approximate waiting time that will be necessary.

Similar courtesy should prompt the purchasing manager to inform unsuccessful bidders when a proposition has been closed as well as to inform the one who receives the order. Small companies, particularly, cannot afford to have a number of proposals outstanding, which would overtax their capacity should all bids be successful. They should therefore be relieved of these tentative commitments of capacity promptly. Furthermore, if the notification indicates in what respect the proposal fell short of the buyer's requirements, it will help the vendor in future negotiations and may lead to the development of a useful source of supply for the buyer. At the same time, it will temper the disappointment of an unsuccessful bidder to know that there was a real reason for the adverse decision.

When a sample is accepted for test, it entails an obligation on the buyer's part to make a fair trial, and it is a courteous gesture to inform the vendor of the outcome of that test, at least in general terms. Some buyers find it easy to terminate an interview by accepting a sample, even if they have no serious intention of giving it a trial. Such practice verges on misrepresentation and in the long run undermines the confidence that is essential to sound business relationships. It is avoided in many companies by a policy requiring that all sample lots for trial be bought and paid for by the buyer's company. This procedure works both ways: It incurs no obligation to the vendor, express or implied, beyond the transaction itself, and it gives the company a definite interest in completing the trial and making a fair evaluation of the product or material thus acquired.

Well-considered policies of this nature build confidence and respect and strengthen the personal relationships between buyer and vendor.

OBLIGATIONS TO SUPPLIERS

In the large sense of obligations incurred in the course of doing business, the law is rather explicit, but there are many cases of interpretation and procedure that involve ethical concepts of this relationship, beyond the strict letter of the law. For example, if business is to be awarded on the basis of bids, the buyer should insist on receiving firm bids within a stated time. If the buyer permits or encourages revisions, particularly at the last moment, the way is opened for sharp dealing on the part of vendors, and the buyer is not free from suspicion of the same fault on his or her own side. *If revisions are to be permitted,* the same opportunity should be frankly offered to all bidders, and *if the specifications are changed* because of an alternative product offered by one of the bidders, all should be invited to bid on the new specification.

The purchasing manager is *not responsible for a vendor's error in calculating a bid.* But if one of the proposals seems excessively low, indicating that an error may be responsible for the discrepancy, it is good practice to ask for a recalculation. If it happens that some item has been omitted from the estimate or that a mathematical error has been made, the purchasing manager is not in the position of taking advantage of such an inadvertent slip to the detriment of the seller. On the other hand, it frequently happens that such a recalculation results in an even lower bid, although this possibility may have been far from the buyer's mind. Naturally, if the bid is accompanied by a detailed breakdown of costs and the error is patent, it would be unethical to hold the vendor to such a proposal, which obviously does not represent the vendor's real intention.

Once an order or contract has been placed on the basis of a legitimate bid, the buyer is *not responsible for assuring the bidder a profit* on the transaction. Sellers occasionally appeal for relief from a contract that turns out contrary to their expectations, but the buyer is under no obligation to surrender or modify his or her own contractual rights if the agreement has been made in good faith. The buyer has an ethical responsibility to his or her own company and to competitive bidders in cases of this sort. If an adjustment can be made, or an alternative source found, without sacrifice of the buyer's position, it may be wise to take such action on the grounds that service and satisfaction will be greater under the new arrangement. But the whole purpose of the contractual agreement is to provide for carrying out the transaction as planned, with a definite allocation of responsibility to both parties, including the risk of unforeseen developments. As a general rule, sellers respect the buyer who stands firmly on his or her rights and prefer to do business on this basis, having the corresponding assurance that the buyer will observe his or her responsibilities under the contract just as conscientiously.

Market Intelligence

Purchasing departments are a vital source of information about suppliers, trends, marketplace actions, and prices. There is nothing wrong with gathering this information and making it available to upper management and marketing.

The method used in gathering is the key issue. For example, when a supplier provides information in confidence, the buyer should respect the request for confidentiality. Reporting price and market-share numbers to one's own marketing department could lead to antitrust problems. Using monetary-position endorsements or coercion to prompt answers from ex-employees is unethical. Likewise using the "next order" as the carrot to lure a supplier into divulging inside information is not a proper intelligence-gathering strategy.[3]

CONFIDENTIAL INFORMATION

The buyer is under no ethical compulsion to answer questions other than those that relate directly to the proposal. Competitive price information is regarded as confidential and should not be disclosed under any circumstances. And although it is generally true that full and frank discussion leads to a better mutual understanding and perhaps to a better purchase, there are circumstances in which factors other than price are also of a confidential nature.

For example, some sellers decline to bid unless they know the use to which their product is to be put. They argue that unsatisfactory performance on a job for which the product was never intended might react unfavorably and unfairly

[3]For a detailed discussion see Alan J. Frankel, "Ethics: Where Do You Draw the Line?" *Purchasing World,* March 1986, pp. 76–98.

against the reputation of the product and the producer, and they prefer to forego a sale rather than risk this unjustified demerit. They point out, quite logically, that with knowledge of what is to be required, they can recommend or prescribe the best materials for the purpose. But sometimes, also, they have a sliding price scale according to the application of identical material, a marketing practice that can be plausibly explained on the basis of special concessions to capture new markets or applications, but for which the logic of purchasing value is somewhat more obscure when one ingot or roll is exactly the same as the other.

However, we are here concerned with buying reasons and policy. Although trade secrets are much less a factor in industry today than they were a generation ago, there are still a number of things that a company may wish to keep strictly "within the family"—little kinks of manufacture that make for the individuality of their product or short cuts that give them a slight advantage in competitive costs. All buyers are well aware that suppliers rarely know the full extent of the uses that their products serve. They have no desire to broadcast the direction of their experimental programs or to have a vendor's sales representatives scurry around to their competitors with the "new idea." Buyers who are reticent about the proposed uses of the things that they purchase need not be concerned over implications that their reticence is unethical. On the other hand, buyers must recognize that under such circumstances they waive the benefits of any implied warranty on a seller's part and have no basis for later expressing dissatisfaction or pressing a claim for unsuitability in their purchase. The seller who is not informed as to the intended use is bound only to the extent of conformance with any specifications that may be set forth in the order.

ENGINEERING SERVICES

One question of ethics frequently raised is the proprietary interest of a supplier in business earned through valuable and extensive preliminary engineering services that produced a design or product adapted to the buyer's need. Is the buyer justified in sending out blueprints of such designs, product samples, or formula specifications for competitive bids, or does the supplier who originated them have a continuing claim upon the business? It is obvious that the seller must recoup these expenses and is legitimately entitled to do so. In the typical case, the service is not of a sort that can be protected by a basic or design patent. It is not a cost that the seller can pass along as a special charge, for the seller is not in the business of consulting engineering except as a means of making sales for his or her production facilities. It is a cost that will normally be reflected in his or her quotation, preferably spread over a reasonable manufacturing quantity, lest the original lot cost be excessively high for the buyer's purpose. Consequently, the distribution and absorption of this cost item frequently contemplate repeat orders to justify the quoted price, and the price is calculated in the expectation or hope of continuing business.

However thoroughly the buyer may recognize the implications of such a position and sympathize with the claims of the seller, the prospect of accepting and maintaining a monopolistic supply situation is contrary to the principles of good purchasing. The buyer cannot conscientiously agree to this solution. There will probably always be controversy as to the fairness of any compromise, but the logical answer, and the one in most common usage, is usually worked out in the form of a liberal term contract: The vendor originating the design or product supplies the buying company's requirements for a year, or more or less, depending on the quantities involved, during which time the vendor is expected to recoup its experimental and development costs in addition to normal production profits. At the end of this period, the business is opened to more general competition, and it is expected that cost to the buyer will be reduced, for these development costs cannot reasonably be expected to be a permanent factor of price. The original supplier, having already profited from its superior skill and from being a step ahead of the field, is still in a preferred position and has a substantial competitive advantage in a year's manufacturing experience as well as, perhaps, in patterns, dies, and tooling, which have been totally depreciated as a cost factor. Except in some very unusual cases, such an arrangement satisfies the buyer's ethical obligation to the vendor.

SHARP PRACTICE

The term *sharp practice,* as condemned in the buyer's code, is best defined by some typical illustrations of evasion and indirect misrepresentation just short of actual fraud. They belong to the old school of unscrupulous shrewdness, when buying was concerned with the immediate transaction rather than the long-range program. These examples would have been commonplace among an older generation of buyers, and sellers in that period were habitually on their guard against such possibilities. In modern procurement and marketing, which are based on mutual confidence and integrity, such practices are frowned upon just as severely by the buyers themselves as by the sales organizations with which they deal.

It is sharp practice for a buyer to talk in terms of large quantities, encouraging the seller to expect a large volume of business and to quote on a quantity basis, when in fact the actual requirement and order are to be in relatively small volume that would not legitimately earn the quantity consideration.

It is sharp practice to call for a large number of bids merely in the hope that some supplier will make an error in the estimate, of which the buyer can take advantage.

It is sharp practice to invite bids from suppliers whom the buyer will not patronize in any case, using these quotations only for the purpose of playing them against the proposals of those who are really acceptable sources of supply. It costs money, time, and effort to prepare estimates and bids. Sellers are glad to undertake the expense in the hope of securing a contract, but the buyer has no right to impose these costs on a seller when the buyer has no intention of giving the seller an opportunity to get the business.

It is sharp practice to misrepresent a market by placing the price of job lots, seconds, or other distress merchandise in ostensible competition with real market prices.

It is sharp practice to leave copies of competitors' bids or other confidential correspondence in open view on the desk while negotiating with a seller, in the knowledge that the latter can scarcely fail to notice them.

It is sharp practice to deal only with "hungry" suppliers and to try to keep them hungry so as to force concessions. More generally stated, this applies to any abuse of purchasing power to the detriment of the seller. Although it is legitimately expected of a purchasing manager to make full use of his or her company's purchasing power, this factor should normally operate to mutual benefit, with the buyer's position strengthened by virtue of being a more desirable customer, offering greater volume, steadier flow of orders, more prompt payment, or similar considerations of value to the seller.

ETHICAL PRACTICES STUDY

To better understand the ethical conduct of purchasers on matters previously discussed, Robert L. Janson undertook a study for the Center for Advanced Purchasing Studies (CAPS). Six of the major conclusions follow.

1. *The great majority of purchasing people are ethical.* If we use an informal standard which says that buyers may accept favors of reasonable monetary value such as advertising souvenirs, lunches, tickets, dinners, golf outings, food and liquor, and holiday gifts and still be considered as acting ethically, 94 percent of purchasing people conduct business practices ethically and within generally accepted purchasing standards.
2. *"Buyers" outside the purchasing department are becoming a serious problem,* since these individuals usually are not subject to the stringent ethical policies that guide purchasing personnel. Sixty-two percent report unauthorized buying in their companies, and 47 percent say that specifications are prepared by other departments to favor one vendor over another. Overall, 44 percent of the dollar value of purchase orders issued in manufacturing, health care, and educational institutions were to vendors selected by persons not in purchasing.
3. *Almost all buyers (97 percent) accept some favors from vendors.* However, only two favors are considered by at least 50 percent of buyers as being ethically acceptable: advertising souvenirs by 72 percent and lunches by 68 percent. Thus, there appears to be a substantial gap between what buyers feel is ethically correct and the way they actually behave. The average annual value of favors actually accepted was approximately $132.
4. *The majority of company sales departments (68 percent) give gifts.* This common business practice is evidently the norm rather than the exception.
5. *Most companies have an ethics policy and it is in writing.* Seventy-two percent of the firms had an ethics policy and 58 percent had a written policy.
6. *The ethical practices in smaller firms tend to be more questionable than those in the larger firms.* For example, in the smaller firms reciprocity is more commonly

practiced, as is purchasing for company personnel. Their ethical practices are less likely to be reviewed than the ones in the larger firms.[4]

Overall, such findings indicate, as have past studies, that purchasing people for the most part conduct their business in a very ethical manner. The NAPM in its new ethical code will punish violators by revoking their professional certification (C.P.M.).

SOCIAL RESPONSIVENESS

A much broader area of ethics involves responsibility to society, often termed social responsiveness. Starting in the 1960s and continuing into the 1990s firms have become subject to many social changes. Government legislation (Occupational Health and Safety Act [OSHA]) has dictated safety in the workplace. The Environmental Protection Agency (EPA) required that plant discharges meet new restrictions. Public Law 95-507 required goals for minority purchases. As can be seen in Figure 3-3 the corporation must face many social responsibilities. The better job it does voluntarily, the less the threat that it will be forced to act under government legislation.

Purchasing finds itself actively involved in many of these areas, through purchase of OSHA-approved safety equipment, minority-supplier programs, and proper disposal of hazardous waste and scrap.

One example of the need for purchasing responsiveness is in the area of hazardous and nonhazardous waste disposal. The cost of properly disposing of such waste will increase dramatically in the future. In 1989 rates rose an average of 37 percent, according to a study.[5] Purchasers surveyed felt new alternatives needed to be explored including:

- Increased recycling
- Finding and substituting less hazardous materials in products
- Setting stricter standards for use and disposal of waste
- Having suppliers take more responsibility for disposing of hazardous wastes from the products they supply

Table 3-1 shows 66 percent worked at a facility that produced hazardous waste, and 61 percent had a shortage of legal disposal sites in their area. As a final note, while only 29 percent listed purchasing as the department responsible for waste disposal, this figure was higher than any other single department mentioned.

The purchasing function is thus in a unique position regarding both selection and disposal of potentially hazardous products.

[4]Robert L. Janson, *Purchasing Ethical Practices* (Tempe, Arizona: Center for Advanced Purchasing Studies, 1988).
[5]"The Hazards of Waste Seep Into Purchasing Department," *Purchasing*, October 26, 1989, p. 26.

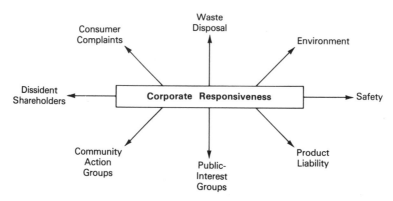

Figure 3-3 Corporate Responsibility

First, the selection process, as always, emphasizes purchasing items from suppliers who meet specification requirements for the purchased product. Often when choosing among products, a safer, less environmentally harmful substance can be selected. And if the product requires something to be purchased that is environmentally hazardous, who better than purchasing to handle its waste disposal safely and effectively?

The destruction of harmful wastes involves contracting with reliable suppliers who take the necessary steps to ensure proper disposal. Purchasers have witnessed the growth of companies in the hazardous-disposal business in the past few years. The reason purchasing is a key player is its ability to select such candidates. Visits to the supplier's facilities, with thorough inspection of disposal techniques, an audit of financial status, and a review of management qualifications, is also necessary. The unanticipated cost of selecting an affordable hazardous-waste-disposal supplier whose methods prove to be unacceptable may be an environmental class-action suit in which you and your company are codefendants.

Table 3-1 The Waste-Disposal Problem

	Percent of Respondents Indicating Yes
Facility produces hazardous waste	66
Shortage of legal disposal sites in area	61
Suppliers recycle, treat, or recover scrap or waste	48
Hazardous waste shipped out of state	39
On-site recycling, treatment, or disposal	36
Purchasing obtains waste-disposal services	29
Difficulty in disposing of hazardous waste	17
Difficulty in disposing of nonhazardous waste	16
Nonhazardous waste shipped out of state	9

Source: "The Hazards of Waste Seep into Purchasing Department," *Purchasing*, October 26, 1989, p. 26.

Careful selection and monitoring of waste-disposal suppliers is a key skill that a purchaser brings to the job. The 1990s will demand that buyers educate themselves about waste disposal. A job that was formerly the province of a beginning MRO buyer has suddenly become a major issue in our society. Purchasers have a big challenge and an even larger opportunity to be socially responsive.

COMBATING UNETHICAL PRACTICES

The subject of business ethics is not one sided. Purchasing managers and buyers are faced from time to time with unethical sales practices, although these are no more representative of selling policy in general than are the occasional instances of unethical buying. There is sharp practice in selling: collusive bidding, restrictive conditions in specifications, artificial stimulation of demand and prejudice among shop operatives, sabotage of competitive products, padding of orders and shipments, use of unfamiliar trade terms and measurements, supposedly sample orders that are magnified into excessive quantities, obscure contract clauses buried in small type, and many others. In most cases these can be avoided by proper selection of vendors but perhaps only after unfortunate experience has indicated the disreputable sources of supply. In dealing with some of the practices, such as collusive bidding, more direct and aggressive action is called for as a corrective measure.

The best defense is competent, objective buying, supported by the necessary follow-through in insistence on contract performance, acceptance testing, and the like. The purchase order or contract in itself constitutes a legally enforceable document. All supplementary agreements, specifications, and special terms should likewise be reduced to writing, using care to see that no ambiguity exists in respect to what is expected of the seller. Reputable sellers respect buyers who are alert, thorough, and conscientious in the conduct of their office, and they respond in kind.

Confidence in a supplier is an essential of any sound purchasing department, but confidence need not be blind. It must be earned and reputable suppliers welcome the opportunity to show that they are worthy of confidence. The purchasing manager is grossly neglectful of his or her own responsibility who unquestioningly accepts the oft-heard advice, "Select a reliable vendor, then trust that vendor to supply the right material and to charge a fair price." The classic admonition, *"Caveat emptor*—Let the buyer beware!" was coined for that individual. No honest buyer apologizes for checking a delivery, making an acceptance test, or analyzing a quotation. These precautions are a test of his or her own judgment and performance as well as of the supplier, and the responsibility cannot be delegated.

POINTS FOR REVIEW

1. Give and defend an opinion as to whether it is ethical for a buyer to accept from a supplier (a) an occasional luncheon, (b) tickets for the theater or for a sporting

event, (c) weekends at the supplying company's hunting lodge or similar facility, and (d) gifts of such items as TV sets and appliances.

2. Discuss the question of whether ethical conduct in purchasing is a matter of morality, good business, or both.

3. Describe top management's role in ensuring ethical conduct in their individual businesses.

4. Discuss the notion that buyers are morally obliged to see that a supplier makes a "fair profit" on a sale.

5. Describe the most widely adopted solution to the problem of compensating suppliers for development and engineering costs incurred in preparing quotations.

6. Define sharp practice as it relates to purchasing and offer hypothetical examples, and describe actual situations involving such practice that you may have observed.

7. Cite examples of how purchasing can favorably impact corporate and social responsiveness.

4

Purchasing Strategy and Policies

Purchasing organizations in the 1990s will be expected to take an ever-increasing role in overall corporate strategy. This evolving role is due to the increasing impact of purchasing on the firm's profits, the acceleration of product development, and the consequent shortening of product life cycles. Getting products quickly from design to market requires that purchasing be involved from the early planning stages. Conversely, a product's salability, availability, and quality is affected by supply-market actions. These actions should be known and should influence overall corporate strategy.

A MODEL OF PURCHASING'S STRATEGIC ROLE

Figure 4-1 provides a model of the role of purchasing in strategy. Many firms develop a *mission statement* or philosophy based on matching the opportunities, constraints, and regulations in the marketplace with their internal capabilities and resources. The mission statement is very broad and may discuss product philosophy or financial parameters. For example, one motor manufacturer's mission statement was this:

> To be the best producer of small and medium motors in our market areas and gain a position of market dominance therein.

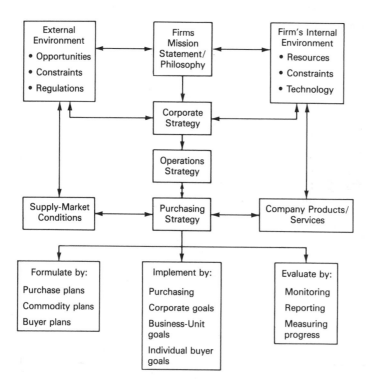

Figure 4-1 A Model of Purchasing's Role in Strategy.

The mission statement is translated into specific *strategic plans,* which are specific to a particular business unit. To illustrate, the same motor manufacturer's strategic plan included introducing a new variable speed motor by first quarter and obtaining a 20 percent market share by the end of the fiscal year. Broad mission statements must be broken down into separate elements.

A useful framework for strategic planning analysis was developed by McKinsey and Company and termed the seven S framework. The seven Ss and a brief description follow.

> Structure—Those attributes of the organization that can be expressed through an organizational chart
>
> Strategy—Actions the organization plans or undertakes in response to or in anticipation of the external environment
>
> Systems—Procedures and processes regularly followed by an organization
>
> Staff—The kinds of specialties or professions represented
>
> Skills—Distinctive attributes and capabilities of the organization and its key people
>
> Style—Patterns of behavior or managerial style of senior managers
>
> Shared values—Spiritual or philosophical principles and concepts that an organization is able to instill into members

Peters and Waterman state that corporate strategists often focus on harder issues of structure, systems, and strategy while overlooking people issues of staff, skills, style, and shared values.[1] Thus planners at corporate level and in the purchasing function need to consider both dimensions when formulating purchasing strategic plans.

Since purchasing supports operations strategy, it is important to tie into and understand operations strategies. Two researchers have classified firms into four stages of manufacturing strategy:

> Stage one: *internally neutral* —Production simply makes product and ships it.
>
> Stage two: *externally neutral* —Manufacturing meets the standards set by competition.
>
> Stage three: *internally supportive* —Manufacturing attempts to become unique from its competition.
>
> Stage four: *externally supportive* —Manufacturing pursues uniqueness of a global scale, becoming a world-class competitor.[2]

Good purchasing strategy will supplement manufacturing strategy in helping a firm achieve cost competiveness.

---

[1]T. J. Peters and R. H. Waterman, Jr., *In Search of Excellence* (New York: Warner Books, 1984), pp. 280–81.

[2]R. H. Hayes and S. C. Wheelwright, *Restoring Our Competitive Edge* (New York: John Wiley & Sons, 1984), pp. 396–403.

PURCHASING STRATEGY

Purchasing's strategic role has lagged behind that of other departments. There are several reasons for this lag: (1) purchasing is seen only as a clerical function; (2) day-to-day operating pressures leave little time for strategic thinking; and (3) management views purchasing as a support function, not a profit contributor.

There are substantial risks to not having the purchasing function included in the strategic-planning process, including:

- Threat to supply assurance
- Improper supplier selection for new products
- Problems with environmental or regulatory constraints
- Improper protection against potential company liability
- Lead time uncertainty
- Price uncertainty

For these reasons and others it is important to include purchasing in the strategic-planning cycle.

Effective strategic planning by purchasing requires that purchasers constantly scan their external supply markets and be aware of corporate plans for new products, product revisions, and deletion of product lines.

Essentially, environmental analysis both internally and externally will lead to the formulation of commodity strategic-action plans.

Environmental Analysis

Environmental analysis consists of searching the environment for signals that may be early warnings of significant change. This is where contacts with key suppliers and reading of market journals in the specific field are useful. The objective is to provide the firm with a larger degree of control over uncertain environmental forces. For example, a long term contract for drills with a major manufacturer may help the wholesale buyer control an uncertain supply variable. Other research has indicated several issues pertaining to environmental analysis that must be studied:

1. Environmental analysis should consider supply, both input side and market output side.[3]
2. Purchasing must determine which trends are relevant to company operations and monitor and evaluate them.
3. Purchasing must develop supply options to fulfill the company's needs.[4]

---

[3] R. E. Spekman, "A Strategic Approval to Procurement Planning," *Journal of Purchasing and Materials Management*, Winter 1981, pp. 2–4.

[4] J. M. Browning, N. B. Zabreskie, and A. B. Huellmartel, "Strategic Purchase Planning," *Journal of Purchasing and Materials Management*, Spring 1983, pp. 21,22.

Key Commodity Planning

From a strategic-planning view there is a need to categorize purchased commodities and services in a way that reflects market realities, such as number or color classifications. In a *number classification,* ones would receive immediate attention; twos not so critical but need monitoring, and so forth. *Color coding* could be done in same manner: red representing critical, and green routine commodities.

One of the authors suggests dividing commodities into two categories based on (1) market stability and (2) internal substitutability.[5] Thus commodities would be classified into a 2x2 matrix, as shown in Figure 4-2. Market stability refers to the degree that one feels supply is uncertain. If supply is ample and the purchaser is buying a standard product, the supply market is stable.

Thus it would be much easier to formulate a hand-to-mouth buying strategy for standard off-the-shelf items with short lead times. Similarly, an unstable market condition may require long-term commitment, to assure availability. Unstable markets also tend to produce larger price fluctuations than stable markets.

The second category is a purchased commodity's internal substitutability. For example, if one is purchasing a special electronic component (CMOS device) on which no substitutions are allowable, the purchaser must assure supply. Combining an unstable market condition with a nonsubstitutable product could lead to serious production stoppages. Purchase products that are in stable supply and can be easily substituted offer maximum flexibility in planning. Cost reductions/substitutions can be freely explored. The buyer has maximum flexibility on these commodities. For nonsubstitutable products in a stable market, the buyer should constantly explore new-product alternatives and negotiate long-term relationships. A sudden change in the stable market condition could push the purchaser into quadrant 3 (critical). Quadrant 3 requires purchasing strategies that assure availability and require constant monitoring. The goal is to move commodities into the quadrant 1 position.

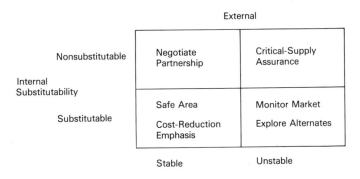

Figure 4-2 Market Substitutability Matrix.

5Ed Bierman, editor, Larry Giunipero, contributing author, The C.P.M. Study Guide, 5th Edition 1988, p. 237.

Strategic-Action Plans

Many alternative strategies are available to the purchasing manager. A climate that encourages creative thinking will help ensure that alternative courses of action are considered. Specific supply strategies include:

1. Realign supplier purchase patterns.
2. Develop new supply sources.
3. Develop international sources.
4. Vertical integration internally.
5. Part ownership of suppliers.
6. Provide supplier assistance, financial or technical.
7. Review product redesign.
8. Develop long-term contracts.
9. Review lease versus purchase.
10. Strengthen inventory control.
11. Encourage supplier stocking.
12. Improve supplier quality control.
13. Stockpiling.
14. Material substitution.
15. Strike hedging.

After strategic-action plans are formulated, steps must be taken to implement them. Implementation involves actions such as developing a new supply source or consolidating the number of suppliers. Finally, an evaluation needs to be made to determine if plans were in fact met. After evaluation, plans typically are modified, revised, or extended, taking into account market conditions and environmental changes.

PURCHASING POLICIES

A corporation's mission statement and strategies lead to its policies. These policies are usually written but may also be unwritten standard operating procedure passed along from employee to employee. They are important in that they influence shared values and the perception employees and outsiders have of the firm. They are also used by auditors who check purchasing's adherence to corporate policies.

Every purchasing department has policies, whether or not they are put into writing. They are one of the administrative tools of departmental management and a reflection of top-management philosophy. The advantages of establishing specific policies and recording them include:

1. An established policy eliminates the necessity for making a new decision every time a comparable situation arises.
2. A written policy assures understanding; it assures that decisions and actions will be consistent and in accordance with the judgment of the responsible department head.

3. An approved policy gives authority to the indicated course of action.
4. An approved policy provides a standard for evaluating performance.
5. An approved policy assists in preparation for audits.

In essence, policies are broad guidelines to management actions. They are different from detailed procedures that guide the individual on how to perform a specific task. A typical purchasing procedure would be processing a purchase order. On the other hand, a typical purchasing policy would be one concerning buying from minority suppliers. Since there is a certain amount of overlap between policies and procedures, some firms title their document Purchasing Policy and Procedures Manual.

Written Policies and Procedures Manuals

It is wise to have policies in writing when they affect activities outside the department, as in the case of interdepartmental relations and vendor relations. A formal statement is desirable for purposes both of record and of communication. The very act of compiling such a manual and committing it to print is a useful project in itself, because it frequently clarifies ambiguities and points of issue; it may also reveal discrepancies or shortcomings in current policy, thus serving to improve departmental standards.

Because departmental policy reflects and is a part of general company policy, the manual must be approved by management authority. To secure that approval, the stated policies must be developed and agreed upon in consultation with those in charge of other phases of company operations who are affected by the rulings. Arrival at this stage of agreement is the most important part of the compilation of a policy statement and is essential to the workability and effectiveness of the policy. These consultations are on the plane of the best interests of the company as a whole, and they involve the whole management philosophy of centralized purchasing.

The scope of the policy manual depends largely on the distribution that is contemplated and the ways it is to be used. Some companies have found it advantageous to supply copies to their entire list of vendors, and it has proved to be a potent means of developing good business relationships and cooperation.

The statements of policy are supported by an explanation of the principles they are based on and of the objectives they are aimed at. In addressing the manual to other departments and to suppliers, it becomes more effective when such reasons are briefly given as a background for the policies stated, which seem less arbitrary when thus presented.

For intradepartmental use, in training work, for indoctrination, and as an administrative guide, this is equally valid. Instructions are better received and better observed when the "why," as well as the "what" and "how," is included. Representative short-form manuals customarily include sections on customer and interdepartmental relationships, ethical considerations, and the like, emphasizing teamwork and cooperation in practical terms. Some of the more extensive manuals contain chapters discussing the principles of proper quality, quantity, price, and value, with applicable criteria, the use of specifications, and the fundamentals of purchase law, contracts, and patent rights.

Of particular importance in any policy manual is a statement from top management that establishes departmental policy as company policy and thus gives the entire code an authority that would otherwise be lacking. While the style of an individual policy manual varies, a brief guideline is as follows:

I. Forward by company president, giving authority to the manual as a statement of company policy
II. A letter by top corporate purchasing officer that describes the objectives of the purchasing function
III. Statement of purpose, which states that policies will be followed on a worldwide basis
IV. Table of contents
V. Information on how to use the manual
VI. Purchasing authority/centralization
VII. Company business practices and standards
VIII. Supplier relations
IX. Purchase orders and contracts
X. Approvals and authorizations
XI. Terms and organizational charts
XII. Glossary of commonly used terms

The remainder of this chapter will discuss some of the more common policies/procedures found in these purchasing manuals.

Centralization of Purchasing

The purchasing function is said to be centralized when the entire function is made the responsibility of one individual.[6] Such a person is then accountable for the performance of the purchasing function. When personnel from other functions (engineering, maintenance, finance) buy, the function is said to be decentralized. The major advantages of centralized purchasing are better control of purchase costs, fair treatment of suppliers, lower administrative expenses, and lower inventories. As previously stated, the purchasing department is given such authority by upper management.

Limits of Authority

While management gives purchasing authority, it also controls expenditures by requiring larger dollar expenditures to be signed by a purchasing manager. For example, at one firm buyers can commit up to $5,000 on a single purchase order; senior buyers, up to $10,000; and the purchasing supervisor, up to $100,000. Any larger amounts must be approved by the purchasing manager, up to an expen-

[6]D. W. Dobler, D. N. Burt, L. Lee Jr., *Purchasing and Materials Management* (New York: McGraw-Hill Book Company, 1990), 5th Edition pp. 32–33.

diture limit of $500,000. Anything over that is forwarded to corporate headquarters.

Company Business Practices

Several policies fall under this category including honesty, conflict of interest, reciprocity, and interdepartmental relations.

Honesty policies essentially state that employees must maintain highest standards of integrity and honesty within the company and with others. Embezzlement or stealing of company funds or property fall into this policy category.

Conflicts-of-interest policies state that individuals should not use their position in a firm for personal gain. Such a conflict occurred when a buyer had a controlling interest in a firm she purchased from. In another case a buyer was placing business with a travel agency owned by his sister. Conflicts or potential conflicts should be declared by the buyer (see Chapter 3).

Reciprocity One of the most troublesome and controversial policy questions purchasing executives have faced is that of reciprocity. The urge to select suppliers on the basis of how much they buy—or may buy—from one's company is both common and understandable. But it generally does not come from purchasing managers, since they buy based on price, quality, and delivery. Most of the effort to promote reciprocal buying comes either from suppliers or from within the buyer's own organization—usually from top management or the sales department.

Under any form of reciprocal buying policy, purchasing becomes less selective, because freedom of choice from among several suppliers is limited. It negates the critical criteria that scientific purchasing calls for in the selection of sources, and it discourages competition among other suppliers, who quickly become aware of its existence. In short, the purchasing manager is stripped of negotiating and buying power.

In recent years, the federal government has taken an increasingly dim view of reciprocity as a business practice. It has charged a number of companies with violating various antitrust provisions of the Sherman and Clayton acts by coercing or attempting to coerce suppliers to purchase their products or products of subsidiaries, under threat of withdrawing their business from suppliers. Various edicts of the Federal Trade Commission have indicated that any pattern of purchases is suspect if it derives from a patronage agreement between companies and not from considerations of quality, price, and service. The FTC attitude has been that reciprocity does not necessarily have to be coercive to be considered in violation of section 5 of the Federal Trade Commission Act; that is, it would be illegal in cases of (1) systematic use by a sales department of purchasing data in communicating with suppliers or (2) a discernible pattern of dealing between supplier and purchaser notwithstanding better price, quality, or service available from competitors.

Internal Relationships

The establishment of a purchasing department is in itself a policy of company management. It immediately entails a whole series of internal, interdepartmental policies relating to lines of authority, channels of procedure, and departmental relationships in general. These policies should be promptly clarified and made a matter of record, for they define the scope and responsibilities of the purchasing function in any particular organization and determine to a considerable extent the effectiveness of the purchasing operation. Neither can they be set by the purchasing manager alone, because they affect the responsibilities and actions of other departments as well. The purchasing manager can suggest and try to persuade, but to have valid force, such decisions must have management approval.

Policies in this category include such matters as the authorizations required on requisitions to purchase, permissions for vendors' sales representatives to contact plant personnel, the final responsibility for specifications, the procedures to be followed in standardization and value analysis recommendations involving engineering changes, and similar points on which conflicts of function and authority may arise. Excerpts from the purchasing manual of a well-known office-products manufacturer provide an example of how purchasing authority and responsibilities, as they relate to other departments, can be defined:

> The methods used by procurement personnel to fill the needs of other company personnel must clearly establish the procurement responsibility to purchase *total value* for the company. This is the basic criterion of all procurement activities. Relations with other company personnel must be established on that premise.
>
> Employees with procurement responsibility shall maintain maximum effort to assure that purchase transactions are processed promptly....[They] are given the prerogative and held accountable to question all purchase requisitions, specifications, and related matters to assure purchase of maximum value for the company.
>
> Procurement personnel shall cooperate fully in assisting other company personnel to obtain information, technical data, samples and visits from suppliers required to permit testing of alternative materials and services.
>
> Data shall be regularly supplied to interested personnel having a need to know regarding production plans, lead times, tooling requirements, shortages, material availabilities, price trends, new-product technical data, supplier engineering and manufacturing capabilities, supplier publications and other information required to maximize effectiveness.
>
> Procurement personnel shall maintain and communicate to those having a need to know pertinent information regarding general economic data, marketplace conditions and other general management information deemed of value. Cultivating close professional association with those involved in the procurement cycle is invaluable. Cooperation is paramount to success and procurement personnel should make every effort to provide desired services required by other company personnel, subject to consideration of obtaining total value in the procurement transaction.[7]

[7]A. B. Dick Company, *Purchasing Manual.*

Supplier Relations

General policy statements about supplier relations are concerned with fair and equitable treatment of suppliers in a professional manner. Supplier relationships today should be characterized by open ethical conduct on the part of both parties to obtain a mutually beneficial relationship. These themes are seen in the policy statement issued by Xerox Corporation (see Figure 4-3). Finally, a statement should state that fair hearing of alternative suppliers currently not supplying will be permitted, provided they might be of value to the company. Other policies typically covered under supplier relations include supplier visits and plant visits, minority buying, and speculative buying.

Supplier Visits   Should the purchasing manager's door be open to every business caller, and is every salesperson entitled to the chance to tell his or her story? Perhaps so, on the first visit; after that it is for the buyer to decide whether the proposal is pertinent and timely from the viewpoint of the company's needs and whether the interview time is warranted. There are three basic methods: (1) see all

---

Balanced Value

Supplier Know-How

Locate, develop and motivate specialty suppliers to make available their technological and commercial know-how to Xerox. Recognize such technical/commercial innovation whenever possible through the placement of Xerox business.
　Communicate new supplier techniques and technologies to potential users within Xerox.

Supplier Service

Obtain a high standard of supplier service in the administration of our potential and actual purchase orders, including rapid communications, short lead times, rapid response time to problems and schedule and engineering changes.

Xerox/Supplier Relations

Create a climate wherein all those who do business or wish to do business with Xerox will respect us for our ethical, fair and considerate treatment of suppliers in addition to our insistence upon our high standards of supplier performance.
　Strict adherence to our corporate ethical conduct policies, including the avoidance of gifts, favors and entertainment, is expected of our suppliers, Xerox Procurement personnel and all Xerox employees. Our buying staff is expected to provide leadership in the field of ethical conduct.
　Conform both to the spirit and letter of existing laws and regulations.

Figure 4-3 Xerox Corporation's statement on supplier relations.

callers, (2) set limitations, and (3) schedule by appointment. Seeing all sellers at their convenience is the most open form for providing others easy access to purchasing. However, it dramatically reduces the efficiency of the purchaser and is typically not done.

An alternative is fixed calling hours. This plan sets aside a block of time (e.g., 2:00 A.M.–4:00 P.M. on Monday and Wednesday) that the buyer can block out for seller interviews. This method improves efficiency but may hinder supplier access owing to out-of-town travel schedules, and the like. Also, depending on order of arrival, salespeople may wait for long periods. Thus appointments seem to be the most popular, since that system maximizes both seller and buyer productivity. Buyers should (except for emergencies) see sellers promptly; their waiting time is valuable also. Some firms designate a certain period to handle most suppliers and general discussions and then make appointments with key suppliers for longer meetings. When possible, out-of-town first-time callers should be met briefly and asked to reschedule within policy.

Finally, to what extent should personal contacts with vendors be cultivated, including visits to vendors' plants? It may be good policy to put visits on a systematic basis and to reciprocate by inviting vendors periodically, individually or as a group, to acquire a personal knowledge of the buyer's plant operations.

Contacts with Suppliers   To be effective, a policy must be clear and definitive, but it need not be arbitrary. Consequently, many policies set up criteria for decisions or methods of handling situations or conditions of action. For example, it is obviously undesirable to grant free access to plant personnel for all vendors' sales personnel, either at their own initiative or at the request of plant managers, for such a policy would negate the principles of centralized purchasing. Yet there are many situations in which such a contract is mutually desirable'and is, in fact, an aid to intelligent procurement. A sensible and commonly accepted policy on this point is to require that such contacts be made through the purchasing department and that in such interviews no commitments are to be made by plant personnel as to preference for products or sources, which might weaken the position of the purchasing department in subsequent negotiations.

Minority Suppliers

Minority purchasing programs, renamed socially and economically disadvantaged supplier programs by some corporations, continue to grow and develop in corporate America. Companies have undertaken minority purchasing programs for a number of reasons, including government legislation, social responsiveness, increased sales, and alternate sources of supply.

Public Law 95-507, passed in 1978, requires that prime contractors who wish to obtain government contracts in excess of $500,000 ($1 million for construction) establish minority sourcing programs. The law mandates that percentage goals for minority involvement be established prior to contract award. It also requires that prospective bidders submit to the relevant federal agency a subcontracting plan incorporating percentage goals and methods to accomplish those goals.

Another law, Public Law 99-661, passed in 1988, requires that the Department of Defense establish a 5 percent minority participation goal in defense procurement. The law also provides for the payment of a premium price to obtain minority business.

Aside from legislation, other reasons for corporate involvement is the social responsibility of being a good community citizen. For while approximately 20 percent of the population is minority, less than 4 percent of all businesses are minority owned. Buying from minorities helps in selling to them. A large oil firm found its center-city service stations increasingly comprised of minority personnel. Buying from the community helped in selling to it.

Firms that have made a commitment to minority purchasing typically have policies on buying from minority suppliers and separate policies on dealing with businesses owned by women. Accounting records of purchases from these two groups are kept separately.

A minority-business policy starts with a definition of a minority supplier as a company in which at least 51 percent of the stock or ownership is held by members of a minority group (socially or economically disadvantaged). Traditional minority-group members are black Americans, Asian Americans, Native Americans, American Eskimos, and Aleuts. A typical policy statement distributed throughout the company by a major manufacturing company reads in part:

> It is the policy of the company to award an optimum portion of its purchase orders and subcontracts to qualified minority business enterprise (MBE) firms consistent with efficient and economic performance of its prime contracts.
>
> In carrying out this policy, purchasing personnel will actively seek new MBE sources for development into qualified suppliers. As practicable, technical and/or management assistance will be furnished to MBE firms not currently qualified to meet our procurement standards, but which have significant potential for doing so.
>
> In no event, however, will any award be made to an MBE firm when doing so would conflict with other contractual provisions, regulations or established company or material policies.

Purchasing executives have been among the most active participants in the minority-business program. The National Minority Supplier Development Council and its various regional affiliates will assist corporate buyers in locating qualified minority suppliers. Also, the National Association of Purchasing Management has adopted a formal policy supporting the concept. NAPM and its local associations have worked closely with a variety of governmental and private-sector agencies created to help minority businesses.

Justifying support for often inexperienced minority companies has been a challenge to purchasing personnel accustomed to selecting suppliers on a purely economic basis. But it is a challenge that has been met successfully by thousands of purchasing departments without harmful effect on basic purchasing policies or relationships and with favorable effect on American society as a whole.

Speculative Buying

The general statement of purchasing objectives limits the purchasing department to procurement for actual or anticipated use. This rules out purchases made primarily for the purpose or in the hope of inventory value appreciation or speculative profits on materials. Such buying—though it may be effected through the purchasing department—is a matter for general management to decide. The outlawing of speculative purchases, however, does not preclude the exercise of purchasing judgment in adjusting the buying and inventory program to economic and market conditions. The purchasing manager may boost purchases in anticipation of rising prices and work closer to actual current requirements when a price decline is in prospect.

Purchase Orders and Contracts

Authorized Requisitions   Purchasers must monitor those signing requisitions to make sure they are rightfully authorized to do so. Most departments have lists stating authorized requisitioners and dollar amounts of requisitioner authority.

　　　This purchase requires authorization, which may be formal or informal. Sometimes it exists only in the form of a manufacturing quota for a given calendar period. The purchasing manager is apprised of this quota and all that it entails in the way of material and supply requirements. Sometimes it is embodied in the bill of materials, either for a standard line of products or for products built to special order. At other times it is expressed in the form of a purchase requisition for required material. For standard materials in common and repetitive use, the purchasing manager usually has some latitude to exercise judgment in purchasing for stock in advance of specific requirements. Decisions are based upon experience, rate of use, sales estimates, and other indicators and are usually in conformance with an established inventory policy. Since the advent of computerized inventory control and materials-requirements planning, however, such decisions are often made jointly by more than one department.

Competitive Bidding

Purchase expenditures over a certain dollar limit, which are not covered by a corporate contract or other agreement, will usually require competitive bidding. In one firm purchase expenditures over $5,000 which have not been quoted for the past twelve months require competitive bids. Those over $2,500 and under $5,000 require annual verbal bids. While the trend to fewer suppliers and long-term contracts dictate less emphasis on competitive bidding, there are still many goods and services purchased under these policies. The aspects of handling competitive bids will vary by firm. These issues typically involve price, bid revision, and late bids.

　　　Should price information be kept confidential? In industrial purchasing, yes. Conversely, the governmental buyer, with a mandatory system of sealed bids and a public bid opening, has no such option. Should vendors be permitted to revise their bids? Only in case of obvious error or in a subsequent negotiating stage if terms, quantities, or specifications are modified so as to warrant a price adjustment. If the stated requirement is changed, should all bidders be given a change to make a new quotation? Not necessarily. If it becomes a new proposal on the buyer's part, a new request for bids may be in order. But if the vendor was selected on merit on the basis of the original proposal, and the terms are altered in negotiation, the buyer will probably stand on the original choice. If the cost-saving changes come at the vendor's suggestion, fair purchasing policy demands that the vendor retain the patronage, with the status of a preferred supplier on succeeding orders. Should unsuccessful bidders be notified? Yes, and with the reasons for the adverse decision, if feasible.

POINTS FOR REVIEW

1. What are some of the reasons the purchasing department needs to be involved in the firm's strategic plan?
2. Select a commodity and discuss environmental factors affecting its supply market.
3. Can you name four purchased items that would fit into each of the quadrants on the market substitutability matrix.
4. Review some of the policy questions to be settled (and the results recorded) before a purchasing department can be assured of operating efficiently.
5. Name at least six aspects of buyer-seller relationships that should be subject to control by policy.
6. Discuss the significance of the minority purchasing program covered in this chapter as it relates to the principles of supplier selection.
7. Differentiate between policy manuals and procedure manuals in purchasing.
8. Comment on the dangers to efficient purchasing inherent in a reciprocal purchasing policy (disregarding the question of the legality or illegality of reciprocity).
9. Discuss the importance of written top-management endorsement of policies and procedures presented in purchasing manuals.

The Basic Purchasing Process

The procurement cycle has several distinct phases: (1) requests for materials, supplies, and equipment from the using departments; (2) selection of suppliers and issuance of purchase orders; (3) follow-up of outstanding orders (expediting); (4) receipt and inspection of materials from suppliers; (5) and in some companies checking of suppliers' invoices. Thus a purchasing department dealing with hundreds of sources for thousands of items has a complex administrative job, in addition to its responsibility for skillful buying. In this chapter we will deal with the basic steps in the purchasing process and the forms, procedures, and systems necessary for proper control of each stage of the process. The advances in computer technology will continue to push purchasers more toward automated systems.

Thus while this chapter contains references to a number of forms and manual procedures, thousands of companies have already computerized their purchasing operations, and many more are planning to do so. It is highly likely that many of the manual methods described herein will be obsolete by the year 2000. However, manual and computerized methods are based on the same basic process and principles. Computers simply speed up the process enormously. Reviewing the essential elements in the procurement cycle will help the reader to understand, better and more quickly, the techniques and benefits of computerized purchasing, which are dealt with in the next chapter.

THE PURCHASING CYCLE

A using department indicates its need for materials on a *requisition*. It uses a *stores requisition* to obtain materials that are in regular use in the plant and carried as normal stock. This requisition goes directly to the stores department, and the requirements are supplied from there. A *purchase requisition* is used for materials that have to be ordered from suppliers. The person who needs the material fills in either type of form with the material name or code identification, the amount needed, and the desired delivery date. Before sending the requisition to either stores or purchasing, the person making the requisition must have it signed by a supervisor authorized to approve the expenditure.

For items of a repetitive nature and for those for which purchases are normally made to replenish stocks, a *traveling requisition* is used. The form is of heavy card stock so that it may be passed back and forth regularly between the requisitioning department, or stores department, and purchasing. A single card is made up for each item, and identification of the item is entered only once—in the heading of the card. But there is space provided for several (up to thirty) requests to purchase. The requisitioner or storeskeeper merely enters the date and the predetermined quantity desired and sends the card to purchasing. When the purchase has been made, it is recorded on the card, which is then returned to stores or the requisitioning department.

In many computerized operations, computer-generated schedules are mailed to the supplier without a purchase requisition being generated. In these cases purchasing will have already negotiated price and terms, usually for one year or longer.

Sometimes purchasing is based directly on a *bill of materials,* which lists every item in a company's end product. When a manufacturing schedule is set by production planning, purchasing is notified and can set up its purchasing schedule or program to correspond with production plans. It receives a copy of the bill of materials, on which are indicated those items that are not on hand or ordered. This tabulation serves the same purpose as a whole series of requisitions. A more automated and sophisticated buying from a bill of materials is done in material-requirements planning (MRP). This system is described in Chapter 17.

ORDERING

The various processes of negotiation and decision making that take place between the time a purchase is authorized and the time the order is issued are covered in Chapters 8 through 14. About the only routine procedure in the process as part of a purchasing system is the invitation to suppliers to bid and the evaluation of bids received. In industry, when such invitations are issued prior to ordering, the form used is generally called a *request for quotation,* and no obligation to buy from the supplier quoting the lowest price is implied. The procedure is employed in one or more of the following situations: (1) The intended purchase would involve relatively high expenditure; (2) not enough price information on the required item is available; (3) the product needed is complex and costly, and the purchasing department has had little or no experience in procuring it; (4) there is intense competition among suppliers of the product or material; or (5) a major contract is up for renewal, and purchasing wants to research the market for competitive prices and service.

In public agencies—governmental and institutional— *invitations to bid* are generally mandatory when a major purchase is planned. Except in unusual cases that require elaborate justification, the business must be awarded to the lowest bidder following public opening of the bids. (Chapter 26)

The *purchase order* is the instrument by which goods are procured to fill a requirement. It expresses in specific language the agreement between the buyer and the vendor. Once accepted, it has the legal force of a binding contract.

The essential information in every purchase order includes name and address of purchasing company, identifying order number, date, name and address of vendor, general instructions (marking of shipments, number of invoices required, and so forth), delivery date required, shipping instructions, description of materials ordered and the quantity, price and discounts, and signature. Terms and conditions are generally printed on the back of the form.

Many companies try to get written acceptance of the order from the vendor. This is sometimes in the form of an extra copy of the order, known as the *acknowledgement copy;* sometimes it is in the form of a detachable stub on the original copy. It is actually more than an acknowledgment; it should constitute legal acceptance of the order. The law of acceptance is discussed in Chapter 14.

Simple purchase order systems usually require at least three copies of the order:

1. The original, sent to the vendor
2. The acknowledgment copy just mentioned
3. A purchasing department file copy

In more elaborate systems, copies may also go to the receiving department, accounting, quality control, and the requisitioner. As more purchasing department operations become computerized, a number of copies of the purchase order may be eliminated. Departments authorized to have access to information on an order can obtain it by means of readouts on the CRT (cathode ray tube) terminals that are part of a computerized system. The computerized system incorporates the same basic steps involved in a manual system.

CLEARING THE ORDER

In some large companies the normal responsibility of the purchasing department ends with the issuing of the purchase order. In such cases the using department or a separate expediting unit follows up for delivery, the inspection department is responsible for acceptance, the stores department takes care of receiving the material, and the accounting department checks invoices and certifies them for payment from its own copy of the order. Usually, however, the purchasing department is involved in all of these duties, on the general principle that procurement responsibility ends only when a satisfactory delivery has been made and materials are actually on hand for use, and when the buyer's obligation to the vendor has likewise been satisfied, completing the contract.

If ordinary expediting methods fail to secure delivery as needed, the buyer who has had contact with the vendor and who made the original agreement is the most effective expediting agent. If materials are not in accordance with specification, the purchasing department must make the adjustment with the vendor. If there are discrepancies in quantity, price, or terms in the vendor's shipment and billing, it is the purchasing department that has the final responsibility for reconciling the matter.

The first step in follow-up is to secure an acceptance-and-delivery promise from the vendor. The vendor's promise is recorded, and provision is made for orderly follow-up without waiting for an emergency to develop if the vendor's promise is not kept.

ROUTINE FOLLOW-UP

Follow-up is selective. A study of prevailing policy shows that less than one third of all companies follow up every order issued for delivery. An additional one third follow up orders classified as "important" or production orders as distinguished from orders for stock. In the other companies, follow-up is restricted to those that are actually and seriously overdue and to special, rush, or emergency orders.

The mechanism for follow-up is a file of open orders arranged in numerical sequence so that those that are longest outstanding are in the front of the file, giving quick visual indication of the oldest ones. This, of course, is not an accurate indicator of the delivery dates requested or promised. Some further coding or signaling device is necessary. (Computerized systems often provide soon-to-be-due and overdue items that are used by expediters for follow-up.)

A common method used in smaller companies is to print a scale of numbers from 1 to 31 across the top of the sheet corresponding to the days of the month. A series of colored tabs, differentiated as to the various calendar months, can then be affixed at the proper point along this scale, on orders for which a positive follow-up schedule is desired. The combination of color and position shows the exact date at which follow-up action is to be taken. The receiving record must be posted against this file daily, and any completed orders must be removed from the file.

Routine follow-up according to such a schedule can ordinarily be effected by simple routine methods. A printed postcard requesting specific delivery information, with reference to date of order and vendor's promise, is the usual first step. A return postcard has been found useful in facilitating the vendor's reply. A somewhat more comprehensive form is sometimes used with provision for asking information on a variety of different points, according to the particular situation.

As the need for expediting becomes more acute, the tone and method of follow-up become stronger and more personalized, the usual sequence being personal letter, telegram, telephone call, and personal interview by expediter or buyer at the vendor's plant. The particular action and the amount of pressure brought to bear are adjusted to the circumstances.

FIELD EXPEDITING

In contrast to such routine expediting is the practice of maintaining a staff of expediters in the field, who keep contact with suppliers on important orders. Such expediters are usually made responsible for all orders placed with suppliers in a given territory; oftentimes they operate from the company's branch offices in these territories, but they report directly to the general purchasing office. Sometimes this function is combined with inspection of materials at the vendor's plant.

The field expediter makes regular progress reports to the purchasing department during the life of the order or contract, and his or her reports, checked with the schedule of requirements, show at all times the prospect of satisfactory fulfillment of delivery dates or indicate in advance the likelihood and extent of any delay that may be encountered.

Buying for heavy construction or negotiating contracts involving long lead times and complex requirements lends itself to field expediting. The expediter must have initiative and native ability to relate to both line and staff personnel in the company and in its suppliers' organizations. In addition, field expediters must also be able to relate to top-level management in supplier companies.

CHANGE ORDERS

It sometimes becomes necessary to make changes in the original order—changes in quantity, scheduling, or specifications; changes authorizing some alternative product; or any other of the scores of possible corrections that may arise with changing design and changing conditions of business. Many companies accomplish changes by correspondence. Others make use of a form known as the *change order,* or *change notice.* It is generally similar to the purchase order in form and is given the same number as the order it revises. In some cases it merely states, "Please change our original order of the above number to read as follows" and lists the requirements as revised. In other cases the body of the form is divided into two parts, the first restating the order as originally issued and the second giving the desired revision.

RECEIVING

The receiving department is usually an adjunct of the stores department, which may or may not be a part of the purchasing department. Its functions are to receive incoming goods, signing the delivery notice presented by the carrier or the supplier in connection with the shipment; to identify and record all incoming materials; to report their receipt to the purchasing department and to the stores, using, or inspection departments as required; and to make prompt disposition of the goods to the appropriate department. Each should be informed of receipt of damaged goods.

To aid in identification of the materials received, the receiving department is advised of all expected shipments by means of a copy of the purchase order.

All incoming materials are reconciled with the receiving department's copy of the purchase order. A record is kept of every delivery, and receiving reports containing this information go to the purchasing and stock-records departments promptly.

INSPECTION FOR QUALITY

Not all materials require formal inspection for quality; in a large proportion of deliveries on a normal procurement program, simple visual inspection meets every practical need. Secondly, many firms today precertify their suppliers' quality. Shipments of material from suppliers who are *certified* bypass incoming inspection and are sent directly to the storeroom or into production.

Where a more detailed examination of quality is required, materials are segregated by the receiving department pending inspection and are not permitted to be placed in stores or go into production until the proper inspection is made. The receiving department notifies the department responsible for inspection that the shipment has arrived and takes whatever samples may be necessary or otherwise makes the material available for inspection. The notification may be accomplished by means of a copy of the receiving slip or by routing the receiving department's copy of the purchase order through the inspecting department on its way back to purchasing. In the latter case the inspection report may be made on the same copy as the receiving report; otherwise, a separate inspection report is required, certifying that the materials are satisfactory or, if not, giving the reason for rejection.

When these two reports are received by purchasing, showing (1) a receipt of materials, including a check on the quantity received, and (2) a certification of quality, they are compared with the purchasing department copy of the order to see that they conform with what was ordered and are attached to it as evidence of proper delivery.

CHECKING THE INVOICE

Meanwhile, an invoice for the shipment is, or should be, received from the vendor, and this, too, must be reconciled both with the original order and with the records of receipt. It is important that the invoice be received and processed promptly, so that the order may be cleared and payment made within the discount period, or so that necessary adjustments may be initiated without delay in case there is any discrepancy. It is customary to ask that invoices be sent in duplicate, one copy to be routed directly to the accounting department and one to the purchasing department. This system allows simultaneous processing from both of these viewpoints in the buyer's company, to be correlated later in the accounting or accounts payable division.

A basic but very graphic illustration of a typical purchasing procedure is shown in the flowchart in Figure 5-1. The company in which it was developed had approximately fifteen requisitioning departments originally, each doing its own buying, inventory control, and stocking. Because their efforts were not coordinated, there were many problems: too many high-cost, low-value transactions, duplication of effort, unnecessary and time-consuming paperwork, lost shipments, and little opportunity to get the benefits of volume buying and professional purchasing. Following the establishment of the coordinated system with eight points of control, the problems were virtually eliminated.

SIMPLIFIED METHODS

The procurement cycle obviously involves a great deal of paperwork and clerical detail. It just as obviously lends itself to simplification and "mechanization" in a number of areas. In those cases when the cost of requisitioning, ordering, receiv-

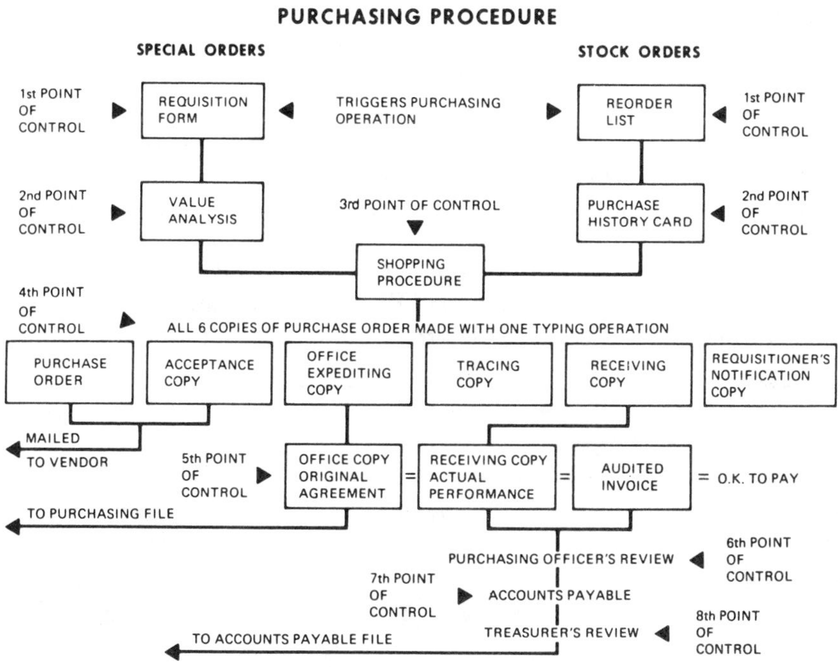

PURCHASING PROCEDURE

Figure 5-1 Flowchart of purchasing procedure at a large metropolitan newspaper shows basic movement of statement of requirements to the purchasing department and then to suppliers.

ing, and accounting for an item, for example, is greater than its value, use of complicated systems to procure it is foolish. This dilemma, known as the small-order problem, is faced by most purchasing departments. Considering the cost of placing a formal purchase order runs anywhere from about $35 to over $75 (depending on the size and type of the company doing the buying and the nature of the material bought), the big advantage to simplified systems is the reduction of administrative cost rather than lower price. As a result, many purchasing departments have set up simplified systems for handling this sort of buying without losing control of it.

The Single Form

One plan is a "small-order" system for the purchase of miscellaneous supplies of low dollar value—usually less than $100. A *single simplified form* is used. A typical small-order form will include requisition, purchase order, receiving report, and accounting copy. Most of the items are picked up by a purchasing department representative from local sources. In some systems the pickup person pays cash; in others, selected vendors are permitted to bill monthly for all purchases picked up during the period. One company has simplified its small-order procedure to the point that it includes a check drawn on a special revolving fund as a detachable stub on the order form. This system eliminates invoices altogether.

Purchase-Order Draft

This simplified approach to small orders is being carried to its logical conclusion and applied to a wider range of transactions by a number of companies. Perhaps the most outstanding development of this kind in recent years is the *purchase-order-draft system* instituted by Kaiser Aluminum & Chemical Corporation that is now widely used in industrial, commercial, and institutional purchasing departments (see Figure 5-2).

Under the system the supplier receives a blank check as part of the purchase order—a detachable portion of the form that is an envelope in addition to being a check. After shipping the order, the vendor puts one copy of the invoice

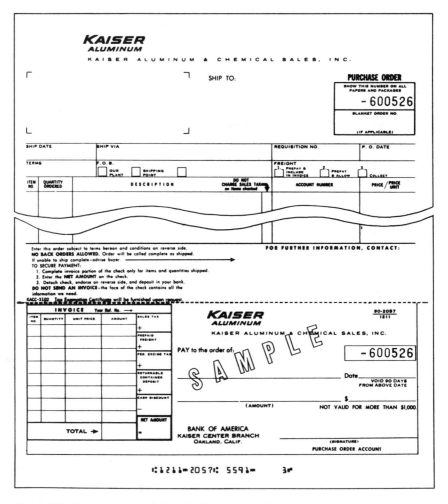

Figure 5-2 Purchase-order draft with blank check attached, used by Kaiser Aluminum Corporation. Courtesy of *Purchasing Magazine.*

inside the check envelope, enters the net amount on the face, endorses it on the reverse side, and deposits it in the bank as an immediate cash payment. The check envelope comes back to Kaiser just as ordinary checks do.

The Kaiser plan was originally intended to cover orders up to $200 in value. But investigation showed that it could be extended to orders up to $1,000. Later, the limit was raised to $2,000; the plan now covers 92 percent of the checks that the company issues for purchased materials. Success of the system has eliminated an enormous amount of filing, retrieving, posting, check writing, stuffing, mailing, typing, and handwriting. Another advantage the buyer receives is lower prices, since the supplier receives cash payment immediately upon receipt of the purchase-order draft.

Telephone Ordering System

Another paper-saving order system in use by a number of companies does away with the purchase order and vendor invoices. This method for handling small orders is commonly called a *telephone ordering system.* Requisitioners indicate the type of material and quantity needed by simply filling in a multiple-copy snapout form that serves all purposes in the order cycle. The requisitioner, in a typical case, removes one copy of the form for his or her records. The rest go to the purchasing department for checking. A buyer selects and calls a vendor, discusses prices and other terms, and places the order orally. No forms are sent to the supplier. The buyer keeps one part of the form as a worksheet and order record and send three copies to the receiving department and one to finance. As soon as accounts payable receives a copy of the packing slip indicating that the material has been delivered, it issues a check to the supplier. The system is used on standard shelf items for which the total purchase cost is $2,000 or less. Price changes, partial or late deliveries, or substitutions of any kind are not permitted.

A significant aspect of the two systems described here is the assumption that both parties to the transaction are trustworthy and reliable and that both are interested in long-term association with each other. This is further evidence of the maturity of purchasing as an industrial function and refutation of the occasionally heard charge that the buyer-seller relationship is necessarily a dog-eat-dog affair. In the blank-check system, the buyer puts full confidence in the supplier; in the telephone ordering system there is mutual trust, because the purchasing department knows the quality of material it is getting, and the vendor knows that he or she will get paid.

Additional Techniques

Numerous other approaches have been used successfully in handling nonrecurring purchases efficiently and with a minimum of paperwork. They are also used on purchases of parts and materials in regular use for which prices and suppliers are established only once a year.

Among the other successful small-order techniques in use in industry are

- Electronic data interchange: This paperless transfer of information from terminal to terminal is discussed in detail in the next chapter.
- Petty cash system: A designated individual visits local suppliers daily, picks up requirements submitted to purchasing the day before, and pays for them with either cash or check.
- Cash on delivery (COD) orders: Buyers call in orders to local suppliers. Upon delivery, the supplier is paid from the petty cash fund by the traffic manager or receiving clerk.
- Supplier stores system: The supplier maintains a stock of commonly used parts in the purchaser's storeroom. Records are kept on issues, and the supplier is paid periodically. The supplier also replenishes inventory levels as required.

Within all simplified systems there are many variations. For our purposes it is sufficient to point out that all of them have the great advantage of eliminating many forms and a great deal of paperwork that in itself can cost more than the material being purchased.

BUYING AGREEMENTS

One of the most effective purchasing devices for cutting both material and administrative costs is the type of buying agreement variously known as the blanket order, open-end order, or yearly order. Essentially, it is an expression of the buyer's intention to purchase all or part of the company's requirements of repetitive items from one supplier during a given period. The requirements may be for a certain class of items (the term *blanket order* is generally used when maintenance, repair, and operating [MRO] supplies are bought this way) or for a specific material or part. Terms are negotiated, and an order is issued for a definite period, usually a year. As the operating departments need materials, they issue simple releases against the order, either through purchasing or directly to the supplier. In the latter case purchasing is kept informed of what releases are issued.

Electronic data interchange (EDI) is used by a number of companies in this type of ordering. In a General Electric system, for example, more than two dozen plants throughout the country can order plant supplies directly from one distributor with whom a master agreement has been made. Buyers dial the supplier's computer direct, and all pertinent information is transmitted from the buyer's computer terminal to the supplier's.

The types of orders discussed above generally carry no guarantee that the buyer will purchase a given amount of material during the term of the contract. It simply designates one company as the supplier for a class of purchased items, for example, plant supplies or office supplies. The order is usually revocable at the will of the buyer, although in practice this rarely occurs. Blanket orders are negotiated only after careful consideration and only when there is some assurance that they will be maintained until the end of the agreement.

Some orders, however, notably those of the *open-end type* used in the automobile industry, authorize the supplier to produce a certain number of items at various times during the life of the contract (for example, ten thousand crankshafts in the first two months, fifteen thousand the second month, and so on). Such instructions then obligate the buyer to pay for the items produced in the specified time, whether or not the buyer is able to use them.

   Vendor stocking agreements, in which the supplier agrees to maintain an inventory of an item, or a family of items and make regular shipments to the customer at specified times, are now widely used. Typical conditions of such orders are described in Figure 5-3. In some cases arrangements are made whereby the

---

MASTER PURCHASE AGREEMENT

This document is a Master Purchase Agreement covering the purchase by BUYER of the SELLER's products set forth in Exhibit A hereof. Except as modified herein SELLER's standard terms and conditions of purchase, as set forth in Exhibit B, shall apply to any orders released against this Agreement.

Ordering and Delivery: SELLER agrees to a daily delivery Monday through Friday to centralized receiving at time convenient to SELLER, with further agreement of delivery to various departments, should the BUYER's decision result in de-centralized delivery at a later date, the number and location of deliveries to be decided by mutual agreement.

Emergency Deliveries: As described in SELLER's operations manual, emergency delivery can be made. In the event of abuse and where the SELLER considers warranted, a charge of $_____ may be made for each delivery.

Stocking: SELLER will stock all items identified in Exhibit A with the guarantee to BUYER that there will be no stock-outs beyond the SELLER's control. Out-of-stock items will be provided with minimum delays; however, under these circumstances the BUYER is free to use other sources of supply to secure out-of-stock items. Delivery of items in Exhibit A are to be completed within 24 hours of order pickup.

Inventory Reduction: SELLER agrees to assist the BUYER in all areas of inventory reductions on all items supplied by SELLER. SELLER further agrees to make available to the BUYER, technical personnel as required to assist in any or all areas of technical service and technical information as required by BUYER's end users.

Price: Prices shown in Exhibit A will remain firm for ___ months. In the event of a general increase in the net cost of one or more items or product lines of the SELLER, the SELLER may increase prices by written notice and acceptance by the BUYER. The SELLER agrees that the BUYER may at any time audit records of the SELLER to determine if increases reflect a true cost to the SELLER. Price increases will become effective the first of the month following notice of increase by SELLER and acceptance by BUYER.

Term of Agreement: The term of this Agreement commences ___(Date)___ and shall end ___(Date)___ .

Other Terms and Conditions:

   • Order Form
   • Packing Instructions
   • Discrepancies
   • Terms and Method of Payment
   • Termination and Signatures

Figure 5-3 Standard terms of a master agreement by which the vendor agrees to carry inventory for the buyer and deliver specified amounts of the purchased product or material at certain regular intervals.

supplier stores and issues materials right in the customer's plant. The supplier owns the material until it is issued and bills the customer monthly.

SYSTEMS CONTRACTING

A more advanced form of blanket or "stockless" purchasing devised by the Carborundum Corporation is known as systems contracting. The company's headquarters buying staff draws up contracts or purchase agreements with suppliers

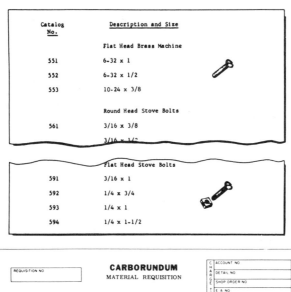

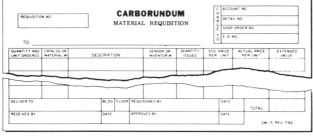

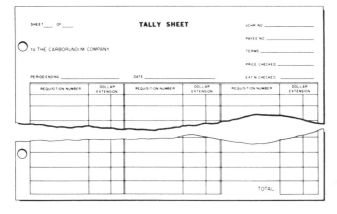

Figure 5-4 Systems contracting procedure includes a catalog (top) of all items bought under the contract, material requisitions that serve as releases and are sent directly by using departments to the supplier, and a tally sheet sent to the buying company's accounts payable department in place of an invoice. Courtesy *Purchasing Magazine.*

covering large groups of materials or supplies generally bought from distributors. These would include office supplies, bearings, steel, mill supplies, and tools. Part of every contract is a detailed catalog of the items covered (see Figure 5-4). Suppliers are required to stock sufficient quantities of all items in the catalog.

Requisitioners in the company's plants are allowed to requisition items directly against the contracts. Material requisitions go directly to the supplier holding a contract rather than to the purchasing department. No invoices are required from the supplier, who simply mails a tally sheet (see Figure 5-4) to Carborundum's accounts payable department every ten days.

The blanket order and similar plans do a great deal more than eliminate much of the paperwork involved in requisitioning, buying, and invoicing. They enable the purchaser to get more favorable discount items on the basis of the increased volume that the company is able to offer the supplier. And the buyer can get this discount without incurring the heavy carrying charges that would be levied if the whole order were brought into the plant at one time. By having material shipped in as needed, the buyer transfers some of the carrying cost to the vendor. This is not so burdensome or inequitable as it seems at first, however. The vendor, with some knowledge of what the customer will need over a given period, is in a better position to plan its own stocks or production and to eliminate the peaks and valleys in supply that often occur otherwise.

Suppliers report periodically to purchasing on what items were ordered and in what quantity. This provides the buyer with an overview of activity that will help in planning future purchasing strategies.

POINTS FOR REVIEW

1. Trace the steps in a typical purchasing cycle.
2. Name the basic forms used throughout the manual purchasing system.
3. Distinguish between routine follow-up of orders and field expediting.
4. Explain the purchase-order-draft system and its advantages for the buyer.
5. Discuss the small-order problem in terms of purchasing efficiency and identify three small-order techniques that have been used successfully in many types of purchasing departments.
6. Describe the advantages of systems contract buying agreements.

6

Information Technology in Purchasing

The automated office has become as much a reality as the automated plant. Applied to purchasing operations, automatic equipment—specifically the computer—has helped to reduce paper-handling costs and free buyers from routine clerical work. The computer has also given the purchasing executive a continuing source of significant operating data not previously available without an enormous amount of hand calculation. The statistical information that the computer produces helps the purchasing manager in long-range planning, inventory control, evaluation of purchasing performance, evaluation of vendor performance, and reporting to management.

No machine can replace personal judgment and decision in purchasing. But the computer is a potent tool for eliminating drudgery and for improving performance in purchasing. The statistical data it provides give added authority to the purchasing manager's decision as to what and how much to buy, and it reduces the possibility of error in reference and calculation.

The computer is in effect a huge file, a superfast calculating machine, and a printer rolled into one. It stores basic data in its memory and translates the data for procurement action. A typical computer used in purchasing operations by an eastern office products manufacturer can compute economic purchase-order quantities, vendor discount, and lead-time information; produce requisitions; write hundreds of purchase orders an hour, if necessary; initiate follow-up orders; audit supplier invoices; prepare payment vouchers and checks. In addition, it turns out a wide variety of operating reports significant to purchasing and other departments as well as to corporate management, such as the status of open orders, commitments, and amount of expenditures. An idea of the amount and type of management information available from a computerized purchasing system can be virtually endless. MIS is a comprehensive computerized data-processing network that encompasses a wide range of individual computer applications that have been in existence for a number of years—for example, payroll, accounts receivable, general ledger, purchasing, inventory control, sales analysis, order processing, production scheduling, plant maintenance, and accounts payable.

There are three basic computer systems for gathering, interpreting, and transmitting information. In the *batch* system, information is collected in various departments during the day in the form of punched cards or tapes and keypunched in a batch into the computer at the end of the business day. An *on-line* system permits any department using a CRT (cathode ray tube) terminal with keyboard to get information on the data previously entered. The information might be as current as reports a few hours old. In a *real-time* system, which also employs the CRT, the information is entered on line, but the data are updated simultaneously so that they are immediately available for display on the CRT of the interested department.

ON-LINE SYSTEM FOR PURCHASING

Computerization of purchasing operations started slowly in the 1960s and 1970s. By the 1980s, however, it was advancing rapidly, even in smaller companies. The advance was in large part driven by the ever-lowering prices for powerful computer equipment. "In 1987 IBM introduced its Personal Systems/2 series, including PS/2 Model 80. The Model 80 had the raw processing speed of a 1975 Model 370/168 (mainframe), which costs $3.5 million."[1] Historically, the computer and the buyer were brought into close contact through the use of two well-established concepts: (1) the CRT (cathode ray tube) terminal, consisting of an integrated typewriter keyboard and a video display unit linked to a computer, and (2) a computerized database. The 1990s will see an accelerated trend toward personal computer (PC based) purchasing systems.

Database Management

Accepting the IBM Corporation's definition of a database as a "collection of data fundamental to an enterprise," a purchasing department could be considered an enterprise in an on-line system. Its database could include such information as buyer names and assignments, vendor names and addresses, descriptive data on repetitively ordered items, and a listing of open purchase orders with current shipping dates. The database retains essential information in the computer and makes it available almost instantly, as already mentioned. The authorized person requiring the information simply enters a required sequence of digits and words on the keyboard, and the requested information is displayed on the screen in a matter of seconds in most cases.

This is in contrast to the situation in which information is stored on paper in conventional files or on tape or disks in off-line computer files. The batch system is characterized by extensive manual effort, heavy paper flow, and lengthy waits for information. A vendor's promised shipment date or a notice of received material might take a week to move through key punching and conversion to tape or disk storage to eventual appearance on a batch-produced report. However, batch processing is still suitable where the volume or frequency of information does not justify installation of a costly, sophisticated system.

External Databases

External databases provide a variety of information that purchasing can use to gain timely information about suppliers and competitors. For example, Polaroid Corporation found in one case that a piece of information that had cost less than $100 resulted in a savings of over $40,000 in material costs.[2]

The firm also found that less than 10 percent of total research time was spent in front of a computer, because the preparation analysis and synthesis of data was far less time consuming when done on line. Databases can access almost any information the purchaser needs. For example, PTS-PROMPT (Predicast Terminal System-Predicast Overview of Markets and Technology) is one of over three hundred databases in the DIALOG (database supplier) system. PTS-PROMPT abstracts significant information appearing in thousands of newspapers, business magazines, government reports, trade journals, bank letters, and

[1]Handley, Cathy, *Pulling the Mainframe Plug, Purchasing,* May 26, 1988, p. 56.
[2]Martin L. Helsmoortel and Warren Norquist, *Purchasing Management,* January 8, 1990, p. 30.

special reports worldwide.[3] Such database information will become ever important to purchasing decision makers in the future.

ROLE OF COMPUTERIZATION

In its planning to computerize the purchasing function, one midwestern company identified the problems that it had hoped to overcome with a new real-time system:

Current purchase-order information was not easily accessible; the process of getting answers to inquiries was time consuming and inefficient; filing operations were often redundant and inconsistent; there was unnecessary duplication in transcription and posting, and errors were frequent; buying personnel were spending so much time on paperwork and clearing up delays in transmission of information that they neglected the most important aspects of their jobs, such as negotiation and planning; management information was difficult and costly to obtain.

The capabilities the company built into the system were as follows: It generated purchase orders, releases against standing orders or contracts, and changes on purchase orders. Up-to-date order information could be both recorded and retrieved when needed. This included order acknowledgements from vendors, deliveries, changes, cancellations, and data on limited inspection and payment information. It permitted identification of received materials by part number, purchase-order number, and supplier. Follow-up and exception reporting of selected purchase-order processes was made automatic. There was a reduction in duplication of effort in the transcription, handling, and resolution of discrepancies that appeared when dissimilar data were used in two or more departments. Handling and filing of the receiving department copies of purchase orders was eliminated. Mistakes or discrepancies in quantities of purchased materials were reduced.

Following the installation of its procurement system, the company was able to report the following operational benefits: Improved accuracy of information permitted faster decision making; duplication of purchase order files, which had been maintained in several places, was eliminated; problems in reconciling documents were reduced; accounts payable information was automatically transmitted; the clerical work load was reduced; paperwork delays were ended and the procurement cycle was shortened; delivered materials were positively identified at time of receipt; potential inventory level reductions were recognized; and commitment reporting was greatly simplified.

The company has repeatedly emphasized two significant points about the new computerized system: First, every action that takes place once the purchase order has been generated is available at all terminals (in this case, purchasing, receiving, receiving inspection, production control, and accounts payable) for reference. Second, information generated and maintained by those departments is immediately available and accessible to them.

[3]Ibid., p. 31.

HOW THE SYSTEM FUNCTIONS

Following, in broad outline, is a description of how the company's computerized system functions.

The specific areas of the procurement cycle involved are the requisition process, the purchase-order- (or release) generation process, the receiving process, the accounts payable process, and portions of the operations report-and-analysis processes. The same information or data involved in the normal procurement cycle, which was discussed in the previous chapter, is the core of the automated system. It has, however, been organized into a formal structure of fields, data sets, programs, processes, and systems. All the information is kept in one place and is available to the various areas that may need it. All the interrelationships that exist in the purchasing cycle have been incorporated into the procurement system data sets; thus data entered by one department affect what happens in other departments. Consequently, no department can work totally independently of another without decreasing the efficiency of the whole system.

The purchasing cycle begins with requisitions for purchased materials and services based on requirements, planning and inventory replenishment, unplanned production manufacturing needs, demand for nonstocked items, capital items, expense items, specialized service requirements, and other types of needs that might arise.

A buyer in the purchasing department checks the requisition, selects a vendor, completes the requisition with the necessary information, and enters all the data including scheduled delivery time in the system. As the purchase order, or purchase-order release or change, is generated, the data are being recorded on the procurement data sets, identified, and cross-referenced. Once all the appropriate information has been entered and verified, the purchase order (or variation) is automatically produced on a printer in the purchasing department.

As soon as the order has been produced, any authorized individual is able to inquire about the status of an order and have the information displayed on the appropriate CRT terminal in one of the departments just mentioned.

Three copies of purchase-order documents are produced: one for the supplier, one for the originator, and one as a permanent record. Meanwhile, scheduled delivery information is recorded for later retrieval.

When a vendor's shipment arrives in the receiving department, it can be identified immediately, either by checking the purchase-order number on the packing slip or retrieving the part number or the vendor's name and address through the terminal (see Figure 6-1). When receiving records receipt of the material, the open purchase-order data are automatically updated. The material is then moved to the inspection department for processing. Disposition of the material (accepted, rejected, partially accepted, and so on) is recorded, and again order records are immediately updated. From inspection the accepted material is moved to inventory.

All information entered is then available to all terminals, including that of the accounts payable department. Accounts payable receives invoices and, upon

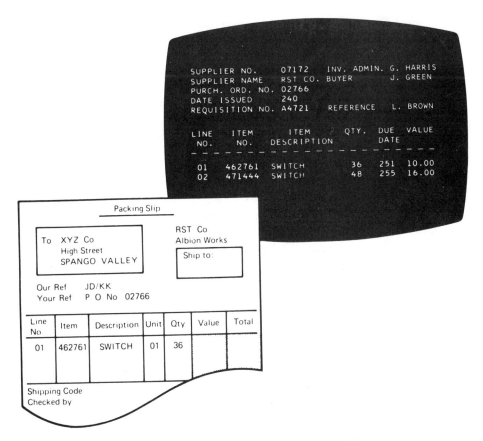

Figure 6-1 Purchase-order details displayed on terminal in the receiving department for verification against packing slip. Courtesy, International Business Machines Corp.

verification, enters a voucher number, the invoice number and date, and any other pertinent information. Payment of invoices is also recorded, thereby indicating completion of the procurement cycle for that order.

PURCHASING USES ITS OWN SOFTWARE

For a time, most of the software available for a fully computerized purchasing system was designed to handle a combination of accounts payable and purchasing—with little emphasis on the latter. That was not satisfactory for one purchasing manager, who felt that such software was geared to paperwork flow instead of to decision making. His solution was a stand-alone system 80 percent designed and programmed in-house, in conjunction with the information systems manager.

The system, which is tied to a mainframe computer, produces four major outputs for decision makers: an automatic requisition, a price-watch report, a commodity-family-analysis report, and complete order-tracking data. In addition, it provides a dozen or so other files and reports on expediting, deliveries, lead times, quality, and administrative activity.

The *automatic purchase requisition* is at the core of the system. The print-out lists part number, description, date that material requirements planning (MRP) generated the requisition, current and historical price data, open and closed purchase-order history, supplier delivery performance history, shipping details, and lead-time data. The requisition helps buyers make decisions by spotting in advance such problems as potential price variances, possible expediting difficulties, and delays in meeting requirements.

The *daily price-watch report* (by buyer) lists items, vendors, purchase-order costs, standard costs, average costs over the past twelve months, and variances. The report helps buyers, supervisors, and the purchasing manager keep score on individual and departmental performance, particularly on cost reductions.

The *commodity family analysis* helps buyers identify negotiation targets. The printout lists each part number and description in a given product category—transistors, for example; the economic order quantity; standard and average cost; forecast quantity and the extended dollar value; last year's quantity and dollar value; and the contract date, where appropriate. This helps buyers to identify high-payoff items where their negotiation skills could be put to good use.

Open order reports, in four versions, are available on terminals to buyers, expediters, and MRP and shop personnel. Only the buyer's copy, however, carries price information. Other users can call up data on any part in the file by part number, by supplier, by buyer, or by purchase-order number. Instead of tracing individual parts as before, expediters, for example, can now see all open orders with one supplier.

The system produces other significant outputs:

- The *dollar-by-supplier report* compares dollars spent with suppliers in various time periods.
- The *expedite priority report* shows expedites by supplier and quantities past due as well as requirements for the next weeks.
- The *estimated time of arrival (ETA) versus required date report* identifies parts on which a supplier-promised date is significantly different from the needed date.
- *CRTs on receiving docks* make receiving, inspection, and storeroom information accessible to all using departments on a real-time basis.
- *Early ship/overship warnings* are available at time of receipt of material.
- The *delivery performance report* shows percentage of late open items by buyer and supplier.
- *MRP performance* can be measured by the profile of lead time allowed by the MRP system.
- *Quality reports* include data on performance by supplier, buyer, and commodity family.
- *Administrative reports* cover dollar commitments by major departments, buyer work load, time taken for requisitions to clear purchasing, identification of unplaced requisitions, and a planned receipts report that aids in cash planning.

Benefits from the computerized system have been numerous. Requisition handling from MRP date to purchase-order date has gone from an average of twenty days to eight days. Expediters can handle more than twice the number of expedites that they handled under the old system. Fifteen percent fewer purchase orders require typing, and typing productivity has doubled from twelve purchase orders an hour to twenty-four through the use of the CRT. Buyers are spending less time as order placers and more time as negotiators and value analysts.

Networked Systems

Buyers operating in multilocation corporations need to be able to see what other locations are doing with a particular commodity. Parker Hanafin Corp. provides their buying locations with this information. Using the company's code system for commodities and suppliers, a buyer is able to access information quickly on the company's 75,000 suppliers. For example, a buyer is able to access supplier ratings by specific commodity groups (see Figure 6-2). Another screen lists all commodities a particular supplier sells. Information is provided by divisions on quality, service and price. Plans call for a completely automated supplier payment process

PURCHASING EXCHANGE INFORMATION
GROUP 01
DIVISION 24 QUICK COUPLING

SEQ	VENDOR CODE	NAME	COMMODITY NAME	PRICE RANK	QUAL RANK	SERV RANK	$ (IN 000)
1	085005170	VENDOR A	0410 ALUMINUM BAR STOCK	3	2	2	
2	034606400	VENDOR B	1410 BRASS AND COPPER BAR STOCK	2	2	1	
3	036940000	VENDOR C	1410 BRASS AND COPPER BAR STOCK	2	2	2	

INQUIRY BY COMMODITY AND VENDOR
- - - COMMODITY - - -
1410 BRASS AND COPPER BAR STOCK

VENDOR	DIVISION	QUALITY	SERVICE	PRICE	$ (IN 000)
VENDOR A	26 INST. CONN.	1	3	2	
VENDOR B	26 INST. CONN.	3	2	2	
VENDOR C	25 PARFLEX	2	3	3	
VENDOR D	24 QUICK COUPLING	2	1	2	
VENDOR E	43 PLEWS	2	3	2	
VENDOR F	24 QUICK COUPLING	2	2	2	
VENDOR G	45 JE CONTROLS	1	1	1	

INQUIRY BY VENDOR AND COMMODITY

COMMODITY	DIVISION	QUALITY	SERV	PR
BRASS AND COPPER BAR STOCK	QUICK COUPLING	2	2	2
	INSTRUMENT CONN	1	2	2
	INSTRUMENT VALVE	2	2	2
	PARFLEX	3	3	3
BRASS AND COPPER FORGINGS	J.E. CONTROLS	1	1	1

Figure 6-2 Networked Purchasing Information Printout
Source: *Purchasing*, Nov. 9, 1989, p. 51.

under a fully integrated manufacturing system that ties purchasing functions into the entire company information system.[4]

Alcoa's network system is called RAPS (RAMIS Access Procurement Program). In this system each plant has its own mainframe but is also able to obtain overall company information.[5] Thus a buyer can obtain data from two important sources to be used in making a cost-effective purchase.

PERSONAL COMPUTERS

As mentioned earlier, personal computers, or microcomputers, have become common in everyday business applications. The purchasing department's use of these tools continues to grow. This growth is being driven by lower prices of hardware (machine) and software (instructional packages), the increasing power and storage capabilities of PCs, and the user friendliness. The term user friendly implies that the person operating the PC doesn't have to be a technical expert. Rather, programs are written in laypersons' terminology for ease of operation and training.

Today's PC-based systems offer users several capabilities including:

- Word processing
- Database management
- Spread-sheet analysis
- External communication
  - External databases
  - Mail systems

Lowering costs of hardware make the PC available to every company. Thus all sizes of businesses can utilize the PC. Table 6-1 lists several of more commonly used terms in PC systems. Selection of both hardware and software applications requires consideration of

- The use for which the system is intended
- The technical support available
- The training required
- The price
- The warranty period
- The performance factors, such as speed and availability of upgrades

Local Area Networking (LANs), used by many firms, permit the user to combine stand-alone feature of the PC with access to more powerful packages by using the PC as a terminal. PCs provide for a variety of uses in modern purchasing operations.

---

[4]How Parker Hannifin Buys, *Purchasing,* November 9, 1989, pp. 47–51.

[5]Tom Stundza, "Alcoa: Taking the Next Step to Computerized Purchasing," *Purchasing,* March 27, 1986, p. 124.

Table 6-1   Common Terms for PC-Based Systems

Applications software	Program operated for specific purposes.
Baud	Rate of data transmission, usually in seconds.
Bit	Smallest unit of magnetically stored information.
Byte	Eight bits equal one byte, and this usually equals one alphanumeric character.
Density	Refers to amount of data that can be encoded in a certain amount of space; typically single, double, or high density.
Disk	Storage device for data.
DOS	Disk-operating-system software, which runs the machine.
Double sided	Both sides of diskette certified 100 percent error free.
Hardware	Physical structure of the computer.
Operating software	Program used to operate the computer.
RAM	Random access memory—typically, internal to computer; can enter information or instructions.
ROM	Read only memory—primarily for storage of data.
Single sided	Only one side of diskette certified 100 percent error free.

Several good micro-computer software programs on purchasing and inventory are available. The capabilities and costs of these programs are reviewed periodically in purchasing publications.

PC APPLICATIONS

In a typical application buyers for a large metals producer use PCs in forecasting, reporting order status, establishing standard costs, and price monitoring. Administratively, the PCs are being used to set up and monitor such activities as departmental budget and salary programs. In some cases problems are defined by buyers, and outside software consultants develop appropriate programs. In others, purchasing department personnel develop their own programs.

In forecasting, the buyer can compute short- and long-range price projections of key alloys used in metals production. Calculations are based on current price data and inflation forecasts made by outside econometric firms. The calculations can be modified by other information that the buyer judges to be applicable. Thus a buyer might develop more than one forecast. The buyer can also project consumption and total dollar expenditure for an alloying material for a given period, using a ratio of material consumption to metals production for a base year.

In a typical forecast of that type, a buyer can complete in about three minutes calculations that would have taken more than four hours when done manually. Automatically printing the data takes another couple of minutes, eliminating typing altogether.

Another software package designed specifically for purchasing brings together in one system all the information that is often scattered around a purchasing department, such as supplier contacts, prices, payment terms, discounts, and comments on vendor performance. Buyers can quickly call up reports on items or vendor history. An advanced version of the package also has special analytical capability; for example, it enables the buyer to compare a quoted price with previous purchases of the same component. It takes advantage of supplier discounts by automatically figuring a discounted dollar amount for each order, checks the order to assure the discount has been taken, and informs the buyer when the quantity purchased reaches a discount plateau. It then prints the purchase order automatically.

ELECTRONIC DATA INTERCHANGE (EDI)

At first, the majority of computer efforts in purchasing were focused within the firm. However, for functions such as purchasing and traffic it made sense to utilize the computer externally as well. Early efforts at such coordination involved an exchange of data supplied on magnetic tapes or punched cards generated by the buying companies' equipment. Suppliers fed the data into their own equipment to produce their internal documents.

Such systems, however, required a certain amount of human intervention—handwritten requisitions and keypunching, for example. In most cases the buyer and seller ended up processing the same information twice, which—as one purchasing manager put it—"the material sits on the shelf or awaits processing."

Thus it was not long before major companies turned to a faster, more accurate, and more efficient method of communication with suppliers, called electronic data interchange (EDI). Simply put, EDI permits a buyer's computer to "talk" to a supplier's computer and transfer purchase orders and related data, despite differences in compatibility. Such interchange requires two major technical elements: a standard message format and a communication protocol.

A standard format calls for data to be strictly organized in a specific manner, so that the content and meaning of the message are clear. There must be agreement on the sequence of the data stream—does, for example, "Date 08-03-85" mean March 8 or August 3? Several sources, notably the American National Standards Institute (ANSI), have produced standards suitable for a wide range of purchasing transactions.

Thus the mission of ANSI/ASC X12 (Accredited Standards Committee X12) was to develop standard communication formats for EDI technology. For purchasing applications ANSI X12 standards will be applicable to accommodate almost any form of purchase order and other documents, such as invoices, shipping notices, freight billings, and acknowledgements. Figure 6-3 shows these as well as other information transfers.

The growth in computer usage, awareness of EDI, and the ANSI X12 standard have resulted in rapid growth for EDI. One source predicted EDI-related expenditures for computer service software and transmissions would reach over $1 billion in 1990. This compared to $38 million in 1985, or a 100 percent annual growth rate.[6] Another source estimates that by 1995 at least 400,000

[6]R. M. Monczka and J. R. Carter, "Electronic Data Interchange: Managing Implementation in a Purchasing Environment," *NAPM,* Tempe, AZ 1987, p. 3.

EDI Buyer-Seller Information Exchanges

Forecasts of future requirements
Purchase order releases
Supplier shipping notification
Overdue purchase orders
Request for quotations
Material certifications
Statistical quality analyses
Order change/cancellation
Invoices

Figure 6-3

companies worldwide will implement EDI. Today there are approximately 9,000 registered users of EDI (Figure 6-4). Proponents also estimate that EDI can produce savings of 3.5 to 7 percent in transport costs and as much as 10 percent in delivered consignment savings.[7]

Communication Alternatives

Communications protocols or procedures are needed to get purchase orders electronically to a number of different suppliers at the right time regardless of differences in the speed, synchronization, sizes, or makes of the computers involved.

There are a variety of methods to transmit electronically. The three major alternatives are (1) terminal to computer, (2) buyer computer to seller computer, and (3) buyer computer to third-party supplier to computer (see Figure 6-5).

In the first case, *terminal to computer,* the seller places a terminal in the purchaser's office, and the buyer uses the terminal to place orders, check inven-

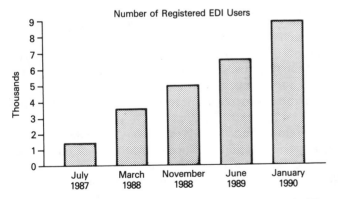

Figure 6-4 Growth of EDI.

[7]Laurie Bradford, "EDI Growth Brings New Breed of Transportation Providers," *Traffic World,* January 1, 1990, pp. 36–37.

Seller's Terminal To Seller's Computer

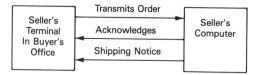

Buyer's Computer To Seller's Computer

Buyer's Computer To Third Party To Seller's Computer

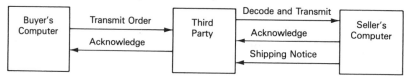

Figure 6-5   Types of EDI Systems

tory, pricing, and the like. This system may require the buyer to have a separate terminal for every EDI supplier. Additionally, information has to be transferred from the buyer's system to the terminal. The advantages of this type of system are security and quick response. A large electronics manufacturer using the terminal-to-computer method stated the following operating benefits:

- The buyer or requisitioner can scan the supplier's inventory level and check contract price and lead time.
- If part number, lead time, and quantity match requirements, the order can be directly entered.
- The buyer can check open order status and shipping information.
- Suppliers can be sent on-line messages.

The second method, *buyer computer* to *seller computer,* represents the closest buyer-seller linkage. Each party establishes a mailbox whereby communications are sent and received. The mailbox ensures security for each party and relieves the purchaser of the responsibility for having to download from its internal purchasing system to a terminal, as in the first case.[8] With the advent of standardized transmission and protocols more users will move towards this mode.

Finally, third-party systems indirectly link the buyer and seller through the use of a third party who performs the interfacing task between buyer and seller for a fee. Several large firms, such as General Electric Corporation, McDonnell Douglas, SCM, and Control Data, offer third-party services.

[8]For a complete discussion see Margaret A. Emmelhainz, "Electronic Data Interchange," in *Guide to Purchasing,* ed. (New York: National Association of Purchasing Management, 1986), pp. 1–10.

Third-Party Networks

Third-party networks permit a buyer's computer to interface with multiple supplier computers in any format, with any communications protocol, greatly expanding the choice of suppliers and commodities.

A third-party network operates as a central communications switch. It accepts a company's purchase orders in a batch, separates them by vendor, and holds those for each vendor in an "electronic mailbox." The messages (purchase orders) are then transmitted to the vendors' computers at predetermined times. The suppliers immediately process the data and ship the buyer's requirements. The major advantages of this system are (1) direct transfer of data and (2) ability to interface with multiple suppliers. The major disadvantage is the batch mode of operation, which slows response time (see Figure 6-6).

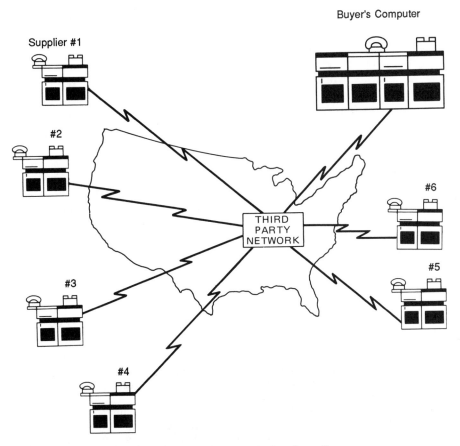

- Accepts RCA computer messages (P.O.S.) in batch mode
- Separates computer messages (P.O.'S.) for each vendor and holds in electronic mailbox
- Matches communications protocol
- Communications timing–window–hours predetermined
- Unlimited vendors

Figure 6-6 Third-party network. Courtesy of *Purchasing World.*

EDI's Advantages

Successful users of EDI report numerous advantages over manual or semiautomatic communication with suppliers:

- Reduced paperwork
- Less keypunching
- Lowered inventory levels
- No "lost in the mail" risk
- No required clerical time
- No forms or printing to be purchased
- No time wasted in telephone calls and conversations

Information is transmitted in minutes or at the most overnight, compared to the average ten-day cycle from the time a purchase order is prepared and mailed to the time the order gets through the supplier's order-entry system. For purchasers operating JIT programs this reduced lead time is a key to lower inventories. It also helps increase communication accuracy with suppliers, a vital step in fostering improved supplier relationships.

Lastly, while EDI reduces paperwork, most firms still tend to utilize two forms: a packing slip on goods, which becomes the carrier's contract for the goods in question and is signed by the buyer's receiving department, and a supplier's invoice. In the future, electronic funds transfer may make the invoice obsolete. EDI buyer-seller interactions can evolve to the transmission of many more buyer-seller information exchanges. These interactions can include drawings, purchase orders, invoices, change notices, bills of lading, etc.

The railroads were among the early adopters of EDI, and many firms use EDI in traffic operations. Certain railroads, for instance, Southern Pacific (SP), will install EDI software for their customers at no charge. Further, SP will pay all telecommunications costs between the shipper and itself.[9] Only when the buyer uses other carriers is there a telecommunications charge for the package.

Implementing EDI

Recent research by Margaret Emmelhainz resulted in an eleven-step implementation model for EDI:

1. The first step in implementing EDI is to establish the need. Given the current and projected growth of EDI, most organizations will be facing a need for EDI in order to remain competitive.
2. Once the need for EDI has been established, a planning committee should be established. The committee should be headed by a person with both interest and competence in EDI. Since the use of EDI usually spans traditional functional boundaries, it is imperative that a strong leader head the committee. Participants in the committee should include representatives from purchasing and materials management, information systems, transportation, legal/audit, accounting, and distribution.

[9]"Railroad EDI Made Easier," *Software Review,* October 1989, pp. 92–94.

3. After the planning committee has been established, an EDI audit should be performed. The audit should address internal factors such as the current status of the internal purchasing and distribution systems, the availability of information systems resources, and the level of interest of personnel. In addition, external factors such as the availability of standards, the level of industry action, current practices of trading partners and competitors, and the availability of support from third-party networks, consultants, and software houses should be examined.

4. Once the EDI audit is completed a plan of action should be presented to top management. The plan should address the need for EDI, the expected benefits and costs, and a timetable for implementation.

5. Once support for an EDI system has been obtained from top management, the type of system to be used must be decided. Decisions must be made on the standards which will be followed, the system configuration to be used, and whether a third-party network will be used. Concurrent with the determination of the system configuration, the transactions, divisions (if applicable), and suppliers to be placed on the system should be selected. Once the specific divisions or departments which will implement EDI have been selected, then a review of internal procedures of these divisions or departments should be made to determine if any changes are necessary to implement the EDI system.

6. Education of potential users and vendors is necessary. This step should be an on-going process and should be started as soon as potential users are identified.

7. Once the potential users are selected and the system parameters are finalized, a final plan and a schedule for the pilot test should be developed and presented to top management. Approval to begin the test should be obtained.

8. Prior to initiation of the pilot test, an EDI contract between the trading partners should be established. The contract should address such issues as covered transactions, third-party networks, allocation of costs, standard terms and conditions which will apply to electronic documents, and any other issues considered important by the trading partners. A project manager at each location should be identified.

9. A pilot test of the EDI system should be conducted. This would usually begin with the transmission of "dummy" data to test the linkages. Then a parallel test of actual data should be conducted, with the same documents being sent both electronically and manually. The pilot test should normally be conducted with a limited number of trading partners and a limited number of transactions until both parties adjust to the system.

10. Upon completion of the pilot test, an evaluation of the system should be performed. Costs and benefits should be examined. Any necessary changes should be made, and a schedule for system expansion should be established.

11. System expansion should be done on an incremental basis. That is, either the pilot transactions should be exchanged with new trading partners, or the pilot trading partners should begin to exchange new transactions.[10]

AUTOMATION THROUGH INFORMATION TECHNOLOGY

Computerized purchasing procedure follows, in general, the very same steps and procedures that make up the standard procedures described in the previous chapter in terms of a manual operation. It does not change the function of a procure-

[10]Margaret A. Emmelhainz, "Strategic Issues of EDI Implementation," Journal of Business Logistics Vol 9, No 2, 1988, pp. 68–69.

ment department, and it is necessarily based on exactly the same data for each purchase transaction and record. The special characteristics of the automated procedure are speed, the elimination of tedious and costly paperwork, and the quick availability of information for almost any purpose desired.

This greater efficiency is in itself a tremendous asset. But even more important than the improvement in procedures is the improvement in management of the purchasing activity that this makes possible. The additional information gives the purchasing officer more tools to work with, a basis for better and faster policy decisions, and the means for extending the constructive aspects of materials and purchasing management. The abilities of the computer are by no means limited to the procedural operations. At least one automobile manufacturer uses the computer to take care of the almost infinite variations in color combinations and accessories that are encountered in purchasing and production for today's highly individualized "standard" models. The appraisal of vendor performance, studies of stock obsolescence, and the preparation of reports to management are other applications that come readily to mind.

Further, automation of all routing and repetitive activities makes possible what is sometimes called management by exception. It has been pointed out in the sections dealing with automated stock control, follow-up, and invoice checking, for example, that it is only the unusual situation—the emergency, the discrepancy or error—that comes to the attention of the buyer once the basic decision has been made. When the routine transactions proceed according to schedule—in perhaps as many as 95 percent of all cases, once the system has been properly installed and adjusted—the buyers' time, ability, and judgment can be concentrated on the research, negotiation, policy, and special-projects phases of procurement.

Purchasing managers must recognize and understand the potential in computers, not only for improvement of their own functions but for complete integration of all an organization's major functions. Thus they should have some general knowledge of computer technology and vocabulary. More important, however, they must be able to see the computer as an overall tool for controlling the total resources of the organization. The use of computerized systems in material and supply management is an executive management issue, not a technical problem. Purchasing and materials managers who want to stay in front of their competition must take the initiative in exploiting the capabilities of the computer.

Thus there is a need to view the computer as an aid to decision making rather than merely a data collector and classifier. In the 1990s purchasers will find computers more useful as decision support systems.

POINTS FOR REVIEW

1. Explain why purchasing operations are particularly suited to computerization.
2. Name the principal elements in a purchasing department database.
3. Describe briefly how an EDI computer-to-computer system works.
4. List the typical operating benefits derived from the computerized system described in the text.

5. Name at least three PC-based software packages and tell how they could be used in purchasing.
6. Discuss the long-range implications of computerization for the purchasing executive.

7

Organizing and Staffing a Purchasing Department

In a small company with a limited volume and variety of purchases, the purchasing department may consist only of the purchasing manager and a clerical assistant. In very large companies the department may have several hundred employees. There is, however, no clear correlation between the dollar volume of purchases and the size of the purchasing staff. That varies widely according to the type of company, the nature or complexity of the product produced and the items that must be purchased, and the scope of the department's responsibility—whether it includes such activities as expediting, inventory control, and traffic management.

As noted, the majority of purchasing departments report directly to a top executive officer—president, executive vice-president, or general manager. This includes plant and divisional departments in multiplant organizations. Here the local purchasing manager is apart from the corporate department at company headquarters and reports to the branch or divisional manager of that operating unit. This situation is discussed in greater detail later in this chapter.

Wherever the head of purchasing reports directly to top management, that person is in the first tier of executives, on the same organization plane with the heads of production, sales and marketing, finance, and engineering. In some companies purchasing is under the jurisdiction of the production or manufacturing division, and the purchasing manager reports to the manufacturing manager. Such arrangements have, however, become relatively rare in recent years.

A third type of organization, used primarily in very large companies and diversified industries operating under a single management, separates the operational and managerial phases of purchasing. Separate buying departments are set up at the divisional level as parts of the division organization plan. A general purchasing department at company headquarters serves the entire organization as a staff facility. It counsels top management on broad purchasing and material policies, conducts general and specific purchasing research programs that are made available to all buyers, sets policies for the guidance of divisional purchasing departments, coordinates purchasing policies and activities throughout the company, and gives assistance on specific purchasing problems where needed. The amount of buying will vary, and it typically does not have responsibility for the details of procurement beyond evaluating purchasing performance at the various divisions and pointing out means for improvement. In most cases it has no jurisdiction over the hiring or firing of divisional purchasing personnel, although it usually sets up the buyer-training programs and has decisive influence in the transfer of persons with superior buying talent to positions of greater responsibility and opportunity among the divisions.

Figures 7-1 and 7-2 show typical purchasing departmental structures in medium and large companies, respectively.

DECENTRALIZED PURCHASING ORGANIZATIONS

In multiplant operations, which are frequently found in enterprises of moderate size and are almost universal among the larger companies, the question arises of whether to do all purchasing for the entire organization at one central point or set up a separate purchasing department for each operating division or plant location, each with a considerable degree of autonomy in buying.

The latter plan is popularly referred to as *decentralization* of purchasing structure. Under decentralized purchasing structures the majority of purchase dollar expenditures are committed at the plant or operating-unit level. If purchasing structure is centralized, the majority of purchase dollar expenditures are committed at a headquarters or central location. Figure 7-3 illustrates an example of a firm that moved from a centralized to a decentralized philosophy. As can be seen in the figure, the firm's divisions and plants make 80 percent of the decisions involving purchase expenditures. Seven years earlier, headquarters purchasing made commitments for 85 percent of the purchase expenditures.

The term should be applied with some reservations, because the decision to centralize or decentralize a purchasing organization reflects the overall philosophy and policy of management. This philosophy can change with time. Centralization or decentralization of purchasing is usually a matter of degree. Furthermore, the system is in no way inconsistent with effective central management control.

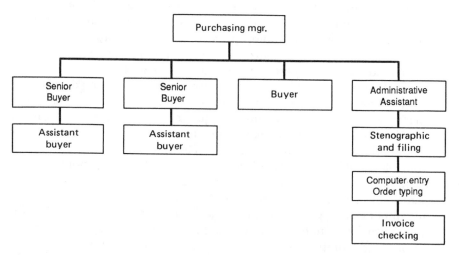

Figure 7-1 Organization plan of a medium-size purchasing department.

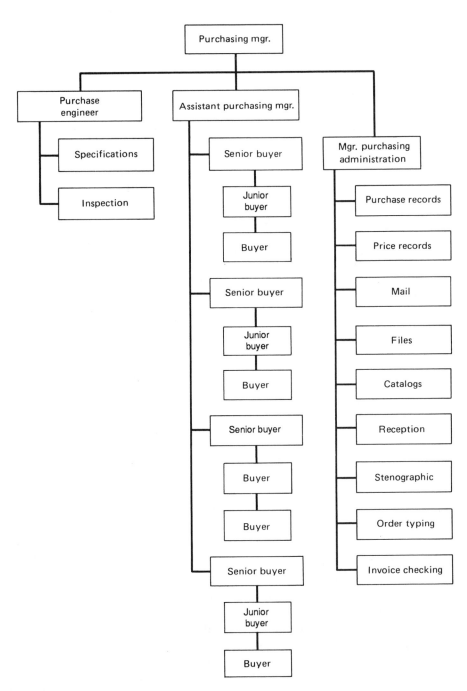

Figure 7-2 Organization plan of a large purchasing department.

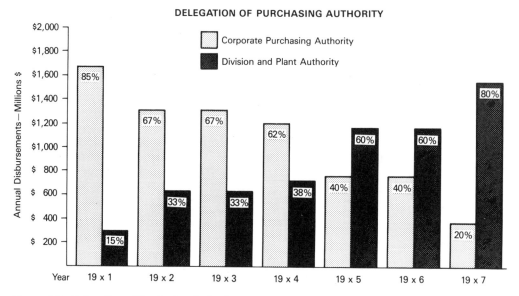

Figure 7-3 Delegation of Purchasing Authority.

The reasons for having a separate (decentralized) plant purchasing organization may be summarized as follows:

1. The plant or division manager is responsible for the profitable operation of that unit. He or she should have jurisdiction over purchasing as well as production, because a large part of costs and a major factor in the efficiency of production is represented in procurement.
2. If the division is large enough to be considered a profit center, it is usually large enough to buy in volume at favorable prices.
3. Each division may have some unique requirements and differences in operating conditions that affect material needs.
4. The public relations aspect of purchasing locally is significant. Goodwill can be fostered by purchasing from nearby sources or through local distributors.
5. Plant purchasing operations can provide quicker, more efficient services in meeting user needs.

CENTRALIZED PURCHASING ORGANIZATIONS

The arguments for complete centralization of purchasing for a multiplant manufacturing company stress (1) the combined requirements of the entire company and the consequent opportunities to leverage these larger-quantity requirements for price advantages and outright purchasing power, (2) the desirability of having a single buying policy and procedure for the whole organization, (3) the need for central controls as a means of evaluating purchasing activities and maintaining high standards of performance, and (4) centralization permits buyers to specialize in a few commodities. Finally, the staff responsibilities of the chief purchasing officer can be handled more effectively through direct administration of all buying.

In this view, plant location in itself is a relatively unimportant detail. The purchasing department is not necessarily located at the plant in any case. It is regarded more as a part of the general executive organization than as a part of the manufacturing operation. Particularly in metropolitan areas, it is not unusual to find a company's executive and purchasing offices in the business center of the city, whereas the manufacturing plants are located in outlying factory sections, sometimes several miles distant. Electronic communication techniques permit the central staff to overcome distance obstacles to plants in other cities and provide efficient buying service.

There are advantages other than mere volume/price in a centralized purchasing program for the entire company. For example,

1. Quality of purchased materials and parts is more readily controlled when they are bought on one contract from one source than when the orders are placed with several unrelated sources by as many different buyers.
2. There is added flexibility, because shipments on existing orders or contracts can be allocated and directed to various plants as needed instead of initiating a new purchase. The transfer of materials from one plant to another may be the quickest and most economical way of meeting an emergency.
3. One plant's surplus may be used to fill another's needs without making an additional expenditure or commitment, at the same time getting a better return on the value of such surplus.
4. Losses from obsolescence of parts due to changes in model or design can be minimized by concentrating the "balancing out" process of manufacture on the existing model in a single designated plant.
5. A higher degree of specialization and consequent purchasing skill can logically be expected in respect to special commodities. This contrasts with a situation in which the same responsibility is delegated to several buyers at the various plants.
6. By consolidating requirements with a minimum number of suppliers, purchasing is able to obtain the best overall value and service because it has greater leverage.

THE CENTRALIZED/DECENTRALIZED MIX

Judging from actual business practice over the years, there is no one best answer to the question of centralization versus decentralization of purchasing. In the period following World War II, complete centralization was generally considered the best form of organization. In the late 1950s and early 1960s American industry, led by such large organizations as the General Electric Company, took a decided turn toward decentralization of operations, including purchasing. A marked return toward some form of centralization began in the late 1960s and picked up momentum through the 1970s stimulated by the energy shortages.

1980s—A Changing Time

The accelerating rate of technical change and the intense competitive pressures in the 1980s made organizations turn to effective management issues focusing on span of control and levels of management. Many firms simply lost touch with the customer and the line worker. Consider the analysis at one major firm: (1) Supervisors and middle managers constituted 30 percent of its employees; (2) 35 percent of the employees were accomplishing the company's total productive effort; (3) there was one manager for every three to four employees; (4) there was one secretary for every two employees; and (5) there were nine levels of management. Faced with an increasingly competitive environment characterized by rapid product changes, management could see why the firm was losing money. Thus the 1980s witnessed severe trimming of middle-management staff. Span of control, which is the number of employees who report to a manager, also grew larger. The result was flatter corporations whose managers had a wider span of control (i.e., more employees working for them).

In purchasing departments these moves resulted in trimming large central administrative staffs. Corporate purchasing staffs were to coordinate the efforts of their multiplant business divisions to gain advantages of centralization and yet keep the decision-making authority at operating levels. One large firm indicated that its information systems would enable it to coordinate purchases with operating units with only buyers and no purchasing managers at the plants. The result of smaller, flatter organizations was that larger firms took a more coordinated approach to purchasing under the centralized/decentralized organization structure. Major forms of these structures include (1) lead division buying, (2) regional buying groups, (3) worldwide buying committees, (4) corporate purchasing councils, and (5) corporate steering committees (see Table 7-1).

COORDINATED PURCHASING

Lead Division Buying

In lead division buying a group of operating units that buy common items, typically because they produce common products, join on a voluntary basis. For example, one firm combined the efforts of several plants that produced transformers and distribution equipment for utility firms. The group first identified common commodities and then appointed a lead negotiator. The lead negotiator was the buyer at the plant having the largest expenditure or having the expertise in the commodity or item purchased.

Table 7-1 Forms of Coordinated Purchasing

Type of Coordinated Purchasing	Primary Basis of Organization
Lead division buying	Similar-type end product(s) produced
Regional buying group	Geographic region
Worldwide buying committee	Major commodity purchased worldwide
Corporate purchasing council	Similar commodity purchased by several buying units
Corporate steering committee	Similar commodity purchased by several buying units

Regional Buying Groups

Regional buying groups are most advantageous where geographic concentration exists within a company. Various plants within the particular region join forces to negotiate with local and regional sources on common commodities (e.g., Pacific Northwest, the Southeast). They generally are responsible for the purchase of large-volume items common to all plants. They also assist individual plants, which may or may not have in-house purchasing personnel to handle local purchases. Regional buying groups make a big impact in their immediate areas, and they facilitate JIT arrangements.

Worldwide Buying Committees

When a key commodity is purchased by many major business units a joint national or worldwide strategy is beneficial. For example, one large diversified firm has a worldwide steel buying committee. Corporate headquarters coordinates this committee, and every plant operation that buys steel has a representative on the committee. Supplier purchase plans and negotiation strategies are established at the meetings.

Corporate Purchasing Councils

With smaller staffs at headquarters and fewer personnel at operating-unit level, purchasing councils were organized by more companies in the 1980s. At a chemical/rubber company councils are formed by purchasing managers at various company divisions. Each member is given responsibility for purchases of companywide requirements for which his or her division is the biggest user. National contracts are negotiated and awarded at headquarters by the council.

Another conglomerate organization has established over forty buying councils. These councils cover specific commodities, such as bearings, tools, and furniture. They work best in environments characterized by good corporate-level and business-unit relations, since council membership is often voluntary.

Corporate Steering Committees

Steering committees are quite similar to councils except that they tend to be more advisory in nature. These committees will meet periodically and discuss strategies on the company's major purchased commodities. Steering committees will also invite large suppliers in for discussions, negotiations, performance assessments, and purchase volumes for the coming year. They provide an opportunity for various operating-unit personnel to meet and discuss buying plans in decentralized environments.

Structured Decentralization

One documented case where purchasing systems allow for coordinated purchasing is at Alcoa.[1] This form of organization places purchasing decision making as close to the actual buy as possible. The corporate staff monitors division performance and gives each buyer within purchasing the ability to access all corporate information. Seventy-five percent of corporate contracts allow local buyer options on pricing. Meanwhile, Alcoa's computer systems allow viewing of all corporate, local, and vendor contracts; inventory turnover, material cost expenditures to date, and so on. The computer data help corporate staffers isolate opportunities for leveraged purchases and consolidation.

Advantages of Coordinated Purchasing

The advantages common to these coordinated forms of purchasing include:

- Leverage for improved pricing
- Big-user prices for small-use locations
- Reduced administrative cost at using locations
- Buying expertise, developed by key individuals

In summary, it enables purchasers to maintain decentralized decision making and gain the advantages of centralization. With more firms putting centralized purchasing information systems in place, the 1990s should see a continuation of these hybrid groups.

FINDING THE BEST MIX

In the final analysis management's decision to centralize or decentralize can be influenced by a number of things: fundamental economic trends, fashions in management philosophy, changes in the structure of business, mergers, and technological developments such as the computer. The computer, for example, has done much to accelerate the trend to centralization in purchasing. It makes possible the compilation and analysis of large amounts of significant purchasing and related data—on activity, volume, prices, inventory status, and so on—so that judgments and decisions can be made speedily and communicated just as quickly to all concerned.

The most widely used arrangement is a compromise designed to obtain the advantages of both methods of organization. As discussed above, this usually takes the form of a decentralized system with centralized coordination and controls. Specific means of developing and maintaining such a system include:

[1]"What Makes Alcoa Our Medal of Excellence Winner," *Purchasing*, June 5, 1986, pp. 58–70.

1. Uniform policies, forms, and procedures at all plants, established through a company-wide purchasing manual; uniform quality standards established by companywide specifications.
2. Continuing review of all purchasing activities by having copies of purchase orders routed to the central office. Systematic monthly reports from all branch purchasing departments, correlated at the central office and redistributed to the branches in a summary report form, with buying recommendations.
3. Dollar value limitation on branch plant purchases. Orders or contracts in excess of the stated limit are subject to approval by the central department. This corresponds to the regulation in many purchasing departments that orders amounting to more than a stated dollar value must be approved by the head of the department or by some higher executive.
4. Certain items, usually major materials in common use at two or more plants, are designated as contract items and are purchased by the central department for all plants. In some cases the initial requirement of a new item is purchased by the plant purchasing department, with subsequent review to determine whether it shall be classified as a contract item. A variation is to delegate the purchase of specified items to a designated plant purchasing department, in which the item is used in greatest volume.
5. Contracts for items in common use are made by the central department, with provision for shipment to all company locations. Branch plant buyers are expected to issue release orders against these existing contracts, but they have the option of buying independently if they can improve on the terms of the contract for their individual plant requirements through special local circumstances or for any other reason. This assures buying on the most favorable terms in all cases and may lead to revision of the central contracts to extend the benefit to all branches.

A previous study to find the best mix of total centralization and total decentralization for a particular company found several complicating factors.[2] They included:

1. The best mix for a company will probably be unique to that company. There is no easy formula that one company can copy from another.
2. The mix will change over time for a particular company. It will be affected by changes in environment, corporate strategies, international conditions, business practices, and specific markets.
3. There will be different mixes for particular raw materials, component parts, and supplies.
4. The best mix of functions probably will not entirely match the company's line structure or the structure for other staff or support functions. This creates a need for effective communication within purchasing and with line management personnel.
5. The mix will not always be popular. Moving responsibility for price negotiations from a local to a higher level takes away some measure of freedom of action. Similarly, a switch of a purchase away from a central group to a local group may imply that central is not doing its job effectively.
6. The mix may be complicated. That calls for much planning and work to make sure that any change is effective. A major effort may be needed to explain how the purchasing program works and how responsibility for purchased materials is assigned on a worldwide, national, regional, or local basis.

[2]George F. Bernardin, "Centralized/Decentralized Purchasing: The Quest for a Perfect Mix," *New England Purchaser and Connecticut Purchaser,* April 1981, pp. 4-6.

CENTRALIZING THE PURCHASING FUNCTION

To this point we have discussed centralization of the purchasing organization. Next we discuss individual needs of the department. This discussion is based on the principle that the purchasing *function* is centralized; that is, one individual or department has buying responsibility. Purchasing responsibility, as with other major management and operating functions, is generally delegated to a specific person or a special department in the company organization (centralization of function). In few concerns of any substantial size today do individual departments do their own buying, of either production materials or operating supplies. In some cases, the specialized purchasing department comes under the jurisdiction of the manufacturing manager. This is a carryover from earlier days, when purchasing was regarded primarily as a service to the manufacturing department. Most companies set up purchasing, or materials management, as a completely separate department, with the chief purchasing officer reporting directly to the executive who has the overall responsibility for profitable operation, that is, the president, executive vice president, general manager, or plant or divisional manager.

The advantages of this system of allocating responsibility and concentrating authority for buying are inherent in the economic principle of the division of labor and in all functional organization:

1. Better control is assured by isolating the materials factor, with one person or department directly responsible to management for handling this function and one complete set of records pertaining to purchase transactions, commitments, and expenditures.
2. Concentration on purchasing develops specialized knowledge, skills, and procedures that result in more efficient and economical procurement.
3. Better performance may be expected in other departments when engineers, production executives, office managers, and other department heads are relieved of the detailed buying responsibility and of the interruptions and interviews incidental to buying. The same principle holds in a nonindustrial organization, such as a hospital, in which the professional staff is often the target of strong selling efforts.
4. Divorcing the purchasing function from the influence or domination of other departments, whose primary interests lie in other directions, afford a greater likelihood that the economic and profit potentials of purchasing will receive more consideration on their own merits and thus may make a greater contribution to overall profitable operation.

PURCHASING-STAFF ASSIGNMENTS

The one-person purchasing department obviously poses no organization problems. All activities are embodied in that person, who generally has an assistant of some type. When the volume of purchasing grows beyond the capacity of one or two persons, organization becomes essential. The buying staff is necessarily larger, and the incidental services and paperwork increase in proportion. Individual buyers cannot efficiently handle the detailed procedures that make up each transaction. They have to give up routine and clerical tasks to concentrate on becoming specialists in buying—usually in one or a few particular commodity groups. The other departmental activities are also divided into specialties and assigned to supporting clerical personnel.

TYPICAL PURCHASING ACTIVITIES

Beyond the basic operating cycle and procedures, operating a purchasing department involves a variety of detailed assignments, of both an administrative and a routine nature. Typical activities of even the simplest purchasing department include:

- Basic information
    - Maintaining purchase records
    - Maintaining price records
    - Maintaining stock and consumption records
    - Maintaining supplier records
    - Maintaining specification files
    - Maintaining catalog files
- Research
    - Conducting market studies
    - Conducting material studies
    - Conducting cost/price analysis
    - Conducting value analysis
    - Investigating supply sources
    - Inspecting suppliers' plants
    - Developing supply sources
    - Developing alternate materials and sources
- Procurement
    - Checking requisitions
    - Securing quotations
    - Analyzing quotations
    - Choosing between contract or open-market purchase
    - Scheduling purchases and deliveries
    - Interviewing salespersons
    - Negotiating and writing contracts
    - Issuing purchase orders
    - Checking legal conditions of contracts
    - Following up for delivery
    - Checking receipt of materials
    - Verifying invoices
    - Corresponding with suppliers
    - Making adjustments with suppliers

- Materials Management
    - Maintaining minimum stocks
    - Maintaining inventory balance
    - Improving inventory turnover
    - Transferring materials
    - Consolidating requirements
    - Avoiding excess stocks and obsolescence
    - Standardizing packages and containers
    - Accounting for returnable containers
    - Making periodic reports of commitments
- Miscellaneous
    - Making cost estimates
    - Disposing of scrap and obsolete and surplus materials

PURCHASING-POSITION TITLES AND DESCRIPTIONS

In the fully organized purchasing department the *chief purchasing officer* (who usually has the title of vice-president of purchasing, director of purchasing, or purchasing manager) is concerned primarily with administrative and executive duties. Figure 7-4 shows typical position titles within a purchasing department.

The chief purchasing officer establishes and directs overall purchasing policies, coordinates the purchasing program and procedures with the requirements of other departments and represents purchasing in various management and policy meetings. The departmental head is directly responsible to top management for departmental administration, morale, training, and performance.

Heads of department may or may not take part in actual negotiation and buying. That participation is usually limited to major contracts and items that involve large volume and dollar value. These usually represent matters of policy as

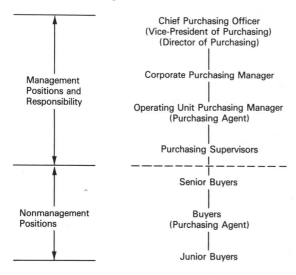

Figure 7-4   Purchasing Personnel Hierarchy—Typical Position Titles.

well as of procurement. Purchasing vice-presidents and directors may also take part in the initial consideration of new suppliers or new materials. But for the most part they are concerned with reports of purchasing activities, order status, and cost trends.

Those next in line—generally *purchasing managers*—are directly in charge of the buying staff and general departmental operations. They assign buying responsibilities and direct the work of the buyers or buying groups. They are concerned with day-by-day purchases, and in many companies all purchase orders pass over their desks for review. Through assistants, they supervise various office services, and where appropriate, such separate sections as expediting, traffic, surplus disposal, and stores.

The title *purchasing agent* still exists in some organizations. Historically, this term referred to the purchasing manager. Today, however, it is more commonly used in conjunction with a nonmanager; thus it equates to a buyer position. *Senior buyers, buyers, and junior buyers* are typically nonmanagement positions. However, in some firms a senior buyer or buyer may have a buyer/planner or secretary reporting directly to him or her.

AUXILIARY FUNCTIONS

In addition to the activities that are distinctly within the province of purchasing, there are a number of responsibilities that are typically shared with other departments by means of recommendations or by decisions reached through conference or committee action in which the purchasing manager or representative has a voice. Among these responsibilities are

- Office practice
- Determination of whether to manufacture or buy
- Acceptance testing
- Materials budget
- Inventory control
- Standardization
- Specifications
- Substitution of materials
- Selection of capital equipment
- Construction projects
- Production programs dependent on availability of materials

A typical position description detailing the functions and responsibilities of an industrial purchasing executive is shown in Figure 7-5.

The list given here is not exhaustive, as activities vary among different companies according to the character or the enterprise and its philosophy of management. Storekeeping and traffic management, for example, are responsibilities of the purchasing department in some companies. Others make receiving and inspection purchasing responsibilities. When the purchasing department's jurisdiction extends into these and other functions—such as materials control, warehousing, and materials handling (or when purchasing along with these functions is put under unified control)—what occurs in fact, if not in name, is the establishment of a type of *materials management* department. The concept of materials management and the different organizational forms that it takes are discussed in Chapter 15.

Position: Manager, Purchasing
Dept. / Divn.:
Reports to:

MAJOR ACCOUNTABILITIES AND THEIR DIMENSIONS

1. Ensure lower prices through programs to inform and educate suppliers of this company's application of their products; by seeking out vendor suggestions for changes and/or improvements in their products to facilitate finished machine assembly; by encouraging vendor representatives to visit this company's manufacturing and testing facilities and thus provide outside expertise in the way of suggestions for material and part substitutions or modifications, and new processes, products, and materials.
2. Locate new supply sources around the world thereby assuring maximum opportunities for complete cost surveys and establishment of best possible supply sources with lowest prices commensurate with on-time deliveries of quality materials, parts and services, whether required for production, service parts, marketing, or burden and capital needs.
3. Locate best United States sources and prices for requirements from this company's overseas operations and then by proper ordering, scheduling, and follow-up assure on-time shipments. Also responsible for domestic company needs, including raw materials, castings, forgings, parts, etc. from sources outside the United States.
4. Encourage and ensure cost reductions and lowest prices through formal purchase cost reduction and purchase cost avoidance programs. Maintain achievement records against established, acceptable, measurable, and reportable goals.
5. Initiate and develop programs for the education and training of purchasing personnel. In cooperation with buyers and managers of company operations initiate, develop, publish, and circulate written policies and procedures to assure constant improvement in the overall effectiveness of the purchasing function.
6. Monitor, analyze, and report annually to management the results and overall effectiveness of the purchasing function.

Figure 7-5 First Page of a Typical Position Description.

One point made clear in our review of the purchasing activity is that the buying operation has a significant relationship with almost every other department in the organization. The closest sort of cooperation must be maintained with production, finance, accounting, engineering, maintenance, sales, office management, and general management.

BUYING ASSIGNMENTS

Buying assignments are usually specific, item by item, with a definite responsibility for each item or commodity classification that is regularly purchased. So far as is practicable, items that are related by nature or by source (rather than by end product or using department) are grouped for buying purposes. In a department of moderate size, in which such assignments are made to individual buyers rather than to a buying group or section, this principle may have to be modified somewhat so as to distribute the work load evenly. But the major classifications at least will be identified with particular buyers—steel buyer, electrical-goods buyer, and so forth—who have direct and sole responsibility for procurement of the stated products. For each such buying assignment it is customary to name an alternate from among the other buyers, who can assist with or take over the buying in a classification other than his or her own as may be required from time to time.

In larger departments assignments are made to commodity-buying sections, each headed by a senior buyer or purchasing agent, with one or more buyers and assistant buyers under his or her direction. When this type of organization is in effect, the commodity groupings and assignments can be completely consistent. Equal distribution of work load among the several buying sections is not essential, because the size of staff in each group can be adjusted to the load, and understudies or alternates are available within the section.

The advantages of organization according to specific, related commodity assignments are the following:

1. Buyers become specialists in a particular field. Concerned with a limited range of items, they can acquire a better knowledge of the materials and products, their characteristics, and their applications, and greater familiarity with marketing practices, economic influences, and sources of supply in that field. All this makes for superior purchasing skill.
2. Duplication and overlapping are eliminated, and situations are avoided in which buyers in the same organization may in effect be competing with each other for supplies.
3. There is greater opportunity to review requirements of related items, sometimes resulting in beneficial standardization and making it possible to combine requirements, gaining maximum-quantity buying advantage, with fewer interviews and purchase orders.
4. Vendor contacts are concentrated, conserving time and effort for both the salesperson and the buyer. The salesperson of a given material or of a related product line usually needs to make only one contact in the purchasing department, and that contact is with a buyer having specific authority.

Some purchasing managers, however, prefer to rotate commodity-buying assignments every year or two, switching a buyer from castings, for example, to plastic extrusions. They argue that rotation

1. Gives buyers a broader view of the overall purchasing operation and prepares them for greater managerial responsibility.
2. Assures smooth functioning of the department by providing capable replacements in the event that "specialist" buyers are absent owing to illness or other reasons.
3. Reduces the likelihood that a specialist will become so bored with the job or so "comfortable" with certain suppliers that he or she has little motivation to seek innovations or cost-reduction ideas.

There can be no standard purchasing classification of commodities that will be applicable to all companies. Requirements vary widely among different industries. The item that is of primary importance and volume in one plant may be used in insignificant quantities, or not at all, in the plant next door. The division and assignment of buying responsibility must be tailored to the individual case.

A representative metal-fabricating company, for example, classifies its purchases in these groups: metals; electrical parts, machine tools and mechanical parts; chemicals, store supplies, and automotive equipment; office and drafting supplies; printing, office machines, and furniture.

These are specific cases, listing only the general group classifications according to which buying duties are assigned. Usually, however, there is a more detailed tabulation of the items in each group. A comprehensive list is given below. Some of these categories may not be applicable in particular companies. Some would be major classifications in one company and subordinate items in another.

- Abrasives
- Accessories
- Automotive equipment and supplies
- Electrical materials and parts
- Electronic parts
- Fabricated parts and assemblies
- Fasteners
- Forgings
- Fuel
- Glass and glass products
- Hand tools
- Hardware
- Instruments
- Insulating materials
- Iron and steel
- Laboratory equipment
- Lubricants, petroleum, products (except fuel)
- Lumber
- Machined parts
- Machinery and plant equipment
- Maintenance, repair, and operating supplies

- Building materials
- Castings
- Chemicals
- Drafting supplies
- Nonferrous metals
- Office machines and furniture
- Office supplies
- Packaging materials
- Paint, varnish, lacquer, and finishing materials
- Paper and paper products
- Plastic parts
- Printing
- Refractories
- Rubber products (except tires)
- Safety equipment
- Screw-machine products
- Services
- Shipping-room supplies
- Stampings
- Subcontracting
- Textiles
- Welding equipment and supplies
- Wood products

The diversity of products in this tabulation reemphasizes the importance of specialization in purchasing, through organization.

Special Commodities

In a number of industries in which the end product is made up largely of a single raw material, as in the case of cotton textiles, the procurement of that material constitutes a distinct activity quite apart from the general purchasing program and department. This is particularly true in the case of products of nature, where the evaluation of quality and the actual purchasing often must be done in markets or auctions at the point of production. For example, in cigarette manufacturing the purchase and seasoning of leaf tobacco may be vested not merely in a separate department but in a separate, affiliated corporation. Large users of wood customarily have a timber agent entirely independent of the purchasing department; the agent buys standing timber or leases timber rights and schedules cutting operations to provide the lumber for manufacturing needs.

Product Purchasing

In companies making a wide variety of products, usually in a number of different plants, the buyer in a plant manufacturing only one product or line of products may be responsible for all major purchased materials and components going into the product rather than specializing in two or three. For example, a company that manufactures vacuum cleaners, waxing machines, and hand tools in several different locations and is constantly bringing out new models will use this system in the interest of time and efficiency. It is particularly useful in cases where there are a number of unrelated products in different stages of development at one time.

Usually, however, provision is made to take advantage of standardization and quantity buying. Items common to two or more products and items that can be bought in relatively large volume are generally assigned to a specialist buyer for purchase.

Project Purchasing

Purchasing for special projects, such as new plant construction or highly complex made-to-order equipment, is frequently set up as a separate division within the purchasing department. This makes it easier to handle special requirements of the project, avoid delays, and obtain cost information in the early planning stages. Project purchasing calls for the use of buyers with a high degree of technical knowledge and training who can work closely with design and engineering departments.

Field operations, such as drilling and laying of pipelines in the petroleum industry, are customarily handled on a project basis. Purchasing for product development and research laboratories, in which requirements are highly specialized and there can be no consistent, continuing materials program, often comes within this category also.

Project purchasing has received its biggest impetus in recent years, however, from military and related procurement. Defense contractors who must bid on such things as complex electronic systems have representatives of the purchasing department participate in the preparation of such bids. A well-known optical company that makes highly complex cameras and reconnaissance systems for the military uses the project-buying approach. Procurement and purchasing engineers assist engineering, sales, and management personnel in the preparation of bids in several ways. They provide cost estimates on new materials and parts, analyze specifications that may cause suppliers trouble, and indicate probable lead times on delivery of materials. Without such specific procurement data, the planning group might make an unrealistic bid, and the company might end up losing money on the job or failing to deliver it on time. Subcontract administrators who handle a portion of a major contract fall into the project-purchasing category.

SELECTION OF PURCHASING PERSONNEL

Entry Level

After specifications for purchasing personnel have been set up, in the form of a list of responsibilities, the next step is to locate personnel. First on the list of prerequisites is a college education. A logical first source then, is college graduates having the necessary academic background. Such persons are regularly cultivated in the standard personnel-recruiting programs of many large companies. Where this method is a part of company policy, the recruiting for purchasing is usually handled as a part of the general program, with the specific assignment to purchasing following a screening and training program during which special aptitudes are disclosed.

College Graduates

In recent years more colleges and universities have established programs for students desiring a degree in purchasing/materials management (P/MM). Research by one of the authors at sixty major corporations found that a bachelor's degree in business administration was favored over a master's in business administration (M.B.A.) or a bachelor's in engineering. The major reason cited was that the undergraduate business degree prepared the student better for work required of purchasing personnel. A specialization in P/MM was most preferred, since it directly prepares students for this area. Typically, purchasing majors take all required business courses plus a core that includes courses in purchasing materials management. These include purchasing, production and inventory control, logistics management, productions/operations management, and advanced purchasing principles.

The authors' research found firms that preferred engineers. These firms emphasized the necessity to understand the technical nature of the product and the importance of a close interaction between purchasing and engineering.

The late Edward J. Bierman, past director of the National Association of Purchasing Management's certification program, suggested the types of academic disciplines useful for students interested in a career in purchasing:

> No one type of educational activity is universally conceded to be best. Qualifications desired will, of course, vary with the type and size of a company and its industry classification.
>
> The ideal college training would probably consist of an undergraduate degree in business, with a major concentration or courses in purchasing/materials management. Engineering and technical courses as part of a B.S. degree in business, or a master's degree in business administration are also recommended.[3]

---

[3]From personal correspondence.

The Certification Board of the National Association of Purchasing Management (NAPM) recommended that the business core of the undergraduate program include the following: accounting, business law, data processing, economics, finance, industrial management, cost accounting, management and organization, marketing, purchasing, materials management, traffic and transportation, production planning and control, inventory control, and statistics.

CERTIFICATION IN PURCHASING

In 1974 the NAPM established a program through which people could earn the designation Certified Purchasing Manager (C.P.M). Candidates for certification are required to take a four-module examination. In addition, they must have a minimum of five years of working experience in the purchasing/materials management profession, or a minimum of three years of experience if they have a four-year college degree. Continuing education and contributions to the profession also count toward certification. Undergraduates are permitted to take the examinations but do not qualify for certification until the experience requirements have been met. Three of the examination modules deal primarily with functional operations in purchasing. The fourth module covers current topics of interest and concern to purchasing professionals.

To assist candidates to prepare for the examination, NAPM has published the *C.P.M. Study Guide,* which follows a format similar to that of the examination. Each module of the study guide is followed by sample questions as well as a bibliography to aid in additional study.

Also available is a diagnostic kit, designed to help in preparing for the examination. The kit enables a candidate to take an actual past examination, score it personally, and isolate areas of weakness that require further study. An explanation of each possible answer to every sample test question is included.

The C.P.M. examination is administered twice a year—in January and June at various testing sites across the country. In addition, candidates take the examination at computer terminals at their convenience. The computer version is also offered at several testing locations.

Full details on the certification program are available from the National Association of Purchasing Management, PO Box 22160, Tempe, AZ 85285-2160.

TRAINING PERSONNEL

Employees first brought into an organization are given "general orientation" on the company, its products, policies, procedures, vacations, pay scales, and the like. After this initial introduction, training methods can include (1) a formal training program, (2) functional training, and (3) a buddy system.

Formal Training Programs

Formal training programs offered by many large firms provide the candidate with a mixture of formal classroom training and assignments in purchasing or other material-related functions. After a period of time (six months to one year), the candidate selects an open position in the company upon approval of the local manager. Most college students are favorably inclined toward companies that offer such a program, viewing the program as an interim step between college and the real world. It also allows candidates to explore several potential functions and locations. Formal training programs are expensive and require time, commitment of operating unit, and headquarters purchasing personnel. They also give the company time to train the new employee to their philosophy and methods of purchasing. Currently such programs are found mainly in larger, Fortune 500 companies.

Sponsor System

In the sponsor, or "buddy," system an experienced employee acts as a mentor to the new employee. Typically the sponsor is someone other than the new hiree's direct supervisor. Sponsors are chosen primarily on the basis of teaching ability and, secondly, on experience. The system is less expensive than formal training and should be combined with coaching from the supervisor or manager. Disadvantages include limiting training to one view or philosophy and the need for sponsors to ensure that their own work does not suffer.

Functional Rotation

This approach involves moving the new employee into related departments for short periods to gain an appreciation for work being performed in areas such as inventory control, quality, engineering, stores, and receiving. This type of training offers the advantage of learning about these departments' different functions and management styles. Also on the plus side, it encourages positive interdepartmental relations. The shortness of the assignment period, however, often makes it difficult to give the new employees meaningful assignments, so they do not contribute immediately to the purchasing department.

Continued Professional Development

One never stops learning. That is true for the employee with two years' or twenty years' experience. Experienced employees will find many avenues open to increase their job skills and long-term career progression. They include the following:

| External seminars | Offered by various educational and professional groups |

Self-training	Evening courses in subjects pertaining to purchasing, product knowledge, or general management skills
On-the-job training	Training programs conducted by the purchasing manager or corporate staff
Job rotation	Rotation into other material functions
Certification preparation	Becoming certified results in recognition and higher pay: certified purchasing manager (C.P.M.) and/or certified production and inventory manager (C.P.I.M.)
Management development	Courses and training in the skills and techniques required to manage a department

CAREERS IN PURCHASING

Purchasing is an occupation of wide variety and interests. The buyer deals with a wide range of materials and products, and these are constantly changing, in themselves and in their economic relationships, through technological developments and progress. The products are procured from many different sources, affording the buyer direct and stimulating contacts and familiarity with a range of supplier industries far broader than the experience of workers concerned only with the internal company operation. In the regular course of their activities, buyers deal with many people—those for whom and from whom they buy—in a variety of business and personal relationships. And the economic conditions under which they buy are constantly changing, so that one day's problems are never quite the same as those of the day before.

Purchasing is a challenging and competitive occupation, with large responsibilities in both the quality of supply service provided and the magnitude of expenditures. It calls not only for knowledge and routine efficiency but also for resourcefulness, for skill in negotiation and good judgment in decisions, and for imagination and initiative in the continuing search for greater value.

Purchasing is a useful, essential part of the company activity. It offers the satisfactions of pride in the end product that embodies purchased materials and in the profit results made possible through wise and effective procurement.

Purchasing is a growing field, soundly established but still in the developmental stage, with many horizons yet to be explored and many opportunities yet to be fully realized and exploited as the function moves toward the broader concept of materials management. The person in purchasing has the opportunity for constructive service to industry and management by contributing to the knowledge and techniques of procurement science, to the broader scope of purchasing service, and to higher professional standards and management status.

Purchasing is steadily winning increased recognition in every progressive company as an integral and important part of industrial management. It has prestige within the company organization. It participates in management councils and policy decisions and has the authority to administer and carry out the programs to fulfill its functional responsibilities. The work of procurement brings the buyer intimately into touch with the requirements and operations of virtually every other phase of the business. The qualities required and developed in purchasing work—analytical skill, foresight, organization and punctuality in meeting responsibility, ability to deal with people, imagination, resourcefulness, and respect for ultimate values—are precisely those that make for success in the broader fields of management. And with increasing reliance being placed upon purchasing as a vital part of profit potentialities, there is little chance that the really competent purchasing person will be unnoticed or overlooked in general management plans.

However, the field is often overlooked by students choosing a career area. The *Wall Street Journal's National Business Employment Weekly* tabbed purchasing as a career area often passed over by graduates that offers bright prospects. In an era of increased competition and tight budgets, the purchasing function is taking on new importance in the business world.[4] Meanwhile starting salaries are among the top for business schools' graduates.

In essence, as stated in a recruiting brochure:

> Purchasing makes you knowledgeable about many different types of businesses and products. You learn about business, not in a narrow sense of statistics, but in day-to-day contact that gives you the broad picture that leads to a comprehensive background for executive management positions....
>
> You assume responsibilities and challenge rapidly....There are few areas that can offer a more stimulating career. Look into this sometimes overlooked path to a high level management career.

POINTS FOR REVIEW

1. Show what factors, in general, determine the size of a purchasing department.
2. Review the arguments for and against completely centralized control of purchasing in the multiplant company.
3. Describe how a compromise system—partially centralized and partially decentralized—is organized.
4. Estimate how well your own course of study might prepare you for a position in a purchasing department.
5. List the requirements that an applicant must meet to qualify for the designation certified purchasing manager.
6. Discuss purchasing as a career in itself, as well as its relation to possible advancement in other corporate functions.
7. Discuss the difference between centralization of the purchasing structure and centralization of the purchasing function.

[4]Michael Kastre, "Opportunity Incognito," college edition of the *National Business Employment Weekly,* *Wall Street Journal,* Fall 1989, p. 9.

8

Purchasing's Responsibility for Quality

The three major factors in every purchasing decision are (1) the quality of the item purchased, (2) the service provided by the supplier, and (3) the price paid by the buyer. Purchasing managers generally state that they consider quality first in importance, service second, and price last. This is another way of saying that unless the quality of the purchased part meets the requirements of the department that uses it, superb service and a low price are next to meaningless.

This point is of utmost importance to industry today. For quality is the route to competitiveness in the 1990s as U.S. business faces ever tougher challenges in response to this issue. Quality expert, Dr. J. M. Juran, has noted that quality is a critical element in international trade, defense capability, human safety, health, and the environment.[1] Companies have been responding to such growth in a number of ways.

1. The scope of quality has broadened to include manufacturing support activities, business processes, and needs of internal customers.
2. Planning for quality has evolved into a formalized approach involving internal participants and joint planning with customers and suppliers.
3. Upper management is increasingly taking charge of managing quality.
4. Training for quality has increasingly been extended into all functions including general management.

These programs, along with others, have affected the purchasing department.

QUALITY, PRICE, AND COST

Quality is *not* measured by price. The assumption that higher price in itself denotes higher quality has been disproved so often and so thoroughly that no thoughtful buyer can proceed on this basis. In every selling field, examples are legion demonstrating that identical material is available at varying prices from different sources and that if a thorough search is made, higher quality can be procured from sources at a lower price than is asked for the lower quality offered by others. The old saying that "you get just what you pay for" is a half truth whose shortcomings have often been learned by the hard and costly method of experience.

Conversely, as higher product quality is demanded by customers, suppliers become a vital part of the quality equation. Thus purchasing can no longer afford to buy based on low price. Instead, analysis must be directed toward minimizing total costs. Consider this hypothetical example:

> Firm A sells an item for a $1/unit that has a 90 percent quality level, resulting in five rejections per year (rejection process costs the firm $250). Meanwhile, firm B's product sells for $1.15/unit and has a 99 percent quality level, which results in one rejection of material per year.
>
> Assume that we buy 10,000 units from each supplier. Then for firm A the actual cost per unit is

$$1/(1 - .10) = 1.111/\text{unit} \times 10,000 + 5(250) = 12361/10,000 = 1.236/\text{pc.}$$

[1] J. M. Juran and Frank M. Gryna, *Juran's Quality Handbook* New York: McGraw-Hill Book Company, 1987, pp. 11–12.

And, for firm B, the actual cost per unit is

$$1.15/(1 - .01) = 1.162/\text{unit} \times 10,000 + 250(1) = 11870/10,000 = 1.187/\text{pc.}$$

In this simplified example we see that poor quality actually cost 24 percent extra (1.00 to 1.24) when buying from firm A. Conversely, firm B, which was initially 15 percent higher on price is 4 percent lower than firm A when evaluating quality costs.

In the 1990s buyers will be required to purchase sophisticated items for products that move from idea phase to customers at a much quicker pace. To be effective in this faster design-to-market cycle requires a commitment up front to quality in design. Thus suppliers will be brought into the process much earlier. Wayne Collins, vice-president of materials operations for Compaq Computer, stated such a philosophy: "We work very hard with suppliers to develop new products with them and introduce our products very quickly. . . If the supplier works well through the design-in and production ramp, then you continue to ride that horse through the production phase."[2] A similar situation exists at Texas Instruments, according to Jerry R. Junkins, chief executive officer. Junkins wants to see more of TI's engineers engaged directly with customers, scientists, and engineers in the design and development of products that use semiconductors and other components made by Texas Instruments.[3]

With such rapid changes taking place, gone are the days when engineering designs the product and then submits it to purchasing for quotes. Today's demands for quality and responsiveness make this process obsolete in most cases. Also, buyers are being asked to operate with less inventory through materials requirements planning (MRP) and just-in-time (JIT) systems. Such programs require good supplier quality, since there is little or no safety stock to fall back on in case of emergency.

CUSTOMER NEEDS FOR QUALITY

Purchasing departments have a primary responsibility in meeting the objective of fitness for use and buying materials and components that add value proportionate to cost of production. For as we require greater precision in quality, the cost to produce increases, while the value added to the customer diminishes. As an illustration, consider a common watch that might cost $20 and provide most of us a great deal of value in keeping time to plus or minus two or three seconds. Time pieces used at track and field events require a much higher degree of precision, to one-thousandth of a second. Of course, the average consumer does not require that level of precision in keeping time. Therefore, the buyer must consider the ultimate need of the customer and correctly specify the proper quality level.

[2]David Roman, "Seconding One Source," *Electronic Buyers News,* September 18, 1989, p. 1.

[3]George Melloan, "Technology Fosters More Corporate Togetherness," *Wall Street Journal,* January 5, 1988, p. 25.

PURCHASING'S ROLE AND RESPONSIBILITY

Purchasing departments have a primary responsibility in meeting the objective of fitness for use by the customer, who perceives value in the product. For materials and component parts have a direct effect on the quality and cost of the end product. Two areas of concern seem to be related directly to purchasing. One is the need for a greater commitment to quality in the design and development stages and in parts and raw materials purchased. The second is supplier quality.

Purchasing needs to ensure that quality is adequately defined for every commodity or product to be purchased, and it is expressed in such a way that

1. The purchasing department knows just what is required.
2. The purchase order or contract is made out with a proper description of what is wanted.
3. The supplier is fully informed of the buyer's quality requirements.
4. Suitable means of inspecting and testing can be applied to see that delivered goods meet the stated standards of quality.
5. Goods delivered in conformance with the quality definition will be acceptable to the buyer's company. Otherwise, the buyer must challenge specifications that are restrictive in nature.
6. The specification enables the supplier to build quality into the product.

Responsibility for the factor of suitability in the quality definition rests ultimately with the departments responsible for product quality and performance and for using the purchased items. This part of the definition should be restricted to minimum essential quality requirements, leaving the greatest possible latitude for considerations of availability and value in purchasing without sacrificing the necessary suitability. If, for any purchasing reason, it seems desirable to modify the basic definition of quality, that is done only with the approval of design and using departments. Thus a primary role of the purchaser is to challenge specifications that are restrictive and where there are potential alternatives. The buyer must justify to the specifier, be it design engineering, maintenance, or a shop floor supervisor, that there are better alternatives. In the preparation of formal specifications, even though they are primarily of a technical nature, the best practice is to approach the matter as a joint project of technical, manufacturing, marketing, and purchasing personnel, so that all phases of quality, use, procurement, and customer needs may be considered from the start and full agreement reached.

QUALITY MUST BE DEFINED

Quality has a special meaning in the purchasing vocabulary. It cannot be characterized simply as "high" or "poor." It is specifically the sum or composite of the properties inherent in a material or product. David Garvin says that product quality has eight dimensions.[4] These dimensions are (1) performance, (2) features, (3)

[4] David Garvin, "What Does Product Quality Really Mean?" *Harvard Business Review*, Fall, 1984, pp. 25–39.

reliability, (4) conformance, (5) durability, (6) serviceability, (7) aesthetics, and (8) perceived quality. Purchasers are particularly concerned with the first six dimensions when buying.

These properties can be measured and defined. The significant ones must be defined so that the buyer knows what to ask the supplier to furnish and knows what is being received. This definition of quality, in greater or less detail, becomes the ordering description for every item—the essence of the purchase order.

Significant elements of quality for materials and components that go into a manufactured product include (1) analysis and dimension; (2) physical and chemical properties; (3) workability; (4) uniformity of analysis and dimension, to ensure uniform results in standard processing and to permit the use of mass-production methods with a minimum of spoilage or readjustment of machinery; and (5) special characteristics tending to increase the salability of the purchaser's product, such as appearance, finish, finishing properties, desirable bulk or weight, and the acquired quality of popular acceptance.

In regard to maintenance and operating supplies, significant properties would include utility, ease of application or use, efficiency, economy of use, and durability.

When dealing with machinery and equipment, one should consider productivity, versatility, dependability, durability, economy of operation and maintenance, and time- and labor-saving features.

ROLE OF SPECIFICATIONS

As in all purchasing, the first step in preparing specifications is to analyze the material or part to determine what function it will fill. Writing the specification around a particular design or merely describing some predetermined quality is the wrong approach. When the quality factors necessary to fulfill the functional need have been determined, they must be described in such a way as to assure the procurement of the proper quality yet allow sufficient flexibility for the application of good purchasing practice. Purchasing managers have a major responsibility at this stage in making the specifications a practical and effective tool for achieving ultimate value as well as precise suitability.

For example, one of the important purposes of using specifications in buying, beyond defining the material, is to provide a uniform quality standard as a basis for comparing competitive bids. Many specifications, however, are so closely written around a particular product that all competition is effectively excluded. Such specifications, of course, should be avoided if at all possible. Generally it is possible, because for the great majority of industrial requirements there are a variety of products or sources wholly adequate for the purpose, and the restrictive features frequently are not essential to the intended application even though they may be entirely consonant with it. Chances are they have been included, either by accident or by design, because the definition was approached from the wrong standpoint—the buyer described a product known to be suitable for the purpose rather than focusing on the basic requirements. Thus an engine may be specified with a prescribed number of cubic inches of piston displacement, which might limit the buyer's choice to a single make, whereas a definition in terms of the power to be developed would be inclusive enough to admit several acceptable alternates as well as this model without sacrificing any significant measure of desired quality. The definition should therefore be rewritten from the viewpoint of the requirement, and all nonessential limiting references should be eliminated. This is also a strong argument for the adoption of standard specifications and established commercial grades, if they are available and suitable, in preference to setting up a new and special definition, even at the expense of some slight compromise in design.

TYPES OF QUALITY DESCRIPTIONS

For purchasing purposes, quality can be defined in a number of different ways, appropriate in varying degrees to various types of purchases.

- Chemical, physical, and dimensional measurements
- Market grade
- Brand name
- Performance/use specifications
- Sample
- Commercial standards
- Formal specifications/drawings/internal specifications

Chemical, Physical, and Dimensional Measurements

Every definition of quality is based on some standard of measurement, understood by both buyer and supplier. Chemical analysis is one method of measurement. Physical tests provide a measurement in respect to various properties (e.g., ductility, elasticity, resistance to abrasion or shock). Dimensional measurements indicate such quality factors as precision finishing and conformance to stated tolerances. Asking that steel meet a 10,000 psi tensile strength or that copper be 99.999 percent pure is an example of such specifications. When such descriptions are used, the buyer must be certain of the application. For if the seller conforms to the asked-for chemical/physical/dimensional measurement, the buyer assumes the responsibility. Secondly, checking the actual quality often requires expensive equipment or use of independent test laboratories.

Market Grade

Market grades apply to commodities graded by government or private agencies. A commodity such as maple lumber is graded into several categories. First and seconds, selects, and #1 common are based on standards set by the National Hardwood Lumber Association. The regulations on commodities like lumber typically allow a wide range of opinion among inspectors. Standards specify a percentage of straightness, clarity, and the like, permitting subjective judgment by the inspectors. The U.S. Department of Agriculture sets market grades on meats, vegetable, grains, and other agricultural goods.

Purchasing by Brand Name

The simplest method of defining quality, although not always the most satisfactory, is to identify a material or product by the manufacturer's own brand name. From the purchasing viewpoint, this method has the advantages of simplicity in ordering, well-organized distribution, and consequently, ready availability. Elaborate inspection and tests can often be eliminated, because the delivery of the specified brand fulfills the obligation of the contract, and it may be assumed that the quality implications inherent in the brand name have been observed. It has the serious disadvantage of limiting procurement to a single supplier, thus eliminating the competitive element except insofar as competition may exist in the distribution of the product.

Even when limited to a specific brand, however, the buyer will often find different prices for the same brand item at competing distributors. Most items and most types of materials and equipment are available in comparable quality from competitive sources or are in competition with adequate alternative items. This is one of the principal reasons for having a special purchasing department: to discover or develop such alternative sources of supply.

When it is desirable, for convenience or any other reason, to use a brand or trade name as the descriptive term or definition for a company requirement, prudent purchasing practice overcomes this restrictive factor by adding the phrase "or equal." On the initial requisition for a material or product that has not been previously used or purchased by the company, design or production personnel may be aware of a particular branded product known to be suitable for the purpose, and they naturally specify that brand. If the buyer lacks time for market search, analysis of products, and the development of a more definitive product description, it is good purchasing practice to order the stipulated brand. But there is no assurance that it is the only suitable material or even the most suitable. It immediately becomes the purchasing manager's responsibility to seek possible alternatives. "Or equal" is the authorization to undertake this responsibility.

Performance/Use Specification

The most obvious measurement of quality in the purchasing sense is the measure of performance. We have pointed out that in each of the foregoing methods the units of measurement of the various properties are primarily useful as a guide or indicator of suitability or performance. They provide a means of comparing degrees of quality. Sometimes it is desirable to use all quality measurements available in evaluating a product. In some cases it may be possible and more practical to measure performance directly rather than to go through the intermediate step of measuring specific properties or quality factors that may be expected to give the desired results.

Performance/use specification is becoming increasingly popular as a method of defining and measuring quality because the desired results can be assured. As a general rule, it is good purchasing policy to inform the supplier or bidder as fully as possible regarding the specific use for which the product is intended, how it is to be applied, and the performance expected. There is no compulsion for the buyer to do this, and there are some cases in which it might not be desirable to do so, as in the case of special applications developed in the user's company or other confidential or competitive situations. However, these are the exceptional cases, not the general rule. Ordinarily, by enlisting the cooperation of the seller and inviting suggestions and advice, the buyer can make a more satisfactory purchase. Another point to be considered is that the law places the basic responsibility on the seller to deliver goods that are reasonably adapted to the purpose for which they are sold; if the seller is not advised of this purpose, however, and if the goods conform to other stated quality requirements, the buyer has no recourse in the event that in use they do not live up to expectations. Two major advantages for the buyer in using performance/use specifications are lower costs of specification writing and the encouragement of supplier ideas. Conversely, purchasers must select suppliers who have excellent reputations, for there is a possibility that a supplier will "cut corners" in the haste to achieve performance.

Thus inviting potential suppliers to prescribe a product or material for a particular purpose does not relieve the purchasing manager of specific responsibility for selection and purchase; the judgment and decision are still a part of the buying function and cannot be delegated to the seller. Nor does this policy condone the purchasing policy often urged by sellers—select a responsible supplier and leave the problem in his or her hands. Up to a certain point the principle expressed in this suggestion has merit, but its acceptance as a complete buying policy is a direct negation of purchasing responsibility.

Machinery is a common example of where performance/use specifications can be applied. For it is possible to describe and define a piece of complicated equipment in terms of dimension and design, given the component elements of each part. As a matter of fact, that is a necessary step for the designer and builder of the machine. But dimensions, design, and structural materials are means to an end, which is performance or productive ability; and it is this characteristic that interests the buyer and is the measure of quality. The buyer is essentially purchasing what the machine will do. All the other factors are meaningless if the equipment turns out to be inefficient or unsuited to a specific purpose. Consequently, performance or guaranteed output is the basic measure of quality, and a proper use specification or description of quality will make satisfactory performance the responsibility of the machine builder rather than mere conformance with the physical factors involved.

Purchasing by Sample

The actual description or definition of quality is sometimes avoided by inviting prospective suppliers to match a sample submitted by the buyer. This may be the simplest method of indicating what is wanted, and sometimes, as a result, it is the lazy buyer's method. Unfortunately, the apparent saving of effort in the first instance may be more than offset by the necessity of detailed inspection and testing to determine that the delivery actually does match the sample. Furthermore, no definite standards are set for the record or for future purchasers.

The practice is justified under certain conditions: in the case of special, nonrepetitive items, or when absolute quality requirements are not a significant factor, or when the size and importance of the purchase do not warrant the effort and expense of formulating a more definitive buying description. It is also justified when used in respect to particular aspects of quality, such as color, which is best defined by comparison with a standard sample. Because of the drawbacks, perhaps the best way to use samples is in conjunction with another form of describing quality. In this case the buyer asks for a sample to a certain specification prior to committing a large order.

Industry and Commercial Standards

Quality parameters set by industry and trade groups to meet the need for consistent quality levels are numerous. Such standards are set by the American Iron and Steel Institute (AISI), the Society of Automotive Engineers (SAE), and the American Institute of Electrical Engineers (AIEE). Because of the cost advantages to manufacturers, the National Bureau of Standards and the American National Standards Institute promote standards from a national standpoint.

Buying to commercial standards has several advantages including:

- Increase in availability
- More supply sources
- Better pricing than special items
- Smaller likelihood of communication errors
- Reduction in the number of specials in inventory

Standard specifications are as easy to use as brand names and are more accurately descriptive and subject to analysis and test. Because they are widely accepted as industry standards, they have the same commercial advantages as market grades in that they are a part of the language of their respective industries or trades and represent materials or products that are directly comparable on the basis of equal quality.

However, because standardization has not yet reached universal or national status, and because there are different sets of standards applicable to various items, some cautions should be observed. One point buyers must watch in purchasing on standard specifications is that some producers will quote on "our equivalent" for the industry standard. That is not necessarily to be interpreted as an indication of inferior quality; it does indicate that there is some deviation from the standard, although there is an implication that the quality is generally comparable and adapted to the same applications.

Formal Engineering Drawings and Blueprints

There are some items, usually of a technical nature, whose quality cannot be sufficiently defined by any of the preceding methods, so that a more formal and detailed specification is necessary. In such cases the engineering or drafting department is called upon to develop a detailed specification. Examples of products requiring drawings include buildings, special machinery, new-product designs, special requirements, and subassemblies requiring more than one of the previously mentioned components. Engineering drawings may reference a number of the other types of quality descriptors, such as brand name, chemical specifications, and commercial standards. Owing to all of the time involved, they are the costliest way to specify quality, but they are the most precise and permit detailed inspection. The vendor, however, assumes no liability for the nonfunctioning of the part, provided it is made to the parameters on the engineering drawing.

STANDARDIZATION/SPECIALIZATION

The savings potential from commercial standards is great, and many firms periodically conduct standardization programs where all purchased items are evaluated for potential savings. Where standardization is accomplished, a further reduction is undertaken through simplification. Simplification involves reducing the number of standard items in stock. Anyone who has assembled a toy swing or a piece of lawn furniture has encountered simplification. Often the extra hardware you receive is the result of a simplification program. It is less expensive for the supplier to stock fewer standards since inventory is lower than shipping extra parts.

Standardization programs permit lower pricing and lower inventory, since fewer items are stocked, and inspection costs are lower. While the benefits of standardization programs are significant, purchasers may encounter resistance from the marketing people, who are seeking unique or name-brand items, and the design engineers who feel their design is better suited than the standard item. Finally, when specifying a standard item, the purchaser is responsible for its proper use in the product applications.

QUALITY THROUGH PROCESS CONTROL AT THE SUPPLIER'S PLANT

As a result of the pressure from competitors and consumers described at the beginning of this chapter, many companies are taking a new stance on the quality of purchased parts and materials. Broadly speaking, their most significant actions include:

- Moving the responsibility—and the cost—for quality measurement back to the supplier

- Demanding from suppliers documentation that statistical process control was used in the production of their requirements (i.e. that quality was measured and assured during, not after, manufacture)
- Raising their own acceptable quality levels to as close to 100 percent as possible.
- Certifying and rewarding suppliers whose quality performance is outstanding
- Educating supplier management personnel in process-control principles and techniques and offering technical assistance in setting up such controls
- Thoroughly investigating supplier plants to determine their ability to meet the buyer's quality requirements (see Figure 8-1).

Much of the credit for moving quality responsibility to the source goes to Edward Deming.[5] Dr. Deming is considered the father of statistical process control. He is given much of the credit for improving Japanese product quality. An American, he lectured in Japan during the 1950's and 1960's and now provides training on quality for many major U.S firms. His philosophy states that we should cease our dependence on mass inspection. Instead, he says we should require statistical evidence that quality is built in. Thus the goal is to eliminate inspection by continually improving the process. Deming advocates the use of several tools to improve a process. Two of the more popular are

- Statistical control charts—charts that plot production and observe variations
- Cause-and-effect diagrams—charts that diagrammatically include sources that create variance

Simply stated, statistical control charts collect samples from a process as it is being run (see Figure 8-2). These samples are recorded on a chart, and if the process remains between its upper and lower limits, the process continues. Should the process exceed its upper or lower control limit, the process is stopped. Efforts are made to discover the source of the error, so that the process produces acceptable parts. When attempting to solve such problems or determine sources for improvement in a process, a cause-and-effect diagram is often used. Basically, this kind of diagram, often called a fishbone, lists the major causes of the undesirable variance. As is seen in Figure 8-3 the surface plating is uneven. Primary causes could be material suppliers, equipment, workers' applications, or employees. Secondary causes for employees include working conditions and supervision. Such charts force systematic thinking about the problem.

A PROACTIVE APPROACH TO QUALITY

In today's highly competitive, worldwide markets, purchasing must play a much more proactive role in ensuring that materials of appropriate quality are received. This means that rather than using the inspection and rejection techniques just described, buyers should work with their suppliers in achieving zero defects in incoming materials and components.

[5]For detailed information see W. Edwards Deming, *Quality, Productivity and Competitive Position*, MIT, Cambridge, MA., 1982.

TECHNICARE

VENDOR QUALITY ASSURANCE SYSTEM SURVEY REPORT

VENDOR NAME

ADDRESS

CITY & STATE

PHONE

SURVEY NO.   DATE

VENDOR PERSONNEL CONTACTED

VENDOR IN CONFORMANCE WITH TECHNICARE
QUALITY CONTROL SPECIFICATIONS:

( ) YES   ( ) NO
( ) PROBATIONARY

DESCRIPTION OF VENDOR'S PRODUCT(S):

CORRECTIVE ACTION REQUIRED: ( ) YES
                              ( ) NO

PURCHASING ASSISTANCE REQ'D: ( ) YES
                              ( ) NO

VENDOR REPRESENTATIVE SIGNATURE & TITLE

SURVEY REPRESENTATIVE SIGNATURE(S):

COPY TO:	YES			NO			SEE REMARK
	INCOMING	IN PROCESS	FINAL	INCOMING	IN PROCESS	FINAL	
1. IS QUALITY CONTROL (INSPECTION) A SEPARATE AND DISTINCT PART OF THE VENDOR'S PLANT ORGANIZATION?							
2. DOES THE VENDOR HAVE QUALITY MANUAL INCLUDING WRITTEN INSPECTION AND TEST PROCEDURES?							
3. ARE INSPECTIONS AND TESTS BEING PERFORMED IN ACCORDANCE WITH WRITTEN INSPECTION AND TEST INSTRUCTIONS, DOCUMENTED, AND AVAILABLE FOR REVIEW?							
4. DOES THE VENDOR HAVE THE LATEST ENGINEERING DRAWINGS AND SPECIFICATIONS?							
5. IS 100% OR SAMPLING INSPECTION USED? HOW IS IT DOCUMENTED? DESCRIBE.							
6. ARE STATISTICAL QUALITY CONTROL TECHNIQUES USED (CONTROL CHARTS, MACHINE CAPABILITY STUDIES, SAMPLING PLANS, ETC.)? DESCRIBE.							
7. ARE INSPECTION AND TEST DISPOSITIONS PROPERLY INDICATED?							
8. DO YOU HAVE PROCEDURE TO HANDLE A SITUATION, WHERE DEFECTIVE(S) ARE FOUND IN A LOT? DESCRIBE.							
9. ARE CONTROLS ADEQUATE TO PREVENT MOVE- MENT OF REJECTED MATERIALS TO STORAGE OR POINT OF USE? DESCRIBE.							
10. ARE REWORKED PARTS AND MATERIALS REINSPECTED AND DOCUMENTED?							

Figure 8-1   Form used to report results of quality audits at plants of current or potential suppliers. Audit team includes representatives from quality assurance, purchasing, and engineering.

Page 2 of 2

	YES			NO			SEE REMARK
	INCOMING	IN PROCESS	FINAL	INCOMING	IN PROCESS	FINAL	
11. ARE PACKAGED MATERIALS CHECKED FOR IDENTIFICATION AND PROPER PACKAGING BEFORE SHIPMENT?							
12. ARE PROPER GAGES, INCLUDING CHECKING AIDS, TEST EQUIPMENTS AVAILABLE AND USED?							
13. ARE GAGES, TEST AND MEASURING EQUIPMENT(S) RECALLED, CALIBRATED, AND RECORDED PERIODICALLY?							
14. ARE ALL MATERIALS PROPERLY IDENTIFIED (ROUTE, TAGS, ETC.)?							
15. DOES THE VENDOR HAVE CERTIFICATION IN: A. WELDING B. N.D.T. C. OTHER? LIST CERTIFYING AGENCY							
16.							
17.							
18.							

REMARKS:	
TECHNICARE'S ENGINEERING COMMENT:	
TECHNICARE'S PURCHASING COMMENT:	
TECHNICARE'S QUALITY ASSURANCE COMMENT:	

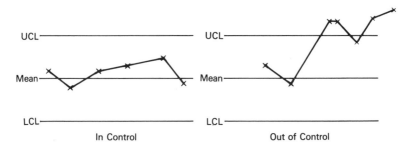

Figure 8-2 Statistical Control Chart.

Jack Reddy and Abe Berger suggest that this goal of zero defects can be obtained when the purchasing department sees itself as the manager of outside manufacturing, responsible for communicating to its suppliers an attitude of 100 percent conformance to specifications. The key in all of this, according to Reddy and Berger, is the development of clear and realistic specifications and working with suppliers in a cooperative mode to ensure their conformance to specifications.[6]

David Garvin has provided a series of guidelines, in the form of questions, that can be used in helping suppliers improve their quality throughout the manufacturing process. These questions are listed in Figure 8-4.

The other major change in measuring the quality of suppliers is the trend toward measuring customer satisfaction. This notion of assessing the satisfaction of the firm's final customer is developed in most programs aimed at quality improvement.

An example of an innovative program is the one developed by Air Products, a major producer of industrial gases and engineering projects. The company has taken as a guide the "essentials and elements of quality improvement" listed by Phil Crosby in *Quality Is Free* (Mentor/New American Library, N.Y., 1979) and

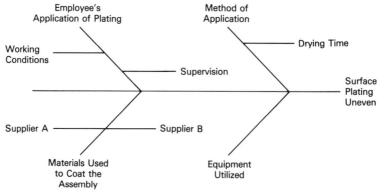

FIGURE 8-3 Fishbone Diagram.

[6]Jack Reddy and Abe Berger, "Three Essentials of Product Quality," *Harvard Business Review.* Vol 61, No. 4. July–August, 1983, pp. 153–159.

Questions You Can Ask a Supplier on Quality Standards

1. How is the quality department organized at your plant?
   Which departments have responsibility for improving product designs?
       —controlling rejects?
       —reducing scrap?
       —resolving field problems?
   What are the roles of engineering, manufacturing, and purchasing in these areas?
2. How is the customer-service department organized? What role does it play in managing product quality?
3. Do you set goals for incoming quality? How are they established?
4. What kinds of data do you keep on rejects, field failures & other kinds of problems?
5. What kinds of things do you do for statistical control analysis of quality? Are acceptable quality levels set? What types of training do you give the work force in these areas?
6. How do you instill a commitment to quality in your work force?
7. What quality programs does your work force practice?
8. Does your firm utilize a total quality-control system? How is it organized?
9. What kind of quality-cost reporting system do you use? What kinds of quality audits?
10. What steps do you take to ensure that your suppliers provide quality components? What steps do you take if they don't conform?
11. Do your people visit your suppliers?
12. What role do your purchasing people play in ensuring quality in their suppliers?
13. How do you usually develop a new product? What are the steps? At what point do customer service, purchasing, and quality departments become involved?

Adapted from David A. Garvin, "Managing Quality," in "The Room Air Conditioning Study," Harvard Business School, 1981–82.

Figure 8-4

used them in conjunction with the highly successful quality-improvement program of the 3M Corporation. The result is the thirteen-point program illustrated in Figures 8-5 and 8-6. The key points in this program purchasing department are, first, the setting of clear expectations of what is acceptable quality and, second, the communication of these expectations to the firm's suppliers.

The value of having clear expectations and good communication can be seen in the following Chrysler, Inc. example.

Managing for World-Class Quality: An Example

When Chrysler Motors was in the throes of its financial crisis in the late 1970s and early 1980s, one of its major problems was its perceived poor quality. In fact, the December 1987 issue of the *American Machinist* stated that Chrysler's vehicles had been viewed as some of the worst-quality products available. But by 1987 this

---

ESSENTIALS OF QUALITY IMPROVEMENT

1. Management Commitment
2. Quality is Consistent Conformance to Customers' Expectations
3. Quality is Attained Through Prevention and Specific Improvement Projects
4. The Objective is Consistent Conformance to Expectations 100% of the Time Rather than Management's Acceptance of Some Error Level
5. Measurements of Quality are Through Indications of Customer Satisfaction, Rather than Indicators of Self-Gratification

---

Courtesy of Air Products and Chemicals, Inc., Trexlertown, Pennsylvania.

Figure 8-5

same article goes on to say, these products are among the most improved.[7] That same year *Purchasing* magazine awarded Chrysler's Procurement and Supply Department with the Medal of Professional Excellence.[8] While there were many reasons for the improvement in Chrysler's fortunes during the 1980s, quality improvement stands out as a key. And a key to Chrysler's quality improvement was the adoption of an aggressive supplier-qualification program. The elements of this program are presented in Figures 8-7 and 8-8, which have been adapted from Chrysler's *Supplier Quality Assurance Manual.*

Again, embedded in this program is the emphasis on ensuring that suppliers know what is expected of them and on working with suppliers to prevent defects from occurring in the first place rather than waiting to "inspect out" defects from products delivered to Chrysler's plants. This effort has paid off handsomely for Chrysler. In 1980, prior to the establishment of the supplier quality assurance program and many other improvements at Chrysler, supplier defects were ranging from 20 to 80 percent. By 1987 these defects were reduced to .5 percent. In addition, there were other benefits, such as (1) reduced costs of inspection, (2) lower inventory investment, and (3) greater use of JIT suppliers.

THE ELEMENTS OF QUALITY IMPROVEMENT

1. Management Leadership for Quality Improvement
2. Organizing for Quality Improvement
3. Education for Quality Improvement
4. Develop Sensitivity to Customer Expectations
5. Quantifying Conformance for Quality Improvement
6. Communication for Quality Improvement
7. Action for Quality Improvement
8. Annual Plan for Quality Improvement

Courtesy of Air Products and Chemicals, Inc., Trexlertown, Pennsylvania.

Figure 8-6

[7]"The AM Award," *American Machinist and Automated Manufacturing,* December 1987, pp. 66–72.
[8]"1987 Medal of Professional Excellence," *Purchasing,* July 16, 1987, pp. 43–65.

Managing for World-Class Quality: An Example, Chrysler Motors
Quality Policy of Chrysler Motors:
The quality policy of Chrysler Motors is "to be the best." This policy requires that every individual and operating unit fully understand the requirements of their customer, and deliver products and services that satisfy these requirements at a defect-free level. Procurement and supply will ensure that all suppliers, both external and Chrysler, are aware of our requirements.
Key Principles:
- Quality is defined as — conformance to requirements
- The performance standard is — defect free
- The quality system is — defect prevention
- Measurement is — cost of quality nonconformance

Supplier involvement — must ensure that all product conforms to Chrysler requirements:
- How this will be accomplished is submitted to Chrysler in a supplier quality system plan
  - describes the quality assurance techniques to guarantee the delivery of defect-free product
  - based on the quality fundamentals presented in the Chrysler supplier quality assurance manual
  - includes continuous quality improvement

Preventive System Benefits:
The use of a quality assurance system based on defect prevention rather than detection will result in improved quality, lower costs, and improved productivity.

Adapted from *Chrysler Motors Supplier Quality Assurance Program: SQA Manual*, 1988 revision, p. 1.

Figure 8-7

When Chrysler executives were asked to explain the dramatic improvement in supplier performance, they indicated that the key was that their suppliers now knew what was expected of them. More than anything else, this approach summarizes purchasing's role in quality—clearly communicating to suppliers what is expected of them and then working with them to ensure 100 percent conformance to expectations. The methods described in this chapter should aid purchasing departments in achieving this goal.

INCOMING QUALITY INSPECTION

While purchasing's goal is to eliminate inspection of supplier material, its traditional role of inspecting purchased items to ensure that their quality is in conformance with the order and is as represented by the supplier will continue to be utilized. Consequently, a provision for inspection and testing is usually included in standards and specifications. More and more, however, companies are turning to another approach to quality assurance that places greater responsibility on the supplier. Before we discuss that change, the reader should be aware at least of the most familiar technique used in conventional inspection: sampling of purchased

---

Chrysler Supplier Quality Assurance System

Key System Concepts:
- Expanded use of the source approval process to select suppliers with acceptable in-place product quality systems.
- Emphasis on preventive quality assurance techniques and the expanded use of statistical process control methods.
- Submission of a quality system plan from each supplier location for review and approval by Chrysler Supplier Quality.
- Establishment of quality and reliability programs where the supplier is responsible for immediate corrective action response.
- On-site surveys by Chrysler quality specialists to verify compliance with system requirements.
- Supplier continuous product improvement planning.
- Ongoing Chrysler assistance in system refinements and reduced product variation efforts.
- Assurance that Chrysler Motors' Suppliers are aware of corporate requirements and are striving to supply defect-free product(s).

SQA System Progression Requirements:
- One-on-one supplier orientation meeting
- System plan submitted
- System plan evaluated
- On-site quality assurance system surveys

Adapted from *Chrysler Motors Supplier Quality Assurance Program: SQA Manual,* 1988 revision, pp. 2–4.

Figure 8-8

goods. The following explanation is adapted from a package program from the Program Aids Library of the National Association of Purchasing Management, *How to Buy Quality* (PAL 42).

Usually the sample is a fraction of the whole lot. In theory, that small segment will indicate what the entire lot is like. The problem is to determine the correct sample size to assure statistically meaningful results and to ensure that the sample is representative of the entire lot. The size of the sample, taken from a variety of published tables, depends on the following considerations:

1. Required level of quality assurance
2. Cost of the item being checked
3. Basic function of the part
4. Quantity of the lot received
5. Required reliability of result
6. History of supplier quality reliability

With the size of the sample established, a target or goal must be established to check against. Normally, this target is expressed in terms of percent defective and indicates the maximum allowable. A target widely used in industry is the acceptable quality level (AQL), which indicates the degree of deviation from a given standard that will be permitted. An AQL of .90, for example, indicates that a buyer will accept a shipment in which 10 percent of the items do not meet the specifications in the purchase order.

On some items the entire lot is tested, but these are usually special cases. Large castings would generally be included in such a category, as would parts for which extreme precision is essential. Rubber safety gloves for use in work involving high voltages would be subjected to individual dielectric tests before acceptance.

Handling Quality Problems

It is probably academic to argue the point of where the technical responsibility lies for acceptance or rejection of a delivery. But it is important to bear in mind these two distinct stages of responsibility—the obligation of the purchasing department to procure materials of the right quality and the obligation of the vendor to deliver in accordance with the order. It is a basic purpose of inspection and testing to confirm or certify the action of the purchasing department and to guide the buyer in his or her decision as to whether the contract requirements have been satisfactorily met in the delivery. The buyer will naturally rely on these findings as an integral part of the procurement process. Certainly any prudent purchasing officer will always consult with technical and using departments in the event of any substantial deviation from specified quality before making a decision as to the disposition of the goods.

Several alternative methods of procedure are open to the buyer in respect to substandard deliveries. These include:

1. *Outright rejection.* The goods are returned to the supplier, at the latter's expense, on a shipping order and invoice issued at the direction of the purchasing department. The supplier is notified of this action and of the reasons therefor. It should also be made clear at this point whether the original purchase order is considered as still in force and unfulfilled or whether the transaction is terminated through default of the supplier.
2. *Return for replacement.* This procedure applies particularly to fabricated parts, but it can be used for materials as well. Accounting procedure is customarily handled through a memorandum invoice or credit memo pending receipt of the corrected or satisfactory delivery.

   At least one company has gone beyond the policy of returning bad castings in exchange for a refund. Ford Motor Company also charges suppliers for its cost of machining the part before it is found defective. Under the Ford program, machining fees are assessed only if a participating supplier's defective rate exceeds 2 percent in a given month. The program includes monthly meetings of Ford purchasing and quality-control personnel with supplier representatives. They determine which castings were scrapped because of supplier mistakes. All parties must agree before a charge is assessed.
3. *Technical or engineering adjustment.* It is frequently practicable for a qualified vendor representative to come to the buyer's plant to make necessary adjustments on faulty equipment or to work out a satisfactory application of nonconforming materials.

TENNANT	**SUPPLIER CORRECTIVE ACTION REQUEST**	NO. _____

VENDOR:	TENNANT® P/N	REF. NSR	DATE
	VENDOR P/N	REQUEST ORIGINATOR	
	PART NAME	BUYER	

REJECT FOUND IN:
☐ INCOMING INSPC   P.O.# _____ QUANTITY _____ NO. INSPECTED _____ NO. REJECTED _____ % REJECTED _____

☐ FINAL MACHINE TEST NO. REJECTED _____ BETWEEN _____ MONTHLY USAGE _____ % REJECTED _____

REQUIREMENT AND NON-CONFORMITY

DISPOSITION OF PARTS
☐ USE AS IS   ☐ REWORKED AT TENNANT®   ☐ RETURNED ON P.O. # _____   ☐ SCRAP AT TENNANT®

☐ THIS CORRECTIVE ACTION REQUEST IS FOR THE VENDORS INFORMATION ONLY.
☐ THIS CORRECTIVE ACTION REQUEST IS DIRECTED TO THE VENDOR FOR INVESTIGA-
TION AND STATEMENT OF CORRECTIVE ACTION. THIS REQUEST MUST BE ANSWERED
COMPLETELY AND ACCURATELY BEFORE _____ .

REASON FOR DISCREPANCY:

STATEMENT OF CORRECTIVE ACTION (ATTACH ADDITIONAL INFORMATION AS REQUIRED)

| EFFECTIVITY DATE: | INVESTIGATOR: | DEPARTMENT: | DATE |

DISTRIBUTION:
White & Green - Return to Originator when completed
Yellow - Retain for use by Investigating and Answering Dept.
Pink - Retain as Originators Copy (for follow-up)
Gold - Retain in Purchasing (for follow-up)

RETURN PART 1 & 2 TO:
Tennant Company
701 No. Lilac Drive
P.O. Box 1452
Minneapolis, MN 55440
ATTN: Q.C. Department

60011181 R

Figure 8-9 Five-part form used to obtain a documented statement of corrective action. The top half of the form is completed by the customer. The supplier is required to complete the bottom half. Courtesy of *Purchasing World.*

4. *Price adjustment.* If goods are usable, although not strictly in accordance with the purchase specification, a price renegotiation in line with the value actually delivered may be the simplest and most satisfactory means of adjustment, although it does not actually correct the condition of a faulty delivery. It should be noted that repeated instances of this nature, regardless of the vendor's willingness to

make the adjustment, are indicators of an unsatisfactory and incompetent source of supply.

Whatever method of adjustment is decided on, two principles should be consistently observed. The vendor must be promptly notified that a delivery is unsatisfactory (see Figure 8–9), and for what reason, and the negotiation or adjustment should be carried on by or through the purchasing department. The procurement is not complete until a satisfactory delivery has been made and accepted. The contractual relationship has been effected through purchasing, and the personal contacts, both with the vendor and within the buyer's own organization, to aid in effecting a proper adjustment or settlement are generally centered on the buyer who placed the original order.

POINTS FOR REVIEW

1. Explain why quality is so important to most firms today.
2. List the eight basic dimensions of and give examples of each.
3. Compare the concepts of suitability and reliability as they apply to purchased products.
4. Explain the meaning of "use specification" and its significance in purchasing.
5. Contrast buying by brand name to buying by specification. Give examples from your own experience with the two types of buying and the reasons for your having employed them in specific instances.
6. Recognize those situations in which deviations from specifications may be necessary.
7. List the alternatives open to buyers when suppliers deliver substandard goods.
8. Describe the approaches to achieving world-class quality discussed in this chapter and compare this to a recent article concerning other firms efforts.

Supplier Selection

Having defined and described the role and organization of the purchasing depart-ment, we turn to its most basic and important job: finding suppliers able and will-ing to provide—consistently—quality, service, and competitive price. To get the best sources of supply for their needs, buyers often can make choices from a num-ber of equally eligible sources. In other cases an extensive search may be required to find one satisfactory supplier or even develop a source where none had previ-ously been available. In either event, purchasing must continually monitor and evaluate supplier performance.

This chapter discusses how buyers choose suppliers. But it should be noted at the start that the principles and methods they use are being applied more intensely today than ever before. As companies are forced by competition to im-prove their products, they, in turn, pressure suppliers to upgrade their perform-ance on quality, service, and price. Some of the effects on the buyer-seller relationship have already been noted. Others will be referred to in appropriate later chapters. They are summarized here to add perspective to the comments on the selection-and-evaluation process that appear later in the chapter:

- The growth in worldwide markets has given U.S. buyers more leverage in pro-moting competition because of the greater number of suppliers available.
- Taking a leaf from Japan's book, U.S. companies are demanding that pur-chased parts come into their plants "100 percent fit for use" if the suppliers want to keep their business.
- Many companies are insistent that suppliers help them with their just-in-time (JIT) inventory programs by making frequent deliveries before parts are needed on the production line.[1]
- Suppliers who meet these relatively new standards are being rewarded with ad-ditional business; those who do not are being dropped. The process is known as narrowing the supplier base—placing business with a few suppliers, where there might have been dozens previously. As one executive put it: "We are bet-ter off with three or four suppliers than with twenty, none of whom cares enough about us to give us the quality and delivery we need."
- With suppliers they can depend on, buyers are increasingly turning to long-term contracts, running from one year up to as many as ten. Both sides benefit: the buyer gets a better price because of the volume involved, plus assurance of supply; the seller has the assurance of continuous volume of business and a chance to plan production more rationally.
- In many instances narrowing the supplier base comes down to placing *all* of a given set of requirements with one supplier. Ford's JIT program requires close integration of the suppliers' and buyers' production systems. In some instances deliveries are made every two hours. Multiple sources of supply would create severe scheduling and integration problems.[2]

Given that kind of environment, purchasing managers must apply basic methods of selection analytically and aggressively.

---

[1] JIT programs actually have many more aspects. This relatively small part is singled out here to high-light the supplier's role in a system. See Chapter 10 and 17 for more details on the JIT concept.

[2] D. N. Burt, "Managing Suppliers Up to Speed," *Harvard Business Review,* July–August 1989, p. 128.

SOURCE-SELECTION MODEL

In the actual process of source selection, there are four stages: (1) the survey stage, in which all possible sources for a product are explored; (2) the inquiry stage, in which the relative qualifications and advantages of potential sources are analyzed; (3) the stage of negotiation and selection, leading to the issue of an initial order; and (4) the experience stage, in which a continuing buyer-supplier relationship is established and suppliers are evaluated on performance (see Figure 9-1).

Survey Stage

As in all purchasing problems, the starting point is the need for a material or product. The exact specifications may or may not be fixed, but the general nature and purpose of the product are known. What is available on the market? Who makes such a product, or who can make it? Who can supply it most satisfactorily and most economically?

The original survey of potential sources should overlook no possibilities, provided they are reasonably accessible and there is some assurance that they meet required standards of quality, service, and price. Trade directories provide comprehensive and well-organized listings of the whole range of manufactured products and manufacturers on a nationwide basis, usually with at least a general indication of size and commercial rating. The *Thomas Register of American Manufacturers* is a national trade directory used by many buyers. Supplementing these are regional directories such as those issued by state chambers of commerce and, on a still more local scale, the classified section of telephone directories. An excellent regional directory is the *Chicago Buyers' Guide,* which lists manufacturers and distributors in the Chicago area. Specialized trade directories list concerns that do not have product lines of their own but provide industrial services, such as foundries, screw machine shops, heat treaters, and custom fabricators of plastic parts. With the continued expansion of world markets, more and more directories of suppliers in foreign countries are becoming available. These include:

Trade Directories of the World, Croner Publications
Asian Sources for Electronic Components, Wordnight, Inc.
World Marketing Director, Dun & Bradstreet
Predicasts F & S Index, Predicasts, Inc.

The buyer's library of manufacturers' and distributors' catalogs is another reference source of prime importance, provided that the indexing system is adequate. Many purchasing managers also have a commodity information file in which they have collected vendors' mailing pieces and data sheets, advertisements, and new-product announcements from business magazines. Some of this information is so new that it has not yet found its way into the standard catalogs, but the alert buyer has it on hand when needed.

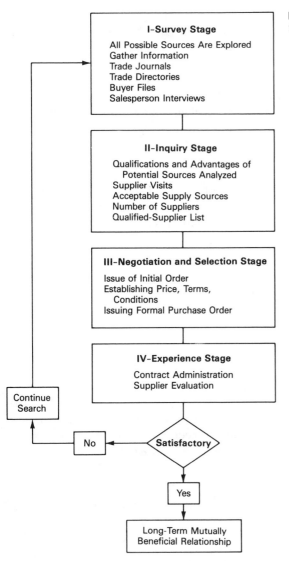

Figure 9-1   Four-Stage Model of Source Selection

I-Survey Stage

All Possible Sources Are Explored
Gather Information
Trade Journals
Trade Directories
Buyer Files
Salesperson Interviews

II-Inquiry Stage

Qualifications and Advantages of
    Potential Sources Analyzed
Supplier Visits
Acceptable Supply Sources
Number of Suppliers
Qualified-Supplier List

III-Negotiation and Selection Stage

Issue of Initial Order
Establishing Price, Terms,
    Conditions
Issuing Formal Purchase Order

IV-Experience Stage

Contract Administration
Supplier Evaluation

Continue
Search

No   ← Satisfactory

Yes

Long-Term Mutually
Beneficial Relationship

Salespersons are an important source of information, both on their companies' products and capabilities and on their application to customers' processes. Experience has shown that the most successful salespersons are those who have not limited their service to buyers to merely selling the product at hand. Their psychology aims more toward meeting the buyer's need, not only with products but also with whatever information, service, and technical advice are available from their companies.

The buyer can build a workable list of likely sources using information from the publications and persons mentioned above. Those who appear to be reliable and stable, have the needed kind of manufacturing capability and experience, and are conveniently located (to keep transportation costs down) are put at the head of the list. Many times the buyer will have the requisite information through reputation or advertising. Those firms that have low capitalization or credit ratings or whose products are not in the required quality range will be excluded.

If the product required is of a routine nature, the buyer may send out a request for bids from such a selected list. If the product is a more important or more complex one or one for which there is likely to be a continuing need, there will be an intermediate stage of inquiry and research.

Inquiry Stage

The inquiry stage involves prequalification of potential sources, which narrows the field from possible sources to acceptable sources. Inquiry at this stage is directed toward developing more specific information on:

- Vendors' production facilities and capacity
- Financial stability
- Product quality
- Technical competence
- Manufacturing efficiency
- General business policies
- Position in the industry
- Progressiveness
- Interest in the buyer's order
- Cooperative attitude

The aim at this point is to find those suppliers who are capable of producing the item in the required quality and quantity, who can be relied on as a continuous source of supply under all conditions, who will keep their delivery promises and other service obligations, and who are competitive on price. Visits to supplier facilities are important in this stage.

Supplier Visits   Particular features to be noted at the plant of a supplier or prospective supplier are:

- Modernity and efficiency of equipment
- Facilities for technical controls and the importance attached to such controls
- Caliber of supervision and inspection
- Evidences of good management and good housekeeping in plant operations
- Practice as to the maintenance of raw-material stocks
- Character of the operation, especially as it relates to purchasing requirements and practices

Personal contacts should also be established with key people in management and production as a very helpful asset in the event that emergency or special requirements need to be discussed later by phone.

When the projected purchase involves substantial expenditure or when the quality of the part to be bought is critical, inspection and evaluation of potential vendors are generally made a team effort. A typical team will include representatives from the purchasing, quality-control, engineering, and production departments, although the makeup of the group may vary. A West Coast manufacturer of complex electronic controls, for example, requires that a team consisting only of purchasing and quality-control personnel check out suppliers of critical parts before they are accepted.

Customarily, supplier survey teams follow a standard pattern of inspection and collection of information. The thoroughness of such inspections is reflected in the form shown in Figure 9-2. Depending on the nature of the item being considered for purchase, the supplier's reputation, and other factors, other teams might give more attention to condition and capabilities of machines, shop methods, inventory, housekeeping, and so on. The inspection can be speeded by having the supplier provide some basic information before the team's visit. One purchasing department, for example, asks suppliers to fill in the vendor capability survey form shown in Figure 9–2 before deciding on how extensive an analysis the evaluation team should make.

The result of the study at this point should be a list of several acceptable supply sources, all capable of furnishing the requirements, with whom the buyer would be willing to place an order. The list is not necessarily in order of preference. It may come very close to that point of decision, but in the orderly process of vendor appraisal and narrowing of choice, there still remains the stage of negotiation in which details and terms are considered, to determine where the best ultimate value lies. Basically this will be in terms of quality, service, and price. Beyond that, it will be influenced by the intangibles of interest, cooperation, and goodwill that enhance the value of all these factors and beyond that, the decision may hinge on special circumstances—the smaller company in which the order will have an importance that is lost in the larger operation, the company that has an engineer or superintendent particularly skilled in that type of production, or the company that has an open spot in its manufacturing schedule to accommodate the order.

There may be no *one* absolute best source. The buyer usually wishes to establish alternative sources for the products that are to be bought, both as an added assurance of supply and to maintain competition. Then the decision as to where the bulk of the business will be placed will be made on the basis of a fourth and convincing criterion—actual experience with the supplier.

Sourcing Alternatives   In considering various potential sources of supply, several basic questions must also be answered.

For instance, should the firm buy direct from the *manufacturer* or go through a *distributor*? The choice is usually dependent on the level of service the firm requires from the supplier. In buying from a distributor, the firm is really buying not only products but the distribution of those products as well. For a firm that has limited warehousing, orders in small volumes, or constraints on the amount of inventory it can hold, a distributor may be an operating necessity. In addition, some products actually cost less through a distributor, as the manufacturer prefers to distribute the product in that manner. An example is the purchase

VENDOR CAPABILITY SURVEY

SURVEY DATE _____

COMPANY NAME _____ □ CORPORATION   □ PARTNERSHIP

ADDRESS _____ □ OTHER _____

PHONE NO. _____ DATE ESTABLISHED _____ STATE OF INCORPORATION _____

SUBSIDIARY OF _____ DIVISION OF _____

CREDIT RATING _____ SECURITY CLEARANCE _____

OFFICIALS (OWNERS)	TITLE	KEY PERSONNEL	TITLE

□ MASS PRODUCTION   □ JOB SHOP   □ MACHINING   □ FINISHING   □ ASSEMBLY

□ TESTING   □ ENGINEERING   □ RES. & DEV.   □ OTHER _____

NORMAL PRODUCTS OR SERVICES	DEFENSE	COMMERC.

CUSTOMER REFERENCES	ITEMS PRODUCED FOR THEM

FACILITIES	SQUARE FEET	OWNED	LEASED	LEASE EXPIRES	PERSONNEL DIRECT	INDIRECT	UNION	NON UNION
OFFICE AREA								
ENGINEERING AND LAB. AREA								
MANUFACTURING AREA								
TOTAL								

UNION AFFILIATION	LOCAL NO.	CONTRACT EXPIRATION DATE

EQUIPMENT:
ATTACH LIST OF MACHINE TOOLS, SPECIAL TEST AND OTHER EQUIPMENT. GIVE GENERAL CONDITION AND INDICATE WHETHER OWNED, LEASED, OR GOVERNMENT FURNISHED.

EQUIP LIST DATED

Figure 9-2 Front side of form used by some purchasing departments in evaluating potential suppliers is filled in by the company being evaluated. If preliminary data warrant further investigation, a survey team will be sent to the supplier's plant for more detailed analysis of operations and capabilities.

of light bulbs, where a large-volume buyer can purchase one case of light bulbs from a distributor for less than it would cost to buy one hundred cases direct from the manufacturer. The distributor is willing to sell at this low cost because it is interested in obtaining additional electrical supplies business from its large customers.

Another issue that must be evaluated in studying potential sources of supply is whether to buy from *local* or *national* vendors. Each has its benefits to offer to the buyer. For instance, the national vendor because of its economies of size may be able to undercut local vendors in price and offer superior technical service. However, because of their proximity, local vendors can, most often, be more responsive. Additionally, they are interested in maintaining a higher level of service. Buying from local services can provide the buying firm with increased goodwill in the community.

An additional consideration concerning the issue of national versus local vendors has to do with the trend toward the greater use of the JIT system. JIT requires frequent and smaller deliveries, which generally means the need to use vendors who are in close proximity to the using facility. This trend may favor the use of local vendors.

One distinction that should be made here is that "local vendors" could include local divisions of national companies. In such a case a buyer enjoys the benefits of both the economies of a large, national vendor and the responsiveness of a vendor situated locally.

One further consideration to make is the size of the vendor selected; that is, should the buyer's firm do business with a *small* or a *large* vendor? A general rule of thumb used in making this decision is to correlate the size of the order with the size of the supplier. The basis for this heuristic is that a buyer should guard against becoming such a significant factor of the supplier's total business that removal of that business could result in the financial ruin of that supplier. Conversely, the buyer wants to ensure that his or her business is important to the supplier and can only do so by giving adequate orders to the supplier. This guards against the possibility of being dropped by the supplier or having delayed shipment when times are tight.

In the past it has been felt that a buyer would not want to represent more than 15 to 25 percent of a supplier's total business. However, with the advent of the move to JIT and single sourcing, this concern has diminished. The move toward becoming a more significant percentage of a supplier's total business means an increasing vigilance on the part of the buyer to ensure that the supplier is continually in a position of assuring supply.

One final consideration to address in the area of evaluating potential sources is the question of whether to buy from *domestic* or *foreign* sources. As noted earlier in the text, international sourcing is becoming a bigger part of many buyers' jobs. Since the process of international sourcing is considerably more complex than buying from domestic sources, it deserves much more attention. International sourcing, including its benefits and obstacles, is discussed in chapter 11. Suffice it to say here that a good purchasing decision will consider all qualified sources, domestic and foreign.

The key point to keep in mind in making all of the decisions discussed above is that the primary goal of all source-selection decisions is the assurance of supply at the lowest total cost. With this in mind, the prudent buyer will consider all possible sources—manufacturer and distributor, local and national, large and small, and foreign and domestic.

Number of Suppliers   Once the number of suppliers is reduced to those qualified, a decision on number of suppliers needs to be made. There is a trend to reduction in number of suppliers. This trend was highlighted during the early 1980s, when Toyota, with a supplier base of 250, purchased a higher percentage of products than GM, with a supply base of 3,500. Recent research with firms using JIT has shown supply-base reductions averaging 30 percent within one year of a JIT program start date. Within two years average supplier base numbers were down 40 percent.[3] Some examples of reported supplier base reduction after five years were

* 5,000 to 300   * 1,000 to 250
* 2,000 to 600   *   800 to 200

Single-source relationships, however, require the highest degree of cooperation and coordination between buyer's and seller's technical staffs, resulting in comprehensive contracts that provide incentives for suppliers. These elements are mainly reflected in long-term contracts that assure suppliers of continued business and reasonable profits. As one auto-industry purchasing executive put it: "To meet our requirements, suppliers will have to put up more bricks and mortar, and they can't be expected to do that with one-year purchase orders." One of the country's largest food processors, for example, has had a single supplier for all its packaging requirements for more than twenty-five years.

Another important factor is that the buyer must maintain greater surveillance of market conditions and technological changes to ensure the supplier remains competitive.

Traditionally, purchasing policy in most companies called for at least two supply sources for any item purchased in volume. The objectives of such a policy are (1) to protect the company's supply lines against supplier shutdowns caused by strikes or acts of God, and (2) to encourage competition among suppliers by implying that one supplier always has a chance to increase its share of a company's orders by outperforming another supplier. Management generally supported the policy as being in the best interests of the company.

It is unlikely, however, that multiple sourcing will be abandoned as basic purchasing policy. Larger companies that use single-sourcing restrict it to very specific items and often for only a specific period (i.e., for critical parts for a given model of an automobile). What can be expected is a continuation and wider use of the policy of narrowing the supplier base. More companies will concentrate their purchases with fewer companies that have proved they can and will meet high standards of quality, service, and delivery—at a competitive price. Table 9-1 lists the traditional differences between multiple and single sources.

[3]L. Giunipero, *JIT Purchasing AME Research Report,* Wheeling, Ill., 1989.

Table 9-1 Advantages of Single Versus Multiple Sources

Multiple	Single
Assurance of supply in case of trouble.	Easier to manage coordination of production schedules and relationships.
Ability to call on unused capacity of several suppliers.	Less time and money spent in training supplier.
Buyer doesn't want to become sole support of one firm. Some limit participation to 20–30% of supplier's volume.	More practical for suppliers to make frequent deliveries.
Lever to guard against price increases.	Less time in evaluation and tracking of performance.
Some suppliers can't handle all of the work.	Vendor feels fully responsible, total obligation.
	Time can be devoted to developing/monitoring one source.
	Leverage over supplier is greater with volume purchases.
	Transportation-cost savings by grouping on different parts.
	Supplier more inclined to do special things.
	Tooling dollars concentrated in one source.

Qualified-Supplier Lists   While the decision on the number of suppliers is often made by the purchasing department, a qualified-supplier list (QSL) ensures that the purchaser will not face a *sole-source* situation. A sole-source situation exists in cases where the buyer must purchase from a certain supplier. In single sourcing the buyer decides to place 100 percent of the business with one source. In sole sourcing the buyer *must* place 100 percent of the business with one source. There is no alternative. Suppliers are added to the QSL through a type of approval process whereby they are approved to supply a certain part or parts. Without a QSL the buyer is always in danger of facing the sole-source problem.

For example, company engineers have designed a product incorporating a common electrical part. For their development work they have selected such a part from a manufacturer's catalog or from an electrical supply house. Their main interest has been merely to find something that will serve the desired purpose. The selected part proves satisfactory and is incorporated in the product design. In drawing up a bill of materials for the first production order, the part is naturally specified by the manufacturer's name and catalog number.

When the purchasing manager receives the requisition to purchase, the manager is bound to conform to this request and does so. However, he or she properly challenges the specification that ties the requirement to a sole source and succeeds in having it modified by the addition of the words "or equal." Now the purchasing manager has leeway for choice on succeeding orders, but because the original part was specified for its known successful performance, the buyer is not to be the sole judge of equality. The buyer is not authorized to make a substitution arbitrarily without the consent of the specifying engineers. In most cases an alternative requires engineering approval in advance of any purchase.

So the buyer promptly starts a search for acceptable alternative products and sources. When a promising new supplier is located, samples are obtained for inspection and test. Assume, for example, that three samples are approved as acceptable alternatives for the specified item. Now, instead of a single source the buyer has an "approved list" of four suppliers and enters their names together with that of the original supplier on the purchase record. It is now the buyer's privilege to patronize any one of the four at his or her discretion. Or the buyer has a mailing list readymade for issuing invitations to bid, with the assurance that any one of the offerings will be acceptable as to quality and suitability.

It is quite likely that the buyer will continue to purchase the bulk of his or her requirement from the source originally named, provided there is a real preference for the product and that the supplier's quality, price, and service are satisfactory. But the buyer will also make some purchases from the others or give them a chance to quote regularly to maintain their interest. An alternative source that is merely another name on a list represents no advantage either to the buyer or the seller. The approved list of supply sources must be used to be useful.

Sentiment in favor of qualified-supplier lists was strongly reinforced by purchasing executives' experiences during the extreme shortages of 1973–74. A nationwide survey of purchasing managers in 1977 showed that 80 percent of the respondents were using approved vendor lists, and of those, 37 percent had adopted the procedure in the previous five years.[4]

One purchasing manager explained his reasons for use of such lists:

> We feel that we must have the proper quality, pricing, and reliability that can be achieved only through the use of preapproved vendors. Reliability is the key—we cannot afford the disappointments of the 1973–1974 period a second time.

Another purchasing executive put his case for the approved list more bluntly:

> There were no good performers during the shortage crisis. But some suppliers were less bad than others. We want to make sure that, if we ever face a similar situation again, we'll at least have the less bad suppliers in our stable.

Two major criticisms are made of the approved-list approach. One is that it is discriminatory and serves to blacklist any supplier that is not included, whereas every qualified seller should be allowed to quote. The other is that it limits buyers and restricts the scope of their choices.

Flexibility and periodic review will overcome both objections. As to the first, it is assumed that all qualified sources have been investigated and given the

[4]"Vendors: Only 'Good Guys' Finish," *Purchasing World*, September 1977, p. 42.

chance to present their story when the list was being built. Further, it assumes that if conditions have changed or if new sources enter the field, the opportunity will be given. If they can at any time give good reasons why they should be added to the list—or replace one or more of the suppliers already included—their claims should get full consideration. The purchasing manager should always be ready to maintain the list at the highest possible standard.

As to the second criticism, the limitation on buyers, if any, is a self-imposed one. In principle, the limitation is set by either of two causes. One is the absence of additional technically or commercially competent suppliers. The other is that there are practical limits to the size of a working list beyond the basic assurance of supply and reasonable competition.

Negotiation and Selection Stage

This third stage leads to issuance of the initial order. The ultimate selection decision can be arrived at in a number of ways. These include published price lists, competitive bidding, and negotiation. Regardless of the method used for selecting the supplier, some negotiation will take place requiring additional discussions with the selected supplier. These discussions ensure that the supplier understands contract conditions concerning delivery, packaging, and payment issues.

Experience Stage

The final stage of supplier selection is experience, which involves following up to ensure that the supplier met the terms and conditions of the contract—conformance to specifications, on-time delivery, and making the buyer aware of any changes at the supplier facility. The formal part of the experience phase involves rating and evaluating supplier performance. Performance ratings provide feedback to supplier on their performance. This feedback allows the supplier to correct any shortcomings and provides a comparative tool for use in negotiations with suppliers. Those with excellent performance may be awarded additional business, while poor performers will lose business and eventually become ex-suppliers.

SELECTING SUBCONTRACTORS

Defense purchasing brought into general business usage a term that had previously been largely confined to the construction industries but is now a permanent part of the vocabulary and the selection policy of procurement. A distinction is made between "prime contractors," whose contract is directly with some governmental procurement agency as buyer, and "subcontractors," who contribute to the fulfillment of that contract but have no direct contractual relationship with the government. Their own specific contracts are with the prime contractors or with "subcontractors of the first tier," as the process of subcontracting is repeated in successive stages down the line. The emphasis in this terminology is on the end product called for in the prime contract.

Essentially, subcontracting is purchasing, and the subcontractor is a supplier. In the defense usage of the term, certain special characteristics of the relationship differentiate it from ordinary procurement and call for special handling. The purchased product is specifically identified with the project and end product of the purchaser; priority ratings on the material used follow through procurement and operations in both plants; and in wartime utilization of the purchased parts or products was definitely allocated. This presents a condition distinctly different from procurement of parts for stock or for application, at the buying company's option, to any need that might arise. Many of the terms of the prime contract are required to be passed along to the subcontract, by reference to the original document, even though there is no direct contractual responsibility between the subcontractor and the government, the ultimate recipient of the product. From the standpoint of the prime contractor's purchasing department, unusually close contacts have to be maintained to see that schedules are properly and positively coordinated with the buyer's assembly program. Altogether, a much larger share of responsibility for the subcontractor's performance rests upon the purchasing manager than in normal procurement conditions. Some variations from normal types of contracts have also been developed. For example, instead of contracting for delivery of a particular part or product, some companies contract for certain machine capacity and machine time in a subcontractor's plant, to be used as the buyer might direct. Under such an arrangement, the buyer furnishes raw materials, schedules production, and provides supervision.

As a result of these special conditions, the typical organization for subcontracting is a special division within the purchasing department for this purpose. In some companies the procedure is considered a separate managerial and administrative function, apart from the purchase of materials for use in plant production operations, and special subcontracting departments are set up outside the jurisdiction of the purchasing department. The reasoning behind such an arrangement is indicated by the fact that such departments are sometimes known as outside-production departments.

In common industrial usage the term *subcontracting* has reference to such parts or products as could be produced with the buyer's own facilities and would normally be manufactured within his or her own organization. Successful subcontracting, as suggested, regards the operations of the supplier as part of a continuous process, leading up to and including the operations in the buyer's own plant. In this concept the supplier's material control, production efficiency, scheduling, and service are definitely the concern of the buyer and his company, to be handled with the maximum of cooperation and mutual assistance. So far as the subcontracts are concerned, the supplier's operations are a part of his or her customer's operation, even though they are carried on under a different roof and a different management.

"BUY" INSIDE THE COMPANY?

In addition to following the source-selection model to find sources outside the firm, the choice of in-house manufacturing exists, although normally, industrial requirements are satisfied by purchase of the needed product or material from some outside source. In fact, a survey in *Purchasing* suggested that companies were moving toward more, not fewer, buy decisions.[5]

However, there is usually the alternative possibility of producing a needed part or product within the buyer's own organization, sometimes with potential advantages in cost, convenience, or control. Where feasible, it should be considered. In a broad sense, the question, Make or buy? must be answered in advance of every purchase, in the form of company policy if not by special analysis. This question may refer to a particular fabricated part for regular product use, or on a broader scale, it may involve the decision of whether the company shall operate its own foundry department instead of purchasing castings or shall have its own printing department or undertake any one of a score of similar operations. It may likewise concern the making of special equipment, such as warehouse shelving, or major construction projects.

THE MAKE-OR-BUY DECISION

The decision to make or buy is presumably made before the requirement ever gets to the stage of a purchase requisition, and it is frequently outside the scope of purchasing department responsibility to find the answer. On the other hand, it is an ever-present consideration in determining the best method of procurement, even after a requisition has been received and regardless of previous practice. Therefore, purchasing is responsible for analyzing the relative merits and advantages of both procurement methods and of making policy recommendations if a change is indicated. Costs and conditions in the supplier industry may be such as to suggest very strongly the advisability of self-manufacture of products formerly purchased. It may also work in the other direction, when the possibility of advantageous purchase arrangements suggests the adoption of this method, even though such action may mean retirement of equipment and facilities formerly used in production. The whole program of subcontracting, discussed earlier in this chapter, is an example of procuring by purchase a wide variety of components, many of which would normally be produced in the purchaser's own plant.

The significance of the question, Make or buy? and the amount of study justified in arriving at a decision depend largely on the dollar volume involved. If it concerns a product representing only a few thousand dollars of annual expenditure, it will not make much difference either way. If the amount reaches hundreds of thousands of dollars, it is frequently a matter of the utilization of existing equipment balanced against the convenience and cost of procurement from outside

[5]Somerby Dowst, "The Winning Edge," *Purchasing*, March 12, 1987, pp. 52–60.

sources. If the amount is more substantial, involving investment in new equipment, a full-scale analysis is indicated, going beyond direct cost considerations into matters of company policy, personnel, labor relations, plant layout, scheduling, and the numerous other details incident to any manufacturing program.

Cost Comparison

The decision of make or buy must be approached analytically and objectively. The company's own facilities must be considered as an alternative source of supply in competition with outside suppliers. A change in policy is not so simple as merely changing from one supplier to another. When it is concerned only with manufacture of a particular part, utilizing surplus capacity or facilities already on hand, it may not be too serious a matter, and the policy can easily be revoked in case the results prove less advantageous than expected. But in respect to larger and more significant items of supply, and particularly when new facilities are to be added or a new line of operation undertaken, it is likely to involve substantial tooling costs, investment in space and equipment, and enlargement of the organization, all of which represent a continuing problem of cost and efficient operation. A basic make-or-buy analysis worksheet is shown in Figure 9-3.

For this reason a comparison of costs is one of the first considerations, though not necessarily the most important. Cost of purchased goods can be accurately determined. Complete cost up to the time of use is the significant figure: price plus transportation charges plus costs of handling and storage. This cost should be calculated on an annual basis and on the entire group of products that would be affected by a change in policy.

Against this figure must be balanced the total estimated cost of production. This figure should include not merely the cost of materials and direct labor but investment and carrying charges, including depreciation on equipment and overhead expenses, with due allowance for the possibility of idle time and production at less than capacity, normal waste and spoilage, and the other usual risks of management that are assumed by the supplier when goods are purchased. These costs should be calculated on the standard basis used throughout the company, because the new manufacturing operation will become a part of the company's general activities and must assume its share of the burden. Only when this has been done is a fair and accurate cost comparison possible. The factor of profit, which is necessarily a part of the supplier's price, is not a proper consideration for the buyer, because the buyer is concerned with costs, and the profit to the company accrues only in the sale of the finished product; however, efficient self-manufacture, elimination of sales expense, and consequent lower cost of components do enhance the profit potential in the eventual sales.[6]

Among the cost factors frequently mentioned as favoring the manufacture of parts rather than procurement by purchase is the possibility of spreading

---

[6]This is a controversial point in accounting. In vertically integrated industries, in which one division of a company manufactures components for another division and also sells to other consumers, it is customary to include a profit factor, with or without a differential in favor of the related plant when the product is transferred. In such cases the individual plants are responsible for their own overhead and must individually justify themselves by profitable operation as separate enterprises.

	MAKE OR BUY ANALYSIS WORKSHEET	DECISION
Dept. No. _____ Project or Part #_____ Quantity Needed_____ Date Needed _____		MAKE ☐ BUY ☐ Date _____ Prepared By_____ Approved By_____

	Purchased Cost	Manufactured Cost
A. Direct Variable Costs - Note A:		
1. Material - Include Variations for Major Products	$ _____	$ _____
2. Labor - Include Variations for Major Products		
Reroute		
Shift Premium		
Incentive Pay		
Etc.		
3. Subcontract		
B. Overhead:		
1. Material Handling		
2. Indirect Labor		
3. Hourly Supervision		
4. Training - Include Special Skills		
5. Set up		
6. Overtime Premium		
7. Vacation and Holiday Pay		
8. Fringe Costs		
9. Other Variable Costs:		
C. Semi-Variable and Fixed Costs - Note B:		
D. Other Costs and Expenses - Note C:		
1. Purchasing, Shipping, Storage, Testing, Etc.		
2. Division Administration		
3. Division Engineering		
TOTALS	$ (NOTE D)	$ _____

NOTES:

A. Separate departmental labor hour and overhead rates may be preferable to the use of composite rates.
Total direct labor standard hours required _____

The divisional rate for overhead applied should be redetermined as substantial amounts of direct labor hours are absorbed in the make or buy products.

B. Semi-variable and fixed costs may be included for specific items.

C. These incremental and out-of-pocket costs are included only when quantities being considered are substantial in amount.

D. Includes vendor's invoice price and adjustments for out-of-pocket non-compensating costs included in the manufactured cost column.

Excess capacity costs should be included.   YES☐ NO☐

Tooling charges should be included.   YES☐ NO☐

COMMENTS:
    (Include vendor reference, delivery time, etc.)

Figure 9-3 Worksheet for analyzing data on which the decision to make or buy is based.

overhead charges over a greater volume of operations. This is more than merely an accounting device, but it is not always a complete answer. Where outside and inside costs are close, as they frequently are, other factors may be decisive. If a company is buying an item at, say, $40,000 but decides to make it at $50,000 to spread the overhead burden, a competitor that is still buying it at $40,000 acquires an immediate advantage that may alter the entire marketing situation.

The results of a complete cost comparison may seriously modify estimates of cost and other advantages based on casual judgment. Almost certainly, it will indicate the prudence of a highly selective approach to the question of make or buy based on detailed analysis of the individual case.

The Quantity Factor

Unit cost is not the only factor to be considered. The quantity of a requirement is important for several reasons. In the first place, it will help to determine whether or not the potential cost saving is sufficient to warrant the undertaking of a special manufacturing project or process. Second, it has an important bearing on actual costs through the economies of mass manufacture and the possibilities of absorbing initial costs. Third, as has already been suggested, it should be sufficiently large to ensure that any facilities that may be established or installed for the purpose will be kept reasonably fully occupied, so that overhead costs for idle time will not offset the unit-cost advantage.

A solution for the latter problem has been found in some cases by setting a basic production capacity that is large enough for economical production yet within the limit of minimum expected requirements. This is calculated to keep the facility running at capacity, any deficiencies being supplied by purchases from the outside. Many company printing departments are set up on this basis. The advantages, in addition to those of cost, include the convenience of having such facilities conveniently available, the possibility of producing rush jobs without waiting for an outside supplier to fit them into the schedule or paying premium prices for extra service, and the possibility of handling short runs and other special and commercially uneconomical requirements on a cost basis.

Any system of partial self-manufacture has the disadvantage of decreasing the desirability and the quantity-purchasing appeal of that portion of the business that must still be procured from outside sources. In such a case the outside vendor is likely to take the position that the buyer's company is a competitor and to give preference to other customers who purchase their total requirements.

Quality Control

The factors considered up to this point have been concerned largely with comparative costs and potential economies. Those are not necessarily the determining factors in reaching a decision. It is quite possible that it will be found desirable to undertake, or to retain, the manufacture of a component part in the buyer's own plant when costs under this method are demonstrably and substantially higher than prices obtainable from outside sources.

Among the conditions that justify such high-cost procurement by manufacture, considerations of quality loom large. It is possible to have the assurance of strict quality control when the processing and fabrication of components are performed and supervised by the organization using them. In general, the greater the control required, either in analysis or in dimension, the more significant this

consideration becomes. Close coordination and a single responsibility are frequently better than divided responsibility, and the guaranty of the end product
means more when control of the entire process and its component parts is in the
maker's own hands.

Furthermore, greater interest and effectiveness in quality development
and improvement can be expected on the part of a producer who is following
through from raw material to end product than from a supplier who is producing
to strict specifications furnished by a customer.

Disadvantages of Self-Manufacture

On the other side of the balance sheet, there are some disadvantages connected
with the self-manufacture of component parts. Once the company is committed to
such a policy, and particularly when special tooling or equipment has been installed for the purpose, an element of inflexibility is introduced into procurement. Freedom of selection is sacrificed, despite possible differences in cost or
other factors. The assurance of supply that is gained by this additional control
must be weighed against the loss of alternative sources.

The hazards of business and changing economic conditions, factors over
which the buyer has no control but that affect markets and procurement, are now
assumed by the buyer's company and may seriously alter the calculations upon
which the decision was originally based. Such influences include cyclical and long-
term trends in the supplier industry, changes in demand for the buyer's product
affecting the nature and volume of requirements, technological advances, and
competitive conditions such as overcapacity in the industry, as well as a variety of
unpredictable random factors such as war, government regulations, and tax
policies.

MAKE-OR-BUY CHECKLIST

One company that has made an exhaustive study of this problem as it applies to its
own operations has compiled a checklist of six major sections to make sure that no
significant factor is overlooked in the final decision. Every question in each category is weighed with the same question in mind, to arrive at these conclusions.
The final step is to recapitulate six answers, to determine where the preponder-
ance of reason lies, and to make the decision accordingly. The checklist asks the
following questions:

1. *Quality factors:* Adherence to specifications? Quality-control setup? Is proper
   equipment available? Experience in this type of work? Who pays for bad parts?
2. *Capacity factors:* Is space available? Is available space obtainable? Is machine time
   available? Must machinery be bought? Are outside finishing operations required? Is sales relationship a factor? Is stability of supplier relationships a factor?
   How much working capital is needed for inventory, and so forth? Is new capital
   investment needed? How much use have we for the new equipment? What return

can we expect? Are our costs complete? Is absorption of internal overhead needed? Would total costs, including overhead absorption, be competitive?

3. *Labor factors:* Would layoffs be created? Would it help us hold the organization together? Must staff be increased? Is special training necessary? Are there union pressures? Is the labor rate competitive?

4. *Scheduling factors:* Can we get all necessary components on time? Have we the capacity to adjust to peaks or slowdowns? Would timing be surer with added sources? Are engineering changes frequent?

5. *Skill factors:* Is the best design experience available? Is the part natural to us? Is this the most profitable use of our executives' time? Is design-assistance relationship a factor? Do we have adequate measures of inside efficiency?

6. *Cost comparison* (on the basis of one hundred pieces): Material cost, operations cost (direct labor, overhead, and profit), setup cost, tools repair allowance and spoilage, packing and shipping costs from outside supplier, tool charge (cost of tools per one hundred pieces based on two years' run).

This is a very complete and scientific evaluation of the problem, dealing principally with the internal company factors involved. Before leaving this phase of the subject, however, it should be pointed out that make-or-buy decisions also have external effects and that there are some long-range considerations of this nature that should also have serious attention. The checklist section on capacity factors recognizes this by querying the effect on sales relationships and the stability of supply relationships.

It is not uncommon, in times of business decline, for manufacturers to switch from buying to making certain parts when excess capacity shows up in their own plants. Even if that is done as a temporary measure rather than as a considered policy based on economy of manufacture, the immediate effect is to leave the suppliers of these parts stranded and to intensify for them the hardships of the business decline. The purchasing manager may well question the wisdom of such use of the make-or-buy alternative, especially if the decision is of a temporary nature. For, when business picks up and the buyer once again seeks parts and service from that vendor, the buyer will almost certainly find that the supplier relationship has deteriorated. In extreme cases he or she may actually have lost that source of supply.

Authorizing the Decision

It is apparent from the many internal elements affected by the make-or-buy policy, that the decision is not one to be made by the purchasing executive alone, even though it is primarily a question of procurement method. It is within the buyer's province to make a recommendation for or against the method in respect to certain requirements of the materials program, and his or her recommendation should be supported with a detailed analysis of available outside sources, comparative costs, and other factors. The company, as is true for any other supplier, has the privilege of judging the profit potential and other advantages and disadvantages of the proposal that will determine whether it is advisable to undertake the production or to relinquish it in favor of outside purchase.

Production executives will naturally be in the best position to pass judgment on the equipment and facilities available or needed and on the practicability of the plan. Production and cost departments will check the purchasing manager's cost estimates. Financial officers will check the advisability of the capital investment involved. Technical and engineering advice will be sought on the advantages of quality control within the organization. Marketing executives are concerned with anything that will enhance the salability of the product and possibly with finding an outlet for surplus production from the new department. The final decision, after all these viewpoints have been presented, is a matter for top management.

POINTS FOR REVIEW

1. List the important criteria used in determining (a) possible sources of supply and (b) acceptable sources of supply.
2. Select a common product (cardboard boxes, paint, and so forth) and develop a tentative plan of what you would do at each step in the source-selection model.
3. Explain the implications of a high turnover among suppliers.
4. List and explain the various sourcing alternatives a buyer can evaluate prior to selecting a source.
5. Differentiate between purchasing and subcontracting.
6. List the major factors to be considered in arriving at a decision to make or buy a product.

10

Supplier Relations, Development, and Evaluation

In the last chapter we discussed how suppliers are selected and various steps purchasers take to insure correct selection. Once a supplier is selected, a relationship develops. Such a relationship can blossom and develop into a mutually profitable one. Alternatively, it can fail for various reasons to meet expectations and terminate. The decision to continue or terminate needs to be based on a fair evaluation system. Many times a purchaser is unable to terminate an unsatisfactory relationship since he or she has not developed other suppliers. In essence, good purchasing requires developing good suppliers who are rewarded for their efforts while dropping those who do not improve. The process is a continuous one making supplier relations, development, and evaluation key parts of a selection process.

ESTABLISHING SUPPLIER RELATIONSHIPS

The aim of careful vendor selection is to find the one most satisfactory source or a group of alternative sources with adequate and reasonably comparable qualifications. Thus succeeding orders for the same item can be placed with these same suppliers with confidence. In other words, the decision as to a source of supply contemplates a continuing relationship.

It is to be expected that this relationship will improve with experience and growth in mutual understanding. The purchasing manager, on his or her part, should make every effort to foster that improvement. The elements that contribute to such improvement include:

- Completeness and clarity of communication concerning the need, the application and usage of the purchased material or product. The scope and limitations of the product itself. The outlook for continued usage and probable quantities required and any special requirements of either a technical or commercial nature.
- Mutual understanding of the conditions and problems of both usage and production, resulting from that communication.
- Mutual confidence in the statements and intent of both parties.
- Mutual consideration—no unreasonable demands, as much notice as possible in the event of changes in schedules or instructions. A fair and open mind in the discussion of differences, and willingness to waive or modify nonessential details of the agreement if the modification does not impair quality of service and is substantially to the advantage of either party.
- A genuine interest in the mutual problem of procurement and supply rather than mere contract fulfillment; for example, suggestions for cost reduction in the product itself and in methods of packing, shipping, usage, and accounting.
- Cooperation—an active effort to fulfill contract obligations, prompt shipment by the supplier to minimize the need for inquiries and expediting action, and prompt processing and payment of invoices by the buyer.
- Continuous improvement of ordering methods and supplier service as the opportunities arise.
- Cultivation of personal contacts in the buying and selling organizations, making for better liaison and goodwill.

Many companies have found it helpful to run suppliers' conferences (or supplier days) annually or more frequently, when vendors are invited to gather at the buyer's plant, to see firsthand how their materials or parts are used, to share in the pride of product, and to be briefed on the reasons for certain buying policies and for the insistence on certain quality specifications. Conversely, buyers find it advantageous to make periodic visits to the plants of their suppliers to see first-hand how the things they buy are produced and to keep in touch with the problems and progress of supplier industries.

Loyalty to Suppliers

A continuing buyer-seller relationship, based on mutual confidence and satisfaction, implies a policy (and, indeed, a responsibility) of loyalty to suppliers. This is the antithesis of opportunism and constant "shopping around" in purchasing. It is true that some cost savings can be made by such methods, but it is usually at the sacrifice of uniformity and continuity of supply and of most of the factors that have been cited as making up good supply service. Especially, shopping around sacrifices the assurance of supply that is the first responsibility in purchasing. Without established and loyal sources of supply, every recurring requirement presents a procurement problem of the first order, and the work of the purchasing department is magnified beyond all reason and proportion.

Experienced purchasing managers are in practical agreement that the long-range considerations of reasonable cost and of satisfaction and value in respect to purchases are best attained through a consistent policy toward supply sources. And a sound purchasing program, like any sound business program, is based on long-range considerations. Buyers who rely on opportunism to gain an immediate advantage make themselves and their companies the vulnerable prey of opportunism in selling.

A high rate of turnover among suppliers suggests either that the purchaser's company is basically an undesirable customer or that wrong decisions as to supply sources have been made in the first place.

ASSISTING AND DEVELOPING SOURCES OF SUPPLY

So far in this chapter we have assumed that adequate sources exist to supply every need and that the purchasing manager's problem is merely one of selection from among the available suppliers. In the majority of cases, and under normal business conditions, this assumption holds true. However, the exceptions to the rule are equally important in the complete supply program and are likely to present difficulties that will put the procurement officer's resourcefulness to a severe test. The buyer's survey and search for the most satisfactory source may result in the discovery that no satisfactory or willing source can be found; yet the requirement exists, and it is the buyer's responsibility to meet it. Thus under any of these circumstances the buyer's responsibility is not to select but to create a satisfactory source.

This supplier development process has been termed reverse marketing.[1] In reverse marketing the purchaser is aware that benefits will accrue to both supplier and purchaser, benefits the supplier may not be aware of. Leenders and Blenkhorn cite the following reasons for reverse marketing:

- High payoffs—an improved quality, price, delivery, etc.
- Market deficiencies—sellers are not aware of all buyers.
- Future considerations—satisfying long-range needs and plans.
- Social political, geographical, environmental concerns—locating [businesses owned by] women and minority businesses, offshore
- Technology—support for supplier, new-product designs
- Recognition and appreciation—shows management purchasing's productive profit contribution
- Current trends—using fewer high-quality suppliers[2]

Other often-cited advantages of supplier development (reverse marketing) include:

- Products or parts that have not previously been made.
- Intricacies of special design.
- Unusual requirements in the specification or difficult conditions of application and use.
- Utilization of new or unfamiliar materials for which there is little precedent in treatment and fabrication.
- The only available sources may be too distant.
- Prices may be exorbitant or out of line with budgeted costs for the product.
- Production capacity may already be fully occupied so that no new customers may be accommodated.
- Potential suppliers may simply be unwilling to bid or uninterested in additional business.

The process in its earlier stages is like that already described. However, the emphasis of the search is placed on qualifications, equipment, and experience in a similar type of operation that might logically be applied to production of the material or part in question. Then, in place of a process of elimination or narrowing of the field, the buyer must concentrate on the most likely sources, persuading them to undertake the desired production and, if necessary, helping to implement their plant and personnel for such expansion or conversion of facilities as may be needed. In such cases, procurement is partly a matter of selling ability, seeking to establish the buyer's company as a desirable customer in the same way that the salesperson normally seeks to establish his or her company as a desirable supplier. Among the incentives offered are (1) the steady flow of guaranteed orders over a period of time at a satisfactory price level; (2) technical assistance in setting up the process on an efficient basis that will result in a satisfactory product; (3) assistance

[1]M. R. Leenders and D. B. Blenkhorn, *Reverse Marketing* (New York: Free Press, 1988), p. 27.
[2]Ibid., pp. 28–33.

in the procurement of raw materials even to the point of furnishing such materials for fabrication only by the supplier, so that risks of waste and spoilage in the initial stages are for the account of the buyer; and, sometimes, (4) costs of new equipment and tooling subsidized until they can be absorbed by the volume of business that develops.

DEVELOPING WORLD-CLASS SUPPLIERS

Progressive corporations expect their purchasing departments to select and develop suppliers that provide their organizations with the best value today and tomorrow. This requires a program that involves suppliers much earlier in the process and seeks to develop longer-term relationships.

Early Supplier Involvement

The quickened pace of new product introduction means that design engineers must consider supplier technology and expertise as well as manufacturability of their design. Attacking these issues during the design phase assures smoother transition from initial design to finished product in a shorter time.

Early supplier involvement requires inviting highly qualified suppliers into early discussions with design engineers. Thus management, quality, technology, delivery, and competence along with cost competence are evaluated prior to approval of the prospective source. According to Gerald Cole, to obtain total quality excellence, timely development of new products, and competitive pricing, buyers will develop close long-term relationships with their suppliers. The focus will be on the buyer's lowest total product cost.[3] Suppliers must be competitive on a worldwide basis. A study by Robert Monczka suggests that CEOs are looking at tangible cost reductions, and while U.S. goals are in the 4–7 percent range, Japanese goals are in the 8–10 percent range. His findings also indicate that the preproduction phase is where the greatest savings are obtainable[4] (see Figure 10-1). Prescreened suppliers are invited to participate as team members with the purchaser's firm in the design process.

Quality Issues

Since these selected suppliers become partners in the design process, they are expected to meet rigorous qualification tests, which are very specific and detailed. Lessons learned from the Japanese approach to supplier selection are becoming popular with U.S. buyers:

[3]Gerald S. Cole, "The Changing Relationship between Original Equipment Manufacturers and Their Suppliers," *International Journal of Technology Management,* 1988, pp. 299–324.

[4]James P. Morgan, "You Can't Separate Quality from Cost Reduction," *Purchasing,* January 18, 1990, pp. 90–94.

Price/Cost Management Approaches

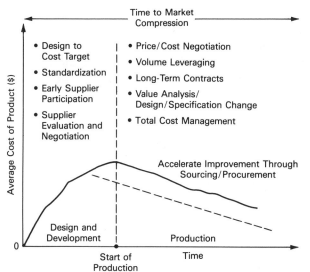

Figure 10-1 Preproduction is the place where purchasing will need to concentrate in order to bring in the kinds of cost breakthroughs that top management is seeking.
Source: James P. Morgan, "You Can't Separate Quality from Cost Reduction," *Purchasing*, January 18, 1990, p. 93.

Mitsubishi Belting Company in Japan reports how inspection teams from the customer plants (buyers) poke their noses into everything from quality-control charts to equipment maintenance records to the food in the cafeteria, and they generally leave a list of as many as 200 demerits that they want corrected. The inspectors particularly demand visual, obvious indicators of quality at every process (total process control), and the indicators must be easy to understand. In effect the customer teams are saying, "You tell us you have total quality control. But where's the evidence?"[5]

Quality education starts at top management levels and is the responsibility of every person in the supplier's organization. The application of statistical quality-control procedures will help increase outgoing quality-control levels. By monitoring each successive process and detecting problems in the process, overall quality levels can be raised. And the increase of outgoing quality levels has allowed some buying firms to skip the incoming check on their prime suppliers' material.

A good example of such a practice is the *certified supplier* program run by Motorola's Communications Sector Group. Basically, a supplier is certified through a two-step program. The first step is an internal-quality investigation, which involves a complete review of a supplier's quality program by Motorola quality engineers. The second step involves an analysis of the supplier's facilities. Meanwhile, incoming inspection is performed for a period of time. If the incoming inspection reveals that there are no defects during this period, the supplier is certified. Certification means that shipments receive no incoming inspection. Also, certified suppliers usually receive a higher percentage of business, according to Ken Stork, Corporate Director of Purchasing.[6]

[5]R. J. Shonberger, *Japanese Manufacturing Techniques* (New York: Free Press, 1982), p. 57.
[6]L. Giunipero, "JIT Purchasing," *NAPM Guide to Purchasing*, Tempe, Ariz., 1986, p. 9.

Supplier Partnerships

These partnerships require thinking of the supplier on a continuing long-term basis, not just as a transaction completed when an order is shipped.

Partnerships require much closer and more open and frequent communication. The supplier's top management becomes involved in the relationship and is usually dedicated to ensuring quality via statistical quality control. Recent research has shown that benefits of partnership include:

- Improved relationship with supplier as witnessed by better communication, sharing of information
- Lower price/cost
- Improved quality
- Greater control over the supplier
- More productive use of buyer time[7]

As with any partnership, there must be mutual benefits. The seller receives the benefits of stable relations and has less need to sell the account; the cost of doing business is less, and there is a basis for investment and improved communication with the buyer. Since selecting suppliers as partners requires much careful upfront analysis, a team approach to selection is recommended. The team needs to include the major functions of purchasing, engineering, quality control, and senior management.

Partnerships require that sellers earn a fair profit that allows for reinvestment in equipment and long-term growth. This necessitates that the buyer become involved in cost and value analyses of the supplier's operation, to assure fair prices in lieu of competitive bidding. Finally, long-term survival of both partners dictates keeping current with changing technology. Thus periodic meetings become important to discuss technology and the way the partners can improve it.

As partnerships grow closer, buyers will become more involved with their supplier's supplier. This is a natural extension of the partnership. Currently, one automotive firm not only schedules its seat supplier but also wants the schedule from the fabric supplier.

Supplier Attitudes

Supplier attitudes must also change. Suppliers are, in effect, told that the burden is on them to supply the production system, or the system will be shut down. In many cases there will no longer be three, four, or five suppliers that share the business on a particular commodity. Instead, there will be only one or two. And it is those one or two who have the responsibility of keeping the buyer's production facility supplied. The previously held notion no longer applies that if supplier number one fails to deliver, either supplier number two or number three will.

[7]L. Giunipero, "Just-in-Time Purchasing in American Industry," Association for Manufacturing Excellence. Wheeling, Illinois, 1989, p. 52.

TABLE 10-1   Key Differences between World-Class and Traditional Purchasing

CATEGORY	TRADITIONAL BUYING	WORLD-CLASS BUYING
Suppliers	Adversaries	Partners
Suppliers	Many: "more is better"	Few: single source
Supplier location	Scattered widely	As close as possible
Supper relations	Short or long term	Long term
Contract period	Short	Long
Quantity delivered	Large	Small
Transportation	Full load, single item	Full load, many items
Deliveries	Monthly	Weekly/daily
Quality	Inspect and reinspect	No incoming inspection
Communications	Purchase order	Electronic/verbal release
Communications	Sporadic	Continuous
Inventory	An asset	An evil—reduce!
Design	Make print, get quote	Seek early supplier input; then make the print
Production	Large lots	Small lots
Storeroom	Large, automated	Small, flexible
Price	Competitive bidding	Cost-based negotiation
Cost improvement	Sporadic	Continuous-driving-material cost down
Seller approach	Selling	Improving product for both parties

Source: L. Giunipero, "JIT Purchasing," *NAPM Guide to Purchasing,* Tempe, Ariz., 1986, p. 8.

There is also a need for a close communication system between buyers and sellers. Frequent deliveries require that both the supplier and the buyer be in constant contact with each other. Any quality problems or schedule changes must be quickly resolved.[8]

Developing world-class suppliers involves similar principles espoused by JIT purchasing. The key difference is that world-class supplier development continuously and unrelentingly reduces costs of doing business. Table 10-1, adapted from a report on JIT-purchasing by one of the authors, summarizes the differences between world-class and traditional buying practices.

DEVELOPING MINORITY SUPPLIERS

The use of purchasing power as a tool in the achievement of certain social objectives came into prominence in the late 1960s and early 1970s. The social unrest of those decades, the growth of consumerism, the awareness of industry leaders that social health was linked to economic health, and the growing intervention of the government in the private sector—all contributed to complicating purchasing decisions that had been based primarily on economic considerations.

Most management policies and government regulations that deal with socioeconomic matters do not require the payment of premium prices, but they do

[8]L. Giunipero, "JIT Purchasing," *NAPM Guide to Purchasing,* Tempe, Ariz., 1986, p. 9.

encourage competitive procedures. That is particularly so in the encouragement and assistance given to socially and economically disadvantaged suppliers, particularly minority suppliers. The objective is to help them be competitive, so that they may remain in the mainstream of the country's economic life.

Minority purchasing programs represent proactive efforts by government and corporations to increase the volume of goods and services purchased from minority-owned businesses. Minority-owned businesses are those businesses in which at least 51 percent of the ownership interest, stock or other, is held by members of socially or economically disadvantaged groups and whose management and daily business operations are controlled by one or more of such individuals.

Traditional minority group members are Black Americans, Hispanic Americans, American Orientals, American Indians, American Eskimos and American Aleuts. *Public Law 95-507* has expanded this definition to include small business concerns owned and controlled by socially and economically disadvantaged individuals. Socially disadvantaged persons are those persons whose ability to compete in the free-enterprise system has been impaired. Economically disadvantaged persons are those persons who have been subjected to racial, ethnic, or cultural bias because of their identity as a member of a group.

Thus minority-owned businesses now can include ownership by the traditional minority groups, the socially disadvantaged groups, and the economically disadvantaged groups. The broadening of the definition has been reflected by the changes that various corporations have made in their program titles—from minority purchasing program or minority supplier development program to disadvantaged-business program.

Companies have undertaken minority purchasing programs for a number of reasons, including government legislation, social responsiveness, increased sales, and alternate sources of supply.

Legal History

In 1969, Executive Order 11485, issued by President Nixon, established the Office of Minority Business Enterprise within the Department of Commerce. The purpose was to mobilize the resources of federal state and local governments and other groups to encourage the growth of minority business enterprises.

To carry out the provisions of the executive order, *Title 41* of the Federal Procurement regulations were amended in August 25, 1971, to include a provision that all contracts greater than $5,000 contain a provision encouraging use of minority suppliers.

Executive Order 11625, passed in October of 1971, gave the secretary of commerce authority to (1) implement federal policy in support of minority business enterprise (MBE) programs, (2) provide technical and management assistance to MBEs, and (3) coordinate participation of all federal departments and agencies in increasing MBE efforts.

Public Law 95-507, passed in 1978, requires that prime contractors who wish to obtain government contracts in excess of $500,000 ($1 million for construction) establish minority-sourcing programs. The law mandates that percentage goals for minority involvement be established prior to contract award. It also requires that prospective bidders submit to the relevant federal agency a subcontracting plan incorporating percentage goals and methods to accomplish those goals. Public Law 99-661, passed in 1987, requires that the Department of Defense strive to reach a goal of 5 percent of purchases from socially and economically disadvantaged businesses.

Social Responsibility/Community Relations

Corporate *social responsibility* implies that corporations should be good citizens within the community. Aggregate figures reveal that the minority community is underrepresented in the business sector.

Seventeen percent of the population is minority, but less than 4 percent of businesses are minority owned, and less than 1 percent of business receipts are collected by minority businesses.

Buying from the minority community *helps in selling* to it. A large oil corporation discovered that its center-city service stations were increasingly comprised of minority personnel, and purchasing from the minority community increased the market share in these areas.

The *competitive benefits* that firms realize from minority sources are not unlike those traditionally experienced when developing a new supplier. More competition for existing business can eliminate sole-source situations, thus improving prices.

As with most efforts in developing a new supply source, success will not always happen immediately, and initial prices may be higher than current prices. However, the development of these additional suppliers will eventually ensure more competition and improved prices.[9]

Establishing a Program

When seeking to conduct business with minority suppliers, purchasers cannot wait to receive sales calls but must seek out those who sell the commodities they purchase.

Second, the purchaser must find businesses with the necessary technical and marketing skills required to establish long-term business relationships. Many firms have tried to find such minority businesses and have failed. The problem lies in the program structure, sourcing, or development techniques.

Minority purchasing programs require top-management support, operating-unit commitment, and measurement of program results against established

[9]L. Giunipero, "Minority Buys Can Boost Competition, Initial Tags," *Electronic Buyers' News*, April 17, 1982, p. 28.

goals. Finally, the program needs to receive visibility within and outside the firm so buyers and minority suppliers realize the commitment is real (see Figure 10-2).

To determine and measure performance, goals are established in total dollars as well as in percent of purchases. Goal setting involves analyzing the commodities and type of procurements within a firm. For example, if a customer specifies a certain computer manufacturer, this is a sole-source procurement, and there are no alternatives. Thus efforts must focus on commodities having potential for minority sourcing. Figure 10-3 shows a typical department's goal for minority purchases.

Members of the National Association of Purchasing Management have been prominent in the work of various organizations concerned with aiding companies owned by socially and economically disadvantaged persons. Local associations have regularly sponsored or cosponsored seminars and workshops designed to guide corporate buyers in developing business relationships with minority-owned firms and assisting such firms with their production and marketing problems.

The National Minority Supplier Development Council (NMSDC) was formed in 1972 with the purpose of fostering minority business enterprise through corporate participation. The organization promotes the adoption and implementation of minority purchasing policies and helps members locate qualified minority suppliers. Headquartered in New York, it has approximately fifty regional councils located across the country. In 1986 the NMSDC reported its 3,700 corporate members spent over $9.4 billion with minority firms. The organ-

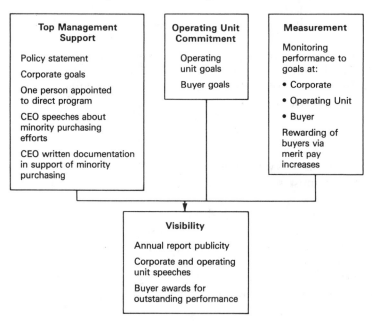

Figure 10-2 Minority Program Structure Chart.
Source: *Electronic Buyers News*, L. Giunipero, "Minority Buys Can Boost Competition, Initial Tags," April 12, 1982, p. 28.

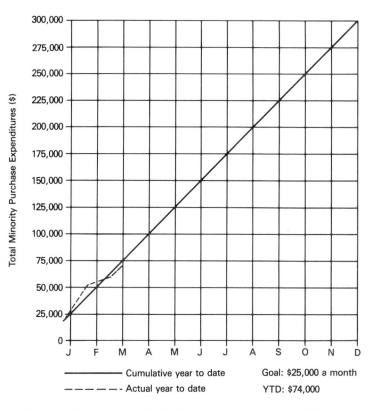

Figure 10-3

Source: *Electronic Buyers News,* L. Giunipero, "Minority Buys Can Boost Competition, Initial Tags," April 12, 1982, p. 33.

——————— Cumulative year to date   Goal: $25,000 a month

— — — — - Actual year to date   YTD: $74,000

ization's councils also have a program to certify minority suppliers. Thus firms are assured they are buying from legitimate minority suppliers.

Other socioeconomic factors purchasing management deals with (1) the use of small businesses as suppliers to government prime contractors, (2) placement of subcontracts in areas of labor surplus, (3) use of non-polluting materials, and (4) placement of business with companies owned by women.

SUPPLIER EVALUATION

The real test of vendor selection is, of course, the test of experience, or satisfactory performance by the vendor once the order has been placed. It was listed in Chapter 9 as the fourth step in selection because it does more than confirm or refute the buyer's judgment and decision. It is the deciding factor in whether the selected vendor will continue to receive the buyer's business or be replaced by another source.

Objective evaluation and rating of vendor performance has gained considerable acceptance in purchasing departments of all types in recent years. But even when sophisticated computerized systems are used to compile comparative statistics on vendor performance, interpretation of those statistics is left to the buyer's judgment.

VENDOR RATING REPORT

J. M. HUBER CORPORATION

COMPANY

Company:	Excellent (4)	GOOD (3)	FAIR (2)	POOR (1)
Size and/or Capacity	4			
Financial Strength		3		
Operational Profit		3		
Manufacturing Range	4			
Research Facilities			2	
Technical Service		3		
Geographical Locations	4			
Management		3		
Labor Relations		3		
Trade Relations		3		
Total 32	12	18	2	

.63 x Total = 20.16

Service

	Excellent (4)	GOOD (3)	FAIR (2)	POOR (1)
Deliveries on Time	4			
Condition on Arrival		3		
Follow Instructions		3		
Number of Rejections	4			
Handling of Complaints		3		
Technical Assistance			2	
Emergency Aid		3		
Supply Up to Date Catalogues, Etc.				1
Supply Price Changes Promptly	4			
Total 27	12	12	2	1

.69 x Total = 18.63

DATE

TOTAL RATING

Products:	Excellent (4)	GOOD (3)	FAIR (2)	POOR (1)
Quality	4			
Price		3		
Packaging	4			
Uniformity		3		
Warranty	4			
Total 18	12	6		

1.25 x Total = 22.50

Sales Personnel

	Excellent (4)	GOOD (3)	FAIR (2)	POOR (1)
1. Knowledge				
His Company		3		
His Products	4			
Our Industry		3		
Our Company		3		
2. Sales Calls				
Properly Spaced	4			
By Appointment		3		
Planned and Prepared		3		
Mutually Productive	4			
3. Sales-Service				
Obtain Information		3		
Furnish Quotations Promptly	4			
Follow Orders		3		
Expedite Delivery		3		
Handle Complaints		3		
Total 43	16	27		

.48 x Total = 20.64

Figure 10-4 In this vendor rating form evaluation categories are weighted according to importance (e.g., "Product" category is weighted 1.25, "Service" is next at 0.69). Individual factors (e.g., quality, delivery) have descending values, from four points for excellent to one point for poor. Total of points in each category is multiplied by the weight for that category.

Rating systems generally involve the three basic considerations in a good purchase—quality, service (delivery), and price—although any one of the factors named may be given more weight than the others. Quality is most important, for example, for a manufacturer of complex components for spacecraft. Price might be given equal weight in an evaluation system used by the manufacturer of highly competitive, "throw-away" items like party novelties. A typical vendor-rating form is shown in Figure 10-4.

Formulas for rating suppliers vary in complexity, again depending on the nature of the item being bought, the quality required, and competition within the supplying industry.

One company that buys its requirements under blanket orders uses a relatively simple system to measure supplier performance on two counts: quality and delivery. (Price performance had already been determined when the contract was originally set up.) Each shipment against the order is rated as follows: by date requested, 100 percent; one day late, 98 percent; two days late, 95 percent, and so on, down to 73 percent for six days late. If quality is to specifications, the supplier is rated 100 percent. If using departments complain about quality of the shipment, the rating drops to 95 percent. For each complaint thereafter, the supplier loses 5 more percentage points.

Suppliers are notified periodically of their performance records. Those falling below the tough new standards of quality and delivery discussed in Chapters 8 and 9 are warned that they are in danger of losing the business. And in more and more cases they are being automatically dropped from the approved list.

Individual Evaluation Measures

Other traditional approaches to measuring quality and delivery of suppliers are listed below

$$1. \text{ Quality} = 100\% - \frac{\text{number of lots rejected}}{\text{number of lots received}}$$

$$2. \text{ Quality} = 100\% - \frac{\text{dollar value of rejected items}}{\text{total dollar value of shipments}}$$

$$3. \text{ Quality} = 100\% - \frac{\text{number of parts rejected}}{\text{number of parts received}}$$

$$4. \text{ Quality} = 100\% - \text{parts per million defective}$$

$$5. \text{ Delivery} = 100\% - \frac{\text{number of late or early shipments}}{\text{number of shipments received}}$$

Measures concerning on-time delivery raise questions of how best to define it. Firms need to decide if they measure

- Purchasing's request date versus actual ship date or
- Supplier promise date versus actual ship date, or
- Supplier promise date versus actual receipt date

The third alternative supplier promise date versus buyer receipt date is quite popular. However, this requires factoring in a transit time. After *on time* has been defined, most firms then establish a "window" (i.e., if the shipment is three days early to two days late it is considered on time).

A study by Hewlett-Packard Corporation found that the greatest hindrance to on-time performance was in the buyer-seller communication process. Buyers and suppliers were clear about what they had agreed on in only 40 percent of deliveries. Many times suppliers were unsure whether the date on the purchase order was a shipment date or delivery date. In contrast, in 90 percent of cases the actual transit times were on schedule. Changes made to clarify the communication process resulted in an increase in on-time deliveries from 21 percent to 51 percent.[10]

Weighted-Point Plan

The weighted point plan is a more comprehensive mathematical vendor-rating formula used by many purchasing departments. It is designed to provide a comparative evaluation of vendor performance in any case in which an item is procured from two or more sources.

This formula is based upon the principles that (1) the evaluation of a vendor's performance must embrace all three major purchasing factors—quality, price, and service—and (2) the relative importance of these factors varies in respect to various items. The first step, therefore, is to assign appropriate weights to each, adding up to a total weighting factor of 100 points. For example, in a given case, quality performance might be rated at 40 points, price at 35, and service at 25, and these percentages are subsequently used as multipliers for individual ratings on each of the three purchasing factors. The assignment of these weights is a matter of judgment. In the company where this system originated, the importance of quality ranges from 35 to 45 percent, price from 30 to 40 percent, and service from 20 to 30 percent.

The quality rating is a direct percentage of the number of acceptable lots received in relation to total lots received.

In rating price, the lowest net price (gross price minus discounts plus unit transportation cost) obtained from any vendor is taken as 100 points, and net prices from other vendors are rated in inverse ratio to this figure.

The service rating is a direct percentage of the lots received as promised, in relation to total lots received.

These three ratings are multiplied by their respective weighting factors, and the results are added to give a numerical "incoming material rating" for each vendor, for a given item. Perfect deliveries, on scheduled time, at the lowest net price earn a rating of 100 points. Any rejections, lapses in delivery, or prices higher than the lowest quotation reduce the rating. At the same time there is an objective basis for determining the extent to which superior quality and service offset higher prices in overall value and satisfaction, or vice versa. A step-by-step

[10]D. N. Burt, *Managing Suppliers Up to Speed*, Harvard Business Review, July–August 1989, p. 133.

analysis of the weighted-point-plan evaluation is shown in Figure 10-5 and discussed below.

Vendor A has delivered 58 lots during the past year, of which two were rejected. The percentage of good lots is 96.5. Multiplied by the weight factor of 40, this gives vendor A a quality rating of 38.6.

The lowest net price from any vendor is $0.93 per unit. A's price is $1.07. By inverse ratio, A's price performance is 86.9 percent. Multiplied by the weight factor of 35, this gives vendor A a price rating of 30.4.

Of the 58 lots delivered, 55 were received as promised. This is 94.8 percent performance. Multiplied by the weight factor of 25, it gives vendor A a service rating of 23.7.

The sum of these figures gives vendor A a total performance rating of 92.7.

Vendor B, who furnished 34 lots during the same period, was the lowest-price supplier at $0.93 per unit, so has a price rating of the full 35 points. However, four of the lots were defective, giving B a quality rating of 35.3. Also vendor B was late with five deliveries, so B's service rating is 21.3, for a total performance rating of 91.6.

In this instance, therefore, vendor A is judged to be the more satisfactory source, and the buyer is warranted in placing the bulk of the business with A in spite of A's substantially higher price. If vendor B could be induced to cut delinquencies in either quality or service by one half, or if the price factor were deemed relatively more important in respect to this item, B would have the better rating.

WEIGHTS		MEASUREMENT
Quality	40%	$\dfrac{\text{Number of acceptable lots}}{\text{Total lots received}}$
Price	35%	$\dfrac{\text{Lowest net price}}{\text{Net price}}$
Service	25%	$\dfrac{\text{Lots received as promised}}{\text{Total lots received}}$

Weights show rank order preference of each factor; for example, in this example, quality is most important!

Let's compare two vendors:

VENDOR A	VENDOR B
Shipped 58 lots/2 rejected	Shipped 34 lots/4 rejected
Price = $1.07/unit*	Price = $0.93/unit*
55 lots received as promised	29 lots received as promised

*Lowest net price

PERFORMANCE RATING	PERFORMANCE RATING
92.7	91.6

Figure 10-5 Weighted-Point-Plan Evaluation

Example of the Cost-Ratio Plan

$$\frac{\text{Total quality costs for item}}{\text{Total value of purchases for item}} = \text{quality cost ratio}$$

$$\frac{\text{Total delivery costs for item}}{\text{Total value of purchases for item}} = \text{delivery cost ratio}$$

Supplier A $50/unit   Supplier B = $51.00/unit
Quality cost ratio 3%   Quality Cost = 1%
Delivery cost ratio = 2%   Delivery Cost = 0%
Total cost ratio (supplier A) = $50 + (3%)($50) + (2%)($50) = $52.50
Total cost ratio (supplier B) = (1%)($51) + (0%)($51) = $51.51

FIGURE 10-6

Cost-Ratio Plan

This plan attempts to capture costs associated with actual supplier performance in the areas of quality and delivery. It is the most comprehensive in terms of a total cost approach to purchasing. Costs uniquely associated with quality, delivery, and price are determined for each supplier. This total is then totaled to produce an overall cost ratio. Quality costs include rework, rejection processing, and the like. Delivery costs include production downtime, expediting costs, higher price substitutes, and so forth. The adjusted price for each supplier in a particular commodity is then compared. Figure 10-6 indicates that it costs less to buy from supplier B even though the supplier is $1/unit higher in price per unit. Not many firms use this approach, since the data-collection requirement is extensive and time consuming. However, with continuing development of personal and hand-held computer systems this evaluation approach will be used more frequently in the future.

POINTS FOR REVIEW

1. Discuss the steps you would take to develop good relations with suppliers.
2. Identify the elements that make for stronger, long-range buyer-seller relationships.
3. Identify key areas you need to investigate prior to developing a partnership relation with a supplier.
4. Discuss some of the socioeconomic developments of recent years that have had an effect on purchasing.
5. Compare the various supplier-evaluation plans in terms of usefulness, cost, and effectiveness.
6. Explain the requirements necessary to establish a cost-ratio plan.

11

Purchasing in International Markets

American buyers, particularly those in big companies, have been dealing with suppliers in leading industrial nations of the world—Canada, England, France, West Germany, and Japan—for many years. Raw-material imports—metals, petroleum, agricultural products, for example—have long been a big factor in U.S. industrial imports. From the late 1970s and continuing into the 1980s, however, there was a tremendous upsurge in U.S. imports—both consumer and industrial—that dwarfed anything that had gone before. There is no appearance that this trend will dramatically reverse itself in the 1990s.

From 1980 to 1988 the U.S. negative trade balance (excess of imports over exports in dollar terms) jumped almost 560 percent. In 1987 it was $160 billion and by the end of 1988 had dropped to $140 million. And the goods were coming from all over the world—including such heretofore "off-limits" nations as the Soviet Union and the People's Republic of China.

The world market has become a reality, and American industrial buyers are increasingly active in it. This buyer activity is illustrated by Figure 11-1, which shows how the U.S. balance of trade deficits have ballooned in the 1980s. The world market has also been spurred by foreign-government restrictions that require buying in the country if one sells to that country. Countries are recognizing this trend and forming alliances to protect trade. Squeezed between the U.S. and Japan, Europe found its domestic markets shrinking and products aimed at global markets failing. The Common Market of 1992 enables European companies to serve a population of 355 million people with a GNP of $5.2 billion and allow for improved international competitiveness.

This relatively sudden development of a worldwide market has important implications for purchasing managers. They now have greater availability of supply and also a greater need for careful selection of sources—some of which are thousands of miles away. That in turn calls for somewhat different buying techniques and more knowledgeable and sophisticated buyers. Dealing overseas requires a certain amount of cultural adaptation as well as new financial skills. This chapter deals with the opportunities and the challenges that face purchasing managers entering the international market.

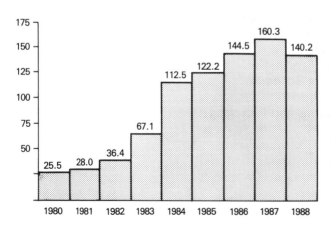

Figure 11-1 U.S. Balance of Trade Current Account Deficit 1980–88
Source: *Economic Indicators* (Washington, D.C.: Government Printing Office), 1989. Prepared by the Joint Economic Committee Council of Economic Advisors.

ADVANTAGES OF INTERNATIONAL SOURCING

Buyers who have turned abroad for a large portion of their purchases cite these reasons:

Cost/Price Benefits.   Generally, offshore sources have been able to offer American buyers lower prices, particularly on manufactured goods, because of lower labor, material, and overhead costs. Total landed costs, including the cost of transportation for thousands of miles in some cases, are often lower than those of U.S. suppliers of a wide range of industrial supplies and equipment. Rising standards of living and pressure from labor may eventually nullify that advantage in developed countries. However, there are several developing countries, such as South Korea, China, Mexico, and India, whose labor rates remain substantially lower than those in the U.S. Finally, during the 1980s a strong U.S. dollar plus weak demand in overseas domestic markets helped keep prices of imports at levels highly attractive to U.S. buyers.

Availability/Continuity of Supply.   Increased worldwide demand for goods made it imperative that new sources of supply be developed. Industry has become sharply aware—particularly since the material shortages of 1973–75 and the oil embargoes of the late 1970s. While key major shortages were not a problem during the 1980s, there is potential for recurrence. For example, experts feel the 1990s could see a reemergence of a powerful Organization of Petroleum Exporting Countries (OPEC). This assumes the current global trends in production and demand will continue, particularly as the great oil fields in the U.S., Great Britain, Canada, and Australia pass their prime, leaving OPEC with approximately 60 percent of the total worldwide reserves.[1]

High-quality Technological Know-how.   For years many people had the notion that foreign producers were generally followers of U.S. industry in quality standards and product innovation. American purchasing managers consistently report the opposite in many cases. Foreign vendors have displayed great flexibility in adapting their manufacturing methods to special requirements: their products—particularly machinery—are often far advanced over their American counterparts; and the quality of many products (e.g., stainless steel, high-tolerance forgings, precision ball bearings) is often superior to that of higher-priced domestic items. It has often been stated that price is the initial motivator for offshore sourcing, and high-quality is a bonus that keeps them returning.

Greater Competition.   The growth of commerce and industry in relatively underdeveloped or politically isolated nations—added to that of the already industrialized countries—has opened up new sources and new productive capacity. Increased competition and availability have a powerful attraction for professional buyers, particularly when they appear to be waning in their normal markets.

[1]"OPEC in a Few Years Is Likely to Reassert Control of Oil Market," *Wall Street Journal,* August 25, 1987, p. 1.

Relative Ease of Communication.   The development of almost instantaneous communication and rapid transportation anywhere in the world has helped promote international trade. A telephone call from New Orleans to Hong Kong, for example, takes little more time than a call between New York and Chicago. FAX machines and electronic data interchange (EDI) allow transmission of purchase orders and drawings in minutes. Air shipments from Europe are made overnight. A New York purchasing manager wishing to visit the Paris plant of a supplier can fly there on the Concorde in less time than it would take to drive to Boston.

Market Entry.   Virtually the whole world is a potential market for goods produced in the United States, so it makes good economic and political sense to buy in that market when it offers competitive advantages. For example, a computer firm wishing to sell its products in Brazil must also buy from Brazil. Second, most multinational corporations accept some responsibility for the economic development of the nations in which they operate. Finally, a foreign country may require a U.S. manufacturer that has a plant there to purchase a certain amount of its product locally. This requirement is called *local content* and was proposed by Congress in response to the flood of Japanese automobiles in the 1980s. However, no formal legislation was passed in the U.S. concerning local content.

COUNTERTRADE PURCHASES

Countertrade occurs when the buyer is required to settle a purchase transaction without paying in cash. Typically the counterpurchase involves the sale of an item to the foreign country and takes place where there are political or balance-of-trade problems or where currency is unavailable.

Forms of countertrade, such as barter, have been used for centuries. Recently countertrade has gained increasing attention, owing to several factors.

- Of the world's 171 countries, 141 demand countertrade in some or all of their purchases.[2]
- Countertrade rose from 2 percent of world trade in 1975 to 10 percent in 1986.
- Countertrade represents $150 billion in today's international economy.
- $7.1 billion of American exports were linked to countertrade in 1984.[3]

Countertrade agreements can be broken into four major categories: (1) barter; (2) offset/counterpurchase; (3) buyback; and (4) switch trading. Barter is the oldest and simplest form of countertrade and involves the direct exchange of goods having offsetting values—an even swap without any flow of money. A major problem with barter is that one party may receive goods it cannot use or it receives less than

[2]Warren E. Norquist, "Purchasing's Role in Countertrade," *Revolution in Purchasing and Materials Management* (Tempe, Ariz.: National Association of Purchasing Management 1989), pp. 262–267.

[3]J. R. Carter and J. Gagne, "The Do's and Don'ts of International Countertrade," *Sloan Management Review,* Spring 1988, pp. 31–37.

the anticipated barter value. However, there have been some innovative barter swaps, as when CBS provided the Chinese with sixty-four hours of programming in return for thirty-two one-minute spots of advertising, which it sold to firms wishing to expand into the Chinese markets.[4]

Offset/counterpurchase refers to a percentage of the goods countertraded in relation to the value of the product being sold. Cash is used to make the individual purchases. Offset/counterpurchase is a form of reciprocal buying. In order to sell in a particular country, the company agrees to purchase a certain amount of product. For example, a major aircraft manufacturer obtains a contract to sell planes to Spain and agrees to purchase products worth 100 percent of the contract value in Spain. That is an illustration of an offset purchase.

Buyback occurs when a firm supplies the technology, equipment, and/or technical advice to build an operating plant in a country and then takes a percentage of the output from the facility. The host country assumes control of the facility after a number of years. To illustrate, a car manufacturer builds a plant in Brazil and takes output as its payment. Buybacks must include enough consideration for supervision and training of the work force and management, or the end product received may lack the necessary quality, thus requiring significant additional investment by the supplying company.

Switch trading involves the use of a third party to dispose of the goods acquired in a countertrade transaction. One of the largest trade and barter information bases is International Business Clearinghouse (IBC), which has a worldwide network of businesses wishing to buy, sell, or trade goods and services. Switch traders frequently receive substitute trade credits, which can later be spent for cash on other products.[5]

Costs involved in countertrade transactions consist of fees paid to agents, such as trading companies, banks, and clearing houses. Additionally, there is a discount from the perceived or negotiated fair market value of the goods versus the value actually received.[6] Purchasing departments are becoming a more critical element in countertrade owing to their input on valuing the products as well as on what products to buy. In most firms Purchasing tends to be the "resident expert" on disposing of surplus or unwanted material. Generally, purchasing and marketing share responsibility for countertrade programs, although recent trends point to more involvement of purchasing.

GENERAL INFORMATION SOURCES

Purchasing in foreign markets is a complex, sometimes very delicate, and often frustrating process. Thus a good start toward success begins with information gathering. There are many sources to which the buyer can turn. Immediately at

[4]Warren E. Norquist, "Purchasing's Role in Countertrade."

[5]J. R. Carter and J. Gagne, "The Do's and Don'ts of International Countertrade," *Sloan Management Review,* Spring 1988, pp. 31–37.

[6]IBID. p. 35.

hand are the finance and traffic departments of the buyer's company, with which the purchasing department should closely coordinate its overseas purchasing efforts. The foreign-trade departments of major banks are an excellent resource. Foreign embassies and U.S. consulates abroad are also a source of help. The U.S. Department of Commerce publishes information on commodities by country of origin. Publications from other sources that are quite helpful are *Foreign Commerce Handbook* and *An Introduction to Doing Import and Export Business,* U.S. Chamber of Commerce; *Export and Import Procedures,* Morgan Guaranty Trust Company of New York; *Exporting to the United States* and *Customs Information for Exporters to the U.S.,* U.S. Treasury Department, Bureau of Customs; and *Export and Import Financing Procedures,* First National Bank of Chicago.

Supplier Information Sources

Locating a supplier—once the determination to buy overseas has been made—can involve something as simple as a telephone call or as extensive as a small research project. Just as with domestic suppliers, buyers can get information on foreign products and producers from a number of sources. Thorough evaluation of the supplier, however, is somewhat more difficult and lengthy, as it may require consultation with other customers of a distant supplier, obtaining and testing samples, or preferably, visiting overseas plants if the producer's reputation is unknown.

Information sources include a variety of publications, from trade journals and newspapers to directories of manufacturers and distributors to trade lists, directory reports, and surveys from the Department of Commerce. One guide to international purchasing procedures lists twenty major directories on international trade. They include such volumes as *The American Register of Exporters and Importers,* published in New York; *Jane's Major Companies of Europe,* published in London; *Dun and Bradstreet's World Marketing Directory,* published in New York; *Directory of Swiss Manufacturers and Products,* published in Zurich; and the *Bottin International Business Register,* published in France, which contains information on companies throughout the world. These and other directories are available in World Trade Center libraries, which have been established in twenty-three major American cities.

The Department of Commerce maintains up-to-date lists of names and addresses of foreign companies dealing in specific products in more than a hundred countries. The lists also identify importers and dealers, along with giving other pertinent information. The department also maintains trade centers in major foreign cities, including Warsaw, Seoul, Milan, Paris, and Sydney. (U.S. district offices in forty-two American cities are also excellent sources of information.)

There are also American Chambers of Commerce in fifty major cities throughout the world, all prepared to help U.S. buyers and sellers. Embassies and consulates are similarly equipped to aid businesspeople seeking to trade in their respective countries.

Banks, airlines, and shipping companies have significant collections of data on businesses in the countries they serve as well as information on local customs and procedures.

Where there is no competitive advantage involved, purchasing managers of other companies experienced in overseas buying are usually willing to help newcomers to the field. Purchasers who are employed by companies with offshore subsidiaries or licenses may find sourcing expertise in the desired country.

Professional associations, such as the International Federation of Purchasing and Materials Management (IFPMM) and the National Association of Purchasing Management's (NAPM) international group can provide assistance. Both groups conduct sessions at their annual conferences, which discuss international purchasing.

DIRECT AND INDIRECT BUYING

Whether to buy directly from overseas suppliers or indirectly through intermediaries depends in large part on the volume and frequency of purchases, the anticipated length of a relationship with a supplier, and the availability of qualified buying personnel.

Small-volume or occasional purchasers most often use a variety of middlemen—wholesalers, brokers, selling agents—for overseas transactions. For a fee (which in the case of selling agents or representatives is paid by the supplier), they will handle the basic details of a purchase, including choice of a supplier when necessary. These agents fall into four classes: (1) merchants, (2) brokers, (3) manufacturers' agents, and (4) independent agents. The buyer must realize that *import merchants* buy commodities from abroad for their own accounts, assume financial risks, and carry inventory. Thus goods purchased through the merchant are quite similar to a domestic purchase. On the other hand, import brokers help buyers locate foreign sources but assume no financial risk and carry no inventory.

Manufacturers' agents are representatives of foreign firms who are located in the United States. They will handle all shipping and customs details but assume no financial responsibility of the principals. Independent agents located in foreign countries will act as agents for a fee. They typically have a good working knowledge of the country and work on a commission basis.

The breadth of services varies widely among these intermediaries, so it is important to know in advance whether their fees (which can run up to 25 percent of the value of the purchase) cover such important elements as research on vendors, shipping costs, insurance, customs, administrative expenses, and degree of financial responsibility. Prudent buyers will also make an effort to determine, preferably from their other customers, the broker's or agent's performance record.

Trading Companies

Trading companies are larger organizations that offer even more comprehensive services than do those of the specialists mentioned earlier. They usually handle a broad spectrum of products from one or more countries, ranging from small consumer goods on up to the most complex types of machinery. Some, Mitsubishi of Japan for one, have offices all over the world and maintain their own transportation and financial services. Countries such as Hong Kong and South Korea have trading companies in major U.S. cities. Many large U.S. firms that established trading companies in the 1970s for export purposes as well as for purchases now offer their offshore expertise to buyers outside their own companies. The Westinghouse Electric Trading Company, located in Pittsburgh, offers this service.

Among the advantages cited for buying through trading companies are greater efficiency and convenience, lower costs, shorter lead times, and assurance of quality inasmuch as inspection is made before shipment and the trading company remains responsible for unacceptable shipments. One criticism is that the prices the companies obtain are seldom established on the basis of costs. Instead, they are based on market levels at the time of purchase, so that the buyer is deprived of the benefits of direct negotiation.

These different points of view underscore the need for extra care and judgment in dealing with new and distant suppliers.

As transportation and communication improvements make the world market even more compact and accessible, middlemen will assume a more specialized role in international trade. Many American companies had well-established networks for buying directly in Europe, Asia, Latin America, and parts of Africa, after years of having sent purchasing personnel abroad on individual buying trips. Some assigned responsibility for purchasing requirements to existing buying departments in foreign subsidiaries; others established separate buying offices that report directly to corporate headquarters.

Foreign Purchasing Offices

Foreign purchasing offices require a long-term commitment to offshore buying. The major reasons are overall expense, foreign-government regulations and legal problems, and difficulties in local staffing. Logistic problems also arise concerning location of the office. For example, possible European sites would include London, Geneva, Frankfurt, and Paris. Foreign restrictions further tighten the restrictions. In Tokyo advance payment of three to five years' rent may be required, while the Swiss limit the number of work permits for foreign nationals.[7] Employee motivation must be through the local value system, and foreign titles and salary structures need to be adopted.

In spite of difficulties, setting up a separate foreign purchasing office has its advantages:

1. Lower operating costs. Foreign purchasing overhead is generally lower than the brokers' fees. Communication is more effective and less costly.
2. Better control. On-site administration provides better control over price, quality, and delivery schedules. The foreign office is also better equipped to handle the intricacies of foreign exchange.

[7]N. A. DiOrio, *An Operational Approach to International Purchasing.* (Tempe, Ariz.: National Association of Purchasing Management, 1986).

3. More-current information. The rules and regulations that govern foreign transactions in overseas countries often change, and an on-site office has access to the
most current legal and economic information.
4. Better understanding. Foreign nationals in such offices can often negotiate better agreements than many U.S. business managers can because of their familiarity with the territory, local business conditions, local customs, and of course,
language.[8]

As previously mentioned, there may be some disagreement concerning
the fourth advantage, since many purchasing managers prefer to place American
supervisors in any type of purchasing organization—subsidiary or separate
office—buying products for use by U.S. plants. In most cases, however, as we
pointed out, on-site nationals have played an important part in the buying process
because of their knowledge. But in recent years nationality as such has become almost irrelevant. Experience has shown that purchasing executives with good professional skills and the ability to adapt to changing conditions can operate almost
anywhere. It is not unusual, for example, to find a Brazilian heading the
Rotterdam purchasing office of a large American firm. Similar situations can be
found in many other functions of business. Managerial competence is the major
requirement.

PROBLEMS

Issuing a purchase order to a foreign supplier does not, however, automatically
guarantee irresistible prices, better service, high quality, bright ideas, and so on.
Suppliers must be as carefully researched—and often more so—as domestic vendors are. Dealing with heretofore unknown companies in foreign markets presents many difficulties and obstacles. Few are insuperable, however, and indeed
present purchasing people with many opportunities for improving their skills in
negotiation, research, finance. Figure 11-2 shows some of the potential problems
buyers will encounter when purchasing offshore. These problems include political stability, cultural and language differences, currency fluctuations, lead times,
inventory, and total cost charges. Buyers must be aware and take steps to protect
against such obstacles if they are to be successful in offshore procurement.

Political Issues

Any analysis prior to the establishment of a long-range overseas procurement program should also include some consideration of political and economic conditions
in the country or region involved. Such a consideration requires a thorough analysis of the country's history. Dimensions analyzed should include government philosophy (i.e., totalitarian, communist, democratic), stability of government, civil
disorders, strikes, and war or conflicts with neighboring countries. The impor-

[8]C. L. Scott and Eddie S. W. Hong, "An Operational Approach to International Sourcing," in *Guide
to Purchasing* (New York: National Association of Purchasing Management, 1975).

Figure 11-2   Obstacles to Offshore Sourcing

Source: Adapted from L. Giunipero, "Evaluating Offshore Purchase Tradeoffs," *Electronic Buyers News, Professional Purchasing Series,* CMP Publications, Manhasset, N.Y., 1984, p. 50.

tance of such research was highlighted after the 1989 Tienaman Square massacre in the People's Republic of China. Many U.S. firms had undertaken active trade with the People's Republic of China, and there were signs of a more open China. However, the suppression of individual rights by the Chinese army changed the buying posture of certain U.S. firms. One director of purchasing stated: "On a personal level I think it unethical to deal with people who act like that," he said, referring to the army's massacre of prodemocracy agitators. "And on a business level I feel that supplier assurance could have been jeopardized. . . . The decision to halt purchasing will stand until something changes over there."[9] However, many others felt the need to try to maintain relations. For example, General Electric's business was not disrupted in China. GE sells its products in China and uses Chinese-made plastic and metal parts that it buys direct. Accordingly, GE remained interested in doing business with China, according to John D. Cologna C.P.M.[10] Had purchasers been familiar with the history of Chinese suppression, dating back to the Ming dynasty, they would have proceeded more cautiously in China.

Cultural and Language Differences

Once the political history, philosophy, and trends are judged acceptable, the culture is studied. Buyers must know and respect the culture and customs of the nationals with whom they deal. A bit of valuable counsel is, know how to communicate with foreign counterparts, preferably in their own language but at least through skilled interpreters. Ignorance or disregard of these matters can lead to embarrassment at best and harm to your own interests at worst.

Examples of misunderstanding abound:

[9]John S. Chester, Jr., China Still in Picture, *Electronic Buyer's News,* October 9, 1989, p. 1.
[10]Ibid., p. 61.

1. In preparing Hertz Rent-a-Car advertisements for the German market, an agency used the then widely known (in the U.S.) slogan, "Hertz Puts *You* in the Driver's Seat." When rendered into German by an unskilled translator, the idiomatic expression, intended to appeal to status-conscious American businesspeople, came out as "Hertz Makes *You* the Chauffeur," which hardly made it appealing to the even more status-conscious German businesspeople.

2. After a few years of doing business with a Japanese company, an American buyer sent the supplier's sales department a letter of cancellation, only to receive a reply stating that they did not know the meaning of the word "cancellation."

3. The purchasing director of a major U.S. company began preliminary negotiations with a Japanese company for the purchase of well over a million dollars' worth of copper-fin tubing. At a critical point the senior supplier representative at the session said flatly, "Mr. R——, tell us the lowest price you are paying any of your current suppliers and I guarantee we will cut that price by 20 percent." Trying to make the point that "auction" buying—that is, revealing other suppliers' prices to obtain leverage in a negotiation—was not the way that he did business, the purchasing director replied, with typical American exaggeration. "Why, I could tell you that I am paying only ten cents a pound" (the average price at the time was about fifty cents).

   The Japanese took the reply literally, and obviously stunned, then highly agitated, they asked for a recess in negotiations. By the time the session was resumed the following day, they had flown in two top officials from Tokyo to add to their delegation. The misunderstanding was quickly cleared when the purchasing director explained that he was simply dramatizing a point. A mutually advantageous contract was worked out, although the purchasing executive came close to missing a substantial reduction in price, and the suppliers a lucrative sale, because of a misunderstanding.

A training visual produced by the International Group of the National Association of Purchasing Management urges offshore purchases to stay well informed on foreign business customs. The following set of "rules" for negotiating in the Japanese market is offered as a guide. The "rules" are, of course, adaptable to purchasing in other foreign nations.

1. Have high-level introductions.
2. Maintain surface harmony.
3. Avoid embarrassments.
4. Understand the importance of appearance.
5. Be patient—progress will be slow.
6. Speak their language—if only a little.
7. Have plenty of business cards.
8. Give little mementos.
9. Be generous with visitors.

"Number 5—patience—is particularly important," the narrator of this training visual says. "Japanese business practice is not to meet and run, but to get to know each other first and to reach some form of consensus among themselves before finalizing a business venture."

Table 11-1   Selected Foreign Exchange Rates, October 1989

	Foreign Currency in Dollars	Dollar in Foreign Currency
Britain (pound)	1.59	.6285
Canada (dollar)	.853	1.17
Japan (yen)	.007029	142.26
West Germany (mark)	.5385	1.857

CURRENCY FLUCTUATIONS

Currency fluctuations can cause problems for overseas buyers. Much of the increase/decrease in costs of buying abroad can be caused by the depreciation/ appreciation of the dollar in international markets. Currencies are valued against one another, and the value of currency expressed in terms of another currency is the *exchange rate*. Rates are published daily in the financial sections of most major newspapers and practically all financial publications, such as the *Wall Street Journal*. Foreign currency is quoted in dollars and dollars in foreign currency. Table 11-1 shows it took $1.59 to purchase one British pound and $.853 to purchase one Canadian dollar in late October 1989.

Currency rates do not remain constant but fluctuate in value against one another based on relative supply and demand for its currency. This demand is influenced by several economic factors including interest rates, inflation/deflation, and relative trade balance. For example, if the United States drastically increased its exports, the dollar would eventually strengthen, since offshore buyers would need to obtain dollars to pay for U.S. exports received. Because drastic currency fluctuations would create havoc in international trade, central banks intervene to buy or sell currency to smooth out drastic fluctuations. These actions by central banks have led to the term *managed float* to describe the exchange-rate system. Currencies fluctuate freely but are managed by central banks.

The fluctuation of currency will create changes in prices for both buyer and seller. For example, if in late October a U.S. firm purchased an item costing $10,000 Canadian, it would have cost $8,530 U.S. As can be seen, when appreciation occurs, the buyer needs fewer dollars to pay for the Canadian goods (price decrease). On the other hand, if the dollar depreciates, the buyer needs more U.S. dollars (price increase) (see Figure 11-3).

Appreciation/Depreciation
    $1 Canadian = $.850 U.S.
    $10,000 Canadian = $8,500 U.S.
Dollar appreciates:
    $1 Canadian = $.80 U.S.
    $10,000 Canadian = $8,000 U.S.
Dollar depreciates:
    $1 Canadian = $.900 U.S.
    $10,000 Canadian = $9,000 U.S.

Figure 11-3

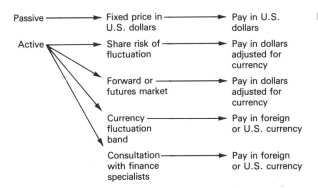

Figure 11-4 Strategies for Managing Exchange Rates

Managing Fluctuations

Given that exchange rates will vary, buyers have several courses of action (see Figure 11-4). The first is to negotiate and pay in U.S. dollars. Advocates of this approach argue that if the offshore price is attractive and the supplier commits for a time period (usually for one year), there is no necessity to get involved with exchange rates. However, the rate risk must either be reflected in the current quote, or the supplier may begin missing delivery and cutting quality to prompt renegotiation if the dollar weakens. Conversely, if the dollar strengthens, the supplier makes extra profits. For those just starting to purchase internationally, payment in fixed dollar is acceptable.

Experienced purchasers tend to move toward more active strategies to manage exchange risks. These include risk sharing, using the forward or futures market, negotiating currency fluctuation bands, and consulting with financial specialists.

Risk-sharing agreements split fluctuations either fifty-fifty or to some predetermined formula between buyer and seller. For example, an item is contracted for $8,500 U.S. and $10,000 Canadian rate. Upon delivery, the dollar has appreciated so that $8,000 U.S. is equal to $10,000 Canadian. The seller receives an extra $250 U.S., and the buyer pays only $8,250. Had the dollar appreciated to $9,000 U.S. equaling $10,000 Canadian, the buyer would pay only $8,750, and the seller would effectively receive only $9,625 Canadian dollars.

Risk sharing may prove to be administratively burdensome in cases where periodic shipments are made. Buyers and sellers can negotiate currency-fluctuation-band clauses, which set a preestablished rate and an upper and lower limit. Where this limit is exceeded, the buyer and seller negotiate a new clause (see Table 11-2).

On one-time purchases with a known lead time, purchasers can look into fixed rates via the forward exchange or futures market. Forward contracts are is-

Table 11-2 Currency Fluctuation Band

Upper limit	150
Fixed rate	140 yen/$
Lower limit	130

sued by major banks and are agreements in which the buyer pays a preestablished rate for currency in the future and bank for providing the service.

Futures contracts may also be purchased through the New York Foreign Exchange Market and the Chicago-based International Monetary Market (IMM). Buyers usually prefer the forward market, since its purpose is to help bank clients conduct international trade, and contract amounts can be matched with the contract. The futures market is primarily used to facilitate hedging and is also used by speculators, and its currency contracts are for set amounts—e.g., $100,000 Canadian dollars or £25,000.

Foreign currency options allow the purchasers an option to buy or sell currency at a fixed rate for a certain time period. Calls are options to buy currency, and puts are options to sell currency at the predetermined rate. Options are used when a purchase is imminent and exchange rates favorable; thus the buyer can lock in this rate for a slight options premium. If the expenditure is approved, he or she exercises the option and buys a futures or forward contract.

Buyers cannot be expected, however, to be financial specialists any more than they can be expected to be engineers and lawyers. When complications in payment terms and currency fluctuations are anticipated, overseas buyers should call on the company finance department for guidance and assistance. A multinational firm is always dealing in several currencies. For example, one firm uses earnings from a West German subsidiary to pay marks for its German purchases for its U.S. plants.

TOTAL COST EVALUATION

The quoted price is the starting point for evaluating a foreign purchase. Additional factors plus price include:

- Tooling
- Transportation
- Customs duty
- Engineering drawings
- Escalation/de-escalation
- Insurance packaging
- Customs broker
- Communication costs (fax, phone)
- Additional inventory
- Fees (documentary, inspection, wharfage, loading port, and terminal)
- Financial fees (letters of credit and bank costs)

Thus getting total cost requires extensive analysis. Unless total costs are carefully considered and monitored, the economic advantage that seemed to exist in a low initial price may quickly evaporate. Rising freight costs, a high rate of reject in items purchased, labor troubles at supplier plants, delayed deliveries, the need for carrying heavier inventories to protect against such delays, and the possibility of having capital tied up in letters of credit are just some of the elements that may affect the final cost of a product purchased abroad.

Additional costs are generated when doing business in national economies that are strike prone, plagued by civil disorder, ruled by unstable governments, or subject to manipulation for domestic and international political purposes. Any one of these conditions, if extended for any length of time, can result in delayed or canceled shipments, revocation of price agreements, and destruction of property. Even the least of those problems—delayed shipments —could require heavy investment in inventory building to guard against plant shutdowns, thereby adding to the total cost of a purchase. In self-defense against such eventualities, some overseas buyers have resorted to double sourcing; that is, they place part of their business with one or more domestic suppliers to assure themselves some supply in the event of trouble overseas. This, however, dilutes the benefits that they would otherwise get from a foreign supplier's lower price.

NEGOTIATING WITH FOREIGN SUPPLIERS

Negotiations with foreign suppliers call for a good deal of understanding and insight in addition to the normal planning required for such sessions. Formal plans are needed, but they are not enough; negotiators must have more than ordinary skills to deal productively with people of different commercial and cultural backgrounds from theirs.

This is not to say that the principles of sound negotiation described in Chapter 14—thorough preparation, development of the negotiating team, precise definition of team members' responsibilities, establishment of objectives, analysis of relative bargaining positions, and so on—do not apply in overseas buying. They definitely do. But some must be modified and others intensified, and in every case they must be adapted to customs, practices, and perceptions that may differ from those found in American business.

Obviously, preparation for negotiation in a foreign country (or anywhere for that matter) begins with the designation of skilled negotiators who have sound judgment and can adapt readily to new or difficult situations. As a backup to basic negotiating techniques, experienced international traders suggest these approaches:

1. Observe local custom in business relationships. In Japan, for example, customers and suppliers customarily get to know each other on a personal basis before getting down to business, so a certain amount of socializing may be expected.
2. Because negotiations in direct overseas purchasing are generally conducted on the supplier's home ground, at least one member of the negotiating team should be fluent in the language and thoroughly conversant with normal business practices of the country.
3. Serious negotiations should be conducted whenever possible only with persons who have the authority to commit their companies. Anyone without that authority may simply drag out the negotiation, wasting valuable time and ultimately leading the buyer to reveal his or her bargaining strengths (and weaknesses) prematurely.

4. Some foreign negotiators measure their success in negotiation by the number rather than the substance of the concessions they win. If they win on more than half the issues, they may consider the negotiation a success. In such a situation, good strategy on the part of the buyer would be to develop as many negotiation points as possible in the advance planning. This would give the negotiator flexibility in making minor concessions without endangering major objectives.

5. Business managers in many foreign countries are extremely status conscious and consider it undignified to deal with lower-level personnel. Negotiating teams, therefore, should whenever possible be composed of—or at least led by—persons whose titles correspond to those of the supplier representatives.

6. Negotiators should avoid peremptory or abrupt actions and decisions that could alienate suppliers (who may also be customers of one or more divisions of the buying company). The kind of blunt talk that is taken quite objectively in American business discussions might be taken as a personal affront overseas. As previously mentioned, maintenance of at least surface harmony is essential.

7. No negotiation should be concluded without mutual understanding and firm agreement on product specifications, delivery schedules, prices, packaging and shipping methods, insurance, and terms of payment. This seems an elementary precaution, but because of language and other differences, carelessness in ironing out details could lead to costly mistakes for both sides. Just the casual use of the term *ton* for example, can cause trouble unless it is made clear what kind of ton is meant: a short ton (2,000 pounds), a long ton (2,240 pounds), or a metric ton (2,204.62 pounds). Similar confusion in describing complex items with close tolerances would present even more serious problems.

TERMS, SHIPPING, INSURANCE, CUSTOMS

Payment for goods purchased overseas can be made in a number of ways: payment in advance; payment after the seller has delivered the purchased materials to the buyer's plant, as in regular domestic buyer-seller transactions; and payment by letter of credit.

The latter method has for many years been the most common form of settlement in the international market. Letters of credit are issued by the purchaser's bank, and the supplier can draw against the credit upon presentation of the required documents. There are two basic types: (1) irrevocable and (2) revocable letter of credit. A revocable letter of credit allows the buyer to change or cancel the letter any time prior to execution without the seller's consent. For these reasons it is seldom used. Irrevocable letters of credit may not be changed or canceled without prior agreement of all parties involved in the transaction. This feature offers great certainty to the seller, and such letters can even be used as collateral.

Letters of credit spell out the total amount of the purchase, the currency in which payments are to be made, and what documents must accompany each draft. Because the foreign supplier is generally responsible for clearance of the shipment, the supplier must submit a bill of lading or airway bill, a commercial invoice, a customs invoice, an insurance certificate, and when required by U.S. Customs, inspection or analysis certificate.

Tariffs/Duties

Duties are assessed on most goods entering U.S. markets. There are three major types of duties: (1) specific, (2) ad valorem, and (3) compound. Specific duties are charged on a specified rate per unit such as $250 per car. Ad valorem is the most popular type and is charged as a percentage of the appraised value. Finally, compound duty is a combination of specific and ad valorem-type duties. These are found in the "Tariff Schedules of the United States," which is part of the *U.S. Tariff and Trade Code*. The *Tariff and Trade Code* contains not only normal tariffs shown above but also a generalized system of preferences (GSP) and Communist bloc restrictions. Major improvements in Soviet American relationships and political freedom for many Eastern Communist countries has led to the United States granting Most Favored Nation (MFN) status to Czechoslovakia and the Soviet Union. Commodities purchased from developing nations or those the U.S. government is trying to help, enter "duty free" under GSP. Products from the Communist-bloc countries face more scrutiny by customs officials.

Customs Brokers

The job of customs broker is to coordinate the paper work and other details necessary to bring the shipment through customs officials. Customs brokers deal with customs officials, file proper documents, advise the buyer about the most favorable tariff rate, and ensure that the shipment doesn't sit on the dock. On medical items, food preparations, agricultural products, and cosmetics they file the necessary documentation with the Food and Drug Administration. Customs brokers also arrange for bonded warehouse storage and immediate transportation.

Bonded warehouses permit the buyer to store material at port of importation and require payment of storage fees. However, duty is not paid until the material is withdrawn. Goods that have high duties are stored in these warehouses.

Goods to be immediately transported enter a port of importation and then are shipped via bonded carrier to another port for customs entry. The advantages are saving time on duty payment and getting goods closer to the buyer's facility.

Foreign Trade Zones

Foreign trade zones (FTZs), also called free trade zones which are located in the U.S., are considered to be outside customs territory and are available for activities that might otherwise be carried on overseas for customs reasons. The Bureau of Customs, U.S. Department of Treasury, describes the function of the foreign trade zones thus in its publication, *Exporting to the United States:*

> On the import and re-export side, no duties are charged on foreign goods moved into zones unless and until the goods or their products are moved into customs territory. This means that the use of zones can be considered for operations involving foreign dutiable materials and components being assembled or pro-

duced here for re-export. Also, in such cases no quota restrictions would ordinarily apply. The facilities are available for operations involving storage, repacking, inspection, exhibition, assembly, manufacturing, and other processing.[11]

In summary, FTZs are used for two broad activities: (1) warehousing and distribution (including repackaging and testing) and (2) assembly and manufacturing. When they leave the FTZ, foreign goods imported into the U.S. are subject to duties. For buyers FTZs provide a ready source of inventory, a display area for foreign products, and a redistribution point. For example, a bearings manufacturer imports bearings, repackages them with U.S. products, then reexports a majority of the bearings but keeps a ready stock for U.S. customers. Information on the zones is available from the Foreign Trade Zones Board, Department of Commerce, Washington, D.C. 20230, or from the nearest Department of Commerce district office.

Duty Drawbacks

When use of a FTZ is not practical but imported products are reexported, buyers can apply for a duty drawback. The drawback provides for a 99 percent refund of ordinary customs duties paid on importation. It applies mainly to goods that contain imported products which are subsequently reexported. Drawbacks require compliance with U.S. customs laws. Time limitations are five years from the date of importation to export of the material and three years after the material is shipped out of the country.

Shipping Terms and Packaging

A number of terms are used in international trade to describe sellers' and buyers' rights, duties, and risks in respect to shipping. A complete list of terms and their definitions appears in the authoritative reference work, *Revised American Trade Definitions,* published by the National Foreign Trade Council. The overseas buyer should, however, be familiar with the following basic expressions:

- *F.O.B. (free on board) your plant:* Supplier makes delivery to buyer's plant on a carrier and bears all risks and costs. F.O.B. the foreign port: Transfer of title occurs when the goods are loaded on the carrier, and buyer assumes costs and risks from that point.
- *Ex works (factory, warehouse, and so on):* Seller makes delivery at port of origin, and thereafter all risks and costs are the buyer's.
- *F.A.S. (free alongside):* Seller bears all risks until the merchandise is placed within reach of the ship's tackle. Thereafter, all transportation risks and expenses are the buyer's.
- *Ex dock:* Seller bears cost and responsibility for placing goods on the dock at port of destination. There, buyer takes ownership and possession and assumes all further risks and costs.

[11]Washington, D.C. Government Printing Office, 1985, p. 31.

- *C.I.F. (cost, insurance, freight):* Seller is responsible for all costs and risks until the ocean vessel ties up to the dock of destination. Unloading is the buyer's risk, as are the costs and risks of all subsequent handling, storage, importation, and transportation.
- *C&F (cost and freight):* Seller does not provide insurance or bear the risk for loss of merchandise while at sea. Otherwise, it is the same as C.I.F.

Proper packaging is an essential element in the safe arrival of overseas shipments. Specification of export packing ordinarily ensures that the goods will be protected despite multiple handling, lengthy in-transit time, and the possibility of pilferage. This should be written into the contract at the time of negotiations.

Several years ago the newly organized International Group of the National Association of Purchasing Management suggested that one of the conditions of the purchase order be the following statement, or one similar to it:

> All goods must be packed in an adequate manner to withstand the handling involved in export shipment by (specify type or carrier). There should also be agreement on the part of the supplier to number each package consecutively, and to indicate on each package the company's name, order number, port of arrival, and country of origin.

POINTS FOR REVIEW

1. List the advantages often claimed for purchasing some requirements overseas. Evaluate them in light of today's conditions.
2. Review the problems that may face buyers entering the international market for the first time.
3. Discuss your personal attitude toward, and experience with, foreign-made products or components, particularly in those cases in which you chose them in preference to domestically produced products.
4. Explain the rules discussed in the text for negotiating in the Japanese market.
5. Give some recent examples of how socioeconomic and political developments can affect American companies' international purchasing programs.
6. Define the following terms as they are used in international trade: F.O.B., ex works, F.A.S., ex dock, C.I.F., and C&F.
7. Discuss how you would handle currency fluctuations on the purchase of a large dollar capital-equipment product from Germany.

12

Price/Cost Analysis

Price Related to Cost
        Zero-Based Pricing (ZBP)
        Analyzing Manufacturing Cost
        Basic Elements of Cost Analysis
        The Learning Curve

Price is, without question, of major importance in any purchase transaction. But at times it has been highly overrated. There are contradictions in people's attitudes to it. Management expects its purchasing department to negotiate and buy at the most favorable prices obtainable. Moreover, it is likely to judge the efficiency of the department on the basis of prices paid. Yet the term *price buyer* as applied to a purchasing manager is considered derogatory. Actually, price is only one of the terms and conditions of a purchase order, neither more nor less important than any of the other terms and conditions.

LOW ULTIMATE COST THE OBJECTIVE

Basically, price is rarely, if ever, considered for its own sake. It is usually used in connection with other factors as a means of achieving economical company operation. A few simple concepts fundamental to all good purchasing should be noted at this point. Some of them have been suggested in previous chapters, but they should be considered specifically in relation to price.

    Low *ultimate* cost is the objective and responsibility of purchasing. Invoice price is one element of cost but not necessarily the determining one. This can easily be seen if a transaction is traced through its various stages. The first stage is when materials are received. That is when delivered cost can be determined. A low price paid to a distant supplier may be outweighed by packing and transportation charges, so that delivered cost of the low-price item is actually higher. The second checking point comes when materials are issued to the using department. The buyer may have paid a lower price by reason of taking larger quantities at a greater discount, but the expense of handling and storage may have outweighed this price differential by the time the materials are actually required, issued, and put to use. The third checking point occurs after the materials have been used or fabricated and incorporated in the end product. Manufacturing costs have now been added, and the extent to which such costs have been increased by reason of inferior workability or difficulties in application must be weighed against a price that would have procured superior materials. At all three stages there is a balance that must be observed, and in considering the original or invoice price, the purchasing manager must aim at ultimate cost rather than immediate unit price.

PRICE AND QUALITY AS ELEMENTS OF VALUE

A common equation used in discussions of purchasing is that *value* equals *quality* divided by *price*. This is not a mathematical formula but rather an expression of the general truth that value varies directly in proportion to the quality received and inversely in proportion to the price paid. It stresses the fact that the amount of investment in materials is less significant than what is obtained in return for the investment. If quality increases more rapidly than price in a series of offerings, the value is greater at the higher price—up to the point at which the buyer would be paying for quality in excess of the need.

As shown in Figure 12-1, the value received increases to a certain point and then diminishes, while the cost to produce increases rapidly.[1] Certain applications require extra attention to maximum value and therefore justify higher prices. A simple water bottle used in the space shuttle must conform to rigid requirements. However, the value of these requirements for the Saturday golfer would not justify the price.

When quality has been defined in a specification, so that it can be considered as a constant in this equation, the comparison of values can be made in terms of price alone, and the lower price would represent the greater value. It should be noted, however, that this attention to price comes *after* quality has been fully considered and decided upon.

It is purchasing's responsibility to keep the company in a favorable competitive position in its field as far as material costs are concerned. This implies that there are prevailing market prices and that the purchasing manager must be familiar with market conditions to buy at or below their levels. Purchasing managers will find differences of price between various suppliers in the same field. They will also find differences according to customer classification and quantity discounts.

Value and Cost Tradeoff

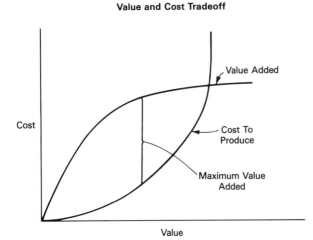

Figure 12-1   Value and Cost Tradeoff

[1]For further discussion of this concept in a quality setting see J. R. Biggs and T. E. Callerman, "Purchasing and Quality Control," *NAPM Guide to Purchasing* (Tempe, Ariz.: NAPM, 1980), pp. 5–6.

Purchasers must therefore insist that suppliers give them the most favorable customer classification thereby qualifying them for the most favorable discounts.

WHO MAKES THE PRICE?

Seller Initiatives

In the philosophy of business, sellers have the privilege of naming the prices at which they are willing to sell their products. In the economics of business, that decision depends on how many buyers can be found who are willing to pay the prices. Otherwise, there is no market. Although in theory sellers are under no compulsion to sell or buyers to buy at any given price level, actually that compulsion exists if business is to be done. Business cannot be conducted on the basis of the irresistible force meeting the immovable object. It is a process of arriving at a mutual agreement that results in sales and purchases. Sellers must find an outlet for their products, and buyers must find the materials their companies need. Markets and prices are not made by quotations or offers but by actual transactions.

Buyers' and Sellers' Markets

Buyers' markets are characterized by conditions of (1) excess capacity and/or supply, (2) reduced lead times, (3) softness in published prices, and (4) a willingness by the seller to negotiate terms, transportation costs, and the like. In a sellers' market the reverse occurs: (1) capacity/supply tightens, (2) lead times increase, (3) published prices are firm, and (4) price increases are sought as well as tougher payment terms. The general overall level of business activity certainly affects these conditions. However, specific markets/commodities react based on their individual factors. For example, in the 1987–88 time period DRAM (direct random access memory), used in electronic applications, more than tripled in price. However, other commodities, such as the personal computers DRAMs were placed in, decreased in price. Thus buyers need to analyze their commodities and assess the relative market conditions at a given time.

It is true, of course, that there are periods when sellers can exert the dominant influence, and other periods when buyers are in the most favorable position. But these "sellers' markets" and "buyers' markets" are basically economic in origin and nature. The resulting price advantages are temporary in that they shift from one side of the transaction to the other as the imbalance is corrected. Realistically, pricing policies follow these changing economic fortunes, but businesses that are built on long-range, continuing supplier-customer relationships do not press the advantage beyond maintaining a normally competitive position. The supplier who consistently sets prices at "all the traffic will bear" forfeits customer loyalty and can expect to fare worse than others when the economic tide turns. The buyer who is primarily an opportunist, looking for the hungriest supplier and capitalizing on that condition, can scarcely ask for consideration in price and service when problems of supply become more difficult.

Market Prices

For most standard materials and products, production costs and competition tend to establish a going market price that is approximately equal among all suppliers at any given time. Prices of freely fluctuating metal and agricultural commodities, such as copper, silver, gold, corn, and wheat, are published in the financial sections of most newspapers (see Figure 12-2).

This system is presumably equitable and mutually satisfactory, representing a fair return to the seller and fair value to the purchaser under prevailing conditions. Buyers frequently test such markets but rarely try to break them. The buyer in not a price censor. A generally established market price level is accepted as one of the economic facts of business life. The rightness of that price, from the buying standpoint, is largely a matter of being sure that regular supply sources are reasonably in line with the going market price and that the purchaser is getting the most favorable terms and discounts warranted by the size of his or her requirements and orders.

Published Price Lists

Sellers spend a great amount of time considering what price to ask for an item. They base this pricing on a number of factors including (1) cost of production, (2) market research on customers, (3) the relative supply/demand situation, (4) competition, and (5) volume and market-share goals, actions, and prices. The data analysis leads to a price. These prices are then formalized via a published price list, which indicates the price and appropriate quantity breaks. When prices are published, the seller is taking a market-based approach to pricing. They are gauging what the market will pay for the product.

In most cases, the price represents what the seller would ideally like to get for the product. For example, the published sticker price on a new car becomes a starting point for negotiations. However, if everyone wants a particular car, a seller may sell it at the best price plus an extra amount. Published prices save sellers from negotiating each particular order, but for most purchasers they represent asking prices.

Obtaining Bids

Competitive bidding is performed for a variety of reasons including: (1) company policy or law (in the public sector) dictates a dollar level or time period for competitive bidding or (2) complex items made to buyer specifications are ordered. Most organizations have a policy requiring that items over a certain dollar value be competitively bid. Additionally, repetitive-use items typically require that bids be updated every year. For example, one large computer manufacturer's policy states that purchase orders with items in excess of $10,000 require written bids. Those between $5,000 and $10,000 must be competitively bid and verbal responses recorded and retained. Quotations must be updated if prices have not remained sta-

CASH PRICES

Wednesday June 27, 1990.
(Closing Market Quotations)

	Wed	Tues	Yr.Ago
GRAINS AND FEEDS			
Barley, top-quality Mpls., bu	n2.60-.85	2.60-3.00	2.85
Bran, wheat middlings, KC ton	73.00	72.00	62.00
Corn, No. 2 yel. Cent-Ill. bu	bp2.78	2.77	2.58
Corn Gluten Feed, Midwest, ton	60.-90.	60.-90.	92.50
Cottonseed Meal, Clksdle, Miss. ton	150.00	147½-150	163.75
Hominy Feed, Cent-Ill. ton	89.00	89.00	77.00
Meat-Bonemeal, 50% pro. Ill. ton	210.-215.	210.00	282.50
Oats, No. 2 milling, Mpls., bu	1.48-.50	1.48-.50	184.50
Sorghum, (Milo) No. 2 Gulf cwt	5.00	4.95	4.57
Soybean Meal, Decatur, Illinois ton	170.-175.	170.-174½	232.50
Soybeans, No. 1 yel Cent.-Ill. bu	bp6.00	6.00	7.12½
Wheat, Spring 14%-pro Mpls. bu	389¼-394¼	392¾-399¾	4.47¼
Wheat, No. 2 sft red, St.Lou. bu	bp3.31½	3.32	4.07
Wheat, No. 2 hard KC, bu	3.33½	3.34½	4.37¼
Wheat, sft wht, del Portland Ore.	3.64	3.63	4.52
FOODS			
Beef, 600-900 lbs. Mid-U.S., lb.fob	1.10	1.11	n.a.
Broilers, Dressed "A" NY lb	x.6355	.6420	.6646
Butter, AA, Chgo., lb.	1.01	1.01	1.30½
Cocoa, Ivory Coast, $metric ton	g1,392	1,397	1,462
Coffee, Brazilian, NY lb.	n.75	.75	1.14
Coffee, Colombian, NY lb.	n.92½	.91½	n.a.
Eggs, Lge white, Chgo doz.	.64-.70	.67-.73	.74½
Flour, hard winter KC cwt	8.85	8.90	11.20
Hams, 17-20 lbs, Mid-US lb fob	z	.83-.86	n.a.
Hogs, Iowa-S.Minn. avg. cwt	61.50	61.00	48.25
Hogs, Omaha avg cwt	61.00	60.75	46.50
Pork Bellies, 12-14 lbs Mid-US lb	.55-.59	.57	n.a.
Pork Loins, 14-18 lbs. Mid-US lb	1.16-1.25	1.17-.20	n.a.
Steers, Tex.-Okla. ch avg cwt	75.50	76.00	72.25
Steers, Feeder, Okl Cty, av cwt	96.65	96.65	90.90
Sugar, cane, raw, world, lb. fob	.1267	.1249	.1398
FATS AND OILS			
Coconut Oil, crd, N. Orleans lb.	xxn.14¾	.14½	.27¾
Corn Oil, crd wet mill, Chgo. lb.	.26c	.26-.26¼	.20¾
Corn Oil, crd dry mill, Chgo. lb.	n.27½	.27½	.21
Cottonseed Oil, crd Miss Vly lb.	a.26	.26	.20
Grease, choice white, Chgo lb.	.12¼	.12¼	.12¾
Lard, Chgo lb.	n.13½	.13½	.14
Palm Oil, ref. bl. deod. N.Orl. lb.	n.14¾	.14½	.20½
Soybean Oil, crd, Decatur, lb.	.2489	.2493	.2068
Tallow, bleachable, Chgo lb.	a.13½	.13¾	.14⅝
Tallow, edible, Chgo lb.	n.14¼	.14¼	.16
FIBERS AND TEXTILES			
Burlap, 10 oz 40-in NY yd	n.2875	.2875	.2860
Cotton 1 1/16 str lw-md Mphs lb	.7970	.8018	.6400
Wool, 64s, Staple, Terr. del. lb.	2.58	2.58	3.50
METALS			
Aluminum ingot lb. del. Midwest	q.72¼-.74¼	.72¼-.74¼	.88¾
Copper cathodes lb.	p1.13⅜-.15	1.11½-.14	1.14
Copper Scrap, No 2 wire NY lb	k.86	.85	.96
Lead, lb.	p.45	.45	.39½
Mercury 76 lb. flask NY	q270-280	270.-280.	302.50
Steel Scrap 1 hvy mlt Chgo ton	114.-115.	114.-115.	114.50
Tin composite lb.	q3.7476	3.7445	6.0191
Zinc Special High grade lb	p.87½	.87½	.80¼
MISCELLANEOUS			
Rubber, smoked sheets, NY lb.	n.46	.46	.50
Hides, hvy native steers lb., fob	.95	.98	.85¼
PRECIOUS METALS			
Gold, troy oz			
Engelhard indust bullion	351.90	350.59	375.04
Engelhard fabric prods	369.50	368.12	393.79
Handy & Harman base price	350.65	349.35	373.75
London fixing AM 350.30 PM	350.65	349.35	373.75
Krugerrand, whol	a359.00	359.00	376.00
Maple Leaf, troy oz.	a363.00	362.75	388.50
American Eagle, troy oz.	a363.00	362.75	388.50
Platinum, (Free Mkt.)	480.50	479.00	502.50
Platinum, indust (Engelhard)	482.50	479.50	506.50
Platinum, fabric prd (Engelhard)	582.50	579.50	606.50
Palladium, indust (Engelhard)	114.00	113.00	156.00
Palladium, fabrc prd (Englhard)	129.00	128.00	171.00
Silver, troy ounce			
Engelhard indust bullion	4.850	4.795	5.300
Engelhard fabric prods	5.190	5.131	5.671
Handy & Harman base price	4.825	4.770	5.290
London Fixing (in pounds)			
Spot (U.S. equiv. $4.8110)	2.7585	2.7705	3.3965
3 months	2.8585	2.8720	3.5130
6 months	2.9625	2.9730	3.6345
1 year	3.1590	3.1735	3.8680
Coins, whol $1,000 face val	a3,475	3,475	3,860

a-Asked. b-Bid. bp-Country elevator bids to producers. c-Corrected. d-Dealer market. e-Estimated. f-Dow Jones International Petroleum Report. g-Main crop, ex-dock, warehouses, Eastern Seaboard, north of Hatteras. i.-f.o.b. warehouse. k-Dealer selling prices in lots of 40,000 pounds or more, f.o.b. buyer's works. n-Nominal. p-Producer price. q-Metals Week. r-Rail bids. s-Thread count 78x54. x-Less than truckloads. z-Not quoted. xx-f.o.b. tankcars.

Figure 12-2 Cash Prices Source: Wall Street Journal—Commodities Section

ble. Other firms require annual bidding on contracts for major commodities. State of Florida purchasing officers are required to obtain written bids for all items exceeding $3,000.

The greater level of buyer knowledge concerning a commodity/product purchase, the more likely a proper supplier will be selected. This knowledge, coupled with attention to the following criteria, will usually ensure the best use of bidding. These criteria include: (1) supplier(s) clearly understands the specifications; (2) there are an adequate number of sellers capable of supplying the product; (3) the purchaser has sufficient time to procure the item; and (4) the total dollar volume of the item is sufficiently high to warrant both buyer's and seller's cost of quotation.

For nonstandard materials—complex fabricated products in which design and manufacturing methods vary and items are made to buyer specification—no ready-made market level exists. Asking for competitive bids is the buyer's simplest way of exploring price under these circumstances and evaluating the rightness of the quoted prices.

Figure 12-3 shows a typical form used to solicit price quotations from suppliers. To establish a right and realistic price, buyers properly insist upon firm bids, that is, the figure a prospective seller will unequivocally state in the bid for the order. If a bid is offered with the suggestion that the seller might revise it subsequently, offering a better price if necessary, the buyer can have no confidence that he or she will in fact receive the best, or right, price offer from that source.

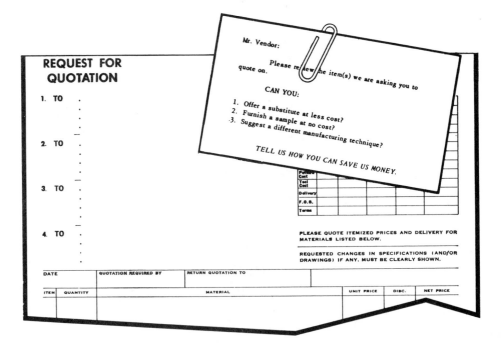

Figure 12-3   Request for quotation with special appeal to suppliers for help on cost reduction.

If there is a wide range in quotations, the excessively high bid is clearly out of line, but the excessively low bid is just as much open to question on the grounds of its economic soundness and reliability. However, a reasonable variation is expected for no two suppliers are exactly equal in manufacturing efficiency and competitive eagerness. If several or all quotations are identical, there is usually a suspicion of collusion to maintain an unjustifiably high price. In the private sector, bids are sent to at least two suppliers and normally three to six.

Having received competitive bids from a representative number of possible suppliers, the buyer can, of course, easily select the lowest price offer. Much of the decision is left to the buyer, the market, and the value of the item being bid. Whether this is actually a "right" price he or she must judge by comparison with the other offers, with past experience, with the prices of similar products, and with his or her own knowledge of prices and markets.

In governmental purchasing a great deal of purchasing of both standard and special items is done on the basis of competitive bids. Since government is very sensitive to charges of favoritism and patronage, this policy is specifically dedicated to the conservation of taxpayers' money. The buyer as a public servant must operate "in a goldfish bowl" for all to see, so the bid system is usually mandatory. When a purchase is contemplated, it is advertised, so that anyone interested may have the opportunity to bid. Sealed bids are received and held, to be opened and made public at a stated time, in the presence of all bidders who wish to come. The order must be awarded to the lowest responsive, responsible bidder. Responsiveness applies to meeting the bid deadline. Responsibility relates to the qualifications of the perspective awardee. If no bids are deemed acceptable, the purchasing officer has no alternative but to reject them all and start all over again, calling for new bids.

If two or more low bids are identical, the purchasing officer may (1) divide the business; (2) request two low bidders to review and resubmit; (3) compute cost factors, such as quality rating, shipping costs, payment terms, and firm price period; and (4) analyze noncost factors, such as lead time, previous experience, and fit with purchasers company.

Identical prices on competitive bid situations involving government-units awards is made by considering: (1) in-state versus out-of-state supplier, (2) U.S. supplier, (3) small or minority business firm. The entire transaction becomes a matter of public record.

Since price is only one criterion of value, competitive bids must be justified on the principle that "all other things being equal," price is the determining factor, and that by making the requirements of quality and service so definitive and clear, there can be no conflict or choice between suppliers on that score. Care must also be taken that the specification is not written so as to be preclusive, admitting only the product of one supplier. On large dollar (or important) purchases a *bid bond* ensures that if the supplier bids the low price, it will accept the business. A *performance bond* is then furnished by the supplier with the bid and becomes the buyer's assurance of quality and service.

Industrial buyers are generally committed to the principle that bid price information is confidential, and they demand greater latitude in deciding where to place orders, so that due consideration can be given to factors other than price. They use the bid system primarily as a means of exploring or fixing the price factor. Frequently it follows, particularly in cases in which competitive products and alternative vendors are adjudged to be equally acceptable, or on standard commercial items on which "all other things" are equal, that business is awarded on the bid basis. But that is not necessarily so. Bids are a useful tool but not the only tool at the buyer's disposal in determining the right price at which to buy.

Buyers and sellers alike are critical of strict adherence to the bidding system for another reason. It gives no weight to past performance and service. Continuity of supply and healthy buyer-seller relationships are important and valuable considerations to both sides. Yet both are disregarded when successive transactions are considered only on the basis of current bids.

NEGOTIATED PRICES

The alternative method of arriving at a price is through negotiation. Negotiation should not be interpreted as "trading" or compromise. It is the process of working out a procurement and sales problem together, to the point of reaching a mutually satisfactory agreement. Negotiation is not at all incompatible with competition. In almost all cases it starts with a competitive bid, a firm bid in respect to the conditions and requirements as known at the time. But it recognizes that this is by no means the last word and that many modifications may be made in all factors to arrive at the most favorable balance of quality, service, and cost. Negotiation can be carried on simultaneously with several suppliers on a given project, maintaining competition right up to the point of decision.

Negotiating Bids

There is considerable debate as to the effectiveness of negotiating competitive bids. Some purchasers feel that negotiating with the low or selected bidder assures the most favorable pricing. Negotiating is particularly useful when bidding on a group of items and one seller is low on eight of the ten items. Discussion may take place to improve competitiveness on the other two. Other purchasers argue that negotiations should take place on issues other than price terms, and they will negotiate transportation and delivery issues prior to awarding the contract. And still others argue that negotiating bids is inefficient and encourages sellers to pad bids, knowing they will be asked to lower them. These purchasers contend that the most effective way to get the seller's best price is to award business to the lowest selected bidder on the first quote. Further, repetitive use of this tactic trains sellers to be competitive on their first quote.

Buyers who negotiate bids argue that they come closer to the right price than do those who merely accept competitive quotations, because all pertinent factors come under analysis and discussion in the course of the negotiation, and details of the requirement can frequently be adjusted to permit price advantages that would otherwise be missed. Many major purchases and contracts in industrial buying are negotiated. Negotiation is more likely on new products for which there is no prior manufacturing experience; otherwise, it is likely that bidders will be impelled to include in their quotations a safety margin for contingencies and unknown manufacturing costs. These extra margins may or may not be warranted in the hindsight of actual experience, but the industrial buyer, unlike the federal government, has no legal recourse through renegotiation after a contract has been completed. Many of these problems can be resolved in the negotiating process.

In its military buying, the federal government has turned largely to negotiation rather than to bid-and-award methods, although recent legislation, such as the Competition in Contracting Act (CICA), indicates a movement toward an increased level of competition. The practice of bid and award has been sharply criticized as extravagant, wasteful, and discriminatory, but such charges are certainly open to debate. The fact remains that the massive, complicated, and urgent requirements in this field could never have been fulfilled by any other method.

Skill in negotiation is an important asset to the buyer. It includes a knowledge of costs and values and the ability to marshal facts logically and convincingly, deal with people, to set realistic price goals, and pursue these goals firmly and persuasively. It is the buyer's responsibility in negotiation to make sure that his or her company receives every price advantage to which it is legitimately entitled. At the same time the buyer must understand and appreciate the seller's position. Although the buyer has no ethical responsibility to safeguard the seller's profits, the buyer is aware that the final price must be economically sound to make the price right for both parties. No purchasing program is stronger than its sources of supply and to drive too sharp a bargain is to weaken the supplier or to eliminate that supplier as a potential, continuing source of supply for future requirements.

A more detailed discussion of the philosophy and techniques of negotiation appears in Chapter 13.

PRICE ANALYSIS

Most often purchasers are faced with a situation where they must evaluate product price without knowing the supplier's cost of producing. In these cases a variety of techniques are used to judge the reasonableness of the price.

- Supply and Demand
- Competitive Factors
- Questionable Low Prices
- Discounts Offered

Supply and Demand

One economic concept is that right price is based largely on the law of supply and demand. As already noted, the operation of this economic law depends on freedom of market action, which has been so modified by modern political and business practices that the action of supply and demand is no longer the decisive factor affecting price, as assumed in classic economic and purchasing theory. Nevertheless, they are influences that cannot be ignored. Prices tend upward when demand exceeds supply and tend downward when supply exceeds demand.

In this equation the purchasing manager represents demand. Individually, the buyer's influence on the situation may be very small. Cumulatively, it may be considerable, but buying policies and action are not a concerted effort except insofar as they represent a common reaction to prevailing conditions. When demand is high, the purchaser must bid up in order to get the goods that he or she wants and needs. The indicated buying policies—to extend forward coverage in times of rising prices and to buy only for immediate needs in times of declining prices—actually tend to exaggerate these price fluctuations rather than to modify or correct them.

In this concept, the rightness of prices at any given time is accepted as being determined by basic economic conditions outside any effective individual control. The buyer's role, then, is to collect and interpret as accurately as possible the facts of supply and demand, the outlook for economic and political conditions, and the psychological temper of the business community, to gauge the probability and reasonableness of prices, current and future.

Competitive Factors

A second theory is that price is determined by competition. It assumes that supply and demand conditions are such as to create a market and to establish a general price level reasonably above the cost of production. Given these fundamental conditions, it is common knowledge that there will be some variations in price—sometimes substantial variations—as between various suppliers. Purchasing managers must discover and understand these variations so that they can place their company's business at the most favorable price that will not jeopardize the equally important considerations of quality and continuity of supply and that will not entail additional costs due to manufacturing or commercial difficulties, excessive spoilage, interrupted production, and so on.

Some of these variations are readily understandable. There may be lower manufacturing costs due to cheaper labor, cheaper power, strategic location in respect to raw materials or markets, better processes or better equipment, more complete mechanization, larger volume of operations, or highly specialized skills. All these are legitimate competitive advantages, in which the buyer can logically share.

Questionable Low Prices

Some low prices are of less desirable origin. The willingness to work on lower profit margins, for example, may be an indication of some essential weakness in the supplier's organization and entails the possible hazard of less adequate inspection or quality control, less attention to progressive research, and less reliable production and service. Low prices attributable to the exploitation of labor are now quite generally outlawed, but it must be kept in mind that any unsatisfactory labor conditions in a supplier's plant are likely to lead at any time to an interruption of supply through strikes and walkouts.

Low prices may be quoted on job lots and off-standard merchandise. This does not condemn the merchandise, which may be entirely usable. There is a legitimate outlet for such goods, but the offerings are generally avoided by purchasing managers who value product uniformity, the assurance of continuing supply from regular vendors, and loyalty in business relationships.

"Buying in," that is, cutting a price to an unrealistic level to win a company's business, is not unknown in a competitive industry. It is done most often to take business away from an established supplier. But the practice—and the acceptance of it by a buyer—can be self-defeating for both sides. Ultimately, the supplier has to raise the price, or cut quality, to recoup the loss from the price cut. Thus the buyer's initial advantage evaporates, and the supplier's good faith and reliability are put in question.

Competition may also be used as a selling weapon, as in the case of a special introductory price to capture a new market or a new customer. This obviously offers no permanent advantage to the buyer, and the temporary advantage may be more than offset by long-range considerations. There is also the vicious and destructive "price war" to discipline a competitor or to drive the company from the field by forcing it to sell below cost to meet price competition, a thoroughly uneconomic procedure and likewise, necessarily, a temporary measure. It can be argued that such situations do establish a market price, though it is temporary and usually limited to a local area, and that the buyer should accept it as such to maintain the company's competitive cost position. In any event, the choice of policy lies between opportunism and stable relationships, and buying decisions are made accordingly.

Purchasing policy, therefore, does not always seek the lowest price obtainable through competition. Yet it does seek competition as one means of evaluating the rightness of quoted prices and of keeping prices right. Competition is maintained by establishing acceptable alternate sources for purchased materials and products; by periodical checking of prices on even common, standard items; by the judicious division of business when quantities warrant; and by inviting competitive bids for comparison and analysis.

DISCOUNTS

There are four types of discounts that concern buyers in their consideration of price.

Trade Discounts

Many companies' pricing systems are set up with a series of discounts, on a graduated scale, that are applicable according to the company's classification of customers, without reference to the size of the particular order. Usually such a system is linked with the policy of distribution through franchised representatives, whole-salers, and local dealers; it makes possible an orderly chain of distribution by pro-tecting the territorial rights, profit margins and incentives, and competitive equality of accredited middlemen. There are also other bases of customer classifi-cation, for example, according to the purpose for which goods are purchased, whether for export, for domestic resale, for fabrication, or for end use. The price, then, depends to a considerable extent upon the classification in which a company is placed, and this involves an element of "rightness" from the purchasing standpoint.

This type of pricing sometimes comes in conflict with the logic of purchas-ing. This is the case when a buyer's purchases of an item are substantially greater than are all the distributor's other sales of that item, when orders are filled by mill shipments so that the distributor's role is only nominal, when the distributor does not actually perform the services associated with a distributor's function, such as maintaining stocks, extending credit, or expediting deliveries, or when such extra services and conveniences are not needed or desired as a part of procurement. The force of these arguments (and of competition) is sometimes recognized by es-tablishing special classifications for large users, by handling them as "house ac-counts" or "national accounts," or otherwise by modifying the discount system to bring prices in line with quantity and service factors.

Quantity Discounts

The practice of offering lower unit prices on larger-quantity orders has already been discussed in connection with the determination of ordering quantities and forward-buying policies. It has its basis in the economies of volume production and the reduction of selling, shipping, and accounting detail, in the added busi-ness assured by the larger orders, and in the large user's importance as a customer.

The buyer's responsibility in this case is primarily an internal one, to ad-just his or her ordering practices to the most advantageous quantity price breaks. It is also a matter for negotiation in getting prices on products made to the buyer's specification, in the instance when quotations are asked on various lot sizes and when cumulative quantity discounts based on total annual purchases instead of in-dividual purchases may be obtained.

Cash Discounts

The cash discount is quite a different matter. It is not a price concession or varia-tion; it is an inducement for prompt payment of invoice charges, and it is earned only when payment is made in accordance with the stipulated terms. Nevertheless, because it affects the net disbursement, the discount is reflected in the total cost of materials, and purchasing must see to it that this potential saving is not jeopar-dized by carelessness in the terms of the contract or delay in the processing of invoices. The saving, though usually expressed in small percentages of invoice amount, is really a very substantial one. A commonly quoted discount, "2 percent, 10 days—30 days net," means that the seller is offering 2 percent for twenty days' use of the capital amount involved, which is at the rate of 36.5 percent a year. Furthermore, discounts are negotiable and have been known to extend as far as 90 days—and in some cases 180 days—on long-term contracts.

Cash discount terms seem very simple, but they must be clearly defined by mutual agreement. For instance, in the absence of any other understanding, most vendors take the stand that the discount period starts with the date of the invoice. The purchasing manager can safeguard the position of his or her company by making it a condition of the order that the discount period shall be calculated from the date that an acceptable invoice is received by the buyer, thus anticipating and avoiding the loss of the discount when invoices are delayed or the lapse of the discount privilege pending necessary adjustments in the invoice charge.

Seasonal Discounts

Producers of products whose demand is seasonal face capacity bottlenecks during peak season. Thus these producers often offer discounts to entice buyers into making purchases during nonpeak periods. These price discounts stimulate demand, thereby enabling the producer to level operating loads and avoid drastic swings in output, which are not cost efficient.

For example, a department store purchasing agent who buys packaging material in July will receive a seasonal discount from the packaging supplier. The supplier realizes that production can be leveled by producing throughout the year and thus is willing to offer a discount for ordering before the traditional holiday season.

MANAGING CONTRACTS FOR PRICE

Firm Fixed Price

After performing a thorough price analysis, the purchaser in most cases prefers to issue a *firm fixed-price* contract, since this locks in the price and puts the incentive on the seller to produce efficiently. The longer the time period between placement of the purchase order and delivery, the more risk each party incurs. If prices are rising, the purchaser is better off with a fixed-price contract, and inversely, if they are dropping, he or she would not desire a fixed-price contract (see Table 12-1).

Table 12-1 Price Provisions on Long-Term Contracts

	Risk to Buyer	
	Prices Trend Up	**Prices Trend Down**
Firm fixed-price contract	Low	High
Fixed price and renegotiation (under extreme conditions)	Moderate	Moderate
Escalation via index	Moderate	Moderate
Price at time of shipment	High	Low

Price at Time of Shipment

Another variation of fixed price, *price at time of shipment*, gives the buyer very little protection when prices are rising but would be of benefit in weak markets.

Given price uncertainties in long-term contracts and for new technology or first-time buys, a sharing of risk often provides a fair method of contracting. *Fixed price plus renegotiation / redetermination* is used when prices and quantities of material and labor are uncertain initially and become known as the contract progresses. Buyers should consider this form of contract when sellers have limited production experience or on the purchase of new items. Maximum price redetermination provides for downward adjustment only.[2] Meanwhile, flexible price redetermination allows for both upward and downward adjustments. Finally, where quantities are known with certainty, certain long-term contracts permit renegotiation under extreme cases. A large smelter had a fixed-price contract to provide billets to a producer of a copper wire. Energy prices soared 25 percent, making it impossible to hold the fixed prices, and the parties agreed to renegotiate.

Fixed Price Plus Incentive

Fixed price plus incentive provides the seller with an incentive to control cost by establishing a target price, a ceiling price, and a variable profit level on the item purchased. For example suppose the buyer and the seller agree to contract on an item at an $1,100 target price. This target is based on the seller's cost estimate of $1,000 and profit of $100. Under a fixed-price-incentive contract, if the seller is able to reduce costs, each dollar of savings will be shared on a predetermined formula. Assuming cost reductions are equally shared and the seller's actual cost is $900, then the final contract price will be $1,000. Conversely, if the seller's cost is higher, his profits will be reduced by the predetermined formula. Assuming the seller's actual cost is $1,100, the final selling price will be $1,150. In any case, under a fixed-price-incentive contract, the buyer pays no more than the agreed-upon ceiling price. Assume in this case that the ceiling price is $1,200, and the supplier's actual costs are $1,200. No profit will be gained by the seller. All seller costs above $1,200 result in losses to the seller. Table 12-2 illustrates this concept.

Table 12-2   Fixed-Price-Incentive Contract

Seller Cost	Based on equal sharing of reductions	
	Profit	Selling Price
$ 900	$100	$1000
1000	100	1100—target
1100	50	1150
1200	0	1200—ceiling price
1300	-100	1200

[2]D. W. Dobler, D. N. Burt and L. Lee, Jr., Purchasing and Materials Management, *Text and Cases* (New York: McGraw-Hill Book Company, 1990), p. 282, 5th Edition.

Escalation/De-Escalation Clauses

Escalation/de-escalation clauses are used in contracts where escalation implies upward price adjustment and de-escalation, downward price adjustment. Since one of the primary purposes of a contract is to fix risk and commitments, escalator clauses should be limited to long-term agreements or contracts involving a long production cycle, as in the case of power-generating equipment or special machinery, in which a period of years rather than weeks or months may be involved in filling the order. Such contracts have been used by purchasers for years. The standard coal contract endorsed by the National Association of Purchasing Agents (now the NAPM) and the National Coal Association contained such a provision, tied in with mine wage agreements, years before the idea was popularized under the descriptive term *escalator clause.*

While these clauses are extensively used, careful planning must be undertaken to determine what procedures govern price adjustment provisions. Key issues to be agreed include (1) what items of labor and materials are subject to escalation, (2) what indices will be used, (3) the dates of the escalation adjustments, and (4) substantiation to ensure correct adjustment. Jay Roman of "Escalation Consultants," states that the lower the percentage of a contract that is held fixed, the more likely it is that engineering and research and development costs will be subject to escalation. In most contracts the unit labor cost and producer price indices published by the Bureau of Labor Statistics are acceptable escalation indices. The key is finding the index that matches the material and labor of the contract. Once the proper indices are identified it is necessary to agree upon the dates when the adjustment are taken. For example, ideally escalation on direct material content should cease once the supplier has the stock or an agreed purchase order price for stock. Last, there must be substantiation, since the risk is transferred to the buyer's account. Provision should be made for downward adjustment on the same basis in the event that costs decline.

PRICE RELATED TO COST

Cost sets a lower limit on the price at which a supplier can afford to make and sell a product. Prices based on cost plus a reasonable profit are fair to the supplier as well as to the buyer, but "cost plus" is a dangerous way to express price in a contract, because it tends to make the supplier careless of costs in the assurance that they will be recovered, plus a profit, in any case. The cost basis of pricing should operate as an incentive for the supplier to reduce costs. Where price directly reflects cost, the buyer can select the supplier having the most efficient management and the most economical production and can share in those lower costs. The buyer can reduce costs by adapting the design and specifications to lower-cost materials and more economical production methods. It is not uncommon for large industrial companies to aid their suppliers in reducing costs by providing technical and management counsel, in the expectation of lower prices resulting from the cost savings.

Zero-Based Pricing (ZBP)

ZBP, developed by Warren Nordquist at the Polaroid Corporation as a method of controlling price increases, illustrates how progressive purchasers seek to control costs. Polaroid buyers are trained to understand cost elements and then to ask suppliers to manage these costs better. Polaroid buyers are trained not to accept material price increases, but rather to ask suppliers to put more emphasis on process control to reduce material usage. Wage increases should be absorbed by suppliers through productivity increase. Profits are not entitlements but should be earned through performance on quality, cost, delivery, and service.[3]

Analyzing Manufacturing Costs

The analyses of supplier prices by ZBP is a form of cost analysis. Cost analysis takes into account both materials and manufacturing costs. The first part is relatively simple, for even a complicated product like an electric motor can be quite accurately broken down into quantitative terms of its major material components— copper, cast iron, and insulation. The spread between material cost and quoted price represents manufacturing cost and profit. To appraise this part of the price, buyers should have a knowledge of manufacturing process and costs and the various operations and handling involved. The cost experiences of their own companies on comparable operations frequently provide rough but useful comparisons.

One of the things that consistent cost analysis shows is that the manufacturing differential is by no means a constant factor; rather, it fluctuates in much the same manner as do materials costs. Sometimes that fluctuation may be justified by circumstances, and sometimes it is open to question. For example, if it is found that the differential is consistently on a percentage basis derived from materials cost, rather than representing a true unit manufacturing cost, the buyer may be justified in challenging the computation, for the percentage markup is not a sound method of estimating the cost of manufacturing operations.

Increasingly, industrial purchasing departments are either establishing their own cost-analysis sections or are using the services of specialists from the accounting or cost-estimating departments to evaluate supplier prices. Automotive and aeronautical companies in particular have pioneered in the establishment of cost-analysis teams that have the capability to estimate what a supplier's material, labor, overhead, and general and administrative costs are. In many cases, particularly in purchases made under government contracts, such data are required of suppliers. In those cases in which suppliers refuse to provide such data voluntarily, the cost analysts use their own experience and judgment as well as cost figures from their own companies' operations, to arrive at what they consider a fair price. This price is then used as a basis for negotiation.

These in-house cost estimates may be made before or after requests for price quotations are sent to suppliers. In some cases a request for quotation is accompanied by a cost-analysis form that the vendor is asked to complete. Even

[3]T. E. Drozsowski, "ZBP Means Saying No to Higher Prices," *Purchasing*, August 2, 1984, pp. 47–49.

when the quoting supplier elects not to complete the form, it has the psychological effect of a reminder that the quoted price will be subject to close analysis.

Basic Elements of Cost Analysis

Five basic items are considered in analyzing supplier cost proposals:

- Materials cost
- Direct labor cost
- Overhead cost
- General and administrative expense
- Profit

These general categories can, however, be subdivided extensively, depending on the complexity of the product, the relative influence of each item on the total cost, and the dollar volume of the order under consideration.

Cost analysis requires a constant questioning—indeed, challenging—of all cost data, whether submitted by the supplier or estimated by the buyer's own plant personnel. Robert Logler, specialist in cost estimating for American Brands, has suggested, in a number of seminars that he has presented, that the following information be sought on the various elements in a cost breakdown.

Direct labor hours.   Is the item being manufactured subject to the learning curve (see Figure 12-4)? Has the same item—or similar items—been built before, and if so, have the labor hours previously required been compared with those in the present quotation? Are there any contingencies in the labor hours? (Contingencies should not ordinarily be considered unless based on known conditions and reasonable estimates.)

Direct labor rates.   What is the basis for rates quoted? Is it the same basis that the supplier has used in the past? If not, why not? What different kinds of labor are required, and are the rates quoted reasonable for the effort involved?

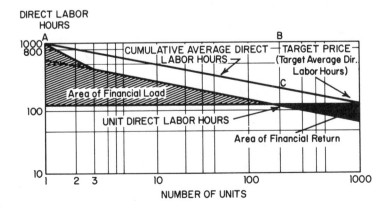

Figure 12-4 Effect of the learning curve on costs.

Material costs.   Are material costs for similar items available? Is a priced bill of materials available? In comparing quantities to blueprint requirements, do they reflect current requirements? Are major dollar items competitively priced? When competition is limited, what is done to assure a fair price? What are scrap allowances and spoilage factors?

Overhead rates.   How are the rates computed? Do indirect loadings reflect current expectations over the period of performance? What are vendors of comparable size and manufacturing capability quoting? Are certain direct costs being included in indirect costs as well?

Profit.   What is the basis for the supplier's profit margin—a percentage of sales? return on investment? How does it compare with that of other suppliers in the industry? Is competition strong enough in the industry to make it negotiable? Will an increase in order size reduce the supplier's unit cost and thereby open the profit margin to negotiation? Can agreement on how the profit margin will be compiled be reached before negotiations begin?

The Learning Curve

Probably the most difficult problems in cost analysis for the purpose of price appraisal and negotiation are those concerning new and nonstandard products for which there is no prior manufacturing experience. This is difficult for the supplier as well as for the buyer, but production-management science has developed some useful techniques for coping with such problems, and the buyer should be familiar with these methods, too.

   The first units of any new product are relatively costly to produce, but experience improves the efficiency of manufacturing methods and the productivity of workers, so that costs come down on succeeding products. The "learning curves" plotting this condition generally show rapid cost reduction on the first few units, then tend to flatten out as methods are standardized but continue downward at a lesser rate as workers steadily gain proficiency. When the curve is plotted on a log-log scale, it approximates a straight line (see Figure 12-4). This is projected to permit establishing a target level of production costs upon which a suitably profitable ultimate price can be predicated. The cumulative average line in this graph is higher than the unit cost line, because it includes the initial high costs, but eventually all these costs are recovered in mass production at the improved rates. The buyer who understands the statistical basis of this phenomenon is likewise able to project a target buying price. That buyer will reject the factual but unrealistically high costs of initial quantities and will base his or her negotiations on total quantities, in which long-run productivity has been established, or insist on a sliding scale, in which the price of successive lots will fairly reflect the lower costs that result from "learning."

   The 80 percent statistical curve shown in Figure 12-4 is fairly representative of average conditions in industrial production and is sufficiently accurate to be used as a starting point in most purchasing calculations. In general, the percentage to be used varies inversely with the amount of manual labor involved in the operation. The practical range for most production processes lies between 70 percent (assembly operations, showing steeper initial decline) and 90 percent (machine work with long runs and few setups). The 100 percent curve (no decline) implies complete automation.

POINTS FOR REVIEW

1. Distinguish between price and cost as they relate to a purchasing departments' responsibility.
2. Differentiate between a sellers' market and a buyers' market, giving examples current or otherwise.
3. Describe the bid system and some of the reservations that industrial buyers have about that method of procurement.
4. Explain the fundamentals of cost analysis. Show how you might apply the technique to estimate what might be a reasonable cost on some personal purchase or expenditure, such as auto repairs, carpentry work, or landscaping.
5. Give a brief explanation of the learning curve.
6. Describe the three types of discounts and explain the purchasing department's responsibility in respect to discounts.
7. Give an example of each type of price contract you might encounter.

13

The Art and Science of Negotiation

Negotiation, briefly discussed in an earlier chapter, was defined as "the process of working out a procurement and sales program together, to the point of reaching a mutually satisfactory agreement." Technically, this definition covers almost any transaction between a buyer and a supplier, from a telephone discussion about the price of a few gallons of lubricant to prolonged conferences on the terms of a major equipment purchase. It is basically a process achieved through bargaining, conferring or discussing an issue. Successful negotiators are those who can effectively manage power, time and information.

In practice, the term is generally applied in industrial purchasing to the more complex situations involving buyers and sellers, in which both make a number of proposals and counterproposals before an agreement is reached. The key word in the definition as far as this interpretation goes is *program,* which implies that something more is involved in the transaction than a simple comparison of bids or the acceptance of a catalog price.

THE NATURE OF NEGOTIATION

The nature of negotiation has been well defined in instructions issued to U.S. Air Force buying personnel:

> Procurement by negotiation is the art of arriving at a common understanding through bargaining on the essentials of a contract such as delivery, specifications, prices, and terms. Because of the interrelation of these factors with many others, it is a difficult art and requires the exercise of judgment, tact, and common sense. The effective negotiator must be a real shopper, alive to the possibilities of bargaining with the seller. Only through an awareness of relative bargaining strength can a negotiator know where to be firm or where he may make permissive concessions in prices or terms.[1]

The process and techniques of negotiated purchasing deserve special attention for two basic reasons. First, the whole concept of negotiation is widely misunderstood, even by persons engaged in purchasing, and in many cases it is suspect. Second, technological change has made industrial procurement increasingly complex, particularly in defense-related industries. Simple, rule-of-thumb approaches to buying one-of-a-kind machines or systems, for example, are no longer adequate. Nor are they any longer satisfactory in the purchase of less complicated items like raw materials and maintenance supplies. The trend toward reduced supplier base and longer-term agreements (see the buying agreements discussion earlier) on these commodities has placed special emphasis on many aspects of the transaction that are open to negotiation. Responsibility for holding inventory, timing of deliveries, methods of transportation, inspection, and prices are only a few of the factors that must be agreed upon before a purchase is complete.

[1]U.S. Air Force, *Air Force Procurement Instructions,* 3-101.50.

Win-Win Concepts

Today's closer relationships with suppliers have moved purchasers to view suppliers as partners rather than adversaries. When the purchaser views a supplier as an adversary, there is an attitude that someone must win and someone must lose.

Progressive buyers view the process as one in which both sides are cooperating to win. Fischer and Ury argue that win-win negotiators search for alternatives that are mutually agreeable to both parties.[2] Win-win negotiations are characterized by interpersonal contact that is spontaneous, responsive, and flexible. Honesty and openness are the keystone of this approach. The parties enter into negotiation confident that they will receive value from negotiation, each comfortable in letting the other party make its case (see Figure 13-1).

Viewing this style of negotiation from a game-theory approach, Luce and Ruiffa described it as a prisoner's dilemma.[3] A matrix of outcomes shown in Figure 13-2 indicate zero-sum (win-lose) and non-zero-sum (win-win) outcomes. As can be seen from the figure, both the buyer and seller receive best outcomes if they cooperate.

While purchasers are moving to win-win situations, this is no excuse for lack of preparation in negotiations. For parties will still be attempting to outmaneuver and outthink each other.

NEGOTIATION DISTINCT FROM BIDDING

There is a distinction between buying by negotiation and buying by competitive bidding that should be emphasized at this point.

In the simplest form of bidding prospective suppliers submit their quotations, or bids, on a given purchase requirement. The bid system is used exten-

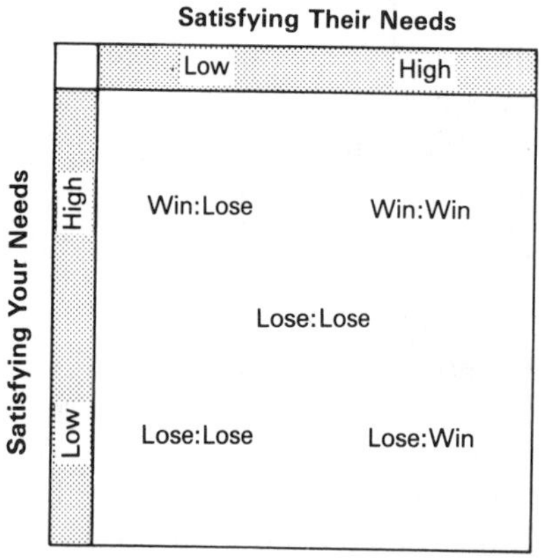

Figure 13-1   Concept of Win: Win

Source: Materials developed by Frank Haluch of Haluch and Associates, Trumbull, Connecticut for use in The Workshop in Negotiating Skills (WINS), a workshop developed by the General Electric Company. Used with permission.

[2]Roger Fisher and William Ury, *Getting to Yes* (New York: Penguin Books, 1983) p. 13.

[3]Quoted in Roy J. Lewicki and Joseph A. Litterer, *Negotiation* (Homewood, Illinois: Richard D. Irwin, Inc., 1985) p. 35.

Figure 13-2 Negotiator's Dilemma Payoff Matrix

Buyer \ Seller	Compete	Cooperate
Compete	S $1.00 B $1.00 Zero-Sum Game	S $0 B $2.00 Zero-Sum Game
Cooperate	S $2.00 B $0 Zero-Sum Game	S $3.00 B $3.00 Non-Zero-Sum Game

Source: Materials developed by Frank Haluch of Haluch and Associates, Trumbull, Connecticut for use in The Workshop in Negotiating Skills (WINS), a workshop developed by the General Electric Company. Used with permission.

sively in government procurement and is often mandatory. An invitation to bid is usually advertised and is open to all qualified suppliers. Bid openings are public and the business is awarded to the qualified supplier who has submitted the lowest bid.

Competitive bidding is used to some extent in industrial and commercial purchasing. But advertising for bids is rare, and public bid opening is neither required nor desired. Nor is the lowest bidder always awarded the business. More often than not, a variation of the bidding method—that is, issuing requests for quotation (RFQs)—is used. Requests for quotation are issued to several, but not necessarily all, prequalified suppliers. The buying company may select the lowest bidder, or simply use the data in a given supplier's quotation as the basis for negotiation. It is, however, a breach of purchasing ethics to use information in suppliers' quotations for "reverse auction" purpose, that is, revealing confidential price data of one supplier to get other suppliers to reduce their original quotations.

When competitive bidding is used in industrial purchasing it usually indicates that there is a market for the item and that some price level has been established. The specifications of the product to be bought are relatively simple and clearly spelled out (see Chapters 12 and 19 for additional discussion of competitive bidding). The major objections to competitive bidding are generally listed as follows:

- Unless the bid contains airtight specifications, the winning bidder may provide a product that meets specifications but does not always provide the performance the buyer expects.
- The winning bidder often is the one who cuts quality to cut the price. The quality producer cannot afford to be competitive and is driven from the market. The buyer is then stuck with inferior merchandise that wears out or falls apart sooner than expected.
- In industries like aerospace and shipbuilding, which depend heavily on government orders, the bidder good enough to get all or most of the government's business may drive competitors out of the field. The winning bidder is then in a position to raise prices practically at will.
- Many economists hold that when an industry is dominated by two or three producers, the result can be an oligopolistic price structure, even without collu-

sion. Producers behave in a rational manner on price, and a follow-the-leader pattern develops. In this case, advertising bidding does not result in competition.

Negotiation, on the other hand, calls for discussion by buyers and sellers to hammer out details of a contract too critical to be covered by an exchange of paperwork. The product under consideration may be one of a kind of special design or competition. There are rarely competitive markets for such items, and certainly no established prices. Negotiation is definitely called for when buyer and seller have different estimates of what it costs to make, deliver, and service a product. Negotiation invariably involves discussions on a range of elements that go beyond price—such as warranties, technical assistance and service, methods of shipment and packaging, and payment terms. Even contracts for standard items that will require large expenditures over a year or more should be negotiated on that basis.

Negotiation as we have defined it—"the working out of a procurement and sales program together"—is generally used in the following situations, assuming that a relatively large amount of money is involved:

- When the purchase involves equipment of a unique or complicated nature that has not been purchased before and for which there is little cost information. A conveyor line for a new, automated food-processing plant would be a good example. Details of the construction, performance, and cost of such an installation would require involved technical discussions before a purchase was actually made.
- When prices on an item are fixed, by custom, "fair-trade" laws, or actual collusion among suppliers. If there are many suppliers in the field, good negotiating tactics are generally successful in winning concessions from one producer who is anxious to get the business.
- When there are few suppliers or only one in the field but the product in question can be made in the buyer's own plant or bought from abroad, or a substitute for it is readily available.
- When a number of suppliers have bid on an item, but none of the quotations is completely satisfactory. None may meet the buyer's requirements as to price, terms, delivery, or specifications. In this situation the buyer must be sure, before he or she attempts to negotiate, that all bids are unsatisfactory in terms of the requirements first placed before the suppliers. It is highly unethical to lead a supplier into committing to a quotation merely to put that supplier into a disadvantageous bargaining position. Responsible buyers will notify suppliers in advance that bids may be subject to negotiation.
- When an existing contract is being changed, and the amount of money involved is substantial enough to warrant discussion. Major price changes on high-volume items, for example, are subject to negotiation.

The nature and purposes of negotiation, however, have not always been fully understood. In the past even some purchasing managers were inclined to put negotiation in the same category as haggling. Some even went so far, years ago, to consider it unethical or vulgar to bargain with suppliers over prices. About thirty years ago the president of the National Association of Purchasing Agents (now the National Association of Purchasing Management) felt called on to correct this notion—which is to some extent shared by certain types of suppliers. His words are today more applicable than ever:

> By negotiation, buyers take the necessary initiative to optimize their position in any given purchase. Without negotiation they are merely accepting the offer given to them.
>
> Vigorous price competition is an essential ingredient of the free enterprise system. To refrain from seeking cost advantages through negotiation is to assume that the item price is right, that it is best for all concerned.
>
> Much of the criticism of negotiation is directed at the methods used. But within the limits of the law and ethics of good business, buyers are obligated by their position to aggresively go after the best price that will mean the least cost under the most favorable conditions available to their firms.
>
> The unspoken criticism of negotiation is more likely to be leveled by suppliers who would like to find some haven for price protection where they would be immune to the results of sound, aggressive and ethical negotiation. They want to protect their weakness of limited sales ability.[4]

MODEL OF NEGOTIATION PLANNING

Figure 13-3 illustrates a model for negotiation planning. It can be seen that negotiators set objectives for their negotiation. These objectives are translated into action based on strategies that depend upon personnel selection, relative power, and wise use of tactics. Additionally, outside influences that have a bearing on strategy

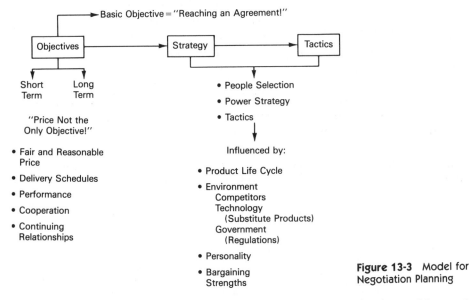

Figure 13-3 Model for Negotiation Planning

[4]Russell T. Stark, Burroughs Corporation, in addresses to local chapters of the association.

and tactics include government regulations, competitors, technology, product-life-cycle stages, bargaining strengths, and the personalities of the parties involved.

Defining Negotiation Objectives

The negotiator without clearly defined objectives is put on the defensive, as it must always be assumed that the other participant in the session has entered the negotiation with some definite goal for his or her company. Uncertainty or confusion over their objectives can lead negotiators into making damaging concessions.

Generalized objectives, such as "getting all we can out of the vendor" or attempting to get "the best possible price," are not much better than no objectives at all. Buyers must define their objectives more precisely in terms of what they and the company hope they can get and reasonably expect to get if the negotiation is skillfully conducted. The objective may be concessions on: price, quality, delivery, or other factors.

The objective should be expressed in specific terms, such as a certain price, but it must always be subject to modification. Flexibility is at the heart of the negotiating art, and all objectives should be hedged by a minimum and maximum position to which a negotiator can move when the opportunity arises, in the first case, and when forced to, in the second case. A buyer going into a negotiation with an objective, or "ideal" price, of $11,500 for a piece of equipment, for example, should have alternative prices above and below that figure that were deemed acceptable before the negotiation began. In the actual negotiation the buyer might use the minimum price the negotiating team agreed upon—$10,000, for example—as a first proposal without any real hope that the supplier will immediately accept it. Conversely, the buyer will be prepared to go to a maximum position—a $12,500 price, for example—but only as a last resort. The objective, maximum, and minimum prices will, of course, have been determined on the basis of cost analysis, need for the equipment, monopoly position of the supplier, or any of the other factors previously mentioned (see Figure 13-4).

As a corollary to having an established objective and alternative maximum and minimum positions, a negotiator must try to estimate the supplier's objectives and maximum and minimum positions. One or more of these may already be apparent in a bid or proposal submitted, or they may have to be deduced from the buyer's own cost analysis or from previous experience with the supplier. In any event, a good negotiator will try to guess where a supplier will make concessions and where that supplier is likely to hold fast to his or her declared position. The

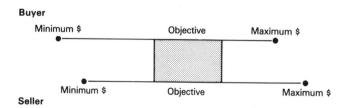

Figure 13-4 The "Heart" or Essence of Negotiation
Source: Paul R. McDonald, Government Prime Contracts and Subcontracts Procurement Associates (Glendora, Calif.:, 1981), pp. F1–18.

negotiator will then prepare to act accordingly in the light of his or her own objectives.

Before entering a negotiation it is advisable for both parties—buyer and supplier—to come to some agreement as to what is being negotiated and put the agreement in writing. This tends to cut down on disagreements and arguments once the negotiation is under way, as reference can be made to a written statement or agenda. Similarly, both sides should clearly indicate who has authority to speak for them in the negotiation and the exact extent of that authority. There is no point in elaborate planning for a negotiation when one side's representative simply does not have the authority to agree on a critical point, such as price.

The strategy and tactics used in purchasing negotiations are similar in many ways to those used in labor negotiations. And both types have been linked to military campaigns in which the adversaries first try to outthink, then to outmaneuver, each other. It should be noted, however, that the phrase "common understanding" used in the air force definition in the beginning of this chapter is critical to understanding purchasing negotiations. Unless both parties to an agreement come away with the feeling that they have made the best deal they could, there has been no real negotiation.

Yet, among people with a win-lose attitude there is a common feeling that someone always gets skinned in a negotiation. Even as astute a politician as John Connally, former secretary of the U.S. Treasury, is reported to have said that in a negotiation one side always comes out a winner and the other side a loser. The fact is that by definition there cannot be a loser when negotiations are successfully completed. A buyer or supplier always has the option of walking away from a negotiation if agreement cannot be reached. Then there is neither winner nor loser—the contest is called off. A purchasing textbook sums it up this way:

> In successful negotiations, both sides win something. But the winnings are seldom equally divided. Invariably, one side wins more than the other. This is as it should be in business—superior business skills merit superior awards.[5]

Thus buyers need to prepare for success keeping a win-win attitude in mind but realizing some negotiations can degenerate into win-lose situations if not controlled.

Also, prior to choosing a strategy one must consider power, people, and tactics. Research has indicated several variables can affect one's strategy. These include people and power. Prominent negotiation expert Herb Cohen says: "Power is the ability to get things done and that much power is based on one's perceptions of it. If you think you have it—you have it. Selecting the right personnel for the negotiation will increase chances of success. Considerations involve who to include in the negotiation from groups such as management, engineers, accountants."[6]

[5]D. W. Dobler, D. N. Burt, and L. Lee, *Purchasing and Materials Management,* 5th ed. (New York: McGraw-Hill Book Company, 1990), p. 297.

[6]Herb Cohen, *You Can Negotiate Anything,* Lyle Stuart, Inc. Secaucus, N.J., 1980. Quoted in Roy J. Lewicki and Joseph A. Litterer, *Negotiation Readings, Exercises and Cases,* R. D. Irwin Homewood, Illinois, 1985, p. 9.

Bargaining Strengths

The basic step in preparing for negotiation is to establish one's own bargaining position, and to the extent possible anticipate the supplier's position. Suppliers' bargaining strength will be affected by how much they want the business, how sure they are they will get the business, and how much time there is to reach an agreement. Buyers' strength will be affected by the amount of competition in the field, how good their price/cost analyses are, how much business they have to offer the supplier, and what kind of time pressures they are under from using departments (see Figure 13-5). Perhaps most important, the buyers' strength will be heavily dependent on the thoroughness of their preparation.

Suppliers anxious to establish themselves with a company or in an industry, for example, may be willing to make price concessions. Buyers pressed for unreasonable delivery dates by their own shops are on the defensive and may be willing to pay a premium for quick delivery. Purchasing managers who have developed alternative suppliers, or who know that a substitute product or material can be used, go into negotiations in a strong position. Sellers who are certain that they have little or no immediate competition (e.g., a dealer with an exclusive franchise in a remote area) know that they will have an advantage in negotiations.

Much of the art of negotiation consists of the ability to determine these strengths and weaknesses in advance and to exploit them to one's own advantage. At the same time, of course, one must try to conceal one's own weaknesses or at least avoid as long as possible having them put to the test.

Negotiating Tactics

Negotiation is often a highly technical matter, but it is always a very human matter as well. Because the essential element in a negotiation is bargaining between individuals, the process involves personalities, human motives, people's strength and weaknesses, and a great deal of psychology. In numerous addresses to purchasing groups, the authors have stressed these general rules for turning the human element in negotiations to one's own advantage:

- *Try to have the negotiation carried on your home ground, according to your own arrangements.* There is a psychological advantage to having the other party come

---

BARGAINING STRENGTHS

Buyer	Seller
Extent of competition	Desire for the contract
Adequacy of cost/price analysis	Certainty of getting the contract
Thoroughness of preparation	Time available for negotiation
Time available for negotiation	
Volume of business	

FIGURE 13-5

to the discussion. It implies that you are in control and have already won one concession. Provide a dignified, comfortable, well-lighted meeting place, free of distractions. Put the leader of your own negotiating team at the head of the table, and try to keep the members of the other team separated.

- *Let the supplier do most of the talking*—at least, in the beginning. Let the supplier give the reasons for his or her demand first. If you use the proper restraint, suppliers may talk themselves into making concessions that were never intended.
- *When your time comes to talk, don't fumble over facts and figures.* Never send out for vital information in the middle of a discussion. Lack of information or lack of confidence puts you at a strong psychological disadvantage.
- *Try to avoid emotional reactions to the supplier's arguments or an emotional approach in presenting your own.* Otherwise, you'll obscure the real purposes of the negotiation and possibly endanger your own position. People who let pride or anger govern their relations with others usually end up by giving away more than they intended.
- *If the supplier has to retreat on a point, let it be done gracefully.* If you spot something wrong in a cost estimate, for example, don't accuse the other side of trickery or ineptitude. Suggest that a revision is in order.
- *Avoid premature showdowns.* You have to come to some sort of a showdown ultimately—that's the reason for the negotiation. But, if you force a supplier into a position in which he or she feels compelled to say, "Here are my terms, take them or leave them," that may end the discussion there. After that kind of an ultimatum it would be difficult for the supplier to give further concessions. So before you make your final concession, be absolutely sure that it is absolutely final.
- *Satisfy the emotional needs of the people with whom you are negotiating.* Most suppliers enjoy selling and persuading, but they are somewhat insecure. Give suppliers a chance to persuade rather than trying to head them off brusquely, and they will be better disposed to make concessions to get your business. And give them the impression that despite your bargaining with them, you respect their position and regard them as members of your corporate team.

Cost-Based Negotiation   When buying a new or complex item or refusing to take the lowest of a number of bids or even negotiating a price change on a regularly bought item, supplier costs are a key area for discussion. Negotiators should come into such discussions with a sound knowledge of costing methods and, if possible, comparative figures from their own cost estimates. Small and medium-size suppliers particularly—and some of the big ones—do not bother to develop accurate and factual records. Their cost figures are often pulled out of the air—on the safe side, of course. Their sales representatives are given a fairly wide range of prices to submit to prospective customers. Too many purchasing people go into negotiations with the rather vague attitude that the supplier deserves a price that includes cost plus a fair profit. But if they do not go after those costs intelligently and aggressively, they may end up giving the supplier a fair profit and themselves an unfair price.

Just because a supplier has lower costs than the next highest bidder does not mean that those costs are low enough. That supplier may still be using his or her plant inefficiently. It is the purchasing agent's responsibility to help the supplier bring down costs to an absolute minimum and still deliver the quality required.

Price-Based Negotiations   Modern industrial pricing, however, is not based simply on costs. If the purchasing manager is unable to determine specific costs on an item under negotiation, he or she can always make certain assumptions about the prices quoted. They may be based on any one or a combination of the following:

- An attempt to get "all the traffic can bear," which is sound economic behavior on the part of a supplier
- Keeping prices just low enough to cut out competition
- Setting a specific rate of return—for example, as a percentage of sales or of capital invested—and pricing accordingly

Any one of these areas is fertile ground for a skilled negotiator.

And even in the case of fixed-price or "fair-trade" items, there is room for maneuvering. A buyer can offer to purchase other items, on which prices are not fixed, from the same supplier if the buyer can get a price concession.

The shrewd negotiator can also use the "unique specification" approach, which makes the component or material that he or she buys different from that bought by all other customers. The classic case is that of the automobile companies that buy tailpipes fabricated to their own specifications. The tube from which the tailpipes are made was selling at the same price to all buyers. But bent into special shapes, it is sold at a lower price than the basic product.

Among the fringe benefits that can be negotiated on industry-priced items are

- The privilege of bulking orders for quantity discounts
- Split shipments to one destination with the price based on total quantity
- Make-and-hold agreements, which may lower the price and provide inventory protection without the cost of carrying it
- Concessions for methods of packaging and palletizing
- Lower shipping costs through a change in carrier
- Terms of payment

PREPARING FOR NEGOTIATION

Before the purchasing manager uses any of these general approaches in a specific negotiation, the manager should plan ahead to obtain maximum advantage. Indeed, preplanning is as important as the tactics of negotiation, because the tactics are based on plans and objectives established before any meeting. Figure 13-6 shows a comprehensive action plan for negotiation.

All good planning begins with the collection of essential *data* —and in the case of negotiation this includes not only economic but engineering, accounting, legal, and financial information pertinent to the particular matter to be discussed. These data should be identified and ranked according to importance.

The collection of *facts* pertinent to the negotiation may involve several different departments, depending on the complexity of the matter at issue. Similarly, the negotiation itself may require the presence of a *team of experts* to participate in the discussions accurately and present the company's position and views.

ACTION PLAN FOR NEGOTIATION

1. *When do you begin to accumulate information?*
   - As soon as you hear about the requirement
2. *Where can information be found?*
   - Trade Associations
   - U.S. Government
   - Old Files
   - People involved in previous negotiations
   - Their engineers, production managers, salesmen, etc.
   - Annual Reports & 10K's
   - Commercial data bases
   - Business publications
3. *Understand your needs*
   - What are you buying/selling (custom—commodity)?
   - What's the time frame (tomorrow—next year)?
   - What's the technology (low—high)?
   - What equals success?
   - What's acceptable?
4. *Understand their needs*
   - Market share or profits
   - Book orders or ship orders
   - Your business key to other business
   - What equals success
5. *Understand their systems*
   - How is pricing generated?
   - How sensitive is their pricing to changes in: volume; labor rates; material costs; process yields; technology (manufacturing and design)
   - How is the product manufactured?
6. *Have you negotiated with them in the past?*
   - What happened?
   - Will you negotiate with the same people?
   - If not, what would be helpful to know about the new players?
   - What issues do you agree on?
   - What issues do you disagree on?
   - What have been the rules of the game?
   - What rules would you like to change?

Figure 13-6
Source: Materials developed by Frank Haluch of Haluch & Associates, Trumbull, Connecticut for use in the Workshop in Negotiating Skills (WINS), a workshop developed by the General Electric Company.

An experienced purchasing executive will always assume that the supplier is sending competent, well informed, and skillful representatives into any substantial negotiation, so he or she will try to match them when selecting a team.

In an involved negotiation, a *team* might be made up of representatives from purchasing, design engineering, accounting, marketing, industrial engineering, and legal departments. They should be thoroughly briefed on the nature of the negotiation and the technical and economic questions involved. They should understand or, even better, participate in the establishment of the company's objectives and alternative positions as described below.

It is absolutely necessary to designate a leader when negotiation involves more than one representative. The leader's authority to commit the company and the limitations on the authority of other team members should be clearly spelled out. Because the basic authority to commit company funds rests with the purchasing department representative, the buyer is generally considered the best choice to lead a negotiating team.

The following guidelines for effective prenegotiation preparation, planning, and documentation are issued to purchasing and materials-management personnel of a large supplier to the automotive and aerospace industries. Note that they are clear and comprehensive.

The effectiveness of negotiation depends largely on the quality and thorough preparation of the prenegotiation effort, and the skill of the negotiation team. Although they are particularly applicable to critical procurements with complex technical and contractual situations requiring negotiation team effort, the basic elements and techniques detailed below apply equally to all procurements requiring negotiation.

The buyer or subcontract specialist responsible for procurements requiring negotiation will, prior to such negotiation:

a. Initiate and develop a proposed plan for the conduct of a negotiation which will consist of but not be limited to the following:

1. Definition of the negotiation objective
2. An agenda
3. Clear identification of all issues involved
4. Designation of the team captain
5. Outline of the apparent prenegotiation positions of both parties
6. Details on the key items and in-house analyses
7. Requests for qualified specialists for evaluation of specific areas

b. Document and submit the proposed negotiation plan, through supervision, to the individual authorized to approve the contractual agreement contemplated.

The size and composition of each negotiation team will vary according to the nature and complexity of each procurement situation. The negotiation team will include qualified specialists who are skilled and experienced in their specific areas to support negotiation.

The chief negotiator will:

a. Select individual members for an effective, well-integrated team
b. Outline individual team member responsibilities in the prenegotiation and negotiation efforts
c. Brief team members on their respective roles in negotiation

The chief negotiator will:

a. Determine and recommend, as a matter of strategy, optimum location and physical arrangements for the negotiation proceedings
b. Incorporate these recommendations for location and physical arrangements into the negotiation plan

The chief negotiator, with the assistance of his team, will make a careful analysis of the relative prenegotiation bargaining positions of our company and the seller. Since negotiation can sometimes be simply a test of strength based on bargaining position, every factor bearing on this position should be identified, understood, and properly evaluated.

After analysis and review of the procurement environment, the chief negotiator will outline the data developed, listing on one side the factors that tend to strengthen his position, and on the other side the factors that tend to strengthen the seller's position, and incorporate this information into the negotiation plan.

At a minimum, prenegotiation analysis should be performed to carefully evaluate the:

    a. Product work statement—to provide complete familiarity with the product and the various processes involved, and to ascertain their effect on cost and their relationship to the specific cost proposal submitted by the seller
    b. Seller's cost proposal—to ascertain the reasonableness of the seller's quoted price and cost breakdowns. The price/cost analysis function should be utilized to clarify all questions that affect costs

The selection and application of appropriate and effective cost/price analysis techniques will be dependent upon how well-defined the specifications are, the extent of competition, the availability of cost and price history data, and the reliability of in-house estimates.

As a final part of negotiation preparation, the chief negotiator and his team should meet to familiarize all members with the plans for negotiation, and the issues, objectives, and data upon which such plans were based. He may conduct a dry run to develop the final negotiation strategy and techniques and to condition the team for the actual negotiation proceedings.

CHARACTERISTICS OF GOOD NEGOTIATORS.

Dean Ammer, a leading authority on purchasing negotiations, has described the attributes of good negotiators as follows:

1. They must be clear, rapid thinkers. The give and take of a complex negotiation requires a person able to think quickly.
2. They must express themselves well and easily. In negotiation what you know may not be as important as what you convey to others. The ability to communicate effectively is an absolute must. Ease of expression does not mean glibness. It comes from a knowledge of the business at hand.
3. They must possess the ability to analyze. They must be able to analyze the statements of others and identify those who favor their position, those who oppose it, and those who favor another solution.
4. They must be impersonal. In the heat of a hard-fought negotiation, it is sometimes difficult to remain calm. But a negotiator must always approach a problem from the basis of the company objective rather than from personal inclinations.
5. They must be patient. Sometimes letting the other persons talk themselves out or explain their positions helps resolve issues without argument.

6. They must be able to consider other persons' ideas objectively. They should be able to place themselves in their opponents' frames of reference, so they can better evaluate those positions.
7. They must be tactful, have poise and self-restraint, like people, and have a good knowledge of human nature.
8. They must possess a sense of humor. You can't win every point in a negotiation. An ability to make concessions and to continue to display good humor will pay dividends in good will, which will help in resolving the remaining issues.[7]

SPECIAL CIRCUMSTANCES

There are times when special circumstances will require a change in the way a buyer approaches negotiations. For instance, what happens when buyers find themselves in a sole-source situation, or what changes are required when buyers negotiate with overseas suppliers?

In the case of a sole-source supplier, in preparing for negotiations, the buyer should be prepared to "help" the supplier find ways to reduce costs. This help may be in the form of technical advice from the buying firm's engineering or production departments. If the buyer is unsuccessful in this attempt to reach mutually satisfactory reductions in cost, then consideration of alternative materials for making the product are sometimes effective strategies. These strategies reinforce the point that very few situations are truly sole source in nature.

In the case of dealing with overseas negotiators, the critical difference is one of culture. Burt, for instance, found in a study on this subject that cultural preparation was a key to success.[8] The ability of a buyer to understand the culture of his or her negotiation partner greatly facilitates the negotiation process and prevents faux pas from occurring or the leaving of dollars on the negotiating table. A good example of such cultural differences has to do with time. Dealing with Europeans or Japanese simply requires more time. For the American buyer that means being more patient.

Negotiation is not, as is sometimes charged, the purchasing department's technique for cutting down the supplier's profits. Nor is it an occult science whose practitioners are exclusively endowed with special gifts. It is the basic process by which competition is furthered in industrial buying and selling. It is the special responsibility of the purchasing agent to negotiate the best possible deal to achieve company objectives—just as it is the special responsibility of sales representatives to negotiate for their companies' objectives.

POINTS FOR REVIEW

1. Explain the difference between buying by bid and buying by negotiation.
2. Describe the situations in which negotiation, as defined in the text, is considered the appropriate method of purchasing.

[7]In a personal communication.

[8]D. N. Burt, "The Nuances of Negotiating Overseas," *Journal of Purchasing and Materials Management,* Winter 1984, pp. 2–8.

3. List half a dozen cost elements other than straight price that are subject to negotiation.
4. Cite some examples of negotiation from your own experience that involved the principles and techniques discussed in the text.
5. Demonstrate, with a theoretical example, the concept of minimum and maximum positions and its application by both sides in a negotiation.
6. Discuss some of the psychological aspects involved in negotiation.

14

The Legal Aspects of Purchasing

Law of Agency
Uniform Commercial Code
Contract Law
    Mutual Assent
    Consideration
    Legality of Purpose
    Fraud/Coercion
Law of Warranty
The UCC and Warranties
Law of Patents
    Copyrights
Contract Cancelations
Waiver of Right
    Cancelation Clauses
    Termination Agreements
Contract Breach
Federal Antitrust Laws
    The Sherman Act
    The Clayton Act
    The Federal Trade Commission Act
    The Robinson-Patman Act
Buyer's Responsibility

A purchasing manager's decisions must be legally as well as economically sound. Sales agreements of doubtful legality can lead to ill will among buyers and sellers, to confusion about the rights and obligations of the parties involved, and to expensive and time-consuming litigation. And unfavorable decisions in such litigation can mean substantial economic loss to the losing parties.

An old adage says that the person who is his or her own lawyer has a fool for a client. This is particularly true today in the highly complicated and ever-changing environment of modern industry and especially in view of the increasing intervention of government in business. The discussion in this chapter should therefore not be considered a substitute for professional legal advice. Its only purpose is to familiarize purchasing practitioners and students of purchasing with the basic principles of modern business law and to suggest ways these principles affect everyday purchasing decisions and operations. In any situation in which the legality of a sales agreement, contract, or business practice seems doubtful or controversial, legal counsel should be consulted.

The majority of disputes are settled without litigation. Buyers must use common-sense judgment of the law and their negotiation skills, realizing that both parties probably want to continue their business relationship and only enter litigation as a last resort.

LAW OF AGENCY

A purchasing manager, or purchasing agent, is, as the name implies, an agent for the company. The word *agent* is common enough in everyday speech—there are insurance agents, real estate agents, and manufacturers' agents. In purchasing law, however, the words *agent* and *agency* have a more limited meaning.

Simply stated, an agent is someone who has been given the power to act on behalf of some other person or some institution. The person or institution for whom the agent carries out a task is called the principal. The extent of an agent's power to act on behalf of the principal is called the agent's authority. Finally, those persons or companies with whom an agent deals as a representative of his or her principal are called third parties.

There are many different kinds of agents, and they differ in the scope of their authority. Some have a very limited scope of authority—they are given the power to perform one specific task, and only that task, on behalf of the principal. Other agents have the authority to make many kinds of decisions on behalf of their principals. Agents may also differ in the kind of relationship that they have with a principal—an agent may or may not be an employee of the principal, for example. Special agents are those who have a very limited authority to perform a specific task. That is, special agents do not have much discretion in determining how to carry out their duties. General agents, on the other hand, have much broader powers and have more latitude in using their own judgment to carry out duties assigned to them by their principals.

Purchasing managers are, for the most part, general agents, and more often than not they are also employees of their principals. A purchasing manager's status as a general agent is important, because it gives a vendor the right to rely on the purchasing manager's written and oral statements. Furthermore, the status of purchasers as general agents give them wide authority to bind their principals to legally enforceable agreements. (The power of special agents to obligate their principals is narrower, and a seller does not have the right to assume that a special agent has a wide range of powers.)

Purchasing managers should keep in mind the fact that salespersons are themselves agents—agents for the vendor. Thus a sales representative, too, may have either a wide or narrow range of powers, depending on whether or not he or she is a general or special sales agent. In most cases, salespersons are special agents. That is, they may solicit orders, but they are not given very wide powers to change prices, to make promises about delivery dates, or to set the terms of a contract.

In dealing with vendor representatives, it is therefore always a good idea for purchasers to have a clear sense of the scope of their authority—the extent to which they may create an obligation enforceable against their own principal, the supplying company.

Agency relationships can be created in several ways. The first and most obvious way is by direct authorization: a principal may directly authorize an agent to perform certain kinds of duties. For example, the purchasing director of a manufacturing concern may authorize a purchasing agent to issue all purchase orders for all lubricants needed by the firm. Such an authorization, which may be either written or oral, is called an *express authority*.

Authority may also be *implied* through what is called the custom of the marketplace—whatever is necessary to carry out specific duties. For example, if it is customary for purchasing agents in this type of manufacturing concern to have the authority to purchase lubricants, then a seller should have the right to believe that the purchasing agent has such authority. Such authority is called customary authority, and a seller must be aware of what is "reasonable" and the "custom of the marketplace," locality, or profession. For instance, the purchasing agent who has the authority to buy lubricants for his or her principal but was not furnished with the cash to do so should have the authority to buy the lubricants on credit.

Finally, agency can be established by any act or acts that can reasonably be construed as creating an agency. Consider again the purchasing agent whose job it is to purchase lubricants for a factory. Suppose the director of purchasing for the factory strictly limits this agent's purchasing authority to no more than $10,000 per month and that in one month the agent signs a purchase order for $16,000 worth of lubricants. In this case the agent has exceeded the actual authority given by the director of purchasing for the firm. However, the vendor (the third party, in this case) has no way of knowing that the agent's authority is limited to purchases of less than $10,000. The purchasing agent, in this case, has the apparent authority to sign a purchase order for $16,000 worth of lubricants. Thus the principal is legally obligated by any such agreement made by the agent, as long as the third party might reasonably be expected to suppose that such authority exists.

The important thing to remember here is that all agreements reached by an agent with proper authority—be it express, implied, or apparent—do create a legally enforceable contract between the principal and the third party.

UNIFORM COMMERCIAL CODE

The Uniform Commercial Code (UCC) has been passed by all state legislatures except Louisiana. It is designed to provide uniformity in law pertaining to business transactions in the areas of (1) commercial paper; (2) sales contracts; (3) bank deposits and collections; (4) letters of credit; (5) bulk transfers; (6) warehouse receipts, bills of lading, and other title documents; (7) investment securities; and (8) secured transactions. Article 2, dealing with sales contracts, is the section of prime concern to purchasers. The UCC will apply to most transactions between buyers and sellers. Buyers need to keep in mind, however, that certain other sources of law will also apply, such as

- Common law formed by past, published court opinions
- Federal legislation
- State legislation
- Public administrative and regulatory boards

In addition, the sale of services is not specifically covered under UCC and thus falls into common law. In deciding whether the UCC or common law will govern the sale of services the primary point, on making that decision is where the majority of funds are spent. For example, if a contract for furnace installation is awarded for $7,700, and the furnace will cost $7,000 and installation is $700, the UCC will apply. If the furnace will cost $700 and installation $7,000, then the common law will apply. Buyers should also monitor contracts for provisions that override the UCC. Last, purchasers must realize that any government body can modify the rules for doing business provided the modifications don't conflict with the regulations of a higher governing body.

The significance of the UCC to purchasing managers has been summed up by a well-known corporate counsel. He points out that the UCC helps the buyer four ways: (1) If a seller makes an offer in writing, the seller has to live up to it for the period of time stated; (2) verbal agreements, if confirmed in writing and no objection is made, are valid; (3) the conflict between a buyer's purchase-order terms and a seller's acknowledgment terms has been generally resolved in favor of the buyer, and (4) as far as warranties are concerned, the purchasing manager can legally rely on the vendor to supply the item needed to do the job. The net effect of article 2 of the UCC, he concludes, is to strengthen the buyer's hand in his or her dealings with suppliers:

> He can now count on added legal protection against trickery. He can more readily believe the express and implied warranties contained in a contract. But, most

important, he can be secure in the knowledge that, in matters involving the four key points in Article 2, the courts will be more sympathetic to the buyer.[1]

CONTRACT LAW

A contract can be most simply defined as a legally enforceable agreement. In their work purchasing managers often must deal with contracts between their principals (the buying companies) and third parties (the vendors). If any purchase order is to have the status of a legally enforceable agreement, it must fulfill the requirements of a contract. The four conditions generally required to make an agreement an enforceable contract are

1. Mutual assent
2. Consideration
3. Legality
4. Competence

Each of these requirements is discussed at some length in the paragraphs that follow.

Mutual Assent

First, a contract must result from the mutual assent of the parties to the contract. Mutual consent consists of an offer made by one party and the unconditional acceptance of that offer by another party. A purchasing manager and a vendor may have long discussions or exchanges of correspondence about a particular sale, and they may discuss the quality, quantity, and price of the goods or services being offered. Such discussions and correspondence, however, do *not* create a contract. They are merely preliminary to the creation of a contract. Price quotations and invitations to trade (such as advertisements) fall within this "preliminary" category. They do not, in and of themselves, create a legally enforceable agreement.

The issuance of a purchase order might very well be the next step after the preliminary discussion or correspondence that precedes a sale. A purchasing manager should keep in mind the fact that the issuance of such an order does not necessarily create a contract—an issued purchase order is really no more than an offer. The purchase order becomes a contract only after it has been accepted by an authorized agent of the vendor. This is the reason for acknowledgment copies, one of which is generally sent along with the purchase order, to be signed and returned by the vendor. It is considered good practice, therefore, to include in the acknowledgment copy the phrase, "We acknowledge and accept this offer." Such an explicit statement of acceptance will leave no question that an enforceable contract is being proposed by the buyer. A purchase order can be an acceptance if it is

[1]John D. Jackson, "Uniform Commercial Code: It's A Bonus for Buyers," *Purchasing*, February 6, 1969, p. 54.

in response to a seller's offer, for instance, when the buyer responds to a seller's written quotation with an order; or if the buyer phones a purchase order in and reaches agreement with the seller on price, quantity, and terms.

Battle of Forms   Suppliers, however, often acknowledge and accept orders on their own forms. Until the adoption of the UCC, any such acceptance that differed in any way from the buyer's purchase order constituted a counteroffer. There would be no contract, because a counteroffer would terminate the original offer and propose in turn a new and different offer. Theoretically, the legal process of offer and acceptance could begin all over again and continue ad infinitum. In practice, that rarely happened, however, and the seller would generally provide what the buyer wanted. But the potential for conflict and litigation was there, and the "battle of the forms" was liable to break out at any time, until the UCC was almost universally accepted. The UCC maintains that

> If parties deal as though they have a contract, then they are deemed to have one. . . . A definite expression of acceptance or a written confirmation—sent within a reasonable time—operates as an acceptance. This is true even though it states terms additional to or different from those offered or agreed upon, unless acceptance is expressly made conditional on assent to the additional or different terms. [article 2, section 207]
> Since additional terms are to be construed as providing proposals for addition to the contract. Between merchants such terms become part of the contract unless a) the offer expressly limits acceptance to the terms of the offer b) they materially alter it or c) notification of objection to them has already been given or is given within a reasonable time after notice of them is received. [article 2, section 207]

Thus if the seller wants an agreement based on his or her terms and conditions, the seller must say so in his or her acknowledgment in words similar to these:

> Acceptance of your order is expressly made conditional on your assent to the terms and conditions stated below and on the reverse side hereof, and we agree to furnish the material described herein only upon these terms and conditions.

If the supplier does not make the acceptance conditional on the buyer's assent, a contract will generally be formed on the buyer's terms.

Prior to the UCC, if a purchasing manager accepted a shipment and there was a dispute concerning the terms and conditions, the courts generally ruled that the seller's terms and conditions automatically prevailed. Acceptance of the shipment by the purchasing manager was considered agreement with the supplier's "last shot," that is, the shipment, which constituted a counteroffer. Under the UCC, the supplier who ships an order—even when his or her terms and conditions differ from the buyer's—is often legally bound by the buyer's terms and conditions. If the supplier insists, in writing, on his or her terms, the buyer still has the choice of accepting the contract or calling it off.

Consideration

Second, a legally enforceable contract must contain the element of consideration. Basically, *consideration* means that each of the parties to the contract makes a sacrifice and each receives a benefit. A one-way, or unilateral, contract, in which one of the parties does not receive a benefit and make a sacrifice, is not legally enforceable. In an ordinary contract of purchase or sale, the vendor agrees to sell and deliver, and the buyer agrees to purchase certain goods or services. Default by either party creates a breach of contract and gives the other party the right to sue for damages. Any promise that is made *without* consideration is called a *gratuitous* promise and is unenforceable.

Quantity   Each party's obligations in terms of *quantity* should be stated as clearly as possible in a purchase order. If the buyer's quantity requirements are not definitely known, the best approximation should be stated, along with a note explaining that the quantity listed is in fact an estimate. In other words, both buyer and seller may create a legally enforceable "estimated" contract by acknowledging, in the contract itself, that exact quantities were not predictable at the time the contract was created. Purchase orders with such ambiguities often state a minimum quantity that shall be bought by the purchaser and a maximum quantity for which delivery can be demanded from the vendor. Thus the ambiguity of the contract can be limited, and the parties to it can share equally in the risk of entering into such an agreement.

    Indefinite contracts for future delivery must also fulfill the requirements of mutuality. If either the buyer or seller has no obligation, the contract is not enforceable. For example, if the buyer's need for certain goods is only hypothetical or conditional, and no consideration for this fact is given to the vendor, the contract is not enforceable. Furthermore, if the time of delivery depends solely on the whim of one of the parties, the agreement is not enforceable.

    The buyer's obligation under a contract is also measured by the quantity specified on the order. A court action involving this point of law brought out the following facts.[2] The buyer in this instance, a building contractor, ordered a specified quantity of roofing tile to be specially manufactured, the order amounting to $2,526, for completing certain of his projects. The vendor's quotation, on which the order was based, was good for thirty days but with the stipulation that the order was to be "subject to the approval of our executive office at Chicago." The vendor acknowledged the order, saying, "We are passing this to our executive department for consideration and attention"; no formal acceptance, however, was issued. Nevertheless, the vendor started manufacturing the tile and made several partial shipments, which were accepted and paid for by the buyer. During the course of the contract, after $1,431.56 worth of tile had been delivered and paid for, it became evident to the buyer that he had overestimated his requirements, and he refused to accept further shipments, whereupon the vendor filed suit to collect for the full amount of the order. The buyer contended that no valid con-

---

[2]*Ludowici-Celadon Company* v. *McKinley,* 11 N.W. 2d 839.

tract existed because of the vendor's failure to make a formal acceptance of the order, and the lower court ruled in his favor. The case was carried to a higher court, however, and this decision was reversed. In holding the buyer liable for payment, the court cited the principle that the shipment itself indicated acceptance, and that shipment of part of the order is acceptance of the whole. "In the instant case," said the court, "plaintiff [seller] manufactured the tile, delivered a part thereof, and tendered the remainder. Had the seller refused to deliver the remainder, the buyer could have recovered damages for the breach of the contract. It must follow, therefore, that the seller is likewise entitled to recover damages because of the buyer's refusal to accept the remainder of the tile." In other words, the obligation is a mutual one. A reasonable variation from the specified quantity, plus or minus, due to manufacturing conditions, is recognized as coming within the meaning of the contract and satisfying its obligations, but this allowable variation is generally limited to a fixed percentage of the specified amount. Trade customs in the various producing industries are usually clear on this point and are accepted as governing in the legal interpretation of a contract.

Price   The purchase order should be quite specific as to the *price* as well as the quantity of goods or services to be delivered. It is not, for example, a good idea to issue an unpriced purchase order unless it is absolutely necessary to do so (as in industries in which the prices of certain commodities fluctuate very rapidly). A purchasing manager who feels that he or she must issue purchase orders without a specific price should give the vendor certain guidelines on notifying the buyer should the price rise above a certain level.

In cases of *unpriced orders,* the UCC states that the supplier may charge a "reasonable" amount when price has not been specified. Additionally, either party may cancel the order if the price is deemed unreasonable. If the buyer refuses to return the merchandise, the seller can collect an amount equal to fair market price at the time the buyer reneged on the contract.

Price in effect at time of shipment is often used in cases where the commodity price fluctuates based on free market or the producers insist on such terms. In these cases buyers are liable for this price unless the supplier ships late or early; then the price on the original contracted delivery date applies. For example, Bethlehem Steel Corporation was to ship buyer Y one hundred tons of cold rolled sheet at $400/ton on December 15. Shipment is not made until January 3, when a new price of $425/ton is effective. In this case the buyer can seek remedy to receive steel at $400/ton.

Delivery   The time of delivery should also be clearly indicated on the purchase order and thus becomes one of the clauses of the contract. Such a schedule becomes part of the vendor's contractual obligation, and if the vendor fails to meet the schedule, that vendor may be held in default of the contract. In certain cases the purchaser may even want to insert in the order a clause stating that *time is of the essence.* Such a clause may relieve a buyer of any and all obligations for that portion of the delivery that was not made during the specified time period.

Inserting *time is of essence* creates a liquidated damages clause. These clauses need to contain a statement of losses incurred by the buying party if the seller does not ship on time. To illustrate: a utility company asks that a transformer manufacturer ship by January 15 or the utility will suffer losses of $250 per day in lost utility billings.

The principle of consideration has been modified in recent years through changes in the law brought about by court decisions and the wide acceptance of the UCC. For example, in some states a party to a contract can be bound to a contract even without receiving consideration merely by stating that it holds itself legally obligated. More important, a party to a contract may, after the contract has been signed, agree to make an additional sacrifice without asking for an additional benefit in the terms of the contract. For example, a purchasing manager who has contracted for a shipment of steel in thirty days may suddenly find that her company desperately needs the steel in fifteen days. The purchaser may at that point call the vendor and ask that the shipment be "hurried up." The vendor is under no contractual obligation to expedite the shipment of steel. However, if the vendor does agree to the advanced delivery date and then fails to meet it, causing a loss to the purchaser's company, the vendor may be held liable for losses that the purchaser incurred. The legal principle involved here is that the purchaser relied on the vendor's promise to expedite delivery and in so relying on the vendor, failed to get the shipment on time. In other words, the purchaser relied on the vendor's freely given promise to her own detriment.

In general, however, the principle of consideration is still a basic requirement of all contracts. Without it, a purchase order is not likely to achieve the status of an enforceable contract.

Legality of Purpose

Third, a valid contract shall not be in conflict with existing federal or local laws and regulations, so that performance of the contract would in itself be an unlawful act. Examples would be agreements embodying discrimination in violation of the Robinson-Patman Act, agreements based on production under conditions in violation of wage and hour laws, and assumption of tax charges by either party in violation of Internal Revenue Service rulings on tax liabilities.

Written versus Oral In addition to legal purpose, the UCC states that a contract with a value of more than $500 is not enforceable unless there is written evidence that such a contract exists. The $500 rule has three exceptions, anyone of which could make an oral contract for an amount greater than $500 enforceable. These exceptions are (1) the goods are made specifically to the buyer's order and are not readily salable to others; (2) both parties behave as if a contract existed; and (3) the parties have always done business on an oral basis.

Thus if a seller makes a set of unique goods for a buyer, the oral contract is binding on the buyer. In the second case, if the seller ships material, and the buyer accepts it and prepares an invoice for payment, no later recourse is available by stating that the contract wasn't valid. Buyers are wise to seek written agreement in these cases, to confirm their actions.

Fraud/Coercion

Fourth, in a valid contract no fraud shall be practiced by either the buyer or seller in arriving at the agreement, nor shall force be used, as parties must willingly enter the contract.

Legal fraud has been defined as any act, deed, or statement, made by either a buyer or a seller *before* the purchase contract is signed or completed, that is likely to deceive the other party. A seller is not liable for fraud if the evidence proves (1) that the seller or his or her sales representative made a false statement *after* the contract was signed, (2) that the seller or his or her sales representative actually did not know that the quality of the merchandise was not as claimed in the sales contract but merely expressed an opinion that he believed the quality to be as represented, or (3) that the purchaser did not believe or rely upon the statements made by the seller or his or her agent. If a purchaser inspects merchandise before entering into the contract, that purchaser is put upon guard and is expected by the law to use his or her own good judgment in respect to the quality and characteristics of the goods; if a purchaser is not sufficiently experienced to judge the quality of the merchandise that he or she inspects and relies upon a fraudulent statement made by the seller, however, the latter is liable.

LAW OF WARRANTY

Warranties are of two sorts: express and implied. If, in the absence of express warranties of quality, fitness, or performance of a product given by the seller, the buyer makes known to the seller the particular purposes for which the goods or equipment are required, relying on the seller's judgment and skill, there is an implied warranty that the goods shall be reasonably fit for that purpose. The inclusion of an expressed warranty covering any of these points renders the implied warranty void, because the latter cannot exist when the seller expressly guarantees his or her merchandise.

Statements made by salespersons are not enforceable as guarantees. Courts have repeatedly recognized the natural tendency of sales representatives to "puff" the virtues of their products for the purpose of making a sale, without imputing to such enthusiastic claims the status of a formal guarantee. An employer is not bound by salespersons' guarantees unless (1) the guarantee is confirmed by the employer or someone in his or her organization authorized to do so; (2) the employer has notified the purchaser that he or she will be bound by guarantees made by the sales representative; (3) the employer has in the past, without such notification, accepted responsibility for such guarantees, thereby implying that the sales representative has this authority; or (4) the guarantee constitutes actual fraud, in which case the employer is responsible for the action of his or her employee even though the employer did not authorize the salesperson to make the fraudulent statement or guarantee, either expressly or by implication.

In invoking the warranty clauses of a contract, the purchaser is under obligation to take action as soon as the deficiency of the goods or the breach of warranty is determined. Many claims based on inferior quality of merchandise delivered under contract have been thrown out of court because of unreasonable delay in ascertaining that such a condition does exist. Many sales contracts, for goods that are capable of inspection on receipt, place a limit on the time within which such claims may be made—usually thirty days—and these limiting clauses have been adjudged valid. There are other types of defects or deficiencies that are not ascertainable until goods have been put into use or until equipment has been installed and started in operation. In such cases "reasonable" promptness is a matter of interpretation, and the buyer must be in a position to prove his or her alertness and promptness in discovering the alleged breach of warranty and taking action to recover. Furthermore, the buyer is not entitled to retain merchandise or to continue to use equipment at the same time that he or she refuses to make payment because of alleged breach of warranty.

THE UCC AND WARRANTIES

The Uniform Commercial Code (article 2, section 2-313) states that express warranties by the seller are created as follows:

> (a) Any affirmation of fact or promise made by the seller to the buyer which relates to the goods and becomes part of the basis of the bargain creates an express warranty that the goods shall conform to the affirmation or promise.
> (b) Any description of the goods which is made part of the basis of the bargain creates an express warranty that goods shall conform to the description.
> (c) Any sample or model which is made part of the basis of the bargain creates an express warranty that the whole of the goods shall conform to the sample or model.

Under the UCC the buyer also has the protection of implied warranties established by law. A warranty of "merchantability" is implied in a contract if the seller is in fact a merchant of the goods involved in a sale. Additionally, there is an implied warranty of "fitness for particular purpose or sale" when the seller at the time of contracting "has reason to know any particular purpose for which the goods are required and that the buyer is relying on the seller's skill or judgment to select or furnish suitable goods."

If a seller wishes to deny an implied warranty of merchantability or fitness, the seller must do so "conspicuously, in language that appraises the buyer of the fact." This requirement of conspicuousness is intended to invalidate the disclaimers of warranty that often appear on the reverse side of sales agreements or vendor acknowledgments in tiny, almost illegible, type—known popularly as boiler plate.

LAW OF PATENTS

A U.S. patent is a monopoly created by law. There are five classifications or bases for patents: mechanical, process, composition, articles of manufacture, and design. The rights of the patentee have been summed up as follows:

> The patentee has the sole right of making, using, and selling the patented articles, and he may prevent anybody from dealing with them at all. Inasmuch as he has the right to prevent people from using them, or dealing in them at all, he has the right to do the lesser thing, that is to say, to impose his own conditions. It does not matter how unreasonable or how absurd the conditions are.[3]

A patent can be extended by improvements on the original device, but after the expiration of a patent (and an expired patent cannot be renewed), the patentee loses all former rights in the patent. Then anyone can make, sell, purchase, or use the invention without any chance of liability. A patentee may obtain another, new patent on some improvement of the original patent when the latter has expired, but this protection covers only the improvement; the original invention is unprotected after the patent period of seventeen years (or a maximum of fourteen years in the case of a design patent).

A person or a company may be liable for infringement of a patent (1) if the person or company uses the patented article; (2) makes it for its use; (3) purchases a part and combines it with other parts, comprising an infringing device; (4) conspires purposely or unintentionally with another and contributes in any manner to an infringement; or (5) purchases and resells an infringing device, although the purchase is made in the belief that the seller had a license from the patentee to sell or use the device.

Copyrights

Copyrights give the author of written work exclusive right to its reproduction. Since 1976 copyrights have been regulated by a federal law entitled the Copyright Act. The major differences between patents and copyrights are that a copyright is not issued by the federal government; rather it is automatically secured when the work is fixed in any tangible medium of expression. The copyright law states that an author must register the work and deposit two copies of it for the right to collect unauthorized reproduction charges in court. In the event the author does not file, he or she still maintains copyright to the material. Generally, a copyright lasts for the life of the author plus fifty years.[4]

[3] *Semler v. Schmicker*, 38 Atl. 2d 831.

[4] Mark E. Roszknowski, *Business Law Principles: Cases and Policy*, (Glenview, Ill.: Scott, Foresman and Co., 1989), pp. 706–7.

CONTRACT CANCELATIONS

The confidence and orderliness needed to do business satisfactorily depends on the sanctity of the contractual relationship, backed up with legal force. A good contract protects the interests and rights of both the buyer and seller, and its obligations are equally binding upon both parties to the contract. Cancelations and defaults in respect to contract agreements cannot be made arbitrarily by either party to the detriment of the other. Therefore, a fair and orderly procedure must be provided to meet the situation involving contract cancelations. Although it is probably true that no contract is actually "noncancelable," this statement does not mean that the existence of the contract in question can be ignored or that the obligation to hold the other party harmless from the consequences of such cancelation can be avoided.

In general, cancelations come within three classifications: for default by the seller, for the convenience of the buyer, or by mutual consent. It should be noted also that, as a general rule, contracts that are indefinite as to quantity or duration can be terminated at will by either party, unilaterally, without penalty, upon due notice to the other party. The very indefiniteness of the terms, in such a case, is construed in law as evidence of mutual consent for termination.

Cancelation for default   The simplest case is that of a default by the vendor in failing to perform as agreed in the contract, in making deliveries that do not come up to specifications, or in failing to meet the specified delivery dates. All the essential factors should be so clearly and definitely incorporated in the terms of the contract as to become a part of the seller's obligation. Then any failure on the seller's part to fulfill the terms is a default on the contract, giving the buyer a cause for redress.

Cancelation for convenience of the buyer   It may become necessary for the buyer to cancel a contract even though the seller is able and willing to perform his or her part of the agreement. In such cases of contract cancelation for the convenience of the buyer, the similar principle holds that the seller should not be called upon to incur any loss through the buyer's default.

Cancelation by mutual consent   Cancelation of a contract is not necessarily a cause for legal action. Just as the making of a contract represents a meeting of minds resulting in an agreement between the buyer and the seller to undertake certain mutual responsibilities, so there may be a meeting of minds in respect to the termination of that agreement without invoking a penalty on either side. There are many instances in the course of business when requirements change, so that a contract or open order is no longer appropriate to the buyer's need. A cancelation is indicated, for the convenience of the buyer. But, if no particular hardship to the seller is involved, for example, if the item concerned is so standard that another outlet can be found, or if it is of such a nature that materials and work in process can be diverted without loss to the orders of some other buyer, the seller may be quite willing to accept a cancelation in good faith as a normal risk of doing business. If an adjustment is in order because of special materials purchased or work done on the contract, a reasonable agreement can be reached through negotiation rather than litigation, based on the equity of the situation.

In each of these types of cancelations, there may be complex ramifications, so that the simple principles mentioned may be subject to different interpretations by the courts. In any event, if there is any considerable liability involved, or if there is any shadow of a doubt as to the liability that may be incurred, it is best to secure competent legal advice in advance of issuing a cancelation.

WAIVER OF RIGHT

A contract is a binding legal document designed to protect both parties, and the legal rights inherent in the contract agreement should be meticulously safeguarded, for they can easily be forfeited by careless action. For example, time of delivery or performance is an integral part of the contract if it is stated, as it should be, in the purchase order or contract. Yet it is a point upon which many buyers are inclined to be lenient, within reasonable limits, so long as systematic expediting is successful in getting deliveries made before the absolute deadline. Now suppose that a certain vendor is chronically tardy with his or her shipments on a continuing contract, requiring an undue amount of expediting effort, until the patient buyer eventually decides to terminate the agreement. The buyer claims breach of contract and has an imposing lot of evidence in the form of late shipments to support this claim. But if the buyer has consistently condoned the lateness of deliveries in the past and has continued to accept overdue shipments, that buyer may find that he or she has waived his or her rights for legal action upon this point. The buyer can still cancel the contract, but the claim for any redress on the basis of the vendor's default has been forfeited.

Cancelation Clauses

Some purchasing departments include a special clause in their purchase orders and contracts, on the subject of cancelation. For the most part, such general clauses add nothing whatever to the rights or protection afforded by the contractual relationship itself. In fact, they may actually destroy the force of the entire contract by making the contract obligations or promises "illusory" in the eyes of the law. For example, the following clause appears in one purchase order, ostensibly to relieve the purchaser of continuing responsibility under a contractual agreement and to reserve the privilege of rescinding or canceling any portion of the order without liability:

The buyer reserves the right to cancel any unshipped portion of this order.

The broad effect, in court, of such a general disclaimer of responsibility for carrying out his or her part of the agreement, however, would probably be a decision that the document is unilateral and that no contract legally exists under such a condition.

On the other hand, some practical advantage may be obtained by specifically stressing a particular phase of delinquency that is to be interpreted by mutual consent as cause for cancelation of an order by the buyer, without penalty. In most cases clauses of this nature are based on the fact that time of delivery is "of the essence" of the contract and that failure to make delivery as promised relieves the buyer of his or her responsibility to accept and pay for goods furnished tardily under the contract. An example of such a clause is the following:

> Should any portion of this order be unfilled at the expiration of 60 days from its date, we reserve the right (notifying you) to cancel said unfilled portion without liability other than to make payments for that portion of the order that has been delivered.

Although it may be argued that this gives the buyer no rights that could not be equally accomplished by specifying a definite delivery date among the terms on the face of the order, it could be invoked in cases in which previous leniency in accepting delinquent deliveries (which would be a normal policy for occasional infractions and if the urgency of the requirement did not require rigid enforcement) was cited as precedent to diminish the force of a delivery agreement. It does serve notice on the seller that the time element is an essential part of the agreement and will be so interpreted. At the same time it provides the means for clearing open-order files with reasonable promptness and for avoiding the accumulation of miscellaneous outstanding commitments.

Termination Agreements

It may be accepted as a basic thesis that a contract is made with the expectation of carrying it through to completion on both sides. But under certain circumstances there may be a strong probability that the buyer may wish to cancel at some stage prior to completion because of contingencies that can be foreseen in principle but not in detail. If ordinary forms of conditional contracts are not appropriate to cover these circumstances, it is highly desirable to have an understanding with the seller as to the procedure to be followed in the event of such cancelation. This agreement may be embodied in a termination clause that is made a part of the contract. Sellers are naturally reluctant to accept termination clauses, and there is no obligation on their part to do so; they are fully entitled to stand on their contractual rights under the principles of cancelation for the convenience of the buyer, as outlined. But if a good, continuing relationship has been established between the contracting companies, and if the contract is an advantageous one so far as it goes, the agreement may frequently be worked out as a part of the negotiation in such a way as to relieve the buyer of the extreme penalties or obligations involved in an ordinary cancelation, without calling upon the seller to sustain any loss by reason of the cancelation.

CONTRACT BREACH

Under the UCC the law expects contracts to be performed by the seller according to the agreed-upon terms and conditions. When that does not occur, the seller has breached the contract. Seller contract breaches may occur for any of the following reasons:

- Seller delivers late
- Seller repudiates the contract, saying the company will not deliver at all
- Seller ships wrong goods
- Seller ships defective goods

Buyers have remedy of cover in these cases. *Cover* is going into the marketplace and acquiring like goods and charging back the difference in price to the original seller. To illustrate: Buyer A has a contract to purchase 1,000 connectors at $1.50 each. The supplier calls and says the company will not deliver. Buyer A calls supplier B and acquires the goods for the price of $1.90 each. Buyer A then recovers the .30/unit from supplier A. In the case of defective or wrong goods, the seller is given an amount of time to "cure" or correct the defect.

While most contract breaches are occasioned by the seller, an anticipatory breach occurs when the buyer suspects the seller will not perform or will deliver inferior goods. The buyer asks for assurance of performance and progress. If these assurances are not forthcoming within thirty days, the buyer can then breach the contract. Such a situation could arise on long lead-time capital equipment where the buyer feels progress is not being made and the seller cannot provide written evidence of such progress. Then the contract may be terminated by the buyer.

FEDERAL ANTITRUST LAWS

Purchasers need to be cognizant of potential antitrust dealings in their relations with suppliers. The four major statutes in this area are (1) the Sherman Antitrust Act, (2) the Clayton Act, (3) the Federal Trade Commission Act, and (4) the Robinson-Patman Act.

The Sherman Act

Passed in 1890, the Sherman Act prohibits contracts, combinations, or conspiracies in restraint of trade. For a violation to occur, an agreement between two or more persons is necessary. It concerns joint activities (agreements) between competitors or between suppliers and their customers that restrict the freedom of any party to make and carry out business decisions entirely on their own. Examples of such joint activity include:

- Price fixing among competitors
- Group boycott by competitors (i.e., agreeing not to buy from a supplier)
- Allocation of customers or markets
- Agreements between a manufacturer and customers that they will not buy competitors' products.

Prosecution of violators can result in a $100,000 fine and imprisonment for three years for individuals and fines of up to $1 million for corporations. "Per se" violations, such as price fixing, are those punishable as a matter of law and deemed illegal without an assessment of their impact on competition.

The Clayton Act

Passed in 1914, the Clayton Act extended the coverage provided under the Sherman Act. In particular, it outlawed tie-in sales. These sales occur when a seller requires the purchaser to buy one product in order to purchase another product. Tie-in sales are expressly forbidden, especially when a manufacturer makes pricing for two items so unreasonably attractive relative to individual prices that the buyer must buy the total package.

The Federal Trade Commission Act

Passed in 1914, this act gave the Federal Trade Commission (FTC) the power to pursue companies that engaged or attempted to engage in unfair competition or deceptive practices. All proposed corporate mergers must withstand the FTC test of unfair competition.

The Robinson-Patman Act

Passed in 1935, it prohibits sellers from discriminating in price when selling the same product to two competing sellers on the same functional level. This prohibition would apply to two competing OEMs or retail dealers. The intent of the act is to prevent large-volume buyers from inducing a discriminatory price from their sellers when no economic justification is present. At a certain point economies of scale become irrelevant. For instance, if company A buys $3 billion of copper a year and company C buys $8 billion of copper per year, economies-of-scale differences are negligible. If C received a lower price, it could use this advantage in the marketplace to drive A out of business. Robinson-Patman is the only antitrust act that makes the buyer guilty for knowingly inducing a discriminatory price. Robinson-Patman also prohibits buyers from accepting brokerage discounts or advertising allowances to which they are not entitled. There are certain factors under Robinson-Patman that allow sellers to grant a discriminatory price. These include:

- A good-faith clause—meeting the equally low price of a competitor
- Differences in seller's costs of production and distribution
- Deteriorating, perishable, or seasonal goods

There have been very few prosecutions under Robinson-Patman, since most sellers prefer not to sue their major customers. It does give sellers a justification, so that they can say, "This is the best price we offer to accounts of your relative size." Additionally, most buyers are aware of, and follow, the law. In fact, buyers should insist they are receiving the seller's most favorable price based on their volume requirements. A recent 1988 court decision on the Robinson-Patman Act allowed price discounting to a particular customer that reflected actual cost savings as a result of quantities or method of sale. The case was based on a charge by the FTC that Boise Cascade had received larger discounts from office suppliers than its smaller competitors had. Since Boise was able to show its actions had not hurt competitors, the discounts were allowed.[5]

BUYER'S RESPONSIBILITY

In essence, buyers should seek to get the lowest price they are legally entitled to and should guard against any inducement of illegal pricing. For it should be remembered that there are many more aspects of law that have a bearing on purchase transactions and purchasing practice. This chapter has merely summarized the points that are most commonly encountered and that should be observed to keep free of litigation or to enhance the prospect of a favorable verdict when litigation cannot be avoided. The cardinal rule of law should be remembered: No one should come into a court of law "with unclean hands," that is, without being sure that his or her own action and intent are lawful and that the breach of legal obligation is not on his or her own part. When the controversy concerns interpretation of an agreement, the court will endeavor to determine the real intent of the parties in making that agreement. But on the whole, the legal principles and requirements are clear and well established, although their interpretation may be modified by the particular circumstances of their application in a given case.

It is important for purchasers to read carefully and to know what they are signing, for it is the evidence of the agreement. Although the courts have in some cases ruled in favor of a buyer who failed to notice some contract clause that was inconspicuously placed or printed in excessively fine print or faint ink, or when the buyer had definitely been led to believe that no such condition was incorporated in the agreement, these are the rare exceptions to the general rule of responsibility for knowing what the contract contains.

Finally, by mutual consent, arbitration can be substituted for litigation. Contract clauses are valid by which contracting parties agree not to enter suit but, rather, to abide by a decision rendered by a disinterested arbitrator. Under such an agreement, the decision of the arbitrator is final and conclusive (unless in making the decision the arbitrator himself or herself is guilty of fraud, misconduct, or such gross mistake as would imply bad faith or failure to exercise honest judgment). Arbitration of contract disputes is encouraged in business practice and is

[5]"Court: Big Buyer Discounts Aren't Necessarily Illegal," *Purchasing*, May 12, 1988, pp. 21–22.

supported by modern higher-court decisions; its legal effect is the practical elimination of litigations.

POINTS FOR REVIEW

1. Explain the law of agency.
2. Distinguish between expressed and implied authority.
3. Name the basic elements of a contract.
4. Differentiate between an expressed warranty and an implied warranty.
5. Discuss the ways in which the Uniform Commercial Code has helped the buyer.
6. Review the major types of contract cancellations.

15

Materials Management

Managing Material Flows
Materials-Management Alternatives
       Buyer-Planner Concept
Advantages of Materials Management
Measuring Materials-Management Contributions
Logistics Management

As we have seen in earlier chapters, purchasing has been given specialized departmental status along with clearly defined responsibilities and authority. But its role in an increasingly complex service and production economy is not fixed, and we can expect to see continued evolution in the function. The main thrust of that evolution is toward interdependence with other functions of business.

As purchasing continues to coordinate its efforts with those of other specialized departments—traffic, inspection, engineering, production, and so on—all these activities will become more integrated than ever before. And the very process of integration may lead to a crossing of lines of authority in certain types of companies and under certain circumstances. This in turn would require new definitions of responsibility and new patterns of organization to administer them properly.

Does purchasing's responsibility in a highly integrated operation end, for example, with the issuance of the order? If purchasing's negotiations with the supplier involve transportation costs, packaging methods, and delivery dates, how far does its obligation extend in these matters? Should purchasing not have some interest in, or even control of, traffic and receiving to see that the supplier meets all requirements that were part of the negotiated price? Similar questions can be asked in regard to other phases of the materials cycle—whether, for example, purchasing's concern with ordering quantities and inventory levels should directly involve it in material control and production scheduling.

Such considerations have led many companies to adopt a broad concept of materials procurement that goes beyond basic buying. Known generally as *materials management,* the concept varies considerably from company to company, depending on the size of the organization, the nature of its products, and the customers it serves. A leading textbook's description of the concept illustrates the point:

> An organization that has adopted the materials management organizational concept will have a single manager responsible for planning, organizing, motivating and controlling all those activities principally concerned with the flow of materials into an organization. Materials management views material flows as a system.
>
> The specific functions that might be included under the materials manager are material planning and control, production scheduling, material and purchasing research, purchasing, incoming traffic, inventory control, receiving, incoming quality control, stores, in-plant materials movement, and scrap and surplus disposal. Not all functions are necessarily included: the ones often excluded are production scheduling, in-plant materials movement, and incoming quality control.[1]

MANAGING MATERIAL FLOWS

Figure 15-1 highlights six factors driving firms toward greater materials coordination. While some of them were mentioned in Chapter 2, these six focus on the need for a more coordinated approach to managing the material flow. Figure

[1]M. R. Leenders, H. E. Fearon, and W. B. England, *Purchasing and Materials Management,* 9th ed. (Homewood, Ill.: Richard D. Irwin, 1989), p. 4.

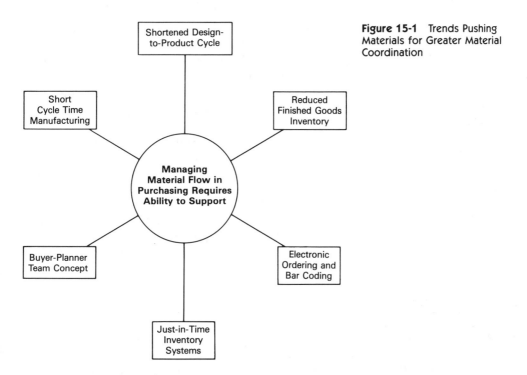

Figure 15-1 Trends Pushing Materials for Greater Material Coordination

15-2 indicates what fast-cycle throughput involves as well as the activities and functional areas involved.

Shortened design-to-product cycles require up-front involvement of purchasing, inventory control, and production planning. Purchasing brings suppliers in early, during the design stage, to discuss ideas with engineers. Meanwhile, production planning is setting up correct times and scheduling receipt of material in the

Primary Objective	Fast-Cycle Throughput					
Involves	Small Quantity Frequent Supplier Shipments	Low Inventory		Flexible Small-Batch Production		Customer Responsiveness
Activity	Supplier Product and Packaging	Shipping	Receiving	Storage	Production	Finished Goods
Functional Areas Involved	Purchasing	Traffic	Receiving	Stores and Inventory Control	Production Planning and Manufacturing	Physical Distribution
Organizational Coordination Structure	Materials Management					

Figure 15-2 Managing the Material Flow for Fast-Cycle Throughput

facility. The new products are run on lines that are geared to produce products in very *short cycles*. Manufacturing's focus today is on getting small batches of products through the plant quickly. This emphasis requires close coordination with planners and buyers. The ability to produce in small batches means the firm is able to match its production output more closely, to accommodate customer preferences. Therefore, fewer finished goods are carried in inventory, necessitating reliable carriers and warehouses who get products to the customer. Meanwhile, raw-material inventories at the start of the supply chain are scheduled on a just-in-time basis and purchased in small quantities in frequent intervals. So great is this coordination requirement that several firms have combined the job of buyer and planner into buyer-planner.

Thus the driving trend toward greater functional coordination in purchasing is fast-cycle throughput. Progressive firms see a competitive nitch in the marketplace where they can meet customer requirements by flexible small-lot production. This quick responsiveness replaces outdated methods of stockpiling inventories and long, inflexible production cycles.

MATERIALS-MANAGEMENT ALTERNATIVES

Before opting for the materials-management concept in its own company, a large electronics corporation surveyed one hundred top manufacturing companies and concluded that there is no typical materials-management organization. Evidently, managers approach the concept pragmatically, the report pointed out, choosing the organization that best suits their needs. On that basis it called materials management a totally integrated approach to control of materials, not a rigorous form of managerial organization.

The survey showed that all but one of the companies using materials management included purchasing in the system. Production control is part of 63 percent of the materials-management organizations; and physical distribution, of 81 percent. Significantly, most of the companies have incorporated a number of other functions: order entry, customer service, quality control, facilities planning, value engineering, customer claims, and sale and disposal of surplus material. Three different types of materials-management organization are illustrated in Figure 15-3.

Even purchasing executives, who are in the most logical position to assume the position of materials manager in the average industrial organization, are not completely in accord as to what materials management covers. Of fifty purchasing executives surveyed by the University of Wisconsin Management Institute, 95 percent said that materials management should include inbound traffic and receiving in addition to buying. But only 60 percent favored bringing outbound traffic, materials handling, and receiving inspection within the scope of the organization. And only 40 percent advocated making production planning and scheduling part of materials management.

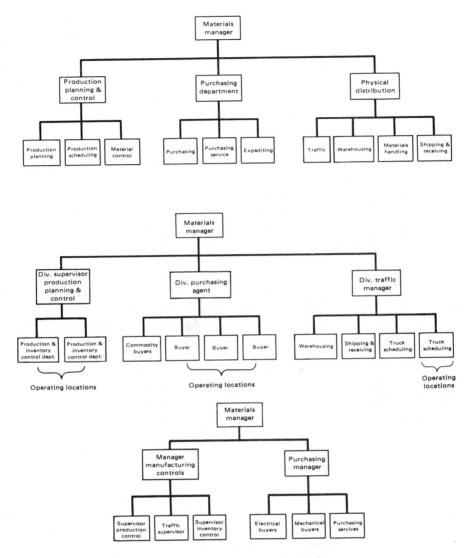

Figure 15-3 Three different organizational approaches to materials management. Courtesy of *Purchasing Magazine.*

A review of typical practical applications of materials management shows how some companies have included the elements mentioned above as well as others—notably physical distribution.

Materials management in one large electronics firm, for example, takes in the functions of purchasing, production and inventory control, and physical distribution. The materials-management organization has the total responsibility to plan, schedule, purchase, store, move, and control goods and services from the supplier through the production cycle to the point of sale.

In this firm, production and inventory control includes production scheduling, forecasting, and planning; inventory-planning measurement and evaluation; stock control and material-requirements analysis; and production and inventory control systems and programs. Physical distribution includes transport of all materials and supplies, receipt and storage of inbound goods, issue and internal movement of materials, operation of the company fleet, personnel travel, and liaison with purchasing and production control to ensure movement of freight at the least total cost.

A division of another electronics firm also has a modified materials-management organization, although it is not designated as such. It is headed by a purchasing agent and includes groups of buyers and a material control group. The latter has responsibility for stores, collating and packaging spare parts and systems for the division's customers, and shipping and receiving.

A third firm's corporate materials-management organization, headed by a vice-president, consists of a director of distribution (under whom is a manager of general traffic), a director of purchasing, and the head of the department of transportation (handling fleet service and travel).

General Electric's materials-management function is responsible for planning and controlling the material resources of the business. A logical nucleus for such a materials-management system, GE points out, is a combination of the materials requirements, materials requisitioning, and purchasing functions. It includes the requirements explosion, detailed production scheduling, and job status and resource loading as part of the system. Receiving, storage, and stockroom also fall within the system, since they relate to the availability of material. Traffic and shipping and billing are generally the responsibility of the marketing department if finished stock is warehoused, but they may be placed in materials management in some locations.

Buyer-Planner Concept

As we pointed out earlier, many firms adopting the materials-management organization have created a new job classification, the *buyer-planner*. Communication links between buyer and planner must be more frequent. Traditional communication went from planner to buyer then to the supplier's sales and then to the

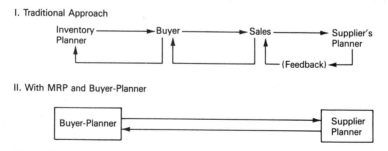

Figure 15-4 Communication Flows—Purchasing to Sales
Source: Morgan, James, "MRP II-That Powerful Tool," *Purchasing*, September 6, 1984, pp. 109–115.

supplier's planner (see Figure 15-4). If a problem arose, the supplier's planner notified the salesperson, who notified the purchaser, who in turn notified the planner. Under MRP the buyer-planner performs the task of releasing the purchase order, working out scheduling, and establishing the appropriate inventory levels. Typically, this position combines the previously separate functions of planning and buying and was created out of the necessity to have closer, quicker communication with suppliers, who are required to maintain MRP priorities. Firms that operate under the buyer-planner concept have buyers who source suppliers, negotiate contracts, and handle long-term aspects of supplier relations. Buyer-planners handle short-term scheduling issues. If a major problem arises with the supplier, the buyer-planner contacts the buyer, who has responsibility for the supplier (see Figure 15-4). Buyer-planners may be assigned to senior buyers or, more typically, to an inventory manager, especially in a materials-management organization (see Figure 15-5). Finally, the jobs of purchaser and buyer-planner have become almost identical, since purchasing is managing what has been popularly termed the outside factory. This means they are managing a factory not physically located in their plant. Thus any supplier changes will affect the buyer and must therefore be closely monitored.

ADVANTAGES OF MATERIALS MANAGEMENT

The great advantage of the materials-management type of organization reported by those companies that have adopted it is the *improved communication* and *coordination* between departments. Materials management provides a central administration where conflicting function or departmental interests can be balanced out in the overall interest of the company. As previously discussed, this centralized responsibility and control also supports *faster flow of materials* from requisition through shipment to customers as finished products.

I. With Buyer-Planner Reporting to Purchasing

II. Separate Purchasing and Planning Functions

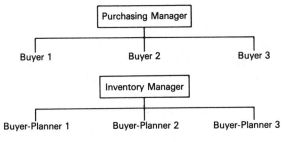

Figure 15-5 Materials-Management Organization Alternatives Using the Buyer-Planner Concept

Among the more specific ways a centrally controlled materials organization has helped a number of companies to improve efficiency and to reduce costs are these:

1. Control of inventories is made easier and simpler. The traditional conflict caused by the efforts of manufacturing, on the one hand, to build up stocks of raw material and parts and of purchasing, on the other, to keep them to a minimum, has been resolved. Production planning and control and purchasing have found it easier to come to agreement on minimum and maximum stocks when they are working more as a team than as separate groups with separate interests. Losses caused by obsolescence or deterioration of surplus materials are eliminated, as are the dangers of shutdowns necessitated by material shortages.
2. Clerical work is sharply reduced. As responsibility for materials moves from department to department, records are almost inevitably duplicated. Many production-control departments, for example, retain file copies of the requisitions they issue to purchasing and in turn demand copies of the purchase order. With production control and purchasing in one office under one individual, a single file copy of either form serves both. Similar reductions in the generation and filing of paperwork can be made in every department involved in the materials cycle, leading in turn to substantial cuts in the clerical force required. (Before the adoption of materials management in an eastern electronics firm, various functions involved in handling materials accounted for 10.5 percent of the total plant work force. A year after the new organization was formed, the percentage had dropped to 7.1. During this time the total work force had increased by 74 percent, but the number of materials personnel had gone up only 18 percent.)
3. Assorted problems of delivery scheduling, emergency orders, and storage are minimized. Purchasing can arrange delivery schedules on the basis of its knowledge of inventory levels and production requirements. Emergency or rush orders are less frequent, because of the understanding between production control and purchasing. Better regulation of the flow of materials into the plant permits better use of storage facilities and coordinated movement of materials into the production line.

Materials management is particularly suited to—and has been most widely adopted by—those companies that manufacture to customers' orders. Such operations often involve fluctuating inventory levels, engineering changes by the customer, and irregular production scheduling. Placing the responsibility for materials in one department enables management to keep informed on the status of every order by checking with one source. In a less coordinated system, basic information about a particular job—what materials have been requisitioned for it, the status of purchase orders placed against the requisitions, the condition of inventories, and manufacturing progress on the job—would have to be gathered from four different departments.

In those companies producing highly standardized items for stock, on the other hand, good communication and coordination between departments handling material have generally been developed by experience. Inventory levels and production schedules are usually established on the basis of sales forecasts and historical usage, and the manufacturing operation is generally more stable and predictable than is the case in the manufacture-to-order companies. In such cases good control has already been built into the materials system, and the plant manager or vice-president of operations or whatever top executive the departments concerned report to is, in fact, a materials manager already.

Another important consideration in the decision to adopt a materials-management organization is the effect that the materials function has on profit and loss. Back when materials management was coming into its own and was being looked on as something of a panacea, Edward A. Stiles, a materials executive, warned against indiscriminate adoption of the concept.[2] He pointed out that in industries in which one or two commodities—textiles, tobacco, leather—represent the major investment the skillful purchasing of these materials makes the difference between a profit and loss in a given year. The in-plant flow of tobacco, for example, however well managed it is, does not have anywhere near the effect of a buying coup or a buying "flop."

It is important to recognize, Stiles said, that just as there are materials-oriented companies, there are production-oriented companies, sales-oriented companies, and service-oriented ones. Rushing into materials management because it may be the fashion is always a serious step—and could be quite a serious error, he pointed out.

MEASURING MATERIALS-MANAGEMENT CONTRIBUTIONS

The ultimate criterion to judge any organizational arrangement is the return on investment generated for shareholders and profitability. In materials management return on investment can be condensed into three major areas: (1) cost reduction, (2) service, and (3) administrative efficiency.

Cost-reduction efforts related directly to profits and effective materials management certainly make a difference. Specific cost-reduction measures include:

- Reductions in material costs
- Reductions in storage space
- Reductions in physical inventory
- Increase in inventory turnover
- Reduction in transportation costs
- Reductions in setup time
- Reductions in cycle times

Second, materials management services other areas of the firm. This service supports the goal of fast throughput and includes:

- Uninterrupted flow of materials
- Assistance to customers—repair, replacement, or delivery
- Reduction in parts shortages
- Average transit time from warehouse to customer
- Minimum of transportation delays
- Accurate inventory counts
- Good forecast accuracy

[2]Edward A. Stiles, "Purchasing's Opportunity in Materials Management," *New England Purchaser,* July 1967, p. 12.

The last area, *administrative efficiency,* covers a variety of measures relating to department efficiencies in operation and development of people. These measures include:

- Materials-management budget target versus actual
- Ratio of materials budget to sales and purchases
- Training and development programs
- Rotation of key people among functions
- Installation of productivity-enhancing systems

LOGISTICS MANAGEMENT

There is often confusion between logistics management and materials management. In practice, many firms use one term or the other to describe the same activity. For example, at Kimberly-Clark Corporation, logistics includes purchasing, planning and traffic/physical distribution. This system would meet the definition of materials management described earlier—planning, organizing, motivating, and controlling those activities associated with the flow of materials. The definition is not very different from the Council of Logistics Management's definition of logistics as "the process of planning, implementing, and controlling the efficient cost-effective flow and storage of raw materials, in process inventory, finished goods, and related information from the point of origin to the point of consumption for the purpose of conformity to customer requirements.[3] Ballou supports the above definition and adds: "for the purpose of providing adequate levels of customer service at a reasonable cost."[4] He goes on to list the key activities as transportation, inventory, maintenance, and order processing (see Table 15-1). Proponents of the view that logistics is more of an all-encompassing term cite its closer tie to the customer as well as to the supplier. Their argument is that materials-management in many firms tends to lose its responsibility once the product is manufactured and needs to consider the customer. Regardless of the term used (logistics or materials management), it is important to check the functions and responsibilities of individuals with the title logistics manager or materials manager.

Table 15-1   Logistics Management

Primary Activities	Support Activities
Transportation	Warehousing
Inventory maintenance	Materials handling
Order processing	Protective packaging
	Acquisition
	Product scheduling
	Information maintenance

Source: Ronald H. Ballou, *Basic Business Logistics* (Englewood Cliffs, N.J.: Prentice Hall, 1987), p. 9.

[3]Ernst and Whinney, *Corporate Profitability and Logistics* (Oak Brook, Ill.: Council for Logistics Management, 1987), p. 2.

[4]Ronald H. Ballou, *Basic Business Logistics* (Englewood Cliffs, N.J.: Prentice Hall, 1987) p. 9.

POINTS FOR REVIEW

1. Review some of the generally accepted definitions of materials management.
2. Describe the flow of a *finished-goods order* and that of a *special order* through a materials-management system.
3. Explain the difficulties in arriving at a universal, authoritative definition of materials management.
4. List some of the advantages claimed for materials management that could not be obtained with the conventional purchasing organization.
5. Discuss why materials management is less suitable in some types of companies than in others.
6. Offer a personal opinion on the future of the materials- management concept in industry and its effect on the status of purchasing.
7. Why is the buyer-planner concept gaining in popularity among firms implementing materials management?

16

Purchasing's Responsibility for Inventory: Management Issues

Purchasing's role in inventory management is complex and changing. The overall objective of this role is to ensure that goods arrive in the desired quantity when they are needed. This role becomes complicated by changing customer requirements and demands; thus it requires the involvement of several management functions. For example, if customer X decides she wants a green widget instead of a purple one, then suddenly the demand for green paint has changed. Or when a large-volume customer calls in and requests that his shipment be moved up by two weeks, the need to change suppliers' shipping dates for material becomes apparent. Figure 16-1 shows the requirements and outcomes resulting from inventory management.

Inventories are considered current assets on the balance sheet. However, having too much or the wrong items can increase the cost of doing business, for inventory not only ties up capital but requires physical space to store it. Thus progressive firms have taken steps to safeguard these assets, while minimizing the number of dollars they have tied up in inventory. During the 1980s the just-in-time (JIT) approach to managing inventories gained increasing popularity among U.S. firms. Under a JIT environment, materials arrive at a plant just in time to be incorporated into the production process. A 1989 study indicated that 37 percent of the firms studied had a JIT program in place, while another 44 percent were in the study or pilot phase of JIT implementation.[1] Materials requirements planning (MRP) systems either alone or in tandem with JIT were used to improve inventory-management techniques.

While these newer techniques gained in popularity, many firms still rely on traditional techniques to manage their inventories. Good purchasers will utilize those systems most appropriate for their particular situations, considering the

Figure 16-1 Requirements and Outcomes of Inventory Management

[1]Ernest Raia, "JIT In Purchasing A Progress Report," *Purchasing,* September 14, 1989, pp. 58–59.

resources and personnel available. Regardless of the inventory system, purchasers need to provide suppliers with accurate and timely information about their quantity requirements, with frequent updates, in order to keep inventory and customer priorities satisfied. In this chapter we will discuss management issues that are applicable to inventory.

OBJECTIVES OF INVENTORY

Inventory is carried for a specific purpose, or otherwise it should be eliminated. Inventory is carried to provide uninterrupted operations in the finished-goods and in-process stages and to provide a level of *customer service* at the finished-goods level. Additional reasons for carrying inventory are *price discounts* for large-quantity buys, *protection* against supplier mis-delivery, poor quality, supply shortages, or material that may be scrapped or reworked in process.

A good inventory policy matches the rate of consumption to the amount of stock on hand or on order. Inventory policy will vary depending on the class of item. Where the cost of the material is low relative to the cost of interrupted production, larger inventories may be maintained. For instance, bottle-making requires large amounts of sand, which is inexpensive compared to the cost of shutting down a facility for lack of sand.

Other specific reasons why one carries inventory include:

- *Lot-size inventories.* Purchases are sometimes made in large quantities, larger than that needed for immediate use. Today many purchasers try to reduce quantities to match consumption.
- *Safety stocks.* These are cushions of inventory held to handle unpredicted fluctuations in demand. Purchasers need to minimize the amount of safety stock.
- *Seasonal/anticipation stocks.* These are needed when goods or materials are consumed on a predictable but changing pattern throughout the year, and when it is desirable to absorb some of these changes by building and depleting inventory rather than changing production rates.
- *Transportation inventory.* This type of inventory results from the need to have inventory on hand to handle the lag time before getting the new shipment. More expensive forms of transportation generally tend to take the least amount of time.

COMPANY POLICY AND INVENTORY CONTROL

The investment in material is a matter of financial policy that may outweigh purchasing quantity and cost considerations. Potential purchase savings may have to be sacrificed for the sake of cash flow or conservation of capital.

Thus it is true that buying policies and inventory policies usually go hand in hand, but they are not one the same. They have the common objective of seeking the lowest practicable ultimate cost of purchased materials. But there are occasions when a company's inventory policy determines or modifies buying policy rather than the other way around. For example, in a market where prices of raw materials or purchased parts are stable, inventory policy will dictate the appropriate buying policy. This is one of the reasons for setting up inventory control as a joint responsibility between purchasing and production planning and control. The purchasing department that has the responsibility for materials control in addition to procurement must have this broader viewpoint of the total materials function and be able to adjust both purchasing and inventory policies to attain overall management objectives.

These policies can often lead to conflicts between various functions in arriving at an overall inventory policy.

Functional Conflicts

Marketing people like to see larger inventories, because large inventories make their job easier. They can sell from stock as opposed to quoting a long lead time. Also, until recently manufacturing's desire for long production runs to maximize labor efficiencies produced larger inventories. Purchasing departments were measured on price and therefore bought in large quantities. The net result was that the finance manager, who preferred lower inventory investment, had conflicts with purchasing and other departments whose objectives often led them to argue for larger inventories. The key to resolving such conflicts is the ability to evaluate the total cost of the decision and subsequent profit and customer impact as opposed to traditional functional measures of low price or selling items off the shelf. Rapid changes in technology and customer preference have led marketers and production personnel to realize the need to maintain reasonable inventory policies. In sum then, the overall objective of inventory management is to maintain assurance of supply, at all levels, while maintaining the lowest possible level of inventory.

QUANTITY DETERMINATION AND CONTRACT POLICY

Mathematical determination of most economical order quantities is a useful device, particularly in respect to inventory items in regular use, and is a guide in all quantity decisions, but it does not automatically provide the answer to the problem of deciding on the right quantity to buy. It is not equally applicable to all classifications of purchased items or to all types of requirements. The decision on quantity may be a matter of policy, in which the economical lot size is only one of several factors to be considered. And there are a number of different buying methods, other than purchasing for the replenishment of inventory, especially adaptable to various types of requirements and having a definite bearing on the decision of how much to buy at a time. A complete purchasing program will probably make use of all these methods, according to circumstances and need. The more important of these are the following:

1. *Definite quantity contracts* with predetermined deliveries scheduled over a period of time. This method is particularly adapted to raw materials and components for scheduled operations and assembly, in which quantity requirements and rate of use are reasonably well known in advance. The contract quantity in this case is the total estimated need for the contract period, usually three months or a year, or a base supply to cover the bulk of estimated needs, to be supplemented by open-market purchases as required.

2. *Continuing contract,* similar to the above but without the specific limitations of quantity and duration, so that it has greater flexibility. In a typical arrangement of this sort requirements are projected three months in advance; firm delivery instructions are issued for the first month, and the supplier is authorized to proceed with the manufacture of the second month's quantity at his or her convenience and to procure raw materials for the third month's estimated requirement. The quantity need is reviewed every thirty days and projected as before, so that in effect there is a firm three months' contract in force at all times.

3. *Term or requirements contracts,* for a specified duration of time but not for a fixed quantity, this being subject to the buyer's needs as they develop. The quantity is usually estimated within stated maximum and minimum limits, with deliveries to be ordered and released as required. The method is used when requirements of a material or product are expected to be substantial, but total quantity and the scheduling of use cannot be accurately known in advance. It is particularly useful in connection with materials that are fabricated in two or more stages.

4. *Open-market purchases,* a method indicated when quantity requirements of an item are either small or variable, when market and competitive conditions suggest the advisability of a flexible purchasing condition, when goods are readily available on short notice, when they conform to industry standards, or when special requirements are known sufficiently in advance to permit ordering and delivery time without endangering the continuity of operations.

5. *Group purchase of related items,* usually those that are used in small quantities as individual items but that make up a substantial order and commitment when combined in a single or "blanket" order to one supplier.[2] It can be done either as an open-market purchase or on short- or long-term contracts. It calls for periodic review of stock by related classifications of items or the review of related items whenever a requisition is received for an individual item. A variation of this scheme is a monthly or quarterly contract on the "requirements" basis as outlined in the third case. This might cover a list of mill supplies or small tools, for example. Bids would be invited, either on an item-by-item basis or in the form of a generally applicable discount from list prices. After selecting the most favorable overall proposal, all requirements for these items are passed along to the successful bidder in the form of memorandum orders to be delivered as needed and billed on a single invoice at the end of the month or contract period. The advantages are that small and relatively unattractive "retail" quantities are consolidated into substantial business and that great savings in clerical and accounting procedures accrue to both buyer and seller, because single small transactions are not made the subject of a formal purchase order and are not carried individually through accounting records.

6. *Special purchases,* applicable to nonrepetitive items—equipment purchases, special parts, items that are not regularly carried in stores, materials and supplies for a particular project. The quantity in such cases is, of course, determined by and equal to the specific need. The method of purchase depends on the nature

[2]Systems contracting is another widely used method. See Chapter 5 for further details on blanket orders and systems contracts.

and size of the project. No generalizations can be made for this broad and miscellaneous category; some of the more important aspects, such as the purchase of capital equipment, are discussed separately.

7. *Purchase strictly for requirements,* as indicated by requisitions received. Quantity is dictated by the individual request. This is the least flexible and least desirable of all purchase policies, affording a minimum opportunity for the application of sound purchasing principles and the development of a planned purchasing program. Except insofar as it includes the classification of special purchases outlined in the preceding paragraph, it is held to a minimum whenever a centralized purchasing organization prevails.

INVENTORY CLASSIFICATION

There is no standard system of inventory classification appropriate for all companies, because of variations in material requirements. There are, however, some general principles that apply. In general, the majority of inventories can be classified into the following categories: (1) raw material and components, (2) work in process, (3) finished goods, and (4) supplies. The type of operation/business determines how many categories of inventory are carried by a particular firm (see Table 16-1).

Raw materials and components represent items that will be further converted by the production process. For example, in a printing shop blank paper

Table 16-1 Type of Operation, Inventory Classification

	Inventory Classification			
	Raw Materials and Components	Work in Process	Finished Goods	Operating Supplies and MRO
Type of operation				
Made to order				
Machine shop	X	X		X
Construction firm	X	X		X
Gourmet restaurant	X	X		X
Custom print shop	X	X		X
Custom dress shop	X	X	X	X
Made to stock				
Fast-food restaurant	X	X	X	X
Service station			X	X
Auto-parts distributor			X	X
General-line grocery store			X	X
Deli/specialty shop	X	X	X	X
Hybrid operation				
Made-to-stock and order				
bakery	X	X	X	X
Copy service	X	X	X	X

and inks are raw materials that are used in the reproduction process to create printed documents. Work in process is inventory that has had some value added to it but requires further processing, assembly, and so forth, before it can be converted into a finished good. Finished goods are inventories that are ready for sale to the customer. Supply inventories support the production process but are not part of the finished product. Operating supplies include spare parts for equipment, oil and grease for machinery, and cleaning compounds. Administrative supplies include pens, pencils, computer paper, stationery, calculators, computers, and the like. As can be seen from Table 16-1, all firms have supplies inventory.

The nature of the business operation and the owner's philosophy will dictate the types of inventories carried. For example, a bakery has raw materials (flour, yeast, water, and so on); work in process in the form of items in the oven or doughnuts waiting to be glazed or cakes waiting to be decorated. It also has finished goods available for purchase by customers. If the bakery owner decided to make pies, cakes, and cookies only on customer order, she would have no finished goods in stock.

As value is added to a process, the inventory becomes more costly to carry. Thus our baker would have a more cost-effective inventory strategy by maintaining more inventory in flour and frostings rather than making ten white cakes and ten chocolate cakes and putting them on the shelf.

Looking at another business, the building contractor has no finished-goods inventory, provided all the projects are taken under contract. When the contractor decides to build a home with no immediate buyer in mind, he has finished-goods inventory until the home is sold.

Purchased-Item Classification

For purchased inventory items major divisions are usually set up for production materials (which are incorporated in the end product and are a direct material cost of that product) and nonproduction items (supplies, which are an operating expense). In some companies, depending on organization and policy, there is a third major division of capital expense items. Inventories of materials in process and of finished goods are typically not a purchasing responsibility.

Nonproduction materials are similarly subdivided. Major headings under this category would include fuels, operating supplies, maintenance and repair items, and stationery.

The process of subdivision is continued until there is appropriate classification for every item. If an item is used for both production and nonproduction purposes—for instance, a common bolt that is a component of the end product and is also used in plant maintenance—it is listed only once, under the major use category. If an item is stocked in several different sizes, each size is treated as a separate item under the appropriate subhead.

INVENTORY RECORDS

The basic inventory record is the perpetual inventory. This is a continuing current record of receipts, disbursements or allocation of material, and balance on hand and on order for every item in stock, showing the complete inventory position.

This information originates in the stores department, and the record is typically kept in that department, with some provision being made to transmit it to other departments as needed. In the small purchasing department, which also has the responsibility for stores and stock control, it is common practice to incorporate the inventory record directly onto the purchase-record card.

In the more specialized and completely organized systems of inventory control, computerized records have almost totally replaced manual methods of record keeping. This has not only eliminated many hours of tedious clerical effort and minimized errors of transcription and calculation. It provides a far more useful management tool by making it possible to present more complete information in analytical form, more quickly and at more frequent intervals. One particular system, for example, makes it possible to furnish the purchasing department with a weekly inventory recap that is automatically subtotaled by commodity groups (for example, plumbing supplies, machine parts, work clothing) together with current, cumulative, and past average-usage data, information on open orders and split shipments, and indicated reorder and follow-up action. This is only a part of the information developed in this particular record. It establishes average prices that are used in pricing withdrawals, calculates inventory valuation, accumulates materials costs on specific job orders, and signals job closing for the invoice department. In providing more and better information of this sort, it has eliminated several individual records and forms previously required and has reduced travel and processing time on others.

All perpetual inventory records are periodically checked against actual stock for accuracy, and any discrepancies are adjusted in the record. In the system just described, the current inventory figure is verified by spot checks of selected items in each classification. In all cases good management requires a complete physical inventory at least annually. The current record is accepted as adequate for control and operating purposes. It does not constitute an audit.

Record Accuracy

Inventory-record accuracy is critical to effective inventory control. Most firms take a complete physical inventory semi-annually or annually to adjust the inventory records. Through the course of a year, the book count and physical count become unbalanced. That is because of errors in issuances, receipts, or unauthorized withdrawals. Major adjustments reflect poor control over inventory stock. Accuracy problems can cause shortages, stockouts, and inventory excesses leading to less-than-efficient operations.

Table 16-2 An Approach to Cycle-Count Frequency

Item Class	Percent of Dollars	Items in Group	Counts/Item per Year	Total Counts/Year
A	80	200	4	800
B	15	350	2	700
C	5	1000	1/2	500
		2000/250 work days/year = 8 counts/day		

Rather than waiting every six months or one year to verify accuracy, many firms have undertaken a *cycle-counting program.* Under cycle counting a selected number of inventory items are counted daily. When a discrepancy is found, it is adjusted, but also the cause of the problem is sought. Once the problem is solved, the inventory accuracy should increase. Cycle counting has provided dramatic improvement in inventory accuracy.

Establishing cycle counting requires determination of (1) count frequency; (2) selection of items to be counted; (3) formation of information and error tolerance; and (4) cutoff control. Count frequency is determined by the item. The greater risk of discrepancy, the more frequently the counts should be made. They are often done through ABC analysis, with A items being counted more frequently. Also, it helps to determine the number of counts made in one day.

Items can be selected by starting at the top of the list and counting eight items per day. Note that only half the C accounts are counted in any one year. If items are grouped into specific storage locations, you count at each storage location sequentially. Table 16-2 is an example of this approach.

The cycle-count form should include part number (item) and the unit of measure. It should also include the book quantity, actual quantity, date, person counting, and the reason for error if there is one. Tolerance determines what error rate can be tolerated. Obviously, the goal should be plus or minus zero percent; however, when a counting program is started, more leeway may be allowed. Additionally, certain accounts will require tighter tolerances than others; for example, precious metals versus washers.

Last, cutoff control implies that the counter knows the exact amount of issues and replenishments on the counted items. That is necessary, since cycle counting, unlike physical counting, is performed without shutting down any operations.

Inventory Valuation

Inventory classification schemes must be developed whereby major inventory groups are assigned a master number and each subgroup a subnumber. Receiving and stores are also aided by bar coding and standard containers. These methods facilitate quick item identification and improve count accuracy. Regardless of the identification scheme, valuing of inventory is primarily handled through *average unit cost* set up, *fifo* (first in—first out), or *lifo* (last in—first out) as standard costs.

To use the average cost method, each item is issued out a weighted average cost of the balance on hand. Each time a new shipment is received, a new average unit price is computed.

Under the fifo method the oldest item is priced and issued first. When the oldest item is used up, the next oldest item is charged out. In periods of rising prices the fifo method understates the costs of goods sold but accurately reflects the value of the inventory in stock.

Lifo is just the opposite of fifo in that the issue is priced from the most recent shipment. In periods of rising prices lifo results in higher costs of goods sold and lower profits. Inventory values are understated in terms of replenishment costs.

STORES/RECEIVING OPERATIONS

Bar Coding

Bar codes are defined as a pattern of alternative parallel bars and spaces, representing numbers and other characters that are machine readable.[3] The major advantages to using bar-code technology in storeroom operations are the reduction in error rate and the improved entry speed and count accuracy.

An executive at Lex Electronics declared that their bar-coding system reduced error rates significantly and increased employee productivity: "Bar coding gives us the benefits of reaching a level of technical expertise that's unmatched by other inventory techniques. We've seen a 70 percent reduction in the error rate over the last twelve months."[4]

Previous studies have shown that humans make one character error every three hundred characters, but bar coding reduces the rate to one error every three million characters.[5] This reduction in error rate and increased speed in shown in Figure 16-2.

While the primary interest of purchasers of bar coding is in inventory and receiving, experts have identified five major areas of use.

1. Information management—allows users to track and access information
2. Materials management—inventory is permanently recorded after coding; thus it can be stored anywhere
3. Production control—in production, codes can identify the part and even the person working on it
4. Time recording—replaces conventional time cards and identifies who is in, when, and for how long
5. Asset control—codes placed on equipment allow management of equipment.[6]

[3]"Some Answers to Questions You May Have about Bar Code Technology," Symbol Systems, Pittsburgh, 1989.
[4]Hugh G. Willet, "Bar Coding Boost," *Electronic Buyers' News,* June 12, 1989, p. 24.
[5]Ibid.
[6]Robert D. Franceschini, "Bar Coding: An Important Technology Comes of Age," *Purchasing,* June 21, 1984, pp. 107–9.

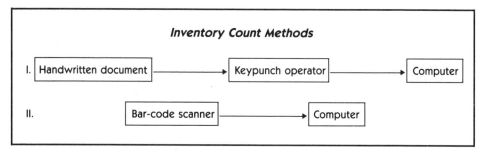

Figure 16-2

Implementing a bar-coding system requires management support, education of personnel, interaction with computer systems, equipment decisions, and feedback/revision. Several equipment-related decisions must be made, including the type of bar-coding equipment; amount of data to encode; printing material; flow of the information; and linkage of scanners, bar coders, and computers.

There are several bar symbologies that have their own specific ways to encode information. Most industries have adopted a standard, or select, code. Three common bar-code symbologies are

Code 39, which is the industry's most popular and widely used, since it is the most versatile. It is used in the health, automotive, and aluminum industries.

Interleaved two of five, which is used by warehouse and distribution functions.

UPC. This bar-code symbology represents only numbers, while the previous two are alphanumeric. It is used by grocery stores and food producers and in vending machines.

Bar-code information has various densities, as shown in Figure 16-3. The density is determined by the size of the package and the scanner used. Currently there are five major types of scanners.

1. Light pens are hand-held devices that emit an infrared light across the bar-code label.
2. Fixed-beam scanners are not portable, and the bar codes must be passed over them. They are less expensive than moving-beam readers.
3. Moving-beam scanners use moving optical beams, usually lasers, which increase reliability but make scanners much more expensive than light pens.
4. The imaging-array, or matrix-array, scanner is a light source that illuminates the bar code, which is then translated by a semiconductor into the bar-code symbol. Such scanners are used where bar-code symbols vary widely in size and printing quality—e.g., supermarkets and large merchandisers like Wal Mart.
5. Hand-held laser guns combine the portability of light pens with the precision of moving-beam laser scanners.[7]

[7]Peter M. Coan, "How to Benefit from Bar Coding," *Inbound Logistics*, July 1986, pp. 29–32.

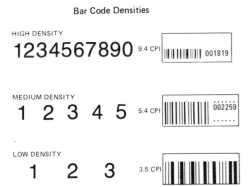

Bar Code Densities

HIGH DENSITY

MEDIUM DENSITY

LOW DENSITY

Figure 16-3   Bar Code Densities
Source: Coan, Peter M, "How to Benefit From Bar Coding," Inbound Logistics, July, 1986, p. 32.

BAR CODE INFORMATION DENSITY AND SCANNING: The characters per inch (CPI)—or density—of information on a bar code is determined by the size of the package and the scanner used. Thus, the denser bar code (top line) is suitable for a small package or product, even though there may be no more information than on the low density code as in 3.5 CPI, while a hand-held light pen is more suitable for reading the high density code.

It appears that purchasers will encounter some form of bar coding in their jobs during the 1990s.

Receiving Operations

Proper and efficient storage and receiving of goods are essential to getting the correct material to the ultimate user. In a manufacturing concern the user is production, and in a retail or wholesale operation the user is the end customer. Effective coordination of stores and receiving with purchasing and inventory control is a necessary operation. Over ordering, excess inventory, and rush orders are often the result of poor receiving and storeroom operations.

Responsibilities   Receiving is the process of identifying, visually inspecting, counting, and recording the receipt of all incoming materials. Proper management is characterized by safe placement, classification, and control of materials. Pilferage, deterioration, obsolescence, and lengthy searches for material are kept to a minimum in a good stores system. This means that carrying costs of inventory associated with deterioration, shelf life, and pilferage are controlled. Direct labor costs are utilized more efficiently if the proper material is provided by a good storeroom system.

Receiving is essentially a clerical operation, but it is an important function in any business. Problem(s) with the purchase transaction or errors should be exposed during the receiving phase. Improper quantities, damaged material, wrong material, and the like, need to be caught prior to getting into the stores. While correcting any problem costs money, the further it gets into the system, the more costly it becomes. Information contained in receiving reports also provides an indication of which suppliers are on schedule and which ones are not providing proper service. Specific steps in the receiving process are

1. Unloading and checking the shipment—checking all of the packages and weights against the carriers' manifest (freight bill). Observation of the crates for external damage should be noted on the bill of lading and freight bill. Otherwise, the carrier is relieved of liability, except for concealed damage.

2. Unpacking and counting the material—checking the supplier's packing slip against the receiving copy of the purchase order. Checks are made for correctness of items and quantities.
3. Recording overages, underages, or damages to the material. Typically, damage report is on a separate form, which is sent to purchasing and accounting departments.
4. Paying or processing freight bills.
5. Filling out the receiving report. (Most often this report is the receiving copy of the purchase order.)
6. Notifying users of material receipt.
7. Marking, labeling, or repackaging.
8. Delivering it to users or placing it in the proper storage location.

Receiving docks contain several types of equipment to improve safety and unloading efficiency. *Dock loaders* are hydraulic or mechanical devices used to adjust the dock to the height of the truck bed. *Truck levelers* lift the truck bed up to the height of the dock. They are expensive but an important item for those who receive fragile/breakable goods. *Shelters* are usually wooden frames around dock areas to surround the truck trailer. *Seals* are large frames made of compressible foam, which form a tight seal around the back of the trailer. Vehicle restraints hold the trailer to the dock by attaching to a bar located on the trailer's bed. *Wheel chocks* or *blocks* are used at docks that are not equipped with restraint bars.

Material Coding and Identification

At a minimum, all businesses need to prepare a stock catalogue listing of all inventoried items. Descriptions should be generic to particular items. For example, a 1" x 20' 1020 grade carbon steel bar and a 2" outside diameter x ⅜" wall could be classified as steel—schedule 40 steel pipe. Also, the groupings in the catalogue should be by similar type items—e.g., steel, fasteners, wood products.

Developing internal codes for parts can be done by (1) arbitrary assignment, (2) numeric or alphanumeric, and (3) drawing or subassembly numbers. Under the arbitrary approach inventory numbers are assigned in sequence as they are added to a store's account. Each inventory item has a separate number, but it bears no relationship to similar items in the account. A ¾" x 2" fastener may have the account number 101 and a ¾" x 2-¼" fastener of the same material may have the account number 202 in this type of system. However, the arbitrary numbering system is easy to set up, and parts can be added quickly. It is a low-cost system and should be used mainly on stores with a small number of items.

The numeric or alphanumeric system is more involved but provides a logical numbering scheme. A typical numbering code might appear as follows:

40
Class of material—resistor
4   3   20
Supplier—AMP
Noun name sequence—400 ohm

An alphanumeric numbering system might include letters as well as numbers.

A third method is the use of drawing numbers or subassemblies. The advantage of this method is that it directly references the technical source for the part. It has the nonsequencing disadvantage of the arbitrary system.

Storeroom Operations

Once a numbering system is established, inventoried items are placed in the storeroom. Material can be stored in two major ways—closed and open. In *closed storerooms* materials are located in a closed or controlled area. An attendant oversees these areas, and issues of material are documents by written release. In *open storerooms* material is stored closest to the position where it will be used or in an open area. Japanese repetitive manufacturers utilize the open system extensively. Their suppliers deliver material to its point of use, thus minimizing inventory, handling, storeroom space, and record keeping. Open-systems storage is also used for bulk items such as tanks of gas, crating lumber, and other bulky items often stored in an open area, either inside or outside the facility.

Storeroom Placement

Once a numbering system is established, it is given a specific location in the storeroom. Stores use a variety of systems, such as racks, pallets, and shelving bins. The key is fitting the item into a proper storage system. Second, good stores minimize the movement of storage into and out of storage in the shortest possible time. General storage guidelines to accomplish the two aforementioned tasks include:

1. Place heavier items close to the floor.
2. If possible, stack heavy items on one another from the floor up.
3. Use bins for small, light items.
4. Place light, bulky items on shelves.
5. Hazardous or odorous items like chemicals should be stored separately and labeled clearly.
6. Items requiring storage at certain temperatures must be stored at those temperatures; otherwise there will be no protection against contamination.

Placement of items in the stores system is often done on the basis of usage. It is desirable to keep the most active items closest to the point of use to minimize handling distance. Another issue related to item location is the utilization of the storage-rack cube. *Fixed location* used in most stores assigns a permanent place for each item. Another approach is to fill the empty space as shipments come into the operation. The *random location* assignment takes full advantage of the cube. The disadvantage of this system is constant renumbering of cube locations and material. Typically, when space permits permanent place assignment is more desirable.

Security

Finally, control over unauthorized issues and potential pilferage needs to be undertaken in effective storerooms. Control can be improved by certain procedures:

1. Use caged closure and tool cribs for valuable equipment, test equipment, precious metals, pharmaceutical supplies, and so forth. Distribute keys to authorized personnel only.
2. Install a checkout system requiring employee's or supervisor's signature.
3. Enclose property with fencing for protection of outside storage.

DISPOSITION OF SURPLUS, SCRAP, AND WASTE

A final objective of stores control is the detection of inactive stock items that increase the inventory investment without contributing any corresponding service or utility. Surplus may arise from any one of many reasons: (1) overrequisitioning, overbuying, or overdeliveries; (2) abandonment of projects or cancelation of sales orders; (3) changes in design or specifications; (4) undetected errors in materials accounting; (5) materials stored in the wrong location and consequently "lost"; and (6) errors in record keeping or breakage.

A distinction needs to be made between surplus, scrap, and waste. *Surplus* has some value. *Scrap and waste* are residues of the production process. The difference is that scrap has resale value—e.g., copper shavings—while waste does not have value—e.g., contaminated oil. Waste disposal requires the purchaser to pay a certified contractor for its disposal.

Particular care must be exercised on hazardous waste or materials. These materials must be properly marked and handled. Improper handling can result in physical damage to employees, citizens, property, and the environment. This material should be separately identified and stored in isolated areas with proper warnings around the area. Additionally, proper disposal of containers and surplus material should be undertaken in conformance with federal and state statutes. In certain states, for instance, Florida, employees must be made aware of any hazardous substances with which they may come into contact.

An alert storeskeeper familiar with his or her stock may notice particular items or lots that are not being called for and may question their place in the inventory. But in dealing with a stock of several thousand items, complete reliance cannot be placed on this chance. A comprehensive system of stores control therefore initiates action, which can be taken in three ways:

1. *Periodic review of stock records* on a systematic basis, taking a specified section each week or month so that the entire list is covered once or twice a year. Items that have not been called for during the past six months or for which the rate of use has fallen off so that stock quantities represent excessive coverage are noted and brought up for analysis and action.

2. *Analysis of physical inventory* at the time the annual inventory is taken. Any material that has actually been in stock a year or more is noted and comes up for review.
3. *Periodic "clean-up" campaigns,* extending beyond the storeroom itself into all departments. They provide for review of materials that have been issued from stores but have not been used for the anticipated purpose, those held in subsidiary stockrooms and tool cribs and thus outside normal stores supervision, and capital items, such as furniture and equipment, that have fallen into disuse or have been replaced by more modern equipment.

Standards can be set to indicate the basis upon which an item should be declared surplus; for example, materials for which there have been no disbursements during the past quarter, quantities in excess of the past six months' requirements, equipment and tools that have not been used during the past year, and materials and supplies in manufacturing departments for which there is no open order.

If there is no reason for holding such items against some future contingency, a decision is made as to the manner of disposition. There are several alternative possibilities:

- Utilization as is, as a substitute for currently standard material or in some other product or model
- Utilization by transfer to another department
- Utilization by chargeout at a percentage discount from standard costs. (An oil company found this method effective in securing acceptance of outmoded models of pumps and other service-station equipment by station managers whose compensation was calculated on the ratio of sales to investment and costs.)
- Utilization by remanufacture
- Return to original manufacturer
- Sale as surplus material
- Sale as scrap

The last three methods of disposal generally come under the jurisdiction of the purchasing department. Whatever disposition is made, it serves to convert a continuing liability into an asset, reduce the investment in stores, maintain a clean inventory, and increase turnover by eliminating inactive items.

POINTS FOR REVIEW

1. Describe the relative roles of top management and the purchasing department in the formulation of inventory policy.
2. Explain how to classify inventory items.
3. Discuss the importance of bar coding.
4. Describe three methods used in a system of stores control designed to prevent accumulation of inactive stock items.
5. Name the methods used in purchasing, by policy, for ordering in quantity.
6. List the ways surplus waste and scrap material and equipment may be disposed of.

17

Purchasing's Responsibility for Inventory: Systems and Techniques

In the last chapter issues pertaining to managing inventory were discussed. This chapter will describe various systems and techniques used to assist management in controlling inventories. The discussion will focus on

1. Identifying costs of carrying inventory, the priority system of ABC analysis, and inventory turnover
2. Utilizing economic order quantity, quantity discounts, and reorder point systems
3. Understanding material requirements planning and just-in-time systems

INVENTORY CARRYING COSTS

Inventory Holding Costs

A major reason for minimizing inventory is that it costs money to hold inventory. It is not unusual to attach a holding cost of 20 to 30 percent to the annual dollar value of the inventory. This means that if a purchaser carries an average of $50,000 in inventory during a given year, the cost to hold this inventory is from $10,000 to $15,000 ($50,000 × 20% to 30%). Holding costs include all expenses incurred by a company because of inventory. These costs consist of interest costs, taxes, insurance, obsolescence, deterioration, storage, and handling charges.

Let's look at each of these elements. *Interest or capital costs* are those monies in inventory that could be invested elsewhere or that in many cases represent the cost of borrowing funds. *Taxes* include any state, city, or county taxes on inventory. Inventories are assets and must be covered by *insurance* policies much like the policies carried for individual homes and their contents. *Obsolescence* refers to inventory, which is no longer desirable owing to customer preferences or design changes. *Deterioration* occurs with a product when the shelf life expires, the dates of sale expire, or the product spoils. If any of these occur, the product must be discarded; thus expense is incurred. *Shrinkage* occurs when inventory is lost, stolen, or otherwise misplaced. Annual inventory counts usually result in adjustments of book figures to actual. *Storage and handling charges* directly relate to the space used to store the inventory and to the personnel time used to track records of inventory, move material, and so forth. Calculating inventory holding costs for a particular operation can be accomplished by obtaining these figures. They represent total inventory costs, which when divided by total purchased expenditures will produce an inventory cost percentage. Finance officers are often useful resource persons from whom much of these data can be obtained.

Information on average inventory carrying cost is more generally available in most accounting systems. As applied to individual items, there will be a wide range of actual carrying costs owing to differences in the physical bulk of various items, the type of storage facilities and protection needed, rates of depreciation, and so on. It would be excessively difficult and would serve no useful purpose to calculate a specific carrying cost for each individual item. But instead of taking one average cost figure of, say, 25 percent on total inventory, it is quite feasible to classify the commodities into three or four groups having similar storage characteristics and to assign an average carrying cost to each group. This cost might range from as little as 10 percent up to 50 percent or more. Applying the appropriate group figure obviously gives added accuracy and value to the calculations requiring carrying costs.

ABC ANALYSIS

ABC analysis is an inventory classification technique in which the items in inventory are classified according to dollar volume (value) generated in annual sales. In inventory, as in many other situations, a small number of items account for a relatively large proportion of annual dollar volume. As a general guideline, *A* items include 10 to 20 percent of all items and account for 50 to 60 percent of the total dollar volume. *B* items include 30 to 40 percent of all items and account for 30 to 40 percent of the dollar volume. The remaining *C* items account for 40 to 50 percent of all of the items, but only for 5 to 10 percent of the total dollar value (see Figure 17-1).

Finding out where the inventory dollars are tied up is important. Perhaps the best way to perform such a task is this *ABC* analysis. To perform such an analysis,

1. Make a list of all the inventory items and determine the dollar value by multiplying unit costs times the number of units sold.
2. Rank the items according to annual dollar expenditures, ranking the highest to the lowest.
3. Calculate the percentage of the total dollar expenditure for each item.
4. Rate the items as *A*, *B*, or *C*. Remember, *A* items as the few top-dollar items that account for most of the dollars spent. *B* items are the middle group and account for a significant number of dollars spent. *C* items are large in volume but small in total dollar expenditure. Figure 17-2 shows a rundown of the analysis.

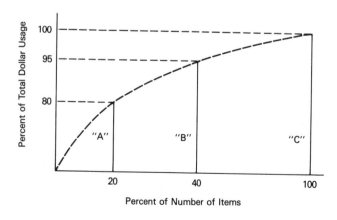

Figure 17-1 ABC Analysis Shown Graphically

Commonly Accepted Measures of Inventory Turnover

$$\frac{\text{Sales}}{\text{Average inventory}} \qquad\qquad \frac{\text{Cost of goods sold}}{\text{Average inventory}}$$

$$\frac{\text{Annual purchase dollar expenditure}}{\text{Average inventory}}$$

$$\frac{\text{52 weeks per year}}{\text{Turnover}} = \text{Week's supply}$$

Figure 17-2

ABC analysis allows one to direct priorities for inventory control. Higher turnover goals should be established for *A* and *B* items than for *C* items. This concept recognizes that each item of inventory is critical and could halt production or sales to a customer. A *C* parts shortage can shut down a line as easily as an *A* parts shortage. The categorization enables one to prioritize control on *A* and *B* items, since higher safety stocks are kept on *C* items.

Typical rules of an *ABC* categorization might state:

A items:	Close control
	Frequent check of schedule revisions
	Little or zero safety stock
	High turnover goals—twelve to twenty-four times annually
B items:	Moderate control
	Check on demand changes
	Moderate safety stock
	High turnover goals—six to fifteen times annually
C items:	Looser control
	Visual check or two-bin system
	Large safety stock
	Low turnover goals—one to five times annually

Inventory Turnover

Inventory turnover is a measure of the velocity at which inventory moves through a particular system. Generally, the higher the turnover, the less inventory one maintains in stock. Turnover in the above case was defined as the annual dollar usage divided by the average dollars in inventory. For example, 300,000 units of annual usage with an average inventory of 30,000 units yields a turnover rate of $300,000/30,000 = 10$. Other commonly used measures of inventory turnover include sales divided by average inventory and cost of goods sold divided by average inventory. Still other firms measure inventory in terms of weeks' supply or days' supply (see Figure 17-2).

ORDER QUANTITY

One of the major questions answered by any inventory system is, How much to buy? Our friendly salesperson likes to sell us a truckload and tell us what a great price we will receive. In certain instances, as for a large promotion on a new item or on a high-usage item, the large quantity may be desirable.

Because quantity is a mathematical figure, there have been many attempts to develop a formula for determining the most economical ordering quantity. Besides the basic need, there are many factors to be taken into consideration—unit cost of the item in various lot sizes, the average inventory resulting from purchases in different quantities, the number of orders issued, cost of negotiating and issuing a purchasing order, and cost of carrying materials in inventory.

A number of practical working formulae have been developed, based on the known factors. The problem can be worked out to determine economic ordering quantity in terms of the number of units per order, the dollar value that this represents, or the number of weeks of coverage at a given rate of use. All of these methods are equally serviceable, because they are merely different ways of expressing the same quantity, and the answers can readily be translated into either of the other two units of measurement, as desired. One such formula that has gained wide acceptance and has proven its effectiveness as a purchasing guide is termed the *economic order quantity.*

Economic Order Quantity (EOQ)

Economic order quantity (EOQ) has been in use for years and is essentially the balance point between acquisition (purchase order) costs and carrying costs. Figure 17-3 shows that carrying costs (holding costs) increase as the quantity of items purchased increases. Meanwhile, the larger the order, the lower the order costs (as fewer orders need to be placed). The balance point represents the point where the sum of the two costs are minimized.

The EOQ formula is represented as follows:

$$EOQ = \sqrt{\frac{2 \text{ x annual usage x order cost}}{\text{unit cost x carrying cost}}}$$

or in abbreviated form,

$$EOQ = \sqrt{\frac{2dB}{cI}}$$

where EOQ = economic ordering quantity
d = annual usage in units
B = order cost in dollars
c = unit cost in dollars
I = carrying cost as a percentage of inventory value

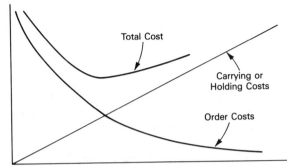

Figure 17-3 Economic Order Quantity

As an example, consider a situation in which the cost of placing an order is $50, the cost of carrying is 30 percent of the cost of the material, yearly usage is 12,000 pieces, and the unit cost is $.10 per item. The economic order quantity, based on the formula, would then be

$$EOQ = \sqrt{\frac{2 \times 12,000 \times 50}{.10 \times .30}}$$

$$= \quad 6,324 \text{ pieces}$$

Remember that carrying cost is expressed as a percentage, not in dollars.

Once the factors of order cost and inventory cost have been determined for any given company operation, the determination of optimum ordering quantity is directly related to a single variable, the total annual usage of the item under consideration.

To give meaning to the formula it is essential, of course, to have reasonably accurate values for the two cost factors. Relatively few companies have detailed information on purchase-order cost. In lieu of an elaborate cost analysis, a satisfactory working value can be found by taking the total cost of operating the purchasing department, including all salaries, expenses, and overhead charges, on an annual basis, and dividing this by the number of purchase orders issued during the year. Ordering costs will, of course, change from company to company and during various phases of the business cycle. As a starting point, many firms today apply an order cost of $50 to $75. Inventory carrying costs (as previously discussed) would be most accurate if applied by category; however, in practice most firms apply one average to all purchased items.

Certain prerequisites underlie the use of EOQ, such as relatively stable usage, fairly constant price, and supply that is not influenced by seasonal factors. It is only in unusual cases that the ordering quantity formula is calculated for each individual order. Once the optimum quantity is established for an item, it is valid until there is some change in one of the variable values—annual usage, carrying cost, or cost of ordering. The appropriate quantity is therefore noted on the purchase order for each item, along with maximum and minimum stock quantities and ordering point, so that the information is immediately available by direct reference when the item is to be reordered.

Limitations of EOQ

The limitations of this kind of formula are readily apparent. Most important is that it does not take into consideration changes in the unit price of the material or product. A change in unit price changes the value of (A) annual usage, in dollars, and consequently changes the economic ordering quantity. This can be adjusted by inserting the revised value in the formula and making a new calculation. But this adjustment does not take care of the more significant fact that the direction of current price trends and the anticipation of price changes may actually be determining influences in purchasing policy regarding the quantity to be bought at any given time. Certainly, they would tend to modify any decisions predicated on a stable price situation. Similarly, the formula does not (except through a recalculation, as in the case of a price change) reflect the price advantages of volume buying and quantity discount schedules.

Even supposing that the price factor is stable and that the formula produces a precise theoretical determination of the most economic ordering quantity, it is quite likely that the resulting figure will have to be adjusted somewhat arbitrarily to bring it into conformity with commercial practice in respect to unit packages, established quantity discount brackets, economic manufacturing quantities, full carload or truckload quantities, and so on. This is somewhat analogous to the classic gibe at engineering practice that calculates a structural strain to three or four decimal places and then adds a 50 percent safety factor.

There are other limitations in which specific materials are concerned. Any formula must be interpreted and applied with common sense, and the ordering quantity formula is no exception. For example, no matter what the formula says, bulky materials like the excelsior, cartons, and filler materials used in the paper and leather industries must be ordered with available storage space in mind, because space may effectively limit the quantity that can be handled. Nor is it sensible to order materials that are subject to deterioration in such quantities that the supply will exceed the shelf life of the material. Portland cement, batteries, photographic paper and film, cellulose tape, and enameled wire are examples of items on which such caution must be exercised.

Benefits of EOQ

Despite the limitations, the mathematical approach has gained widespread acceptance and usage, for sound policy reasons and because of the savings and benefits it produces when used properly and consistently.

It has already been noted that the decision on best quantity is quite a complicated one if all the pertinent factors are considered, and the list of purchased commodities typically runs up to thousands of items. Without some sort of approved mathematical procedure to simplify the calculations, an excessive amount of time and effort may be expended on this one aspect of the purchase for the larger and more significant items, whereas scant attention may be given to any accurate determination of best quantity for the great majority of items on the list. There will be a tendency to rely on other, less scientific standards of quantity, such as mere precedent. Experienced buyers may make a quick, intuitive appraisal of the factors and come fairly close to the right answer most of the time. The improved performance that results from using mathematical methods suggests that intuition is far from reliable when ordering quantities are concerned.

The ordering quantity formula substitutes fact for judgment. It establishes a definite relationship between the significant variables in the situation and eliminates the variable of personal judgment, so that quantity decisions are consistent and are in accord with policy. It can be used on computers or converted into tabular form for direct reference. Thus the scientific method can be applied to every item on the list with a minimum of effort.

For the great majority of stores and supply items the mathematical method can be relied on completely. The buyer is relieved of all responsibility on this score and is assured of having made correct decisions, which are reflected in superior performance. For example, the purchasing department of the Bell Telephone Laboratories, as early as 1940, devised a series of conversion factors based on the formula that made it possible to reduce inventories automatically by 28.5 to 42.0 percent of dollar value while supporting the same volume of requisitions and maintaining a superior standard of service, as compared with the situation in which stock control, ordering point, and order quantity were based on the judgment and decisions of experienced stockkeepers and buyers. Thus the often neglected area of operating supplies and standard parts, representing a great number of different items that must be purchased and stocked, sometimes in relatively small amounts but in substantial total volume, is readily brought under scientific purchasing control.

For production materials and other items in which the final determination of ordering quantity involves a consideration of price trends, seasonal factors, advance coverage, or other elements not provided for in the mathematical calculation, the formula nevertheless furnishes a useful starting point. Under stable conditions it may be directly applied. In any case the necessary modifications may be made more intelligently, and with a clearer understanding of costs entailed, than if there were no basic standard of optimum quantity.

In addition to these uses in quantity decisions, the formulas have established some important and hitherto unrecognized principles of costs and cost relationships in respect to inventory control, which is inseparable from the problem of how much to buy. Among these are the following:

1. Total cost is at a minimum at the point at which ordering cost is equal to carrying cost for a given quantity.
2. Within reasonable variation of order size (plus or minus 20 percent), the total cost varies very little; beyond these limits total cost goes up rapidly either way.
3. Ordering too little usually costs much more than ordering too much.
4. A change in the cost of carrying stock has a much greater effect on the most economical order size than does a change in the cost of restocking. (Mathematically

speaking, optimum size of order varies in inverse proportion to the carrying cost and in direct proportion to the square root of the reorder cost.)

Quantity Discounts

Most price schedules provide for quantity discounts. Quantity discounts are conventionally quoted in terms of price breaks or brackets. Quantity discounts are presumed to reflect demonstrable differences in the cost of manufacturing or handling rather than the purchaser's economic power. "Cheaper by the dozen" pricing is a common practice in industrial distribution as well as in retailing, and the price differentials may be substantial and alluring. If the optimum quantity indicated by formula comes close to the point of such a price "break" or bracket, common sense would dictate adjusting the quantity purchased so as to take advantage of this extra saving. But if the formula does not actually give the answer to this problem, it does suggest that the lower unit cost must be balanced against the extra investment and the extra cost of carrying inventory over a longer period, to determine whether the lower unit cost thus earned represents a real saving to the purchaser.

When facing a price schedule, the purchaser must first calculate the EOQ for each price and then analyze the total acquisition costs. Figure 17-4 shows a typical price-break schedule. Calculating the EOQ at the price break shows quantities of 167–69, which puts the purchaser at $15 per unit. Next an evaluation of the total cost must be made. The total cost formula includes the annual purchase cost, inventory carrying cost, and ordering cost. Using these formulae, we find our total cost is lowest when buying in a quantity of 201 and paying $14.75 per unit. One must consider, however, that the buyer may not have sufficient space to store 34 more items.

Quantity Discount Worksheet

Each case of quantity discount must be individually considered. A simple mathematical approach for determining the return, or "profit," on the larger quantity purchased is shown in worksheet form in Figure 17-5.

Here is an example of how to use the worksheet. Consider a tubular item priced at $42.20 per 100 feet in small lots and at $33.60 in lots of 1,000 feet or more. It is used at a rate of about 150 feet per month and is generally requisitioned in lots of 500 feet, or about three month's supply. Problem: to determine whether it would be more economical to buy nearly seven months' supply at the lower price. The applicable inventory carrying rate is 12 percent per year, or 1 percent per month. Freight charges amount to $4.00 on a shipment of 500 feet and $7.50 on a shipment of 1,000 feet.

Following the calculations on the worksheet, we find:

1. Total cost of an order for 500 feet is $215.00.
2. Total cost of an order for 1,000 feet is $343.50.
3. Additional investment entailed by ordering 1,000 feet at one time is $128.50.

Calculating EOQ and Total Costs from a Price Schedule

Price Schedule

Quantity	Price/Unit
0–200	$15.00
201–400	$14.75
401–1000	$14.60

Other data: Carrying cost—24%
Order cost—$50
Annual demand—1,000 units

$$\text{EOQ} \,(\$15) = \sqrt{\frac{2 \times 1000 \times 50}{.24 \times 15}} = 167$$

$$\text{EOQ} \,(\$14.75) = \sqrt{\frac{2 \times 1000 \times 50}{.24 \times 14.75}} = 168$$

$$\text{EOQ} \,(\$14.60) = \sqrt{\frac{2 \times 1000 \times 50}{.24 \times 14.60}} = 169$$

EOQ at the $14.75 and $14.60 prices are unfeasible, since the quantities of 168 and 169 bring a price per unit of $15.00, owing to the price schedule. Therefore, look at the total cost (TC).
TC = annual purchase cost + annual inventory cost + annual ordering cost
= demand × unit price + order quantity/2 × carrying cost × unit price + demand/order quantity × cost/order
TC (15) = (1000)(15) + (167/2)(.24)(15) + (1000/167)(50) = $15,600
TC (14.75) = (1000)(14.75) + (201/2)(.24)(14.75) + (1000/201)(50)
= $15,354
TC (14.60) = (1000)(14.60) + (401/2)(.24)(14.60) + (1000/401)(50)
= $15,412

Figure 17-4

4. Total cost of 1,000 feet, ordered in two lots of 500 feet, is $430.00.
5. Cost saving on 1,000 feet, ordered at one time, is $86.50.
6. Additional period for which the additional investment must be carried is (approximately) four months.
7. Additional inventory carrying cost is $5.30, making the total cost of additional investment $137.80.
8. Cost saving (5) divided by total cost of additional investment (7) represents a return of nearly 65 percent on the additional investment over a seven-month period.

Because this return is many times greater than the normal return on investment, it would probably be advisable in this case to buy the larger quantity and take advantage of the price discount. There may be other considerations, such as

QUANTITY DISCOUNT ADVANTAGE WORKSHEET

TPFC 1135

MATERIAL	DIVISION	DATE

VENDOR	ADDRESS

1. COST TO BUY REQUISITIONED (SMALLER) QUANTITY NOW:	2. COST TO BUY RECOMMENDED (LARGER) QUANTITY NOW:
SMALLER QUANTITY	LARGER QUANTITY ....
TIMES: UNIT PRICE ....PER............	TIMES: UNIT PRICE ....PER............
EQUALS: COST OF GOODS	EQUALS: COST OF GOODS ....
PLUS: FREIGHT	PLUS: FREIGHT ....
EQUALS: TOTAL COST	EQUALS: TOTAL COST

3. ADDITIONAL INVESTMENT REQUIRED TO PURCHASE LARGER QUANTITY NOW:	4. ULTIMATE COST TO BUY LARGER QUANTITY, BY MEANS OF SMALLER QUANTITY RE ORDERS:
TOTAL COST FROM 2 ABOVE	QUANTITY (FROM 2 ABOVE) ....
MINUS: TOTAL COST FROM 1 ABOVE	TIMES: UNIT PRICE (FROM 1 ABOVE) ....PER............
EQUALS: ADDITIONAL INVESTMENT	EQUALS: ULTIMATE COST ....
	PLUS: FREIGHT (EST. FROM 1 ABOVE) ....
	EQUALS: TOTAL ULTIMATE COST

5. SAVINGS WHICH WOULD RESULT FROM BUYING LARGER QUANTITY NOW:	6. PERIOD OF ADDITIONAL INVESTMENT:
ULTIMATE COST TO BUY LARGER (RECOMMENDED) QTY. (FROM 4 ABOVE)	LARGER (RECOMMENDED) QTY.= ....MOS. SUPPLY
MINUS COST TO BUY SAME QUANTITY NOW (FROM 2 ABOVE)	LESS: SMALLER (REQ'ND.) QTY.= ....MOS. SUPPLY
	EQUALS: MONTHS ADDITIONAL INVESTMENT MUST BE CARRIED MONTHS

7. COST OF CARRYING INVENTORY IF LARGER QUANTITY IS PURCHASED NOW:	8. RATE OF RETURN ON INVESTMENT:
ADDITIONAL INVESTMENT (FROM 3 ABOVE) X.01 (CARRYING COST PER MO' 1% OF INV.),.......................... TIMES: MOS. ADDITIONAL INVESTMENT MUST BE CARRIED (FROM 6 ABOVE)	DIVIDE TOTAL SAVINGS (FROM 5 ABOVE) $ BY TOTAL COST OF ADDITIONAL INVESTMENT (FROM 7, AT LEFT)
EQUALS: CARRYING COST OF INV.	EQUALS: O _____ EQUALS _____ % RATE OF RETURN ON
PLUS: ADD. INVESTMENT (FROM 3 ABOVE)	INVESTMENT
TOTAL COST OF ADDITIONAL INVESTMENT	

THE PERCENTAGE FIGURE DEVELOPED IN BLOCK 8 IS THE RATE OF RETURN ON THE EXTRA INVESTMENT REQUIRED TO PURCHASE THE RECOMMENDED LARGER QUANTITY NOW. IT SHOULD BE COMPARED WITH THE PREVAILING RATE OF RETURN ON INVESTMENT IN THE DIVISION CONCERNED, TO DETERMINE THE ADVISABILITY OF PURCHASING THE LARGER (RECOMMENDED) QUANTITY.

PREPARED BY_____

Figure 17-5   Worksheet for calculating quantity discount advantage

maintaining inventory balance, or greater fluidity of assets, or conserving working capital for other essential purposes in the business. It is part of the purchasing responsibility, however, to determine the most economical buying policies and follow them, consistent with its authority and budget.

ORDER TIMING

Having determined the quantity, we need to establish *when to order*. Ordering too early results in extra inventory, while delaying an order can mean a stockout.

The reorder point (ROP) provides information about when to order. ROP systems trigger a new order when the stock on hand plus the stock on order falls below a certain point. The reorder point is usually calculated by multiplying *average demand* by the *lead time*. For example, let's look at a company that uses 500 batteries per year (usage is uniform) and works 250 days per year. The supplier lead time is 20 days, and the firm's order quantity is 100. As shown in Figure 17-6, under the assumption that there is no safety stock, the reorder point in 40 (20 days lead time x 2 batteries per day usage). If the lead time or usage changes, the reorder point will be adjusted. For example, the supplier calls and indicates that the lead time has moved to 30 days. The reorder point also moves to 60 (30 days x 2 batteries/day usage).

Two other popular inventory policies can also trigger reorder points: a min/max setup and the two-bin system. The first establishes definite minimum and maximum levels for inventory accounts. Minimum points will trigger a purchase order regardless of the reorder point. Maximum levels are set as a check against overzealous purchasing for a short-term price savings. Unless supply is threatened, the maximum level is not to be exceeded.

The second technique, the *two-bin system,* provides visual review for small-dollar items. Stock is kept in two separate bins. The second bin contains enough stock to cover demand over the lead time of the replenishment order. Once the first bin is empty and the material in the second bin is in use, an order is placed for a replacement of the first bin.

Periodic Replenishment

All of the order-timing methods previously discussed are termed *fixed-order quantity* models in that the quantity reordered is usually fixed; however, the time between replenishment varies. Certain items may be better controlled by periodic checks on their inventory level. This type of reorder system is called a *fixed-order period* and is characterized by a constant time period between reviews. Once a review of stock on hand is made, a decision to reorder is made, to bring stock back to a predetermined level. Purchasers operating under fixed-order-period models will see variable quantities from order to order.

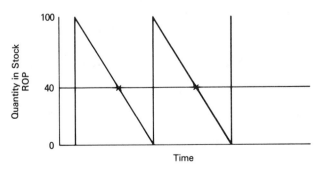

Figure 17-6 Illustration of Reorder Point

SIZE OF SAFETY STOCK

As discussed in the previous chapter, safety stock represents inventory held for emergency requirements. Keeping safety stock to a minimum without disrupting production or service is important. Typically, firms add a layer of safety stock in their parts inventory to cover demand increases, supplier delivery delays, or quality problems. The level of safety stock should be reviewed for each item or categories of items. The lower the safety stock levels are, the less money is tied up in inventories.

Safety stock levels are established by reviewing the lead-time variation and the demand variation. An estimate of criticalness of the item is made, and the amount of safety stock is calculated. Each firm determines safety stock differently; many companies operate on "gut feelings." Safety stock is best established on an account-by-account basis.

Additional questions that should be explored when establishing safety stocks include:

- What was the number of stockouts experienced this past year? If there were few, safety stock could be reduced; and if there were many, then better planning or increased stock levels may be necessary.
- How can a purchaser plan and communicate better with suppliers? Improved planning and communication can result in short lead times and more reliable deliveries.
- What is the total dollar level of safety stock carried in inventory?
- When can we remove safety stocks from well-managed, stable usage accounts and from accounts where stockouts do not create problems?
- Based on a review of past history, what was the reason for stockouts? Was it increased demand or supplier error, or a problem of not ordering soon enough?
- Are safety-stock levels reviewed at least annually?

Probablistic Approach to Safety Stock

A policy based on probability implies the calculated risk of stockouts, which inventory control specifically seeks to avoid. This risk is kept low by having safety, or reserve, stocks. The lack of even a small item—a certain type of fastener, for example—can halt production just as quickly as the lack of a heavy stamping. So it becomes more important to have safety stocks for items controlled by formula than for the larger items that are under continuous individual attention.

Determining the proper size of the reserve stocks is a basic problem. If too large, they represent a wasteful expense and can be a serious item. Although safety stocks may represent a relatively small percentage of the total value that passes through inventory over the course of a year, they can amount to 60 percent or more of inventory content at any given time, which is the basis of inventory carrying cost. On the other hand, too-small safety stocks defeat the purpose.

The first step, then, is to determine the degree of protection desired, that is, not to exceed one stockout in two years, five years, and so forth. From this starting point, the calculation of necessary reserve stocks is a rather complicated statistical process. The number of demands per month, over a period of a year, is plotted on a Poisson distribution curve to establish a frequency-of-occurrence ratio, and from this an inverse accumulation ratio is calculated (see Figure 17-7). In this example, with an average, or expectation, of three demands per month, the inverse accumulation ratio table shows that 0.034 of the area of the curve (shaded area) lies to the right, or above six demands per month. This means that, 96.6 percent of the time, the number of demands will be six or less, and 3.4 percent of the time there will be six demands or more. Assuming a restocking period of one month, then, to limit the chances of a stockout's occurring more than 3.4 times in 100, the time to place a restocking order is when the stock balance reaches the equivalent of six demands, and the safety stock would also have to be six demands' worth, or three in addition to the expected three demands during the restocking period.

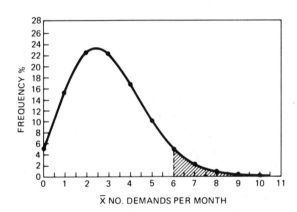

Frequency of Occurrences of Poisson Dist.
X = 3

No.	Frequency of Occurrence Ratio	Ratio (Inverse Accumulation)
0	.049	.951
1	.149	.801
2	.224	.577
3	.224	.353
4	.168	.185
5	.101	.084
6	.050	.034
7	.022	.012
8	.008	.004
9	.003	.002
10	.001	.001
∞	∞	∞

Figure 17-7 Poisson distribution curve for determining safety stock requirements

MATERIAL REQUIREMENTS PLANNING (MRP)

Material requirements planning (MRP) is a management technique that goes beyond the traditional bases for determining quantity requirements discussed earlier. Thus it directly affects purchasing schedules. In an MRP system the (dependent) demand for components of a manufactured product depends on the forecasted (independent) demand for the finished product. Thus demand for components is calculable based on demand for the end product. If we forecast selling 1,000 wagons, we need 4,000 wheels, 1,000 bodies, 2,000 axles, and so forth.

Although statistical methods of inventory control—economic order quantities, safety stock, and reorder points—were part of early MRP methods, they are generally considered invalid by proponents of the more sophisticated MRP techniques that have been developed. The basic difference between the statistical methods and the MRP method of controlling inventory is that the former assumes relatively uniform usage of components and gradual depletion of inventory.

Proponents of MRP point out that no such assumption can be made about dependent demand components of assembled products. Inventory tends to be "lumpy," with periods of heavy demand alternating with periods of almost no demand, because end products are usually made in lot sizes to keep setup costs down rather than in a perfectly continuous flow. If order points (which are based on averages and assume a uniform demand for dependent components) are used to replenish inventory independent of the timing of end-product fabrication, the results can be either severe shortages or overloaded inventories.

If, for example, a dependent demand item (say, a small-horsepower motor) that is bought according to traditional statistical inventory methods is required in two or more end items (a variety of home appliances) simultaneously, a shortage can occur, and frantic expediting in purchasing will be necessary. What is perhaps a more prevalent problem in companies that use the traditional order point system is unnecessarily high inventories, with consequent higher costs.

The MRP process begins with the production plan (a statement of production in aggregate units). This plan is then broken into a master production schedule (see Figure 17-8), which is basically a detailed statement of requirements for end items, by date (planning period) and quantity. End items are generally finished products, but they can also be major assemblies or parts used at the highest level in the product structure (e.g., replacement or service parts for the end product). Levels refer to the complexity of the product. The end item is a level O; and subassemblies, level 1; components are at lower levels (see Figure 17-9).

The next step is to explode manufacturing *bills of materials,* which list all components, including subassemblies, finished parts, raw materials and purchased parts that go into a given product or end item, and the amount of each required in each unit of that item. The *gross quantity required* in each time period, less the projected on-hand and on-order quantities, is the *net quantity* that is required and is to be ordered at that time. In calculating net requirements, the computer takes into consideration common usage of components in multiple

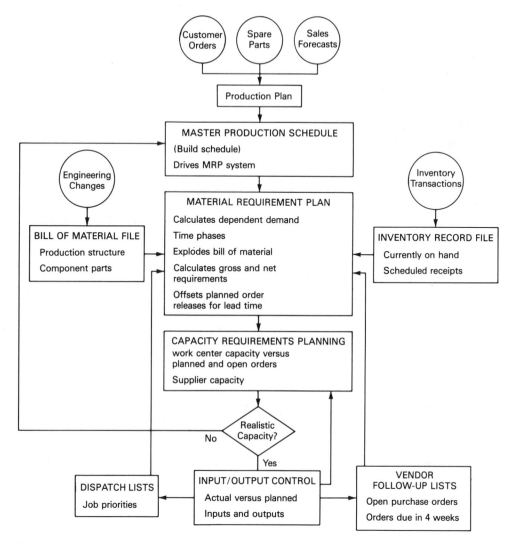

Figure 17-8 Flow chart for a model material requirements planning system
Source: *McGraw-Hill Yearbook of Science and Technology, 1982/83,* Sybil P. Parker, ed. (New York: McGraw-Hill Book Co., 198), p. 508.

products, changes to bills of materials, manufacturing and purchasing lead times, and order status. The requirements provide input not only to inventory planning and control but to capacity requirements planning and shop floor control. Orders are then offset for lead time—i.e., they are moved back in time to determine when they need to be ordered.

In brief, MRP produces "planned orders" that tell inventory planning and control what and how much to order, when to order, and when to schedule delivery; capacity requirements planning determines capacities which will be required by work center, each period, to meet the production plan; and the shop floor con-

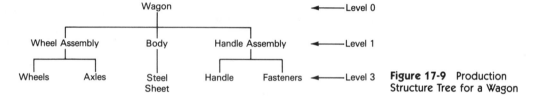

Figure 17-9 Production Structure Tree for a Wagon

trol module ranks the priorities of the orders in the shop allowing for improved efficiency of material and labor.

Basic Steps in MRP

Fundamentally, material requirements planning is a precise refinement and formalization of basic management techniques that have been used in manufacturing planning for many years. To quote the American Production and Inventory Control Society's MRP training aid:

> The techniques of MRP are not difficult or new. In fact, many of the techniques seem, on inspection, so simple that one might wonder why all manufacturing companies haven't always used them. The problem lies in the fact that the application of MRP rules to thousands of inventory items was not feasible until the computer was introduced into the manufacturing systems area.... The main function of an effective manufacturing control system is to have the right materials, in the correct quantities, available at the right time to meet the demand for the company's finished products. The objective of MRP is to determine requirements accurately and quickly to enhance management's control over the complete manufacturing process. It does this by calculating the components needed to meet the master production schedule. On the basis of production and procurement lead times, the MRP system calculates the time periods in which these components must be available. Traditional inventory management approaches could not go beyond the limits imposed by the information processing tool available at the time. With the introduction of the commercial computer with its ability to store data, manipulate it, and produce information at speeds previously unimaginable, industry now had a tool that could respond to our dynamic business environment.

Following are some of the key concepts and terms of MRP:

Dependent demand—that demand quantities for all but the O level (end item) are calculated.

Bill of materials—forms the basis for calculating gross requirements of dependent demand items.

Gross-to-net requirements—inventory on hand is deducted from gross requirements to arrive at net.

Time phasing—takes the net requirements and moves them back in the time horizon by the appropriate lead time. If the MRP shows an item will be required in week six and it has a four-week lead time, then an order needs to be placed in week two.

Product structure tree—represents a schematic diagram of the production process making the end item.

MRP II

During the 1980s MRP was extended to include business and financial-planning data. For in the 1970s MRP had been primarily a stand-alone system used by planners at the operational level. MRP systems incorporating these additional planning data are called MRP II, manufacturing resource planning, or closed-loop MRP. The new systems have the effect of extending the MRP scheduling into all major functions of the firm. The dictionary of the American Production and Inventory Control Society (APICS) defines MRP II as "the method for the effective planning of all the resources of the manufacturing company."[1] With MRP's increased scheduling accuracy, companies realized they could use these numbers in their business and financial plans. There was no longer a need for two sets of numbers, since executives could now use MRP numbers in developing business plans, cash-flow reports, inventory projections, production volumes, and sales-mix decisions. All key functional groups are tied into the planning cycle through the MRP II system. For example, marketing can use data from the master production schedule to promise customer orders. If engineering drawings are not completed on time or are changed, a schedule delay will be visible throughout the organization.

MRP II systems are applicable to all sizes of firms, including those with sales of less than $1 million. One source estimates that software prices range from $500 to $300,000. Hardware prices also vary; however, most MRP II systems are run on minicomputers or mainframes.[2] Computer advances have allowed MRP II to function effectively by manipulating massive amounts of data to keep scheduling up to date and priorities in order and valid. Wight cites the characteristics that distinguish MRP II from other resource planning systems:

1. A top-down system—everything begins with the strategic business plan.
2. A common data base—there is only one set of files in the firm.
3. What-if capability—simulation capability to evaluate alternate plans.
4. Total company system—as previously mentioned, it ties in all formal groups.
5. System transparency and validity—users work within the system and follow its logic.[3]

A study of leading firms using MRP II systems found multiple benefits from MRP II. All cited substantial reductions in manufacturing inventories, fewer stockouts, and improved delivery.[4] These benefits are common to "stand-alone" MRP systems. There were, however, other benefits mentioned, unique to MRP II.

[1] Thomas F. Wallace Editor, *Dictionary, (Terms and Definitions)* Washington, D.C.: American Production and Inventory Control Society, 1980, p. 16.

[2] L. Giunipero, "Material Resource Planning," in *Yearbook of Science and Technology,* ed. Sybil P. Parker (New York: McGraw-Hill Book Co., 1990), pp. 506–10.

[3] Oliver W. Wight "MRP II Unlocking America's Productivity Potential," Book Press, Brattleboro, VT., 1983, pp. 57–58.

[4] S. Melnyk and R. Gonzalez, "MRP II: The Early Returns Are In," *Production and Inventory Management,* first quarter, 1985, pp. 124–37.

1. Rationalization of production—in multiplant operations, product lines were shifted to improve operating efficiencies.
2. Leveling employment—increased the ability to keep employment levels of the work force relatively constant.
3. Managing labor disputes—"what-if" simulation capability allowed for an evaluation of the effect of strikes or walkouts and the development of contingency plans plus rescheduling customers.
4. Managing product development and introduction—since MRP II planners and design engineers during prototype and preproduction-model development, coordination and approval of problems were handled much more quickly. It also planned corporate resources necessary to finance the new line.
5. Managing the firm during recession—making decisions based on good-quality data enabled firms to control costs.
6. Manufacturing viewed as an asset—through its ability to deliver on time.
7. Improving the manufacturing environment—reducing conflict through better communications.
8. Linking functional areas—which facilitates joint decision making.
9. Formalizing the management and use of information—some good-quality information in the database is essential.
10. Formalizing the strategic plan—through its requirement of top-down, bottom-up involvement in tying strategic and operation plans.[5]

MRP and Purchasing

Oliver W. Wight, consultant on production and inventory control and a recognized authority on material requirements planning, explained the significance of MRP for purchasing in these terms:

> When the computer came along, people were delighted to be able to use it to do requirements planning, but for many years it remained just an ordering technique. Then two significant developments occurred. . . .
> We began to recognize that MRP could be used not just as a way to order, but as a way to reschedule. The simple logic of MRP could be used to determine if the due dates on existing purchase orders were correct or needed to be pulled up or pushed out.
> Later on it was recognized that MRP is really a closed loop system where the master schedule must be constantly kept up to date to represent what really will be done, rather than what we planned to do sometime "or would like to do."[6]

Wight used a simple example to show how the system affects purchasing (see Figure 17-10). The top chart, "MRP Used for Ordering," *shows projected gross requirements, which are usually exploded from the bill of material.* In this example 90 bicycles are to be built in period 1, and the projected gross requirement for handle bars for the period is 90.

The second line shows scheduled receipts or *open purchase orders.* The next line shows the projected available balance, which in this case is the on-hand figure. Line four shows the planned order releases, which generate lower-level

[5]*Ibid.*

[6]Oliver W. Wight, "MRP: An Aid to Professional Purchasing," *National Purchasing Review,* November-December 1978, p. 16.

MRP Used for Ordering

		WEEKS					
		1	2	3	4	5	6
PROJECTED GROSS REQUIREMENTS		90	80	100	110	90	110
SCHEDULED RECEIPTS	300						
PROJ. AVAIL. BAL.	250						-30
PLANNED ORDER RELEASE			300				

MRP Used for Reordering

		WEEKS					
		1	2	3	4	5	6
PROJECTED GROSS REQUIREMENTS		90	80	100	110	90	110
SCHEDULED RECEIPTS					300		
PROJ. AVAIL. BAL.	250	160	80	-20	170	80	-30
PLANNED ORDER RELEASE			300				

Figure 17-10 Basic method of computing requirements for ordering and reordering using the MRP system

material requirements and the requirements for shop capacity planning. In each succeeding week gross requirements are subtracted from the sum of the schedule receipts and the 250 currently on hand, and by week 6, a negative, or net, requirement occurs. Used this way MRP indicates when to order.

The bottom chart shows how time phasing the scheduled receipt (i.e., showing the due date on the purchase order) permits the MRP computation to tell if that due date is correct when circumstances change—at the manufacturing level, for example. In the example at least 20 of the 300 scheduled receipts should be moved from period 4 to period 3, or the assembly scheduling call for 100 handle bars will not be met.

If the circumstances change on the purchasing side—for example, a vendor is unable to deliver the 300 required in week 4—the system is programmed to change the due dates on all other matching components of the bicycle, such as wheels, gears, and so on, once the information on the delayed delivery is fed back to the master schedule. As a result, purchasing will not be wasting time expediting things that are not needed when they could use the time to expedite things that are needed. When schedules are not properly updated, it is not always easy for purchasing to find out what is needed first.

MRP can not only predict shortages week by week, according to Wight, but when information on changing circumstances is fed back into the system, it can repredict week by week. "As anyone who has worked in purchasing knows," he says, "if they could be working this month on next month's shortages, it would end a lot of the living from crisis to crisis that has become a way of life in so many companies."

Comparing the traditional "order launching and expediting" system with material requirements planning, Wight says that with the old system the following conditions prevail:

- Thirty percent of open purchase orders are typically past due.
- Purchase commitment reports are grossly overestimated in the early time periods.
- Vendor performance reports mean very little—the shortage list is the real schedule.
- The bulk of the purchasing effort is spent firefighting and expediting.

With MRP, he claims,

- Less than 3 percent of the open purchase orders are typically past due.
- Purchase commitment reports represent what actual commitments to spend with vendors are.
- Vendor performance reports become a useful, realistic tool.
- The bulk of the purchasing effort is spent in buying economically, doing value analysis, developing better sources, and so on.

Material requirements planning, it should be remembered, is not simply a method of inventory management but an entire system. It requires an enormous amount of planning, highly accurate bills of material, complete and up-to-the-minute inventory records, and a precisely realistic master schedule. It must be co-ordinated with the organization and operation of several other departments in the company.

MRP's Benefits for Purchasers

The allocation of time in the typical purchaser's day also changes under MRP. Studies at Steelcase, and the Tennant Corporation have shown that the portion of the day spent expediting drops significantly, while time spent on interviewing salespeople, cost-reduction negotiation, and value analysis activities increase (see Table 17-1).

Table 17-1   Typical Time in Buyer's Day

	Before MRP	**After MRP**
Expediting	50%	15%
Order processing	20%	20%
Sales interviews	15%	15%
Other communication	15%	20%
Cost reduction/negotiation/other projects		30%

Source: Adapted from Morgan, J.P., "MRP Breaks with Past Patterns of Failure," *Purchasing*, July 24, 1980, p. 51.

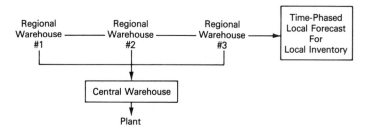

Figure 17-11 Distribution Requirements Planning

Since MRP enables priorities to remain current, a new term, *deexpediting*, has entered the purchasing jargon. Deexpediting is moving the delivery date back in the time schedule, since the material won't be required as soon as originally thought. Buyers must educate suppliers about their production process and also learn as much as possible about the supplier's production process.

Major benefits resulting from MRP include the following:

- Reductions in inventory.
- Improved productivity. (The material is more likely to be there when needed.)
- Reduction in parts shortages.
- Improved inventory accuracy levels.
- Better planning and communication of future needs to suppliers.
- Improved distribution efficiency.

Distribution Planning

Once MRP or MRP II is installed, firms with distribution centers will extend it to these centers. Under distribution requirements planning (DRP) each warehouse develops its equivalent of a master schedule of future demands, which is the feedback to a central warehouse or manufacturing plant (see Figure 17-11).

JIT AND INVENTORY MANAGEMENT

Just-in-time (JIT) as applied to inventory management has been misunderstood, not only by some purchasing managers but by a great number of suppliers as well.[7] JIT is not simply a form of inventory control. It is actually an operating philosophy and strategy that has significant *effects* on inventory control, purchasing, and suppliers.

JIT *does* involve efforts to reduce inventories to an absolute minimum and to eliminate safety stock. It does call for delivery of components and materials as they are needed. And it is, in some instances, the basis for having suppliers locate plants close to customer facilities to achieve on-time delivery. All three elements,

---

[7]JIT has been described as producing only the minimum necessary units in the smallest possible production-run quantities at the latest possible time with the objective of achieving plus or minus zero performance to schedule.

however, are by-products of internal application of JIT. As a corporate position paper on the subject says:

> Through schedule discipline, coordination and synchronization of all operations and materials flow, excess inventory cover is rendered unnecessary. JIT thus goes beyond production and inventory control. It is a way of managing the total business. This results in significant improvement in inventory performance, as well as productivity of the total operation. JIT drastically reduces investment, as well as total cost of operation.

The paper lists these as key factors of an effective JIT program:

- *Engineering:* Ideally, the JIT process starts as early as the product design phase with identification of opportunities for use of standard components, reducing parts proliferation, and manufacturing processes lending themselves to smooth flow, automation, and in-process quality checks. Design and processes are to be stabilized prior to manufacturing release with minimal and well-controlled subsequent changes.
- *Inventory management:* Inventory is considered an unnecessary expense of both space and money and all efforts are made to eliminate it. It is created as a buffer for fluctuations in marketing demand, accuracy of stock balances, and processing time for material movement and production. The goals, in the long run, include:

  Minimum safety stock—approaching zero

  Small/standard lot size (daily/hourly requirement)

  Standard container use

  No receiving/no inspection (supplier to line)

  No (or small) stores (on-line supply)
- *Supplier quality:* Operating with a safety stock near zero and purchased material arriving just in time provides no allowance for material that is incorrect or defective. The supplier must develop and demonstrate its ability to provide a product that consistently meets the requirements of production with an extremely low defect rate, in the ppm (parts per million) range.
- *In-process yield and quality:* All of the processes must be statistically capable and consistently provide an output that

  Meets requirements

  Has a low defect rate

  Does not scrap items from previous processes

  Does not require time- or material-consuming rework
- *Manufacturing discipline:* The entire manufacturing operation is to be organized to ensure smooth continual *flow of material* with minimal bottlenecks. All *operations* are to be *balanced.* Each operation, component, and subassembly line is to feed the next work center with exactly what it needs, when it needs it. Changes in the shop *floor layout,* coupled with a cost-effective automated material movement system, facilitates the balancing of operations.
- *Setups:* Objectives are set for quick changeover of tooling, including intense programs to have single-digit-minute changeovers. The smaller the setup time (and cost), the smaller the quantity. Uncontrolled fluctuations and unpredictable factors in the total process have to be minimized.

MRP AND JIT

Proponents of JIT point out that it is not a program to displace material requirements planning. One vice-president for materials calls it "more of a marriage to existing systems." He points out that MRP is still needed to translate a forecast into a material requirements plan, to create a master production schedule, to do capacity planning, to monitor bills of material, to schedule vendor material, and so on. If JIT replaces any part of MRP, it is in the shop floor control area—the execution of the schedule on the factory floor. MRP does the planning, JIT does the execution.

Inventory-Control Results

By the mid-1980s JIT "success stories" began to appear. General Motors had JIT programs in a number of midwestern plants and was trying pilot programs in others. GM's Buick facility in Flint, Michigan, cut its inventory on hand and in transit from $48 million to $25 million. General Electric had programs in forty of its locations, and some companies reported inventory cuts up to 70 percent.

One of the purchasing manager's most important contributions to a JIT program will be to persuade important suppliers to participate. The purchasing manager in charge of negotiating long-term "materials as needed" contracts for Harley-Davidson Motor Company has compiled the following list of benefits to answer the inevitable question from suppliers, What's in it for me?

- A long business relationship with Harley-Davidson
- Reductions in paperwork
- Three- and five-year contracts for specific part numbers
- A schedule for each part number sent on a monthly basis, allowing for planning for more efficient work schedules
- Elimination of final inspection costs
- Standardized packaging and shared expenses[8]

Finally, in a study by one of the authors of this book, researching firms that had implemented JIT purchasing reported inventory reduction as JIT's greatest benefit.[9] When asked to rate improvements that resulted from JIT implementation, respondents listed the top five as follows:

1. Higher inventory turnover
2. Timely deliveries
3. Increased assurance of a steady supply
4. Faster delivery in critical situations
5. Improved quality

[8]Drew Winter, "Just-in-Time Works!" *Production,* January 1984, pp. 39–41.

[9]L. Giunipero, "Just-in-Time Purchasing," Association for Manufacturing Excellence, research report, Wheeling, Illinois, 1989, p. 73.

POINTS FOR REVIEW

1. Apply the economic order quantity (EOQ) formula discussed in the chapter to a real or hypothetical situation.
2. Discuss the limitations of the EOQ formula.
3. List the benefits derived from use of the formula.
4. Briefly explain what material requirements planning (MRP) is.
5. Name the benefits that accrue to purchasing from the use of MRP.
6. Briefly describe the just-in-time (JIT) concept and its significance for purchasing.
7. Explain how inventory carrying cost affects decisions on quantity to purchase. Find a local firm's carrying cost.

18

The Purchase of Transportation Services

In a report on the activities of its purchasing and transportation departments a large manufacturing company listed expenditures of $686 million for materials. Its outlay for transportation services (primarily inbound and outbound freight charges) was $78 million. Cost-reduction efforts of the purchasing group resulted in savings for the year of $25.7 million, or approximately 4 percent. Those of the transportation section amounted to $6.9 million, or almost 9 percent.

The figures are significant to anyone interested in purchasing because they dramatize a number of facts that are not always appreciated by many who otherwise show great concern about the cost of materials.

1. Transportation costs represent a substantial part of the price of purchased product—and thus of the average company's expenditure on materials and services. (This holds true in governmental and institutional buying as well.) In the case above the amount is slightly more than 10 percent. This in turn is a little over 5 percent of the company's yearly income, assuming that materials and services account for about half the company's sales dollar. Such costs require careful analysis.

2. Use of transportation services involves a form of purchasing. Recognition led the company mentioned above to combine the two functions—purchasing and traffic and transportation—into a single department. The trend to this type of organization has been strengthened by the deregulation of the transportation industry in the early 1980s.[1] The move greatly spurred competition in the field, since rates are no longer controlled and fixed. As a material transportation executive with Union Pacific, Wayne W. Mattson, put it:

   Our goal is to have professional purchasing of transportation services. It should not be an afterthought of the purchasing function. We're actively promoting transportation management, especially inbound management, as a means of providing better service to the internal customers of each firm—the manufacturing department.[2]

3. The purchase of transportation, therefore, should involve the same techniques discussed in earlier chapters: careful evaluation and selection of suppliers, price analysis, value analysis, aggressive negotiation, and so on. A corollary is that knowledgeable personnel, using those techniques, can effect substantial savings and, just as important, obtain greatly improved service from suppliers. As one expert has put it, because the basic purpose of the purchasing function is to secure goods and services in the most cost-effective manner, skilled purchasing professionals should apply their skills to the service that transports the goods. It makes no sense, he points out, for a buyer to record a $100 savings obtained through negotiation, only to have part or all of it vanish because of improper carrier selection.

This approach to transportation costs, reflected in a special report issued by the National Council of Physical Distribution Management in 1982, is useful

[1] Although the term *deregulation* is commonly used, transportation has not been totally deregulated. More precisely, the government has relaxed regulation of carriers, permitting them to do things that just a few years ago were not allowed. The so-called deregulation has given carriers more freedom to compete and more opportunities to operate more efficiently. It has changed but not eliminated government regulatory restraint. See page 324 for additional details.

[2] Quoted in "Professional Profile," *Purchasing*, September 14, 1989, p. 49.

today. It suggested a number of strategies to shippers and receivers who want to stay competitive in the changing transportation market. Among them are a number of familiar purchasing methods: cost analysis and negotiation, long-range contracting, and concentration of business with a limited number of suppliers. Among its specific recommendations:

- Use more analytic and negotiating skills in buying transportation services.
- Stress the *management* of transportation, with emphasis on planning, budgeting, and communication.
- Place business with a limited number of carriers to obtain the best volume discounts.
- Consolidate shipments to build traffic volume.
- Negotiate more contracts to minimize uncertainties in service, equipment supply, rate escalation, and spot markets.

RELATIONSHIP OF PURCHASING AND TRAFFIC

Large organizations generally have separate traffic departments; others have some form of materials-management system (see Chapter 15) in which traffic and purchasing are closely related parts. Even as late as the 1970s, however, a leading trade journal reported that most companies did not have professional traffic departments. Often, it was said, the traffic "department" is staffed by a shipping clerk whose only knowledge of transportation is the telephone numbers of local carriers and the names of carrier sales representatives who call. A warehouse foreman who keeps goods moving on and off the shipping dock may also be considered part of the "department."

Purchasing personnel generally have little difficulty working with existing traffic departments. Nevertheless, it is important that they continually press their case for help on inbound shipments. Because the bulk of the transportation dollar is usually spent on outgoing shipments, particularly in industry, the tendency is to pay more attention to that area. Given the proper motivation, a traffic department can be of great assistance to purchasing on such matters as supply routes and rates for inbound shipments; routes, rates, and classifications for potential suppliers; rate adjustments; tracing, expediting, and reconsigning shipments; advice on the most economical size of orders from the standpoint of freight charges; pooling of inbound shipments; auditing freight bills; changes in freight rates and classifications; and filing claims for loss and damage.

With the big increase in international trade, the traffic department can be of even greater help, particularly in regard to shipping and clearance documents, tariff and custom regulations, and various forms of overseas transportation.

A purchasing manager intent on getting utmost value for the dollars that the purchasing department spends has a problem—and an opportunity—in those cases in which the traffic department, if it exists at all, is not much more than a couple of clerks. The problem is that responsibility for traffic is generally dispersed among the accounting, sales, and purchasing departments, so that in the end no one is really responsible, and significant cost savings are passed up. Purchasing and sales specify the carriers that they want for their shipments; accounting audits the freight bills; and no one bothers with the fine points of procurement, such as negotiation. Purchasing's opportunity in such cases is to assume full responsibility for setting up an organized traffic activity of some kind—be it under direct purchasing control or not—so that the company can get the full benefits of a "transportation purchasing" program.

CONTROL STARTS WITH FUNDAMENTALS

In some ways the field of transportation is exceedingly complex: the number of carriers (and the specialized equipment and services available) is huge; federal, state, and local regulations are voluminous. Buyers or purchasing managers, however, need not be authorities on every phase of the subject to exercise the same control over transportation costs that they do over material costs. Buyers can start with a working knowledge of fundamentals. Thereafter, they have access to a wide variety of information and help. The literature on traffic and transportation is extensive, and several authoritative trade journals in the field keep their readers current on all significant developments in the industry. We have already spoken of existing traffic departments as an excellent source of guidance and assistance; lacking that source, the purchasing manager can always call on the services of outside professional traffic consultants.

Leading transportation companies—railroads, airlines, and truckers, for example—have staffs equipped to provide all kinds of assistance, for general or for specific problems. Despite the element of self-interest that is involved, the knowledge and expertise that they make available is very valuable. In a more general way associations—the Air Transport Association, the American Trucking Associations, and the Association of American Railroads, to name a few—also offer help on a wide range of transportation problems.

A basic approach in coming to grips with transportation is to avoid leaving too much control over shipments in the supplier's hands. Vague purchase-order specifications or instructions as to what mode and what carrier to use in shipping purchased goods are almost always open invitations to costly abuses, often unintentional but still harmful to the buyer's interests. Buyers who take the easy way out and limit instructions to "Ship best way" and "Ship soon as possible" simply take too much for granted. To a supplier's shipping department, "best way" could mean whatever is the easiest, rather than the most efficient, way. It could also mean shipping by a friendly carrier who is generous at Christmas but costly and unreliable every other day of the year. The term could also be interpreted quite innocently as the fastest way at premium rates, even though the buyer may have had exactly the opposite in mind. An open-ended expression like "Ship as soon as possible" is also open to obvious misinterpretation. Buyers should be specific about the mode of shipping—and carrier, if possible—and exact about delivery dates. Suppliers are specialists in making certain products; there is no assurance that they are specialists in transportation.

F.O.B. TERMS

Title to Purchased Goods

Making a purchase involves a transfer of title to the merchandise from the seller to the buyer. It must be assumed—or ascertained, if any doubt exists—that the seller has a clear title to the goods in the first place. The time and place of the actual transfer of title are important, for ownership entails responsibilities and risks, and this point is the source of frequent legal controversy. Thus the designation of an F.O.B. (free on board) point has a much more far-reaching effect than indicating whether the seller or the buyer is responsible for paying the transportation charges.

If goods are sold and shipped F.O.B. seller's location, the purchaser automatically takes legal title to the goods at the moment the shipment is delivered to the carrier. By doing so, the purchaser assumes full responsibility for all accidents, contingencies, damage, loss, and delays occasioned by the carrier. The purchaser is responsible for seeing that suitable insurance is carried on the goods while in transit and for recovering from the carrier any damages for which the latter may be liable through its negligence or other reason. (It has been ruled contrary to public interest for a shipper to agree to relieve the carrier of liability for loss or destruction of goods through negligence of the carrier, and such contracts have been held invalid.) The buyer or consignee is responsible for payment of the transportation charges to the carrier and for payment for the merchandise to the shipper, even though the shipment is lost or destroyed in transit.

In shipping F.O.B. the seller's location, the title having passed, the seller cannot regain possession of the goods during transit even though the seller receives definite information before the goods have reached their destination that the buyer is insolvent. On the other hand, the seller is obliged to exercise ordinary prudence and good judgment in protection of the purchaser. In one leading case a buyer was adjudged to be not liable for payment for a shipment lost in transit, even though the terms of the contract were F.O.B. seller's city, because the seller had used poor judgment in making a nominal declaration of value ($50) to the carrier, when for a few cents additional the seller could have listed the true value ($500) of the merchandise.[3] Similarly, a seller defaults and assumes liability if it fails to follow the buyer's shipping instructions regarding the route, the carrier, packing equipment, date of shipment, or other reasonable instructions issued by the buyer. This law is applicable regardless of the usual law pertaining to shipments ordered F.O.B. the seller's location. When the testimony shows that a seller breached any competent clause or element in a valid contract, the buyer is relieved of responsibilities, including those arising under F.O.B. shipment rules of law.

If goods are sold and shipped F.O.B. buyer's location, title passes to the buyer at the time when goods are delivered to the buyer by the carrier. Under these circumstances the buyer does not assume the responsibilities outlined above,

[3] *Semler* v. *Schmicher*, 38 Atl 2d 831.

but they are for the account of the seller so long as the latter retains title to the merchandise.

Transportation Charges

Buyers should have a basic knowledge of commonly used transportation terms, particularly F.O.B. (free on board). Many people assume that the term simply indicates that either the seller or the buyer of the item is responsible for transportation charges to the buyer's plant. As previously discussed there is more to F.O.B. than just freight charges. However, every purchase involves a transfer of title to merchandise from seller to buyer, assuming that the seller has title to begin with. When and where the transfer of title takes place are important because of possible legal complications over such things as damage and loss. There are several variations of F.O.B. terms, and the choice of a particular term will be influenced by trade custom, the nature of the item, the amount of money involved, and the buyer's analysis of what costs are involved in each method—for example, would it eliminate paperwork, save time, and so on to simply have the supplier handle everything up to delivery at his or her plant? Following are the choices of terms of sale:

1. *F.O.B. origin, freight collect.* Title passes to buyer at the seller's plant or warehouse. Buyer owns the goods in transit, pays freight charges, and files claims, if any.
2. *F.O.B. origin, freight prepaid.* Title passes to buyer at the seller's facility, but freight charges are paid by the seller. Buyer owns the goods in transit and files claims, if any.
3. *F.O.B. origin, freight prepaid and charged back.* Same as item 2 but seller collects freight charges from buyer by adding the amount to the invoice.
4. *F.O.B. destination, freight collect.* Title passes to buyer upon delivery to the buyer's plant, and buyer pays the freight charges. Seller owns the goods in transit and files claims, if any.
5. *F.O.B. destination, freight prepaid.* Seller pays the freight charges, owns the goods in transit, and files claims, if any. Title passes to buyer upon delivery.
6. *F.O.B. destination, freight collected and allowed.* Seller owns goods in transit and files claims, if any. Title passes to buyer on delivery. Buyer pays the freight charges, but charges them back to the seller by deducting the amount from the invoice.

Table 18-1 summarizes these descriptions.

Larger companies generally prefer to buy F.O.B. the seller's plant, because their traffic departments (and often purchasing departments) are better equipped to do an effective job of carrier selection and routing. Smaller companies may not have the staff or the expertise to exercise that kind of control over transportation costs and service and, in a sense, may be forced to turn that responsibility over to the suppliers. Passive acceptance of such a policy weakens their whole purchasing stance, however. The fundamental criteria of right price and right quality at the right time apply to transportation just as much as they do to materials, and any or all of them may be affected adversely by improper packing and shipping.

Table 18-1 Common F.O.B. (Free on Board) Terms Defined

		Effect	
Terms of Sale	**Title Passes to Buyer**	**Buyer**	**Seller**
F.O.B. Origin or Factory, Freight Collect	at origin or factory	pays freight charges bears freight charges owns goods in transit must file claims for loss, damage or overcharges	
F.O.B. Origin or Factory, Freight Prepaid and Allowed	at origin or factory	owns goods in transit files claims	pays freight charges bears freight charges
F.O.B. Origin or Factory, Freight Prepaid and Added	at origin or factory	bears freight charges owns goods in transit files claims	pays freight charges collects freight charges from buyer by adding to invoice
F.O.B. Destination, Freight Collect	at destination	pays freight charges bears freight charges	owns goods in transit files claims
F.O.B. Destination, Freight Prepaid and Added	at destination	bears freight charges	pays freight charges owns goods in transit collects freight charges from buyer by adding to invoice files claims
F.O.B. Destination, Freight Prepaid and Allowed	at destination		pays freight charges bears freight charges owns goods in transit files claims

Source: Florida Purchaser

MODES OF TRANSPORTATION

The transportation industry offers a wide variety of modes to move goods of every size, shape, and weight to practically any point in the country. (*Mode* is an industry term meaning a particular form of transport.) Regardless of mode the bill of lading becomes the contract document between shipper and carrier. Four legal categories of transportation firms operate in the U.S.: (1) private, (2) common, (3) contract, and (4) exempt.

Private carriage describes company-operated as opposed to carrier-operated transportation. Technically, private carriage includes the operation of company-owned railroads, barges, ships, and aircraft, but in general use the term refers to trucks, both local and long distance. An estimated nine of every ten trucks in use are engaged in private carriage.

Companies operating their own trucks use them to supplement for-hire transportation. The reason most often given is that by running its own trucks the company can obtain transportation equipment or service not available from for-hire carriers or superior to what they offer.

Yet companies who require neither special equipment nor special service also operate their own trucks. They find they can provide the same or better service at substantially less cost. Few companies who make the decision to operate trucks ever stop using them.

Common carriers are the backbone of the transportation system and serve the public. They cannot discriminate in selecting shippers or receivers.

Contract carriers move freight under contract for certain shippers or receivers. The commodity carried tends to be specialized. For example, there are many contract carriers in the Midwest that haul steel from mills to customers under contract.

Exempt carriers are free from Interstate Commerce Commission regulation for rates, routes, services, and financial stability but not excluded from safety requirements.[4]

Rail Freight

Rail freight is the basic mode for large shipments, and it still accounts for almost half the freight shipped in the United States. Most railroads are considered as common carriers and must serve the general public. Rates for full carload (CL), which run approximately 30,000 pounds and up, are generally lower than those of other modes, with the exception of pipelines. Less than carload (LCL) rates are less competitive. Use of rail freight requires either a rail siding at the buyer's plant or an easily accessible freight yard or similar facility (in which case pickup by truck adds additional costs). Once at the buyer's facility, a rail car can be retained for forty-eight hours beyond the next 7:00 A.M. free of charge. Holding rail cars beyond this forty-eight-hour period results in a charge to the buyer. This charge is called *demurrage*. Good coordination between purchasing and traffic can minimize demurrage charges. Faced with tough competition from other modes, railroads are continually upgrading their procedures, rolling stock, and special equipment for moving and handling, in an effort to retain the business of large shippers. The normal time for a rail shipment to move from New York to San Francisco is at least five days; times between other points vary proportionately.

Roadrailers One example of new equipment is roadrailers. Roadrailers are completely integrated intermodal vehicles that contain both a two-axle highway wheel set and a single-axle rail wheel set. When on the open highway the rail set is re-

---

[4]For further discussion see Joseph L. Cavinato, *Purchasing and Materials Management* (St. Paul: West Publishing Co., 1984), pp. 190–91.

tracted, and when on tracks the road tires are retracted. Roadrailers offer numerous advantages over *piggyback*. In piggybacking the truck/trailer is placed on the rail car, which is then referred to as a trailer, on flat car (TOFC). Some of the specific advantages of roadrailers are the following:

- It eliminates need for the flat car to haul the truck trailers, cutting locomotive horsepower requirements for the same cargo.
- Lower weight means quicker acceleration, faster train speed, and the ability to stop in half the distance of a TOFC.
- Terminal cost of equipment and labor is lower.
- Cranes are no longer necessary for loading and unloading trailers.
- Railroad clearance problems are nonexistent.[5]

Software   Since time is longer on rail shipments, customers' ability to trace the status of a particular shipment is important. One example of such a software system is LIBERATOR, offered by the Southern Pacific (SP). This system is put in at no charge for SP customers. It requires a personal computer modem and DOS operating system. The system enables shippers to transmit bill of lading information directly to SP and other railroads. Other program fields have capabilities for conforming to the weight and special-handling standards set by the Standard Transmission Commodity Codes (STCC). Additionally, the system provides for communication with SP and other railroads via Western Union's Easy Link. Thus telegrams, mailgrams, and faxes can be sent or received as well as entry into other data bases. SP pays all telecommunication costs between itself and the shipper.

Motor Freight

Truckers carry the greatest percentage of freight billings in the United States. The extensive interstate highway system makes it convenient and economical for shippers to specify the trucking mode. However, the 1990s will pose challenges for the trucking industry. Thomas Donahue, president of the American Trucking Association, has described six challenges shaping the transportation system and cost of distribution in the 1990s:

1. *Congestion.* The interstate highway system contains only 1 percent of the nation's lane miles yet 21 percent of the traffic. This 21 percent is much greater than original designers planned. It is anticipated that expenditures of $60 billion annually are required to maintain and improve the interstate system.
2. *Pollution.* Regulating truck hours to control pollution and congestion would hurt most businesses. Alternate fuels, which will be environmentally safe, are being studied.
3. *National transportation policy.* The attractiveness of various shipping modes will be influenced by this policy. Donahue feels truckers have won a large share of business based on price and service.
4. *Fuel taxes.* They should be left at current levels, or cost of transportation will increase for all modes.

[5]Kevin P. Keefe, "A Horse of a Different Color," *Trains,* June 1989, pp. 28–33.

5. *Changes in work force and technology.* Such changes will lead to a trucking industry with more women, minorities, and immigrants.
6. *Globalization of competition.* This will mean more consolidations of business as well as increased use of such modes as containerized shipments. Donahue estimated that three million containers moved through U.S. ports, and one million of these were overloaded.[6]

Motor freight carriers handle either truckloads (TL) of approximately 33,000 pounds or less than truckloads (LTL), which are considerably more expensive. The advantages of this mode include great flexibility in short hauls and door-to-door service (most plants are equipped with docks for loading and unloading trucks). Generally speaking, truck freight moves faster than rail freight on short hauls, and it is competitive on a time basis on many long hauls.

Other Modes

Surface freight forwarders appeared on the scene as an economic response to the difficulty that shippers have had in getting railroads and trucks to move small (LCL and LTL) shipments at what they consider reasonable cost. Surface freight forwarders pick up relatively small shipments from a number of customers, consolidate them into carload or truckload lots, and arrange for their transport by rail or truck. The largest and best known surface freight forwarder is United Parcel Service. UPS also carries a large volume of the small freight shipments.

Air freight, looked at in terms of total cost, can often be competitive with rail and truck freight, despite its higher rates. Deliveries by air reduce the need for large inventories of certain types of products; packaging requirements are simpler and less costly; delivery is fast (New York to San Francisco: five to six hours).

The airlines have steadily increased their share of the freight market with innovative ideas in packaging and handling as well as the addition of enormous carrying capacity in the new jumbo jets.

Airline counter-to-counter parcel service, offered by the leading carriers, provides for fast movement of small packages (25 pounds or less and no larger than 90 inches in length, width, and girth combined). Packages must be delivered and picked up at the airport. The airlines guarantee that a shipment will go out on the next available flight.

Air freight forwarders provide the same types of services as their surface freight counterparts. They consolidate small shipments, move them by air at quantity rates, and through use of trucks at origin and destination can provide door-to-door service overnight to many points. Forwarders now offer service to about 8,000 communities. Rates are high but competitive in terms of total cost.

Parcel post is a popular choice for inbound shipments of 70 pounds or under. Major problems associated with this mode are the general deterioration in postal service, shippers' or buyers' difficulty in determining delivery schedules, delays that occur during holiday periods, and the high rates of loss and damage in shipments.

[6]Rupert Welch, "Top Transportation Challenges Are Highway Needs, Congestion, Pollution," *Traffic World,* September 1989, pp. 25–26.

Express mail, developed by the U.S. Postal Service, offers guaranteed overnight delivery of letters and packages weighing up to 70 pounds. Items delivered to an express mail post office by 5:00 P.M. are available for pickup the next morning or can be delivered directly to the addressee before 3:00 P.M.

Air express package service has been inspired by the success of Federal Express in the overnight package delivery market. Other carriers, including Emery Worldwide, Purolator, and Airborne Express, are offering a similar overnight service. Service is door to door, as opposed to the airline counter-to-counter parcel service. In some cases carriers use their own or leased aircraft. In others they use the major scheduled airlines, charter aircraft, commuter airlines, or combinations of these. This is the fastest-growing segment of the transportation market. Shipment weight limits vary among carriers but are increasing. Some weight limits are as high as 150 pounds, up from 70 pounds just a few years ago.

Bus package express provides transport of relatively small packages between approximately 25,000 communities on the routes of major buslines. Total transit time on short runs—for example, New York to Boston—is comparable to that of air freight. Service is generally available twenty-four hours a day, seven days a week. Packages must be brought to and picked up from bus terminals. Table 18-2 shows a comparison of various minimum and maximum shipping weights for small deliveries.

Inland waterways transportation—by barges and scows drawn by towboats and tugs—has been enlarging its share of the freight market for a number of reasons: rates are considerably cheaper than those of any other mode, carriers have superior equipment for handling low-value bulk commodities and semifinished items, the number of industrial centers linked by navigable rivers has increased, and delivery is often as good as that of rail freight.

Piggyback and fishyback are neologisms for shipping methods developed by combining two of the modes just described. As previously discussed, the first method involves pickup of a special trailer at the shipper's facility and then transport of the trailer to a rail facility, where it is loaded on a flat car. The longer part of the haul is then made by rail. The trailer can be delivered directly to a plant with a rail siding, or it can be moved again by tractor truck to its destination. Fishyback is a variation of piggyback, except that it combines movement by truck and water carriers. The combination of two modes permits reduction in handling

Table 18-2 Small-Shipment Weight-Limit Chart (in pounds)

Carrier	Overnight	Two Days or More
Federal Express	150	No limit
Emery Air Freight	No Limit	No limit
Greyhound	100–150	100–150
Parcel Post/ Express Mail (U.S. Post Office)	70	70
UPS	70	70
Airline Counter to Counter	25	25

Table 18-3 *General Modal Comparisons*

Characteristic	Water	Rail	Truck	Air	Pipeline
Speed	Very slow	Moderate	Fast	Fastest	Slowest
Rates	Very low rates	Low rates	Moderate to high rates	Highest rates	Lowest rates
Typical weight	50,000 and up	30,000 and up	20,000 to 30,000	Varies	n/a Continuous flow
Typical products	Large volume Raw materials	Large volume Raw materials Manufactured goods	Moderate volume Manufactured goods Raw materials	Low volume Low weight High value Perishable products	Oil/natural gas Slurry

costs as the handling of one unit—the container—is faster and more efficient than handling a large number of individual items.

Even more efficient is the shipment of containers without vehicle chassis and wheels, popularly known as containerized freight. Special flatbed trailers are used to haul the containers to and from railroad loading ramps and port loading facilities.

Pipeline transportation. Although technically they are common carriers and in terms of dollar value carry a significant percentage of the nation's freight, pipelines transport natural gas and petroleum products and on rare occasions coal slurry—crushed coal suspended in water. Unlike other common carriers, pipelines usually handle the products of their owners, oil and gas producers. They are regulated by the Interstate Commerce Commission to protect the small producers or refiners who must use the pipelines of others to transport their products.

On a cost per barrel/mile basis, pipeline transportation is more cost efficient than any other form of transportation, with the exception of the largest supertankers.

A summary comparison of the general characteristics of several modes is shown in Table 18-3.

FREIGHT RATES AND CLASSIFICATIONS

Contrary to a widely held belief, freight rates are not established and controlled by the ICC or any other government agency. The role of the ICC had been to determine that the rates proposed by carriers and shippers are just, reasonable, and nondiscriminatory. Rates are more easily open to negotiation following deregulation of the transportation industry.

Classification of materials or products being moved is the basis for setting rates, that is, the higher the classification, the higher the rate. Plastic articles transported as LTL shipments, for example, have been classified as "Less than six pounds per cubic foot, class 200; six pounds per cubic foot, but less than 12 pounds per cubic foot or over, class 85." The rate for class 100 is approximately one half that of class 200; the rate for class 85 is about 15 percent lower than that for class 100.

Classes are printed in two publications that are essential parts of the business library of anyone involved in specifying or paying for various types of shipping: the *National Motor Freight Classification,* published by the American Trucking Associations, Washington, D.C., and the *Uniform Freight Classification,* published by Tariff Publishing Officer, Chicago.

To be sure that they are charged the correct freight rates—and that they do not violate any federal or state laws—shippers should thoroughly acquaint themselves with the descriptions of articles in the tariffs under which they ship. Commodity descriptions in shipping orders and bills of lading should conform to those in the applicable tariff, including packaging specifications, because there may be different rates for the same articles that are shipped in different types of packaging.

Precise descriptions of purchased items to be shipped to buyers are essential, then, if buyers are to get full value from their "transportation dollars." Because higher classes are shipped at higher rates, it is important that the buyer not assume that shippers or rate clerks will automatically protect the buyer's interests. Suppliers will often ship at the higher rate when there is some doubt about the exact classification to protect themselves, as there are legal penalties for falsifying billing. Similarly, rate clerks assess a shipment on the basis of what is on the shipping order and will often go to the higher rate to protect themselves.

Table 18-4 provides a few simple examples of how incomplete descriptions of purchased items can result in higher freight costs and ultimately higher total product cost.

Examples abound of how analytical purchasing and traffic managers have reduced costs through changes in classification. Two from a large manufacturer of electrical equipment are typical. The company had been paying higher rates on electric meter sockets than on cable terminals and other items with similar transport characteristics. Application for a change in classification to the lower class and lower rate was successful, and costs were cut substantially. In another case the company, like many other companies that discover their product descriptions are incomplete or slightly inaccurate, asked for a change in classification of certain components of their generators from "electric generator parts." The traffic department had found that the components could more accurately be classified as structural steel parts. The change was agreed upon, and the rates went down.

Table 18-4 Shipping Costs Rise When Descriptions Are Incomplete

Specific Product	If Shipped with This Incomplete Description:	Is Rated:	Should Be Rated:
Cotton work shirts	Cotton shirts	Class 100	Class 77.5
Crude sulfate of soda	Chemical	Class 100	Class 50
Cotter pins, iron, or steel	Hardware	Class 70	Class 50

Source: Courtesy of *Purchasing Magazine.*

Negotiation of freight rates is somewhat different from the type of negotiation described in Chapter 13. Efforts to obtain changes in rates begin with the shipper and the carrier. If agreement is reached on a new rate, the carrier proposes it to the appropriate freight rate bureaus that the transportation industry has established in various parts of the country—for example, the Southern Motor Carriers Rate Conference or the Southern Freight Tariff Bureau. If after a public hearing, the appropriate bureau approves the change, the tariff is published and filed with the ICC, to become effective in not less than thirty days. The ICC reviews the tariff and unless the commission believes it to be unreasonable or unjustified, or unless interested parties, such as other shippers and carriers, object, no further action is taken.

An executive of a large eastern trucking company has offered the following basic suggestions to purchasing managers without immediate access to traffic information or training, who nevertheless want to purchase transportation as economically as they purchase materials and equipment.

1. Keep the freight classifications that apply to your purchases in your purchasing library. Local carriers will help in identifying which classification you need and where you can get it.
2. Determine if density is a factor in the rating of any commodities that you buy. If so, instruct suppliers to specify density on all such shipments.
3. Whenever a "released value" provision applies to your purchased commodities (the information appears in the classification), make sure the supplier takes advantage of the provision.[7]
4. Make sure that your purchase order carries the complete classification description and insist that the supplier describe the shipment in the same way on any shipping documents.
5. Never permit incoming merchandise to be described by trade name. Very few classifications list trade names, so the shipper may be assessed higher charges.
6. Whenever more than one item is shipped on a bill of lading, see that a weight breakdown is furnished for each item. A basic rule of rating shipments is that whenever a weight breakdown is not furnished for each item, the entire shipment is rated at the highest rating that applies to any one article in the shipment.

DEREGULATION OF TRANSPORTATION

Deregulation of transportation, which broadly speaking is aimed at reducing the maze of rules governing carriers and at introducing greater competition into the industry, began in earnest in the 1970s. Some of the major provisions of the laws passed follow.

— The Airline Deregulation Act of 1978 made it easier for new carriers to enter the field and allowed carriers to raise or lower rates within certain limits without permission from the Civil Aeronautics Board.

[7]The ICC permits shipments of certain commodities at "released value," that is, at less than their actual value to limit the carrier's liability. The carrier in turn can offer a lower rate to the shipper. The "released" provision sets the maximum for which a loss or damage claim will be paid. However, many shippers who take advantage of the provision carry insurance policies to cover damage above "released value."

— The Motor Carrier Act of 1980 made entry of newcomers into the business easier, permitted existing carriers to expand operations and raise and lower rates within certain limits without permission from the Interstate Commerce Commission, and permitted companies with private trucking operations to haul freight for subsidiaries and charge for the service.

— The Staggers Rail Act of 1980 gave railroads more freedom to compete by reducing railroad regulation and loosening restraints on railroad management. It provided for long-term rail contracts between carriers and customer. It also exempted piggyback and container-on-flatcar service from ICC regulation. Rate changes, based on cost increases and decreases, were permitted within certain limits, without being subject to ICC approval.

— The 1984 Shipping Act provided for more competition in ocean transportation. Ocean conference members can now publish their own rates, within certain limits. The act also permits service contracts between carriers and customers. These can cover rates, transit time, and other conditions of service. The bill does away with special rates a carrier could offer a shipper who moves all freight by conference carriers. The act also provides that groups of smaller shippers can pool their freight and negotiate lower rates with ocean carriers.

Deregulation and Private Carriers

Recent changes in Interstate Commerce Commission (ICC) policy make private carriage more attractive, and these changes are expected to spur the growth of private carriage. These changes are designed to save fuel and make maximum use of the nation's transportation fleet. They help private carriers by giving them more freedom to cope with a classic transportation problem—how to achieve a balanced operation or how to have a truck fully loaded in both directions for every trip.

Private carriers are now permitted to haul for the public, for hire, once they have applied for and obtained operating rights from the ICC. They can also haul, for hire, for subsidiaries of parent companies. These restrictions were initially placed on private carriage to protect the markets of the ICC-regulated carriers.

No long-distance fleet can operate at a profit if it has freight moving only in one direction and must return to its base empty. Here is where purchasing, by pairing deliveries to customers with pickups from suppliers, can help make a private fleet operation profitable and reduce inbound transportation costs at the same time.

This need to provide a two-way loaded movement before a private carriage operation can be profitable is why companies use their private fleet for only part of their transportation needs. The unbalanced one-way moves, both outbound and inbound, are turned over to a common carrier on the assumption that the common carrier will have other customers offering freight to be shipped in the opposite direction.

General advice to companies considering the move to private carriage is to analyze the pros and cons of the move by factoring in present transportation costs, the probability that balanced movements will be available, the cost of equipment, availability of labor, operating expenses, and so on. Some transportation consultants specialize in fleet proposal analysis.

The full effect of deregulation is difficult to predict, but proponents have generally predicted these long-term benefits to users of transportation services:

- New and improved services for effective product flows
- No regulatory constraints on services
- Cost-based pricing for competitive sourcing
- Cost-oriented services and pricing
- Terms that give purchasing strength in relations with vendors and carriers[8]
- Movement of freight under contractual agreements
- Commodity shipment rates set according to the market place instead of by rate bureau tariffs and classifications

Reregulation

For the most part deregulation results have been beneficial; however, in the late 1980s certain groups argued for reregulation of the transportation industry. Following is a brief review of some of the major points raised by reregulation proponents.

1. Despite motor carriers' best efforts and regulatory changes allowing them to carry bigger loads and pull longer trailers, productivity has declined since deregulation in 1980. In 1989, motor carrier rates were up about 18 percent from 1985.[9]
2. Airlines have witnessed sharply diminished competition, higher fares and increased congestion at airports that are dominated by a single carrier. Reregulators argue that this more concentrated industry is dominated by megacarriers who dictate fares and routes locking out potential new competitors.
3. In the railroad sector rates have increased, while service has decreased.
4. Small users and those in remote regions don't receive competitive pricing.
5. High turnover in industry, particularly trucking, results in price and service variations.

Despite the reregulation attempts, most sentiment favors continued deregulation. In the trucking industry overcapacity is a major problem, since deregulation has meant more trucks. However, there has not been a corresponding increase in freight, and truckers have been left with carrying smaller-than-average loads. In the airlines industry, Transportation Secretary Samuel Skinner testifying before Congress in February 1990 cited overall results of a nine-month study, which indicated that airline passengers did have more choice to more cities at lower rates than before deregulation. According to Skinner, "A lot of these people are complaining because they don't understand what the alternative is." The alternative is substantially higher fares.

It does appear that a few very large carriers will dominate nationwide in all modes under deregulation. Thus, regulation proponents argue, a regulated ol-

---

[8]See Joseph L. Cavinato, "Buying Transportation," *NAPM Guide to Purchasing* (Tempe, Ariz.: National Association of Purchasing Management, 1986), p. 3.

[9]"Lost Highways: The Trucking Shakeout Continues," *Purchasing*, November 9, 1989, pp. 31–32.

igopoly has been replaced by an unregulated oligopoly.[10] Smaller carriers must develop a local, regional base or a market niche.

PURCHASING TRANSPORTATION

It appears that a deregulated transportation environment will continue into the 1990s. Thus purchasers will need to continually monitor several areas in making effective transportation purchases. Four major areas are - (1) services, (2) pricing, (3) evaluation, and (4) cost-reduction opportunities.

Services

Many different innovative transportation services are available to buyers. We have already discussed roadrailers and computer tracing. Others include:

- Daily and mixed shipment, small lot, just-in-time deliveries from many vendors
- Delivering material directly to production line
- Warehousing material at less cost than using in-house space
- Flexible rates that are higher for faster deliveries and lower for slower deliveries[11]

Pricing

Carrier pricing under deregulation is established by negotiation between buyer and carrier. A common strategy employed by many firms is to take control of inbound transportation from the seller and then negotiate contracts with a few carriers in exchange for favorable rates and improved service. One materials manager reduced his carrier base from thirty-five to five, saving $200,000 in traffic expenses. Delivery-time clauses are also inserted in some contracts. These clauses state that delivery is guaranteed within a certain time frame, and that if the shipment is late, the carrier's price is decreased by a certain percentage. For example, one firm has a guarantee of on-time delivery between St. Louis and Detroit to plus-four hours from noon of the scheduled arrival date. If the driver arrives after 4:00 P.M. the company loses 25 percent of the agreed upon-rate. In the past freight rates were priced at cost per hundred pounds. Today rates can be assessed by pound, square foot, cubic foot, and so on. As opposed to commodity, descriptions rates can be set by freight all kinds (F.A.K.).

Evaluation

While pricing is an important variable in carrier selection, it is not typically ranked number one. Consistent service and the ability to meet precise schedules seems to rank first in most studies. For example, the ease of entry and exit into the trucking business makes the best rate not always the most desirable.

[10]"Commerce Predicts Growth in Transportation Sector," *Traffic World,* January 9, 1989, p. 25.

[11]See Cavinato, "Buying Transportation," p. 4.

Other areas needing evaluation include:

- Financial stability and history
- Carrier profitability
- Management stability
- Special equipment available
- Ability to serve specific geographic areas
- Tracing systems
- Ability to handle claims promptly
- Rating and billing efficiency
- Computerization, EDI/software support
- Size of the carrier and other customers

Cost Reduction

While adequate evaluation will help make the transportation buy cost-effective, purchasers must continually look for improvements. Some of the more popular methods include:

- Freight bill audits. These audits ensure accuracy of freight bills and also correct freight cost. Claims for overcharges may be submitted up to three years after date of receipt.
- Monitoring demurrage. Proper scheduling reduces the time rail cars sit on company site. Some firms negotiate average demurrage agreements whereby the receiver is given one demurrage credit for each rail car released in the first twenty-four-hour period.
- Packaging review. Reusable, lighter, or more efficient methods of packaging can result in lower charges and less weight. One firm substituted light reusable plaster pallets for wood ones, saving weight and spare costs.
- Good carrier relations. Inviting carriers to discuss methods of improving transportation services and costs is useful. Additionally, good relations help in obtaining shipments when they are required on a rush basis.
- Outsourcing. This is the sourcing out to third-party logistics-services companies all or part of a company's transportation or logistics needs. Outsourcing is similar in concept to a typical make-or-buy study, that is, focusing on what one does best helps to optimize profits. Other advantages include achieving (1) more customized services, (2) cost reduction, and (3) improved carrier-customer relationship through EDI and satellite trailing.

  An outsourcing company and a customer company working together can minimize the manufacturer's transportation costs and provide needed services.[12]

THE IMPORTANCE OF PROPER PACKAGING

Packaging is an important consideration in the transport of products and materials because it can affect the price, the quality, and to a degree the delivery of the purchased product. The buyer should be aware of these facts: (1) items should have adequate protection against jolting, rough handling, accidents, and all the

[12]Thomas F. Dillon, "Outsourcing—More Than Another Buzzword," *Purchasing World,* February 1989, p. 31.

other dangers inherent in the movement of goods—particularly when more than one carrier is involved; (2) excessive packaging can add unnecessary freight charges, because it adds weight to a shipment; and (3) properly designed packaging and containers not only minimize the problems mentioned here but can reduce handling costs at points of origin and receipt as well as in the customer's storage and production areas.

Whenever possible, agreement on the types of packaging and containers to be used for shipping the purchased products should be made at the time that the purchase itself is negotiated. The better carriers respond positively to appeals for assistance in holding down total purchase cost, just as reliable suppliers of materials and equipment do. Most of the innovations and improvements in packaging and handling that have been developed over the years were inspired by competition, which in turn is spurred by buyers of transportation, either in traffic departments or in purchasing departments.

The experience of a midwestern company that had to truck heat exchangers about 150 miles to another division for plating provides a good example of close carrier-customer coordination in overcoming problems and cutting costs. Protective packaging was needed on the units when they were shipped to the plating facility and when they were returned to the plant. But the packaging was costly and time consuming. Working together, carrier personnel and company personnel from both the traffic and production departments devised special equipment that would permit safe shipment of the heat exchangers without any packaging at all. But the group did not rest with that improvement; using skids and racks, they refined the system so that the heat exchangers could be moved from the plant to the trucks, from the trucks right into the plating process and then back out on the trucks for movement back to the plant, without being removed from the equipment.

DAMAGE CLAIMS

Despite advances in transport packaging and handling, damage during shipment continues to plague the transportation industry and its customers. Buyers should be particularly concerned about early detection of damage to inbound freight, not only because of the possible monetary loss but because damage to production materials, for example, could disrupt tightly scheduled manufacturing operations. Goods should be inspected as quickly as possible, both to ascertain the need for immediate replacement and to determine carrier responsibility, if any. If there is an indication that the carrier is at fault, claims should be made promptly, because even the most efficient and cooperative carriers can take up to several months to settle claims. Supporting evidence should always accompany claims.

POINTS FOR REVIEW

1. Discuss the similarities and differences between conventional purchasing of materials and supplies and procurement of transportation services.

2. List some of the problems that can be caused by indifference as to how products are to be shipped and by vague or incorrect instructions regarding shipment.

3. Differentiate between transportation *modes* and *carriers* and give several examples of each.

4. Describe some of the major changes brought about by *deregulation* of transportation, and explain why the term often appears with quotation marks.

5. Discuss the means available to purchasing managers without a background in traffic management for controlling the cost of transportation.

6. Explain the importance of proper packaging with respect to both inbound and outbound shipments of freight.

19

Purchase Planning and Forecasting

Some successful businesses have been launched on a hunch, but few have survived solely on the instinctive genius of their founders or managers. If an enterprise is to continue to be profitable, it must be operated according to some plan. And the plan, in turn, must be based on some estimate of the future—of the demand for the company's products, of the size of its markets, of its requirements for materials, machines, and personnel. Whether this attempt to gauge future conditions is called forecasting or, less elegantly, educated guessing, it is essential in business. Good managers narrow the range of probabilities they face and plan what action they will take to meet them.

Purchasing, as a management function, has a responsibility to participate in company planning and forecasting. The scope of its responsibility may vary, depending on the ratio of material cost to finished product cost and on the relative position of the purchasing executive in the managerial group. Regardless of the exact position of the purchasing department in the corporate hierarchy, however, the results of purchasing planning or lack of it have a very definite effect on overall company planning and the realization of company profit objectives.

The importance of planning can be seen even in purchasing's most basic activity: forward buying to meet expected requirements for a given period. It is even more evident in view of the trend to long-range contracts noted in previous chapters. When purchasing managers make three- to five-year commitments with fewer and fewer suppliers, they must plan to allow for certain contingencies.

On the one hand, material will be on hand when it is needed; requirements can be pooled to get lower prices through volume buying; economic ordering quantities and other cost-reducing formulas can be applied; and material costs will be stabilized over a stated period. On the other hand, purchasing managers must negotiate contracts that do not extend their companies' financial commitments. They must avoid costly inventory charges by working out just-in-time or similar programs for controlling inventories (see Chapters 16 and 17). They should also make provision for periodic review and revision of buying plans. The company saddled with a fixed commitment could be in a difficult situation if market conditions changed drastically.

MANAGEMENT'S NEED FOR GUIDANCE

These points alone would justify the need for purchasing departments to make some organized effort at forecasting and planning. There are others, however. The most important is the value to top management of knowing the probable future course of major materials, prices, and availability. Decisions on how to price manufactured products are much easier to make when material costs can be reasonably estimated. The significance of such information is obvious: tire manufacturers, for example, must have some indication of price and supply trends in the rubber industry. Producers of equipment—mechanical or electronic—find accurate forecasting of trends in materials and components of great value in pricing their products.

Informed estimates of materials supply and availability of substitutes also aid management in its planning. Although studies of substitute materials and other technological developments that may lower costs or improve the quality of manufactured products are logically the concern of other departments, they often are the by-products of purchasing department forecasting.

Purchasing forecasting can be used in setting up departmental plans—setting materials budgets, setting up cost-reduction goals, particularly for the long range—and the establishment of reliable, competitive sources of supply needed for future company expansion and growth. Purchasing in many companies, both large and small, also participates in forecasts of the general economic situation and their implications both for the purchasing department and for the enterprise as a whole.

Regular access to at least a summary report of new orders received by the company is important to good purchasing planning. Trends in this figure often provide a useful indicator of future operating rates in advance of actual changes in manufacturing schedules. For longer-range planning, the purchasing department should be kept informed of company sales quotas and forecasts.

Purchasing planning for production materials begins with what is essentially a short-term production forecast—the manufacturing schedule. The schedule indicates to the buyer the nature and volume of material requirements and the expected rates of use. In a large and highly organized company, it may come to the buyer in tabulated form from the production-control or planning department. In the smaller company the information may come to the buyer informally from the plant manager or superintendent. The schedule indicates the approximate volume and flow of materials that the purchasing department will be expected to provide. It should be communicated to the purchasing department systematically, for purchasing policies and plans must be keyed to it. Conversely, the purchasing agent should be informed of any changes in the anticipated operations, so that buying plans can be adjusted accordingly.

In job-shop manufacturing operations the purchasing department is often called in before the bidding stage to supply cost estimates on parts and materials. This advance knowledge of probable requirements enables buyers to begin planning earlier than would be the case if they had to wait until the business was in the house and bills of material and requisitions all prepared. The collection of cost data in itself is an element in their planning. And without committing the company, they can begin to look for additional sources and alert regular suppliers to the possibility of new orders.

ANNUAL OPERATING PLANS

Corporate plans are put into financial terms by way of annual budgets. In multiplant operations these budgets are complex, covering operating units, divisions, and plants as well as corporate headquarters. Figure 19-1 shows a typical budgeting process. The various components include administrative, operating, research

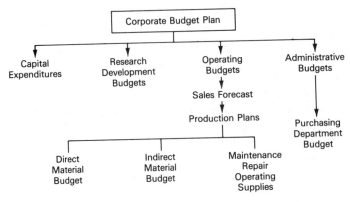

Figure 19-1   Flow of a Typical Corporate Budget Process

and development, and capital budgets. Since budgets involve expenditures with outside firms, purchasing gets involved with buying capital items and supports research and development. Funds for operating the purchasing department come through the administrative budgets. *Purchasing administrative* budgets include salaries, computer expenses, telephone, training, and travel.

The *direct-material* budget accounts for all materials traceable to the finished product. The purchasing department is responsible on an annual basis for setting *standard costs*. Standard costs are typically set late in the final fiscal quarter and are established in two ways.

In the first method, called forecasted variance, the buyer sets the price on the last price in the final period and forecasts a variance depending on anticipated inflation, cost reductions, volume, and the like. Comparisons are made between forecasted variance and actual variance. In the flexible budgeting approach these variances are adjusted for production volume fluctuations. Table 19-1 shows a simple example of the forecasted-variance approach. Note that the buyer anticipates an increase at the start of the second quarter. In the second case, called the *zero-variance* approach, the buyer anticipates what the price will be averaged throughout the year, so a zero variance is the goal. In this case the buyer may run a

Table 19-1   Standard Cost-Setting Approaches

I. Forecasted-Variance Approach

| LAST PRICE PAID | STANDARD COST | VOLUME | TOTAL $ | Variance | | | | |
				1Q	2Q	3Q	4Q	TOTAL
$1.00	$1.00	100,000 units	100,000	0	1334	1333	1333	(4000)

II. Zero-Variance Approach

| LAST PRICE PAID | STANDARD COST | VOLUME | TOTAL $ | Variance | | | |
				1Q	2Q	3Q	4Q
$1.00	$1.04	100,000 units	$104,000	1000	0	0	(1000)

favorable variance early in the year and unfavorable later. The end result is a zero variance.

While purchasers forecast the prices, production personnel control the quantity of material used. Indirect material includes items that can't be billed to a specific unit—heat, light, water, or oil. The MRO budgets all maintenance and support items.

Material and other budgets involving purchased items give the department time to plan ahead and establish strategies to optimize material costs and give executives an idea about product-pricing strategies. Partnerships with suppliers, early discussions about standardized equipment, and blanket orders all can be established when purchasing has access to, and input into, budget plans.

BASIC STEPS IN PURCHASING PLANS

Collection and orderly presentation of pertinent information—including objectives—are fundamental to purchasing planning. Figure 19-2 shows some of the questions that might be asked in preparing a procurement plan for raw materials. The checklist, compiled by an industrial-purchasing executive, is offered only as a sample of the kinds of information required for good purchasing planning; it can be adapted for specific planning programs involving a wide range of products or materials.

Once significant data have been accumulated, they must be so organized that they can be put in written form in logical sequence for review and reference. A basic presentation for a purchase plan on a relatively simple commodity is outlined in Figure 19-3. It should contain—at a minimum—all the information shown in the figure.

This relatively simple outline would, of course, be considerably more comprehensive when used in planning for more complex or more critical items. In any case, the plan is not complete until it has been presented, in written form, to key persons whose departments would be affected by it (see Chapter 4 for strategic plans). Those might include the production manager, production planner, maintenance manager, or master mechanic, depending on what products or materials the plan covers. They may be able to provide additional data or opinions that would make the plan more accurate and more complete. More important, the review will help them to determine whether or not the plan reflects their needs. This in turn leads to a clarification of what their objectives are and how well they match up with the objectives of purchasing. Other departments that can help in rounding out a purchasing plan are receiving, accounting, and design engineering.

BENEFITS IN "PLAN OF PURCHASE"

The experience of a well-known chemical company illustrates three important points about purchasing planning: the need for close cooperation between the using and purchasing departments, the variety of techniques available to pur-

QUESTIONS TO BE ASKED IN DEVELOPING A WRITTEN PROCUREMENT PLAN FOR RAW MATERIALS

1. What are the short and long-term objectives of the business involved?
2. Quantity required at each using location—by months for the next one to two years?
3. What specification applies at each location? What alternative might be considered?
4. Storage capacity available at each location? What ideas do we have on how much inventory to carry? Is inventory limited by storage facilities, working capital, deterioration with age?
5. Method of delivery preferred at each location? What alternative methods of delivery can be considered without new investment or with new investment? What is the maximum quantity per delivery?
6. Consumption and price by location, by month, for previous one or two years?
7. Current suppliers at each location, price being paid, and quantity supplied for previous one or two years? Production Department performance evaluation of current suppliers?
8. Prospective suppliers, their plant locations, capacities and processes? Desirable features of prospective suppliers relative to current suppliers? Is supply regularly available or subject to seasonal or other factors?
9. Total industry capacity/demand ratio for the product for past one or two years, with estimate of expected demand in next few years, by end use?
10. Supplier labor review—renewal date on labor contract?
11. Process economic data, such as estimated production cost, raw material cost, co-product values, batch sizes, yields, make-vs-buy? Rank suppliers from lowest to highest cost producers. Relative profitability of suppliers?
12. Objectives for value improvements sought in new buying period?
13. Preferred quantity statement in new agreement, i.e., fixed quantity or percent of requirement, or fixed monthly minimum or fixed monthly maximum?
14. Specifications and methods of analysis to be described in contracts for use in receiving and accepting materials?
15. Preferred length of contract period? What alternatives might be considered?
16. Is any option desired for contract extension?
17. Preferred terms of payment?
18. Method of invoicing?
19. What points of discussion must be explored between technical production men in buyer or seller organization?
20. What technical service might we require?
21. Who will provide transportation equipment? What alternatives should be considered?
22. Are suitable freight rates currently in effect? Do any new rates have to be established? Evaluate for each supplier.
23. Will all material move in bulk equipment or will some be required in containers? If so, how should it be packed?
24. Will purchases be negotiated or determined by bidding?
25. Distribution cost from the various suppliers' plants to each consuming location?
26. Do we want multiple suppliers for each consuming location?
27. How do we want to write our inquiry?

Figure 19-2
Source: Courtesy of *Journal of Purchasing and Materials Management.*

Ten-Step Basic Commodity Plan

1. Description/specification of item commodity
2. Historical and expected future demand
3. Size of total market
4. Major producers/suppliers
5. Current suppliers' purchase percentage and dollar splits by supplier
6. Supplier strengths—price, quality, service
7. Supplier weaknesses
8. Contract type, length, method (e.g., blanket releases)
9. Short-term plan—one year
   Long-term plan—five years
10. Quality improvements and cost reductions resulting from plan

Figure 19-3

chasing in developing a plan, and the benefits that can accrue from good planning.

Forecasts for chemical raw-material needs were not given to the purchasing department of this company until after annual budgets were established in November and December. As a result, chemical buying for any year ran into the second quarter of that calendar year. Inevitably, there were delays in delivery; buyers spent much of their time trying to expedite shipments; and there was little time to investigate cost-reduction possibilities, better sources, or supplier and buyer performance.

With the cooperation of the production planning department, purchasing was able to get forecasts of consumption for twelve months at each midyear—from July 1 of the current year to June 30 of the following year. Production planning also agreed to revise the forecast annual rate on a quarterly basis. This gave the buyers at least three months more to complete their planning.

Buyers now use two approaches in planning their purchase. A "plan of purchase" is made up on all raw materials and chemicals with an annual purchase volume above $50,000. The buyer outlines the type of purchase that he or she plans—spot, contract, and so forth—and how the business will be split among various suppliers, both by quantity and by dollars. The buyer indicates the terms and past performance for each supplier and gives a brief description of supply conditions for the item, a price forecast, and data on previous price changes.

A more elaborate approach is used on all production materials costing more than $100,000 annually or on which there is only one supplier. A buyer complies with the following instructions in preparing a plan of purchase for the head of the department:

- *Raw-material significance:* State percentage of raw-material costs and manufacturing costs for the item and its function in the manufacturing process.
- *Market condition:* Describe availability, price, economic factors of the market, and significant changes in supply-and-demand relationships that have taken place or are expected to take place in the foreseeable future.

- *Production:* Show total world production, domestic and foreign, broken down by supply company, if possible.
- *Buying objectives:* What will be done to improve company profits on this item? Show what improvements, if any, can be made in relations with suppliers.
- *Significant changes from previous plan:* Indicate change from previous plan—in price, quantity, business split, suppliers, terms, and so forth, and their effects on supplier relations, profits, and method of purchase.
- *Reasons for business split:* Explain the basis for split of business among suppliers and indicate what contributions suppliers have made to improve our profits.
- *General:* Indicate unusual contractual liabilities or advantages and any other information pertinent to buying the particular commodity. When plan does not conform to plant recommendations, explain why.

The immediate results of the planning program were better performance in cost reduction and service to the operating departments. With more time available, buyers were able to complete twice as many cost-improvement projects during the first year of the program as in the year before. The number of rush orders issued by the purchasing department was cut considerably, and relations with other departments improved accordingly. In addition, purchasing managers are now better able to appraise both buyer and supplier performance against the stated objectives of the purchase plan.

FORECASTING

Except in the larger companies, forecasting future price and availability trends is not generally a highly organized activity. Planning is often done on the basis of an informal forecast, often developed within the purchasing department itself. Increasingly, however, companies have turned to formalized forecasting, done either by their own economists or research departments or by outside consultants. Forecasting is identified as an educated assessment of the most probable course of events or a range of probabilities; planning is deciding what to do about them if they occur. (Someone once offered this simple analogy: a weather forecaster tells the radio audience to expect a cloudy morning followed by clearing skies and a sunny afternoon; some parents who are planning a picnic for the kids pack raincoats and check the programs of local movie houses, just in case.)

Purchasing managers are, in fact, in a good position to act as company economists in situations that do not warrant a full-scale planning department. With a little extra effort they can collect and interpret basic information of the kind by which professional economists and forecasters try to anticipate future developments. However, we are concerned primarily with forecasts directly related to purchasing costs and availability of supply in listing the following elements that provide data for forecasting:

1. *General overall business conditions and the rate of growth in the economy.* A rising population and a steady and substantial rise in the gross national product obviously put pressures on supply and prices, for example.

2. *Growth and technological change in specific industries.* Activity in the automobile industry has long been an important indicator of the direction of supply trends in various materials. Booming auto sales push up demand for steel, rubber, copper, and plastics. As auto makers try to cut engine weight and meet emission-control standards, their consumption of aluminum and platinum, for example, will rise, with subsequent effects on the markets for those metals. Conversely, a slump in auto sales and output will have the opposite results.

3. *Labor conditions.* Strikes and costly labor pacts have a direct effect on supply in the first case and prices in the second. Anticipated labor turmoil in an industry—particularly the major ones, such as steel, aluminum, and other metals—poses problems for buyers, who must weigh the risks of overbuying against the risks of production halts because of materials shortages. Once- or twice-removed strikes against the suppliers of a buyer's suppliers can be a matter of concern. These and other possibilities call for close attention to the labor situation throughout industry.

4. *Expansion or contraction of supply.* Major plant expansions in a given industry generally indicate greater availability of supply. But by the same token, closing of plants or dropping of product lines by major suppliers generally decreases availability. Changes in tastes or styles can push up the demand for substitute materials—witness the tremendously increased use of plastic materials in household furniture.

5. *Cost trends in an industry* (and in that industry's suppliers). These are of obvious significance. Improvements in productivity, usually through the installation of new equipment, can often be a matter for negotiation.

6. *The buyer's own "feel" of the market.* The buyer's abilities to judge suppliers' expectations for the future are intangible but extremely important elements in a purchasing forecast. This is particularly true as U.S. buyers encounter growing markets and advancing technology in their efforts to develop offshore sources.

NAPM Report on Business

The monthly report on business published by the National Association of Purchasing Management (NAPM) is one of the best macroforecasting tools available. This report is widely quoted by such respected sources as the *Wall Street Journal, Business Week,* and *Barron's.* The survey results are also carried in major daily newspapers, and a copy of the report is mailed by the Business Survey Committee to the chairman of the Federal Reserve System. The Federal Reserve System controls money supply, and its policies affect interest rates, which affect economic activity. It is important to understand the report.

The report is compiled from monthly replies to questions asked of over three hundred purchasing executives in industrial companies. These executives are located in all fifty states and represent twenty-one Standard Industrial Classifications (S.I.C.). The number of respondents in each of the twenty-one industries is in direct proportion to that industry's contribution to Gross National Product (GNP). Twenty-one industries in fifty states are represented on the committee.

Survey responses cover six major indicators: (1) new orders, (2) production, (3) vendor deliveries, (4) inventories, (5) employment, and (6) prices. Respondents are asked to indicate if business in these areas was better, the same, or worse than during the previous month. Vendor deliveries are reported as faster, the same, or slower. These responses are then compiled into a chart showing the percentage reporting in each category (see Figure 19-4). An overall index, the

Figure 19-4

Report On Business®

Economic Decline Eases in February; PMI Rises to 48.3%

FEBRUARY REPORT

Analysis by the National Association of Purchasing Management Business Survey Committee; chair, Robert J. Bretz, C.P.M., director of materials management, Pitney Bowes, Inc.

The economy declined in February for the 10th consecutive month, but at the lowest rate of decline since June 1989, say the nation's purchasing executives in their latest **Report on Business.** New Orders increased for the first time since May 1989. Production also registered an increase for the first time since June 1989. Both New Export Orders and Imports continued to show increases. Employment declined for the 12th consecutive month, although the rate of decline was the lowest since June 1989.

Supplier Deliveries (formerly Vendor Deliveries) were faster for the 10th consecutive month at a significantly greater

rate than in January 1990, when many shortages developed as a consequence of the record cold weather experienced in December. The improvement in Supplier Deliveries was reflected in Inventories, which declined for the 15th consecutive month at the greatest rate of decline since December 1986. Prices declined for the ninth consecutive month at the greatest rate since December 1982 and a significant decline from January 1990, when the shortages and slower deliveries resulting from the severe weather conditions in December caused many prices to rise.

The **Report** was issued by Robert J. Bretz, C.P.M., chairman of the National Association of Purchasing Management's Business Survey Committee, and director of materials management at Pitney Bowes, Inc. Said Bretz, "The manufacturing economy declined in February, however, the rate of the decline was the lowest in eight months. Although the first increases registered in Production and New Orders since mid-1989 are encouraging, the continued improvement in Supplier Deliveries and significant decline in Prices suggests a lack of any underlying strength in the economy."

PURCHASING MANAGERS' INDEX

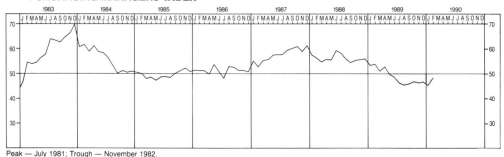

Peak — July 1981; Trough — November 1982.

PURCHASING MANAGERS' INDEX (PMI)

February '89	53.7	September '89	46.0
March '89	51.0	October '89	46.9
April '89	52.7	November '89	46.4
May '89	49.8	December '89	46.7
June '89	48.8	January '90	45.2
July '89	46.2	February '90	48.3
August '89	45.5		

The **Purchasing Managers' Index** (PMI) rose to 48.3% in February, up from 45.2% in January. Although February is the 10th consecutive month of decline, the 48.3% reading is the highest since June 1989 (48.8%). A reading below 50 indicates that the manufacturing economy is generally declining; above 50, that it is generally expanding. Bretz added, "Although the increase of over three points in the PMI from the low January level looks impressive, it appears that much of the improvement is attributed to the additional production required to make up for weather-related production curtailment in December and early January, and the severe auto industry cutbacks in January."

B U S I N E S S

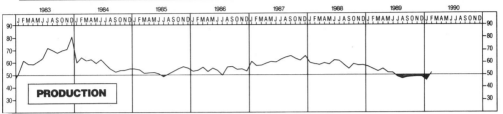

Peak — July 1981; Trough — November 1982.

Production increased in February for the first time since mid-1989. The Production Index rose to 51.5%, up sharply from 45.4% in January and the highest since June 1989 (51.5%). The significant improvement from January appears to be a correction from much lower production activity in January, particularly in the auto industry and industries affected by severe cold weather conditions during the coldest December in recorded U.S. history.

Production	%Better	%Same	%Worse	Net	Index
February	27	53	20	+ 7	51.5
January	18	56	26	− 8	45.4
December	17	58	25	− 8	48.4
November	19	56	25	− 6	48.4

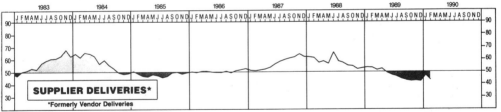

Peak — July 1981; Trough — November 1982.

New Orders increased in February for the first time since they declined in June 1989. The New Orders Index rose to 51.8%, up from 45.8% in January. The sharp increase appears to reflect a rebound from the severe reductions in auto production in January and weather-related problems during December.

New Orders	%Better	%Same	%Worse	Net	Index
February	29	48	23	+ 6	51.8
January	23	50	27	− 4	45.8
December	17	56	27	−10	49.4
November	20	52	28	− 8	48.2

Peak — July 1981; Trough — November 1982.

Supplier Deliveries were faster in February for the 10th consecutive month. The Supplier Deliveries Index fell to 43.3% in February, down significantly from January (47.2%). The improvement from last month reflects the increased production in February and fewer shortages than in January which resulted from the extreme cold weather in December.

Supplier Deliveries	%Slower	%Same	%Faster	Net	Index
February	3	80	17	−14	43.3
January	7	82	11	− 4	47.2
December	4	78	18	−14	42.5
November	5	75	20	−15	43.0

IN SHORT SUPPLY

Bearings — 19th consecutive month, a consequence of anti-dumping suits; **Castings** — 14th time in 18 months; **Electric Motors** — 6th time in 11 months; **Acrylic Acid** — 17th time in 20 months (used in manufacturing plastics); **Caustic Soda/Soda Ash** — 33rd consecutive month (used heavily in paper-making, petroleum refining and soap-making); **Hydrogen Peroxide** — 3rd consecutive month (increasing demand exceeding supply because of switching from chlorine use by paper makers to avoid dioxins; used as a bleaching agent and, in solution, as a topical cleansing agent and antiseptic; **Sodium Chlorate** — 9th consecutive month (increasing demand exceeding supply because of switching from chlorine use by paper makers to avoid dioxins, used heavily in paper-making and dyeing); **Titanium Dioxide** — 31st consecutive month (increasing demand exceeding supply because of switching from chlorine use by paper makers to avoid dioxins, a lead-free pigment used as a whitener in coatings, paints, paper and other industrial applications); **Polyethylene Resins** — Primarily as a consequence of an explosion at Phillips Petroleum plant reducing about 8% of U.S. polyethylene resin output until mid-1990 (used heavily in making packaging materials and paper coatings).

UP IN PRICE

Rhodium — 2nd consecutive month (used heavily as an alloy with platinum and as a corrosion-resistant electroplate for protection of silverware from tarnishing); **Caustic Soda/Soda Ash** — 39th consecutive month, primarily as a consequence of lower demand for co-produced chlorine by paper-makers (used heavily in paper-making, petroleum refining and soap making); **Methanol** — 2nd consecutive month (used heavily as a solvent and in synthesizing other chemicals); **Toluene** — Used heavily in making explosives, dyes, and benzoic acid; as a solvent in paint, and as a gasoline additive; **Freon** — 4th consecutive month (used as a refrigerant); **Polystyrene** — Used chiefly in making synthetic rubber, plastic resins and plastic; **Coal; Corn**

Figure 19-4 (cont.)

Report On Business®

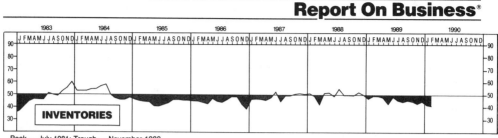

Peak — July 1981; Trough — November 1982.

Inventories declined in February for the 15th consecutive month. The Inventories Index fell to 40.8%, down from 41.8% in January, and the lowest since December 1986 (38.4%).

Inventories	%Higher	%Same	%Lower	Net	Index
February	18	50	32	− 14	40.8
January	14	56	30	− 16	41.8
December	15	55	30	− 15	44.5
November	13	53	34	− 21	42.8

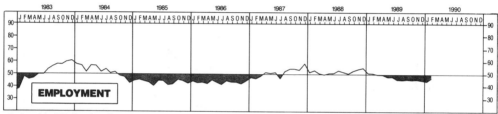

Peak — July 1981; Trough — November 1982.

Employment declined for the 12th consecutive month in February, but at the lowest rate since mid-1989. The Employment Index rose to 46.7% in February, up from 44.1% in January, and the highest since June 1989 (47.7%). A number of members continued to report layoffs, hiring freezes and early retirement programs.

Employment	%Higher	%Same	%Lower	Net	Index
February	11	69	20	− 9	46.7
January	8	71	21	− 13	44.1
December	8	69	23	− 15	44.9
November	12	65	23	− 11	45.4

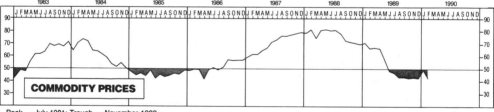

Peak — July 1981; Trough — November 1982.

Prices declined in February for the ninth consecutive month. The Price Index fell to 42.2%, down sharply from 49.7% in January and the lowest since December 1982 (39.1%), which was the beginning of our current economic recovery. All of the items, which were reported higher priced in January because of weather-related shortages, are on the February list of items reported down in price.

Prices	%Higher	%Same	%Lower	Net	Index
February	13	59	28	− 15	42.2
January	24	56	20	+ 4	49.7
December	10	63	27	− 17	42.7
November	10	64	26	− 16	43.1

Products — Corn starch (used heavily in both food processing and paper making) and corn sweeteners (used in food processing).

DOWN IN PRICE

Aluminum — 11th consecutive month; **Aluminum Products** — 4th consecutive month; **Brass**; **Copper** — 4th consecutive month; **Nickel** — 9th consecutive month (used heavily in making stainless steel, plating metals and batteries); **Steel** — 6th consecutive month; **Steel Scrap** — 4th consecutive month; **Stainless Steel** — 3rd consecutive month, after being reported up in price for the 15th time in 20 months in July 1989; **Zinc** — 9th time in 10 months (used heavily in metal alloys and as a protective coating for metal); **Corrugated Shipping Containers**; **Printing Paper** — 7th time in 8 months; **Acetic Acid** — Used in making various acetates, plastics and rubber in tanning, a preservative in foods and a solvent for gums, resins, volatile oils, etc.; **Benzine** — After being reported up in price for 3rd consecutive month

in December 1989 (used heavily in making medicinal chemicals, dyes, varnishes, lacquers and resins); **Chlorine** — 6th time in 11 months, primarily a consequence of lower demand by paper-makers switching to alternatives to avoid dioxins while demand for co-produced caustic soda continues (used heavily in bleaching paper and fabrics; purifying water; and, in making synthetic rubber, plastics and other chemicals); **Ethylene Glycol** — Used heavily in making antifreeze, brake fluid, plastic paint and ink; **Ethylene Derivatives** — 3rd consecutive month; **Plastic Resins** — 2nd consecutive month (used in making plastic products); **Rubber**; **Gasoline** — After being reported up in price in January 1990; **Diesel Fuel** — After being reported up in price in January 1990; **Fuel Oil** — After being reported up in price in January 1990 for 4 consecutive months; **Natural Gas** — After being reported up in price in January 1990 for 4 consecutive months; **Propane** — After being reported up in price in January 1990; **Eggs.**

BUSINESS

BUYING POLICY

Lead times for Production Materials shortened slightly in February. The number of purchasers reporting lead times of 60 days or less rose to 85%, up from 83% in January.

Lead times for Capital Expenditures in the important six months or longer category was unchanged (51%) in February. However, the number of

Report On Business®

members reporting lead times of 60 days or less rose to 34% from 32% in January.

Lead times for Maintenance, Repair, and Operating (MRO) Supplies shortened in February. The number of members reporting lead times of 30 days or less rose to 89% up from 86% in January.

PERCENT REPORTING

Production Materials	Hand to Mouth	30 Days	60 Days	90 Days	6 Mos. and Longer	Capital Expenditures	Hand to Mouth	30 Days	60 Days	90 Days	6 Mos. and Longer	MRO Supplies	Hand to Mouth	30 Days	60 Days	90 Days	6 Mos. and Longer
February	17	40	28	12	3	February	10	8	16	15	51	February	42	47	8	1	2
January	17	41	25	11	6	January	11	8	13	17	51	January	41	45	11	2	1
December	17	40	27	13	3	December	11	6	15	18	50	December	42	48	7	3	0
November	18	35	28	14	5	November	11	7	13	17	52	November	42	43	12	2	1

PRODUCTION MATERIALS

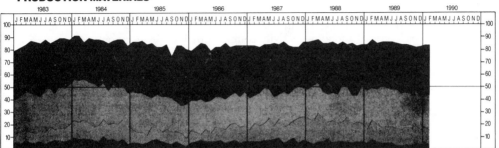

NEW EXPORT ORDERS

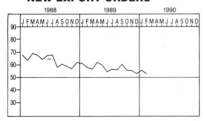

New Export Orders continued to show relatively strong growth in February. The number of members exporting (71%) is slightly higher than the overall average of 1989 (70%). The New Export Order Index fell to 53.0% in February, down slightly from 55.5% in January. The overall average of the index for all of 1989 was 57.5%.

NEW IMPORTS

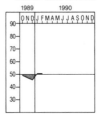

Imports increased in February for the second consecutive month. The Imports Index (not seasonally adjusted) in February (50.5%) was unchanged from January and remains the highest in the five-month history of the index. The 77% of members importing in February was down somewhat from 82% in January, but within the average for the past four months.

	%Better	%Same	%Worse	Net	Diffusion Index	%Exporting
February	14	78	8	+ 6	53.0	71
January	17	77	6	+11	55.5	73
December	15	76	9	+ 6	53.0	72
November	16	79	5	+11	55.5	69

	%Better	%Same	%Worse	Net	Diffusion Index	%Exporting
February	12	77	11	+1	50.5	77
January	12	77	11	+1	50.5	82
December	5	81	14	-9	45.5	78
November	8	78	14	-6	47.0	76

DATA AND METHOD OF PRESENTATION

The **Report on Business** is based on data compiled from monthly replies to questions asked to purchasing executives in over 300 industrial companies. Membership of the Business Survey Committee is diversified geographically, based on value added by state, and by Standard Industrial Classification (SIC) category, based on each industry's contribution to Gross National Product (GNP). Twenty industries in 50 states are represented on the committee.

Survey responses reflect the change, if any, in the current month compared to the previous month. For each of the indicators measured [New Orders, New Export Orders, Imports, Production, Supplier Deliveries (formerly Vendor Deliveries), Inventories, Employment and Prices], this report shows the percentage reporting each response, the net difference between the number of responses in the positive economic direction (higher, better and slower for Supplier Deliveries), and the negative economic direction (lower, worse and faster for Supplier Deliveries), and the diffusion index.

Responses are raw data and are never changed. The diffusion index includes the percent of

positive responses plus one-half of those responding the same (considered positive). The resulting single index number is then seasonally adjusted to allow for the effects of repetitive intra-year variations resulting primarily from normal differences in weather conditions, various institutional arrangements and differences attributable to non-moveable holidays. All seasonal adjustment factors are supplied by the U.S. Department of Commerce and are subject annually to relatively minor changes when conditions warrant them. A sufficient history is not yet available for the New Export Orders and Imports Indexes to determine seasonal adjustment factors. Therefore, these two indexes are not seasonally adjusted. The Purchasing Managers' Index (PMI) is a composite index based on the seasonally adjusted diffusion indexes for five of the indicators (New Orders, Production, Supplier Deliveries, Inventories and Employment) with varying weights applied.

Diffusion indexes have the properties of leading indicators and are convenient summary measures showing the prevailing direction of change and the scope of change. An index reading above 50% indicates that the economy is generally expanding; below 50%, that the economy is generally declining. The distance from 50% is indicative of the strength of the expansion or decline.

Purchasing Managers' Index (PMI), was developed in conjunction with personnel at the U.S. Department of Commerce. When the PMI is above 50 percent, the manufacturing economy is generally expanding and below 50 percent, it is declining. Each of the six indicators also have indexes, computed by taking the percent of those reporting better plus one-half of those reporting the same, times a personal adjustment factor.

The report provides data in a timely fashion, since it leads similar government data by three to four weeks and has been shown to coincide quite closely with government data. It should be summarized and presented to management monthly, as it can provide overall indicators to management about the status of the economy.

Other useful information obtained from the Report on Business is the following:

- Commodities in short supply
- Commodities up in price
- Commodities down in price
- Buying policy (commitment length)
- Regional economic activity compiled by local associations
- Special commodity reports
- Special studies, such as forecast of economic activity for the ensuing six months

Purchasing Price Forecasting

By tracking and forecasting materials prices, purchasing can provide the marketing, sales, and accounting departments, as well as general management, with essential information. With that type of data on material and component costs, marketing can update the pricing of company products to protect profit margins. It helps accounting to set cost standards and to update them more rapidly and accurately. It gives management greater flexibility in planning cash flow and helps the sales and marketing team in their negotiations with company customers.

TRW has a particularly effective price forecasting system in its purchasing department. It makes use of both sophisticated mathematical techniques of forecasting and a consensus technique that relies heavily on the skill and judgment of its buyers. Thus it is flexible enough to meet the needs of the smallest of TRW's 175 operating units.[1]

Forecasts are made for an entire bill of material (an itemized list of the components for each manufactured product, including the name, part number, and amount of the component required). The methods, or models, used are as follows:

Price tracking.   Prices actually paid, or contracted for, on representative items are monitored periodically. Using those data, TRW is able to develop indexes for

---

[1] Much of the material on price forecasting is drawn from *Purchasing World* articles by Sanford A. Jaffe, Steve Nakashige, and Stanley D. Sibley on the TRW system.

the individual items and a composite index for the entire bill of material. Actual prices can be extrapolated to obtain short-run forecasts of prices. The approach can be used successfully if price changes are expected to move in one direction, up or down, during the forecasting period. The data can also be used in long-range forecasting. Patterns of past price movements help the forecaster to understand the causes of the price changes and to anticipate further changes. The price patterns can also serve as a basis for choosing statistical forecasting methods.

Consensus forecasting.   Twice a year buyers estimate the price changes that will occur on representative items during the coming three years compared to previous periods. Proper weighting of the forecast prices to reflect their relative importance enables TRW to calculate a composite price index for the bill of material. This index can then be compared with the actual prices that have been tracked.

Forecasting by regression.   Regression analysis is a statistical technique for forecasting future trends of a key dependent variable (e.g., the price of copper) on the basis of what is expected to happen in other "determining" or independent variables (e.g., copper demand, copper industry labor costs). Using this technique, TRW forecasts its future costs (the dependent variable) on the basis of Bureau of Labor Statistics price indexes (the independent variables). Those projections are supplied by an outside service, Chase Econometrics.

TIMING OF PURCHASES

Depending on forecasting scenarios, buyers will adjust the timing of purchases. In this section timing refers to length of commitment made by buyers on purchased goods and services. In practice, buyers will often contract for an extended time period (e.g., 1 year) and schedule shipments in smaller quantities as required.

Hand-to-mouth buying is purchasing in small quantities that are necessary to keep production running. Just-in-time systems indicate hand-to-mouth ordering. Firms also tend to purchase MRO items and office supplies in this manner. It is necessary to establish a streamlined or electronic or verbal ordering system when timing purchases in this manner, or administrative costs will outstrip inventory savings.

In *current-requirements* purchasing, purchases are committed to support volumes on the books. This strategy allows quantity consolidation but does not extend buying commitments further than the actual order backlog.

A third timing strategy is *forward buying,* which is buying in quantities greater than current requirements but less than foreseeable requirements. Forward buying permits buyers to commit volumes based on historical or expected volumes prior to the company's actually booking these volumes. However, if there is historical precedent—say that sales averaged 15,000 widgets for the past five years, and each widget requires a sprocket—then the buyer might negotiate with a supplier, in this case for an approximate volume of 15,000 sprockets. Forward buying permits the purchaser to negotiate volume pricing and perhaps lock in a fixed price at an opportune time. If the purchaser takes the contracted volume for a one-time inventory, storage costs will offset some of the savings.

Contracting Policies in Fluctuating Markets

When negotiating to buy commodities that fluctuate in price, the purchaser faces the question of what time period to lock in for favorable price advantage. *Deliberate volume timing* involves buying forward when prices are on the upswing and buying hand-to-mouth on the downswing. Effective utilization of this strategy requires excellent forecasting.

Rather than attempt to forecast market changes, some purchasers prefer to commit a fixed amount at regular intervals in approximately equal dollar amounts, this is termed *dollar budgeting*.

Hedging   Hedging is the purchase or sale of a futures contract in a specific commodity to offset the purchase, sale, or inventory of a cash commodity. In essence, a hedge is similar to an insurance policy, which protects you against loss by paying you an amount of money.

For insurance protection, you incur a premium. With hedging, you incur a cost in placing an order on the futures market and are required to put up an amount of money to cover the commodity contracted. This amount of money is called *margin* and varies depending upon the commodity.

Therefore, hedging is a way not only to reduce your risks in the face of price fluctuations but also, in some cases, to ensure supply. The objective of hedging is to protect yourself against price risks, not to take physical delivery of the commodity. In short, hedging offers purchasers protection, since they sell or buy on the cash market and do the opposite on the futures market.

The cash, or spot, market refers to the current price—what you would pay today for purchasing commodities. In earlier times cash-market places were meeting places for buyers and sellers. It was from these early cash-market places that contracts developed for future deliveries.

Several commodities are traded on the futures markets—the major items are agricultural commodities (wheat, sugar, corn), livestock (cattle, pork bellies), and selected metals (copper, gold, silver).

The two primary metals markets are the Commodity Exchange (COMEX), located in New York, and the London Metals Exchange (LME), located in London.

Other national exchanges include the New York Mercantile Exchange and the Chicago Board of Trade. There are several large regional exchanges that specialize in specific commodities.

Buying and Selling Hedges—Examples   There are two major types of hedges—a buying hedge and a selling hedge. The buying hedge offers protection against price fluctuation when a fixed-price sale is made for delivery at a future date (see Table 19-2). For example, company A agrees on May 1 to sell 10,000 motors to

Table 19-2 Buying Hedge

Cash Market	Futures Market
May 1990 SELLS 50,000 lbs. copper at $.77/lb.	BUYS 50,000 lbs. January 1991 copper at $.84/lb.
October 1990 BUYS 50,000 lbs. copper at $.82/lb.	SELLS 50,000 lbs. January 1991 copper at $.89/lb.
Loss ($.05/lb.)	Gain $.05/lb.

company B at a fixed price for a December delivery. The price for the motors is based on May copper prices. At 5 pounds of copper per motor, 50,000 pounds of copper is needed.

Company A has three major alternatives for satisfying its copper demand: (1) It can order the copper immediately and then store it; (2) it can order the copper prior to fabrication and absorb the subsequent increase or decrease in price; or (3) it can hedge.

Assuming company A chooses to hedge, the hedge would work as follows:

In May the buyer purchases a January futures contract at $.84/lb. the current cash price is $.77/lb. and during the next four months the price of copper rises to $.82 a pound, which would have cost the firm $2,500 in profits on the order if unhedged. However, the futures prices also rises by $.05 a pound, and thus the purchaser's company makes this amount on the transaction.

On the other hand, should copper decrease in price, the purchaser would have gained in the cash market and lost in the futures market. The only cost incurred in this hedge is the commission and lost interest on the margin put up by the buyer.

The selling hedge is primarily used to protect the value of inventory in a declining market. For example, a capital-goods manufacturer has 100,000 pounds of copper in inventory and is committed to receive another 50,000 pounds. However, a major customer for whom the copper was to be used has put a six-month delay on the order, and fabrication will not begin for another four months.

The purchaser could either do nothing, except hope that copper does not decline in value, or use a hedge to protect against a potential decline.

A simplified example of a selling hedge is shown on Table 19-3. Here the invoice for the cash-market transaction is billed at the current copper price of $.72 a pound, bringing the cash loss to $7,500 ($.05 a pound x 150,000 pounds). However, the futures market saw a gain of $.05 a pound.

The major premise of the previous two examples is that the cash market and the futures market generally move by the same amount. However, that is not always true, since supply and demand factors and speculators' positions, for example, can change during the course of a hedge. The difference between cash and futures prices is the *basis*.

The theoretical price differential for the basis is due to carrying charges. The further into the future a contract is placed, the larger the basis.

Table 19-3 Selling Hedge

Cash Market	Futures Market
BUYS	SELLS
May 1, 1990 OWNS	May 1, 1990 150,000 lbs.
150,000 lbs. copper at $.77/lb.	January 1991 copper at
	$.84 lb.
SELLS	BUYS
October 1990 use copper	150,000 lbs. January 1991
150,000 lbs. copper at $.72/lb.	copper at $.79/lb.
Loss ($.05/lb.)	Gain $.05/lb.

As you approach a specified date, the carrying charges disappear, and the spread between the cash price and the futures price narrows. This can cause either a greater gain or a greater loss in the futures transaction.

In real-world markets factors like supply and demand and speculator reactions to current events will also affect basis. Speculators are individuals who take a position (either buy or sell) in a futures contract and hope to profit on a commodities price movement. The speculator stabilizes the market for the hedgers by taking alternate positions and providing sufficient volume to allow the exchange to operate efficiently. Speculators' primary concern is to sell high and buy low or buy low and sell high. These actions can cause a market to be inverted. An *inverted* market occurs when the futures price is less than the cash price. In the large percentage of future sales, actual delivery is not called for, and the transaction is closed by issuing a transfer notice. The major reason buyers do not take delivery is that the quality level is a very common (basic) or merchant quality. Buyers with more demanding specifications cannot use such material.

Benefit and Drawbacks of Futures The primary benefit for purchasers using the futures markets is the protection from wide swings in prices. The major drawbacks to futures trading are (1) the limited number of commodities traded, (2) the quality of the material, and (3) a perception on the part of many managers that it is speculation. While it is true that individual trades result in a loss or gain over a number of trades, these even out.

Speculative Purchasing

In general, speculative purchasing refers to buying material in excess of current and future requirements with the intention of profiting on price movement. Such actions are generally left to decisions of upper management. Profit and risk are primarily the responsibilities of management. It has already been noted that inventory profits, though resulting from purchasing action, do not customarily accrue to the credit of purchasing in the company audit and accounts. Purchasing seeks at all points to minimize risk—risk of shortage or surplus, of physical or financial depreciation, of overextended investment in materials. In many cases, the purchasing manager's authority to take risks is definitely circumscribed by the placing of a monetary limit on the value of orders that may be issued without specific authorization of a superior officer.

Management, however, can and does take risks for profit. In respect to materials procurement, in addition to the routine review and authorization of large purchases, such risks include decisions to risk shortages by deferring purchases in the expectation of lower prices or, at the other extreme, decisions to invest a large proportion of the company's financial resources in materials inventories, perhaps at the expense of other business purposes.

Usually such decisions are implemented through the purchasing department, but the policy and responsibility lie with management. In some special cases, as when one or more key commodities are inherently volatile in price behavior, characterized by short-range fluctuations or wide market swings, when their role in the cost structure of the purchaser's product is significant and correspondingly volatile, speculative purchasing may be indicated as the rule rather than the deviation. It is in such commodities that the greatest problems, opportunities, and hazards of speculative purchasing occur. Because the objectives and techniques of this sort of buying have little in common with the general purchasing program, such procurement is sometimes set up as a separate assignment, handled by a commodity specialist close to management or by an executive in the management group, where the responsibility for speculative risk actually lies.

Most cases and those most pertinent to a study of general purchasing principles arise in connection with items that would normally be bought in the course of regular purchase procedure. Here a situation may develop that in the judgment of the purchasing manager calls for forward buying beyond the scope of her established policy and authority and justifies the additional risk. The common-sense way of handling such a situation is for the purchasing manager to make a recommendation to the general manager or other executive to whom she is responsible, with the reasons as to why she considers the extraordinary expenditure advisable. If management concurs in this judgment, the purchase is authorized and made through regular purchasing channels. The ultimate decision reflects both purchasing and management judgment and objectives.

Some companies have established purchasing committees, consisting of the purchasing manager and top executives in general management, sales, and finance. The function of a purchasing committee is not to buy. It is to review and set purchasing policies on major requirements. Members usually concern themselves with only a dozen or so particular commodities that are critical to the business. They determine the period of coverage that is desirable or make specific purchase authorizations.

RESEARCH IN PLANNING AND FORECASTING

Forecasting plays an important part in the system described on page 338, but it is not explicitly given that label. In that program the buyers interpret market conditions and production outlook in their own studies of conditions. In other companies, particularly the larger ones, a research section might develop the necessary data and leave the interpretation of the facts it collected to the buyers and their supervisors. The extent to which research groups make specific forecasts followed by recommendations as to action varies widely. The smaller the company, the more likely it is that the buyer or purchasing manager is his own researcher and forecaster. In the larger organizations it is generally a joint effort between purchasing research and the buyers. Figure 19-5 shows a format for informal monthly forecasts by a purchasing department.

In at least one large multiplant organization, the research organization is specifically charged with forecasting and making recommendations. The reports that it makes are, of course, the work of large numbers of highly trained specialists and therefore outside the scope of the small purchasing department. But the principles on which they are based can be used in modified form even in the smallest purchasing department. In the case of the small department the reports would be prepared by, rather than for, the purchasing manager and directed to his management rather than to the buyer.

- *Materials-situation bulletin:* an analysis of the current market situation for each of the major materials purchased by the company, accompanied by a short-term recommendation as to forward coverage
- *Price-information bulletin:* market-price history of key purchased materials and short-term forecasts of price movements

PURCHASING DEPT. MONTHLY REPORT _____

Purchase Orders (in 1000$)

SUMMARY	Drug Chem	Pkg Matl	Equip Supp	Total	FORECAST	Drug Chem	Pkg Matl	Equip Supp	Total
Open as of 10-1-	000	0000	000	0000	To be placed in Nov.	000	000	000	0000
Placed in Oct.	0000	0000	000	0000	Deliveries in Nov.	000	000	000	0000
Deliveries in Oct.	000	000	000	0000	" " Dec.	000	000	000	0000
Open as of 11-1-	000	0000	000	0000	" next 6 mos.	0000	0000	0000	00000
COMPARISON									
Total 10 Mos. 19	0000	0000	0000	0000					
Total 10 Mos. 19	0000	0000	0000	0000					

COMMENTS

VOLUME - Chemicals - The value of new orders and deliveries made in October were within 5% of our buyers' prophecy. November is expected to be about 15% less than October.

Packaging Materials - The value of new orders increased sharply over the projection, chiefly due to hedging against shortages that were developing in suppliers inventories as a result of steel and glass strikes. Deliveries were nearly 20% greater than normal thus securing many important raw materials against possible shortage.

INVENTORIES - Current inventories are obviously increased some and normal operations can be expected for some time. However, we recommend continued additions to our inventory of steel items (caps, drums, band and wire) to protect against tight supplies expected for several months after steel production is resumed.

PRICES - In spite of buyers' resistance to price increases, there is no evidence that prices will hold at present levels indefinitely. All indications are that labor costs will continue to contribute to some inflation and reflect in possible increased prices in many of our materials.

Figure 19-5 Format for a short-term, informal monthly forecast by a purchasing department

- *Advance ordering and inventory bulletin:* a list of suggested ordering lead times and inventory levels in the light of current general economic and market conditions

The group also issues long-term forecasts—sometimes as far ahead as ten years—on basic materials like steel and aluminum. It also maintains price indices on all key materials.

POINTS FOR REVIEW

1. Explain why the importance of purchasing planning extends beyond the purchasing department itself.
2. Construct a set of preparatory questions to be asked in preparing a hypothetical procurement plan for a product or material—one with which you are familiar or one that may be designated by the instructor.
3. Distinguish between planning and forecasting, giving examples of each as they are employed in a purchasing department.
4. List the major elements to be considered in forecasting for purchasing.
5. Name and describe three types of reports that a purchasing manager, even in a small company, can submit that would be of value to company management.
6. Explain hedging in the futures market.
7. Describe the difference between hand-to-mouth and forward buying techniques.

20

Value Analysis/ Standardization

We have already suggested that the value concept breaks across the lines that divide functional responsibility and prompts a new purchasing activity—value analysis. To measure value we balance what we get in our purchase against what we must pay. We get from the supplier what we ask the supplier to furnish; thus we start with the quality definition and apply all our purchasing skills to procure that quality at a minimum cost. The essence of the quality definition is suitability. But as soon as we enter the realm of price analysis and negotiation, we may find that a part of what we are paying goes for quality features that do not contribute substantially or proportionately to suitability of the material or product purchased. To that extent the expenditure is wasteful. This brings us to a study of the purpose or function for which the item is purchased. That study includes a review of the specification for a possible revision of the quality requirement that may permit us to reduce costs without impairing suitability.

This process of study and review—value analysis—is not simply a routine part of the buying process. It takes time, special attention, and special talents. It is essentially a staff service to the buyer. In some situations, particularly in smaller companies, one person may have the dual role of value analyst and buyer. But any full-scale value analysis program is most effective when the purchasing department has its own staff analyst or analysis section or has a leading role in any companywide value analysis program. However, in all cases the buyer must act as a value analyst challenging product specifications so as to ensure that the company receives the best value for its purchasing dollar.

A SECOND LOOK AT THE SPECIFICATION

Value analysis (VA) is variously defined. One simple definition describes the process as "engineering unnecessary cost factors out of a purchased item." A more elaborate definition states:

> Value analysis is the study of the relationship of design, function, and cost of any product, material, or service with the object of reducing its cost through modification of design or material specifications, manufacture by more efficient processes, change in source of supply (internal or external), or possible elimination or incorporation into a related item.[1]

Carlos Fallon, at the time a materials specialist on the RCA corporate staff, defined value analysis in an internal memorandum as follows:

> Value analysis is a performance-oriented scientific method for improving product value by relating the elements of product worth to their corresponding elements of cost, in order to accomplish the function of the product at least cost in resources.

[1]Dean S. Ammer, *Materials Management and Purchasing*, 4th ed. (Homewood, Ill.: Richard D. Irwin, 1980).

DEVELOPMENT OF VALUE ENGINEERING

Originally, value analysis was intended to apply primarily to parts already in production. It soon became obvious, however, that the study of function could begin early in the design stages of a part or product. Gradually, the scope of value analysis was expanded and refined to include preproduction functional analysis, which in turn became known as value engineering (VE).

The Department of Defense (DOD), which enthusiastically adopted the value concept in the early 1960s, describes value engineering as

> A systematic effort directed at analyzing the functional requirements of systems, equipment, facilities, procedures, and supplies for the purpose of achieving the essential functions at the lowest total cost, consistent with the needed performance, reliability, quality, and maintainability.

The DOD goes on to state:

> Although there are numerous other published definitions of VE, most are merely minor variations of this definition and none appears to contradict it. Others may refer to their value improvement efforts by such terms as value analysis, value control, or value management. There may be some subtle differences between these other programs and VE, but the basic objectives and philosophy appear to be the same for all.[2]

Thus the various terms are generally considered interchangeably and are used so in this text.

Value analysis by purchasing does not encroach upon the functions or prerogatives of other departments. The cost-reduction possibilities that it discloses are initially presented as recommendations—perhaps only queries—to those who must ultimately define the need. Wherever changes in material, design, or process are involved, approval by engineering or manufacturing departments is essential before a specification can be changed. If a suggestion has merit, the actual changes are often worked out in those departments. If a suggestion is impracticable, or if there are other factors that outweigh the cost consideration, it can be rejected. In short, purchasing can challenge a specification but cannot change it without the approval of the using department.

The application of value analysis to existing specifications is in no sense a derogation of the engineering skill and judgment represented in the original statement of need. Rather, it adds another criterion in defining right quality. It gives recognition to the fact that in design and specification, as in every other field, there is an ever-present possibility of improvement and that the only way to achieve that improvement is through continuous, systematic effort directed toward that end. Characteristically, if any part or material is doing its job satisfactorily, and if the specification satisfies the requirement of suitability, there is no inclination on the part of the user to disturb the situation.

[2]Department of Defense, *Value Engineering*, Handbook 5010.8–H (Washington, D.C.: Government Printing Office).

Value analysis also recognizes the fact that in mass production, no unit saving is too small to merit respectful attention, because small unit savings multiplied thousands of times in the total production program quickly mount up to impressive dollar figures. The Ford Motor Company, a pioneer in promoting value analysis activities in purchasing, used a slogan pointing out that with an annual output of millions of vehicles, "the difference of one cent per car represents a saving or loss of tens of thousands of dollars per year." Changing one small component from a forging to an equally serviceable screw-machine product saved four-tenths of a cent per unit—an insignificant figure standing alone. But sixteen of the parts were used in every car. Annual saving: $64,000. Typical savings through value analysis actually run many times greater than this very modest example. Savings of up to 3 or 4 percent of total purchasing expenditures have been reported from a number of companies.

Where accurate records of value analysis savings are maintained, experience has shown that every dollar spent on the activity is returned many times over. In one dramatic case the Black & Decker Manufacturing Company reported that it had saved $1.2 million dollars in a value analysis program that required only a $12,000 additional departmental expense.

In most cases the savings are repeated in succeeding years' purchases. In companies that have had an intensive value analysis program for ten years or longer there is no indication of reaching the point of diminishing returns. Instead, the habits of mind engendered throughout an organization by this approach to value buying give added momentum to the program, with ever-increasing results. Value analysis is an integral, sound, continuing element of scientific purchasing. Such experience, more than any other factor, has brought about the realization that purchasing is, in fact, a profit-making function. This is particularly true at manufacturing firms facing increased competition. "Global competition will not allow anything less than continuous value improvement," according to a representative of John Deere Corporation.[3]

ELIMINATING UNNECESSARY COST FACTORS

Value analysis is a more fundamental and far-reaching concept than the simple process of price analysis in that it goes to the causes of cost. Further, it has the practical objective of applying direct corrective action to minimize these causes and reduce costs, instead of leading only to comparisons and negotiation on the basis of existing costs.

The supplier's basic costs of manufacture are largely fixed by the design, materials, and methods specified by the buyer for production of the purchased item. It may be that the item itself, which the buyer is asking the supplier to produce, represents an unnecessarily high cost for the intended purpose. If that is the case, and if it is recognized, the buyer and his or her associates can attack that hard core of basic production cost, seeking to eliminate or modify the unnecessary fea-

[3]Lea Tonkin, "John Deere Harvests the Fruits of VA," *Purchasing*, June 16, 1988, pp. 82–87.

tures of design and manufacturing operations. In this way they should arrive eventually at a part or specification that truly represents the most economical product to satisfy the end-use requirements. It is obvious that this concern for value adds a new and important dimension to the buyer's definition of "right quality."

From the standpoint of economical product cost, it would be difficult to over-emphasize the significance and benefits of such an approach. Over a long period of years, the constant trend of economic factors has been to build additional costs into the basic cost structure of manufactured products in the form of higher labor rates, more expensive raw materials, and higher taxes and costs of doing business. Meanwhile, each increment in basic cost of manufacture reduces cost flexibility and tends to perpetuate the higher price plane. Under these circumstances, anything that can be engineered out of basic cost as a direct, item-by-item saving is doubly significant. Such savings permanently eliminate cost factors and conserve productive effort. They are repetitive, multiplied many times over in quantity requirements.

From the standpoint of purchasing practice and supplier relationships, the value analysis approach also has much to commend it in that it does not attempt in any way to "squeeze" the supplier, to reduce his or her normal margins of profit, or to exert extraordinary competitive pressure in dealings with that supplier. As a matter of fact, the supplier's own suggestions and cooperation may be enlisted in this effort, to mutual advantage. It is one of those happy situations in which everybody wins.

CHECKLIST FOR VALUE ANALYSIS

This approach to the problem of cost is well summarized in the checklist of ten "Tests for Value" originally compiled and used in the purchasing department of the General Electric Company and widely adapted throughout industry and the Department of Defense. This code, which has been widely circulated throughout every division of the company, among engineering and manufacturing as well as purchasing personnel, follows.

Every material, every part, every operation must pass these tests:
1. Does its use contribute value?
2. Is its cost proportionate to its usefulness?
3. Does it need all of its features?
4. Is there anything better for the intended use?
5. Can a usable part be made by a lower-cost method?
6. Can a standard product be found which will be usable?
7. Is it made on proper tooling, considering quantities used?
8. Do material, reasonable labor, overhead, and profit total its cost?
9. Will another dependable supplier provide it for less?
10. Is anyone buying it for less?

Examples of this type of analysis, with a representative application of each listed test to a purchased component (most of the components were bought in the hundreds of thousands), were cited early in the GE program, as reported in *Purchasing Magazine* for May 1951:

Test 1. (Condenser used across contacts of a relay to provide arc action as contact opens.) When cobalt became available after World War II, an alnico magnet was used to provide snap action. Analysis disclosed that the condenser was no longer necessary with this magnet—it did not add value to the product—and it was eliminated. The saving was 500,000 condensers per year, at 10 cents each.

Test 2. (Spacer hub for mounting light aluminum disks.) Considering the simple function of this part in the assembly, the cost of 90 cents per unit was out of proportion to its usefulness. The cost was high due to undercutting to reduce weight, which was an important factor. Analysis showed that, by making the part of aluminum, the undercutting could be eliminated, the weight still further reduced, and identical performance provided at a cost of 20 cents per unit. The saving was 77 percent.

Test 3. (Stainless steel disk used in dispensing machine.) These washers were formerly chamfered on one side. Analysis revealed that the chamfer made no contribution to value—the part did not need all of its features. Eliminating the chamfer reduced the cost from 18 cents to 5 cents per unit, a saving of 72 percent.

Test 4. (Mica stack used for insulation.) By changing from sheet mica to molded Micalex, the parts of the assembly were more rigidly mounted, resulting in a better assembly, and cost was reduced from $40 to $34 per thousand, a saving of 15 percent.

Test 5. (Hub assembly.) This part was formerly made as a two-part riveted assembly, at a cost of $30 per thousand. Study showed that it could be made as a one-piece casting, eliminating the assembly operation and simplifying production. At the same time, cost was reduced to $10 per thousand, a saving of 67 percent.

Test 6. (Stud contact.) This part had been made to special design, at a cost of $27 per thousand. Purchasing search discovered a standard-design stud, available at $14 per thousand, that provided identical performance. The saving was 48 percent.

Test 7. (Stainless weld nipple.) Because of relatively small quantities required, the former procedure had been to purchase a standard stainless fitting and machine away a part of it to provide the desired weld embossing. Cost by this method was 20 cents each. Value analysis disclosed the fact that production requirements had increased to the point where another process should be considered. It was subsequently produced in quantity on an automatic screw machine at a cost of 5 cents each. The saving was 75 percent.

Test 8. (Stainless dowel pin.) This part was purchased in large quantities, made to special design and specifications with close tolerances required. The cost of $3 per thousand seemed out of line with reasonable standards, but was justified by the vendor's costs. The manufacturer was invited to confer on details of the specification, manufacturing process, and inspection. As a result, some wastes of material and labor were eliminated from the manufacturer's operation. The identical part, produced to the same close tolerances, was subsequently produced at $2 per thousand, a saving of 33 percent.

Test 9. (Bushing.) Exploration of the market disclosed that this part, purchased from an established source of supply at $18 per thousand, could be procured from an equally reliable supplier at $13.50 per thousand, a saving of 25 percent.

Test 10. (Button.) This part, used by one division in large volume, was being purchased at $2.50 per thousand. Research within the purchasing department revealed that another division was using a similar button costing $1 per thousand. The latter was found to be applicable to the use under study, with equally good performance, at a saving of 60 percent.

The monetary values in the GE examples are, of course, not particularly meaningful in light of today's prices. But the percentages of savings are still impressive, and the value techniques and principles on which they are based are more valid than ever.

THE ROLE OF PURCHASING

Value analysis for cost reduction is everybody's business and is more effective when its principles are applied throughout the organization, wherever requirements and specifications originate. But there are five important reasons why it is logical for the purchasing department to initiate and promote this activity (as in the case of standardization, which is one of the tools of value analysis, indicated in test six of the checklist.)

1. Regardless of how much cost-reduction activity is carried on in other departments of the company, it is still a responsibility of the buyer to seek maximum value when a product requirement comes up to the point of purchase. It is his or her duty to challenge wasteful and avoidable costs inherent in the things that he or she is asked to buy. Thus it is inescapable that a large share of whatever value analysis work is done will be done by the buyer or in the purchasing department in any case.

2. Purchasing, more than any other department, must be cost conscious in respect to the materials and parts that go into the company's end product. This is a desirable attribute in every department, but it is an integral part of the buying responsibility. The purchasing manager is brought face to face with the cost factor in every transaction. Even when value analysis is not organized for special consideration, it is practiced to some degree, as a matter of course, in every purchasing comparison and decision.

3. Purchasing is costwise through experience in price analysis and comparisons, evaluation of alternative materials and methods, and the handling of many comparable items. The buyer learns why some products cost more than others and what features in a specification make suppliers' quotations higher. This knowledge is enhanced by the buyer's daily exposure to the product offerings and sales presentations of vendors, which can be directly related to his or her own requirements and often can reveal how cost reductions are being effected in other companies having similar needs.

4. Purchasing is objective in its attention to costs, to a degree that is difficult for the person or department whose first concern is the utility or performance of a product and whose judgment is understandably influenced by creative pride of design.

5. Purchasing is a natural focal point at which each individual requirement and specification, from whatever source in the company, must pass in review. It is therefore in a strategic position to apply the experience gained in connection with one item to other similar items, to recognize the areas in which intensive value analysis gives greatest promise of effective and profitable results, and to carry on such projects as part of a specific, comprehensive, and continuing program.

Thus beyond its own direct value analysis activities, the role of purchasing is to initiate and organize; to promote cost consciousness in all departments of the company, keeping this topic in the forefront of their thinking; to point out opportunities or to raise questions as to the possibility of cost reduction in purchased items; to develop practical techniques for product and value analysis; and, upon request, to train personnel of other departments in the application of these techniques, giving whatever assistance may be required.

TECHNIQUE OF PRODUCT ANALYSIS

The techniques of product analysis are as varied as the problems in this field, but particular attention should be directed to one method that has been exceptionally resultful. The examples previously cited have been concerned with individual components or small parts of a larger assembly. The more comprehensive approach starts with the complete assembly, considered as the sum of its parts.

A widely used technique is to take such an assembly, dismantle it, and mount it on a panel board of plywood or other suitable material in such a way that each of the component parts, down to the smallest screw or other fastening device, is shown in relation to all other parts. With this visualization, analysis is facilitated and the pertinent questions are more readily framed, leading to better and more economical practice.

A variation of this technique is to mount adjacently on a panel board, in corresponding position for direct comparison, the disassembled components of competitive or alternative products (e.g., dashboard clocks) so that their relative designs and merits and costs may be analyzed, resulting in a revised specification that literally embodies the best and most economical features of each.

Still another technique that has produced excellent results is the "brainstorming" session. A problem or product is presented to a group of people for consideration. They need not be experts in the particular subject. If they represent a variety of special interests and experience, such as purchasing, engineering, and manufacturing, so much the better. The meeting is totally unrehearsed. The group leader presents the problem, stressing the function to be served by the product and showing current design or practice. The leader then invites suggestions for improvement. Each person makes whatever suggestions come first to mind, however unorthodox or impracticable the ideas may seem to be. These are listed and grouped, and when the first flow of ideas has slowed down, they are explored in greater detail, again in open discussion and with the invitation for further ideas that may have been prompted by some aspect of those already presented.

In relatively large-value programs, involving a number of specialists, a planned and systematic approach is generally more productive than an unorganized idea-swapping session. A popular procedure for analysis calls for a logical progression, moving from the collection of information, to speculation as to the function of the part or material, to consideration of substitutes or alternatives, then all the way through to recommendations and action. Called the VA/VE job

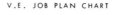

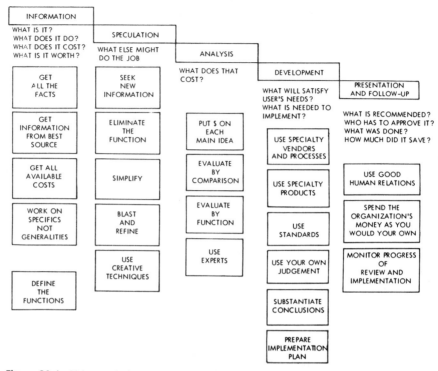

V.E. JOB PLAN CHART

Figure 20-1   Value analysis-value engineering job plan

plan, it is widely employed in industry and the Department of Defense. The basic principles on which the job plan is built can, of course, be adapted even when value analysis is carried out on a smaller scale, for example, by the individual buyer.

A diagrammatic explanation of the job plan is shown in Figure 20-1. A more generalized example of how an end product can be value analyzed component by component is presented in Figure 20-2.

SCOPE OF VALUE ANALYSIS

The scope of value analysis is not limited to factors of design and manufacturing method. In chemical manufacturing industries, for example, the product is inherently and rigidly defined in its composition and grade, and variations or alternatives are obviously ruled out of consideration. Nevertheless, value analysis has been effectively applied in this field in respect to reagents, solvents, plasticizers, containers, bulk handling and distribution, and other elements in the process that substantially affect product costs.

The last three items in the General Electric Company's checklist for value relate exclusively to purchasing policies and methods and are applicable to any items of use in any company.

Because the concept of value is compounded of both quality and cost, the subject is not complete without reference to the criteria of buying at the right price (Chapter 12). Many of the methods used in that determination are properly included in the broad field of value analysis. The same is true of decisions on whether to make or purchase a part or item (Chapter 9) and, as will be shown, the whole field of standardization (see the separate discussion of standardization later in this chapter).

In the early days of value analysis the function was generally performed by buyers themselves, particularly in small and medium-size companies. It soon became clear that this arrangement was unsatisfactory because of the additional load it placed on personnel in terms of time, paperwork, and follow-up. As value analysis became more widely accepted, more formal types of value analysis organization developed. Among these are the following:

- Full-time analysts, generally assigned to the purchasing department, whose major responsibility is the study of purchased parts and materials offering the greatest potential for improvement or cost reduction.
- Value analysis committees made up of representatives of various functions, including purchasing, design engineering, manufacturing engineering, and accounting. The purchasing representative is generally the department's staff analyst, who acts as chairperson.
- A variation of the value analysis committee made up of representatives of all functions in the plant. The purchasing agent or manager is generally the chairperson of the committee.
- Value analysis by project, in which VA teams are organized to work full time on specific VA objectives. When the project is complete, the committee is disbanded.

The use of value analysis techniques is not exclusively a matter for full-time specialists, according to L.D. Miles, who set up the first value analysis program in the 1950s at the General Electric Company.

"Much good value can be achieved by everyday use of the techniques," he says, "and large amounts of unnecessary costs will still be unidentified, however. Value activities must be enhanced by the use of a specialized skill and knowledge.

"Obviously, the prevailing philosophy of a company's management, and the size and scope of the business, will determine the appropriate provision for value analysis effort."[4]

REPORTING ON VALUE ANALYSIS

The results of the analyst's work are in the form of reports and recommendations. They are supported in every case by cost comparisons and the projection of anticipated savings, because saving money is the goal of value analysis. The reports are

[4]Miles, a columnist for *Purchasing World,* was widely known as the father of value analysis for his pioneering work and continuing contributions to the discipline. The quotation is from his book, *Techniques of Value Analysis and Engineering,* 2nd ed. (New York: McGraw-Hill Book Co. 1972), p. 24.

How to analyze a product

Even a good product
can be made better.
Value analysis provides
the approach.

PRE-CONCEIVED IDEAS are the biggest obstacle to value improvement. The design of the portable vacuum cleaner illustrated here is a good one—but even a well-made product can be improved.

The value analyst goes beyond normal buying steps and evaluates the total concept: from the standpoint of sales, engineering, production, cost. A fresh look can turn up additional savings.

No line of inquiry should be ruled out. Every question should be answered. Sometimes the "dumb" question is the one that triggers the best result.

Here's how a VA brainstorming session —designed to develop ways to improve the vacuum cleaner—might work:

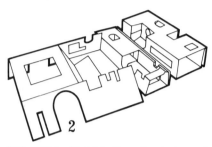

Parts must be fitted into three die-cut pieces of board. Would a molded plastic shell cut down packing labor? Can we redesign the spacers into a one-piece carrying caddy for the accessories?

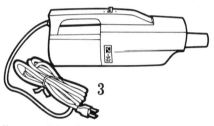

Vacuum unit has three-piece housing. Can this be made as two pieces? Why not mold the nameplate into the part instead of applying it in a separate operation? Could a standard metal tube replace the special molded housing?

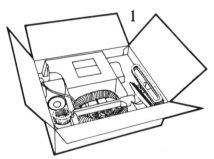

Interior packaging hides the product. Can it be redesigned for better visual display? Can the number of assembly operations be reduced in packing? Why not design the carton so that it can be used as a wall storage box?

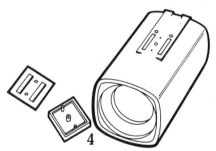

Seal for handle attachment must be assembled from inside housing. Can extra plastic piece be eliminated? Is there another way to achieve airtight closure?

Figure 20-2 A basic approach in value analyzing an end product begins with identification of the function of parts and materials and consideration of alternatives. Courtesy of *Purchasing Magazine*

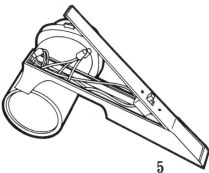

5

Plated metal handle requires extra operation. Can we use stainless or spun aluminum and cut out finishing operation? What about the switch? Can we buy it cheaper from a specialty supplier?

8

Rubber diaphragm on nozzle is fastened with metal plate and two screws. Can we mold protrusions on plastic and heat seal to eliminate screws? What purpose does the metal plate serve?

6

Blower assembly has too many parts. Why not combine into one? Do internal spacers have to be finished? Only purpose is to separate fins.

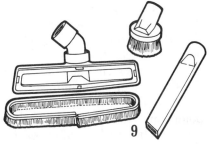

9

Brush housings and cleaning attachments are made from two types of plastic, rigid and soft. Can we standardize on one material? Washer in floor brush is brittle. Is there a better material? Nylon brushes set in metal rim; can they be all nylon and set in plastic? Do bristles have to be removable or can entire part be replaced? Two spring clips hold movable brush for upholstery cleaner. Is there a better way?

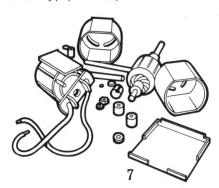

7

Is motor overdesigned for the job? Can we recheck the specifications? Is it possible to use a lighter housing to reduce weight? Can a standard base plate be used in place of special?

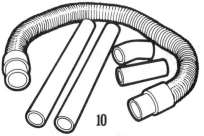

10

Two pieces of metal tubing must be chamfered on one end. Can they be made from rigid plastic, molded to shape? Flexible hose has wire core; what gage wire is needed?

made to the purchasing manager and only through the purchasing department to other personnel or departments affected. This is the orderly channel of procedure and communication, because decisions based on the recommendations, involving changes in specifications, manufacturing methods, or shop practice, must be made at the executive level. To inject a third, independent factor and personality into interdepartmental problems of value and utility tends to confuse the issue, to give the impression of meddling, and in general to weaken the force of the recommendation and the consideration that is given to it. By contrast, a purchasing proposal based on the ideal recommendation and within the buyer's legitimate province of purchase cost reduction, must be weighed on merit even though the proposal may not be adopted for other reasons.

In addition to actual research and analysis projects, an important part of the program is to promote cost consciousness throughout the entire organization, whether materials are specified and used. The publicizing of improved practice and lowered costs, through bulletins and employee publications, helps toward an understanding of what value analysis tries to accomplish and generates enthusiasm for the program. Cost reduction must be a team effort. When it is accepted that value analysis is not critical of previous decisions but is predicated on the principle that almost everything is capable of improvement, progress is made toward getting everybody on the team. A second step is to make available training in value analysis techniques. That is best done with small groups, in "workshop" sessions. Engineering, manufacturing, and other specifying departments, as well as buyers, should be invited to participate. The mixed group presents various viewpoints on the value and fosters understanding of the common objective.

The chief qualification for a successful value analyst is an imaginative, questioning mind, backed with enthusiasm and perseverance. A knowledge of cost accounting and of manufacturing processes is desirable. The value analyst must have the ability to work with people and the willingness to share credit. Nothing can kill a value analysis program more quickly than a "credit-grabbing" attitude.

ENLISTING SUPPLIER ASSISTANCE

One of the most fruitful sources of information and help in value buying is the cooperation of suppliers. Here buyers have at their disposal the advice of specialists who are expert and experienced in their respective fields to a degree that buyers, concerned with many different products, can rarely hope to attain. The purchasing manager who can establish a relationship with suppliers in which they make the buyer's problems their own, and will work with the buyer toward the objectives of cost reduction, enlists the technical resources and manufacturing experience of an entire industry. Such a relationship is, of course, predicated on the assumption that the cooperative supplier will be the preferred supplier and will profit through greater sales. This policy in itself represents a sound concept of value in purchasing. Figure 20-3 shows a checklist used by one company to solicit value analysis help from vendors.

ALLIS-CHALMERS PURCHASING DIVISION _____ Works	VI$_2$P* SUPPLIER CHECK LIST FOR VALUE IMPROVEMENT

A-C PURCHASE ORDER OR INQUIRY NO. _____ BUYER _____

PART NAME _____

A-C PART NO. OR DRAWING NO. _____

WE ARE CONTINUALLY ANALYSING OUR PRODUCTS FOR VALUE AND SOLICIT YOUR HELP THROUGH ANSWERS TO THE FOLLOWING QUESTIONS THAT MAY BE APPLICABLE TO THE PART IDENTIFIED ABOVE. OUR AIM IS TO ELIMINATE UNNECESSARY COSTS WITHOUT ADVERSELY AFFECTING THE FUNCTIONAL INTEGRITY OF THE PART; WE WANT YOUR SUGGESTIONS!

QUESTIONS	CHECK YES | NO	SUGGESTIONS
1. DO YOU UNDERSTAND FUNCTION PRODUCT IS TO PERFORM?	☐ **	
2. COULD COSTS BE REDUCED BY RELAXING REQUIREMENTS AS TO: ● TOLERANCES? ● FINISHES? ● TESTING? BY HOW MUCH? _____	☐ ☐ ☐ ☐ ☐ ☐	
3. COULD COSTS BE REDUCED THRU CHANGES IN: ● MATERIAL SPECIFIED? ● ORDERING QUANTITIES? ● MFG. PROCESS USED? I.E., CASTING, FORGING, STAMPING, ETC. BY HOW MUCH? _____	☐ ☐ ☐ ☐ ☐ ☐	
4. CAN YOU SUGGEST ANY OTHER CHANGES THAT WOULD: ● REDUCE WEIGHT? ● SIMPLIFY THE PART? ● REDUCE OVERALL COSTS? BY HOW MUCH? _____	☐ ☐ ☐ ☐ ☐ ☐	
5. DOES IT APPEAR THAT ANY OF THE SPECIFICATIONS OR QUALITY CONTROL REQUIREMENTS ARE TOO STRINGENT?	☐ ☐	
6. IN SUPPLYING THIS PRODUCT, WHAT IS THE GREATEST ELEMENT OF YOUR COST THAT WE MIGHT POSSIBLY HELP ALLEVIATE?		
7. DO YOU HAVE A STANDARD ITEM THAT COULD BE SUBSTITUTED FOR THIS PART SATISFACTORILY?	☐ ☐	WHAT IS IT? _____ WHAT DOES IT COST? _____

8. OTHER SUGGESTIONS?

SUPPLIER (COMPANY NAME)		ADDRESS
SIGNATURE	TITLE	DATE

* "VALUE IMPROVEMENT IN PURCHASING" AT ALLIS-CHALMERS
** IF ANSWER IS "NO," OBTAIN FUNCTIONAL INFORMATION FROM BUYER INVOLVED

Figure 20-3 Form used to solicit supplier help in a value analysis program.
Courtesy of *Purchasing Magazine*

In organized value analysis programs, this source of help is cultivated by means of "supplier clinics." A representative group of suppliers is invited to come to the buyer's plant, usually for a two-day meeting, at which materials requirements, problems, and policies are explained to the group as a whole and sometimes in private conferences. The visitors are not salespeople in the ordinary sense but are drawn from the higher-ranking management and operating officers of the supplier companies. A focal feature of the clinic is a comprehensive display of the company's important products and the purchased parts that go into them. Here suppliers can see firsthand how their own products are used in the buyer's assembly, which is not always clear from the specification or blueprint. It shows the reasons underlying certain terms of the specification, the need for close tolerances at one point or of extra strength at another, and the relationship of each part with other sections that may be procured from other sources. It stresses the idea that the parts manufacturer is in fact a participant in making the end product and that its quality, utility, and cost (and hence its marketability) are really the concern of all.

This is good education, but the clinics also have a more immediate and practical objective. When the suppliers inspect the parts on display, they are invited to indicate those that they are equipped to furnish to best advantage and on which they would like to quote. At the same time it is made clear that the company is receptive to any suggestions as to parts design or manufacturing method that will improve quality or reduce cost or both. Suppliers are furnished with blueprints and specification sheets on the selected item, for further study and estimates.

STANDARDIZATION: A TOOL FOR VALUE

Mass-production techniques are predicated on the principle of uniformity and interchangeability of materials and parts. To this extent the vast majority of manufacturing companies are committed to the policy of standardization in their product lines. This commitment is reflected to some degree in the standardization of their purchase requirements. When this principle is carried one step further, to coordinate these "standard" requirements with the standard product lines and quality grades of supplier industries, additional advantages accrue in the form of quicker availability, alternative sources, and, again, in the economies of mass production.

These advantages are obviously of primary importance in purchasing and value analysis. Theoretically, it is possible to determine and define the ideal quality—in terms of composition, dimension, physical and electrical properties, and other attributes of a material or product—for each individual purpose. This ideal quality could be procured, at substantial cost of money and time. In some special instances procuring the ideal quality may be necessary, but in most cases it is both impractical and unnecessary. Industry has found the answer in standardization of materials and products. Thus the selection may be made not from an infinite number of possible qualities and sizes but rather, from a more practicable range, broad enough to meet the majority of requirements satisfactorily, yet sufficiently limited and well established as to acceptance and use to permit mass production and ready availability. Even so, there is a great deal of designing, manufacturing, and purchasing done on the basis of special specification, when reasonable standards could be adopted with no sacrifice of utility or satisfaction and with substantial advantages of economy and convenience.

Good purchasing practice extends the concept of standardization by promoting the consolidation of similar requirements into a single specification, wherever possible. For example, fewer types of cleaning compounds or fewer grades of lubricants than are ordinarily requested for specific applications might adequately serve the plant's maintenance needs. If so, there would be fewer items to buy and carry in stock, and those that are required could be purchased in larger quantities to better advantage. The same principle can be applied to production materials, as for example, fewer sizes of fasteners, tubing, bar stock, and an endless list of other items.

Engineering Standards

The buyer's interest in standardization is of direct importance as it affects product fabrication. Standardization of screw threads makes possible the use of stock machine screws and bolts in standard tapped holes. Standardization of pipe fittings makes it possible to install plumbing and heating fixtures in existing piping systems and to alter or expand these as required. The list could be extended to great length, touching on many materials and products in common use in our daily living.

Standardization has also been applied to the composition of materials. A typical example is the SAE steels, a series of alloys of specified composition and known properties, defined, identified by numbers, and recognized by all buyers and producers of steel. The number of possible varieties of such steels, the nature and proportion of component elements, and the particular properties attained are almost infinite.

Typically, such standards are developed through the cooperation of producers and users, taking advantage of the experience and technical skill of both groups and coordinating these efforts through various national technical societies or governmental agencies.

Among the agencies that have actively sponsored the development of industrial standards are the American National Standards Institute, the American Society for Testing and Materials, the Society of Automotive Engineers, the American Society of Mechanical Engineers, and the National Electrical Manufacturers' Association. The federal government has also taken an active and effective interest in such projects through the National Bureau of Standards and various procurement agencies.

The American National Standards Institute (ANSI) catalog of standards lists almost three thousand standards currently in force. A *Directory of Standardization* issued by the National Bureau of Standards (NBS miscellaneous publication 288) lists by product name more than five hundred organizations concerned with standardization.

Government Standards

The federal government has contributed greatly to industrial standardization. As mentioned, it has placed the services and facilities of the National Bureau of Standards at the disposal of industry, on request, as a coordinating and sponsoring organization for the development of standards. This service is reinforced by the promulgation of such standards and by the sponsorship of a certification plan indicating adherence to standards by manufacturers, which substantially lessens the burden of individual tests. Figure 20-4 is a list of the benefits provided by the federal government's specifications and standards.

Second, as a large consumer and buyer of a great variety of products, it has developed standards for its own purchases. These standards originate with the various procurement agencies, principally the armed forces and the Federal Bureau of Supply.

BENEFITS
PROVIDED BY
GOVERNMENT
SPECIFICATIONS
AND STANDARDS

1. Elimination of unnecessary types, varieties, and sizes of supply items, thereby reducing capital investment in inventories and storage space.

2. Utilization of nationally known and recognized technical industry standards.

3. Simplification of procurement procedures, better delivery service, and reduced procurement costs.

4. Utilization of regularly produced supply items to the maximum extent practicable.

5. Assurance to Federal agencies that the product being purchased has the characteristics and quality determined essential to the agency's requirements and will best satisfy the intended use--price and other factors considered.

6. Participation by large and small suppliers on an equal basis in supplying Government requirements, thereby broadening sources of supply and assuring greater supplier participation.

7. References to related specifications and standards, such as marking and packing requirements, by which the references become an integral part of the requirement.

8. Sampling, inspection, and test procedures for use in determining that requirements have been met, in addition to clear and accurate descriptions of the technical requirements for the material, product, or service, including design and construction, and component parts.

9. Purchase of supply items which will result in maximum value being received for the public funds expended.

Figure 20-4   Advantages of specifications and standards as outlined in a U.S. government booklet for business managers

An Industry Advisory Council has been established, collaborating with the Standards Division of the Federal Supply System to bring government standards and procurement practices more closely into line with industrial purchase requirements and prevailing manufacturing practices. The membership of the council includes representatives of the American National Standards Institute, the American Society for Testing and Materials, the Society of Automotive Engineers, the Manufacturing Chemists' Association, the American Society of Mechanical Engineers, the National Electrical Manufacturers' Association, technical experts from a number of leading industrial companies, and significantly, the general purchasing manager of a large manufacturing corporation to represent the industrial purchasing viewpoint.

Another contribution of government to standardization has been the compilation of a directory of all standard specifications, including nongovernmental standards—those of the technical societies, and of individual large manufacturers—for the benefit of the producing industry and purchasing executives. The advantage of knowing what work has been done and what results are available is that duplication of effort is avoided and a multiplicity of similar but not identical standards is eliminated. The cause of overall standardization is thus advanced.

STANDARDIZATION CUTS PRODUCT COSTS

Standardization, then, can be a potent tool of purchasing and value analysis. An adopted standard is essentially a definition of quality that becomes the purchasing manager's ordering description for the item. A standardization project or program must be effected through those in the company organization who design the product, thereby creating the need for specific materials and parts, and those who requisition and specify materials and supplies for plant use. The initiative and pressure for standardization, however, may logically come from the purchasing department, which has the responsibility for economical procurement and is in the strategic position of being a clearinghouse for the requirements of all departments, so that variations in usage and specification among various departments can be most readily detected here.

The most convincing argument for specifying and purchasing standard products rather than items of special manufacture is the factor of cost. A survey of representative manufacturers of industrial products revealed the following significant cost comparisons: 23 percent of the manufacturers estimated that special items cost from 10 to 15 percent more to produce than comparable standard items; 47 percent estimated the additional cost at from 25 to 50 percent; 17 percent estimated that the extra cost ran even higher than 50 percent. Only 12 percent reported that no substantial extra cost was involved. The type of product and the supplier's facilities and organization for handling special work naturally influenced these calculations, but the general conclusion is clear that deviations from standards mean higher costs and less value received for the purchaser's dollar.

This is confirmed by value analysis studies that show many instances where simply switching from a specially fabricated part to a standard part of equal utility has resulted in cost savings of as much as 75 percent.

Along with this cost advantage is the factor of greater availability and more prompt delivery. Standard items are normally "shelf items" that can be promptly furnished from manufacturers' or distributors' stocks or those that have a regular place in the supplier's production schedule, so that delays are minimized. Special items, on the other hand, must be fitted into the production schedule, often involving a delay of weeks or months. Thus the normal procurement cycle or lead time is lengthened by the addition of scheduling procedure and the actual production cycle. Procurement of emergency fill-in quantities becomes excessively difficult, if not impossible.

STANDARDIZATION CUTS INVENTORY COSTS

One of the chief benefits of standardization is the possibility of reduced material and supply inventories. With fewer types and sizes and quantities of items to be carried in stock, a smaller total inventory can support the manufacturing program. The prudent quantitative safety margin on a single item protects requirements for all its various uses or applications. There is greater flexibility in meeting the demands of changing rates in the usage of any given item, and the danger of incurring losses through obsolescence is minimized. Reduced total inventories release working capital for other, more productive purposes. This is a constant objective of management.

At the same time stock turnover is faster, so there is less accrued carrying cost to add to the real cost of material up to the time of use.

STANDARDIZATION PROGRAMS

An effective company standardization program depends upon definite assignment of responsibility and continuing attention to the subject. In some companies it is set up as a function in itself, under the supervision of a standards engineer or of a director of standards. More common practice is to undertake standardization as a committee activity. This is perhaps the more logical procedure, because standardization is essentially a process of securing agreement among those responsible for specification and use of materials, those responsible for product design, and those charged with the procurement of the needed items. All these factors should be represented in any form of permanent committee organization, with provision for participation on particular projects by individuals or department heads directly affected. Where no standardization committee has previously existed, the purchasing department frequently is the one to initiate such an activity; often as not, the purchasing representative serves as its chairperson.

One of the first objectives of the program is to establish standard nomenclature for all materials used. Analysis of stockroom inventories often reveals instances of duplication in which identical items may be carried under two or more identifying descriptions. Duplication can easily happen when an item is requisitioned by and purchased for different departments, each of which uses its own term to describe the item; or if a part is identified by the manufacturer's part or catalog number or by the company's own part number for a particular end use in product assembly, it is often the case that two or more such parts are actually identical and interchangeable, although they may be independently requisitioned, purchased, and recorded. Effective standardization of materials cannot be achieved without standard means of identification.

Analysis of stockroom records reveals other pertinent information: excessively slow-moving items and materials carried in a multiplicity of sizes and grades. Data of this sort can be the starting point for study regarding the feasibility of standardization in particular areas. Another starting point may be found in purchase records. Not all materials pass through a central stockroom and appear on stores records. But in the usual organization of a purchasing staff by commodity groupings related items are generally handled by one buyer, and it is usually a simple matter to detect similar products used by several departments, excessive varieties of a single basic product purchased, and deviations from normal usage.

Aims of a standardization program are (1) adoption of companywide standards for materials used for like or similar purposes, (2) correlation of these company standards with established industry standards to the greatest possible degree, and (3) reduction in the number of varieties and sizes to be purchased.

The Standard Stock Catalog

The work of a standardization committee generally results in decisions as to which materials and supplies are to be carried in stores as standard stock items. This information is frequently incorporated in a standard stock list or catalog, often a computer printout showing all stock items, identified by standard nomenclature with whatever cross-reference may be required, detailing all sizes of each item regularly carried in stores. Requisitions are expected to conform to this list, and users can expect immediate supply of listed items. The list is revised as new items are added by action of the committee or as standards are changed in view of changing requirements and usage. On common supply items, requests for nonlisted varieties are automatically questioned and are procurable only under exceptional circumstances, for good reason.

POINTS FOR REVIEW

1. Give a brief definition of value analysis and explain the distinction, if any, between value analysis and value engineering.
2. Name the "ten tests for value" discussed in the text.

3. Use some or all of these tests in a simple value analysis of some product (and its components) that you use or are familiar with.
4. List the reasons for giving the purchasing department a leading role in a company's value analysis program.
5. Discuss the supplier's role in customers' value analysis programs. Explain how a supplier might take the initiative in helping to organize a value program in a company that does not have one.
6. Explain why standardization is an important element in value analysis and standardization, employing, when possible, examples of standardization in some products that you use.

21

Purchasing Services

Numerous articles have been written about how the United States is becoming a service economy. Figures now show that services account for 71 percent of the gross national product and 68 percent of the work force is employed in services versus 19 percent in manufacturing.[1] According to the U.S. Department of Commerce during the 1980s the service sector and retailing accounted for almost 80 percent of all new private-sector jobs. The service sector now contributes 58 percent of the Gross National Product (GNP) averaged worldwide.[2] Compounding this trend were the employee cutbacks (downsizing) that took place at many firms. Thus jobs previously performed inside were now being subcontracted out and in some cases to ex-employees who now acted as external consultants. These changes require that purchasing departments contract for a broader variety of services and spend more dollars.

The difference between product and services are sometimes blurred, and the distinctions are debatable. Figure 21-1 shows a list of twenty services that typical organizations might acquire. Webster defines *service* as "any result of useful labor which does not produce a tangible commodity."

Viewed in another way, services involve efforts of people that are usually labor intensive, involving the delivery or investment of people's time as opposed to an end product. This doesn't imply there are not end products, because there

---

Twenty Typical Services Purchased by a Firm

Health Maintenance Organizations (HMO)
Employment agencies
Corporate travel
Consultants
Advertising
Contract labor
Construction services
Computer assistance
Janitorial
Maintenance
Car rentals
Hotels
Food services
Vending machines
Freight forwarders
Water treatment
Relocation services
Pest control
Landscaping
Security

Figure 21-1

[1] *The Economist World Atlas and Almanac,* (Englewood Cliffs, New Jersey: Prentice Hall, 1989).
[2] John E. G. Bateson, *Managing Services Marketing,* Dryden Press, Hinsdale, Illinois, 1989, p. 4.

usually are, but we are paying for time as opposed to materials, equipment, buildings, and other physical assets. Certainly, some products have characteristics of both goods and services, and these are often termed *mixed purchases.*

SERVICE-PRODUCT COMPARISONS

Table 21-1 shows a comparison of products and services. While a product can be held and inspected, a service often cannot. Thus "prompt, friendly service" is difficult to describe. But sellers of services will stress such benefits. For example, keeping a facility's grass cut and shrubbery landscaped contributes to improved community and customer perceptions of a business. Second, products can be inventoried, services cannot. Thus scheduling services becomes a more critical job. Third, manufacturers can service all types of markets from local to international at a single facility. In addition, manufacturers realize economies of scale, while services by their nature tend to be smaller and operate in local markets.

Most products (excepting retail) are delivered to the buyer, but the customer often comes to the service. For example, most fork-truck service-repair contracts require that the work be performed in the dealer's service center. Other services are brought to the buyer, for instance, landscaping, water softening, pest control, janitorial services.

In making a product, manufacturers gear their process to produce with minimum variation from specification. The impact of labor intensity and smaller operations make this more difficult for service operations. To illustrate, one branch location of a print shop provides excellent service and quality, while the second branch is always late. This variability makes it difficult to establish standards and to ensure that they are met. Finally, many services are completed through mental or physical actions. The management consultant who develops a plan to improve management efficiency and the office cleaning crew are examples of this mental or physical effort. Meanwhile, purchased goods are physically received by the receiving department.

TABLE 21-1   General Comparison of Service and Product Characteristics

Service	Product
1. Intangible	Tangible
2. Noninventoriable/perishable	Can be inventoried
3. Local in scope	Local, national or international in scope
4. Customers come to service or it is delivered	Product delivered to customer
5. Variability in output due to personnel	Output homogeneous/consistent
6. Standards difficult to establish and measure	Standards can be established and tests done to check conformance
7. Is received by an action, physical or mental	Is physically received

SERVICES-PURCHASING CYCLE

For purchasing, the activities of buying services still involve requesting competitive bids, analyzing quotations, placing purchase orders, and following up. It is important, however, that purchasers impress upon users the need to clearly communicate the scope of the service. The major steps in the contracting process are

- Statement of work
- Solicitation of bids
- Supplier selection
- Follow-up and measurement

Statement of Work

The statement of work is the key to the service contract, as the specification is to the product contract. A good statement of work will outline the specific services the contractor is expected to perform. It should indicate the *type, level,* and *quality* of service. While complete descriptions are necessary, overspecifying will result in increased costs and limit competition. To illustrate, one cleaning contract was written to "clean and wax floors using Johnson's floor wax and a Tennant floor scrubber with #2 buffing pads," while another was written to "shine and polish floors weekly using three coats of wax."

Where possible, all jobs should be performance oriented. *Performance-based* statements of work describe the *duty,* the *method,* and *frequency,* thereby allowing the contractor the maximum flexibility in selecting methodologies. An example of a performance standard is, "Floors shall show no dust or dirt streaks after cleaning." *Design-based* statements of work state more specifically the desired results and how the job will be accomplished. Such specifications are used when the user or buyer desires greater control over specific methods of performance. Again, this approach can lead to higher costs, less competition, and higher administrative costs to ensure that the contractor is following directions.

Solicitation of Bids

Finding service suppliers is done in the same way as finding other suppliers (see Chapter 8). Trade directories, company records, other purchasers, and local Chamber of Commerce directories can prove quite helpful. A key item that should be compiled prior to or during the bid cycle is a list of employee qualifications. This information is particularly important when the work will require advanced skills. The list should include a résumé of the qualifications and accreditations of each employee, length of employment, and names of specific personnel assigned to your project. Medical certification stating that they are free from contagious diseases should also be requested. Other issues to be included in the solicitation include:

1. Work schedules
2. Emergency response periods—inquiry on availability and response time in case of emergencies
3. Length of contract
4. Special terms, such as liability insurance, workmen's compensation, wage provisions, and liquidated damages provision

The offer solicitation should provide sufficient time for service suppliers to respond to bid. Since there is a potential for misunderstanding, a prebid conference is often held to allow suppliers to ask questions. Such conferences are often held a few weeks prior to bid deadlines. Additionally, it is worthwhile to allow prospective suppliers to inspect facilities, grounds, or equipment for which the services are required.

Selecting Service Suppliers

Establishing a fair price is often difficult for service purchasers. Often there is no baseline for comparison; as more services are performed, however, records can be developed as bases for evaluation. Some of the price analysis techniques include:

- Comparison to a previous contract
- Comparison to a standard
- In-house estimates
- Comparison to other quotes
- Work-measurement studies

A useful tool is the General Services Administration's (GSA) *Custodial Manager's Handbook,* which includes a listing of the typical custodial tasks and the amount of work an average laborer can accomplish.

Purchasers will often negotiate with service contractors prior to contract award. From a supplier-relations standpoint, it is important to treat all equally in negotiation. However, negotiation provides flexibility in permitting (1) innovative ideas, (2) use of flexible contract arrangement; (3) evaluation of factors other than price; and (4) examination of contractors' costs.

One tool used by firms to evaluate service contracts is a weighted-factor evaluation plan. An example is shown in Table 21-2. Quality, price, and previous experience are the highest-rated factors in the particular plan shown. Final analysis reveals bidders to be quite close in total evaluation.

After a proposal analysis, a decision on price or a cost-based contract is made. If the contract is cost based as opposed to a fixed-price contract, a target cost needs to be established with a "not to exceed" (ceiling) price and an auditing procedure to verify costs. Such cost-type contracts are usually issued for maintenance and overhaul of industrial equipment.

Prior to selection, all supplier bonding and insurance requirements must be current and up to date. Finally, payment terms need to be discussed, since, as we mentioned earlier, service shops are often small, and local suppliers often expe-

Table 21-2 Services Contract—Weighted-Factor Evaluation Plan

	Maximum Points	Supplier A, Rating	Supplier A, Points	Supplier B, Rating	Supplier B, Points
Base price	25	7	175	5	125
Quality of work	30	6	180	6	180
Worker qualifications	15	5	75	6	90
Management team	5	7	35	7	35
Quality-audit program	5	6	30	7	35
References	5	5	25	7	35
Insurance/liability	5	7	35	7	35
Previous experience	10	5	50	6	60
Total	100		605		595

Scale: 7 = outstanding
      4 = average
      1 = poor

rience cash-flow problems. The seller can facilitate the payment process by carefully preparing the invoice and breaking out materials from services, as some states apply tax only to materials.

Follow-Up and Measurement

Making sure that the selected supplier meets the agreed-upon requirements is the final phase of service purchasing. One way to visualize this process is on the basis of input, throughput, and output (see Figure 21-2). The first phase is accomplished by measuring compliance to inputs (specifications), work, and meeting of outcomes. To illustrate, a janitorial firm was contracted to "remove dust from all surfaces of the interior of a forty-two-hundred-square-foot office building each Monday evening." Records showed that the work had been performed each Monday as per contract (throughput) stipulations. After four weeks a physical-inspection check at 6:00 A.M. Tuesday showed that the output was in compliance with the statement of work.

All too often service contracts are not regularly or randomly inspected for compliance with the contract. The result is that action is taken only in response to complaints by those who are affected by the service.

An example of a past performance evaluation process is provided by Ms. Laura Dereberry of St. Thomas College:

> Evaluations are conducted in written form by both the purchasing department and the end user. In some cases we also ask the supplier to complete a preprinted evaluation.
>
> Our evaluations can be done at the end of a project, quarterly (waste disposal, travel), during phases of a contract or project (architectural services, design services), or six months to two years after completion of a project. Evaluations have three sections that are rated either numerically 1–10 or Poor, Fair, Good, Excellent; and the third section asks for objective comments.[3]

[3]Julie Murphree, "Evaluating Service Buys," *NAPM Insights,* June, 1990, p. 13.

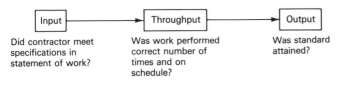

Figure 21-2 Measurement View of Service Process

Input	Throughput	Output
Did contractor meet specifications in statement of work?	Was work performed correct number of times and on schedule?	Was standard attained?

LEGAL ISSUES

Owing to their nature, commercial service contracts frequently require the contractor to provide insurance or bonds to protect the buying company. Contractor liability insurance is usually required when contract work is performed on company premises. The contractor often will assume temporary custody of the buying company's property when repairing equipment and reworking damage to property resulting from improper maintenance procedures. With regard to personal liability, contractors are required by law to contribute to workman's compensation. Buyers should also request that sellers sign a "hold harmless agreement," which releases the buyer from financial injury charges if the supplier's personnel are injured while on the buyer's property.

Termination/Delays

In order to terminate a contract, buyers must notify suppliers of the intent to cancel and must give reasons. The service contractor can respond by (1) showing that excusable delays have occurred that would extend contract completion or (2) prove that there are no defects in performance or that the defects have been corrected so performance is no longer in question.

UCC Applicability

The purchase of many services also involves the purchase of goods. For example, is the purchase and installation of a piece of machinery a contract for services or goods? The reason for concern is that the Uniform Commercial Code (UCC) applies to transactions for the purchase of goods. Thus sales of goods would fall under UCC. Meanwhile, sales of services are governed by common law. The question then arises as to which law is applicable when both goods and services are purchased. In these mixed contracts the applicability of the law is determined by the predominant purpose of the contract. If the predominant purpose is goods, the UCC is applicable. If it is services, then common law is applicable.

POINTS FOR REVIEW

1. What are the primary differences between products and services?
2. Why are purchasers seeing an increase in the amount and type of services purchased?
3. Why is the statement of work so important when buying services?

4. Describe the input-throughput-output cycle for a service.
5. Why would you schedule a prebid conference for services?
6. Whom should the buyer consult with to identify the component tasks or elements of a service activity?
7. Develop a typical list of multiple evaluation criteria you would use when selecting a contractor.

22

Purchasing's Role in Capital Expenditures

Manufacturers of machine tools and other types of major equipment are extremely competitive, but the competition is usually based on individual features of design and application. Competing makes are therefore not always directly comparable or interchangeable. In such cases the practice of buying from alternative sources of supply or from approved lists of suppliers is not always applicable. In other respects the purchasing procedures and problems are similar to those used for any other requirement. The selection and purchase of major equipment is by nature a special project rather than a continuing program. Thus the decision involves the judgment of many persons.[1]

More executives participate in the selection of machinery and similar equipment than in the purchase of materials, components, and supplies. The purchasing department rarely *initiates* such a purchase. But it is brought into the transaction when technical, cost, and delivery data are collected. Assembling these data is more than a routine action, because it provides the facts necessary for an evaluation. It also requires a knowledge of the work to be performed and the various types of equipment available. It is the point at which alternatives are explored for best value and greatest usefulness.

In large companies that use much equipment there is usually a specialized machinery buyer in the purchasing department. In those companies that have large numbers of certain types of machinery—lathes, for example—there is likely to be more repetitive buying of machinery. For example, once the decision has been made to replace or expand a battery of lathes, the procedure is distinctly a purchasing one.

QUALITY AND COST FACTORS

As is the case with all industrial purchases, the requirement fundamentally consists of a purpose to be served or a job to be done rather than the material or machine to do the job. Quality, in the sense of suitability for the purpose, therefore means the ability of equipment to do a particular job satisfactorily and efficiently over a period of time. The chief factors in selecting heavy machinery include (1) economy, (2) productivity, (3) dependability, (4) saving time or labor, (5) durability, and (6) service level.

The six buying motives should be analyzed in some greater detail. They are all operating characteristics and are concerned with costs of use after the purchase, not with costs in the purchase price. But because the purpose of this procurement is the use of the machine rather than the machine itself, they constitute a cost increment that must be considered in the ultimate cost of performing the job. As an element of production cost, they frequently outweigh many times over the significance of the purchase price. Therefore, these characteristics of the equipment are constituents of quality and of value, in which the purchasing man-

[1]Buying construction is another type of capital expenditure in which purchasing departments are becoming increasingly involved. Frequently, the purchase of equipment and the purchase of construction are closely related, as in the building and equipment of a new plant or the expansion of an existing one. Procurement for that type of project is discussed later in this chapter.

ager is vitally interested. The final decision is not entirely within the manager's jurisdiction in this case, but it is highly important that these characteristics be interpreted in terms of the buying motives, without which no satisfactory selection can ever be made.

Economy of operation means that the added costs per unit of production will be held to a minimum. This is a generalization covering all sorts of factors that contribute to the end result; and other considerations are more specific.

Productivity, or efficiency of equipment, means that more units will be produced or more successive operations performed within a given period of operation, with the same result of lower cost per unit plus the advantage of faster production.

Dependability means low maintenance cost and continuity of production, with a minimum of idle productive time due to breakdown. It is the assurance that the requirement will actually be satisfied and the continuity of use will avoid the increment of overhead charges without corresponding output against which they can be applied. It should be supported with adequate service from the supplier in respect to replacement parts and whatever special mechanical adjustment may be required.

Time- or *labor-saving* features of equipment point to the fact that important production costs are involved in addition to the cost of the equipment itself and its operation and that they may vary with different types of equipment. These costs may not be directly allocated to the equipment, but their effect on the overall cost should be given full consideration. Machines exist primarily to increase the productivity of human labor, and the ability of a machine to operate with a crew of three workers instead of four or to increase the output of a single operator 5 percent or 10 percent as compared with that operator's production at another machine is perhaps the most significant measure of the machine's efficiency and advantage as an investment.

Durability refers to the service life of equipment at high efficiency. This means a greater total output, a greater return on the investment, and more units of product over which the cost of the machine may be spread. As a matter of cost-accounting policy, it is probable that this cost will have been fully depreciated before the useful life of the machine has been exhausted, but that does not alter the basic economy of durable equipment.

Servicing

Servicing the equipment is a major consideration in capital-equipment purchases. In most cases the seller will service the equipment during the initial start-up phase and through the warranty period. During this initial period service is usually provided free of charge or at a reduced rate. However, after the warranty expiration date a decision must be made to contract for such service or do it with in-house personnel. Training of in-house personnel in maintenance can be part of the initial contract provision. Finally, during contract negotiations the seller may offer an extended warranty. Usually for a flat fee the seller will perform a periodic preventative check and also cover emergency breakdowns. In these cases the buyer pays for the cost of parts.

While service insures safety, buyers must make sure that suppliers meet all applicable and federal safety codes. Requirements of the Occupational Health and Safety Act (OSHA) must be met, or severe fines will be imposed.

Life-Cycle Costing

A technique for evaluating the total cost of a piece of equipment, developed by the Department of Defense and gaining in usage in industry, is life-cycle costing. It is a method used to compare and evaluate the total cost received in bids, based on the expected life of the product. All costs are evaluated as a package: research, development, production, operation, and maintenance of the product or system.

The maintenance aspect of life-cycle costing has been used particularly successfully by the city of Chicago. For example, prior to buying refuse trucks with a lifetime guarantee of maintenance, the city spent an average of $293 per month to maintain each vehicle. When trucks were bought, by competitive bidding on a life-guarantee basis, the monthly average was reduced to $183.69, a total fixed-unit cost for the life of each unit of equipment.

The emphasis on operating costs does not imply that initial cost can be disregarded. As a matter of fact, it is highly important in that initial cost is the factor against which productivity, dependability, and durability must be weighed in seeking purchase value. Furthermore, as a capital investment, initial cost has a direct bearing on ultimate costs, because it involves carrying charges, determines the cost chargeable to depreciation, and provides the basis on which profitable operation must be calculated. Just as in figuring the true cost of materials certain factors, such as transportation and handling in and out of stores, must be added to the invoice price, the total cost of equipment includes transportation, cost of installation, any extra foundations or other special expenses, and the costs of accessories and tooling.

Return on Investment

The position of investments in machinery as a part of a company's capital structure has an important bearing on the purchase of such equipment. It brings financial departments and policies more intimately into the picture than is the case with purchase of production and supply items. And it has important effects on real cost, owing to taxes and the possibility of write-offs in the capital account.

Like all capital investments, major equipment purchases should earn a return. The financial department is basically responsible for analyses of return on investment, but purchasing managers should, nevertheless, be familiar with the most widely used techniques.

Among the methods of calculating and evaluating capital-equipment expenditures listed in the purchasing handbook sponsored by the National Association of Purchasing Management are payback, return on investment, present worth, and MAPI (Machinery and Allied Products Institute) (see Figure 22-1).

MAPI Form (First Page)

PROJECT NO. _____   SHEET 1

SUMMARY OF ANALYSIS
(SEE ACCOMPANYING WORK SHEETS FOR DETAIL)

I. REQUIRED INVESTMENT

1	Installed Cost of Project	$_____	1
2	Disposal Value of Assets to be Retired by Project	$_____	2
3	Capital Additions Required in Absence of Project	$_____	3
4	Investment Released or Avoided by Project (2 + 3)	$_____	4
5	Net Investment Required (1 − 4)	$_____	5

II. NEXT-YEAR ADVANTAGE FROM PROJECT

A. OPERATING ADVANTAGE
(USE FIRST YEAR OF PROJECT OPERATION)*

		Increase	Decrease	
6	Assumed Operating Rate of Project (hours per year)		_____	6
	Effect of Project on Revenue	Increase	Decrease	
7	From Change in Quality of Products	$_____	$_____	7
8	From Change in Volume of Output			8
9	Total	$_____ A	$_____ B	9
	Effect of Project on Operating Costs			
10	Direct Labor	$_____	$_____	10
11	Indirect Labor	_____	_____	11
12	Fringe Benefits	_____	_____	12
13	Maintenance	_____	_____	13
14	Tooling	_____	_____	14
15	Supplies	_____	_____	15
16	Scrap and Rework	_____	_____	16
17	Down Time	_____	_____	17
18	Power	_____	_____	18
19	Floor Space	_____	_____	19
20	Property Taxes and Insurance	_____	_____	20
21	Subcontracting	_____	_____	21
22	Inventory	_____	_____	22
23	Safety	_____	_____	23
24	Flexibility	_____	_____	24
25	Other	_____	_____	25
26	Total	$_____ A	$_____ B	26
27	Net Increase in Revenue (9A − 9B)		$_____	27
28	Net Decrease in Operating Cost (26B − 26A)		$_____	28
29	Next-Year Operating Advantage (27 + 28)		$_____	29

B. NON-OPERATING ADVANTAGE
(USE ONLY IF THERE IS AN ENTRY IN LINE 4)

30	Next-Year Capital Consumption Avoided by Project:		30
	A Decline of Disposal Value during the Year	$_____	A
	B Next-Year Allocation of Capital Additions	$_____	B
	TOTAL	$_____	

C. TOTAL ADVANTAGE

31	Total Next-Year Advantage from Project (29 + 30)	$_____	31

*For projects with a significant break-in period, use performance after break-in.

Figure 22-1 Part of the form that the Machinery and Allied Products Institute (MAPI) uses for analyzing proposed capital-equipment expenditures

The most common approach, according to the handbook, is to calculate the return on investment:

$$\text{Simple return on investment} = \frac{\text{savings/year}}{\text{investment}}$$

The common approach is computation of average cash flows (less depreciation) per year divided by the average net book value of the assets over the project life. Here is an example to illustrate the method:

> A proposal to procure a special baling machine requires a present outlay of $10,000 and has expected cash inflows of $2,000 at the end of one year and $4,000 at the end of each succeeding year for the next four years. Straight-line depreciation for the $10,000 investment over its 5-year life is $2,000 per year, assuming no salvage value. Cash flows after depreciation are zero after the first year and $2,000 in each of the next four years ($4,000 − $2,000 − $2,000). The average cash flow therefore is 1/5 (0 + $8,000) = $1,600 per year. The average net book value of the assets is 1/5 ($8,000 + $6,000 + $4,000 + $2,000 + 0) = $4,000. The accounting rate of return is 1,600/4,000 = 40 percent on net book value, if taxes are ignored.[2]

Payback Method   In the payback method the cost of the equipment is divided by the savings per year. This method gives the number of years it takes a piece of equipment to pay for itself. Thus a machine costing $20,000 and generating a savings of $4,000/year would have a payback period of five years ($20,000/cost divided by $4,000/year savings). The payback method is the inverse of simple return on investment. In the above example the return on investment is 20 percent and 1 divided by the payback period (1/5) also equals 20 percent.

Net Present Value   Net present value (NPV) is perhaps the most complex analysis; it considers the time value of money. For savings in future years are not equal to savings in the current year and must be discounted back to present-day dollars.

To illustrate, the machine in our previous example cost $20,000 and generated $4,000/year in savings. Its useful life was five years. As can be seen in Table 22-1, the machine will not pay itself off in the five-year life. At 8 percent the

TABLE 22-1   Example of Net Present Value

Year	Present Value Tables 8%	Present Value Tables 10%	Facts
	Present Value Tables		**Facts**
Year	8%	10%	
1	.926	.909	$20,000 Investment Today
2	1.783	1.736	5-year life
3	2.577	2.487	8% cost of capital
4	3.312	3.170	0 salvage value
5	3.993	3.791	$4,000/yr. savings

$4,000/year savings × 3.993 (8%) = $15,972 (this is less than $20,000)
$4,000/year savings × 3.791 (10%) = $15,164 (this is less than $20,000)

[2]G. W. Aljian, ed. *Purchasing Handbook*, 4th ed. (New York: McGraw-Hill Book Co., 1982), pp. 16–19 and 16–20.

machine yields a present value of $15,972, and at 10 percent the present value is $15,164. Thus we are spending $20,000 to obtain $15,972 or $15,164. One also might note that as the interest rate increases, the net present value decreases, since the opportunity cost of investing funds is higher.

NEW VERSUS USED EQUIPMENT

Not all buyers may be in a position to acquire new equipment because of cost considerations. In such cases used equipment may provide an alternative. Used equipment may also be the appropriate alternative when time is a consideration, either in terms of delivery or usage. Used equipment is frequently available, and as a result, the long lead times usually associated with the acquisition of capital equipment can be reduced substantially. Or if a piece of equipment is to be used for only a brief time, buying used equipment may make more sense.

When to Buy Used Equipment

Aljian's *Purchasing Handbook* suggests that in the following six situations acquiring used equipment may be the preferred alternative.

1. When price is of prime importance and the difference in cost between new and used equipment is significant and/or the buyer's funds are limited.
2. Where equipment will be used for a limited time or where the equipment will be idle much of the time.
3. Where equipment will be used for training or for pilot or experimental purposes.
4. Where equipment is to be for auxiliary operations or services such as maintenance.
5. When better delivery is an essential fact, or
6. Where used machines can economically be converted to satisfy the need.[3]

Considerations When Purchasing Used Equipment

Regardless of why a buyer chooses to buy used instead of new equipment, there are a number of considerations that must be taken into account.

For one thing, buying used equipment involves to sources very different from the original manufacturer, where one buys new equipment. These sources include the original owner of the equipment, used-equipment dealers and brokers, and auctions. In any case, before buying used equipment the buyer must know the market, to be able to determine value.

Additionally, it is often difficult to determine the condition of piece equipment and, since most sellers of used equipment provide little or no warranty, great care must be taken in inspecting the equipment before purchasing it. It may be that the buyer will have to enlist the help of a production or maintenance engineer to assist in such inspections.

[3]Ibid., p. 16–2 .

Finally, in writing the contract for the purchase of used equipment, the buyer should make sure that the seller will warrant the following items:

1. Marketable title
2. The absence of any liens or encumbrances, and
3. That no litigation or other proceedings questioning the seller's title are pending or threatened.[4]

THE BUYING TEAM

On the basis of the requisition and the comparative data and costs assembled by the purchasing department, the problem of selecting the right equipment is a matter for joint consideration by the plant engineer, the chief production executive, the head of the department in which the equipment is to be used, the purchasing manager, and a representative of general management. Expressed in functional terms, these are the individuals responsible for setting up the process, for overall efficiency of operation, for using the equipment, for economical procurement, and for the company's capital policy.

In the small company the conference will probably be an informal one, leading directly to the purchase authorization. In the large company it will lead first to a recommendation, requiring authorization by some designated officer of the company before the purchase can be made. For the purposes of this recommendation, a more formal analysis must be made and put into writing. It is presumed that if the request is well founded and based on demonstrable need, the required authorization will be granted; nevertheless, there is a distinct value in going through this procedure. Putting the recommendation and supporting data into writing is evidence that an adequate analysis has been made and that the pertinent questions have been considered and answered. As a record of what the equipment is expected to accomplish, it provides a standard against which actual performance can later be measured. If this later comparison proves disappointing, and it is too late to do anything about the particular purchase, the analysis will still be a guide to judgment in later decisions, indicating whether too much or too little weight has been given to certain factors of selection, or whether excessive optimism or aggressiveness or superior selling ability on the part of any individual connected with the selection has prejudiced the decision to the disadvantage of the company as a whole. Such circumstances can be guarded against in later selections.

A typical form for analysis and recommendation consists of a letter-sized sheet printed on both sides, with space for such pertinent data as the following:

- Operation for which equipment is to be used.
- Part or product to be produced.
- Estimated annual requirements of this part.

[4]Ibid., pp. 16–21.

- Estimated number of machine-hours that new equipment will expend in a year.
- Is equipment to provide additional capacity or for replacement of present equipment?
- How is the part now being produced?
- Present cost of producing part.
- Cost of procuring part from outside sources.
- Estimated cost of part produced on the new equipment.
- Total installed cost of new equipment.
- Itemized list and cost of accessories required.
- Age of present equipment.
- Salvage value of present equipment.
- Remarks: advantages expected from new equipment.
- Recommendations for purchase.
- Signatures of plant manager, chief engineer, purchasing manager, and department head.

Machine size and power requirements, while not specifically part of the performance specifications, should be carefully defined in relation to a plant's layout and utility systems. These requirements are sometimes overlooked by suppliers. One company emphasizes their importance with a special amendment to its purchase orders for capital equipment (see Figure 22-2).

THE ONE-OF-A-KIND BUY

Increasingly, purchasing departments are getting involved in the procurement of unique capital items. Specially designed power generators for paper mills, made-to-order, large-scale materials handling equipment for steel companies, sophisticated pollution-control devices for all types of industry, and robotics for automakers are just a few examples.

A former executive who is responsible for capital-equipment acquisition at a major steel corporation, has pointed out that this kind of developmental or prototype buying presents special problems for purchasing managers charged with the job. He identifies these problems as follows:

- *Delivery:* Most supplier predictions about their ability to manufacture and deliver a new item are wide of the mark. Consequently, the buyer has to build protection into the contract or agreement in various ways. These include provision for liquidated damages; escalation clauses tied to promised delivery; rejection of goods delivered late; assurance of future business, contingent on timely delivery; promotional efforts on behalf of the supplier's product in the buyer's plant, contingent on the seller's meeting promised delivery dates.
- *Acceptance:* The danger in prototype buying is that the buyer may view the purchase in the traditional light and pay for it on receipt. To do so would be to give up leverage—i.e., hold back payment until he is satisfied the new equipment will perform as expected. The agreement should clearly define what constitutes performance and how tests to verify performance will be conducted.
- *Warranty:* A warranty commencing upon delivery could result in the warranty's running out before much useful life has been received from the product. If

EQUIPMENT SPECIFICATIONS

Date_____

TO:_____   (MAIL TO VENDOR
   _____   IN DUPLICATE)
   _____

           SUBJECT: P.O. # _____

Gentlemen:

The equipment being purchased from your company on our order # _____
is to be furnished according to the following special information and specifications
which are made a part of the Purchase Order. Where compliance is impossible,
you are to notify the Rheem Manufacturing Company in writing of the variations.
They must be approved by our Plant Engineer before work can proceed.

1. Building Limitations
   A. Minimum Ceiling Height   _____
   B. Maximum Door Width   _____
   C. Maximum Aisle Width   _____

   Equipment must be built to dimensions which will permit
   movement to installation through our Plant in accordance
   with these minimum and maximum dimensions, unless
   otherwise specified.

2. Utilities
   Power   _____   Volts
   Air   _____   Pounds Pressure
   Water   _____   Pounds Pressure
   Gas
           Natural _____
           Mixed   _____   BTU _____
           Mfg.   _____   BTU _____

3. Paint
   Paint all body, frame and other fixed parts   _____
   Paint all guards   _____
   Paint all exposed moving parts   _____
ACKNOWLEDGED
_____   SIGNED:_____ Plant Engineer

_____   _____ Materials Manager

Figure 22-2. Special instructions added to equipment specifications that
accompany purchase orders for capital items.

acceptance of a new item requires complex testing procedures as a requisite,
the beginning of the warranty period should be tied to acceptance.
- *Documentation:* Dates, costs, events, minutes of meetings, complete correspondence should be recorded—such documentation is critical in developmental
purchasing. A fine-tuned awareness of events related to the order is also essential. The buyer's ability to reconstruct events that occur during a purchase may
have a significant effect on later negotiations.[5]

[5]M. J. Fowler, "Buying What's Never Been Bought Before," *Purchasing World,* April 1983, p. 60.

WHO SETS TERMS AND CONDITIONS?

The high value, technical complexity, and distinctive design features of many capital-equipment items often complicate negotiation for purchase of such equipment. In requesting bids, purchasing departments forward their company's terms and conditions. Suppliers traditionally insist that their product has special features and that they are in a better position to evaluate its performance technically and in terms of experience, and they acknowledge the order using another set of terms and conditions. Consequently, a certain amount of haggling and byplay are often involved before the transaction is complete.

One large steel company has taken the initiative in setting terms and conditions from equipment suppliers and put it into the hands of its buyers. It has set up "Standard Conditions for Equipment Purchase Agreements" that are sent out with every request for quotation involving equipment or construction work costing more than $100,000. A broad range of subjects is covered. Particular emphasis is placed on terms of payment, indemnity for patent infringement, and warranties. In addition to the warranty against defects, for example, the company insists on a performance warranty with this clause:

> Seller acknowledges that Crucible has informed seller of the specific purpose for which Crucible will use the equipment. Seller expressly warrants and guarantees that the equipment is merchantable and is fit and suitable for the specific purpose for which Crucible intends to use the equipment.

Despite some initial resistance, suppliers have generally accepted the idea that their proposals will not be considered unless they agree to the standardized terms and conditions. The benefits for the company have been (1) more simplified analysis of bids, as identical terms make price and technical details a common denominator for competing vendors; (2) stronger negotiating position; and (3) reduction in negotiating time.

CONSTRUCTION BUYING

Buying construction is a relatively new—but growing—purchasing responsibility. In view of purchasing's successful experience in major equipment procurement, many larger companies have added specialized construction buyers to the departmental staff. Accelerating the trend is the fact that the two buying responsibilities often go hand in hand, as in the building and equipping of a new plant or the expansion of an existing facility.

Admittedly, construction buying can be more difficult and complex than the conventional repetitive type of purchasing. Yet that should be only another challenge for the professional buyer. As the head of the contracting services group in Union Carbide Corporation's purchasing department wrote several years ago:

The purchase of services is frequently approached with fear and trembling by those who perform other procurement activities with a cool analytical mind. They often accept quotations from contractors without questions and qualifications, whereas they dissect, analyze, and review in depth quotations received from MRO or equipment suppliers. Yet a buyer can apply the same techniques used for commodity buying of raw materials, equipment and supplies to the purchase of contracting services for new construction, renovation, alteration or maintenance. Contractors should be viewed as suppliers. Their quotations can be analyzed and negotiated. The receipt of competitive fixed price quotations and the subsequent award to the low responsive bidder is not necessarily the best procurement action.[6]

In a typical project—construction and equipping of a new, $10 million chemical plant, for example—a team approach would undoubtedly be used. The team would be made up of project, facilities, chemical, electrical, and instrumentation engineers plus the manager of capital purchases. Other specialists might be added as the project progresses, such as legal personnel when contracts are being drawn. In an earlier time only project engineers and chemical engineers would have had total responsibility for new plant projects of this type. Generally, such teams follow procedures similar to those that follow.[7]

One of the team's first responsibilities is to define the project. In the case of construction, as with equipment, the user's needs must be precisely determined—the purpose of the building, space requirements, equipment and systems placement, and target date for completion. Then clear and detailed specifications should be drawn up by the team or outside specialists or both. An in-house technical staff (e.g., engineering) is usually better able than buyers and requisitioners to interpret specifications and bidders' responses to them. Contracts for construction usually require the architectural or engineering firm to provide this type of support.

Bids should be requested only from experienced, financially sound contractors. One technique for evaluating bids is to rate potential suppliers on those factors considered essential to a successful project. A typical list might include the following:

- *Base bid price:* The lowest bid price should be rated 10. Other bids should be rated lower according to their relationship to the lowest bid.
- *Unit price for additions and reductions:* Rating to be on the same basis as that for base bid price.
- *Supervision:* How important is first-rate supervision of the project?
- *Location:* How important is it to have the supplier geographically close to the project?
- *Vendor presentation:* How well prepared was the vendor for an interview?
- *Compatibility with present system:* How adversely will a change in vendors or methods affect the business?

[6]Donald J. Sullivan, "Purchasing of Contracting Services," *Journal of Purchasing and Materials Management,* Spring 1975, p. 23.

[7]Descriptions of these procedures are based largely on an article, "Put More Competition into Capital Buying," by John J. Kiernan, C.P.M., purchasing manager of Bard-Parker, Lincoln Park, N.J., which appeared in the November 1982 issue of *Purchasing World.*

- *Management team:* Does the vendor's team show evidence of providing support and ability to perform?
- *Quality control:* How effective is the vendor's quality-control department?
- *Client reference reports:* What do other customers say about the vendor?
- *Prior experience:* How many projects similar to this one has the vendor successfully completed; is he or she a rookie or an old hand?

Each factor is assigned a numerical value between 1 and 10 to show its relative importance (see Figure 22-3). More than one factor may have the same

Factors	Value	A	B	C
RATE VENDORS				
Base Bid	10	6 / 60	8 / 80	9 / 90
Unit Prices For Additions And Deductions	10	8 / 80	7 / 70	9 / 90
Supervision	7	6 / 42	5 / 35	8 / 56
Location	4	8 / 32	10 / 40	7 / 28
Vendor Presentation	3	7 / 21	7 / 21	8 / 24
Compatibility With Present System	4	8 / 32	4 / 16	10 / 40
Management Team	8	9 / 72	7 / 56	8 / 64
Quality Control	8	8 / 64	6 / 48	9 / 72
Client Reference Reports	5	7 / 35	6 / 30	8 / 40
Prior Experience	9	8 / 72	8 / 72	9 / 81
Totals	68/680	510	488	585
Rank		3	6	1
Percent of Maximum Score		75.0	68.8	86.0

Figure 22-3 Vendors are rated, also numerically (1 to 10), on their ability to satisfy each requirement. Rating is shown in upper half of boxes. Factor value multiplied by rating gives the vendor's score

Source: John J. Kiernan, "Put More Competition Into Capital Purchasing," *Purchasing World,* November 1982, p. 42.

value. Each vendor is judged on each factor and given a rating between 1 and 10. The rating is multiplied by the value of the factor, and the total scores are tabulated. If the vendor who gets the highest score is not the lowest bidder, judgment comes into play. The team must determine if the difference in prices is more or less important than the differences in the vendors' abilities. In one company use of the method over two years resulted in choice of the low bidder in half the projects, the second low bidder in 40 percent, and others in 10 percent.

LEASING CAPITAL ITEMS

According to the American Association of Equipment Lessors (AAEL), eight out of ten U.S. companies use leasing to supply some or all of their equipment needs. The chief advantage of leasing is that it enables a company to obtain the use of an asset without borrowing or using internally generated cash. This helps cash flow, conserves working capital, and provides 100 percent financing. It is also a hedge against the risk of equipment obsolescence. Further, it is a way of avoiding administrative, maintenance, and service costs and problems that owners of equipment must cope with. Finally, leasing provides certain tax advantages. The main disadvantages are that it is a high-cost form of financing and the lessee surrenders the residual value of the assets leased (i.e., the value at the end of the lease).

Items most often leased, according to a survey among major U.S. and Canadian companies are passenger vehicles; other vehicles; duplicating equipment; buildings; land; typing and other office equipment; and production equipment.[8] Accountants point out that the lease-purchase decision is really a financing one, that is, it is considered only after the decision to invest has been made. The study mentioned above, however, showed that most requests for lease evaluation involved treasury, controller, legal, engineering, and purchasing personnel.

The Caterpillar Corporation's leasing company has developed a checklist of questions to be asked by customers considering lease arrangements for lease of any capital equipment. A lease plan evaluation form that summarizes those questions appears in Figure 22-4. Caterpillar Leasing Company also suggests that the answer to the lease-or-purchase question be predicated on three points:

1. *The current financial condition of the business.* Generally speaking, good cash flow and profitability will make outright purchase more attractive. If cash flow is squeezed, leasing will be more desirable.
2. *Business condition forecast.* Businesses that face a future of reasonable certainty of profit and sustained profitability will find purchase more attractive. For more cyclical businesses, such as machinery, autos, and forest products, leasing provides an "escape valve." A major expansion or acquisition plan may project heavy demands on cash flow and make leasing more attractive.
3. *Maintenance and downtime costs.* Generally speaking, most owners of equipment keep it too long, resulting in a 25-to-50-percent "cost waste" in excessive mainte-

[8]W. L. Ferrara, J. B. Thies, and M. W. Dirsmith, *The Lease Purchase Decision* (New York: National Association of Accountants, 1982).

Lease plan evaluation

Lease

	Plan 1	Plan 2	Plan 3
Lease term (months)			
Monthly payment ($)			
Advance payments (number)			
Security deposit ($)			
Purchase option (price)			
Balloon payment at end of lease ($)			
Residual guarantee (yes/no)			
Amount of guarantee ($)			
ITC to lessee (yes/no)			
ACRS to lessee (yes/no)			
Other costs not covered in lease payments:			
Freight ($)			
Taxes ($)			
Insurance ($)			
Loan origination fees ($)			

Maintenance

	Plan 1	Plan 2	Plan 3
Maintenance & repair ($/mth)			
Frequency of inspection (hours)			
Hour limitations (hours)			
Overtime charges ($/hour)			
Extras (identify) ($)			

Remarks: _____

Figure 22-4. Form for comparing competing lease packages. Courtesy of *Purchasing World.*

nance. Unless a company has a fairly sophisticated maintenance, repair, and replacement program, leasing can help manage these aspects of costs through planned replacement and, if desired, a maintenance-and-repair program.[9]

Types of Leases

There are two basic types of leases: operating and financial. The operating lease is short term and for a period considerably less than the asset's useful life. Financial leases run for the full life of the equipment.

Operational leases are useful in cases where the lessee (party who leases the equipment) has short-term needs, or obsolescence is a factor. Lessors (owner of the asset) frequently don't make a total profit on the initial lease but seek to make additional profits on subsequent leases or sale of the equipment.

While lessees frequently terminate operating leases, financial leases often contain noncancelable provisions. Thus many banks and other third-party lenders are willing to loan funds to underwrite financial leases. The rate charged by a les-

[9]D. Butler and D. Colbert, "Take Another Look at Leasing," *Purchasing World,* March 1984, p. 60.

sor on a financial lease is comprised of (1) prevailing interest rate, (2) depreciation rate determined by length of lease, and (3) lessor's fee.

EQUIPMENT DISPOSAL

Worn, obsolete, or replaced equipment needs to be properly disposed of. Purchasing usually handles such duties, since that department is knowledgeable about markets and supplies.

Several methods exist for disposal and include:

- Trading in for new equipment
- Shifting the equipment to another location within the plant or company
- Selling to a used-equipment dealer or broker
- Disposing of equipment as trash

The most useful and profitable course of action for the company is using the equipment within the firm. If scrap dealers or brokers are solicited, payment should be required via certified check and the equipment sold on an "as is, where is basis" with no warranties. If the equipment is discarded, it should be destroyed to ensure that no future liability will be incurred through unauthorized use. For example, a large utility company in the Northeast cuts the bucket off its lift units prior to salvage to make sure the equipment will not be reused.

POINTS FOR REVIEW

1. Explain why the purchase of capital equipment is handled differently from that of materials and supplies.
2. Name and discuss the chief factors to be considered in selecting heavy machinery.
3. List the advantages and disadvantages of buying used equipment.
4. Trace the steps involved in the purchase of capital equipment from the time that the need is known until the purchase order is ready to be placed.
5. List the items, other than price, that purchasing can negotiate with suppliers of capital equipment.
6. Discuss when leasing capital equipment or buildings could be more advantageous than buying them outright.
7. What are the major methods used to dispose of equipment?

23

Measuring Purchasing Performance

Purchasing and management executives alike would welcome some reliable yard-stick for the measurement of efficiency and effectiveness in purchasing. Consequently, a great deal of serious thought has been given to the problem. It has been the subject of continuing study for several years by the National Association of Purchasing Management.

SOME COMMON FALLACIES

It is easy to oversimplify when trying to measure purchasing performance. Probably the most common fallacy is to set a standard of efficiency by expressing *departmental operating cost as a percentage of total purchase expenditures.* (See Figure 23-1) This percentage is necessarily an average figure, for it is obvious that there is a wide disparity between the purchasing cost for orders of relatively small value, for hard-to-find items, and for those that are required only occasionally and the cost of procuring standard and familiar materials from established sources in substantial volume. Examples can be found of purchasing costs ranging all the way from 0.75 percent of expenditures to 2.0 percent or more, each of which could conscientiously be described as efficient performance for the particular company and conditions concerned. Independent purchasing services operate on percentages ranging from 2.5 percent to 5.0 percent and are able to demonstrate savings as compared with unorganized and inexpert purchasing. A reasonable average figure would be in the neighborhood of 1.5 percent to 2.0 percent, but this is the broadest sort of generalization and has little meaning for the individual company; a variation of 0.5 percent on any substantial purchasing program runs into significant dollar figures.

Simple mathematics shows the fallacy of that standard: To reduce the cost, all one would have to do is pay more for purchased materials and supplies—the greater the expenditure, the lower the cost as a percentage of that outlay. That, of course, would be inefficient purchasing..

The late Albert D'Arcy, then of Union Carbide Corporation, demonstrated the difficulty in generalizing about purchasing costs as a measurement of efficiency. He said that the data he and his staff had accumulated over the years showed very little consistency in cost figures from various companies. It appears, he said, that there is no simple, ready-made formula to tell what purchasing cost should be in a given company or industry.

D'Arcy went on to point out that company organization, accounting methods, objectives, definitions of costs, and company and departmental objec-

$$\frac{\text{Total purchasing department cost}}{\text{Total purchase expenditures}} = \begin{array}{l} \text{cost to purchase} \\ \text{\$1 worth of goods and services} \\ \times\ 100\% = \text{percent of administrative cost} \end{array}$$

Figure 23-1   Cost to purchase a dollar's worth of goods

tives vary widely. Straight cost analysis in respect to purchasing may not always give the right answer, as the purchasing department may be producing other benefits for the company—balanced inventories, innovative ideas, and so forth.

Purchasing operating costs should be tracked, he concluded, "but it is important that management evaluate cost performance in the proper perspective."

Another method sometimes advocated is the measurement of cost per order.

$$\text{Cost per order} = \frac{\text{purchasing department administrative costs}}{\text{Total number of purchase orders}}$$

This has the virtue of being tied to actual operations performed rather than to the incidental (though highly important) factor of funds expended. It is subject to the same sort of criticism, however, because cost per order can be reduced by issuing more orders for smaller quantities, whereas real purchasing efficiency may lie in the other direction.

EFFICIENCY AND EFFECTIVENESS

The positive principle to be deduced from these analyses is that there is a dual job of measurement to be done—efficiency in departmental administration and efficiency in procurement. There is the cost of operation and the cost of materials to be considered before performance can be truly evaluated. The first factor, administrative cost, is relatively manageable, since management science has developed standards and measures that can readily be applied. The second factor, cost of materials, is more difficult; it can be approached through the type of information included in purchasing department reports to management—inventory ratios, material costs related to current market levels, savings effected through good purchasing practice, adherence to material budgets, and the like, all tending to demonstrate specific accomplishments or performance in the actual procurement function.

The most satisfactory measurements are those in which the two phases are separately considered. For convenience, they may be designated as *efficiency* and *effectiveness,* both of which are important to the company. Management consultant Peter Druker has stated that effectiveness is doing the right things while efficiency is doing things right. Effectiveness is more related to specific professional skill in procurement, which is the function of the department. Furthermore, cost of materials is the factor that embraces total expenditures and product costs, whereas departmental administration represents only a small percentage of total cost. No really useful purpose is served by trying to force a relationship between administrative costs and material costs, however each need to be measured. Thus both effectiveness and efficiency are necessary in a professional purchasing department.

Benchmark Ratings

One of the best ways to measure efficiency on administrative issues is through a comparison to other firms. The Center for Advanced Purchasing Studies (CAPS) has begun to collect performance data on an industry-by-industry basis. To date CAPS has collected from petroleum, food-service, semiconductor, and telecommunications industries and plans eventually to reach a total of thirty industries.

Figure 23-2 shows the data collected from the petroleum industry group. It should be noted that there are no legal problems with collecting such data, since it is related to the purchasing department's methods and nonpricing practices. Each industry's practices vary, and such a comparison allows firms to gauge their results in comparison to industry averages. For example, in the oil industry, crude-oil and gasoline purchases are not acquired by purchasing professionals. Also, no purchases of electricity fuel and utilities are included.[1] Benchmark studies should prove extremely useful to purchasing executives wishing to compare their methods to those of others as well as to monitor trends over time. In industries like semiconductors comparisons are available between domestic and foreign-owned

---

Major Conclusions: Petroleum Industry Benchmark Study

1. Purchasing (the dollars spent with vendors) accounted for 9 percent of sales revenue.
2. The expense of operating the purchasing function was only 8/100 of a cent per dollar of sales revenue.
3. It cost less than one cent to purchase a dollar's worth of goods or services.
4. There was one purchasing employee per 171 company employees.
5. There was one purchasing employee for each $104 million of sales.
6. There were $8.5 million in purchases made by the purchasing department per employee in purchasing.
7. Each professional purchasing employee handled $13 million in purchases.
8. There were 102 active suppliers per purchasing employee.
9. Each professional purchasing employee managed 171 active suppliers.
10. Each supplier received $96,000 in company orders in 1988.
11. The purchasing department spent $58,000 with each supplier in 1988.
12. The number of suppliers decreased by 7 percent from 1987 to 1988.
13. Minority-owned suppliers received 2.8 percent of total purchase dollars.
14. Female-owned suppliers received 1.6 percent of total purchase dollars.
15. Inventory of purchased items accounted for 12 percent of total purchase dollars.
16. Inventory of purchased items accounted for 1 percent of sales revenue.
17. Inactive inventory (which has not moved in at least three years) was 21 percent of total purchased inventory.
18. The purchasing department made 69 percent of the total goods purchases.
19. The purchasing department made 44 percent of the total services purchases.

Figure 23-2

[1]The center's complete report is available from Center for Advanced Purchasing Studies, PO box 22160, Tempe, AZ 85285-2160.

firms. All data are kept confidential, and no one company is specifically identified in the report.

Administrative Cost Efficiency

Administrative costs are used as a measure of efficiency, and it does not necessarily bear any fixed ratio to the amount of purchase expenditures. Another point to be kept in mind is that although the effort should be made to keep department expenses at the practical minimum, this attitude should not be emphasized to a degree that would suggest or encourage doing without such departmental activities as research, training, cost analysis, and fieldwork by buyers at the company's plants and those of suppliers. During periods of economic turmoil (e.g., in 1973–74, when shortages placed enormous burdens on purchasing departments), administrative costs may skyrocket. In 1973–74 the real measure of purchasing performance was its ability to get the material needed to keep production lines operating.

The measure of departmental costs should, therefore, be made against a budgeted standard cost developed by an analysis of activities; the volume of specific operations, such as the number of requisitions handled and purchase orders issued; an allowance for incidental functions and special projects, recommendations and budget requests of the department head; and a proportionate share of general administrative overhead. This budget should be liberal enough to include personnel and facilities for carrying on a complete and progressive program of procurement—"spending money to save money." It should be close enough to represent prudent management, efficient work production on clerical and other processing operations, and good administrative control. In short, it should be a realistic appraisal of the job to be done. It should be adjusted from time to time as conditions change and as the department head can demonstrate the need for such adjustment. Evaluation of this phase is based on adherence to budget, with proportionate credit for keeping expenses below the estimate and proportionate debit for expenses above this figure.

A fair measure would be the ratio that general company overhead bears to total manufacturing cost, because that is essentially what the figure represents.

Variables in Purchasing Effectiveness

One of the basic difficulties in devising a standard method of measuring purchasing effectiveness is that so many variables are involved. This fact is apparent in the widely differing scope and character of requirements in various types of operations in which the *value of purchased materials* may range all the way from 20 percent to 80 percent of total expenditures, with a corresponding variation in the relative importance of the purchasing function. Thus the first principle of evaluation is that it must be done on an individual company basis. Comparisons are significant only to the extent that the type of industry and the size of the unit are comparable. In addition, price comparisons can lead to *legal issues* that influence antitrust legislation.

There is a further variation in the *functional organization* of individual companies and the responsibilities assigned to the purchasing department, which may range all the way from simple clerical detail to complete materials management in companies of similar size within the same industry.

Price is a major purchasing variable. Price alone is not a proper measure of performance, because it is frequently subordinated to other considerations, so that better procurement may be effected by paying more for materials. It is, however, an important factor. In evaluating price performance, it must be considered against the variable standard of changing market levels or against adjustable standard costs as established in cost-accounting procedure. Purchasing problems and effort vary with market conditions. Costs rise rapidly when intensive expediting is required to assure delivery or when constant research is needed to develop satisfactory sources of supply.

Inventory ratios and turnover are widely and understandably accepted as an indication of the efficiency of the purchasing policy and program. Here again, standards will vary according to conditions, as noted in the discussion of proper purchase quantities, for purchasing policy may call for the accumulation of greater material reserves and greater advance coverage in times of advancing prices, which would result in less favorable turnover. In using such a yardstick, therefore, the condition at any given time could be seriously misleading, but the average of a month-to-month record over the period of a year would give a reasonably fair measure of accomplishment. Additionally, JIT systems warrant very high turnover for key items where some manufacturers maintain stock in terms of hours of supply.

THE FUNCTIONAL APPROACH

No attempt will be made here to propose a formula capable of application in every case to measure the efficiency and proficiency of purchasing. But an approach to such a solution can be outlined. Throughout this book emphasis has been placed upon the functional considerations of procurement. That is also a sound basis upon which to measure purchasing performance.

The functional responsibility of a purchasing department is to provide a steady flow of materials as needed, at lowest ultimate cost. This involves many factors—the right material, the right quantity, the right time, the right source, and the right price—that interact with one another, so that each decision of what is "right" in a given case depends upon what is "right" in respect to some or all the other factors. A compromise or balance must be achieved to arrive at the best end result. In the same way the measure of accomplishment is to be found in terms of the end result, in which these various measurable factors are contributory elements, to be reconciled in the final accounting.

The system of measurement should focus attention and effort upon performance rather than upon the details of rating, and the department head should have confidence that it will fairly reflect his or her accomplishments.

The system should conscientiously segregate the factors for which each department is directly responsible, so that the credits and demerits may be equitably applied. It should never be permitted to set up the type of interdepartmental competition that might discourage fullest cooperation toward the common aim of the most economical and profitable overall operation.

Cooperation is often influenced by perceptions, as one research report indicated. Perceptions that nonpurchasing personnel have of purchasing shape purchasing's image. Major components affecting these perceptual dimensions of purchasing performance were

- Output of purchasing through experiences personnel have with purchasing's services
- Interactions with purchasing by role or personality conflicts
- Observations of purchasing in ethical behavior, as judged by outsiders
- Reputation of purchasing in terms of perceived esteem held for the department by others
- Expectations of purchasing relating to how nonpurchasing managers perceive its contribution to firm's mission, profits, etc.[2]

STANDARD COST AS A BASIS OF MEASUREMENT

The end result of purchasing is product cost, and the measurement of purchasing performance can logically be based on that consideration. The direct responsibility of the purchasing department is the net cost of product materials up to the point of use, excluding the cost of maintenance and operating supplies. The standard of measurement is standard cost, arrived at by careful and detailed analysis of the complete bill of materials, with normal margins for waste and spoilage, corresponding to the standard costs used in accounting and in sales price estimates, and adjusted monthly to market fluctuations with the assistance of the purchasing executive. These costs will take into account the quality specifications representing the grade of material required to satisfy the company's standards of product and operation. The standard cost is expressed as one overall figure, either cost of purchased materials per unit of product or a percentage of total product cost, although the figure is made up of carefully itemized elements. The single figure is used partly to simplify accounting and evaluation, but even more as recognition of the facts that flexibility is essential in working out the purchasing program and that attention should be focused on the end result rather than on the details. And the end result is total product cost.

Besides being adjusted periodically to market conditions, the standard cost is revised for any changes in product design, bills of material, or manufacturing policies at the time at which these changes are made. For example, if it is decided to purchase a component part in fabricated form rather than to manufacture it in the plant, in the interest of greater ultimate economy or for better utili-

[2]Joseph L. Cavinato, "Purchasing Performance: What Makes the Magic?" *Journal of Purchasing and Materials Management,* Fall 1987, pp. 10–16.

zation of facilities, a cost adjustment is in order. In this case purchase cost will necessarily be higher, because outside manufacturing services are now being purchased while the company's own manufacturing operations are being reduced. The same principle would apply if the decision were reversed. The object at all times is to reflect fairly the specific cost responsibility of both departments.

Such standard costs, which are in effect a purchase budget for product materials, provide a practical and significant basis for the measurement of purchasing performance in respect to the largest and most important phase of the procurement function. A large part of many buyers' evaluations are based on comparing actual cost and standard cost. A more complete analysis is presented in Chapter 19.

SPECIFIC EFFECTIVENESS MEASURES

There are a number of other factors involved in the complete purchasing operation and the responsibility that goes with it, affecting full evaluation of performance. These factors can be considered separately and the results, properly weighted, applied to the overall evaluation (see Figure 23-3). A discussion of these factors follows.

1. Cost Savings Cost savings result from paying less for a product or material than previously paid. There are several methods by which a firm can realize a cost savings. These include:

- Substituting a less costly material
- Finding a new source of supply at a lower price
- Negotiating a more favorable contract with a current source
- Using a standard item for a special corporate or multiple unit
- Negotiating the agreement
- Achieving savings in transportation, packaging, or terms

Such cost savings are tangible savings, which directly affect the company's bottom line.

Less visible but still important are *cost-avoidance* savings. These savings are the result of delaying a proposed price increase or avoiding it. Cost avoidance can be achieved by taking action prior to a published price increase, eliminating or reducing escalation clauses, negotiating a lower price increase than proposed by the supplier, and delaying the date of a price increase. Since these figures are less tangible, certain "purists" feel they don't represent savings. Firms that track avoidance compare it to a general market inflation rate to see how successful their program is. Cost savings are definitely preferred; however, cost avoidance takes an increased importance in inflationary markets.

2. Inventory Performance. Continuity of operation, to the extent of having materials on hand when needed, is a purchasing responsibility. JIT and MRP systems

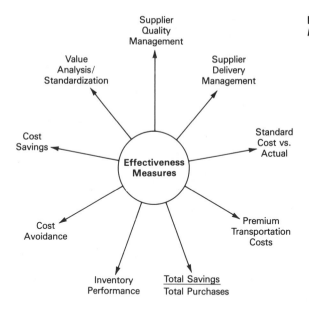

Figure 23-3 Purchasing-Performance Measures: Functional Effectiveness

recognize that this requires holding a minimum of working inventory, which minimizes carrying charges and space. The size of this inventory, in relation to current operating rates, is set in conjunction with inventory planners. If the approved policy is to carry a week's supply, the inventory should amount to one fifty-second of the amount of annual expenditures; if it is a two-week supply, the inventory would be one twenty-sixth of annual expenditures. This variable standard should be adjusted according to prevailing policy, and it should be measured in total dollar value. The cost of carrying inventory, which is calculated upon experience by standard cost-accounting methods, ranges from 20 to 35 percent in most industrial companies (see Chapter 17).

If by efficient planning, scheduling of purchases, and stores management, continuity of operation is maintained with a turnover of inventory every thirty days instead of every forty-five days, average inventory is reduced by 25 percent, and purchasing performance should be credited with the carrying cost of 25–35 percent on that amount. If the inventory runs high because of overbuying or inefficient materials control, resulting in a slower turnover, a corresponding debit should be applied.

Turnover is not the only measure of inventory performance. Losses due to obsolescence (unless due to change in design or other causes outside purchasing's jurisdiction and control), production delays due to lack of standard materials that should have been in stock when needed, and unnecessary extra transportation charges incurred for faster and more expensive means of delivery indicate poor performance. Obsolescence losses may be offset by credit for salvage operations and sales of scrap and surplus items. This group of factors does not lend itself to evaluation on a strictly quantitative or percentage basis and may call for a prorating with other departments, because the delays and emergency shipments may be caused by rush requisitions, changes in specifications, or abnormal and unforeseen demand. They should be noted, however, and a point rating assigned to fit the circumstances. It should be kept in mind that such demerits are not a serious reflection on purchasing performance unless they occur too frequently and run into large amounts.

3. Quality Factors   The purchasing department is responsible for procuring materials of adequate quality, in accordance with approved specifications. Failure to do so is an indication either of faulty buying or of selection of the wrong supplier. Today's quality standards require minmax rejects. In evaluating purchasing performance, demerits are in order for rejects in excess of the allowable margin and for the cost of working substandard items to make them usable and up to specification.

4. Supply Management   This measure is related to the supplier base and includes factors such as number of suppliers, multiple sources, single sources, supplier relationships (long-term or short-term partnerships), reliability of supplier, location of manufacturer/distributor, minority and female ownership, and shipping policies.

5. Generating Supplier Ideas.   Suppliers are experts in their materials and components. Their ideas and suggestions should be solicited and evaluated and implemented when appropriate.

Rather than solicit supplier information in a sporadic manner, many firms are beginning to use a more systematic concept called supplier days. During supplier days vendors are invited to the buyer's plant to discuss ideas, including cost-savings proposals. Successful proposals often result in an increased volume of business for the supplier.

A record of cost-improvement ideas contributed by vendors should be kept by buyers to be used in future vendor-selection processes.

6. Electronic Data Interchange (EDI)—Blanket orders, systems contracts and stockless purchasing   Fasteners, mill suppliers, office supplies, tools, and other low-value items are best acquired through EDI blanket orders or systems contracts. The low-value order is a costly one for purchasing, since the value of the order, unlike its price, does not increase.

EDI blanket orders and systems contracts provide the purchaser with savings in order-processing costs, time spent contracting for small-dollar items, and time spent locating suppliers, as only a one-time search of the marketplace is necessary. Such orders and contracts also "lock in" favorable prices, thus affording price protection.

Stockless purchasing is a system whereby a supplier ships material to a purchaser's plant at no immediate cost to the purchaser. The purchaser does not pay for the material until it's issued for use in her company's manufacturing operations, thereby permitting savings in inventory and stocking charges.

7. Value Analysis   This systematic and scientific approach identifies and eliminates unnecessary costs from a product, material, or service while monitoring or improving the function of the part. The objective of value analysis is to maintain or improve consumer value of the product at the same or a lower production cost. (See Chapter 20.)

While a value analysis program can be carried out by the purchasing department alone, such a program is generally more successful when purchasing is part of a team comprising representatives from purchasing, design engineering and other departments. Contributions to profits can be made through refinement in design, material specifications, and manufacturing processes.

8. Anticipatory Purchases   Buying extra quantities in anticipation of a price increase or prior to a preannounced increase saves money. However, the savings prior to the price increase must be balanced against the cost of carrying the material. Figure 23-4 shows how a purchaser saved $8,000 by purchasing prior to a price increase.

9. Transportation Improvement   Purchasers have excellent opportunities to decrease transportation costs by negotiating changes in tariff classifications, consolidating shipments, and having the seller assume the freight charges.

In cases where the supplier will not assume freight costs, the buyer should compare the supplier's average freight cost over the last few years with the average market rate. It could be, the supplier is shipping at premium rates rather than at lowest-cost, freight rates.

Amount purchased:	100,000 lbs. at $1/lb. = $100,000
Material usage:	25,000 lbs./week
Terms:	Net 30
Average inventory:	25,000 lbs.
Cost of carrying inventory:	24% year = 2% month
Announced price increase:	$1.10 lb.
Material savings	= (new price unit − old price unit) × quantity = ($1.10 − $1) × 100,000 = $10,000
Incremental carrying costs	= amount purchased × standard cost × carrying cost/month = 100,000 × $1 × 2% = $2,000
Net savings	= material savings − incremental carrying costs = $10,000 − $2,000 = $8,000 effective cost savings

Figure 23-4 Effecting Cost Savings by an Anticipatory Purchase

USING A RATING SYSTEM

The total evaluation of purchasing department performance consists of a basic rating on product cost, which is the real test of the department's performance, and modifying factors representing various phases of departmental responsibility and accomplishment. Three of these factors—cost reduction, inventory dollars or ratios, and administrative cost—are measurable on a scale and can be given a weight commensurate with their importance on a logical mathematical basis.

Certain firms attempt to weight dimensions and quantify on a scale such as setting a 100-point standard in the various sections of the measurement and in the total rating that represents an object to be attained, it does not necessarily follow that it is attainable under all conditions or that a lower rating is an indication of incompetence. Rather, it is an index of performance that can be interpreted as showing the department is falling short of expectations and not making its fair contribution to profitable company operations. On the other hand, it might show the department is coming close to the standards of performance that the company can reasonably expect in this phase of its business and is therefore doing a competent job.

Second, it must be recognized that the standards in each case are based on judgment that may or may not be accurate and realistic in its expectations. Measurements of both performance and the standards against which it is rated that are consistently above or below the stated standards may show that management is expecting too much or too little of its purchasing division. This discovery in itself is highly important; it may suggest and demonstrate that the estimates of material costs or administrative costs or policies of procurement should be revised to conform more closely with actual performance, but the competitive and profit factors of doing business must be based on actual performance. And for purposes of the rating itself, the standards and the expectation must be reasonable in relation to the conditions, both internal and external, under which purchasing is done.

Third, the ultimate rating provides a *comparison of performance* not only in relation to the stated standards but also in relation to performance in previous periods. This ratio is important for management to know. However, the rating is not a measure of comparison with purchasing performance in other companies or a definitive percentage measurement of excellence. There are too many variables in the type of materials purchased, the volume of purchases, and the specific organization responsibility, as well as variables of judgment in setting standards, to permit any such general interpretation.

These qualifications do not imply that the measurement and rating are inaccurate or of little value. Rather, they constitute a warning against a too superficial or arbitrary acceptance of a numerical result as the ultimate figure.

RESEARCH IN PURCHASING PERFORMANCE

A National Science Foundation (NSF) provided a substantial grant for a nationwide study of purchasing performance.

In an executive summary of the study the following points were noted.

1. Eighteen leading U.S.-based organizations participated in the study, and more than 200 managers and buyers were interviewed. *More than 200 purchasing performance measures* were identified [italics added].
2. The key measures in purchasing appeared to be price effectiveness, work load, cost savings, administration and control, vendor quality and delivery, and material flow control. The survey showed, however, that there are important differences in the ways in which the companies measure performance in each of the areas named.
3. Several important principles related both to systems and to people were suggested by the research:

   - A few narrowly defined measures are more effective than several loosely defined and partially understood ones.
   - Every measure must be based on a valid and comprehensive database used by all individuals in the purchasing organization.
   - There is no one best way of measuring purchasing performance; each organization must tailor its own.
   - Standards for purchasing performance cannot be fixed but must be adapted to changing conditions.
   - One overall measure of purchasing performance is not feasible.
   - The performance measures and database must be reviewed periodically.
   - The cost of purchasing-performance measurement must be weighed against the benefits.
   - Purchasing-performance measurement is not a substitute for good management.
   - Communication is of paramount importance in creating an effective measurement system; expected performance levels and the use of measures must be clearly understood by all.
   - The measures should be used to motivate and direct behavior, not to punish individuals.[3]

JOB ANALYSIS AND EVALUATION

Many experienced purchasing executives who are convinced that no practicable performance-rating system can be applied to purchasing have turned to job analysis and evaluation. The method sets forth specific responsibilities of the function and the minimum qualifications of education, training, experience, personality, and ability to fulfill the requirements of the position. On this basis, with suitable relative weights assigned to the various items, a rating of individual competence and performance can be made. It is a workable method, and it can be applied to all grades of personnel in a purchasing department, as in other departments.

[3]Robert M. Monczka, Phillip L. Carter, and John H. Hoagland, "Purchasing Performance: Measurement and Control—Executive Summary," unpublished study, School of Business Administration, Michigan State University, East Lansing, Mich., January 1978.

A somewhat similar approach involves the use of a series of check points for evaluating performance. Included would be such inquiries as the following:

1. What are the *personal characteristics,* ability, and organizing skill of the department head that have a particular bearing upon competence in the performance of the function and value in serving the overall company interests? This question recognizes the principle that departmental efficiency largely reflects the competence of the department head. The evaluation would necessarily be made by a superior management executive or by a professional management engineer.
2. Does the purchasing department have a broad statement of *policy,* preferably in written form? Is it a good policy? Is the policy observed in practice? Has the policy been brought to the attention of all suppliers?
3. Does the purchasing department have a standard *procedure,* preferably in the form of a written manual? Is it a good procedure? Is it efficiently carried out in practice? What checkpoints are used to determine adherence?
4. Is the performance of the purchasing department satisfactory in securing the delivery of *quality* material at the time needed?
5. Are materials secured at the right *price?* Measurement of this factor may be against the standard of market price for buyers in a comparable industrial position and for a comparable volume of purchases, or against "standard cost" prices as established in the accounting procedure of the company. The most practicable method of determining this point is by a systematic spot check or audit of the more substantial purchases, including an examination of the method of inquiry and choice of supplier as supporting evidence of whether the right prices are being obtained.
6. What is the *cost of operating the department?* It may be judged in relation to the departmental administrative budget or measured by the cost of placing an order or by what it costs to spend a dollar in purchasing.
7. To what extent does the purchasing department create or dissipate *goodwill* for the company? The general reputation of the purchasing department in the trade and among its suppliers has a bearing on this point.

A variation and expansion of the job analysis concept is used by a midwestern company to judge individual buyers' performance. The company's system has two elements: the job-dimension rating and the buyer-performance evaluation. A dimension rating, when multiplied by the performance rating, provides a composite rating. This rating enables department management to evaluate the relative contributions of buyers within a comparable purchasing discipline (see Figure 23-5).

The job-dimension rating provides a profile of a specific buyer's job, as seen by the department manager. The profile comprises twelve criteria, which are to be rated as to degree of difficulty or scope on a scale of 1 to 10, with 10 as the highest rating.

The criteria and the significance of higher ratings (7, 8, 9, 10) are as follows:

- *Dollar value of purchases:* The buyer has authorization to commit company funds in excess of the sum permitted the average buyer.
- *Decision making:* Buyer has to make frequent unilateral decisions and/or contribute to shared decision making.

- *Market volatility:* Buyer is responsible for items that are subject to fluctuations, erratic availability, and difficulty in making price projections.
- *Technical expertise required:* Job requires relatively higher levels of technical knowledge of item(s) being purchased.
- *Level of contact—suppliers:* Job requires or involves interface with upper management.
- *Level of contact–other departments:* Job requires or involves interface with upper management.
- *Number of items purchased:* Number of items is above average. The complexity of items purchased must be considered.
- *Number of current suppliers:* Buyer has more than average. Complexity of dealing with each must be considered.
- *Government constraints/regulations:* Buyer has more than average involvement with items that may be affected by government actions.
- *Number of division product lines*
- *Number of purchase orders/frequency*
- *Foreign sourcing:* Buyer has more than average involvement with foreign suppliers.

These criteria are, of course, related to the special requirements of the company and its divisions. Purchasing managers in other types of companies will have different objectives. The total of all ratings (a possible 120) is a means of comparing the content of each buyer's job with any other.

The buyer-performance evaluation provides for an objective numerical rating of a buyer's strength and weaknesses in thirteen performance criteria. Seven are objective performance criteria (what was accomplished) as follows:

- Purchase price versus market
- Cost-savings performance
- Inventory control
- Minority sourcing
- Attainment of personal objective
- Vendor relations
- Ethics

The other six are subjective criteria (how accomplished):

- Creativity
- Interpersonal skills
- Initiative
- Judgment
- Administrative ability (organization and planning)
- Technical experience

Each manager responsible for rating buyers is provided with a guide. The guide describes each criterion and the various expectations it reflects. The rating scale goes from highly effective (10) to highly ineffective (1). Different ratings along the scale are defined by examples of the kinds of behavior that could typically be expected from a buyer at these levels of effectiveness.

JOB DIMENSION

Division/Plant: _____ Incumbent: _____

Title: _____

Major Area of Purchase: _____

Job Dimension Criteria	Rating Last Year	Rating This Year	Reasons for Change
Value of Purchases			
Decision Making			
Market Volatility			
Technical Expertise Required			
Level of Contact—Supplier			
Level of Contact—Other Departments			
Volume of Items Purchased			
Number Current Suppliers			
Government Constraints/Regulations			
Number Division Product Lines			
Purchase Order Frequency			
Foreign Sourcing			
Total Rating			

All criteria to be rated according to degree of difficulty or scope 1 through 10, with 10 as highest rating.

Other comments on the job dimension or content of this position: _____
_____
_____
_____
_____
_____

Rated by: _____

Date: _____

Reviewed by: _____

Date: _____

Figure 23-5a Job-dimension rating

BUYER PERFORMANCE EVALUATION

Incumbent: _____ Title: _____

Division/Plant: _____ Major Area of Purchase: _____

Objective Performance Criteria (What Accomplished)	Last Year			Actual This Year		
	Rating	Weight Factor%	Weighted Rating	Rating	Weight Factor%	Weighted Rating
Purchase Price vs. Market						
Cost Savings Performance						
Inventory Control						
Minority Sourcing						
Attainment of Personal Object						
Vendor Relations						
Ethics						
Subjective Performance Criteria (How Accomplished)						
Creativity						
Interpersonal Skills						
Initiative						
Judgment						
Adm. Ability (Organ. & Planning)						
Technical Expertise						
NET RATING		100%			100%	
X Dimen. Rating						
= Composite						

Other comments on the evaluation of this individual: _____

_____

_____

_____

Rated by: _____

Date: _____

Figure 23-5b Buyer-performance evaluation

Under the purchase-price-versus-market criterion, for example, at a level of 10 the buyer could be expected to make a thorough and accurate market evaluation prior to making a purchase, to ensure the best value over an extended period of time (not a single "spot" purchase). At the level of 1 the buyer could always be expected to buy at premium prices without receiving premium quality or service, or when the latter two are not required.

Purchasing Human Resource Audit System Evaluation (PHRASE)

The National Association of Purchasing Management developed PHRASE to improve purchasing performance by enabling firms to target specific training and development needs.[4] The intent of the program is to enable managers to pinpoint the strengths and weaknesses of each individual, as the overall company purchasing operation. PHRASE is broken into three stages: (1) job analysis, (2) diagnostic evaluation, and (3) employee development.

In the job analysis phase a questionnaire addresses industry needs and results in company-specific job descriptions for each job level within the purchasing department. The critical duties are shown in Figure 23-6, with national norms for positions of manager, senior buyer, buyer, and junior buyer. The benefits of the first stage include: (1) staff needs and time allocations are addressed; (2) it allows for planning of strategic objectives; (3) it allows employees and managers to match their perceptions of time use; and (4) it permits comparisons to national norms.

The diagnostic evaluation measures the individual's comprehension of key duties surveyed in the job analysis. Thus it enables the manager to pinpoint employee strengths and weaknesses and then extend these findings to the department as a whole. Figure 23-7 shows a typical report and illustrates where training is needed. The data are presented on raw score, percent of items correct, z score (positive better than norm, negative worse), and training factor. The higher the training factor, the more training required by the individual. In our example Jane Smith's greatest training needs are in the area of planning and forecasting. Ranges and average scores of many individuals within a firm provide results that can be extended to the department and to corporations for in-house training programs.

In the final phase, employee development, targeted training programs are developed for the company and its employees. This phase is the most critical in terms of increasing the effectiveness and productivity of the purchasing department.

POINTS FOR REVIEW

1. Identify the inconsistencies in the argument that purchasing performance can be judged by purely quantitative standards, for example, by departmental operating costs.

[4]For a complete discussion see Edward J. Bierman and Lisa J. Marinelli, *Guide to Purchasing—PHRASE 3.18* (Tempe, Ariz.: National Association of Purchasing Management, 1985).

Duties

**Average
Percent of
Time Spent**

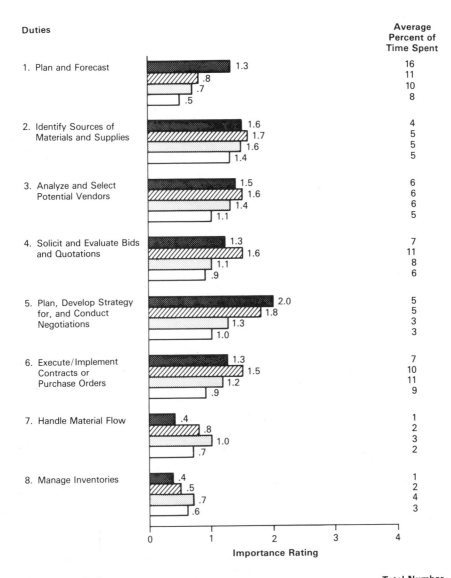

1. Plan and Forecast

1.3
.8
.7
.5

16
11
10
8

2. Identify Sources of
Materials and Supplies

1.6
1.7
1.6
1.4

4
5
5
5

3. Analyze and Select
Potential Vendors

1.5
1.6
1.4
1.1

6
6
6
5

4. Solicit and Evaluate Bids
and Quotations

1.3
1.6
1.1
.9

7
11
8
6

5. Plan, Develop Strategy
for, and Conduct
Negotiations

2.0
1.8
1.3
1.0

5
5
3
3

6. Execute/Implement
Contracts or
Purchase Orders

1.3
1.5
1.2
.9

7
10
11
9

7. Handle Material Flow

.4
.8
1.0
.7

1
2
3
2

8. Manage Inventories

.4
.5
.7
.6

1
2
4
3

0   1   2   3   4

Importance Rating

Importance Scale:

0 = Not Important
1 = Somewhat Important
2 = Important
3 = Very Important
4 = Extremely Important

Key:

▨ = Manager
▨ = Senior Buyer
☐ = Intermediate Buyer
☐ = Junior Buyer

**Total Number
Surveyed**

111
218
85
55

Figure 23-6

Source: *NAPM Guide to Purchasing PHRASE 3.18* (Tempe, Ariz.: National Association of Purchasing
Management, 1985), p. 8.

Name: Jane Smith
                              1024 Smith Street
                              Columbus, OH 44691
Company: Company X
Employee No.:   0371
Position: Senior Buyer
Grade: 17

Duties	Raw Score	Percent	z Score	Training Factor
1. Plan and forecast	10	20	−1.5	1.8
2. Identity sources of materials/ supplies	5	55	0.8	0.0
3. Analyze and select potential vendors	6	60	1.9	0.0
4. Solicit and evaluate bids/quotations	3	30	−0.8	1.1
5. Plan, develop strategy for, and conduct negotiations	2	25	−1.3	1.5
6. Execute and implement contracts or purchase orders	5	50	0.5	0.0
7. Handle material flow	8	60	1.3	0.0
8. Manage inventories	4	75	1.8	0.0
9. Evaluate performance of vendors and resolve contract or vendor quality problems	9	80	2.1	0.0
10. Manage human resources	8	60	1.2	0.0
11. Perform communications activities	9	75	2.0	0.0
12. Perform administrative activities	15	85	2.3	0.0

Key:
Raw score—actual number correct
Percent—percent of items answered correctly
z score—how individual performed in relation to average performance (positive is better than norm; negative worse)
Training factor—how much training is needed in each area

Figure 23-7 Individual Phrase Diagnositc Report (Step 2)

Source: *NAPM Guide to Purchasing PHRASE 3.18* (Tempe, Ariz.: National Association of Purchasing Management, 1985), p. 11.

2. Discuss the difference between measuring purchasing efficiency and purchasing proficiency, and give an opinion on how the results of each measurement should be interpreted.
3. Name five other factors that can be considered in evaluating purchasing performance.
4. Describe the concept of standard costs and its use in determining the effectiveness of the purchasing department.
5. Make your personal evaluation of the system for gauging the performance of a purchasing department described on pages 405–407.
6. List the key measures in evaluating purchasing performance as determined by the study funded by the National Science Foundation.

24

PURCHASING IN RETAIL ORGANIZATIONS

Over one-third of all professionals involved in purchasing in the United States are in the retail/wholesale trade sector, so it is important that we include a discussion of buying for resale. It is the purpose of this chapter to show just how different merchandise buying is from the industrial buying process while at the same time identifying enough similarities between the processes to reinforce the notion that there is a common body of purchasing knowledge that applies to buying in all sectors of the economy.

MERCHANDISE BUYERS AND INDUSTRIAL BUYERS: ARE THEY SIMILAR?

For years students in purchasing classes have been told that there were basically two types of purchasing: purchasing for resale and purchasing for consumption or conversion. Most purchasing texts are concerned only with this latter category, the industrial or institutional buyer. The role of the first category of buyer, the merchandise buyer, is described by Dobler, Burt, and Lee as follows:

> Today's merchants determine what consumers want, buy it at a price to which they can add a profitable markup and sell it to the customer at a satisfactory level of quality and service.[1]

Dobler, Burt, and Lee further suggest that the role of the industrial buyer is more complex in that their actions must be more closely integrated with other functions of the firm. In today's world, however, it may well be that merchandise buyers must also act in closer coordination with other activities of their stores. For instance, each store tries to create its own distinct image, and merchandise bought must be in concert with this image. This requires close coordination between buyers and other functions in the store, such as display, sales promotion, training, receiving and marking, distribution, and the store's purchasing department. This last department is particularly important as it is responsible for ensuring that the appropriate packaging is available for the merchandise being sold. In addition, retailing is a highly competitive industry, and buyers must be made acutely aware of the financial picture of the firm in making merchandising decisions that will have an impact on inventories and other expenses. In the past merchandise buyers were evaluated primarily on gross margin. Today, however, their evaluation is more representative of the total profitability of their buying decisions. There has to be closer control of expenses other than the cost of merchandise. In this sense the merchandise buyer's and the purchasing agent's goals are becoming increasingly similar—to increase the profitability of the firm!

Other authors have also commented on the similarity of the two buying processes. For example, Ettenson and Wagner define retail buying as the decision-making process through which the retail buyer identifies, evaluates, and selects

---

[1]Donald W. Dobler, David N. Burt, and Lamar Lee, Jr., *Purchasing and Materials Management,* 5th ed. (New York: McGraw-Hill Book Co., 1990), p. 4.

merchandise for resale to the customer. They also suggest that retail buying is really a special case of industrial buying:

1. Both retail buyers and industrial buyers act as brokers for their respective customers.
2. Both are affected by short-run and long-term goals.
3. Both have extensive training and experience and are expected to be well informed about their merchandise selections.[2]

This is not to say that the two roles are identical. At the International Purchasing Conference held in New York, May 3–6, 1987, David F. Miller summed up the major differences this way: "In retailing buyers have the responsibility not only for buying *finished* products but for selling them as well." In this sense merchandise buyers are both buyer and seller, and this is where their role differs significantly from their industrial counterparts.

In addition to this basic difference, other goals of these two types of buyers are also different. The merchandise buyer is primarily concerned with fashion as opposed to utility. As a result, merchandise buyers must be much more flexible and be prepared to adapt to a volatile marketplace. Their markets are characterized by rapid changes and short selling seasons. While strategic planning is becoming more important in the retail business, it is the seasonal plan that is critical for the merchandise buyer.[3] This shorter planning cycle causes the merchandise buyer to buy production time and hold off in committing to specific sizes and colors. Thus while their industrial counterparts are making long-term commitments to their suppliers, merchandise buyers must hold off to the latest possible moment before making commitments to their resources.

Beyond these major differences, however, there are numerous similarities between the two roles, as a review of the merchandising buying process will illustrate.

THE MERCHANDISE BUYING PROCESS

The main similarity between merchandise buyers and industrial buyers lies in the buying process used by both groups. Lewison and DeLozier suggest that the merchandise buying process consists of six steps: identifying, surveying, contacting, evaluating, negotiating with, and buying from sources of supply.[4] This process is similar to that described in many purchasing textbooks. For instance, Zenz describes the purchasing process as follows: recognition of need, description of

[2]Richard Ettenson and Janet Wagner, "Retail Buyers' Saleability Judgements: A Comparison of Information Use across Levels of Experience," *Journal of Retailing,* Spring 1986, p. 42.

[3]Therese M. Maskulka, "An Examination of Strategic Planning in Retailing" (doctoral dissertation, Kent State University, 1987).

[4]D. M. Lewison and M. W. DeLozier, *Retailing,* 4th ed. (Columbus, Ohio: Charles E. Merrill Publishing Co., 1986), p. 476.

need, selection of sources, price determination, placing the order, follow-up of the order, maintenance of records, and vendor relations.[5] While the process described in purchasing texts goes beyond the source-selection process that Lewison and DeLozier outline, these authors suggest that many of the other activities listed by Zenz are part of the procurement process that occurs after the order is placed with a given vendor. In their text on retailing Lewison and DeLozier claim that the procurement process consists of the following activities: ordering and following up, receiving and checking, marking and stocking, and paying and returning. It may well be that what Lewison and DeLozier have separated into two functions, buying and procurement, is what Burt and others call procurement.[6] In any case, it is apparent that the processes used by both merchandise buyers and their industrial counterparts are similar.

Another major difference between these two groups of buyers is the source of the impetus for the recognition and description of need for each item purchased. In the case of merchandise buyers this impetus clearly lies with their resources. The design capability of a particular resource becomes an important evaluation factor when choosing a resource, as design is a critical factor of success for apparel retailers. While design capabilities of industrial suppliers are important, they are not as critical. Most often in the industrial arena, it is the buying company that takes responsibility for the design of commodities purchased. In fact, as suggested by Burt, the better purchasing agents take a proactive role by getting involved in the design stage of most items bought by their companies.[7] Their early involvement in the design stage ensures that specifications are functional and that utility becomes the predominant goal. As we said earlier, fashion, not utility, is the key to successful merchandise buying. This significant difference between merchandise and industrial buying cannot be overlooked.

Another major difference between these two sectors is the responsibilities of buyers. As noted above, the merchandise buyer is not only a buyer but a seller as well. Diamond and Pintel indicate that the responsibilities of the merchandise buyer include:

1. Merchandise selection, that is,
   - what to buy
   - how much to buy
   - from whom to buy
   - when to buy
2. Advertising
3. Merchandise pricing
4. Management of the sales force
5. Management of the department[8]

[5]Gary J. Zenz, *Purchasing and the Management of Materials,* 6th ed. (New York: John Wiley & Sons, 1987), pp. 7–10.

[6]David N. Burt, *Proactive Procurement* (Englewood Cliffs, N. J.: Prentice-Hall, 1984), p. 3.

[7]Ibid., p. 23.

[8]Jay Diamond and Gerald Pintel, *Retail Buying,* 3rd ed. (Englewood Cliffs, N. J.: Prentice-Hall, 1989), pp. 7–9.

As can be seen from this list, the buying responsibilities of the merchandise buyer are exactly the same as those of the industrial buyer; however, the merchandise buyer is responsible for a good deal more than buying. In other respects, however, the merchandise and industrial buyer are alike. For instance, Diamond and Pintel suggest that the merchandise buyer must secure the cooperation of others in the store to be successful. And like their industrial counterparts, merchandise buyers are evaluated on total cost.[9]

Additionally, retail buying is in many respects organized in a similar fashion to industrial buying. It is a combination of centralization and decentralization. However, with the exception of food chains in which the buying decisions are heavily centralized, there is a great deal of autonomy at the divisional level. The reason, according to Diamond and Pintel, is that as chains expanded, the buyer became too removed from the local market.[10] The retailing counterparts to the corporate purchasing departments in the industrial sector are the resident buying offices, which are located in major markets like New York, Dallas, Los Angeles, and selected overseas locations.

These resident buying offices may be either independent, corporate, or cooperative in nature. Diamond and Pintel give examples of each, including Felix Lilienthal, a now-defunct buying office that represented a number of small independent department stores across the country; the corporate buying offices of May Merchandising, which is involved in the buying of private labels for the May Department Store chain; and Associated Merchandising Corporation, a cooperative made up of many large department stores throughout the country.[11] This last association is akin to the buying groups and cooperatives in the institutional and governmental sectors (see Chapter 25). The purpose of these buying offices is the same as in any centralized purchasing organization; that is, they hope to increase purchasing effectiveness through greater buying volume and increased product and market knowledge gained by specialization and greater standardization.

According to the *NRMA Buyer's Manual,* buyers in most department stores are highly specialized along product lines, buying, for example, just men's shirts and ties or just small kitchen electronics. Each buyer normally has responsibility for product selection, specifications, vendor selection, contract commitment, catalog copy and presentation, and acquisition of product sales-training materials.[12] Again, there are a number of similarities in the responsibilities of buyers in the retail and the industrial sectors. But again, a major difference is that merchandise buyers are also responsible for selling the products they buy.

While significant differences do exist between merchandise buyers and industrial buyers, many of the actual buying decisions are similar. For instance, the merchandise buyers, like their industrial counterparts, must decide whether to buy direct from the manufacturer or from a middleman. The reasons for

[9]Ibid., p. 2.
[10]Ibid., p. 33.
[11]Ibid.
[12]R. Patrick Cash, *The Buyer's Manual* (New York: National Retail Merchants Association, 1979), p. 100.

choosing either direct shipments from a manufacturer or store-door deliveries from a wholesaler are essentially the same for a retailer as they would be for an industrial firm. Just as in the industrial sector, the decision is based on whether the retailer chooses to perform the distribution function. In the case of smaller retailers this simply may not be a choice owing to space constraints. A larger chain, such as J. C. Penney, because of the sheer volume of its purchases and its extensive distribution system, chooses to buy direct from the manufacturer for most of its purchases.

Other reasons for choosing to deal with a wholesaler include such things as a faster response time and smaller deliveries. A recent study by Levy and Van Breda found that lead times from a wholesaler were substantially smaller than when buying direct. In their study they found the average lead time from a wholesaler to be seven days, while that from a manufacturer was twenty-eight days.[13] These benefits of reduced lead time and smaller orders mean that the average inventory held by the retailer will be smaller, with a corresponding reduction in inventory carrying costs. In addition, many wholesalers in a retail distribution chain will provide marking services, which in turn allow for labor savings for a retailer. Finally, the use of some wholesalers allows for consolidation of deliveries. With receiving space at a minimum at branch stores, this may be a significant benefit. All of these reasons are similar to those used by industrial buyers in making a decision to buy from a distributor as opposed to buying direct from a manufacturer.

Another decision must be made by the retail buyer—whether to maintain a large vendor base to ensure innovation and competitiveness or to limit the number of vendors and increase leverage with them. And just as with their industrial counterparts, retail buyers must weigh the advantages and disadvantages of each of these strategies. The key to making this decision in the retailing sector, as in any of the other sectors discussed above, is the need to maintain a strong, loyal vendor base that will be willing to respond to emergencies, provide innovative designs, and keep the firm competitive in a fiercely competitive industry.

The *NRMA Buyer's Manual* suggests one way of achieving this goal is by building key resource or partner relationships. These relationships will result in greater bargaining power for the store as well as many other advantages.[14] The reason is that the store becomes important to a few key resources. The manual points out that, "in a time of dynamic change in the wholesale marketplace, successful retailers are giving high priority to developing and maintaining strong relationships with their vendors."[15]

One way to build these strong relationships, suggested by the *NRMA Buyer's Manual,* is to split the volume of key products between two or three key vendors.[16] This will ensure fast response to the store's needs. Additionally, concentration with fewer resources means better terms, lower buying expenses, and preferred treatment. Once again, the argument for single sourcing or sourcing

[13]Michael Levy and Michael VanBreda, "How to Determine Whether to Buy Direct or through a Wholesaler," *Retail Control,* June–July 1985, p. 42.

[14]Cash, *Buyer's Manual,* p. 64.

[15]Ibid., p. 127.

[16]Ibid., p. 130.

with a smaller vendor base is no different for retailers than it is for industrial firms. The problems associated with a smaller vendor base are also the same as they are in the industrial sector. Specifically, overdependence on a single source could result in disaster if something were to happen to that source—bankruptcy, fire, strikes. What is required with the sourcing decision is a balance between too many sources and too few sources.

Another way of looking at the size of the vendor base is to check the costs in dealing with too many suppliers. As suggested by Crooks, too many vendors can have a negative effect on profits by increasing costs associated with ordering, freight, and receiving. Crooks, again, echoes the sentiment expressed earlier of the need to become important to your vendors.[17]

In an interview with one of the authors of this book J. C. Penney executives discussed the size of the vendor base. They said that the need to establish exclusive private labels in order to compete with fashion specialty stores required Penney to increase its vendor base. The reason is that few vendors produce both brand and private labels.

In addition to these concerns of channels and the size of the vendor base, the merchandise buyers are concerned with negotiating the best prices. That includes making sure the store receives all the discounts to which it is entitled and the best transportation costs available. In essence, retail buyers, like their industrial counterparts, are interested in obtaining the lowest possible prices for the merchandise they buy. In order to achieve the lowest net price for a given product, the retail buyer uses price and cost analysis based on his or her knowledge of the market and product. One major difference for a retail buyer, in contrast to industrial buyers, is the negotiation of advertising and promotional discounts.

Other procurement functions are also important to the merchandise buyer, such as expediting orders and ensuring that goods are received, inspected, properly marked, and properly stored and that invoices are properly paid. All of these actions are similar to those engaged in by most industrial buyers.

Actual source selection by merchandise buyers is also similar to the process used by many purchasing agents in that both use evaluation criteria in selecting suppliers. In both cases these criteria are a combination of price, quality, service, and delivery. However, they are weighted differently. In retailing, for instance, it is not the price itself that is critical but, rather, the potential markup. In addition, the return policy of a particular vendor is extremely important to a merchandise buyer as well as the markdown policy of that vendor. Other criteria used by merchandise buyers in choosing vendors include those given by Woodside: previous experience with the vendor, gross margin, strength of vendor advertising, potential sales volume, and intuition. Woodside suggests that of these, previous product sales success, supplier reputation, and advertising support may be the most important.[18] It is important to note here that the major goal of merchandise buyers

[17]Edwin Crooks, "The Case for Concentrating Purchases," *Journal of Retailing*, Spring 1966, pp. 14–18.

[18]Arch G. Woodside, "Reseller Buying Behavior: Some Questions and Tentative Answers," in J. H. Summey and R. D. Taylor, eds., *Evolving Marketing Thought for 1980: Proceedings of the Annual Meeting of the Southern Marketing Association*, (New Orleans November 19–22, 1980), p. 495.

is to sell what they buy at the greatest profit possible, and the criteria suggested by Woodside reflect that goal. Here, then, is another major difference between merchandise and industrial buyers, but in general the selection criteria are quite similar.

Again citing Lewison and DeLozier, the general criteria used by merchandise buyers in selecting vendors include merchandise (quality), distribution (delivery), price, promotion, and service. These are similar to the criteria of price, quality, service, and delivery used by industrial buyers.[19]

A more complete listing of source-selection criteria used by merchandise buyers can be found in the *NRMA Buyer's Manual:*

1. Merchandise desirability—the right merchandise for your customer
2. Bargaining position on prices and terms
3. Deliveries
4. Vendor distribution practices—e.g., exclusive arrangements and first offers
5. Promotional aids
6. Vendor's reputation for reliability[20]

One final set of source-selection criteria detailed in Diamond and Pintel demonstrate specific areas of concerns for retail buyers:

1. Suitability and availability of merchandise offered
2. Distribution policies that include such things as limited sales and specials
3. Pricing policies including such things as price maintenance and fair trading (now illegal, which has led to an increase in private labeling)
4. Promotional merchandise policies
5. Shipping and inventory maintenance policies including size of orders and timeliness of deliveries
6. Pricing policies including issues such as the fullness of the line versus the cost
7. Profitability including potential markups, preticketing of merchandise, markdown and return policies[21]

A specific example of the use of source-selection criteria is the J. C. Penney approach. Quality, price, and delivery are all important to Penney buyers. In buying fashion items, quality becomes preeminent, and in buying commodity items, price becomes more important. Timing is critical in a retailing environment, because a customer who does not find what he or she is looking for is likely to leave the store and not return. As a result, delivery reliability is crucial, and Penney penalizes late deliveries by deducting a penalty from the price of the product.

Again, what can be seen in these criteria is how closely intertwined the buying and selling processes are in a retailing firm. Where an industrial buyer purchases a commodity or component part that is converted in the production process, the retail buyer sells what he or she buys. This closeness between the two

[19]Lewison and DeLozier, *Retailing*, pp. 487–89.
[20]Cash, *Buyer's Manual*, pp. 128–29.
[21]Diamond and Pintel, *Retail Buying*, pp. 149–54.

processes may really be what separates the retail buyers from their industrial counterparts. This difference is also reflected in the source-selection criteria used by both sets of buyers.

While it does not appear that merchandise buyers have developed the sophisticated vendor-evaluation schemes used by many industrial purchasing departments, some attempts have been made in this direction. Perhaps one of the more sophisticated evaluation methods developed for merchandise buyers is Berens's. It uses a decision-matrix approach to vendor selection.[22] However, this is not to say that retail buyers do not evaluate their resources. The two sets of vendor-evaluation criteria below indicate what is considered important to the retail buyer in regard to vendor performance.

The first list was compiled by Diamond and Pintel:

1. Number one concern is margin
2. Number of customer complaints and returns
3. Accuracy of quantity shipped and billed
4. Ability to meet promised delivery date
5. Pricing accuracy
6. Unauthorized substitutions
7. Returns to vendor and reasons for returns
8. Terms and allowances provided
9. Compliance with shipping instructions
10. Adherence to special instructions such as packaging and marking[23]

The second set of criteria for evaluation of vendor performance comes from the *NRMA Retail Buyer's Manual:*

1. Sales analysis—what's selling?
2. Periodic examination of stocks
3. Personal comments from customers and salespeople
4. Customer requests noted on the selling floor
5. Markup as compared to comparable merchandise
6. Markdowns—why are they occurring?
7. Was merchandise received in time for peak selling period?
8. Were alteration, refinishing, or repair costs excessive?
9. Were credits excessive?—Why? Customer complaints?[24]

Both lists emphasize that realized gross margin is the critical criterion in evaluating vendor performance.[25] While this emphasis might not be as clearly seen in the industrial sector, it is nonetheless there. In a proactive procurement environment industrial buyers will be critically aware of the effect their purchases have on the ability of their firms to compete in the marketplace. Additionally, more and more purchasing departments are being evaluated on the basis of the

[22]John S. Berens, "A Decision Matrix Approach to Supplier Selection," *Journal of Retailing,* Winter 1971–72, pp. 47–53.

[23]Diamond and Pintel, *Retail Buying,* p. 159.

[24]Cash, *Buyer's Manual,* pp. 131–32.

[25]Ibid., p. 132.

cost of poor quality. A primary measure used in evaluating this concept is feedback from the customers of the firm in the form of complaints, returns, and field warranty expense. While industrial buyers are not as close to the final customer as their retail counterparts, they are being forced to ensure that what is bought satisfies the firm's customers' needs. This suggests a need for the industrial buyer to become more familiar with the final customer of the firm.

It is also clear that retailers are as concerned with developing minority business enterprises (MBEs) as their industrial counterparts are. A good example of the efforts being made by retailers in this area is the development by J. C. Penney of their minority business base. In 1987 Penney placed business in excess of $250 million with MBEs. Not only does Penney place business with MBEs but it helps build and support such enterprises. It is active with the Minority Business Development Council (MBDC) and has contributed millions of dollars to the MBDC fund. This fund lends up to $250,000 to MBEs, which are then required to pay the fund back at prime rates. The success of J. C. Penney in this area can be measured by the success of their MBE suppliers. One such supplier now receives in excess of $62 million from Penney business.

This review of the merchandise buying process indicates that there is good support for the premise that the jobs of the merchandise buyer and industrial buyer are similar enough to warrant the inclusion of the former group in this book. This conclusion is further supported by the results of a survey of a small sample of merchandise buyers, conducted by one of the authors, discussed in the following section.

A SURVEY OF MERCHANDISE BUYERS

Questionnaires were sent out as part of a class project at Florida State University. Although there are a number of problems with the instrument itself, the results provide some interesting data. Most important, the questionnaire was based on areas of concern to the industrial buyer. Yet it would appear that the merchandise buyers who responded to survey had no problem identifying with these concerns. That in itself might speak to the similarities in the buying processes of these two sectors.

Even with the problems in the study, these results represent a significant contribution, as there is little existing research on the behavior of retail buyers. The point is made rather emphatically by Mazursky and Hirschman, who decry the scant attention this subject has received in spite of the fact that the behavior of the retail buyer can have such a dramatic effect on the profitability of the firm.[26] Sanford Zimmerman, former chairman of Abraham & Strauss, is quoted in the *NRMA's Buyer's Manual:* "The buyer is the critical factor in the success or failure of any retail venture."[27] Given this importance, it is surprising that there is such a

[26]David Mazursky and Elizabeth Hirschman, "A Cross-Organisational Comparison of Retail Buyers' Information Source Utilisation," *International Journal of Retailing*, January–February 1987, p. 44.
[27]Cash, *Buyer's Manual*, p. 42.

paucity in the literature. The study discussed below, then, is just a small step in filling this void.

Sample

The sample for the survey was drawn from buying personnel at sixty department stores located across the United States. Over three hundred questionnaires containing items pertaining to purchasing techniques, buyer training, and buyer-performance evaluation were mailed out, and thirty-six completed responses were returned. While this sample is small, it does represent a diverse group of buying personnel who are geographically dispersed, employees of both independently owned department stores and department store chains, and at all levels of the buying hierarchy in department stores. Chains included in the sample were the May Company, Federated Department Stores, Allied, Macy's, Gimbel's, Emporium Caldell, and Associated Dry Goods. Job levels represented in the sample ranged from buyers to senior vice-presidents responsible for merchandising. Product lines bought by the respondents in this study included home furnishings, cosmetics, lingerie, men's furnishings, women's accessories, fashions, men's sportswear, toys, and candy. Respondents' buying experience ranged from one to thirty-six years with an average of a little over twelve years. All in all, the sample obtained from the survey appears to be representative of department store buying personnel.

Results

While this survey was only an exploratory study aimed at determining some of the characteristics of merchandise buyers and the merchandise buying process, the results obtained from the survey are instructive and useful for comparison with traditional purchasing practices. For instance, the survey revealed information pertaining to criteria used for vendor evaluation, price determination, professional affiliation, vendor relations, use of long-term contracts, MRO procedures, buyer training, centralization of the buying function, foreign purchasing, other materials functions, use of the computer, and buyer-performance evaluation. Each of these is reviewed briefly below.

Factors used for vendor evaluation. Respondents were asked to rate the importance of the following factors in selecting vendors: quality, timeliness of delivery, price, service, warranty policy, and a miscellaneous category of "other." These criteria are similar to those used by most purchasing agents and, in light of our review of the merchandise buying process, would not seem to be an all-inclusive list. However, most respondents seemed to be able to answer without much difficulty. In only six cases was the "other" category used. The most frequently used "other" response was a comment relating to fashion. This ties into our discussion on the importance of fashionability in merchandise buying. In addition, it appears that a number of respondents felt that fashionability was part of the quality factor, the factor that was most frequently chosen as most important.

On a scale of 1 (least important) to 5 (most important), quality had a mean rating of 4.11 among this sample of department store buyers. Timeliness of delivery followed with a mean rating of 3.89. Service had a mean rating of 3.69, followed by price with a mean rating of 3.56. Warranty policy received the lowest mean rating with a score of 2.71. Had this item been worded to reflect the importance of returns and markdowns, it is likely to have received a higher rating.

What all of this says is that quality is extremely important to this sample of buyers. However, these results also suggest that delivery, price, and service are also important and, where quality is standardized, become controlling factors in the selection decision. This conclusion is based on the observation that each of these three items had more total ratings of "moderate" (3) and above than did quality.

These results also dovetail with what is happening in the industrial sector. A greater emphasis is being placed on quality in the source-selection decision but not to the exclusion of price, delivery, and service. As in the industrial sector, some retailers are consolidating their vendor base to ensure more consistent quality in the merchandise they buy. Sears executives are quoted in *Stores* magazine as intending to "commit their buying strength to fewer and fewer sources, with the emphasis on those that share our concern for intrinsic quality and will work with us on the development of rigid product specifications."[28] The same type of philosophy is being pursued by those industrial firms that find themselves in a just-in-time environment.

Price and vendor selection.   This sample of retail buyers more often than not chose vendors on the basis of brand name (64 percent) and only infrequently used competitive bidding in selecting resources (11 percent). Another important price factor used in selecting vendors was negotiated discounts (36 percent). Again, the merchandise buyer is not only a buyer but also a seller of merchandise, and how well an item will sell is of paramount importance. Brand names sell and in many cases prices on such items are not negotiable. So while buying on the basis of brand names is frowned upon in the industrial buying office, it would appear to be standard practice among retail buyers. It is interesting to note, however, that in many of the larger department stores buyers are insisting that manufacturers create exclusive private labels for them, ensuring a competitive edge against the increasing number of specialty stores in the retailing industry. This proliferation of specialty stores may result in the adoption of the strategy being used by Sears that we referred to earlier. Sears selects a few vendors who are willing to work with rigid specifications and exclusive arrangements. This strategy is similar to the one being pursued in the industrial sector, where many firms are purposely reducing their vendor bases to ensure better control over quality and delivery.

Professional affiliation.   One of the more interesting results obtained from this survey of department store buying personnel was that there were no true profes-

[28]"NRMA News", *Stores*, January–February 1980, p. 58.

sional buying associations to which these buyers belonged. When asked, "Do you or any member of your staff belong to a professional buying association?" the respondents answered by citing the buying group or chain to which they belonged. It is interesting to note that none mentioned NRMA (National Retail Merchants Association), a group that better fits the description of a professional association and that most department stores belong to. What is apparent from the responses to this question is that there is no professional purchasing association for merchandise buyers.

Vendor relations.   Part of the questionnaire dealt with the issue of ethics. The responses seemed to indicate that merchandise buyers had the same concerns as their industrial counterparts do regarding relationships with vendors. Diamond and Pintel emphasize that there is an increasing concern with the ethical practices of retail buyers.[29] A recent study by the Center for Advanced Purchasing Studies (CAPS) on ethical practices demonstrates that it is a common concern shared by all buying professionals.[30] The *NRMA Buyer's Manual* points out that ethical practices can have an effect on the ability of a store to compete: "The practice of ethical business principles and courteous dealings with vendor representatives can mean having the edge in a highly competitive business."[31]

All respondents indicated that their stores had policies relating to professional ethics. Social interaction between buyer and vendor was limited to lunches and dinner, a practice acceptable to 33 percent of the sample. Sixty-four percent of the respondents also felt that accepting token gifts, such as pens and pencils, was acceptable. There were limits as to what constituted acceptable gifts from vendors, however, as none of the respondents felt it was ethical to accept the gift of a weekend retreat from a vendor. In short, merchandise buyers appear to have ethical standards similar to those of industrial buyers.

The responses in this sample of merchandise buyers mirror reports in the *NRMA Buyer's Manual* that most stores have a policy on gifts. The *Buyer's Manual* cautions that the acceptance of gifts could be at worst illegal, as such acceptance could be construed as commercial bribery and, at best, unethical. The manual concludes that the best gift a vendor can give a buyer is well made, salable merchandise.[32] This sample also mirrors the responses contained in the CAPS study of a wider purchasing population.

The *NRMA Buyer's Manual* goes on to delineate what constitutes good and bad ethical practices:

General good business practices:

1. Written confirmation of orders
2. Good faith in business dealings

[29]Diamond and Pintel, *Retail Buying*, p. 166.

[30]Robert L. Janson, *Purchasing Ethical Practices* (Tempe, Ariz.: Ernst and Whinney/Center for Advanced Purchasing Studies/National Association of Purchasing Management, 1988), p. 10.

[31]Cash, *Buyer's Manual,* pp. 132–33.

[32]Ibid.

Practices to be avoided:

1. Undue pressure for cooperative advertising
2. Taking of unauthorized or unearned discounts
3. Cancellation of definite orders before delivery date
4. Returns that are not justified or [are] in poor condition
5. Pirating of merchandise designs or dealing in pirated designs
6. Buying of designer/trademarked merchandise that is actually an illegally copied design[33]

As we noted several times during the general discussion on retail buying, the success of retail buyers depends in large measure on the relationships they develop with key vendors. Ethical treatment of those resources is clearly one way to ensure good relationships. As noted in the *NRMA Buyer's Manual,* "Good manners and fair courteous treatment should prevail irrespective of how large the order."[34] This advice would well be heeded whichever sector the buyer is operating in.

Use of long-term contracts.   As might be expected, because of the volatile nature of fashion items, long-term contracts were not used for such items. However, the survey results did indicate that 50 percent of this sample used contracts of a year or more for the following commodities: men's ready-to-wear, major appliances, MRO items, and cosmetics. As noted earlier, there may be an increasing trend in the use of long-term contracts as retailers attempt to gain greater leverage over their vendor base and establish exclusive merchandise contracts.

MRO purchasing procedures.   The responses to the question of how MRO purchases were handled by the store indicate a general lack of awareness by merchandise buyers of such items. The reason is that in most stores these items are under the control of the store's purchasing department or maintenance department. There is a distinct dichotomy between merchandising and operations in a department store, so this lack of awareness is not surprising. Most department store purchasing departments have established blanket orders or system contracts for maintenance items and other repetitive supplies purchases. More details concerning the operation of a department store purchasing department were reported in a *NAPM Purchasing Guide.*[35]

Buyer training.   Responses to questions relating to training for both new and experienced buyers indicated that while training was considered extremely important for new buyers, there was little or no formal training for more experienced buyers. This void in training has been noted elsewhere. For instance, Forrester states that "the retail trade at large still has not recognized the vital importance of

---

[33]Ibid., pp. 130–31.

[34]Ibid., pp. 129–30.

[35]Michael G. Kolchin, "Purchasing for the Department Store," in *Guide to Purchasing* (Oradell, N. J.: National Association of Purchasing Management, 1987), Section 2.15.

training buyers to buy."[36] He further states that this is particularly true in the area of negotiation, and he points out the value of such training to the profitability of the store.[37]

Centralized buying.   Like their industrial counterparts, merchandise buyers make use of centralized buying agreements where it is beneficial to their store. In the case of a multibranch store almost all the respondents (75 percent) centralized the buying function in the downtown or headquarters store. In addition, 67 percent said they used corporate buying agreements of some form or another when these agreements offered value to the store. Many of the arrangements were in coordination with the import buying office of the parent company or buying group. This situation closely parallels the one found in many multidivision or multiplant industrial firms.

Foreign buying.   Department stores are extensively engaged in foreign buying. Seventy-nine percent of the respondents in this sample bought offshore. An examination of the factors that influenced these buyers to look overseas for merchandise, showed that they were essentially the same as for any other buyer. Respondents in this survey indicated that the most important reason for turning to offshore suppliers was quality, with fourteen of the thirty-six respondents ranking this factor as most important. It was followed by availability and price, which were ranked as most important by twelve respondents.

The results of this study are similar to those reported by Diamond and Pintel, who list the following reasons why merchandise buyers turn to offshore resources:

1. Lower costs
2. Quality
3. Greater profit opportunities
4. Prestige
5. Unavailability of merchandise domestically
6. Searching for fashion trends such as haute couture and avant garde fashions[38]

In their study of international purchasing by industrial firms Monczka and Giunipero found similar factors.[39] Both industrial and merchandise buyers turn offshore, because they can find better quality (or perhaps style in the case of merchandise buyers) at more reasonable prices, which in turn allows these buyers to be more competitive in their markets at home.

Buyers reported that their greatest problem when buying offshore was the increased lead times involved with foreign purchases. Next on the list was

[36]R. A. Forrester, "Buying for Profitability," *Retail and Distribution Management,* May–June 1987, p. 25.

[37]Ibid., p. 26.

[38]Diamond and Pintel, *Retail Buying,* pp. 200–204.

[39]Robert M. Monczka and Larry C. Giunipero, "International Purchasing: Characteristics and Implementations," *Journal of Purchasing and Materials Management,* Fall 1984, pp. 2–9.

problems with communication, followed by varying quality standards and currency fluctuations.

Diamond and Pintel cite similar problems:

1. Delivery—increased lead times and possible dock strikes
2. Quality variations
3. Reorders are hard to fill because of lead times
4. Necessity for early selection of colors—usually don't get "hot" colors in time to purchase foreign goods
5. Size discrepancies
6. Money allocation—require partial payment at time order is placed, which ties up capital
7. Time involved in foreign buying
8. Capital risks as a result of currency exchange-rate fluctuation
9. Determining the actual cost—need to determine the landed cost of foreign merchandise
10. Cost of promotion—foreign goods often unfamiliar to customers and foreign suppliers rarely give promotional allowances[40]

Again, these problems are like the ones encountered by the participants in the Monczka and Giunipero study. The results once again point to the similarities in the two buying processes.

Other materials functions.   Earlier we pointed out that retailing texts generally note that many materials activities are separate from the buying process itself.[41] It appears that this sample of merchandise buyers would agree with this approach. The survey showed that others in the store were responsible for such activities as transportation, expediting, and receiving. In particular, the traffic department was responsible for these activities in most of the stores represented in this sample. Additionally, in most department stores the traffic manager reports to the vice-president of operations, a nonmerchandising function.

Use of the computer.   The computer is used extensively in the retailing business. In the merchandise buying function it is used for inventory control, maintaining vendor lists, vendor evaluations, and purchase-order status. The most heavily used function for the computer is in the area of inventory control. Thirty-four of the thirty-six respondents in this sample indicated that their store used computers for this function. Knowing what is in stock is critical for a merchandise buyer, as it is necessary to ensure availability of merchandise in order to make sales. Nothing turns customers away from a store more than not being able to find the merchandise they seek. The inventory-control systems in use in many department stores are highly sophisticated, and industrial buyers could probably learn a great deal from their retail counterparts in this area.

Buyer evaluation.   Performance evaluation is an important topic for merchandise buyers as well as industrial buyers. In the past merchandise buyers have been

[40]Diamond and Pintel, *Retail Buying*, pp. 204–8.
[41]Lewison and DeLozier, *Retailing*, pp. 474–525.

evaluated on the basis of their gross margin. While all thirty-six respondents in this study indicated that their stores used gross margin in evaluating buyer performance, other measures are now becoming as important. The survey showed that other activities that affect total store performance are also being taken into account, including such measures as inventory turnover, cost-versus-sales ratios, and operating costs. These measures are analogous to effectiveness measures now being used to measure industrial buyer behavior. The move away from evaluating retail buyer performance solely on this basis of gross margins parallels the move away from measuring savings as the primary indicant of industrial buyer performance.

Other studies in the retailing literature have looked at what determines whether a retail buyer will be successful. One such study by Martin concluded that successful buyers were more aggressive, more self-confident, and willing to take a leadership role in merchandise trends.[42]

Diamond and Pintel identify the following traits as qualifications for successful merchandise buyers.

1. Education
2. Enthusiasm
3. Analytical excellence
4. Ability to articulate
5. Product knowledge
6. Objective reasoning
7. Dedication
8. Leadership—not only with people but in fashion
9. Appearance
10. Flexibility[43]

These traits are similar to those required by industrial purchasing professionals who take a proactive role in the procurement process in their firms.

SUMMARY

Hirschman and Mazursky suggest that the goals fundamental to the success of a retailer are customer satisfaction and profitability.[44] Clearly these requirements for success are similar for any firm whether it be in the retail or the industrial sector. Critical to the success of any retailer are the actions of its merchandise buyers, for as noted in the *NRMA Buyer's Manual*, "successful retailing depends on locating profitable sources of supply and maintaining dealings with them as long as a profit is shown."[45]

[42]Claude R. Martin, Jr., "The Contribution of the Professional Buyer to a Store's Success or Failure," *Journal of Retailing*, Summer 1973, p. 79.

[43]Diamond and Pintel, *Retail Buying*, pp. 13–16.

[44]Elizabeth C. Hirschman and David Mazursky, "A Trans-Organizational Investigation of Retail Buyers' Criteria and Information Sources," New York University Institute of Retail Management, working paper no. 82–8, Graduate School of Business Administration, 1982, p. 44.

[45]Cash, *Buyer's Manual*, p. 132.

As industrial firms continue to increase the amount of dollars expended on the purchase of goods and services—some firms are already spending 65 percent of their total sales on these items—the role of their suppliers in their success can only increase. This trend means that the role of the industrial buyer in a firm's success is also increasing. And as noted by Dobler, Lee, and Burt, buyer success is clearly a function of the success of the firm's suppliers.[46]

In this review of the merchandise buying process, we have seen that many of the methods used to ensure success are similar in both sectors. Diamond and Pintel point this out in their description of what it takes for a merchandise buyer to be successful. They indicate the importance of strong supplier relationships, which can be achieved by placing significant volumes with a few suppliers and by treating these suppliers, as well as all suppliers, fairly and ethically.[47] This call for fair and ethical treatment of suppliers is applicable to all buyers regardless of sector.

So while there may be some critical differences in the buying processes in these two sectors, there does appear to be a number of similarities in the two processes. The common thread that runs through the buying processes in all the sectors is that good buying is good buying regardless of sector.

POINTS FOR REVIEW

1. Tell how the merchandise and industrial buying processes are different and how they are similar
2. Determine what is most critical to the success of a merchandise buyer.
3. Tell how the success of a merchandise buyer is measured and how this differs from an industrial buyer.

[46]Donald W. Dobler, Lamar Lee, Jr., and David N. Burt, *Purchasing and Materials Management,* 4th ed. (New York: McGraw-Hill Book Co.,1984), p. 4.

[47]Diamond and Pintel, *Retail Buying,* p. 167.

25

INSTITUTIONAL PURCHASING

Since institutions are becoming a larger part of our economy, it is important to include this sector in a textbook on purchasing. What is meant by institutions? The term used here includes such organizations as hospitals, colleges and universities, banks and other financial institutions, certain portions of the food-service industry, and similar organizations. As a means of exploring buying processes and concerns in the institutional sector, three particular institutions will be examined: (1) hospitals, (2) food-service operations, and (3) educational institutions. In each case only a brief review is included, but it will be enough to give the reader a feel for the buying processes and concerns in each of these categories.

HOSPITALS

Health-care institutions are coming under great scrutiny today because of rapidly increasing costs. Since a major portion of these costs are paid by the federal and state governments, there is significant pressure on hospitals to control costs. One area that is under particularly close scrutiny is the purchase of goods and services by hospital materials managers. Next to labor costs, materials management is the next most significant cost accounting for 20 to 30 percent of most hospitals' operating budgets, according to figures provided by the American Society for Hospital Materials Management.[1] To put this into perspective, U.S. hospitals spent in excess of $8 billion in 1982.[2] More important, perhaps, is the rate at which these costs are rising. For example, in 1975 Dean Ammer, a respected expert in hospital materials management, estimated that the costs of purchased goods and services amounted to $7,000 per bed.[3] By 1983 Ammer estimated that these costs had risen to over $14,000 per bed and were increasing at double the rate of inflation.[4] However, until recently materials management was not an area that received long-term attention by hospital administrators. Evidence was the low esteem in which the materials function was held and its low position in the organizational hierarchy of most hospitals.

Prospective Payment System

But this is all changing, as the federal government is putting increasing pressure for cost containment by hospitals and other health-care providers. This pressure is coming in the form of new procedures for reimbursing health-care providers for Medicare-covered charges. In 1982 the federal government switched from a retrospective reimbursement system of payment for these charges to a prospective

[1]"Purchasing," *Hospitals,* January 20, 1987, p. 100.

[2]David S. Greisler and Sumer C. Aggarwal, "Hospital Materials Management: Potential for Improvement," *Journal of Purchasing and Materials Management,* Spring 1985, p. 18.

[3]Dean S. Ammer, *Purchasing and Materials Management for Health-Care Institutions* (Lexington, Mass.: Lexington Books, 1975), p. 2.

[4]Dean S. Ammer, *Purchasing and Materials Management for Health-Care Institutions,* 2nd ed. (Lexington, Mass.: Lexington Books, 1983).

payment system (PPS).[5] PPS places ceilings on reimbursement amounts by placing each individual case into one of 467 diagnoses. Each diagnosis has a single national rate of reimbursement. If a given hospital can provide service for less than this rate, then it is entitled to keep the difference. PPS is also being adopted by third-party providers, and this change is forcing a new philosophy on hospital administrators. They must now be concerned with cost containment as well as revenue generation.

Prudent Buying

This concern with cost containment has spilled over into the purchasing area, since it is one area where costs can be controlled through more effective procurement practices. Again, the thrust for this effort to contain costs comes from those who provide reimbursement for patient services. Third-party providers are now insisting that hospitals follow prudent buying principles in the acquisition of goods and services. Where prudent buying practices are not followed, third-party providers may refuse payment in excess of the lowest-priced supplier unless the institution is able to justify higher costs.[6] The burden of proof lies with the hospital in demonstrating that it is in fact, a prudent buyer.[7]

Prudent buying has been described by Henning as follows:

> Prudent buying is the organization and administration of all forms of purchasing in the hospital applying uniform policies and procedures designed to assure cost-conscious purchasing practices within the meaning of sections 2102 and 2103 of the *Provider Reimbursement Manual*. Purchasing is prudent when product costs as shown on invoices and hospital costs directly related to the acquisition and use of these products—storage, distribution, processing, and disposal—are the lowest that the support of quality patient care permits.[8]

Prudent buying seems to be no different from good procurement practices. Just as industrial organizations have recognized the importance of good purchasing, so now do nonprofit institutions, such as hospitals. And hospitals, like their industrial counterparts, attempt to improve their purchasing function by turning their attention to the principles of good procurement practice. For example, Greisler and Aggarwal, in their study of hospital materials management, identified the following opportunities for savings:

1. More sophisticated price negotiations
2. Effective use of economically sized reorders

[5]Greisler and Aggarwal, "Hospital Materials Management," p. 17.

[6]J. P. Widman, "Development of a Prudent Purchasing Program," in Charles E. Housley, ed., *Hospital Purchasing: Focus on Effectiveness* (Rockville, Md: Aspen Publications, 1983), p. 96.

[7]M. H. Goodloe, "The Effects of the Prudent Buyer Concept on the Supplier," in Housley, *Hospital Purchasing*, p. 110.

[8]W. K. Henning, "Application of the Prudent Buyer Principle to Purchasing Administration," in Housley, *Hospital Purchasing*, p. 100.

3. Attainment of volume-based price discounts when possible
4. Sizing inventories at optimal levels
5. Control of inventory damage, waste, and obsolescence
6. More efficient use of storage space
7. More effective utilization of Hospital Shared Services approved price lists
8. Improvement in accuracy of inventory records; error rate below 5 percent
9. Minimization of materials handling costs by conducting materials flow analyses
10. Improvement in paperwork processing and manpower utilization by utilizing methods studies and process analyses of materials management operations
11. Improved training for materials management personnel[9]

Holmgren and Wentz also identified a number of potential cost-saving opportunities for hospital materials management.

1. Value analysis
2. Make or buy analysis
3. Group purchasing
4. Reducing inventory
5. Standardization
6. Competitive bidding
7. Centralization of purchasing
8. A materials management orientation
9. Back-up stocking by vendors
10. Educating other departments on methods for reducing materials costs
11. Increasing average inventory turnover
12. Consignment arrangements
13. Issuing instruments from one central location
14. Utilizing ABC inventory systems
15. Establishing criteria other than brand name for selecting equipment
16. Negotiating agreements that will take account of fluctuating markets
17. Educating medical staff in cost containment
18. Improving maintenance agreements and maintenance of equipment to avoid rapid replacement[10]

The primary goal of hospital materials management, according to Frommelt and Schanilec, "is to support the health-care delivery system through efficient use of the hospital's limited resources. Thus materials management considers the cost of supplies, personnel, space, and time without compromising quality."[11]

Again, all of these goals seem to be standard for any buying function and do not seem to differ between the profit and nonprofit sectors of the economy. The goal in both sectors is the most effective procurement possible while maintaining quality levels desired by the clients of the organization. And as in the profit sector, improved purchasing effectiveness in the nonprofit sector can be achieved by evaluating the structure, process, and people associated with the purchasing function.

[9]Greisler and Aggarwal, "Hospital Materials Management," p. 20.

[10]J. H. Holmgren and W. J. Wentz, *Material Management and Purchasing for the Health Care Facility* (Ann Arbor, Mich.: AUPHA Press, 1982), pp. 6–7.

[11]J. J. Frommelt and J. L. Schanilec, "The Integration of Central Services into Material Management," in Holmgren and Wentz, *Material Management*, p. 167.

Centralization of the Purchasing Function

In the health-care organization there has been much discussion relative to the structure of the purchasing function. Most of this discussion has revolved around the need to centralize the purchasing function in order to better control the cost of purchased goods and services. And according to Holmgren and Wentz, more centralization is taking place in hospitals than in industry.[12] Additionally, many hospitals have long since gone to a materials management form of organization. As illustrated in a study conducted by Giunipero and Stepina, more than half of their sample held the title of materials managers and had purchasing, receiving, inventory control, distribution, materials handling, and transportation reporting to them.[13] Holmgren and Wentz suggest that materials managers of larger hospitals not only had these traditional materials functions reporting to them but had such areas as reusables and disposables, laundry, dietary, print shop, escort services, all internal and external shipping and distribution, and communications reporting to them as well.[14]

However, just as there has been resistance to the move toward greater centralization of the purchasing function and materials management in the industrial sector, there is a resistance to such movement in the hospital sector. This resistance comes as a result of questioning purchasing's technical competence in the procurement of specialized supplies and equipment, especially in areas such as pharmaceuticals, food service, maintenance, radiology, and other laboratory supplies and equipment. This resistance can be overcome by following the advice given by Hayas on how to establish centralized purchasing in hospitals. He suggests the following:

1. Obtain full hospital administrative support
2. Sell the benefits of centralization in order to receive their cooperation
3. Establish purchasing department's credibility through a slow, yet steady, implementation process[15]

The benefits of a centralized purchasing function must be sold to the customers of purchasing if such an organization is to be established. That is true for all sectors, institutional or otherwise.

Group Purchasing

Hospitals have also sought to become more effective purchasers by evaluating the buying process itself. One of the ways to reduce the cost of purchased goods and services is to buy in larger lots. However, a major difference between the institu-

[12]Holmgren and Wentz, *Material Management*, p. 4.

[13]Larry C. Giunipero and Lee Stepina, "Executive Summary: Hospitals Materials Management Survey" (manuscript, Florida State University, September 1985), p. 12.

[14]Holmgren and Wentz, *Material Management*, p. 5.

[15]S. Randolph Hayas, "Total Centralized Purchasing: Can It Ever Be Achieved?" in Housley, *Hospital Purchasing*, p. 31.

tional and industrial sectors is that institutions can group together and enter into group purchasing agreements and, according to Holmgren and Wentz, some 50 to 70 percent of the voluntary hospitals in the United States have turned to group purchasing as a means of reducing prices for purchased goods and services.[16] These group purchasing agreements have the potential for lower prices because of the increased buying power offered by the groups. This potential has not been reached, however, as only about 10 percent of the average hospital's purchases are made through group purchasing programs. Housley identifies the following barriers to group purchasing:

1. Lack of commitment on the part of both purchasing and vendors
2. Lack of credibility of the value of group purchasing
3. Group purchasing is seen as a threat to the hospital purchasing agent
4. Lack of effectiveness on the part of the directors of the group
5. Vendors fear loss of profits
6. Failure to share pricing information with the group
7. Lack of leadership on the part of the group
8. Conflicts that arise between hospitals and vendors[17]

Another problem that renders the groups less successful than they might otherwise be is the phenomenon of dual group memberships. As noted by Moore, dual members "shop around" between the two groups, and that ends up diminishing the buying leverage of both groups.[18] A last problem that makes group purchasing less than effective is lack of product standardization. In order for a group purchasing organization to be truly effective, it must be able to group together a large number of standard products. Unfortunately, there may be resistance on the part of group members because of a preference for certain brands.

Despite these problems, it appears that group purchasing organizations, are here to stay. That is true if for no other reason than the pressure put on hospitals to justify their costs of materials by government agencies. It is clear, however, that there is likely to be a shakeout among these group purchasing organizations, with the larger ones the survivors.

Hospitals are also beginning to use the computer more in managing their materials functions. In addition, hospitals, like their industrial counterparts, are becoming more involved with electronic data interchange. Hospitals are also following the lead of their industrial counterparts in looking at the value of single sourcing as a means of reducing their materials costs. This latter point is evidenced by the development of the prime supplier contract, which is being evaluated by a number of hospitals. A prime supply contract places orders for all supply categories with one vendor.[19]

[16]Holmgren and Wentz, *Material Management,* p. 276.

[17]Charles E. Housley, "Overcoming Barriers to Group Purchasing," in Housley, *Hospital Purchasing,* p. 227.

[18]C. W. Moore, "Group Purchasing: Past, Present and Future," in Housley, *Hospital Purchasing,* p. 243.

[19]Charles E. Housley, "The Prime Supplier Contract: Getting the Most For the Hospital's Supply Dollar," in Housley, *Hospital Purchasing,* p. 125.

As can be seen by this brief review of the buying process in hospitals, there are a number of similarities with the industrial sector. There are, obviously, some differences. For instance, the hospital materials manager does get involved in some unique purchases, such as monitors, linens, disposables and reusables, and stretchers.[20] But, even in these purchases, there are many similarities in the process. For example, in evaluating linens, there is a classic make-or-buy decision to be made. Should the hospital own and launder its own linens or should it use a linen-rental service? In regard to disposables and reusables, hospitals probably have significantly greater experience than their industrial counterparts. That is particularly true in the area of disposal of hazardous waste materials. It may well be that hospital materials managers could teach their industrial counterparts a good deal in this most critical area.

While there are a number of differences between these two sectors, there is at least one common thread to purchasing effectiveness in both sectors. That is the need for reliable suppliers. Holmgren and Wentz put this need very clearly:

> Responsible suppliers are an essential link in providing high quality medical care. In addition to delivering needed supplies and equipment, suppliers research products before marketing them; explain new technology; promote, distribute, and, in some cases, represent an assortment of products; transport products; visit potential customers; negotiate; hold inventory (thus partially financing the eventual sale); train personnel in product use; and provide repair and follow-up services.[21]

Hospital materials managers are recognizing the importance of a good vendor base and have established fairly well-developed vendor-evaluation systems, allowing them to reward good vendor performance and eliminate poor vendors.[22] This also is an indication of the similarity between the institutional and industrial buying processes.

FOOD SERVICE

While it is not clear that food-service organizations can be described as institutions, it is clear that this segment of purchases represents a significant portion of the total goods and services purchased in our economy.

Similarities to Industrial Buying

Recognition of the importance of food-service purchasing led to the commissioning of a study by the Center for Advanced Purchasing Studies (CAPS) on the purchasing practices of large food-service firms.[23] This study, published in the spring

[20]Holmgren and Wentz, *Material Management,* p. 73.

[21]Ibid., p. 25.

[22]Goodloe, "Prudent Buyer Concept," p. 114.

[23]R. Dan Reid and Carl D. Riegel, *Purchasing Practices of Large Food Service Firms* (Tempe, Ariz.: Center for Advanced Purchasing Studies/National Association of Purchasing Management, 1989), p. 76.

of 1989, collected data from sixty-one multi-unit food-service firms from across the United States. The findings of this study identified a great many similarities between industrial purchasing and purchasing for the food-service organization.

For instance, like their industrial counterparts, food-service organizations have purchasing organizations that are a combination of centralization and decentralization. Products like meats, poultry, and major capital equipment are bought under a national account agreement negotiated by a corporate purchasing function, while products like dairy and produce are bought locally.

Food-service purchasers are also heavy users of written specifications, as are their industrial counterparts. In the CAPS food-service study, the authors found that 62.7 percent of their sample used formal, detailed, written specifications.[24] A survey of industrial purchasers by Dobler, Lee, and Burt showed that 82 percent of their sample used either brand names, commercial standards, or written specifications in buying products for their firms.[25] All of these are, in essence, forms of detailed specifications.

The CAPS food-service study also highlighted the fact that 85 percent of the food-service purchasing organizations that participated in the study were involved, to some degree, in the strategic-planning process in their respective organizations.[26] As indicated in an earlier CAPS study on purchasing organizational relationships, participation in corporate strategic planning was increasingly becoming an added responsibility of the corporate purchasing department.[27]

In addition, food-service operations are very involved in value analysis. The critical issue, however, in most value analysis studies of food-service operations is the question of yield. Yield can be defined as the amount of usable product generated by each pound of food purchased.[28] In addition to studies pertaining to yields of various food products, food-service operators are also concerned with issues such as functional analysis of specifications, lease-versus-buy considerations, and alternate product considerations. All of these analyses are concerned, ultimately, with the question of price versus value. In this respect, buying in the food-service sector is no different from buying in the industrial sector. The goal for both is the attainment of maximum value for each dollar expended.

This concern for value also extends into the area of vendor evaluation. As with their industrial counterparts, food-service buyers have developed criteria for supplier selection based on important characteristics of what they perceive to be "good" suppliers. In the CAPS food-service study, the characteristics that were deemed most important were accurate and on-time delivery, consistent quality with reasonable prices, and a willingness to work together.[29] Again, as in the in-

---

[24]Ibid., p. 20.

[25]Donald W. Dobler, Lamar Lee, Jr., and David N. Burt, *Purchasing and Materials Management,* 4th ed. (New York: McGraw-Hill Book Co., 1984), p. 55.

[26]Reid and Riegel, *Purchasing Practices,* p. 18.

[27]Harold E. Fearon, *Purchasing Organizational Relationships* (Tempe, Ariz.: Center for Advanced Purchasing Studies/National Association of Purchasing Management, 1988), p. 16.

[28]Hugh J. Kelly, *Food Service Purchasing: Principles and Practices* (New York: Chain Store Publishing Corp., 1976), p. 184.

[29]Reid and Riegel, *Purchasing Practices,* p. 23.

dustrial sector, the "good" supplier is one who provides a combination of price, quality, and service. These characteristics would appear to be the common thread among the buying processes in all sectors of the economy.

Another commonality between the food-service sector and the industrial sector identified by the CAPs food-service study is in the area of ethical practices. Ethics is a big issue in the economy generally and in purchasing particularly. In the CAPS food-service study, 61.7 percent of their sample had a company-issued code of ethics.[30] This compares to the 72 percent who had a written policy concerning ethical practices in an earlier study of ethical purchasing practices sponsored by CAPS in 1988.[31] As with the 1988 study, the food-service study found some disagreement on what constitutes unethical behavior by buyers. For instance, in accepting gifts it was the value of the gift rather than the act of accepting the gift that seemed to be important. In both the ethical-practices study and the food-service study, keeping gifts up to the value of twenty-five dollars was acceptable. Also, in both groups the divulging of another vendor's price was seen as clearly unethical. Both these studies suggest that ethics is a generic concern to all purchasers, regardless of the sector to which they belong.

While there are many similarities in the buying practices in the food-service and industrial sectors, there are a number of differences as well. For instance, certain characteristics of goods and services purchased take on more importance in food-service than in industry. As an example, one major issue in the purchase of most foodstuffs is that of perishability. Specifically, a critical aspect in any specification involving food is shelf life, which is, perhaps, one of the reasons that produce and dairy products are bought locally. Additionally, the handling and storing of food products come under very close scrutiny by public-health agencies.

In other purchases the level of vendor service becomes paramount. A good example is in the purchase of coffee. It is not only the coffee that is being bought but also the equipment and the service of that equipment. The situation is the same with the purchase of sanitation supplies for the kitchen. In this case the particular service that is most critical is the adjustment of chemicals and cleaning equipment to ensure proper cleanliness levels given water conditions in the local area.

Use of Master Distributors

One element in the CAPS food-service study that differed from the industrial sector was the size of the vendor base. More important, it was the trend that was different. While the industrial sector is significantly reducing the size of its vendor base, the CAPS study showed that just the opposite is occurring in the food-service sector.[32] However, the conclusions drawn by Reid and Riegel may be somewhat

[30]Ibid., p. 26.
[31]Robert L. Janson, *Purchasing Ethical Practices* (Tempe, Ariz.: Ernst and Whinney/Center for Advanced Purchasing Studies/National Association of Purchasing Management, 1988), p. 10.
[32]Reid and Riegel, *Purchasing Practices,* p. 21.

misleading, as their study neglected to discuss the role of master distributors in the food-service industry, and while food-service organizations may use a number of vendors to supply their requirements, most of what they actually receive comes from master distributors, such as Sysco, CPC Continental, Kraft, Sexton, Martin Brower, and Rycoff. These distributors provide a wide variety of grocery products and minimize the number of deliveries made to the individual operating unit. Since space, especially receiving space, is at a premium, this service is a necessity.

EDUCATIONAL INSTITUTIONS

As a final example of institutional buying, what follows is a brief review of the buying process in institutions of higher learning.

Increasing Cost Pressures

The buying process in the educational sector does not differ significantly from that in the industrial sector. One difference is the setting in which educational buyers find themselves. Their clients, the faculty, are considerably more resistant to using the purchasing department than their counterparts in industry. Many professors feel they know what they want and think that going through purchasing for their needs only slows down the process, or worse, that it results in the purchase of inferior products bought solely on a price basis. Yet there is increasing pressure for more effective purchasing in the educational sector as resources become scarcer and budgets become tighter. With spiraling tuitions, the public is clamoring for better cost control by educational institutions. One area where costs can be controlled is in the purchase of goods and services.

In an article reviewing how colleges and universities might contain costs, Bernard and Beaven identify purchasing management as an area where costs might be controlled.[33] They state that during the ten-year period 1974–84 the cost of supplies and materials purchased by universities and colleges rose by over 120 percent.[34] Attempts to control some of these costs by switching to the use of contracted services was largely unsuccessful, as the cost for these services doubled during the same period.[35] Bernard and Beaven suggest in their article that educational institutions can save 10 to 15 percent by following four basic good purchasing practices:

1. Increasing the use of competitive bidding to achieve the best prices and best vendor support
2. Coordinating closely with accounts payables to assure that payment terms for key vendors are as favorable as possible to the institution

[33]Clark L. Bernard and Douglas Beaven, "Containing the Costs of Higher Education," *Journal of Accounting*, October 1985, pp. 78–92.

[34]Ibid., p. 78.

[35]Ibid., p. 80.

3. Promoting purchasing as a service-oriented, rather than control-oriented, department to users
4. Establishing and maintaining good vendor relations so that vendors value their business with the institution and are willing to make some concessions[36]

They also cite what they call symptoms of poor purchasing management:

1. Increasing number of "emergency" orders
2. Low levels of competitive bidding
3. Vendor complaints about slow payment
4. User complaints about poor vendor support and service
5. Little standardization of commonly purchased items to facilitate competitive bidding[37]

Once again, what is being recommended is the use of effective purchasing principles, which are applicable to all types of buying. The difference in the educational sector, perhaps, is the need for purchasing to be seen as even more of a service department than its industrial counterparts.

In the case of the educational institution the prospective client of the purchasing department is a faculty member, research scientist, or university administrator. While they are experts in their chosen profession, they have little feel for the commercial aspects of purchasing. Yet this doesn't preclude them from specifying a specific brand or entering into negotiations with a particular vendor before indicating the need to the purchasing department. The net result is that the purchasing department is inhibited from performing its task of obtaining the maximum value for each dollar expended for supplies, equipment, and services for the institution.

More Effective Purchasing

As in the industrial sector, if institutional purchasing is to be effective, it must become involved in the procurement process at an earlier stage. And just as in the industrial sector, the only way that institutional purchasing will be able to accomplish this is by providing a "service" to the academic community. This service might be to make academic departments aware of new products or to show them how to stretch their shrinking budgets by more effective purchasing.

Ritterskamp, Abbott, and Ahrens pick up on the first "service," providing market and product knowledge, in their text on educational institutional purchasing:

> In educational institutions, the purchasing agent serves as the liaison between rapidly changing industry and the faculty member who may have become cloistered in the classroom, laboratory, or library.[38]

[36]Ibid., p. 84.

[37]Ibid.

[38]James J. Ritterskamp, Jr., Forret L. Abbott, and Bert C. Ahrens, *Purchasing for Educational Institutions* (New York: Bureau of Publications, Teacher's College, Columbia University, 1961), p. 39.

The second "service," stretching shrinking departmental budget dollars, might be provided by demonstrating how different departments could coordinate purchases to increase the buying leverage of the university. In one example cited by Bernard and Beaven a university saved $250,000 annually by coordinating the purchase of supplies for its five science laboratories.[39] Another way to save university dollars is through the centralization of purchases. For example, Bernard and Beaven cite the example of Columbia University, which saves $323,000 annually by centralizing maintenance of more than forty different types of university-owned equipment through one on-site service company.[40]

In any case the institutional purchasing department will become truly effective only when it is perceived as a service department and not a department that seeks to wrest control of purchases from using departments. It must be able to convince using departments that they will be better served by using central purchasing and not simply be caused to suffer additional paperwork and delays. Bernard and Beaven make this point succinctly when they conclude: "a service-oriented purchasing manager quickly realizes that the key to cost reduction in this area is to provide excellent service to the users, who will then rely on central purchasing."[41]

Ritterskamp, Abbott, and Ahrens suggest that one way of achieving this reliance on central purchasing is by involving the faculty and others in the procurement process.[42] For instance, enlisting the help of the faculty in developing specifications or in testing products might help.

Cooperative Buying

Another means available to educational institutions to increase their purchasing effectiveness, one that is not available to their industrial counterparts, is the buying cooperative or group. Use of such an organization allows the individual university or college to increase its buying power by banding together with other institutions and negotiating attractive pricing arrangements with vendors. The buying groups used by educational institutions are either the same or similar to those discussed earlier in the section on hospital buying groups. The advantages that hospitals find in these groups apply to educational buying cooperatives as well.

The largest buying cooperative used by educational institutions of higher learning is the Educational and Institutional (E&I) Cooperative Service, which was established some fifty years ago when a small group within the National Association of Educational Buyers (NAEB) banded together to purchase jointly a few commonly used products. Since that time E&I has evolved into a $100 million organization that provides its membership with access to over seventy-five negotiated furniture, supply, and service contracts. An example of such a contract is the

[39]Bernard and Beaven, "Costs of Higher Education," p. 84.
[40]Ibid., p. 90.
[41]Ibid., p. 86.
[42]Ritterskamp et al., *Purchasing for Educational Institutions,* p. 203.

one for steel office furniture and related steel products with Steelcase. Another example is the national account agreement with Hertz for discounts on car rentals. Membership in E&I is open to tax-exempt institutions of higher learning and health-care institutions. In fact, hospitals expend 25 percent of their total dollar volume through E&I contracts.

In addition to the E&I cooperative, many universities belong to other cooperatives that have been established along state jurisdictions or other common characteristics. For example, state-supported universities in Ohio have formed the Inter-University Council, and members of the Big Ten have banded together to contract for a number of products and services. In Arizona the University of Arizona, Arizona State University, and Northern Arizona University have established a cooperative and purchase such items as steel office furniture, uniforms, athletic tape, and scientific instruments as a group.

Also, state-affiliated universities may participate in state contracts. In some states, state-affiliated institutions are mandated by law to participate in such agreements. However, in most states decisions to participate are left to the individual institution.

In any case a number of cooperative arrangements are available to educational institutions that allow them to increase their individual buying power and thereby improve their purchasing effectiveness. These arrangements are available to educational institutions because of their tax-exempt status, although there have been a number of challenges to such arrangements by vendors who feel they have been excluded from a growing segment of business. Among these challenges were an unsuccessful one against the Inter-University Council in Ohio and a challenge to the contract entered into with Xerox by the universities in the Big Ten. As with the ones regarding the status of hospitals, these challenges are likely to continue in the future because of the size of this sector and its importance to the economy. In 1987 the cost of U.S. education at all levels amounted to over $282 billion.[43] In 1986 the cost of providing health care in the U.S. was over $458 billion.[44] It is estimated that the cost for purchased goods and services for these organizations ranges from 20 to 30 percent.[45] The size of this sector alone will attract greater government scrutiny as can be evidenced by the recent attention to charges of price fixing leveled at a number of prestigious universities throughout the country.

Improved Purchasing Practices

Colleges and universities have also adopted improved purchasing practices in an attempt to control their costs of supplies and services. Like their industrial counterparts, educational institutions are heavy users of systems contracts. In addition, educational institutions have turned to other purchasing-productivity-

[43]Bureau of the Census, *Statistical Abstract of the United States: 1988*, p. 119.

[44]Ibid., p. 88.

[45]Donald W. Dobler, David N. Burt, and Lamar Lee, Jr., *Purchasing and Materials Management*, 5th ed. (New York: McGraw-Hill Book Co., 1990), p. 660.

improvement processes in an effort to contain payroll costs in the purchasing department. Such processes include:

1. Check-with-order—payment is authorized and sent to the vendor with the purchase order.
2. Speed-order systems—the requisition is sent directly to data entry and the purchase order is cut and sent to the vendor.
3. Direct-order entry—the order is placed with an approved vendor by the using department.

Used properly and with the appropriate controls in place, these processes can free up a buyer from time normally dedicated to routine, repetitive purchases. As an example of how extensively these processes are used by some educational institutions, the experience of the University of Arizona might be useful. At the University of Arizona half of all requisitions go directly to data entry for processing. The upper dollar limit on such requisitions is $500. Half of all requisitions are in the check-with-order category. These orders amount to only 3.5 percent of the total dollar volume of purchases made by the University of Arizona. The benefit of such processes is apparent. They reduce the paperwork and processing involved with a large number of small-dollar-volume requisitions. Direct-order-entry programs are prevalent in the scientific-instrument industry.

Educational institutional purchasing offices, like many of their industrial counterparts, have a number of functions reporting to them. A listing of such functions might include motor pool, telephone and other communication services, mailroom, print shop, travel, bookstore, food service, and construction. These are, of course, in addition to the traditional functions of the acquisition of all goods and services and the receiving, storing, and distributing of the purchases. One major difference from their industrial counterparts is that the bookstore and certain food-service operations make purchases for resale.

Like their industrial counterparts, educational purchasing managers are concerned with a number of pressing issues. These issues pertain to the structure of the purchasing department; that is, To whom does purchasing report? and Who reports to purchasing? In too many instances purchasing in the educational sector is still a low-level function, and forward-thinking purchasing professionals are concerned with how to increase purchasing's influence as a means of helping their respective institutions control costs.

These issues also pertain to the purchasing process. Progressive institutional purchasing directors are eager to see a more proactive purchasing process at their colleges and universities. They want to play a larger role in the strategic planning process. They are interested in greater utilization of computerization in purchasing and the use of EDI where possible.

And these issues pertain to people. A recent survey conducted by the University of Arizona showed that while the work load of twenty top university purchasing departments increased significantly over the period 1979–86, the number of people assigned to these departments had not increased dramatically. Requisitions during this period increased from an average of 31,188 to 40,557, and purchase orders increased from an average of 30,399 to 38,120. At the same time the number of full-time equivalents assigned to the purchasing departments only increased from an average of 9.26 to 10.82.[46] While purchasing directors at these universities have been able to increase the productivity of their people by using many of the processes described earlier, they feel that, with more people, they could be even more effective in helping their respective universities contain costs.

Unfortunately, for many institutions the resources are not available to upgrade their purchasing departments so that they could be truly effective cost controllers. This dilemma brings into question whether the importance of this function has been recognized by many university administrators.

SUMMARY

Institutional purchasers follow practices similar to those of their counterparts in the industrial sector. As noted by Dobler, Burt, and Lee, good purchasing principles apply to all sectors: industrial, institutional, and governmental. The differences between sectors is only a matter of emphasis.[47] Perhaps the biggest difference between the industrial and the institutional sectors is the lack of a profit motive in the truly not-for-profit institutions. Ritterskamp, Abbott, and Ahrens sum up this thought:

> With no profit motive involved in educational procurement, purchasing indiscretions will not be so readily apparent, and the primary mission of buying efficiency will be judged on how far the tax dollar can be stretched or the budget amplified, as the case may be.[48]

What applies to the educational institution applies to other institutions as well. In this chapter we have demonstrated that public scrutiny can result in action in the form of legislation or outcry pushing for increased purchasing efficiency and effectiveness. This public scrutiny, which is also a hallmark of the governmental sector, is the major difference between the institutional sector and the industrial sector.

POINTS FOR REVIEW

1. Explain what replaces the profit motive in containing costs in the not-for-profit segment of our economy.
2. Explain what is unique to purchasing in the institutional sector.
3. List the factors common to good purchasing in all sectors of the economy.

[46]Unpublished survey conducted by Gerald F. Evans, director of purchasing and stores, University of Arizona, Tucson, Ariz., 1987.

[47]Dobler, Burt, and Lee, *Purchasing and Materials Management*, p. 616.

[48]Ritterskamp et al., *Purchasing for Educational Institutions*, p. 22.

26

GOVERNMENTAL PURCHASING

In this chapter we will show that the buying practices followed in the governmental sector are basically no different from those followed by industrial buyers, except in three important respects.

MAJOR DIFFERENCES

One difference is that government agencies are spending taxpayers' money, and as a result, their procurement practices are subject to close public scrutiny. In the federal sector this need for scrutiny has resulted in over four thousand pieces of legislation regulating the procurement process. This extensive regulation leads to a much more inflexible procurement process than is found in the private sector.

Another important difference is that government agencies attempt to carry out social policy through procurement. Legislation pertinent to government procurement attempts to accomplish such things as the development of domestic and local businesses through laws like the Buy American Act and local preference laws; the development of small and disadvantaged businesses through set asides for such businesses or awards to businesses in areas of labor surplus; and the development of minority- and women-owned businesses by requiring that a percentage of contracts let by the Department of Defense go to such businesses.

The other major difference between the procurement processes in the governmental and industrial sectors is that government is a sovereign power. This means, basically, that it can change the rules on how it chooses to do business with its contractors. It can do so because of its size and relative buying power. In some respects this situation sometimes prevails in the private sector as well, as when a large buyer does business with a small supplier who depends on the buyer for a livelihood. But as in the private sector, an abuse of this power can result in a diminishing of the supplier base, since more and more suppliers will choose not to do business with the government.

SIZE OF THE GOVERNMENT SECTOR

One has to be impressed with the sheer size of the volume of purchases in the governmental sector. Estimates vary, but consider some of the numbers.

In an article illustrating how big a market opportunity the government sector is, Holtz estimated the total purchases made by all levels of government, federal, state, and local, at $650 billion annually. Of this total he estimated that the federal government spent $200 billion; the rest was spent by approximately 80,000 autonomous or semiautonomous governmental units at the state and local levels. These estimates were obtained from Census Bureau figures, which identified 79,913 autonomous or semiautonomous governmental units, including 3,042 counties, 35,684 cities and towns, 15,174 local school districts, 25,962 special districts, plus the federal government and the 50 state governments.[1]

[1]Herman Holtz, "The $650 Billion Market Opportunity," *Business Marketing*, October, 1986, p. 88.

Page, in his text on public purchasing, estimated that over 20 percent of GNP was represented by the goods and services purchased by the public sector. In the 1979 fiscal year, he estimated, the total amount spent by this sector was approximately $500 billion—$200 billion at the federal level and $300 billion at the state and local levels. Page also pointed to the large numbers of people involved in the overall procurement process in the governmental sector. He estimated that 417,000 people were involved at the state and local levels and 139,000 at the federal level. These figures were based on 1979 fiscal year estimates.[2]

Not only is the sheer size of these figures impressive but the rate at which they are growing is impressive as well. For instance, the Council of State and Local Governments reported in 1975 that expenditures by state and local governments in 1963 were $25.3 billion and by the federal government, $38.9 billion. By 1973 these figures had increased to $75.7 billion at the state and local levels and $53.8 billion at the federal level.[3] By 1979 the federal government's level of expenditures had risen to $94 billion, and by 1983 this figure had risen to $168 billion. This amount represented twenty-one million contract actions by federal procurement personnel.[4] In 1987 this level had risen to over $197 billion, representing more than twenty-two million contract actions, according to data reported in Dobler, Burt, and Lee.[5]

These estimates of the size of government procurement activity attest to the importance of this sector to the health of the U.S. economy.

FEDERAL PROCUREMENT

While there are many agencies that have purchasing responsibility within the federal government, this discussion will concentrate on the practices of contracting officers in the Department of Defense (DOD). Of the approximate $200 billion spent by the federal government annually, DOD spends approximately 80 percent. The department was in the public eye in the recent past because of rumored scandals within the agency.

An example of this notoriety was the cover story of the July 4, 1988, issue of *Business Week*, "The Defense Scandal."[6] In this article accusations were thrown back and forth among federal contractors, legislators, and government personnel. *Business Week* suggested that the fallout from all this controversy over the procurement process in the federal government would be an increase in legislation, further regulating an already overregulated activity. The discussion continues. Many industry pundits are saying that more legislation is exactly what is not needed. In

---

[2]Harry Robert Page, *Public Purchasing and Materials Management* (Lexington, Mass.: Lexington Books, 1980), p. xiii.

[3]*State and Local Government Purchasing* (Lexington, Ky.: Council of State Governments, 1975), p.1.1.

[4]Stanley N. Sherman, *Government Procurement Management*, 2nd ed. (Gaithersburg, Md.: Wordcrafters Publications, 1985), p. iii.

[5]Donald W. Dobler, David N. Burt, and Lamar Lee, Jr., *Purchasing and Materials Management*, 5th ed. (New York: McGraw-Hill Book Co., 1990), pp. 678–79.

[6]"The Defense Scandal," *Business Week*, July 4, 1988, pp. 28–33.

fact, what is really required is the removal of many of the already existing regulations and a move to force DOD contracting officers to act more like their procurement counterparts in industry. There is a need, critics argue, for the Pentagon to treat contractors in a less adversarial fashion. And there is a continuing cry for greater centralization of the defense procurement process, which would eliminate some of the red tape associated with defense contracting. These issues are similar to the ones dealt with by industrial purchasers during the last several decades.

In order for the reader to obtain a better perspective of what is entailed in the defense procurement process, we will describe the process itself, its scope, and the similarities to and differences from the buying process used in the industrial sector.

The Federal Procurement Process

The federal procurement process as developed by the Office of Federal Procurement Policy (OFPP) is actually a fifteen-step process that is divided into two basic categories, preaward and postaward activities:

Preaward Activities

Step 1: Requirement determination
Step 2: Requirement specification
Step 3: Procurement requests
Step 4: Procurement planning
Step 5: Solicitation
Step 6: Evaluation
Step 7: Negotiation
Step 8: Source selection
Step 9: Award

Postaward Activities

Step 10: Assignment
Step 11: System compliance
Step 12: Performance measurement
Step 13: Contract modifications
Step 14: Payment
Step 15: Completion/closeout[7]

In addition to these fifteen steps, the OFPP has delineated 112 activities that may be required. What exists, then, is a detailed, well-defined series of activities to be carried out during the procurement process in the federal sector.

Page describes procedures in some larger federal organizations, where the responsibilities are divided among two different contracting officers.[8] The

[7]*The Federal Procurement Process* (Washington, D.C.: U.S. Office of Management and Budget, Office of Procurement Policy, Task Group Number 3, Executive Committee on Federal Procurement Reform, November 16, 1983).

[8]Page, *Public Purchasing*, p. 262.

preaward activities up to and including the award of a contract fall under the duties of a purchasing contracting officer (PCO), and the postaward activities are administered by an administrative contracting officer (ACO). In addition, Page describes a number of purchasing-related positions that are listed in the handbook *Qualification Standards for White Collar Positions under General Schedule*, published by the U.S. Office of Personnel Management:

1. Supply program management (GS 2003)
2. Inventory management (GS 2010)
3. Contract and procurement (GS 1102)
4. Purchasing (GS 1105)
5. Quality inspection (GS 1960)
6. Traffic management (GS 2130)
7. Distribution facilities and storage management (GS 2030)
8. Property disposal (GS 1104)
9. Logistics management (GS 346)[9]

As can be seen from this description of various civil service positions involved in federal procurement, many of the functions performed by the industrial sector are performed by the government sector as well.

Sherman has simplified this rather detailed process by developing a ten-step, generic procurement model:

1. Needs perception
2. Make or buy decision
3. Requirement definition
4. Resource allocation
5. Solicitation and award
6. Performance and administration
7. Completion, delivery, and acceptance
8. Payment and discharge
9. Application and utilization
10. Disposal[10]

In Sherman's model it can easily be seen that the buying process in the governmental and the industrial sectors is basically the same. But what is also evident from our brief review of the federal procurement process is that it is much more complex and detailed than the process in the industrial sector. In fact, as noted by Cook and others, the federal procurement process is too detailed and procedurally oriented. Cook suggests in his review of the process that it was these complexities that led the commission to the OFPP in 1979 to study the process.[11] The conclusions drawn by the OFPP were as follows:

> [The process is] so complex that users of products and services often do not get what they want when they need it. . . . The statutory base is outdated; regula-

[9]Ibid., p. 9.

[10]Sherman, *Government Procurement Management*, p. 222.

[11]Curtis R. Cook, "A Study of Decision-Making Processes in the Practice of Federal Contract Management" (doctoral dissertation, George Washington University, July 1987), p. 11.

tions are voluminous and complex; meaningful standards of performance are lacking; flow of authority and responsibility is not clear; and there is a lack of accountability for results. . . . the procurement process is cumbersome, costly and frustrating.[12]

As noted earlier in this discussion of the federal procurement process, this inflexibility dictated by procedural detail is one of the major differences between the federal and industrial sectors. Later in this chapter this level of bureaucracy is discussed further.

Scope of DOD Procurement

There can be no doubt of the sheer size of federal procurement, as was demonstrated by the figures cited earlier. *Time* magazine calls the acquisition process for DOD the largest business enterprise in the world, an enterprise made up of 170,000 employees who sign some 56,000 contracts daily resulting in $170 billion in expenditures for goods and services annually.[13] Sherman refers to the federal government as "the largest single buyer of commercial products or modified commercial products."[14]

Most of the actual contracting in DOD is carried out by about 22,000 civilian and 3,000 military contracting officers spread through more than 800 buying offices around the world.[15] To put this in perspective, AT&T has some 1,700 people involved in the purchasing and traffic functions, and this company is one of the larger industrial purchasing organizations.

The organization of the procurement process within DOD is a combination of centralization and decentralization. For instance, items purchased for use by all branches of the military are procured by the Defense Logistics Agency (DLA), but items that are specific to a given branch are acquired by branch commands, such as the U.S. Army Material Development and Readiness Command (DARCOM) or the Navy's Ships Parts Control Center (SPCC).

The major purchases in DOD are for the research and development and acquisition of new weapon systems. This can be seen by the fact that only 2 percent of the contracts awarded represent over 90 percent of total contract dollars awarded.[16]

An interesting side note to these facts and figures concerning the size of the federal procurement process is the predominant type of contract used by the federal government. Conventional wisdom often criticizes the federal government for its overuse of cost-plus contracts. Yet data provided by the Federal Procurement Data System Standard Report suggest a predilection toward the use of

[12]U.S. Office of Management and Budget, Office of Federal Procurement Policy, *Proposal for a Uniform Federal Procurement System* (Washington, D.C.: Government Printing Office, 1982), p. v.

[13]Bruce van Voorst, "Mission: Just About Impossible," *Time,* February 1, 1988, p. 44.

[14]Sherman, *Government Procurement Management,* p. 27.

[15]Summary of DOD Procurement Process prepared for Robert B. Costello, assistant secretary of defense for acquisitions and logistics, by the Office of the Assistant Secretary of Defense, for Acquisitions and Logistics (Policy), 1987.

[16]Sherman, *Government Procurement Management,* p. 20.

fixed-price contracts. The report for the fiscal year 1983 cited in Sherman shows that the 81.2 percent of the contracts noted in the preceding paragraph were of the fixed-price type. These contracts represented 70 percent of total dollars expended.[17] What is demonstrated by these figures is the same preference for fixed-price contracts that is found in the industrial sector.

Similarities and Differences

This description of the federal procurement process shows a major difference between federal and industrial sector purchasing—the sheer magnitude of purchases. To further emphasize this point, Schill reports that in 1980 DOD spent more than the combined net incomes of the top 130 firms in the Fortune 500.[18] But the real question is how different the processes used by buyers actually are.

The main difference cited by contractors who do business with the federal government is that the federal procurement process, by law, requires extensive use of formal advertising and competitive bidding. This law has left the impression that the federal government buys only from the lowest bidder. Yet that is not always the case, as in the many instances where the low bidder is deemed not capable of fulfilling the requirements of the bid. The notion of a "qualified" low bidder is similar in all sectors. For the government, like its industrial counterparts, is interested in obtaining reliable sources of supply and reasonable prices. So, as noted by Sheth, Williams, and Hill, a more complex answer to the question, Is government purchasing really different? may be that on a procedural level government buying may differ from industrial, but on a conceptual level they are similar.[19] In both government and industry, buyers are trying to obtain the right material, in the right amount, at the right location, at the right time, and at the right price.

The myth of sole reliance on the competitive bidding process is further shattered by Dobler, Lee, and Burt, who report that there has been greater emphasis on negotiation in government procurement and that only 12 to 16 percent of all government procurement use the formally advertised bidding process.[20] Sherman reports that 65 percent of the procurement dollars awarded in 1983 were awarded on a noncompetitive basis. In fact, under the Armed Services Procurement Act (ASPA) of 1947 seventeen exceptions were provided where the government could use methods other than formally advertised sealed bids. The Competition in Contracting Act (CICA) of 1984, while reducing the number of exceptions for noncompetitive awards, did broaden the definition of competition and abandoned the preference for formally advertised sealed bidding as the means of awarding government contracts. The tenor of this particular act sug-

[17]Ibid., p. 334.

[18]Ronald L. Schill, "Buying Practices in the U.S. Department of Defense," *Industrial Marketing Management,* October, 1980, p. 291.

[19]Jagdish N. Sheth, Robert F. Williams, and Richard M. Hill, "Government and Business Purchasing: How Similar Are They?" *Journal of Purchasing and Material Management,* Winter 1983, p. 8.

[20]Donald W. Dobler, Lamar Lee, Jr., and David N. Burt, *Purchasing and Materials Management,* 4th ed. (New York: McGraw-Hill Book Co., 1984), p. 647.

gested a balance between formal advertising and negotiation in the awarding of business to federal contractors.[21]

In this regard the federal government is attempting to achieve goals similar to those sought by any buyer. Dobler, Lee, and Burt state these similar goals as follows:

1. Support operations
2. Buy competitively and wisely
3. Keep minimum inventories
4. Develop reliable sources
5. Hire and train competent personnel[22]

But Sheth, Williams, and Hill argue that government and industrial buying are different in terms of goals as well, since the federal government is also interested in achieving political and social goals.[23] They also mention a number of other technical and procedural processes, briefly reviewed below, that differ in government and in industrial buying.[24]

1. *Size of purchase.* As we have pointed out, Sheth, Williams, and Hill note that the average purchase made by the federal government is large and usually complex. This often limits the number of potential vendors capable of fulfilling contractual requirements.
2. *Legal restrictions.* As noted earlier, the federal government is a heavy user of formally advertised, sealed bids. In addition, the federal procurement process is constrained by budgetary limitations and a strict accountability for the expenditure of funds. Also, as a result of the reliance on the formal advertising process, the government holds strictly to standardized product specifications. The best example of these standards may be the use of military specifications (Mil Specs). Most notably under the category of legal restrictions, the potential contractor of federal government business is subject to a number of statutes that dictate how business with the federal government will be conducted. Sherman has referred to these numerous pieces of legislation as "a statutory cornucopia."[25] A historical sketch of federal procurement legislation is presented in Table 26-1. This table was derived from Appendix B of the 1982 OFPP report, *Proposal for a Uniform Federal Procurement System.* An even more detailed description of the acts passed to achieve social policy through the federal procurement process is contained in Sherman's text on government procurement management.[26]

    Since 1982 a number of important pieces of legislation and executive orders have been enacted that have had significant impact on the federal procurement process, including the Competition in Contracting Act (CICA) of 1984. CICA is discussed more fully later in the chapter.

    In addition, ASPA (Armed Services Procurement Act) has been amended twice, with DAR (Defense Acquisition Regulation) and, later, FAR (Federal Acquisition Regulation). FAR also amended the Federal Property and Administrative Services Act (FPASA), which had controlled procurement for all civilian

---

[21]Sherman, *Government Procurement Management,* p. 52.

[22]Dobler, Lee, and Burt, *Purchasing and Materials Management,* p. 669.

[23]Sheth et al., "Government and Business Purchasing," p. 12.

[24]Ibid., pp. 9–12.

[25]Sherman, *Government Procurement Management,* p. 121.

[26]Ibid., pp. 367–75.

Table 26-1 Brief History of Federal Procurement and Related Legislation

1775	Second Continental Congress established a commissary general.
1792	Second Congress passed a law requiring that all purchases be made by the Treasury Department.
1861	Congress enacted a law (Civil Sundry Appropriations Act) requiring advertising for government purchases except in matters of public exigency (established formal advertising).

Section 3709 of the Revised Statutes
- Amended in *1910.*
- Applied to the military until *1948.*
- Applied to GSA until *1949.*
- Applied to other executive agencies until *1965.*
- Still applies to purchases not in the executive branch.

WWI	*War Industries Board*—relaxed or eliminated many procurement procedures (restraints returned after the war).
1926	*Air Corps Act*—allowed the government to encourage design innovation so that quality aircraft would be available for purchase (first formal recognition that sealed bids were not always appropriate).
1934	*Vinson-Trammel Act*—imposed profit limitations on contracts for aircraft and naval vessels.
1941	*Renegotiation Law*—allowed government to renegotiate certain contracts to eliminate excessive profits.
WWII	*War Production Board*—eliminated the statutory requirement for formal advertising.
1947	*Armed Services Procurement Act* (ASPA)—stated a preference for formal advertising but authorized the use of negotiation under seventeen justifiable exceptions.

- Generated *Armed Services Procurement Regulation* (ASPR) (now known as Defense Acquisition Regulation [DAR], which governs military procurement, sets limitations on the use of certain types of contracts, and underscores the importance of small-business participation in government contracting.

1949	*Federal Property and Administrative Services Act*—established a statutory basis for the procurement procedures of civilian agencies.

- Control of procurement policy conferred upon General Services Administration (GSA).

1959	*Federal Procurement Regulations*—published by GSA, which set up civilian agency procurement policies and procedures.

- Augmented by individual agency procurement regulations.

1962	*Truth in Negotiations* (P.L. 87-653)

- Amendment to ASPA.
- Strengthened safeguards and clarified procedures pertaining to negotiated procurements by defense department.
- Emphasized use of incentive-type contracts.

1970	*Cost Accounting Standards Board*—required defense contractors to account for certain costs in a consistent manner.

- Disestablished on September 30, 1980.

Socioeconomic Goals and the Procurement Process

1931	*Davis-Bacon Act*—set minimum wages on federal construction contracts.
1933	*Buy American Act*—promoted both business and labor interests by giving preference to domestic sources for federal purchases.
1934	*Copeland Act*—prevented salary kickbacks on federal construction projects.

1935   *Miller Act*—required payment bonds to protect subcontractors and material suppliers on federal construction jobs.

1936   *Walsh-Healy Act*—upgraded wages and conditions on federal supply contracts.

1938   Congress ordered federal procurement of products made by workshops for the blind.
   • Expanded in *1971* to include other handicapped persons.

1938   *FLSA*—required that federal contractors abide by minimum wage and work hours.

1955   *SBA*—provided for small-business and labor-surplus-area assistance and preference programs.

1965   *E.O. 11246*—EEO established requirements for federal contractors ($10,000+).

There are many other pieces of legislation that can affect procurement; e.g., EPA, wage and price controls, OSHA.

Reviews of Government Procurement

1894   Dockery Commission

1940s   Hoover Commissions

1969   *Commission of Government Procurement* (COGP)—charged to study the federal procurement process and to make recommendations to improve its efficiency.
   • Office of Federal Procurement Policy Act (OFPPA) *P.L. 93-400* created OFPP (OFPP).
   • OFPP charged with carrying out COGP's recommendation.
   • *P.L. 96-83*—reauthorized OFPP.
   • *P.L. 96-178*—established new system to address statutes, regulations, the procurement work force, and procurement research.

1982   *Prompt Payment Act (P.L. 97-177)*—directed that payment be made within thirty days after receipt of a proper invoice.

Source: Adapted from Appendix B, "A Brief History of Government Procurement and the Statutory Mandate for this Proposal," *Proposal for a Uniform Federal Procurement System*, OFPP, 1982.

agencies in the federal sector. According to the OFPP, FAR is meant to be, "a single, simplified, government-wide regulation."[27]

3. *Compliance reviews.* The federal government establishes tight specifications for products and uses the General Accounting Office as a watchdog to ensure that these standards are met. The GAO also ensures that all proper procedures are followed in the procurement process.

4. *Solicitation of vendors.* Sheth, Williams, and Hill point out that ASPA requires the use of formal bid advertising except where specifically otherwise noted. As we mentioned earlier, ASPA does allow for seventeen exceptions to this requirement. Under CICA, formal advertising is replaced by sealed bidding and the number of exceptions have been reduced. However, as illustrated in Sherman's discussion on this subject, sealed bidding is to be used only when the following criteria are met:

   a. When there is more than one qualified supplier willing to compete for and to perform the proposed contract
   b. When the requirement is adequately defined allowing bidders to bid on the procurement on an equal basis
   c. When sufficient time is available to allow the purchase to be accomplished through an orderly solicitation and award process
   d. When price can be used as an adequate basis for determining the source to be awarded the contract[28]

[27]*Proposal for a Uniform Federal Procurement System*, p. 13.
[28]Sherman, *Government Procurement Management*, p. 240.

Are these criteria any different from those that would be used to determine when competitive bidding would be appropriate in the industrial sector? Apparently not, as they are similar to the criteria listed in Dobler, Burt, and Lee.[29] The major difference, perhaps, between these two sectors in regard to the subject of competitive bidding is the justification process that must be used when competitive bidding is not used. Again, because of the scrutiny required in the public sector, it is substantially more difficult to justify noncompetitive actions in the federal procurement process. However, as noted earlier, it is not impossible, as over 65 percent of the awards made in 1983 were made on a noncompetitive basis.[30]

5. *Security.* Sheth, Williams, and Hill also state that all bidding or negotiation information is open to public review, except in cases where national security is involved. This particular element of the federal procurement process is particularly nagging for many potential government contractors, as they do not want information contained in their proposals to get out to their competitors. Consequently, they decline to bid on government business, leaving the government a smaller group of potentially qualified suppliers from which to draw upon.

6. *Diffusion of authority.* The federal government is a maze of agencies and departments, all of which have some buying authority. Sheth, Williams, and Hill suggest that this diffusion of buying authority often makes it difficult to determine which agency or which contracting officer has the appropriate authority to let specific contracts.

7. *Leverage.* Sheth, Williams, and Hill also point to an interesting irony in the rigidity and procedural detail found in the federal procurement process. While it would be assumed that the government was able to exercise leverage in the buying-selling relationship with its contractors, this insistence on compliance to rigid specifications prevents leverage. As long as the government contractor has followed specifications, the government procurement agency is required either to accept delivery or to provide a contract adjustment for any required change. This would be akin to the case in private industry where the buyer uses design specifications, and the supplier's only obligation is to meet what is written in the specifications. Unlike their industrial counterparts, however, government contracting officers often find themselves in a situation where there are few or no alternatives to the current supplier, and hence the supplier has a position of leverage not often found in the industrial sector.

Sherman points out another problem with rigid specifications and compliance to procedural detail. He claims that this process results in several suboptimization problems by eliminating the use of commercially available products that would better fill the procurement need at more competitive pricing.[31] This failing was recognized in the enactment of CICA, which now allows greater use of functional specifications.

8. *Procedural detail.* As we have emphasized, a major difference in doing business with the federal government is the procedural detail involved. In fact, Sheth, Williams, and Hill claim that the most frequent complaint registered by suppliers doing business with the federal government is the amount of paperwork involved. Just as irritating are the complexity of forms involved and the confusion created by this jungle of paperwork. This insistence on procedural detail results in increased costs and time for the supplier interested in doing business with the federal government and, hence, higher procurement costs.

9. *Instrument of social policy.* As discussed earlier, the federal government sees the procurement process as a means of carrying out social policy. This is clearly the

[29]Dobler, Burt, and Lee, *Purchasing and Materials Management*, pp. 204–5.
[30]Sherman, *Government Procurement Management*, p. 52.
[31]Ibid., p. 235.

case in the area of developing businesses owned by women and minorities. Recent legislation enacted by the government literally forces government contractors to seek out these firms as subcontractors in fulfilling the requirements of federal contracts. Examples of such legislation include Public Laws 95-507, enacted in 1978, and 99-661, enacted in 1986. The first provides for set asides, percentages of federal contracts that must be placed with small and disadvantaged businesses, and the latter requires that 5 percent of contracts entered into with DOD must be placed with minority business enterprises (MBE). Sherman suggests that these laws act as a restriction on a contracting officer's ability to place business in a competitive manner and in a sense conflicts with the overall objectives of the procurement process.[32] Such conflicts, however, are inevitable as the federal government attempts to balance social and economic objectives. Still unanswered is the question, At what cost will these social objectives be achieved if, in fact, they are achieved at all?

10. *Government power.* Finally, Sheth, Williams, and Hill reiterate the point made by many other authors that the federal government is a sovereign power that can dictate the terms and conditions under which it conducts business. In short, because of this power, it is very difficult to sue the government for breach of contract unless the government chooses to be sued. Additionally, for many of the items the federal government buys, it is a monopsonist operating in a technical monopoly.

Sheth, Williams, and Hill conclude that many of these differences in the government procurement process arise from basic differences in objectives and philosophy from those of the private sector. These differences include a higher degree of accountability, more stringent disclosure rules, and significantly greater procedural detail.[33] In short, the federal procurement process is very large, very bureaucratic, and very diffused. However, Sheth, Williams, and Hill also conclude:

> While there are indeed significant differences in the public and private sectors, there are also striking similarities between the two sectors, both in the purchasing decision process itself and in the types of purchasing decisions made.[34]

Schill also notes these similarities when he suggests in his discussion of DOD procurement that government buying is merely a subset of industrial buying.[35] And, as noted earlier in this discussion, the prime similarities are in the basic objectives of both processes. In essence, both governmental and industrial buyers are looking for suppliers who will provide them with quality products, good service, and reasonable prices. Such suppliers are referred to in CICA as "responsible sources," which the act describes in the following manner:

A responsible source:

1. Has adequate financial resources to perform the contract or the ability to obtain such resources;

[32]Ibid., p. 376.
[33]Sheth et al., "Government and Business Purchasing," pp. 12–13.
[34]Ibid., p. 7.
[35]Schill, "Buying Practices," p. 294.

2. Is able to comply with the required or proposed delivery or performance schedule taking into consideration all existing commercial and government business commitments;
3. Has a satisfactory performance record;
4. Has a satisfactory record of integrity and business ethics;
5. Has the necessary organization, experience, accounting and operational controls and technical skills or the ability to obtain such organization, experience, controls, and skills;
6. Has the necessary production, construction, and technical equipment and facilities or the ability to obtain such equipment and facilities; and
7. Is otherwise qualified and eligible to receive an award under applicable laws and regulations.[36]

Except for the legal disclaimer at the end, these criteria seem identical to those that might be used by an industrial buyer in evaluating a potential supplier before awarding business to that supplier. Procurement success in the federal sector is a matter of effective contracting, just as in the industrial sector where buyer success is dependent on supplier success.

In addition to the need for a reliable resource base, there are a number of other similarities between governmental and industrial buying. For instance, both engage in make-or-buy analyses, and in both cases the trend in these decisions is toward buying. And, as in the industrial sector, there are constraints as to the amount of outsourcing that is possible. The typical make-versus-buy decision in the governmental sector revolves around the issue of services. The major constraint on these decisions is the restrictions placed on them by civil service regulations. These restrictions are similar to those placed on industrial firms by union contracts. As in industry, the key to such decisions is to make the most economical use of resources. Consider, for instance, the general guiding principle published by the Office of Management and Budget (OMB) in its Circular A-76 of 1967:

> It is the general policy of the administration that the federal government will not start or carry on any commercial activity to provide a service or product for its own use, if such product or service can be procured from private enterprise through ordinary channels.[37]

Sherman sees the issuance of this directive, as well as the ensuing legal battles over its intent, as affirmation of the principle of the least costly method of performance.[38] Again, as in the industrial sector the make-versus-buy decision is basically an economic one but one that is often constrained by political issues.

The government procurement sector is also greatly concerned with other basic procurement techniques, such as value analysis and cost analysis. In fact, government buyers are even more forceful in these areas than their industrial counterparts through their insistence on accompanying documentation demonstrating that these activities have taken place.

[36]Sherman, *Government Procurement Management,* pp. 139–40.
[37]Ibid., p. 154.
[38]Ibid., p. 159.

The government, although greatly constrained, also engages in international sourcing. The main constraint in this area of procurement is the protection of domestic industry and can be seen in such legislation as the Buy American Act of 1933. More recently, however, the government has enacted legislation that has made it possible for government contracting officers to look overseas for their needs under certain conditions. Executive Order 12260 issued in 1980 and the Trade Agreement Act of 1979 both attempted to address this issue by setting the following as their objective:

> To achieve equal treatment of foreign and domestic suppliers of designated nations, and to provide them equal opportunities (on a reciprocal basis in both magnitude and quality) to compete for contracts awarded by specified government entities.[39]

While there are many exceptions noted in these pieces of legislation, their very enactment suggests an effort on the part of the federal government to allow more economical procurement.

What can be seen from this brief identification of a number of similarities is that the federal government procurement process is, in fact, very much like its industrial counterpart except for a few significant exceptions. One of these exceptions has to do with the source and timing of funding for government contracts. In many instances projects are not fully funded when they are awarded. This requires great diligence on the part of the contracting officer, who must keep on top of the funding process for ongoing projects. In the next section we discuss this issue and other areas of needed reform.

FEDERAL PROCUREMENT REFORM

Ever since there has been a federal procurement system, there have been calls for its reform, starting with the Second Continental Congress and its establishment of a commissary general in 1775 to the reforms that abound today. The goals of the system in 1775 are really no different from those of today's federal procurement process: "To maximize competition, obtain fair prices and assure accountability of public officials for public transactions."[40] A review of these reform activities are included in Table 26-1, (458).

Unfortunately, many of the attempts at reforming the system have had just the opposite effect. Legislation pertaining to the federal procurement system has evolved in a piecemeal fashion, responding to specific issues of a particular time and resulting in a bureaucratic maze that inhibits effective procurement. Congress's reaction to most problems in federal procurement is to pass yet another law that further inhibits government contracting officers from fulfilling their mission of obtaining maximum value from taxpayer dollars expended. As a

[39]Ibid., p. 357.
[40]*Proposal for a Uniform Federal Procurement System*, p. 133.

result, there are now in excess of four thousand pieces of legislation pertaining to federal procurement.

More recent calls for reform have attacked this legislative morass as unnecessary and argue for a procurement system that is more flexible, looks upon its suppliers as partners rather than adversaries, and is run by a cadre of procurement specialists who possess the ability to effectively carry out the goals of purchasing. In short, these critics argue for a system that is more competitive than the current one. A good summary of this argument was given by the then secretary of defense, Caspar Weinberger in his annual report to the Congress for the fiscal year 1988:

> A myriad of laws and regulations prevent buying in the same manner as the private sector, but we are reviewing our policies where possible to encourage more stable long-term contractual relationships with responsible sources. This in no way compromises our attempts to generate more competition and eliminate noncompetitive contracts wherever possible. Rather, it will complement our efforts to acquire more commercial and nondevelopmental products.[41]

This theme of competition is one that has been carried out through the reforms instituted since the end of World War II. These reforms have addressed the process itself, that is, making it more like the industrial sector; the structure of the federal procurement process, making it more centralized; and the procurement work force, making it more professional. These areas are briefly reviewed below.

Process

Starting with the recommendations of the Commission on Government Procurement in 1972, the thrust of more recent reform legislation has been toward simplifying and unifying the process while ensuring that the essence of the process was based on competition. The Commission on Government Procurement specifically proposed "the creation of an integrated system for the effective management, control, and operation of the federal procurement process."[42] This recommendation laid the groundwork for the establishment of the Office of Federal Procurement Policy (OFPP) and the Federal Acquisition Regulation (FAR), which covers both military and civilian procurement.

Ten years later, in 1982, the OFPP published its *Proposal for a Uniform Federal Procurement System* (UFPS), which proposed a greatly simplified procurement system that would be more responsive to the needs of the country.[43] One of the major recommendations of this proposal was that a single, simplified government regulation be issued with a goal of making it easier to do business with the government. In tracing the history of legislation pertaining to government pro-

---

[41]Report of the Secretary of Defense Caspar W. Weinberger to the Congress on the FY 1988/FY 1989 budget and FY 1988–92 defense programs, January 12, 1987, p. 103.

[42]Sherman, *Government Procurement Management,* p. 100.

[43]*Proposal for a Uniform Federal Procurement System,* p. v.

curement, the OFPP found that the existing patchwork of laws created a procurement system that could be described as follows:

> The current federal procurement "system" is not an integrated system but, rather, a collection of statutes, policies, organizations and operations that are sometimes inconsistent, ineffective and uneconomical in satisfying agency mission needs in a timely manner.[44]

One specific example of the inconsistencies that were apparent in federal procurement legislation were the sixteen inconsistencies found between the Armed Services Procurement Act (ASPA) and the Federal Property and Administrative Services Act (FPASA), the two main regulations governing federal procurement in the military and civilian sectors.[45] These inconsistencies resulted in a call for a uniform regulation pertaining to all government procurement.

This proposal led to the issuance of Executive Order 12352, which sought ways of implementing the recommendations proposed by the OFPP. One such action was the enactment of the Federal Acquisition Regulation (FAR). Page cites the goals of this regulation in his text on public purchasing:

> It is the policy of the United States that the acquisition of property and services by the federal government shall be performed so as to meet the public needs at the lowest total cost, maintain the independent character of private enterprise by substituting for regulatory controls the incentives and constraints of effective competition, and encourage innovation and the application of new technology by stating public needs so that suppliers will have the maximum latitude to exercise independent business and technical judgments in offering a wide range of competing alternatives.[46]

Again, the stated goal of government procurement, the acquisition of goods and services at the lowest total cost obtained through the workings of the market system, is identical to the stated goal of industrial purchasing departments. However, FAR really puts the burden on sellers to create this environment of competitiveness by controlling their actions. The Competition in Contracting Act (CICA) of 1984, on the other hand, placed more emphasis on government actions that would ensure a greater degree of competition in the federal procurement process. While more broadly defining competition and moving away from an insistence on sealed bidding and formal advertising, CICA narrowly defined instances where noncompetitive awards could be made. This act was a response to critics in Congress and elsewhere in and out of government who were demanding greater use of competition in government contracting.

Unfortunately, like many of the other congressional attempts to legislate a more competitive federal procurement process, CICA also constrains contracting officers from acting like their industry counterparts. As noted by Sherman, CICA has increased the level of time and effort required to issue a government

[44]Ibid., p. 6.
[45]Ibid., p. 110.
[46]Page, *Public Purchasing,* p. 35.

contract, with an even greater insistence on procedural detail.[47] Preston states this problem even more emphatically in the conclusion to her 1986 review of the federal procurement process:

> In the last three years Congress has reacted to specific problems with very detailed legislative proscriptions about how DOD manages the contracting process. Although legislation itself is not to blame for the problems that beset defense contracting today, congressional activities over the last few years have not fostered an environment that promotes accountability and a willingness to make judgmental decisions. Changes made by the Competition in Contracting Act and other provisions of law perpetuate the penchant for establishing a paper or bureaucratic trail of reviews to ensure that decisions are made "objectively." While ensuring that anyone who wants to sell to the government has a fair chance to do so, such legislative proscriptions promote an organization that is oriented towards ensuring that the process of objectively choosing a contractor is followed correctly, not one whose goal is to buy the best product at the best price.[48]

This problem described by Preston is also addressed by Sherman when he suggests that CICA has "a concern of creating competition strictly for the sake of competition regardless of other effects."[49] This insistence on competition in government contracting has stirred great debate among both advocates of CICA and its detractors.

For instance, in a recent article in the *Journal of Purchasing and Materials Management,* Williams and Bakhshi conclude: "If Congress originally intended DOD to compete as the private sector does, it should know that CICA is not leading to this result."[50] These authors further suggest that the federal sector procurement process is already as "competitive" as it may get and, in fact, is more competitive than its industrial counterpart. They cite figures that show that DOD competed 82 percent of its contracts for 57 percent of its dollars, while industry competed only 56 percent of its contracts for 58 percent of its dollars.[51] Williams and Bakhshi suggest that maybe it's time to slow down the increase of competitive restrictions being placed on this process and time to measure the actual benefit of CICA-type prescriptive legislation.[52]

The other predominant argument against further legislation requiring more competition in DOD contracting is that insisting on competition in a noncompetitive market simply won't work. Colvard and Beck, as well as many others, suggest that the government is a monopsonist buying in a technical monopoly.[53]

---

[47]Sherman, *Government Procurement Management,* p. 121.

[48]Colleen A. Preston, "Congress and the Acquisition Process: Some Recommendations for Improvement," *NCMA Journal,* Summer 1986, p. 24.

[49]Sherman, *Government Procurement Management,* p. 134.

[50]Robert F. Williams and V. Sagar Bakhshi, "Competitive Bidding: Department of Defense and Private Sector Practices," *Journal of Purchasing and Materials Management,* Fall 1988, p. 34.

[51]Ibid., p. 33.

[52]Ibid., p. 34.

[53]James E. Colvard and Alan W. Beck, "Cost of Object or Object of Cost?" *The Bureaucrat,* Winter 1985–86, p. 19.

In such a constrained market, they argue, the forces of competition are unable to work, and it would be better to learn how to manage this market more effectively rather than arguing that more competition is needed.[54]

Beltramo argues that the enforced competition in DOD contracting has never been demonstrated to have the desired effect of reducing costs of acquisition.[55] He also argues that the government is a technical monopsonist and that there are really very few contractors who choose to do business with DOD because of all the restrictions, which lead to greater risks and lower profits. Beltramo sees much of the legislation in the area of DOD procurement as "competition for competition's sake" without any measurable benefit to national security. In fact, he cites the fact that the air force has over one thousand individuals assigned to competitive advocacy roles and that if the government were to reduce this force substantially, greater cost reductions than could ever be achieved by legislative restrictions would be forthcoming.[56]

In the same article DeLuca, who at the time of publication was the air force's competition advocate general, responds to Beltramo's criticism by citing several examples where dual sourcing has resulted in significant cost savings to the air force in the procurement of major weapon systems.[57] While agreeing that there are significant problems associated with DOD contracting, DeLuca suggests that DOD contractors need to be more selective in their dealings with DOD and, rather than fighting competition, they should let competition enhance their role in this process.[58]

Platt, who was DeLuca's counterpart in the Navy, picks up on this argument concerning the contractor's role in improving DOD contracting by suggesting that what is really needed is for military contractors to become better salespeople.[59] They will need to do this, argues Platt, to deal with the aggressive customer DOD is becoming—a customer that is forcing its supplier to become more efficient and effective and, hence, more competitive.

And the argument rages on! What is clear from this review of the reform of the federal, and especially the DOD, procurement process is that the government, like its industrial counterparts, is interested in obtaining the best products at the lowest cost. It is in how it attempts to achieve this goal that it differs from industry. What is not clear, however, is whether legislation alone is an effective way to achieve more proficient procurement. Changes must also be made in the structure of the procurement process and the people who perform the procurement tasks if the process is to be truly improved.

[54]Ibid., p. 22.

[55]Michael N. Beltramo and Anthony J. Deluca, "Is Competition Hurting Technology?" *Military Logistics Forum*, pp. 42–49.

[56]Ibid., p. 48.

[57]Ibid., p. 44.

[58]Ibid., p. 49.

[59]"Rear Admiral Stuart F. Platt, the Navy's Costbuster," *S&MM*, March 10, 1986, pp. 45–47.

Structure

One reform that is consistently heard concerning federal procurement is the need to centralize the process. These calls for centralization culminated in the establishment of a "procurement czar."[60] Such a position, it was felt, would centralize all procurement authority for DOD under one individual, the undersecretary of defense for acquisitions. The first appointee to this position was Richard Godwin. Upon assuming this position, Godwin found an organization, the Pentagon, that was highly decentralized and filled with rivalries between the armed services. More critically, all parties were happy with the way things were and were not anxious to give up their individual procurement authority. And, more important, Godwin was not given authority to override the service chiefs without first obtaining their agreement. What Godwin found was that without the support of the secretary of defense, reforms of the nature recommended by the Packard Commission were not likely to occur. Godwin did not enjoy such support from Caspar Weinberger.[61]

What all of this demonstrates is the difficulty of reforming a process that is highly politicized. While the changes Godwin was trying to accomplish were those recommended by a presidential commission, they were changes that did not appeal to those in whom purchasing authority currently resided. As reported in *Electronic Buyers' News,* Godwin's proposed changes were seen as "an assault on their turf."[62] This article quotes one of the members of the House Committee on Armed Services, John Kasich (R-Ohio), as saying, "What we had here was open warfare between those who wanted to protect their turf and the new kid on the block."[63] In the final analysis, Godwin was not able to achieve what he had been charged to do and resigned. His successor as "procurement czar" was Robert Costello.

One advantage Costello enjoyed over his predecessor was the support of his boss, Frank Carlucci, secretary of defense. Costello seemed to have greater success in this role not only because of this support but also because of his more consensus-oriented management style and his greater emphasis on improving the productive and technical capabilities of the defense industry.

These most recent struggles in reforming the Pentagon procurement process come as a result of recommendations made by the Presidential Blue Ribbon Commission on Defense Management (also known as the Packard Commission) and as part of Executive Order 12352, which called for the designation of a procurement executive with agencywide procurement responsibility for each agency of the federal government.[64]

---

[60]Van Voorst, *Mission,* p. 44.

[61]"Defense Procurement: Killed in Action," *The Economist,* October 17, 1987, p. 33.

[62]Diane Norman, "Godwin Says He Lacked Clear Mandate for Reform," *Electronic Buyers' News,* September 29, 1987, p. 1.

[63]Ibid.

[64]The President's Blue Ribbon Commission on Defense Management, *A Formula for Action: A Report to the President on Defense Acquisition* (Washington, D.C.: Government Printing Office, 1986 and Executive Order 12352 of March 17, 1982), p. 137.

The presidential commission in its report, *A Formula for Action: A Report to the President on Defense Acquisition,* recommended reorganization of defense procurement along the lines of what typically is found in industry, which is highlighted by the following characteristics:

1. Clear command channels
2. Stability
3. Limited reporting requirements
4. Small, high-quality staffs
5. Communication with users
6. Prototyping and testing[65]

To this end the commission made recommendations as to how such a reorganization might be accomplished. These recommendations were spelled out under the following seven categories:[66]

A. *Streamline Acquisition Organization and Procedures.* It was under this section of the commission's recommendation that the position of undersecretary of defense for acquisitions was created. The commission called for the establishment of service acquisition executives for each branch and also reiterated the need for a single, greatly simplified statute, revamping procedures to go along with the proposed new organization.
B. *Use Technology to Reduce Cost.* This section of the commission's recommendations called for the greater use of prototype systems before engaging in the full-scale development of new systems.
C. *Balance Cost and Performance.* This section calls for greater coordination between the undersecretary of defense for acquisitions and the joint chiefs of staff in looking at joint programs and attempting to identify tradeoffs between cost and performance in defining new weapon systems.
D. *Stabilize Programs.* This section called for the institutionalization of baselining for major weapon systems and the expansion of multiyear procurement for high-priority systems.
E. *Expand Use of Commercial Products.* This section suggested greater use of commercially available products and the design and development of new products only when commercially available ones were clearly inadequate to fill the needs of the military.
F. *Increase the Use of Competition.* Called for greater use of commercial-style competition that emphasized quality and performance as well as price.
G. *Enhance the Quality of Acquisition Personnel.* Called for the development of a defense acquisition corps similar to the foreign service.

While these more recent reforms have emphasized centralization of the federal procurement process, they are just the most recent in a series of battles between the proponents of centralization and those of decentralization. And while it may appear that the forces for centralization have been successful, it may well be that although there is now greater centralization of authority in DOD, accountability has been greatly diluted. And as aptly demonstrated by Godwin's quick exit

[65]Ibid., pp. 12–13.
[66]Ibid., pp. 15–16.

from the position of undersecretary of defense for acquisitions, authority on paper is effective only as long as those reporting to you accept that authority. It may also be that attempting to force industry norms on procurement management methods in a bureaucracy like DOD is a futile exercise unless there is a commitment from above to ensure compliance. This commitment is unlikely because of the political instability of these elected positions. As concluded by Page some years ago, the old conflict between efficiency and political expediency once again rears its head.[67]

People

All the reforms cited above have indicated a need for the upgrading of the federal procurement work force. The general thesis behind the call for an upgraded work force is that with more competent procurement personnel, there would be less need for the plethora of legislation pertaining to federal procurement. Sherman captures this notion well when he concludes:

> Although the trend in government policy is to increase regulatory requirements and investigation personnel in an attempt to cause improvements in procurement practice, an alternative that could potentially gain more for the overall benefit of the public is enhancement of personnel capabilities.[68]

Colvard and Beck draw similar conclusions when they state that what is needed is more technically competent procurement personnel, not more legislation.[69] And, as noted earlier, both E.O. 12352 and the President's Commission on Defense Management call for the enhancement of federal procurement work force and provide steps for improvement.

Attempts have been made to address the need to improve the capability of the federal procurement work force. For example, the National Contract Management Association (NCMA) developed a training program that contains sixty-eight modules pertaining to a common body of knowledge in government contracting.[70]

In 1986 *The Acquisition Enhancement (ACE) Program Report II* recommended the establishment of a Defense University of Acquisition Management (DUAM) as the means to achieve such improvement.[71] This was followed by the development of a training curriculum and associated training blueprints by the Federal Acquisition Institute (FAI).[72] More recently legislation has been proposed

[67]Page, *Public Purchasing*, p. 7.

[68]Sherman, *Government Procurement Management*, p. 383.

[69]Colvard and Beck, "Cost of Object?" p. 22.

[70]National Contract Management Association (NCMA), *Education and Training Program Structure*, January 1985.

[71]Department of Defense, Acquisition Enhancement (ACEII) Study Group, *The Acquisition Enhancement (ACE) Program Report II*, vol. 1, December 1986.

[72]Federal Acquisition Institute, Office of Acquisition Policy, General Services Administration, *Government Wide Study of Procurement Training*, September 1987.

that would create a defense acquisition agency (S. 1202) and defense acquisition university (H.R. 2897). These bills are aimed at "creating an elite corps of procurement specialists within DOD to conduct all contracting to ensure a stronger and more capable procurement staff."[73]

In addition to these actions to improve government contracting, periodic seminars are held by both the NCMA and the FAI at which current improvements in defense contracting process are discussed.

There can be no doubt that there is an active movement afoot to improve the capabilities of the federal procurement work force; however, it is not enough simply to improve the training and educational requirements of federal contracting officers. Salaries for these positions must also be upgraded if there is any hope of attracting truly qualified purchasing professionals to procurement positions in the federal sector. While there has been some improvement in this area, it is clear that federal compensation is significantly lagging behind compensation offered in the industrial sector. For example, a GAO report showed that in 1985 federal procurement salaries were as much as 37 percent behind the averages found in industry for similar positions.[74] Current salaries for entry-level positions in the federal sector are in the mid-seventeen-thousand-dollar range, while industry is offering up to the mid-twenties for similar positions.[75] It is clear from these figures that the federal government still has a long way to go before parity can be achieved between the federal and industrial sectors.

In summing up this section on federal procurement reform, it should be pointed out that simply improving the quality of people working in the federal sector is not enough. As stated by Cook, it is the process more than the people that is the cause of poor performance in the federal sector. He cites a statement from the chairman of Martin Marietta that the federal procurement process

> has grown to the point of being so complex, so regulated, so overseen, so detailed, and so documented that it is difficult to do it right even when one tries his very best.[76]

Cook concludes that these regulations "shackle" government contracting officers and prevent them from employing the appropriate decision-making processes to achieve effective procurement. Therefore, Cook states, it is not enough to get better people.[77] What this suggests is the need to deal with all three parts of the system, the process, the structure, and the people, if any reform of the system is to be successful.

[73]"Civilian Procurement Corps Proposal Boosts Job Chances," *Impact*, September 1989, p. 1.

[74]United States General Accounting Office, Report to congressional requesters, *Procurement Personnel: Information on the Procurement Workforce*, November 1987, p. 19.

[75]"C.P.M. Status Gives Purchasers an Edge When Seeking GS-1102 Positions," *Impact*, December 1989, p. 2.

[76]Cook, *Federal Contract Management*, p. 13.

[77]Ibid., p. 153.

ISSUES FACING FEDERAL PROCUREMENT

One thing becomes clear in describing the federal procurement process: It attempts to achieve similar goals to those espoused by its industrial counterparts, but its methods in achieving these goals are very different. In many respects, however, federal procurement faces many of the same issues facing industrial purchasing.

For instance, the federal sector is obviously concerned with ethics in purchasing and has gone to great extents to ensure compliance with both laws and practices deemed to be ethical. Because of public scrutiny of the process, ethical practices may be a more critical issue to government contracting officers than to their industrial counterparts, but nonetheless the issue of ethics cuts across all sectors of purchasing.

In addition, supplier relations is as important an agenda item in the federal sector as it is in the industrial sector. In fact, Robert Costello, the then undersecretary of defense for acquisitions, spoke of the importance of good supplier relations in federal procurement in a speech at the National East Coast Educational Conference of the National Contract Management Association in 1987:

> In addressing the third area of concern, buyer-seller relationships, I can wrap it up in a nutshell: a reliable, effective defense for our nation depends on a vigorous, productive, and growing defense industry unencumbered by a tense atmosphere and strained working relations between government.[78]

What Costello seems to be saying is that successful federal procurement depends in large measure on a healthy and technologically competitive supplier base. Costello further expanded on this notion when he was quoted in *Electronic Buyers' News* as proposing a variety of methods to the House Armed Services Committee for improving defense procurement, including the fostering of a competitive environment, sustaining U.S. technology and manufacturing leadership, improving quality, and establishing mutual trust between government buyers and suppliers.[79] These goals are similar to those expressed by any industrial purchasing department. In order to implement these goals, Costello invited a number of industrial, academic, and government procurement specialists to Washington to discuss how the U.S. could improve its industrial base and what role DOD should play in such improvement. What is clear from these initiatives is the fact that DOD, like its industrial counterparts, is turning to its suppliers to improve its competitiveness in meeting the national security needs of the nation.

The issues identified by Costello for the DOD procurement process are like those that are important to all procurement processes regardless of sector. They are as follows:

1. Simplify procurement laws and regulations
2. Improve the industrial base

[78]Speech presented by Robert B. Costello, assistant secretary of defense (production and logistics), at the National East Coast Educational Conference of the National Contract Management Association, November 6, 1987, p. 18.

[79]"Costello Hits DOD Buying," *Electronic Buyers' News,* November 23, 1987, p. 1.

3. Improve the quality of products
4. Improve the acquisition work force
5. Improve relations with industry[80]

The question remains, however, whether these goals can be accomplished. Particularly, can the process be simplified? It may be instructive in this regard to look what has been accomplished within the United States Postal Service, a quasi-public organization. When John Davin became the assistant postmaster general for procurement and supply, one of his first tasks was to greatly simplify a system that had become similarly overbureaucratized. One of his first acts was to reduce the procurement manual from over a hundred pages to forty pages. In the overview of the new manual, Davin states his intent "to emphasize significant policies and processes rather than detailed procedures."[81] Davin further states in this overview that the manual adopts commercial procedures wherever possible and provides guidelines rather than detailed procedures to aid contracting officers in obtaining quality supplies and services in a timely manner. While it may not be possible to obtain such drastic changes in DOD, these changes do show that it is possible to bring reform to the government procurement process.

STATE AND LOCAL GOVERNMENT

As noted at the beginning of this discussion of governmental purchasing, state and local governments spend some $300 billion annually for the purchases of goods and services. These expenditures are made through more than eighty thousand buying entities. More important, perhaps, is the fact that these purchases are likely to grow as the federal government continues to push responsibilities for services down to the state and local levels. In fact, a study by Chase Econometrics in 1985 predicted an annual growth rate of 9.1 percent for state and local spending.[82] In addition to spending more money than the federal sector, the state and local sector is more widely dispersed. This means that there is no one state and local sector but, rather, some eighty thousand separate buying entities, all of which have their own goals, rules, and procedures governing the procurement function. This makes a review of this segment of purchasing extremely difficult, but an attempt will be made to highlight some of the commonalities in the buying processes used by these jurisdictions.

State and local purchasing is in many respects similar to federal procurement. And, as indicated above, public purchasing does differ in many respects from private-sector purchasing. Page summarizes these differences in his text on public purchasing as follows:

[80]Office of the Assistant Secretary of Defense (Policy), *DOD Procurement Process—Overview*, February 1987.

[81]*A Guide to the New United States Postal Service Procurement Manual*, United States Postal Service, October 1987, p. 1.

[82]Carla S. Lallatin, "Sales Opportunities in State and Local Government Markets," *Agency Sales Magazine*, February 1987, p. 51.

1. Funds being expended are public funds, not those of a business proprietor or a corporation, and thus may be expended only as prescribed by law. Rigid budgetary restrictions and public auditing procedures apply.
2. The process should be conducted in full public view.
3. Public purchasing is a much more rigid system with limited flexibility.
4. The system is subject to censure by the public and the press.
5. The government can and does act in a sovereign manner.[83]

Given this background, Page goes on to state the following two challenges faced by public purchasing officials:

1. Maintaining the integrity of the operation by making every effort to forestall waste and fraud and thus protect the public interest and treasury.
2. Maintaining the responsiveness of the operation, within the resources provided, by making every effort to respond to the needs of the jurisdiction; to provide the needed item of proper quality, at the right price, at the right time.[84]

Once again, the stated goals of all buying functions are similar. The major difference between the private and public sectors is that public buyers are buying in a fishbowl fully exposed to public scrutiny. While this exposure may ensure accountability for the expenditure of public funds, it does restrict public buyers in carrying out their functions efficiently and effectively.

While purchasing at the state and local levels has many similarities to federal procurement, there are a number of differences.

For instance, the size and structure of state and local purchasing departments vary from jurisdiction to jurisdiction. The 1983 procurement survey conducted by the National Institute of Government Purchasing (NIGP) reported that a majority of its respondents were in purchasing agencies that had one senior purchasing professional and five or more operating-level professionals.[85] In its 1989 survey the NIGP reported that more than 50 percent of its sample were in agencies with four or fewer buyers, and only 16 percent of that sample had more than twenty people assigned to the purchasing department. In that same study the NIGP reported that 70 percent of the respondents spent less than $30 million annually.[86]

Another difference from the federal sector is that state and local purchasing tends to be much more centralized. An August 1981 revision to the 1979 study by the National Association of State Purchasing Officials (NASPO) showed that all states had some form of central purchasing activity; however, only twelve states have this central purchasing authority vested in an individual whose title has purchasing in it. The rest were included in areas such as general services, finance,

[83]Page, *Public Purchasing*, p. 1.

[84]Ibid., pp. 8–9.

[85]*Results of the 1983 Procurement Survey* (Falls Church, Va.: National Institute of Governmental Purchasing, 1983), p. 2.

[86]*Results of the 1989 Procurement Survey* (Falls Church, Va.: National Institute of Governmental Purchasing, 1989), p. 3.

administration, and budget.[87] This same study found that it was a trend toward greater centralization of purchasing activity in thirty-six states. The 1983 NIGP study indicated that the majority of chief purchasing officers in this sample had responsibility for material and supply purchases, equipment purchases, and equipment leases and rentals.[88] The 1989 NIGP study found that almost 96 percent of its 620 respondents had purchasing activities that were centralized. This sample also had associated responsibility for the following areas:

1. Printing, including contracting for printing services
2. Mailing
3. Stationery stores
4. Central warehousing
5. Risk management
6. Data processing
7. Traffic, public safety
8. Inventory management
9. Surplus
10. Inspection
11. Real estate[89]

This trend toward greater centralization of purchasing activities may well be the result of recommendations contained in documents published by the Council of State Governments, such as *State and Local Government Purchasing: A Digest* and *State and Local Government Purchasing*. In the first document the following principles are set forth:

1. Purchasing authority and responsibility should be clearly set forth.
2. A central purchasing authority should have overall responsibility for the purchasing program.
3. Provision should be made for waivers of competitive bidding and for the delegation of various functions.
4. Central purchasing authority should be management oriented.
5. The internal organizational pattern for the purchasing program will probably vary among state and local governmental units.
6. Central purchasing authority should occupy a place in government which provides the status necessary to effectively coordinate and deal with other departments and agencies and which attempts to preclude direct political pressure.[90]

The second document suggests that there should be a central authority responsible for ensuring the integrity and effectiveness of the purchasing pro-

[87]Council of State Governments, *State and Local Government Purchasing*, 2nd ed. (Lexington, Ky.: Council of State Governments/National Association of State Purchasing Officials, 1983), pp. 186–87.

[88]*1983 Procurement Survey*, p. 2.

[89]*1989 Procurement Survey*, p. 5.

[90]*State and Local Government Purchasing: A Digest* (Lexington, Ky.: Council of State Governments, 1974), pp. 4–5.

gram.[91] What both of these documents are recommending is the centralization of the purchasing activity for a given jurisdiction so that greater effectiveness and accountability can be maintained. The specifics for establishing the responsibility for a central purchasing authority were detailed in the Model Procurement Code (MPC) developed by the American Bar Association on behalf of the Council of State and Local Government in 1975.[92] It is interesting to note that while most state and local jurisdictions have established statutes pertaining to central purchasing authority, the 1989 NIGP survey reports that only 27 percent of the respondents' jurisdictions had adopted the MPC as of 1989. Only another 14 percent were considering adoption.[93]

The 1983 NIGP survey also reported that 74 percent of its sample has developed policy and procedure manuals that guide the operation of the purchasing agency in their jurisdictions.[94] The majority of these manuals were written since 1980, which again may be a result of the recommendations made by the two main associations involved in state and local purchasing, NASPO and NIGP.

Also, while the federal sector is going away from the use of formally advertised sealed bids, that is still the primary method of procurement at the state and local levels. A 1979 survey of top state purchasing officials conducted by the National Association of State Purchasing Officials (NASPO) found that all but five states have a legal requirement for sealed bids.[95] The threshold amount for requiring sealed bids ranged from $300 in Pennsylvania to $10,000 in Oregon and Wisconsin. The 1983 procurement survey conducted by the NIGP found in its sample of 262 governmental purchasers that 61 percent operated under laws that required sealed bids.[96] Similar to the NASPO survey, the NIGP survey found that the threshold amounts for sealed bidding ranged from $1,000 to $10,000. The NIGP survey also showed that newspaper advertising was still the primary method of formal advertising, as 72 percent of its sample were legally required to use this method of bid advertising.[97] In the later NIGP study conducted in 1989, 75.6 percent of the sample of 620 governmental purchasers indicated that sealed bidding was required by law in their jurisdictions.[98] Even where not legally required, this method of procurement was used by over 90 percent of this sample. In addition, essentially all of these purchasers were required to use some form of formal advertising.

Another issue that seems to be important to both the NASPO and NIGP is the use of local preference. Both organizations have come out strongly opposed to such legislation because of its inhibition on good purchasing. This message seems to be getting across to the members of these two organizations—these sur-

[91]*State and Local Government Purchasing* (Lexington, Ky.: Council of State Governments, 1975), p. 2.1.

[92]*State and Local Government Purchasing*, 2nd ed., p. 17.

[93]*1989 Procurement Survey*, pp. 4–5.

[94]*1983 Procurement Survey*, p. 3.

[95]*State and Local Government Purchasing*, 2nd ed., p. 124.

[96]*1983 Procurement Survey*, p. 3.

[97]Ibid.

[98]*1989 Procurement Survey*, p. 18.

veys indicate minimal use of local preference in state and local purchasing. The NASPO survey indicated that only eleven states had local-preference legislation.[99] In the 1983 NIGP survey 58 percent indicated that local preference was neither legally required nor practiced. In those cases where local preference was practiced it usually amounted to less than a 5 percent differential between low bidder and the local supplier.[100] This percentage compares to the range of 1 to 25 percent cited in the NASPO study.[101] In the later 1989 NIGP study the percentage not having a legal mandate for local preference dropped to 53.2 percent of the 617 responses to this question. The amount of preference was approximately 5 percent, although the predominant preference was to award business to local bidders in the case of tie bids.[102]

One other major difference between the federal and the state and local sectors is the lack of socioeconomic legislation at the state and local levels. For example, the 1983 NIGP found that over 65 percent of the respondents in that study had no minority business enterprise (MBE) requirements, and 45 percent were not active in that area.[103] The 1989 NIGP study showed that only approximately 9 percent of the sample has legislation permitting set asides for small businesses, and only a little over 12 percent had any special provisions for MBE/WBE businesses.[104] Given the government's role in enacting social policy, this seems to be a low percentage of jurisdictions with legislation that would encourage doing business with small and disadvantaged businesses.

Another area where the state and local sector is attempting to be different from its federal counterpart is in the use of most-favored-customer (like the federal most-favored-nation) clauses in contracting for goods and services. Such a clause is a requirement at the federal level and has in many cases discouraged contractors from doing business with government agencies. Again, both NASPO and NIGP are opposed to such clauses as a constraint on effective procurement. In the 1979 NASPO study only three states reported using most-favored-customer clauses in their contracts.[105] Seventy-nine percent of the respondents in the 1983 NIGP survey indicated that they did not use such a clause.[106]

State and local purchasers are also frequent users of cooperative purchasing when it is of value to their individual jurisdictions. In this respect this sector is similar to the institutional sector discussed earlier. In fact, some of those institutions could easily be included in this section of comparative buying, because they are government entities. Cooperative purchasing provides a great opportunity for good purchasing. Not only can cooperative purchasing provide lower prices to smaller governmental entities, but it can also provide purchasing expertise that might not otherwise be available to them. Because of its possible advantages, many

---

[99]*State and Local Government Purchasing,* 2nd ed., p. 140.

[100]*1983 Procurement Survey,* p. 3.

[101]*State and Local Government Purchasing,* 2nd ed., p. 140.

[102]*1989 Procurement Survey,* p. 13.

[103]*1983 Procurement Survey,* p. 4.

[104]*1989 Procurement Survey,* p. 16.

[105]*State and Local Government Purchasing,* 2nd ed., p. 153.

[106]*1983 Procurement Survey,* p. 4.

state legislatures and the Model Procurement Code (MPC) have established guidelines that allow for the establishment of cooperative purchasing among different local government purchasing organizations.

Research into this area seems to indicate a high usage of cooperative purchasing to save taxpayer dollars expended in the purchase of goods and services at the state and local levels. For instance, in its 1981 revision of its 1979 procurement study NASPO reported that forty-two states participated to some degree in cooperative purchasing.[107] The 1983 NIGP study reported that only 10 percent of total dollars expended were spent through such agreements but that over 40 percent participated in piggyback contracts or joint-bid cooperative agreements. Most respondents in this study felt that participation in such cooperative arrangements provided overall savings to their jurisdiction.[108] Almost two-thirds of the respondents in the later 1989 NIGP survey indicated that they participated in cooperative purchasing programs. These respondents also indicated that significant dollars were saved by all jurisdictions that participated in such agreements.[109]

The first cooperative agreement was established in Hamilton County, Ohio, in 1931 and is described by Page in his text on public purchasing. This description illustrates both how such arrangements are formed and how they operate:

Example of a Cooperative Purchasing Agreement: The Cincinnati Plan

1. Started in 1931 by the city of Cincinnati and Hamilton County and is still in existence.
2. Administered by a coordinating committee of purchasing agents of Hamilton County.
3. Comprised of the purchasing agents of:
   — Cincinnati Board of Education
   — City of Cincinnati
   — Public Library of Cincinnati
   — Hamilton County
   — University of Cincinnati
4. Strictly a voluntary cooperative effort.
5. Savings have averaged 14 percent and have ranged as high as 50 percent.[110]

The key to the effectiveness of such agreements is not only the presence of enabling legislation but also the commitment of elected officials to active participation in these agreements.

While there are many differences between federal and state and local procurement, there are a number of similarities. As we have noted, the government sector is substantially behind its industrial counterpart in salary. The most recent NIGP survey shows that this gap is narrowing, but there appears to be a long way to go. The narrowing gap is particularly evident in the lower ranges of salary. The number of chief procurement officers in the 1989 sample who made below

[107]*State and Local Government Purchasing,* 2nd ed., p. 229.
[108]*1983 Procurement Survey,* p. 3.
[109]*1989 Procurement Survey,* p. 7.
[110]Page, *Public Purchasing,* p. 317.

$30,000 had declined from 33 percent to 16.7 percent, while the number making below $40,000 had dropped from 72 percent to 48.9 percent from the previous survey in 1985. However, the NIGP reported little improvement in the over-$70,000 salary range, where only 3.8 percent of this sample of chief procurement officers were included.[111] Only 15.3 percent of the 1989 NIGP sample had salaries in excess of $55,000, while a contemporaneous study of the NAPM membership reported almost 25 percent of that sample had salaries in excess of $51,000.[112]

Closely tied to this issue of salary is the desire of the entire government sector to improve the professionalization of its procurement work force. At the state and local levels both NASPO and NIGP have worked hard to provide guidance, in the form both of training and policy recommendations, to aid local jurisdictions in attaining this goal. It would appear that their attempts in this direction have not been totally successful to this point. One indication is the fact that NASPO reported in its 1981 revision of its 1979 survey that only four states felt that certification was an important qualification in hiring procurement officers.[113] The 1989 NIGP survey reported that only 3 percent of the jurisdictions in its sample had a mandatory requirement for certification of its procurement work force.[114]

Another issue related to professionalization is that of ethics. It is a particularly sensitive issue for public purchasers because of the importance of perceived fairness in awarding government contracts. The NASPO 1981 revised study reported that twenty-nine states required their procurement personnel to sign conflict-of-interest statements; thirty-six states had policies prohibiting personal purchases; and forty-nine states had regulations prohibiting back-door selling.[115] It is interesting to note that these three issues are important to the broader purchasing profession as well. In the 1988 Center for Advanced Purchasing Studies (CAPS) study on ethical practices 68 percent of the sample indicated that their companies had confict-of-interest policies; 84 percent of the sample said that their companies prohibited personal purchases; and 62 percent of that sample indicated that back-door selling was a problem at least some of the time.[116]

In spite of the fact that all government buyers have the reputation of buying strictly on the basis of low bids, that is not the case. In the 1981 NASPO study forty-five states reported that they allowed for the award of business on criteria other than price.[117] In all cases awards are given to the lowest responsible bidder. In fact, both the federal and the state and local sectors stress the importance of responsible bidders. A responsible bidder is defined at the state and local levels in

[111]*1989 Procurement Survey*, p. 12.

[112]David Chance, *Profile of the NAPM Membership*, (Tempe, Ariz.: The National Association of Purchasing Management), January, 1989, p. 3.

[113]*State and Local Government Purchasing*, 2nd ed., p. 237.

[114]*1989 Procurement Survey*, p. 12.

[115]*State and Local Government Purchasing*, 2nd ed., pp. 218–20.

[116]Robert L. Janson, *Purchasing Ethical Practices* (Tempe, Ariz.: Ernst & Whinney/Center for Advanced Purchasing Studies/National Association of Purchasing Management, 1988), pp. 26–27.

[117]*State and Local Government Purchasing*, 2nd ed., p. 213.

the same manner as in the federal sector. The *State and Local Purchasing Digest* defines a responsible bidder as one who has business integrity and financial capability and has demonstrated the ability to perform.[118] Once again, the government sector relies on qualified suppliers to ensure purchasing effectiveness just as the industrial sector does.

And like their industrial counterparts, public buyers are adopting new technology to improve the effectiveness of the purchasing function. An example is the use of computers, which has greatly facilitated the access to cooperative purchasing for local jurisdictions. One such application in this direction was the development of the Supplynet system in British Columbia, which contains information on vendors and commodities and allows for the consolidation of purchases for a large number of local entities throughout British Columbia.[119] The 1989 NIGP survey identified another area where technology has improved the efficiency of the purchasing function at the state and local levels. Its survey reported that 77 percent of the respondents accepted requests for quotations by way of facsimile machines (FAX), and another 18 percent accepted sealed bids by FAX. NIGP's conclusion from these results was that the FAX was the most significant productivity improvement for its members since the advent of the personal computer.[120]

AN EXAMPLE OF LOCAL CITY PURCHASING

While it would appear that the state and local government sector attempts to achieve goals similar to those espoused in the industrial sector, it would also appear that it is unable to obtain these goals because of the conflict between purchasing effectiveness and political expediency. Perhaps the best way to explain this dilemma is to describe the process for a major city. Comments presented here were obtained in an interview with the former purchasing manager for the city. In order to protect the identity of this particular city, it is referred to simply as the City.

Procurement in the City

Procurement is controlled by the home-rule charter enacted in the early fifties. In short, this legislation requires that all purchases of $2,000 or more must be advertised for two weeks in local newspapers. In addition, all bid proposals for $2,000 or more require bid surety bonds.

The stated purpose of the procurement department is as follows:

> The Procurement Department is the central purchasing and materials management agency for the City. Its purpose is to purchase, store and distribute all materials, supplies and equipment as well as contract for all services provided by the city charter.

---

[118]*State and Local Government Purchasing: A Digest,* p. 20.

[119]Janice Davis, "B. C. Launches Supplynet System," *Computing Canada,* September 4, 1986, pp. 1–2.

[120]*1989 Procurement Survey,* p. 19.

The objectives for the procurement department are as follows:

The principal responsibility of procurement is to acquire the materials, supplies, and services with the best quality at the lowest cost. Because both quality and cost are important, the city charter mandates that all purchases be made through a competitive bidding process.

Organization of the Procurement Function

The Procurement Department is headed up by the procurement commissioner, with two deputy commissioners. The organizational chart (see Figure 26-1) is our construction, not an actual organizational chart.

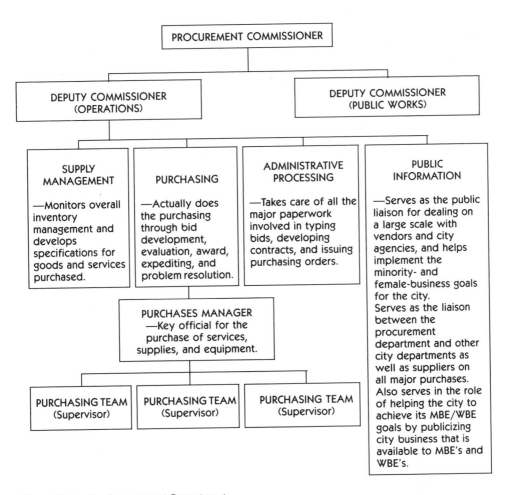

Figure 26-1   City Procurement Department

Scope of Operations

The operations division (not including public works or capital assets) is responsible for the purchase of $120 million annually of services, supplies and equipment and the overall management of $125 million in supply and property inventory. This involves more than four thousand contracts per year and more than twenty thousand purchase orders.

These contracts are let on the basis of proposals received in response to bid invitations (on contracts in excess of $2,000) advertised in local newspapers. Advertised bids are of two varieties: (1) general market bids, which are open to all eligible bidders; and (2) sheltered market bids, which are open only to members of sheltered markets (minority- and/or women-owned businesses).

Current Problems

The following are a few of the problems faced by the procurement department in attempting to perform its duties in an effective manner:

> *Procedures.* Because of the procedural detail involved in the procurement process, it takes 90 to 120 days to write a purchase order after receipt of a requisition. This problem is being addressed by a purchasing/procurement system that will speed up routine and repetitive purchases.
>
> *Policy.* A major policy objective of the city is to increase the participation of minority- and women-owned businesses. The problem with this objective is that there are not many qualified businesses in this category that are bondable. Additionally, the restriction of bids to the "sheltered" market has resulted in the development of a number of brokers—minorities or women who bid on city business and who, when successful, turn around and buy the materials from a nonsheltered business. The result is that the city pays higher prices, and minority and women employees are not helped.
>
> *Personnel.* When the purchasing manager took over his current position, there were two distinct groups of employees in the Procurement Department. The older group was mostly less educated and more apathetic. The city is in the process of trying to upgrade these positions by including education and certification requirements in the job specifications for these positions. In addition, there is a need to develop a policy manual to help new employees learn their responsibilities.
>
> *Other Problems.* The payment process, because of its verification requirements, is so cumbersome that it causes problems for vendors in paying their bills. This is a particular problem for small and minority businesses.
>
> In addition, the city imposes on vendors who do business with the city taxes and other restrictions that are so burdensome that many vendors choose not to do business with the city. This "robs" the city of many excellent sources for its requirements.

Relationship to Other Agencies

The city can buy from state contracts, but in most cases vendors don't want to participate because of the taxes imposed by the city.

While there are no local-preference laws in the state, there is a reciprocity law that states basically, that if another state has a local-preference law, vendors from that state will be treated in a similar manner when they sell here. However, this proviso is easily circumvented by establishing a sales agency in the state.

In some areas the city operates jointly with the school board in selecting vendors and negotiating contracts. An example would be heating-oil requirements for both entities.

Professional Development

The city is active in both the NAPM and the NIGP and pays for the purchases manager's dues for both these organizations. In addition, all new professional staff members are required to attend the NAPM basic purchasing courses and will be required to meet certain education criteria for promotion.

Differences between City and Industrial Purchasing

Prior to assuming her current position, the purchases manager held a similar position for a large industrial firm. When asked to describe the differences between the two positions, she responded, "In the city, we don't engage in purchasing, we simply push paper."

In further explaining what she meant by this statement, the purchases manager made the following observations:

> In essence, the procurement process is dictated by procedure and allows for very little judgment by purchasing personnel. A bid request is typed, mailed out to the bidders' list, returned, and opened. The award is made to the lowest bidder with only a few exceptions, such as no bid bond or a bid bond not paid properly.
>
> The inefficiency of the process can be seen by the fact that typically five hundred bid invitations are sent out, and only three or four proposals are received. Vendors are not prescreened, so that bid requests are often sent to unqualified bidders. This results in much wasted time and effort and added cost.
>
> Additionally, there is no reason for salespeople to call on purchasing, as the procedure dictates who will win the award. The better route for salespeople is to call on using departments and encourage users to specify their products. In many cases specifications are simply copies of vendors' promotional data.

The purchases manager concluded her assessment of the differences between city and industrial purchasing by stating: "While the objectives of both the industrial purchaser and the city purchasing manager are the same—obtaining a quality product in a timely manner at the least possible expenditure—the process in both sectors differ. In industry, judgment prevails, while in city purchasing, procedure dictates."

The purchases manager indicated that the city may eventually adopt the model procurement code (MPC) in the future. This would begin to correct a number of discrepancies between the industrial and city purchasing processes.

This example once again demonstrates that while the goals of the two processes are similar, it is much more difficult to achieve goals of effective purchasing in the state and local sectors because of the constraints placed on public purchasers. It also demonstrates that attempts are being made to improve this situation. Specifically, both NASPO and NIGP have made great strides in providing policy recommendations and training that, if heeded, should go a long way toward improving state and local purchasing. Finally, it should be pointed out that the city purchasing department described above is not meant to be taken as a typical city purchasing operation. Rather it is meant to highlight some of the difficulties encountered in attempting to purchase effectively in a city environment. As in the industrial sector, there are good purchasing departments and not-so-good ones.

SUMMARY

Perhaps the basic conclusion to be drawn from this rather extensive review of governmental sector purchasing is that the public sector has substituted legislation for managerial judgment in ensuring effective purchasing. The reason is the need for accountability and fairness in public purchasing. The question that remains, however, is whether legislation is a perfect substitute for good judgment. More specifically, will legislation that requires competitive bidding to the exclusion of all other means of selecting suppliers achieve the goal of optimal purchasing, or does it, in fact, prevent the attainment of this goal? As the review of the federal sector clearly indicated, the use of competitive bidding cannot work across the board. The federal government has recognized this and has defined competition more broadly to include negotiated contracts. It would appear that the state and local sector has been slower to move in this direction, but even in this sector there has been recognition that good purchasing is not served by the award of business strictly on the basis of low bid. The notion of responsible bidders has clearly been accepted by public buyers at all levels, and in this respect the buyers are similar to their industrial counterparts in recognizing the need for qualified suppliers. Effective purchasing in the government sector is a function of successful contracting, as in the private sector, where buyer success is dependent on supplier success.

Beyond the need for a qualified supplier base, there are a number of other similarities between public and private-sector purchasing. In both sectors there is increasing recognition of the vital role purchasing plays. James E. Holhouser, Jr., then governor of North Carolina, acknowledged this role in the preface to the first edition of *State and Local Purchasing*:

> Sound purchasing operations contribute greatly to the economical and effective operation of our governments and, perhaps of even greater importance at this time in our national history, they are basic to public confidence and trust in government. Furthermore, purchasing is an important, although underutilized, resource for improved program planning and evaluation and for policy and management generally.[121]

[121]*State and Local Government Purchasing,* p. ix.

The State and Local Purchasing Digest further emphasizes the importance of good purchasing to good government but also points to the major difference between public- and private-sector buying:

> Responsible purchasing is fundamental to responsible government and, in contrast to industrial or private buying, the price of goods purchased is not the overriding indicator of performance. More important in public purchasing is how the price is obtained. Here, fairness and openness are paramount. There is no room for partiality, secretiveness or deception. Good government and good purchasing are found together.[122]

Points for Review

1. Describe the major differences between governmental and industrial purchasing.
2. Describe the major differences between federal and state and local procurement.
3. Explain why federal procurement reform has been so ineffective.
4. Explain why it is so difficult for a government purchaser to be effective in attaining the goals of good purchasing.

[122]*State and Local Government Purchasing: A Digest,* p. 30.

Case Studies

CHAPTER 1
BERGMAN'S SONS FURNITURE COMPANY

Harold Bergman was the owner of a relatively small but thriving furniture manufacturing business. The basic products were various types of wooden garden furniture. To supplement this business, which was somewhat seasonal, Bergman took contracts or subcontracts for such items as home workbenches and hotel and institutional furniture. As a matter of policy (Bergman's personal decision), the market was limited to a rather small geographical area. He felt that this enhanced the company's local business relationships and to some extent relieved him from the pressures of strong outside competition.

The company's profit position was good. The principal raw material was lumber, for which several reliable supply sources had been developed over the years. This item represented about 40 percent of product cost. Other materials and supplies represented an additional 15 percent. Because sales and administrative costs were low, Bergman was able to add a comfortable 40 percent markup on the standard lines. One of his business axioms was that so long as lumber was bought right, the company had no cause for worry. On contract business, generally more competitive, the margin was not so great, but it was still satisfactory, because he was highly selective in the type of contracts he accepted.

Eventually, Bergman decided to retire and turn the business over to his two sons, then in their thirties. Both had worked for him for a number of years.

When George and Edward Bergman assumed full control over the business from their father, they found it in excellent shape. The cash balance was large and materials inventories high in asset value. Plant and office were staffed with experienced older employees. The vogue for "outdoor living" continued to bring more orders for garden furniture. Also, the growing popularity of do-it-yourself projects was creating a steady and promising market for home workbenches. The brothers decided to add these items to the regular line, and their hardware and department store customers showed great interest in the new numbers. This gave better diversification and balance to the company's operations. The younger Bergmans gradually went a little farther afield to extend their market. At the same time they continued the policy of seeking some contract work to keep manufacturing volume at a high level.

As the business grew, they leaned heavily on Fred Wilt, who had been general manager under their father. They left all procurement and production responsibilities to Wilt, while George took charge of sales and Edward concentrated on finance and personnel. Wilt was a competent, conservative executive, as the elder Bergman had been, and was completely loyal. He was considered an expert in all types of lumber and woodworking processes. He took pride in quality of product and in high standards of service. To maintain these principles, he believed in dealing only with established suppliers whom he considered loyal and in having "plenty of materials" on hand at all times. And he tolerated no slipshod methods of workmanship in the plant.

In his search for contract business George Bergman took a small order to do some laminating of plywood and plastic panels for a specialty packaging company. The project was experimental for both companies, but it turned out very satisfactorily. Within a year additional orders came in steadily, and this phase of the business boomed until it accounted for nearly 25 percent of all Bergman sales. That meant a rapid increase in plant personnel, a buildup in inventories, and an expansion in purchasing, both in dollar volume and in the number and diversity of items purchased. Plastics, adhesives, and metal trim were a few of the new items added to the buying list.

With expanding business, the Bergmans realized that a larger executive staff was needed. Among other things, they saw the need for a purchasing manager to relieve Wilt of the growing burden of procurement details. Wilt felt that goal could be accomplished more simply by adding one or two persons to his own staff. The brothers, however, aware that manufacturing problems, too, were becoming more complex and demanding, and looking ahead to further growth, decided to follow their plan for a separate purchasing department. Temporarily, at least, the new purchasing manager would double as officer manager, a responsibility heretofore carried by Edward Bergman. For this position they settled on Frank Parvis—like themselves, in his thirties. Parvis was currently employed as purchasing manager for a book publishing concern. He knew the Bergmans only slightly, but he came to their company highly recommended by close mutual friends.

In a general way the Bergmans looked upon Parvis as one of a small group of "comers" who could help build the company into a substantial enterprise. He was given a good salary and assurances that he would receive generous bonuses based on annual profits. He was told that he had a free rein in organizing and running a complete purchasing department—except that "for the time being" Fred Wilt would continue to purchase the major raw material, lumber.

Parvis set up the new department and procedures on the basis of his experience in his previous purchasing position. He took on two young men from within the company as buyers. One had been a clerk under Wilt and had handled the routine buying of shop supplies. The other had served in various positions in the plant, with a consistent record of promotions in recognition of his capacity to accept additional responsibility. Both men had been with the company for upwards of five years. Both had two years of college education, and the first one was attending evening classes to complete his work for a degree in business administration.

Except for the normal problems encountered in building any organization from scratch, Parvis had no great difficulties. Wilt seemed quite cooperative, even to the point of expressing relief that the detail of buying had been lifted from his shoulders and gratification that two of "his boys" were to be in the buying positions. At the same time he made it clear that he considered lumber buying to be his prerogative and had no intention of surrendering it, for two reasons: his expert knowledge of the material and his continuing responsibility for quality of product. Although, nominally, he turned over the rest of the buying to Parvis, he continued to see most of the regular suppliers who called at the plant, and occasionally he would call Parvis or send him a memo requesting favorable treatment for a certain supplier. Early in his experience at Bergman's, Parvis learned the expediency of tending toward liberal margins of safety in ordering and inventory, merely to forestall Wilt's outspoken anxiety over possible shortages of "minor" nonlumber materials, and he took pains to see that no actual shortages developed. The implied criticism, he felt, was of policy rather than of fact.

The situation was not intolerable for Parvis, but he did feel frustrated by having to share a divided buying responsibility. He felt that neither his personal nor his departmental performance could be fairly evaluated on the basis of a partial purchasing program, especially because the material excluded from his control was, in terms of dollar expenditure, the largest single factor of total purchases. Personally, he got along well enough with Wilt and had no desire to raise the issue of organization on personal or theoretical grounds. Objectively, he considered Wilt's position to be a roadblock to good, professional purchasing. He realized, too, that he had his own position to establish and prove before he could effectively challenge management's organization plan. The Bergman brothers, with complete confidence in Wilt, were not aware of any shortcoming or conflict. Meanwhile, Parvis was so occupied with other details, both of purchasing and of office management, that he tried to live with the situation until he could have his own organization fully developed and could talk with the Bergmans about centralizing all purchasing in his department.

In preparation for such a proposal, Parvis made an intensive study of the entire materials and procurement situation, documented so far as possible by actual purchase records and specifically related to the criteria of product cost and overall company interest. Among the points he noted were the following:

1. With extended markets and the introduction of new products, the company is meeting with harder competition, so that the markup and profit margin are narrowed. To date, increased volume has maintained total profits and has enabled Wilt to effect some manufacturing economies. The materials factor of product cost has not changed significantly. The profit squeeze is intensifying, and the point of breakeven volume is steadily rising.
2. With diversification of product beyond the simple garden furniture line, lumber is no longer the unique and dominant item of purchased material cost in the same degree that it had previously been. The company is buying more lumber than before, but instead of the previous 40:15 ratio, it is now just about equal in dollar expenditure to the sum of other materials.

3. In view of both the above-mentioned factors, the theory that "right buying" of lumber is the answer to all materials cost problems must be discarded. Query: What is "right buying" of lumber?

4. Prices paid for lumber have risen sharply over the past year, corresponding to the general advance in the lumber market. On new materials purchased since product diversification, there is no basis for comparison, but contracts now in force assure that the present level will hold for another six months. On materials previously used, and now bought by the purchasing department, a modest saving of 3 percent overall can be shown, despite rising markets. There are a variety of reasons in respect to individual items; in general, the saving can be attributed to the closer attention given to these so-called minor items. Query: Is it reasonable to assume that similar savings could be made on lumber through specialized purchasing attention?

5. On nonlumber items, economical order quantities, scientifically calculated, average forty-five days' supply; inventory quantities average three-weeks' supply. On lumber, order quantities are usually dictated by the carload unit, and inventories are maintained at sixty days' supply. This adds a substantial carrying cost at time of use. Query: Could scientific methods of determining order quantities, closer scheduling of deliveries, and inventory control be applied to reduce carrying cost by half? Could broadening the base of supply provide the assurance of ample material now provided by reserve stocks?

6. Concede Wilt's expert knowledge of lumber and Parvis's lack of experience with this material. Buyer number two, with excellent experience in working with lumber in varied shop operations, is (or can become) well qualified for lumber procurement. Standards set by Wilt or with his approval, and observed in purchasing, can give the needed assurances of quality.

7. The company now has no consistent purchasing policy. It has two policies, independently developed and administered. There should be a single policy, with the authority of executive approval.

Before Parvis had the opportunity of presenting this brief and argument to his management, the Bergmans announced plans to acquire a small electronics company in a nearby city. This concern produced control mechanisms in small lots. Its annual sales volume was about half as great as the Bergmans'. The company was highly engineering oriented. It had two buyers, both graduate engineers, working under a vice-president responsible for product development as well as for procurement.

QUESTIONS

The Bergmans called in Parvis, explained the new venture, and asked him to submit a report covering three points. If you were Parvis, how would you respond?

1. What kind of purchasing organization do you recommend for the company, including the furniture, laminating, and electronics divisions? How should present personnel be assigned? Will more people be needed?
2. Write a statement of purchasing policy applicable to the entire organization.
3. How would you evaluate purchasing for all divisions, and how can we, as owners and managers, be kept informed?

CHAPTER 2
NEARFRANK ROLLER COMPANY

Nearfrank Roller Company manufactures a wide variety of steel rolls used on industrial machinery, ranging from small printing presses to large food-processing equipment. Its purchasing department buys a relatively small number of items—quality steels, several types of components, and maintenance supplies—but the critical nature of the materials requires a high degree of skill in the buying staff.

Harry Fenlon, the director of purchases, had reorganized his department two or three times in the fifteen years that he had held the position. In the last reorganization, eight years ago, he had settled on an arrangement that paired a buyer and a clerk-typist in a "buying team." The clerk-typist's responsibilities under this arrangement were quite broad. In addition to typing orders, he or she acted as the buyer's secretary and handled all routine follow-up of orders, answered requests for delivery information from operating departments, and occasionally handled the purchase of nontechnical, noncritical items, office supplies and janitorial equipment. Several of the more competent clerk-typists were recognized unofficially as assistant buyers and were considered capable of handling many of the buyer's responsibilities in his or her absence. There were six buyer-clerk-typist teams in the department, one receptionist-file clerk, an accounts payable clerk, and a part-time clerk who helped check invoices and handle overload work.

Harry was quite satisfied with the arrangement and had no reason to believe that his department's performance was considered anything but good by the company's management. When the president called in a management consulting firm to study the operations of major departments of the company, he cooperated wholeheartedly in the project. He instructed his departmental personnel to provide the consultants with information on their jobs, work habits, allocation of time, and so forth. He discussed the activity of the department and its individual members with the consultants.

To Harry's surprise, the management consulting firm's final report included a strong criticism of the purchasing department organization and recommended a drastic change. Excerpts from the section dealing with the purchasing department follow.

> The team basis for buying is not acceptable, as within my knowledge no other company of comparable size is using it. . . . In the team arrangement the clerk-typist acts as a crutch for the buyer, thus weakening the buyer to a point where he or she delivers less in the way of productive effort rather than more.
>
> Many purchasing departments are handling your ratio of orders per buyer without the use of a buying team.
>
> Under the team setup each clerical member of the team reports to the director of purchases, but organizationally clerical workers are well removed from direct supervision. As a consequence, each member sets his or her own pace.
>
> The entire clerical group is a functional one, as distinct from the line group of buyers. Their function is to handle all paperwork and record keeping. This func-

tion should be handled separately from the line group in a centralized arrangement.

Labor is a commodity. You are paying too high a price for it in the purchasing department. There is not enough awareness of the productive capacity that a dollar will buy.

We recommend that the department be reorganized with all clerical help grouped together under a clerical supervisor who should be appointed immediately. At least two and possibly three members of the clerical force could then be let go or moved to other departments, because work loads would be more evenly distributed and more efficiently handled.

The president called Harry in and handed him a copy of the section of the management consulting firm's report that dealt with the purchasing department. "They're pretty outspoken in their comments, Harry," he said, "and I want you to be the same in your answer—which I'd like to have right away."

Harry dictated a point-by-point reply to the criticisms listed. Then he wrote the following general memorandum and sent both documents to the president.

The consultants support the concept of a strictly functional approach. I still support a combination functional line approach.

Every company designs its own purchasing facility to fit its own needs, with the objective of developing a strong, well-trained profit-making group. Therefore, broad statements about what should be done about reduction of clerical costs or changes in organization must be considered along with their effect on our ability to carry out major objectives.

The consultants are well qualified to determine practical clerical work loads. But they seem unwilling to give our buyers the assistance they need to perform their functions—that is, to give good service to the shop, save the company's money, and continually increase their knowledge of the products they buy. Buyers have to have time to review requirements, get the most out of sales interviews, and make visits to suppliers' plants. They have to be free to attend conferences away from their desks and to take on another buyer's responsibilities in case of sickness or absence for some other reason. And above all they must have plenty of time for the preparation and conduct of negotiations.

We must not reduce our clerical personnel until we are able to reduce the clerical work accordingly. We are adopting some changes and considering others and expect to effect other improvements as we go along. Some of these will require the cooperation of other departments.

Our present organization and clerical procedure were adopted owing to the shortcomings of the functional-type operation previously followed. I believe we have made good progress and would resist any backward steps in this respect. We have no intention of making any changes that would hinder the buyer or his or her ability to perform his or her proper function.

QUESTIONS

1. Write a point-by-point answer to the management consultants' criticisms and recommendations based on your understanding of the nature and scope of the purchasing function.

2. List specific changes and improvements that could be carried out to improve the efficiency of the purchasing department.
3. Describe and explain the need for each.

CHAPTER 3
BESTON FOOD PRODUCTS COMPANY

Jean Hopkins was in her second year as director of purchasing for Beston Foods. She had come to the company after eight years as purchasing manager of a division of a major steel company to succeed a man retiring from the post after thirty years' service. In her first year with the company she had concentrated on improving her understanding of those areas of food industry purchasing for which her experience in heavy metals had not prepared her—primarily, the technical and commodity-market phases. When she felt sufficiently grounded in the basics of these specialized areas, she began turning her attention to some of the broader phases of procurement common to all industries—including such aspects as administrative procedures, purchasing policies, vendor relations, and buyer training. She had had no other mandate from the food company management other than to see that the department was kept "up to date" and at a high level of efficiency.

In the process of reviewing procedures and policies in the Beston Company's purchasing manual, which had not been revised in several years, Jean came across a section that read:

> We believe our vendors carry out their responsibilities to us when they provide us with good service and high quality at lowest possible cost. Any effort on their part to go further than this through the giving of gifts or gratuities is unnecessary and should be courteously but firmly discouraged.

The policy on gifts and gratuities in Jean's former company had been written at company headquarters and was much more precise and stronger. It had specifically forbidden any employee to accept gifts of any kind, other than advertising items, or to accept entertainment or lunches from suppliers. It pointed out that any employee accepting gifts was, at worst, involving himself or herself in commercial bribery and, at best, violating company policy. Jean had personally endorsed the policy, and she and her buyers scrupulously followed it.

Jean had no desire to try to force this stricter code on her new company or even on the purchasing department. Yet she felt there was an obvious contradiction between the Beston Company's policy and the practice of her department. During her first Christmas season with the company she had seen a few gifts—a bottle of liquor, a box of cigars, and similar items—on her buyers' desks. She knew also that at least two buyers had attended World Series' games as guests of one of the Beston Company's best and most respected suppliers.

Jean decided to bring some consistency into the situation. She called her supervisory buyers together for a frank talk about this phase of vendor relations.

To her surprise and gratification, they were not only glad to discuss the matter but indicated that they would welcome a more specific prohibition of gifts and entertainment. "They're more bother than they're worth" was the consensus; such gifts were accepted only to avoid embarrassing reputable vendors of standing. Several pointed out that they were aware of the statement in the manual but had never heard of anyone trying to implement it.

They agreed that a letter should go out over Jean's name to the Beston Company's entire vendor list, explaining a new purchasing policy on gifts and gratuities and asking the recipients to refrain from offering them to members of the purchasing department. The following letter was prepared for mailing right after Thanksgiving:

> In recent years employees in our department have received Christmas gifts from some of our suppliers. They generally have been modest tokens of the esteem and friendship we know exist between our organization and those with whom we do business. We feel, however, that it would be in the best interests of all if we kept our relationships on a strictly business basis.
>
> We have therefore decided on a policy of not permitting any member of this department to accept personal gifts from any firm or individual doing business with our company. We sincerely hope you appreciate our position that quality, service, and price should be the only considerations in our buying.

Meanwhile, the Beston sales department was aggressively merchandising a new line of canned luxury foods—pâté de foie gras, vichyssoise, smoked oysters, and similar delicacies. Pictures of the foods were displayed by the company's reception room and mentioned in a new "welcome booklet" for visiting sales representatives. A small selection of several items had even been mailed as gifts to all Beston Company stockholders at the end of the last fiscal year with a note encouraging them to recommend the delicacies to their friends.

During the fall season the sales manager had what he considered a brilliant idea. Among the many reports run off on the company computer that were available to his office was one listing every supplier with whom the Beston Company was doing business, together with their addresses. Here, he reasoned, was a captive audience on which he could try a first-rate merchandising idea. Without informing the purchasing department, he sent a letter addressed to the sales manager of every Beston supplier during the first week of December. It read in part:

> During the coming holiday season, what better way could you find to express your gratitude to customers for their business during the past year than with a gift of fine food? And what finer food is there than Beston's Gourmet Specialties? . . . Remember your special business friends with a boxed selection of Gourmet Specialties. . . . Available beautifully gift wrapped in $10, $25, and $50 sizes.

It did not take long for Jean to discover what had happened. Within a few days she had one mildly sarcastic letter from a supplier, containing copies of the letter on prohibiting Christmas gifts and the one promoting Beston products as gifts. Which one, he said in effect, am I supposed to believe? Jean, furious, went directly to the executive vice-president and complained of the embarrassing situation she and the company had been put in. The executive vice-president called in the sales manager, who seemed only slightly amused by the whole affair.

Questions

1. Was the director of purchasing justified in complaining?
2. Had her approach to the problem of gifts been too arbitrary or naive?
3. What other methods might she have used in establishing a no-gift policy that would have avoided the situation described above?
4. What do you think of the sales manager's tactics; were they businesslike, ethical, and do you think he should have had free access to the purchasing department's vendor lists?
5. Assuming you were the executive vice-president, what actions would you take to solve the problem?

CHAPTER 4
DALTON-FRANKEL CORPORATION

Dalton-Frankel Corporation is a large producer and marketer of building materials. Its products include asphalt tile, roofing paper and composition shingles, caulking compounds, wallboard, and insulation. The company is organized according to product divisions, with a strongly centralized administration, including finance and accounting, sales and advertising, and purchasing.

The company's policy has been to conduct its manufacturing operations in relatively small plants devoted to a single product, located individually in small and medium-size companies throughout the territory it serves. There are fourteen such plants in four adjoining midwestern states. None of the product divisions or plants are dominant in their respective fields, but collectively they form a large and influential organization in the building-materials sector. Similarly, the combined purchasing power is substantial, and centralized purchasing capitalizes on this fact. Despite the diversity of materials purchased, the company is able to deal to advantage with the larger companies among its supplier industries; it has, in fact, the status of a national account.

The reasons for decentralizing manufacturing operations in smaller cities are chiefly concerned with labor relations—a more stable labor supply, generally lower wage rates, better environment, and smaller employee groups. But there are also sales advantages. The scattered plants provide an opportunity to maintain good warehouse stocks of the entire line at strategic points throughout the company's marketing area. This in turn promotes the feeling among the building trades that Dalton-Frankel is essentially a local industry, even though a specific product of the company may be manufactured several hundred miles from the point of use.

With both these objectives in mind, Dalton-Frankel's management has developed an active program of local public relations, stressing community pride and service and participation in community affairs wherever its plants are located.

The director of public relations suggested to the purchasing manager that the company's purchasing policy was not consistent with the overall company program. He said that purchasing might be able to contribute a great deal to the effectiveness of the public relations efforts without compromising purchasing principles. Because the company was interested in the economic prosperity of the areas in which its plants were located, he pointed out, buying more from local sources would tend to create and stimulate markets for Dalton-Frankel products. While recognizing that a strict "buy-at-home" policy was probably impractical in respect to the various plants, he contended that diversified suppliers—including minority suppliers—could be found within the area as a whole, of a size and character to constitute satisfactory sources. This situation, he added, could be capitalized on to promote the public relations program.

QUESTIONS

1. Was the public relations director's suggestion sound and feasible?
2. As a purchasing manager, how would you respond to such a proposal?
3. What steps, if any, would you take before making a decision on the proposal?

CHAPTER 5
AYERS COMPANY

The Ayers Company fabricates metal parts and uses considerable quantities of abrasive compounds in its finishing operations. For a number of years brand A compound had been purchased and used exclusively for one stage of the process, because that was the product the finishing department foreman had insisted on having. Price of the product was $1.92 a pound, but there were several competitive brands available in a price range from $1.60 a pound and up, which the purchasing manager considered suitable for the operation. The specification calling for brand A had the usual modifying phrase "or equal," but the words were practically meaningless, as the foreman declared that the other brands were not equal. The production manager supported the foreman on the grounds that he knew the operation and was responsible for results in his department: brand A was known to be dependable, and a substitute material might slow operations or affect the quality of the finished product, offsetting the small saving on price. The purchasing manager argued that 16 percent was not a small saving. The production manager was not impressed. "On 6,000 pounds it comes out to less than $2,000 at best—and I think that's a small price to pay for assurance of quality—and a satisfied foreman." The purchasing manager also concluded that the amount did not warrant making an issue of the matter, so he let it drop.

Some months later the production manager moved on to another company and was replaced by a man accustomed to conferring with the purchasing department on material specifications and buying practices. The purchasing manager eventually brought the matter of abrasive compounds to his attention and he responded by suggesting tests of the lower-cost compounds.

Several brands were tested on the basis of one shift's operations. "The foreman was right," the new production manager said. "Nothing you've shown us does the job as well as brand A, but it slows down the process so that we get fewer pieces per machine-hour. Here are the brands that come closest. Brand B turns out almost as many pieces per pound. Brand C keeps the machines up to speed, but they eat up about 10 percent more compound. However, you have a point, too. We can save some money. Here's what the cost comparisons show, figuring machine time at $14 an hour." He presented the following figures:

Brand A—$1.92 lb, 120 pieces produced

8 hr machine time	$112.00	per piece	0.933
10 lb compound	19.20	per piece	0.160
Cost of operation per piece			1.093

Brand B—$1.80 lb, 115 pieces produced

8 hr machine time	$112.00	per piece	0.974
10 lb compound	18.00	per piece	0.156
Cost of operation per piece			1.130

Brand C—$1.60 lb, 120 pieces produced

8 hr machine time	$112.00	per piece	0.933
11 lb compound	17.60	per piece	0.147
Cost of operation per piece			1.080

"Machine time is the big factor," he continued. "Frankly, even if brand B had shown a cost saving, I'd have turned it down, because we need full output to keep our production lines in balance. I'd be interested in anything that would speed production—even at a higher cost. Brand C does the job. The real saving comes out to about half of what you estimated, but on about 60,000 pieces a year I'm not knocking them. Let's try C."

After using brand C for a few weeks, the foreman complained that he was able to turn out only 110 pieces each shift and he was using up to 15 pounds of compound to do it. His costs were up nearly 16 percent. Switching back to brand A didn't help much. Less compound was used—about 12.5 pounds per shift—and production remained at the lower rate.

Analysis of the problem revealed that although the same type of steel was being used for the part, one of the changes instituted by the new production manager was in the heat treatment prior to finishing, which resulted in greater surface hardness but slowed down the finishing process.

The foreman gathered other data from finance and personnel departments to support and further his analysis. These included:

- The plant worked a five-day week (eight hours/day) and ran two shifts, with daily output at 240 pieces/day (120 pieces/shift) and was shutdown for two weeks in July.
- The procedural change resulted in a slightly better finish but had no impact on customer perception of quality.
- Selling price per unit currently averaged $2. It was now a seller's market, and all output was being sold.

The purchasing manager resumed his search for a suitable compound but concentrated on those that offered faster cutting properties. He bought a trial lot of a premium-priced compound—brand D at $2.21 a pound. This made it possible to bring production up to the required 120 pieces per shift, using 15 pounds of brand D. Unit finishing cost was still up about 11 percent compared with the original operation. But on the hard-surfaced steel unit cost was less than with either of the other compounds, despite the fact that brand D was substantially more expensive than either. The important thing was that the production rate had been restored.

The purchasing manager was still not convinced that the best solution had been found. As he now saw the problem, there were still three alternatives that would satisfy the requirement:

1. Use brand D on the surface-hardened steel, 120 pieces per shift. Estimated unit finishing cost: $1.21.
2. Finish the parts before hardening, using brand C as before, and heat treat after the finishing operation. Estimated unit finishing cost: $1.08.
3. Assuming that brand D, used on the parts before hardening, could step up output to 125 or more pieces per shift, use brand D and heat treat after the finishing operation (using only 12 lb.). Estimated unit finishing cost: $1.11. This cost is lower than one and higher than the other of the above, but it does assure a higher production rate, which is one of the production manager's objectives.

QUESTIONS

1. Should the production department in this case have been required to justify its reason for certain product references?
2. Which department should have the final decision on what should be purchased, and is purchasing justified in questioning, by implication, manufacturing policy in presenting alternative solutions?
3. How can purchasing judge the factor of production rates when no monetary valuation has been put on them?
4. Which brand would you recommend and why?

CHAPTER 5
BLESTING COMPANY

As part of a planned program of acquisition and diversification, Futura, Inc., a Chicago-based publishing company, bought out the Blesting Company, manufacturers of heavy-duty lift tables used primarily at loading and receiving docks and in metalworking operations. Blesting, located near San Diego, had annual sales of about $80 million. Previous Futura acquisitions included a bookbinding company in New York City and a small chain of hardware stores on the west coast.

Viola Dopple, Futura's director of purchasing, had visited Blesting shortly after the company was acquired. She met with Hayward Blesting III, vice-president of operations, and Sheila Yardavis, a longtime employee who was both secretary of the company and its manager of purchasing and services. They explained the division of purchasing responsibility in the company: Hayward was responsible for negotiating most of the major purchases, such as machinery, steel plate, castings, fittings and hose, and motors; Sheila, with a clerical assistant, handled the paperwork on those purchases and also bought all other items, primarily maintenance, repair, and operating (MRO) supplies. Annual expenditures for purchases averaged about $35 million and between three hundred and four hundred purchase orders were issued each month. They had no specific figures on the cost of operating the purchasing function. Both were of the opinion that some additional help was needed in purchasing but said they were so busy with their assorted duties that they "just hadn't had time to get around to doing anything about it."

Viola, short-handed and pressed for time herself, suggested no great changes in the Blesting purchasing system but did ask that one copy of each purchase order issued be sent to her office. Hayward and Sheila agreed to that arrangement. They told Viola they would cooperate in any way and looked forward to working with her to improve their own purchasing.

Blesting's purchasing system was conventional: a six-part purchase order was typed for every requisition received in purchasing: the original and an acknowledgment copy went to the vendor; one copy went to the receiving department; another went to the requisitioner; and two remained in the purchasing department, to be filed alphabetically by vendor and by item. (Sheila saw no problem in having one of purchasing's two copies go to Futura's purchasing department as requested by Viola.)

When orders were delivered, the Blesting receiving and stores clerk prepared a three-part receiving notice—one copy for purchasing, one for accounting, and one to remain in receiving. All vendor invoices came to purchasing for checking and were then sent to accounting for payment.

Several months after Viola's visit to Blesting, a Futura management trainee with a B.S. in business administration, was assigned to her department for a four-month period. The trainee, Angelo Tobias, had spent time in the marketing and financial departments. During his original interview he had expressed interest in a career in finance or purchasing and materials management.

In his first two months in purchasing Angelo showed considerable aptitude, and the director decided to send him on temporary assignment to the Blesting plant. "I have talked to Hay Blesting and Sheila Yardavis about you," she told him. "We have agreed that you should get some actual buying experience there, but we also want you to study their procedures and possible personnel requirements and get your opinion about what, if anything, might be done to improve their efficiency. They are cooperative people, both executives, and open-minded to new ideas. When you're ready with your recommendations, report to me first. Then we'll sit down with the Blesting people to discuss them."

Shortly after his arrival at Blesting Angelo undertook a thorough study of the company's complete purchasing cycle. He began with an analysis of all purchase orders for the previous year. Concurrently he reviewed order-related activities with requisitioners, receiving personnel, accounting personnel, and several suppliers of MRO and office-equipment items. On occasion he sat in on sales with Sheila and was an observer during two major negotiation sessions conducted by Hayward.

In his procedure analysis he found that almost three-quarters of all purchase orders had a value of less than $500, and of those just over half were for less than $200. He concluded that on the average Sheila and her clerk spent as much or more time placing and handling the less-than-$500 orders as they did on larger orders. The amount of paperwork required in issuing, receiving, and paying for the smaller orders was the same as for the larger ones.

Angelo concluded that the major problem facing the Blesting purchasing department at the time was the disproportionate burden of the relatively small and less important orders that Sheila, with limited help, had to handle, as well as the cost of processing the paperwork on those orders at every stage of the purchasing cycle. Although he had three weeks to go in his assignment, he felt it was time to make his recommendations to Viola.

QUESTIONS

1. Assume that you are Angelo. What recommendations would you make in regard to purchasing procedures and personnel requirements? Be specific about changes or innovations you feel are necessary, and explain in detail how they should be implemented and what results can be expected from them.

CHAPTER 6
ELECTRONICS, INC.

Paul Smith had to prepare for an important meeting to decide whether the company should proceed with its fledgling EDI program or to fax its purchase-order requirements to its suppliers.

As he prepared for the meeting he thought about the company's EDI efforts over the past twelve months. Electronics, Inc., a division of a major Fortune

500 company, was considering the implementation of an electronic data interchange system for its purchasing department. The firm placed an average of four hundred orders per day and a study revealed that 50 percent of these orders were for amounts less than $500. It was thought that EDI could reduce these administrative costs by 80%. Paul hoped to reduce the time that it took to place a purchase order. On average the manual purchase order cycle at Electronics, Inc. took five to twenty working days, from generation of requirements to the confirmation, signature, and mailing of the order. It was expected that EDI would reduce that time to three to five days. Additionally, much less clerical time would be spent on purchase orders. Currently, processing of fifty purchase orders averaged twenty-four man-hours; it was expected that EDI would reduce this to three hours.

A just-in-time (JIT) inventory system was in the process of implementation and it was expected that EDI would facilitate this program. The EDI transmission could be sent to suppliers who were not necessarily geographically close to the plant. For example, a distant supplier could be utilized without the necessity of a nearby facility. The logic behind this was that sending a purchase order electronically would permit the supplier to release the material upon demand.

Paul, manager of purchasing for the division, indicated a strong desire to push the project forward. His plan was to start the project slowly and gradually extend it to more commodities.

The electronics division purchased many commodities, including semiconductors, electro-mechanical parts, integrated circuits, labels, printed circuit boards, as well as copper wire and cables. It initially appeared that the commodity group of semi-conductors would be selected for the pilot project. The semiconductor commodity group was selected due to its purchase expenditure volume. In addition, the semi-conductor supplier had expertise in the area of EDI and was willing to pilot an EDI program with Electronics, Inc.

The next decision faced by Paul was deciding whether to use a computer-to-computer system using a value-added network or a personal computer (p/c- to-p/c) application. A report by the corporate office listed the advantages of these systems.

Computer to computer was possible, but the supplier and buyer would have to do their own ANSI translation or buy the service from a value-added network. P/c-to-p/c involved rekeying data for both the buyer and supplier which could result in poor data integrity. Legal considerations concerning applicable contract terms and conditions; proper signature authorization approval as required by policy; record accuracy and record retention; as well as audit and security criteria were also issues that needed to be addressed and solved.

Pilot testing of orders began in April using the computer-to-computer system. The first transmissions uncovered several problem areas. These included interpretation differences regarding the ANSI X 12 standard and change-order functionality since the buyers' auditors required a paper trail. It was also found that two full-time positions would be required if EDI were fully implemented—a systems-resource person and a full-time person in the purchasing department. The additional cost, including wages and benefits, was estimated at $50,000 per position. However, it was also projected that three full-time clerical support personnel could be moved elsewhere in the organization at an estimated savings of $30,000 per position since the filing, mailing, and inputting of data were not needed. Paul also had read that firms that were truly committed to EDI often had the backing of upper management and a full-time EDI manager.

At the end of the first year of pilot testing the following results were obtained. Savings in clerical personnel were realized on the EDI parts, inventory turns increased on EDI parts, and purchase order processing savings were realized. However, it was found that the transfer of purchase orders only did not offset the investment and time required to conduct an EDI program. It only saved the internal processing time which could be accomplished by faxing orders. However, it was felt that providing forecasted demand to EDI suppliers could reduce lead times by 35–50 percent. Buyers would have to agree on a firm period during which no cancellations would occur in exchange for the leadtime reductions. The buyer's advantage in providing such forecast data would be increased inventory turns. To provide forecast information accurately there was a need for a cross functional team to work the issues of the master schedule, production control, purchasing, and finance. Finally there would be a need to obtain top management support in order to change standard buying practices.

QUESTIONS

A decision had to be made on the next phase of EDI at Electronics, Inc.

1. Assume you are Paul Smith. What is your next step in the EDI process for his firm?
2. Discuss the Electronics, Inc. approach to EDI implementation. What, if any, approaches would you change?
3. Estimate the potential costs and benefits of the system selected by Electronics, Inc.

This case was prepared by Larry Giunipero with the assistance of Ms. Maxine Austin.

CHAPTER 7
JACKSON CORPORATION

The Jackson Corporation, producers of electronic communications equipment, was founded primarily to supply the U.S. Air Force with certain highly specialized items. The company has, however, steadily sought to develop some less complex commercial business as a hedge against technological change or a sharp cutback in defense spending.

Jackson Corporation's purchasing department has grown along with the company, adapting itself to expansion and changing conditions. At the beginning purchasing decisions were made by the engineer-owners, and the administrative operations of ordering were carried out by clerks. Gradually, a full-scale purchasing organization developed to handle the rapidly increasing material requirements resulting from military orders during the defense buildup for the war in Vietnam. Production was limited to a few important items, and the four buyers brought into the purchasing department soon became familiar with the relatively complex parts and materials that they were buying. With only slight assistance from the engineering department, they were able to handle all procurement efficiently.

The company's business picked up during the space-exploration program. The purchasing manager, Archer Dix, continued to expand his department, to the point at which he had eight buyers working for him. Four of the buyers were college graduates, of whom three had business administration degrees. One had an undergraduate engineering degree and a master's degree in business administration. Four of the buyers had been with the company from the start and had been brought into purchasing from the manufacturing and stores departments. Two trainees, both with B.S. degrees in electrical engineering, joined the department a couple of years later and were used as expediters and general backup for the buyers.

Space-age production and procurement problems were more complex than those associated with production of relatively standardized military equipment, however, and the Jackson Corporation purchasing department felt the difference. Most of the products ordered for use in spacecraft were custom built for a particular mission, and output was in terms of one to five units, in contrast to the hundreds and thousands turned out during the war. Technological change was much more rapid. Components and materials satisfactory for one satellite were obsolete a few months later. Designers increasingly called for patented or proprietary items or highly specialized products available from sole sources.

Under these complex, swiftly changing conditions, the buyers were not so quick to learn as previously, and their dependence on the components engineering department was much greater. The components engineers had responsibility for analyzing customer requirements, acting as liaison between customers and the design engineering department, and testing. They set the specifications for all purchased products that went into Jackson products. Increasingly, vendors with new ideas or suggestions for changing specifications would find themselves referred to the components engineering department after pleasant but unproductive visits with purchasing department personnel.

When the contradictions in the organization became apparent, General Manager Walter Walsh asked his operations manager to make a careful analysis of the situation. It showed that the components engineers were making more and more actual buying decisions, although they had no clearly defined authority to purchase. They were also providing special services—testing, collecting technical data, and making recommendations on design—yet they had no direct responsibility for cost reduction. Further, they were spending as much time with vendors as the buyers were, with the result that sales personnel were obligingly making two calls—one to the buyer and one to the engineer—and wasting everyone's time.

Walter decided that a revamping of the whole procurement operation was needed. He was able to get Sam Harmin, manager of materials of a recently acquired Jackson Corporation subsidiary, temporarily attached to his staff to undertake the job. Sam was a brilliant young executive with broad experience in manufacturing and cost accounting and a master's degree in business administration. He was considered one of the bright lights of the Jackson organization.

After a six-week study, Sam came up with a number of recommendations. The entire components engineering group should be moved into purchasing, because they are in effect already selecting vendors as well as specifying components. They should be called *procurement engineers,* or *materials engineers,* to indicate that they have buying authority as well as responsibility.

One of the present buyers (with the engineering degree) should be retained as a procurement engineer. One buyer should be given a special assignment as a packaging specialist, working with packaging vendors and with components suppliers on packaging of Jackson purchases. Two buyers should be assigned to buying other nontechnical, nonproduction items.

The four younger buyers should be grouped into an inventory-control buying group with responsibility for determining inventory levels and order quantities, handling all administrative details of ordering and expediting. He proposed renaming this group buyer-planners. They would report to the purchasing manager and on a dotted-line basis to the appropriate commodity buyer.

The trainees should be transferred to another department, preferably manufacturing. The clerical help should be absorbed elsewhere in the company.

He made no recommendation concerning Archer Dix.

QUESTIONS

1. Do Sam Harmin's recommendations offer a solution to the basic procurement problems of Jackson Corporation?
2. As manufactured products grow more complex, should there be a corresponding increase in the technical knowledge required of buyers?
3. Is there a risk of wasting or misapplying engineering talent by giving technically trained people buying responsibilities?
4. If you were Mr. Dix how would you reply to Mr. Harmin's proposal?

CHAPTER 7
RSX, INC.

In April 1990, Jack Daniel, vice-president of finance for RSX, Inc., headquartered in Los Angeles, was reviewing a proposal to restructure his purchasing organization. He was considering what action, if any, he should take on the proposal.

GENERAL COMPANY BACKGROUND

RSX was a high-tech research and policy corporation established in 1971 by two physicists who had left the Rand Corporation. Currently, major research emphasis was in the areas of high-pressure technology (HPT) and plasma physics. By 1989 sales had grown to $56 million, and purchases were approximately $12 million. There were six hundred employees.

The company's only customer was the Department of Defense (DOD). The annual report summarized its mission: "We conduct technical and military analyses to assess system feasibility and utility, and for specific systems, to develop and demonstrate prototype hardware." Accomplishing this mission required an environment that stressed independent and creative thinking.

Personnel were highly educated and included all major scientific and engineering disciplines. Of the technical staff 40 percent held doctoral, 30 percent master's, and 30 percent bachelor's degrees. The average professional on the staff had over twenty-two years of experience. A large number of the staff had retired from high-level government positions prior to working for RSX.

The overall organization was headed by Ed Diaz, a retired four-star general (see Exhibit 1). Prior to Diaz's leadership the company was run by its founders. During 1988 RSX was acquired by SOFCOM, a provider of electronic systems and high-technology services to the government, with sales of $200 million. Realizing RSX's "think-tank" nature, SOFCOM interfered very little in its operations.

THE PURCHASING ORGANIZATION

Prior to 1989 purchasing was centralized in Los Angeles. A corporate purchasing manager and a staff of senior buyers handled all purchases except for maintenance, repair, and operating supplies (MRO) as well as materials under $1,000.

In mid-1989 Washington Research Laboratory (WRL) was decentralized and allowed to purchase all its requirements. The major reasons for this change were the benefits of quicker response to scientists' needs and shorter lead times through use of local suppliers. Rita Young, purchasing and facilities manager at WRL, detailed the extent of such problems prior to decentralization in a report to corporate management.

> All capital-equipment purchasing is performed at the corporate level plus all contract-purchased items over $1,000. This centralized organization interferes with meeting our program goals. These goals require obtaining items such as camera systems, pumps, laboratory equipment, and office furniture on time. When purchasing highly technical equipment, I feel it necessary that we have control rather than communicating with an office 3,000 miles away. For example, in March 1988 we tried to set up an agreement with Cybernet Services. On March 19 we sent the requirements to Los Angeles purchasing for approval. Inquiries to Bob Kopper, director of purchasing, were met with promises that he would provide status reports. On April 30 Los Angeles decided they could not handle the contract, and it was turned over to WRL. It took Los Angeles a month to decide they would not handle the job. In another case WRL sent a requisition to the Los Angeles office for furniture in April 1984. The majority of desks, chairs, and file cabinets were not received until January 1988. The items received were of wrong color, incorrect style, and configuration. It took ten days and nine phone calls to the California supplier, the Los Angeles purchasing office, and the manufacturer's representative to clarify one part number for a desk.

Exhibit 1   Organization Chart for RSX, Inc.

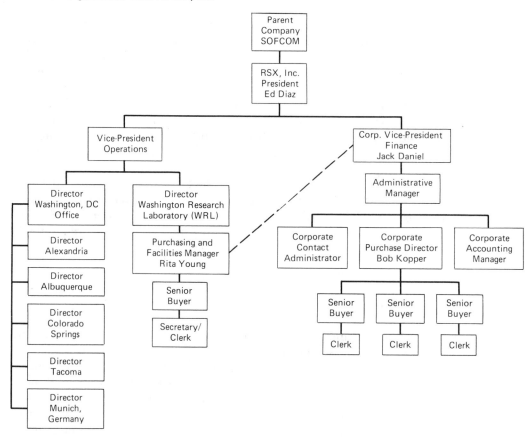

Owing to such examples, Mr. Daniel allowed Ms. Young to procure requirements for the WRL subject to a $10,000 limit of authority. Any orders over this amount would be approved by him. Despite this change, all non-MRO purchases at other company buying locations were handled from Los Angeles (for locations see Exhibit 1).

REGIONAL PURCHASING PROPOSAL

According to Ms. Young, since the decentralization in 1989 WRL had provided good service to its requisitioners, and there were no major supply problems. Inventory was also controlled, as purchases of materials and electronics components were targeted for six turns per year. During late 1989, funding cutbacks at DOD had reduced WRL's sales from $5 million in 1989 to a forecasted level of $2.5 million for 1990. Ms. Young felt this reduction would result in budget pressures for staff reductions. WRL's purchasing staff was mostly paid through direct expense, a charge generated from specific government contracts. Indirect expense was allocated from general corporate overhead. Ms. Young felt a regional buying approach would protect her department from the variations in contract levels by providing a larger portion of her budget from indirect overhead.

More important, she felt that purchasing efficiencies could be gained by including the Alexandria and Washington, D.C., offices under WRL. Efficiencies would result from increased buying volumes, improved supplier relations, and use of GSA price lists. "There are problems with suppliers at both these locations, since the clerks don't have professional buying expertise," she stated.

Mr. Daniel was also aware of a financial problem with increasing petty cash use at the Alexandria and Washington office locations. According to Ms. Young, the reason was that accounts payable problems forced many suppliers to stop doing business with the two East Coast offices. Currently, copies of the packing slip, purchase order, and invoice were sent to Los Angeles for payment. "I don't have problems with payment to my suppliers, since we keep our records in order and I travel to the West Coast once or twice a year to keep communications open," Rita stated.

In deciding on the regional buying proposal, Mr. Daniel needed to address the various benefits and drawbacks. Secondly, would it solve the petty cash problem; and third, what impact would it have on the corporate purchasing staff, who still had strained relations with Ms. Young over the recent decentralization? He wanted to resolve the issue before Rita Young's forthcoming May visit.

QUESTIONS

1. How do purchasing objectives differ in a Research & Development (R&D) environment from a production environment?
2. As Mr. Daniel, what factors would you consider in deciding on the type of purchasing structure at RSX, Inc.?
3. What form of purchasing structure should Mr. Daniel adopt for RSX, Inc.?

This case was written by Larry C. Giunipero during the Case Writing in Purchasing Workshop. Copyright © 1987 by the National Association of Purchasing Management. Reprinted by permission.

CHAPTER 8
PLACIDO ENGINE COMPANY

It was four o'clock on Friday, October 12, 1989, and Ronald Penson, senior buyer-castings, for the Placido Engine Company of Detroit, Michigan, had just finished a telephone conversation with an upset supplier. It was the fourth such call Ronald had received in response to a letter he had sent to his magnesium-castings suppliers concerning a severe corrosion problem. All four had told Ronald that they could not adhere to his request without a significant increase in their costs.

THE COMPANY

The Placido Engine Company was a division of the General Products Corporation, a $2 billion company that enjoyed a worldwide reputation for quality and leadership in aviation, aerospace, and industrial products. In its nearly four decades of operations, Placido had built more than forty-five thousand gas engines for a wide variety of commercial, industrial, and military applications. While the most significant part of Placido's sales was in the commercial and general aviation markets, the company was attempting to move toward a balance between commercial and military sales.

THE EXECUTIVE CORROSION TASK FORCE

During the summer of 1989 Placido started receiving complaints from their customers concerning corroded gear boxes on engines. The problem was significant and serious enough to warrant the attention of Fred Thompson, senior vice-president of the company. In order to resolve this problem and find a permanent solution, Fred created an executive corrosion task force. This task force immediately solicited inputs from purchasing, quality assurance, manufacturing, engineering, production control, materials, and the Magnesium Corrosion Task Circle[1] for suggested solutions to the corrosion problem as well as recommendations for implementing suggested programs. The Executive Corrosion Task Force was under extreme pressure from Fred Thompson to take immediate steps to resolve the corrosion problem.

THE CORROSION PROBLEM

Upon investigation, it was determined that a large part of the corrosion problem was in the Turbo 110 engine and its magnesium castings. It was also found that a significant proportion of these castings were already corroded upon receipt from Placido's suppliers. However, instead of rejecting these castings, quality assurance was processing them through for rework. The basis for this action was the need for parts to meet production schedules. It was believed that the delay encountered by rejecting unacceptable castings would be more costly than the cost of reworking them internally.

The task force decided that this process of reworking unacceptable castings was no longer desirable and directed the purchasing department to take immediate steps to ensure that corrosion-free magnesium castings were received by Placido. As a first step in this direction, the purchasing department was further instructed to notify its castings suppliers that strict adherence to the previously issued Mil Spec-M-3171 and the cleaning and corrosion prevention procedure

---

[1]The Magnesium Corrosion Task Circle was established in 1986 to deal with the general problem of magnesium corrosion. It was part of Placido's reliability circles program.

prescribed by Placido would now be required. Failure to meet these specifications would result in rejection of unacceptable castings, or in cases where Placido elected to reprocess unacceptable castings in lieu of rejection, the supplier would be debited for the cost of the reprocessing work involved.

The responsibility for notifying the castings suppliers of this decision fell to Ronald Penson, who was the senior buyer for castings for Placido. Given the urgency of the situation and the political sensitivity of the issue, Ronald thought it best to send a letter to his current magnesium-castings suppliers immediately (see Exhibit 1).

Exhibit 1 Letter Sent to Castings Suppliers Concerning Corrosion-Free Castings

An intense corrosion-prevention program for magnesium castings has recently been undertaken at Placido Engine Company. An integral part of this program is the assurance that castings are corrosion-free upon receipt of shipment from our suppliers. Your strict adherence to Mil-M-3171 and the following is requested:

CLEAN & CORROSION-PREVENTION PROCEDURES PER MIL-M-3171 AND AS FOLLOWS:

- After penetrative inspection, following heat treat, castings will be alkaline cleaned and hydrofluoric acid pickled.
- After hydrofluoric acid pickle, castings to chrome pickle treatment, rinse and bake to dry at $250°$ F $+ 25°$ F.
- Dip castings in 7220 rust oil B and package for shipment.
- Package to ensure castings do not come into contact with each other, subsequently rubbing away protection.

The responsibility to deliver corrosion-free magnesium castings per casting drawing, engineering blueprint, or M.O.T. is placed with you, the supplier. Failure to do so necessitates an immediate rework at Placido to stop the corrosion process that may ultimately scrap parts. The cost incurred for the rework will be passed on to you in the form of a debit initiated by an Inspection Transfer Report (I.T.R.). The I.T.R. will also have a negative effect on your quality rating.

Your support in this effort is imperative. Please forward the aforementioned procedure to the appropriate personnel in your company.

Direct any questions regarding processing to Robert Dear, Quality Assurance Engineer, (405) 876-1241.

Thank you.

Ronald Penson
Senior Buyer

RP:rr

cc: Executive Corrosion Task Force members

NEGATIVE REACTIONS FROM SUPPLIERS

Ronald was not prepared for the quick—and negative—responses he received from his suppliers. The general sense of the comments was that they were already properly treating the castings to prevent corrosion and disagreed with the procedure Placido was requiring. Furthermore, they all told Ronald that if they were required to follow the procedure prescribed by Placido, it would be necessary for them to expend considerable amounts of time to retool their current processes and to purchase new equipment. These actions would result in substantially higher costs in producing the castings, which would be passed on to Placido.

Ronald was now facing a serious dilemma and was not sure what to do. One thing was certain. He had to act quickly, as Fred Thompson was demanding an immediate solution to the corrosion problem.

QUESTIONS

1. What is the immediate issue facing Ronald Penson?
2. What would you recommend Penson do to deal effectively with this situation?

This case was written by Michael Kolchin during the Case Writing in Purchasing Workshop. Copyright © 1984 by the National Association of Purchasing Management. Reprinted with permission.

CHAPTER 8
TEMPLE DRUG COMPANY

Temple Drug Company is a relatively small manufacturer of a number of proprietary items that enjoy good reputations. Temple Toothpaste, for example, has had good sales for many years at a premium price. Much of its success has been due to a distinctive flavor that appeals to many people and to an aggressive merchandising campaign among dentists.

About two years ago, the purchasing manager, Arthur Kaplan, had worked out a highly successful program for improving the quality performance of suppliers of packaging materials. The Temple Company buys several hundred different packaging items, including over a dozen varieties of collapsible tubes for its toothpaste and other extrudable products. The production department had complained that it was having trouble with various shipments of tubes: off sizes would cause machinery breakdowns, spillage, and general disruption on the packaging line. There were also other complaints of faulty packaging, but the problem of the tubes was the most troublesome one. Arthur decided that a complete review of the company's procurement and use of packaging materials was needed.

He sought the cooperation of the company's development section, representatives from the production department, and quality-control engineers. Together they reviewed the company's packaging requirements, its packaging specifications, and the performance of packaging suppliers. At Arthur's suggestion, they invited supplier representatives to a number of their meetings and frankly discussed their problems with them. Several of the committee members just as frankly expressed their suspicions that the suppliers were completely at fault for the quality problems that the company was facing.

Ultimately the facts came to light and, as usual, indicated that blame for poor-quality performance could be shared by both sides. In its growth from a two-person manufacturing operation in one corner of a warehouse to a good-sized manufacturing company, the Temple Company had been satisfied with an informal approach to a number of functions. Its packaging department, for example, was a relatively recent development. Over the years the company had relied on suppliers' suggestions and drawings in buying its packaging materials instead of developing its own.

In the case of collapsible tubes existing suppliers had changed manufacturing methods, and new suppliers had taken their own approach to design. As a result, little "gimmicks" or variations in size or shape had gradually crept into the designs of the tubes. Instead of buying a standard tube from a number of suppliers, the company was in effect purchasing a large number of specials. Eventually these variations began causing trouble on the highly automated packaging line, which requires a high degree of standardization.

With the help of its suppliers the company's package development group worked out a program for supplying its own drawings and setting acceptable quality levels for all major items. An interesting phase of the cooperative effort between buyer and suppliers was the program of reciprocal visits to permit representatives from the Temple Company and its packaging suppliers to see each other's manufacturing plants in operation. In one of the first visits arranged under the plan the production manager of a bottle manufacturer was able to suggest a change that immediately cleared up a problem on the Temple Company bottling line.

A year later Arthur decided to try a slightly different approach to the problem posed by the rising number of complaints from the processing department about the quality of raw materials. He thought he would do some of the basic research himself in advance rather than take the valuable time of a whole group of executives. He began by calling in vendors, discussing complaints about the quality of their products, and asking their advice. Several of the suppliers indicated that the problems were caused by the casual approach taken to specifications by Temple Company operating and procurement personnel. They pointed out that the company assumed too much knowledge on their part as to what was required and that specifications were often vague or incomplete. As a result, the suppliers would occasionally take advantage (consciously or unconsciously) of the general specifications to ship off-quality material.

On the basis of his own findings, and the comments and recommendations of major raw-materials vendors, Arthur drew up a memorandum to Fred Schulte, superintendent of the processing plant, and Morton Dunn, the chief chemist. In it he suggested that his chemical buyer, a chemical engineer, be named coordinator of a program to review and organize the company's raw-materials specifications. The buyer could work with the laboratory and the using departments as well as with suppliers in this project. As a start he suggested taking USP

(United States Pharmacopeia) minimum requirements as the basic Temple Company specifications.

"Up to now," he wrote, "different suppliers have practically been using the trial-and-error method to meet our requirements. I think we'll all agree that it's time to change this situation." He asked Fred and Morton to call him.

Instead of a call, he received an answering memorandum from Morton the following day, indicating that a carbon copy had also gone to the president, Michael Baker. In summary, it read:

> Any program of this type will only lead to further deterioration of quality. Vendors will try to get us to lower our standards, so that they can sell us standard or lower-quality items that they are making in volume for other suppliers, at greater profit to themselves. We must force them to meet our specifications, or we run grave danger of losing the small but loyal market for such products as our toothpaste, one of the big features of which is its distinctive flavor.
>
> USP standards are inadequate for us, as they specify chemical purity. We make no compromise with purity, of course, but we do have special processes and special ingredients that differentiate our products from others—in color, taste, and texture. I believe we need more crackdowns and less cooperation with suppliers in this matter.

A short while later Arthur had a call from the president asking him to come into his office to discuss the situation.

QUESTIONS

1. Assess Arthur Kaplan's handling of the raw-materials quality problem. Was his failure to get immediate cooperation from Morton Dunn the result of a fundamental mistake on his part, or was it merely a matter of timing and handling?
2. Outline an approach that might have produced a more favorable reaction from Morton.
3. If Arthur's plan is essentially sound, how should he attempt to salvage it and get Michael Baker's support for it?

CHAPTER 9
TEMPLETON ENGINE COMPANY

The Templeton Engine Company, located in eastern Wisconsin, was a major producer of aircraft jet engines. On December 15, Dave Giltner, sales manager for precision cutting tools, called Neil Carlson, a purchasing supervisor for Templeton, to tell him that Precision planned to increase its prices 6 percent across the board on February 15. When he replaced the telephone, Neil wondered how to respond to this news in view of Templeton's plan to reemphasize its cost reduction program in January.

THE COMPANY

The Templeton Engine Company produced turbojet and turboprop engines for use on small and medium-sized jet aircraft. It did not compete in the commercial jet engine market, although it did produce smaller engines used to power auxiliary equipment on commercial airliners. Templeton's sales totaled approximately one billion dollars per year, divided roughly 80-20 among private and governmental purchasers. The firm employed 6,200 people, including approximately 50 professionals in the purchasing department. Because of the technical character of its products, over the years the company had developed a strong engineering orientation which pervaded all aspects of its operations.

PURCHASING ACTIVITIES

Templeton spent approximately $600 million a year for materials, most of which were used in producing its finished products. All buying activities were based on material specifications generated in the firm's various design engineering departments. As a general rule, technical factors were the controlling considerations in specification development.

When considering potential new suppliers for major purchases, the purchasing department coordinated an extremely thorough investigation of the operations and capabilities of each firm reviewed. In addition to an investigation of the normal commercial and service considerations, personnel from Templeton's quality-assurance and manufacturing engineering departments carefully analyzed each vendor's production and quality-control operations. The objective was to evaluate both effectiveness and efficiency, as well as compatibility with Templeton's requirements. After selection, when a supplier proved its ability to meet the buyer's requirements consistently, Templeton frequently utilized a vendor certification program that allowed the supplier to perform a great deal of its own part inspection and acceptance.

Templeton's buyers used both competitive bidding and negotiation techniques in determining price, depending on the prevailing buying and market conditions. Since some of Templeton's products were sold to federal agencies, buyers had to follow government regulation, which stipulated the use of competitive bidding and negotiation and set the guidelines for their use. The Defense Contract Audit Agency periodically audits such purchases to ensure compliance. Once a vendor is selected, however, buyers frequently negotiate numerous contract details and service arrangements with the vendor.

An additional complication faced by some buyers stemmed from a Federal Aviation Agency (FAA) requirement. Each of Templeton's products and related components produced by specific suppliers had to be tested and certified initially by the FAA. Whenever a new supplier for such a part was used, Templeton was required to subject the new item to a rigorous and costly 150-hour operating test. Hence, buyers did not change suppliers without considerable analysis and effort to rectify problems with existing suppliers.

Like many major firms, over the years Templeton's purchasing philosophy evolved to view suppliers as partners that, in reality, functioned as extensions of its own production operations. Thus, while buyers evaluated a supplier's performance rigorously, they worked closely with the supplier to optimize the benefit of the relationship for both organizations. When it was advantageous, buyers liked to utilize long-term contracts—often up to three years in duration—to assure compliance with quality and pricing objectives. As a rule, Templeton's buyers had responsibility for the full range of activities involved in their respective transactions—everything from market research to expediting.

COST AND QUALITY

For obvious reasons quality requirements in the jet engine industry were stringent and extremely important. No producer of shoddy work survived for long. At the same time, however, competition among major producers had become increasingly intense. Consequently, the incentives to keep costs down were substantial. For this reason, buyers at Templeton diligently sought out potential opportunities to reduce material costs without jeopardizing quality. The company, in fact, was currently in the process of reemphasizing its corporatewide cost reduction program.

THE PURCHASE OF TOOLING

The Templeton manufacturing organization used approximately one-million dollars worth of tooling each year. Because of the tight tolerances required in the manufacturing process, tooling that performed with precision and reliability was essential.

The special tooling supplied by Precision Cutting Tools was a major dollar item for Templeton. In addition, after extensive testing Templeton's design engineers specified the Precision organization as a sole-source supplier.

As Neil Carlson pondered the pending 6 percent price increase on Precision's special tooling, he was acutely aware that he had less than sixty days to resolve the problem.

QUESTIONS

1. What alternatives does Neil have in responding to the price increase announced by Precision?
2. What constraints does he face in choosing the most appropriate course of action?

This case was written by Donald Dobler during the Case Writing in Purchasing Workshop. Copyright © 1984 by the National Association of Purchasing Management. Reprinted with permission.

CHAPTER 9
DIJON, INC.

Dijon, Inc., makers of engineering and drafting supplies, a family-owned company for more than ninety years, was bought out by Lizco Corporation, office-equipment manufacturers. Lizco gradually placed a new management team in the acquisition, including Horace D. Kombit as purchasing manager. Kombit had had a good record as a senior buyer in one of Lizco's larger divisions.

One of Kombit's first moves was to undertake a review of Dijon's relationships with its major suppliers—who they were, what they supplied and in what volume, and how they were performing. What he found in his first look at the records was interesting but hardly helpful. Many of the suppliers, he noted, were like Dijon—old, established companies with a reputation for fair dealing. They appeared to have had comfortable relationships with Dijon, some of them for a considerable time. He found few comparative data, however, on these suppliers' quality, price, or service performance. And preliminary inquiries among using department heads produced not much more than agreement that "they've done pretty well by us."

Kombit concluded that a lot more in-depth research was needed—both of Dijon's records and suppliers' records. He gave the assignment to Tim Shenko, a buyer he had brought with him to the new job. He instructed Shenko as follows:

- Collect as much hard data as possible on each major supplier's overall performance in the past three to five years.
- Compare each supplier's prices for a representative group of items with those of competitors.
- Visit each supplier's plant (with a company engineer when appropriate) and check equipment and facilities as they relate to Dijon's requirements.
- Consult with each supplier's top management and key personnel to determine how well they understand Dijon specifications and the need to adhere strictly to them.
- Evaluate the supplier's management team and financial condition.
- Determine how much business Dijon is placing with the supplier and what percentage of the supplier's total sales that business represents.
- Draw up a report on each supplier, giving your opinion and recommendations relative to the suitability of the company as a major, long-range supplier to Dijon.

Shenko's first report, on the Saltzman Company, contained the following information:

The company is family owned and has been in business since 1927. The president, Leon Saltzman, who inherited the company from his father, has two sons, one of whom is a physician. The other is a professional musician. Leon Saltzman appears to be in good health and in complete charge of operations.

Most of the twenty-three nonunion employees have been with the company for several years—and the three top supervisors for an average of twenty years. A Dun & Bradstreet credit report indicates that the company is in sound financial condition.

Saltzman has been competitive on most prices over the past five years and has a generally good reputation among Dijon's shop personnel for quality and delivery. They report occasional late deliveries that "caused no harm." A severe problem arose about four years ago when delivery on a critical item was held up for more than a week, causing a Dijon customer to cancel a substantial order in turn. In that case Saltzman had difficulty in getting parts for an older machine that had broken down.

Saltzman's production equipment has been in operation, on the average, for ten to fifteen years, and three of their fifteen units are less than five years old. All machines appear to be in good condition, and plant maintenance and housekeeping are good. Packaging and shipping facilities are excellent.

The products supplied by Saltzman represent about 90 percent of Dijon's requirements and approximately 25 percent of Dijon's total annual purchases. The Dijon purchases account for about 80 percent of Saltzman's sales.

QUESTION

1. Assume that you are Tim Shenko. Prepare a report on Saltzman as requested by Horace Kombit, explaining fully the reasoning behind your opinions and recommendations.

CHAPTER 10
RIPLEY ENGINE COMPANY

In early 1990 Tom Kemp, procurement specialist for R&D at Ripley Engine Company, Birmingham, Alabama, and a three-man team were responsible for recommending which potential suppliers should receive a request for proposal (RFP) for an important new component for small turbine aircraft engines. One of the four potential suppliers in the market, Aerolog, Inc., had been disqualified as a supplier to Ripley in early 1988. Tom wondered whether to include Aerolog, Inc., on the RFP list.

RIPLEY ENGINE COMPANY

In its nearly four decades of operation, Ripley had built more than forty-five thousand turbine engines for a wide variety of commercial, industrial, and military applications. Annual sales in 1989 were about $1 billion. Major product lines included aircraft propulsion systems, compact and powerful gas turbines for power generation systems, and larger, more-rugged turbine systems for high-precision industrial applications. Noted for its research and development and innovation, Ripley led the very profitable market for small gas turbines. The company had a reputation for high quality and had always leaned on its suppliers for both quality products and on-time deliveries. The product lines all had worldwide applications in existing markets. Major customers looked to Ripley for research and development activities to improve overall operations.

In the mid 1980s, Ripley initiated actions to miniaturize the fabricated metallic components of certain engines to reduce both their weight and size. Several of these special efforts had progressed to the design and procurement phase.

PROCUREMENT AT RIPLEY

Procurement operations for turbo machinery projects were divided into four major activities under the management of David Nelson (see Exhibit 1).

Procurement to support research and development projects was accomplished by eight procurement specialists under the supervision of Joseph Moncreif. Typically, this work to support R&D was completed in very close coordination with the engineers and quality-control personnel responsible for the research project. Indeed, for major projects, a two-step supplier-selection process was used. Step one involved selecting potential suppliers to receive the RFP, while step two involved evaluating the supplier proposals actually received.

The two-step process was completed by a team of specialists representing engineering, procurement, and quality assurance. The procurement specialist was usually the team leader.

Exhibit 1   Organizational Chart for the Ripley Engine Company

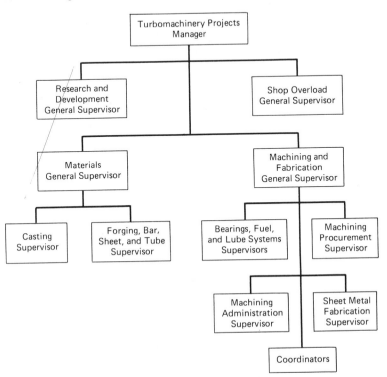

In early 1990 a vendor-selection team was appointed to select suppliers for a RFP for a highly complex fabricated metal component for small turbine engines for the aircraft market. The team was headed by Tom Kemp of R&D procurement. The other members of the team were two engineers and a representative from quality control. The members of the team brought this expertise to the task:

Tom Kemp, team leader, had been with the company about two years. He graduated from Whittier College in 1975 with a major in physics. After college, he worked two years with the committee to reelect President Ford and then was a lobbyist in Washington, D.C. A contact with business led to a major job in purchasing with a California firm. In 1988 he moved to the Ripley Company in Birmingham, Alabama.

George Smith, the senior engineer on the team, had been with the company for fifteen years. He was a highly respected R&D engineer. He held an undergraduate degree from MIT and had done graduate work at Cal Tech.

Fred Brown, the other engineer, had been with the company about ten years. He held an engineering degree from Purdue University and had been an R&D engineer at Ripley since leaving college.

Paul Logan, quality-control, had been with the company about four years. He was a quality-control engineer by training with an M.B.A. from Case Western University. Paul had a reputation for being a very tough man when quality was in question.

PROCEDURES FOR SELECTING SUPPLIERS FOR THE RFP

Typically, the RFP team responsibilities included:

1. Identifying all potential suppliers.
2. Developing a detailed analysis of each potential supplier.
3. Recommending the potential list of suppliers to a corporate-level review board, consisting of the vice-president of engineering, the director of purchasing, and the program manager. The board decided which firms were to be on the RFP list.
4. Conducting the analysis of the proposals actually received from the firms on the RFP list.
5. Recommending a firm for contract negotiations.

COMPLEX METAL FABRICATION INDUSTRY

The team discovered rather quickly and somewhat to their surprise that the industry capable of supplying the needed fabricated metal components consisted of only four firms. Their initial research uncovered the fact that one of these four firms, Aerolog, Inc., had been disqualified three years earlier as a supplier to Ripley for both quality and delivery problems. The Aerolog incident had required extensive litigation in 1987–88. Aerolog had a bad reputation with the old timers at Ripley.

The team listed these facts about the firms:

1. Aerolog appeared to be fully qualified as a bidder based upon the criteria developed for technology, plant capacity, utilization rates, managerial team, and finances.
2. Two other firms, Reck Aerospace and Crum Aerospace, also appeared to be fully qualified.
3. The fourth firm, Northeast Machine Works, was questionable from the context of plant capacity and utilization rates. The firm appeared to have a superior managerial team.
4. Many senior managers, engineers, and others were strongly opposed to considering Aerolog for anything at Ripley.
5. Word that Aerolog might get its foot back in the door spread throughout R&D, engineering, marketing, and quality control like a prairie fire.
6. Phone calls and comments to the team all seemed to say "not again," or more specifically, "You will be sorry you did that!" and "It's been nice knowing you."
7. See Exhibit 2 for comparative data on the suppliers developed by the team.

Exhibit 2   Comparative Data on Potential Suppliers

	Aerolog, Inc.	Reck Aerospace	Crum Aerospace	Northeast Machine Works
Technology (scale 1 to 50)[a]	48	47	49	46
Capacity				
Sufficient	Yes	Yes	Yes	Yes
Utilization rate	80%	82%	79%	90%
Financial status				
Current ratio	2.36	2.22	2.02	2.56
Quick ratio	1.35	1.10	.93	1.50
Debt to equity	.75	.73	.76	.76
Sales—1989	$41,759.9	$18,653.0	$9,653.4	$7,543.8
Sales growth over past year	10%	9.8%	11%	3%
Cost of goods sold	89.6%	88.7%	90.3%	89.3%
Change from last year	−3%	−.5%	+2%	+3.5%
Managerial team (scale 1 to 10)	9.4	9.2	9.1	9.6
Quality reputation[b]				
Long term (scale 1 to 10)	5	9	8.5	9.3
Last two years	9.5	9	8.7	9.4

[a]All scales are based on big being best.

[b]Based on information collected from other customers.

As Tom and the team met early on July 21, 1990, they knew they had to bite the bullet on this issue. Should Aerolog be included on the list for the RFP? Their list and analysis was to be presented to the corporate review board at 9:00 A.M. on July 23, 1990.

QUESTIONS

1. Based on the vendor-selection team's analysis of the four (4) possible suppliers' capabilities, how would you rank each of the four suppliers?
2. Should Aerolog be included on the RFP list?

This case was written by Robert A. Kemp during the Case Writing in Purchasing Workshop. Copyright © 1984 by the National Association of Purchasing Management. Reprinted with permission.

CHAPTER 11
TRUETEST, INC.

Truetest, Inc., a manufacturer of sophisticated testing equipment, was founded in the mid-1970s by five former employees of a much larger California company that made similar products. The Truetest owners—two engineers, two marketing executives, and a production manager—established their business in Texas, where they felt that the oil, aircraft, and space industries as well as industry in general presented them with an unusual opportunity to prosper and grow.

They were correct, and business moved ahead smartly in their first few years. But along with increased sales came increased difficulties, in the form of service and quality problems with the suppliers of precision parts—particularly precision castings, which Truetest bought by the thousands. Parts suppliers in the area, most of them relatively new enterprises set up from five to ten years before Truetest, were hard put to keep up with demand in the rapidly expanding economy of the Southwest. They tended to favor their well-established customers in regard to service and technical assistance. Because of the critical nature and high prices of the parts that Truetest bought, Tom Whitnow, the owner, who had overall supervision of manufacturing and purchasing, was uneasy over the relative indifference of local suppliers to quality problems that seemed to be arising more frequently.

Whitnow decided to discuss the situation with Mike Baumrose, whom the owners had hired away from the California company (where he had been a senior buyer) to become Truetest's purchasing manager. In the discussion Whitnow stressed the need for the company to develop more and better sources. Baumrose said that he had been in contact with a number of suppliers in other parts of the country but had not gotten much satisfaction. Prices were generally higher than what Truetest was paying, shipping costs could be considerable, and there was a surprising lack of interest in taking on a new accounts.

"I don't think we should stop there," he told Whitnow. "As soon as I get my desk cleared of some of this detail, I'm going to try to get a line on some foreign suppliers. I've heard that a representative of several Yugoslavian companies, including a couple that make the kinds of parts we need, has been very actively looking for business in this area. And he's apparently getting it. I thought I might call him in and talk with him."

Whitnow's eyes popped a bit. "Yugoslavia?" he said skeptically. "That's kind of way out, isn't it? I mean the idea of buying from some company we have never heard of—and a Communist one at that. Do they really know anything about precision casting, for example? What would some of our customers around here think about our buying components in a place like Yugoslavia? And how would we pay people like that—in rubles or something?"

"Whoa," said Baumrose, "I haven't decided to buy anything. I just want to know how you feel about looking into the matter of buying overseas. We're actually in the middle of a world market, and we should be seeing what it has to offer us. In fact, we may be trying to *sell* in some of these countries before long if we keep growing the way we have up to now."

"Okay," said Whitnow, who was a responsible, astute businessperson despite his blustery manner. "Talk to the guy if you can locate him. But don't even hint at committing us to anything. Meanwhile, I'll discuss the idea with the others at our management meeting on Monday."

Baumrose called in the Yugoslav representative, Peter Pavelic, discussed Truetest's requirements with him in a general way, and asked for sales literature and some particulars on the two companies that Pavelic represented—Bosniatec and Kosovo Specialties. Baumrose was impressed by the sales literature and their list of European customers—including Saab of Sweden and Rolls-Royce of England.

Their discussion on prices was inconclusive; Pavelic was reluctant to be specific about them until sample parts could be sent back to Yugoslavia for study. He was most emphatic, however, that the companies that he represented could not only meet U.S. prices for many parts but could also come in lower on some.

Baumrose declined to give him any sample parts, thanked him for the information he provided, and said he would get back to him after discussing their conversation with Truetest's top management some time during the next few weeks.

A couple of days later, Whitnow met Baumrose in the hallway and said, "The other fellows showed some interest in the idea of buying overseas. They'd like you to fill them in on things, including your talk with that guy from Yugoslavia. We'd like to get together with you in a day or two and get the whole picture. Can you meet with us in the conference room at 10:30 on Friday?"

Although he hadn't expected to be asked to report so soon, Baumrose agreed to be there. His interview with Pavelic had further stimulated his interest in the possible use of foreign sources, and he had intended to do a more extended study of the subject. He felt, however, that he should not muff the present opportunity to (1) let the owners know he was actively trying to help solve one of their pressing problems and (2) provide them with information that they would need to judge—if not make decisions on—various aspects of buying internationally, as it applied to Truetest.

QUESTIONS

1. Presumably, Baumrose would have about ten or fifteen minutes to give an informal report of the type he had presented on similar occasions. If you were in his position, what points would you cover?
2. Which, if any, would you treat more extensively than the others?
3. Describe how you would go about getting pertinent information in the limited time available to you.
4. What suggestions or recommendations would you make to the owners at this time?

CHAPTER 11
THE CANADIAN OFFSET

On March 13, 1987, Peter Bennett, vice-president/procurement for the Government Products Group of MegaSystems, International, of Columbus, Ohio, discovered that a major error had been made in a report to top executives of MegaSystems regarding a large international contract. Bennett pondered his next step.

MEGASYSTEMS GENERAL BACKGROUND

MegaSystems, International, had recently been formed by the merger of two large computer and electronic corporations. Staff reorganization was not complete, nor were new communications channels firmly established among the five new product groups (see Exhibit 1). Although the groups were autonomous, coordination of overall business was the responsibility of a corporate staff headed by the president, chief financial officer, and the vice-chairman. This group, known as the unholy triumvirate, had a reputation among MegaSystems management for rapid, decisive, and drastic action.

The four commercial groups were organized along their product lines. However, because of the dynamic nature of business in the Government Products Group (GPG), program management offices were established, each reporting to a Systems Division (see Exhibit 2). Bennett recognized that each of the Aero Space Division program managers had dual reporting responsibility to both division and group executives.

THE CANADIAN CONTRACT

GPG established a program management office in 1983 in Hamilton, Ontario, to coordinate a $950 million MegaSystems subcontract with a Canadian partner and the Canadian government. Aerospace Division would deliver complex electronics packages for integration by the Canadian partner into an advanced aircraft. By the time the contract ended in 1992, MegaSystems had to spend an amount equal

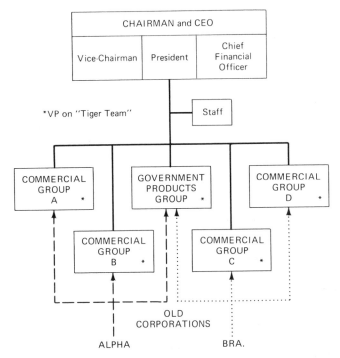

Exhibit 1 Organization Chart for MegaSystems, International

to contract value in Canada. To ensure that this offset industrial benefits program was met, the Canadian Government insisted upon a penalty matrix (see Exhibit 3) in the contract. If spending goals in any cell of this matrix was missed, additive penalties could cost MegaSystems up to 25 percent of contract value.

On February 27, 1987, the MegaSystems president visited the Hamilton office. He discovered that projected shortfalls in the offset program by 1992

Exhibit 2 Organization Chart for Government Products Group

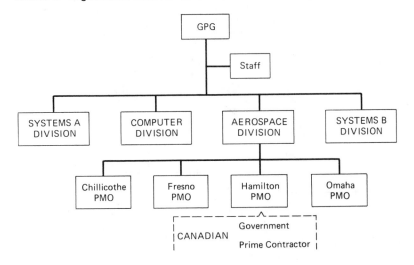

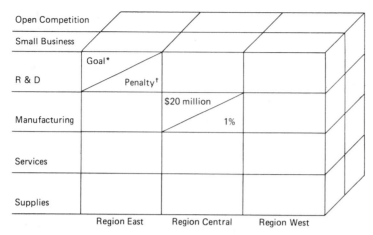

Exhibit 3 Framework of Goal/Penalty Matrix for Industrial Benefits

*Each cell has a goal assignment.

†Failure to meet the specific cell goal will incur a percentage penalty even if overall goals (region, type, etc.) are met.

would cost MegaSystems $71 million in penalties. Further, a sole-source follow-on procurement of $1.2 billion was to be held by Canada until the industrial benefits projections were met. He immediately formed a "tiger team" of VPs from each group to resolve the problem. A deadline of three weeks was imposed. Bennett, as the GPG representative, was given primary responsibility.

Exhibit 4 Offset Industrial Benefits

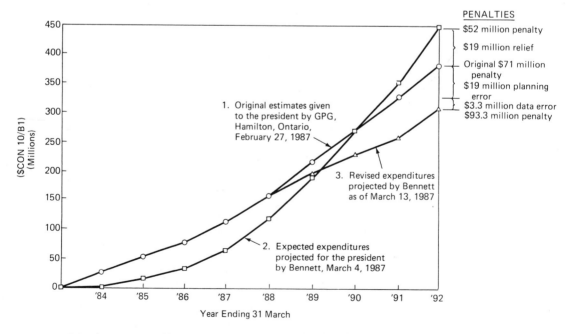

On March 4, Bennett checked data in the Hamilton office. He noted that a cost overrun of $100 million on the contract would provide a penalty relief of $19 million. This was reported to the president, who passed the news to the Canadian government. As Bennett checked the data on the final report on March 13, he found that the $71 million was actually $74.3 million. Further, the $19 million relief had already been credited before the $71 million figure was computed. The real penalty shortfall was thus $93.3 million (see Exhibit 4).

After receiving the initial report, the president had assured the government that the solution was already well underway. Bennett knew that a meeting with the Canadians was scheduled for early the following week. He also knew that the president didn't like unpleasant surprises and that the head of the "tiger team" had reminded him, "This is a GPG problem." Bennett had only a short time to decide upon his course of action.

QUESTIONS

1. What alternatives could you suggest to help Peter Bennett reach his offset goal?
2. Write a detailed plan to Mr. Bennett listing your specific plan of action.

This case was written by Clarence M. DeYoung during the Case Writing in Purchasing Workshop held at George Washington University. Copyright © 1987 by the National Association of Purchasing Management. Reprinted by permission.

CHAPTER 12
STICKNEY CORPORATION

Dave Peters, manager of purchasing for Stickney Corporation, faces a dilemma regarding quality standards for trueing wheels that are sourced and which are critical to production needs. Constraints dictated by management require "keeping the line running" to ensure timely delivery of products to their customers. Stickney Corporation, a subsidiary of Auto Corporation with headquarters in Hartford, Connecticut, is an established component supplier to the automotive industry. Recent consolidation of Stickney operations has included relocating production and administrative offices from Illinois and Indiana to Macon, Georgia. The firm employs approximately 225 people at the new facility.

Stickney Corporation is recognized as the world's leading supplier of slipper tappets. Tappets are part of hydraulic lifter assemblies used in automobile engines. They consist of seven parts. Management strategy calls for penetration into related automotive markets utilizing the techniques of their past success, namely, innovative technological applications, flexibility to meet customer demand, and stringent quality standards in all facets of production.

Production capacity at the Macon facility for slipper tappets is 100,000 per day utilizing a three-shift operation. Stickney's major customer for slipper tappets is one of the largest auto producers, who take an average of 40,000 per week. Organizational structure at Stickney includes a purchasing department responsible for procuring all production and administrative needs. As the manager of purchasing, Dave Peters is responsible for the timely procurement of raw materials (castings and spring wire), component parts, and MRO items (maintenance repair and operating). Peters starts each day meeting with people from various functional areas of the company. These meetings include the production supervisor and inventory-control personnel. During the meeting Peters is informed of quality problems on the production line and various other urgent situations. Any "hot" items are acted on immediately to ensure that problems are resolved as quickly as possible. An MRP system is used at Stickney to provide a daily reorder report to Peters.

Peters currently utilizes local sources for 25 to 30 percent of Stickney's purchases. When feasible, multiple sourcing is the preferred method of purchasing. In addition, a small percentage of materials are sole sourced. Quality concerns are handled by the quality standards department at Stickney. The quality manager at Stickney is currently working on a vendor certification program. Incoming inspection for defects is the quality method employed now. A major problem for Stickney is delivery of consistent, high-quality, defect-free components from vendors. Because of management's concern for resolving quality problems, the purchasing department's guidelines states evaluations should be based on the lowest total cost. All relevant factors are taken into account when awarding a contract, which ensures that the problems associated with "low price only" are avoided. For example, one key factor in awarding contracts is the ability of suppliers to work within Stickney's lead-time constraints. Raw-material lead times can be as long as twenty-two weeks, and component lead times as long as thirteen weeks. Inventory for critical "A" customers is held on a one-month level. Other customer's materials are held for a ten-day period.

For several years Stickney has purchased a diamond trueing wheel from the Allen Grinding Company at a unit cost of approximately $100. Trueing wheels are used to clean slipper tappets. After each tappet operation a separate tool clears any cuttings away. This deburring tool is in turn cleaned by a trueing wheel. Thirty-two machines depend on the proper operation of this wheel. Each tappet is processed through one of these machines.

A supervisor has approached Peters and informed him that the last few orders of trueing wheels were not performing as well as previous lots. The wheels are lasting half as long as they should and are creating geometric problems with the tappets. They are also visibly different from previous shipments received. The wheels can be used, but because of the problems, the reject rate has increased, resulting in decreased production of tappets owing to rework time.

When Peters contacted the Allen Company, he was told that the wheel was now being manufactured at a new location. Further, the production process had been changed. Allen was the sole source for trueing wheels. Until the past few shipments the production supervisor had been quite pleased with Allen's wheels. If the problem continued, however, it could jeopardize Stickney's quality reputation.

QUESTIONS

    1. What are some of the alternatives Dave Peters needs to consider?
    2. What is the effect of poor quality of indirect materials such as trueing wheels on finished product?
    3. What is the best way to specify quality for trueing the wheels?

This case was prepared with the assistance of Dave Peters, Dave Mrus, Curtis Dawkins, and Teresa Moss.

CHAPTER 12
JOSEPH'S COLORANTS, INC.

Polysil represents a substantial part of the end product cost of an item made by Joseph's Colorants, Inc., and sold to the tobacco, packaging, and toy industries. Polysil is a specialty raw material with high research-and-development and technical-service costs and a high profit margin. It is a trade-name item, generically no different from the product sold by other producers, and is a member of a broad family of products that have FDA approval.

Joseph's, using about a million pounds a year, is one of the three or four larger buyers of Polysil. Joseph's prime concerns in respect to its end product are color stability, gloss, and resistance to abrasion. Sacrifice of any of these characteristics for a saving in the cost of Polysil, or any other intermediate advantage, would endanger the company's market position.

The price of Polysil is firm at twenty-five cents per pound, delivered in 30,000-pound truckload lots in nonreturnable polyethylene-lined drums (550 pounds net per drum). Historically the material, which is very hydroscopic, has been delivered in sealed, vacuum-packed, open-head drums rather than in bulk.

Joseph's plant is in South Chicago and is supplied by two vendors: Alpha Chemical in St. Louis and Gamma Chemical in Cincinnati. Joseph's has excellent transportation facilities, including a rail siding, and it ships to its own customers by common carrier. Both suppliers have warehouses in the Chicago area.

Senior buyer Jim Sands and chief engineer Tolley Nettles were discussing raw-material requirements one day.

"It's tough making projections on a multifunctional product like Polysil," said Sands, "but our sales volume looks as though it's going to increase rapidly, and we're going to need a lot of that stuff. But that sales increase will be based on our ability to stay competitive. Sunrise Chemicals for one is going to give us a real run for our money from now on. So that means we've got to get better value on our Polysil buys."

Nettles agreed. "But where do we get it?" he asked. "Any real price reduction is out—that's a high-risk item, and both Alpha and Gamma have got to cover their investments. We've run cost estimates on them a number of times, as you know, and they don't have much room to maneuver. And we don't want to fool with quality, although we might be able to ease up somewhat on specifications. Packaging might be an area in which we could do something, but I don't know. We're probably paying well for those drums—yet we can't afford to have that stuff kicked around by some of the help we've got to live with these days. Let some of that material get contaminated and we're in trouble."

"I think we ought to call Gamma's people in and talk to them," said Sands. "They've been cooperative in the past, and they should be able to come up with some ideas. There are a number of possibilities for better value—in specs, packaging, transportation, receiving, storing—all kinds of things. Why don't we ask them in and go over some of these points? Tell them we want ideas—real ideas—that we can really dollarize."

Four producers share a total market of approximately forty million pounds as follows:

- Alpha—50 percent
- Gamma—25 percent
- Beta—15 percent
- Delta—10 percent

Joseph's business (one million pounds annually) is split two ways:

- Alpha—60 percent
- Gamma—40 percent

Engineering studies have shown that bulk delivery of Polysil is practical, with a 10 percent reduction in price as a feasible goal. However, the initial investment in a receiving and handling facility would be about $200,000, preferably borne by the supplier.

Joseph's long-range goal is a 15 percent increase in net sales. Their colorants are presently attractively priced at $8 per gallon and buyers are still finding new uses for them.

Sands knows that Gamma is capable of handling all his company's requirements for Polysil with the same high standards of quality and service they are now providing. He is willing to switch a substantial part of his business to either supplier on the basis of an attractive reduction in total cost. He decides to approach Gamma first.

QUESTIONS

1. Assuming that you are Sands, discuss the strategy and tactics you will use to achieve your company's objectives.
2. Describe in detail your approach to getting better value on your Polysil buys and your purchase volume allocation by supplier.

CHAPTER 13
BRISTOL MOTORS CORPORATION

Bristol Motors Corporation is a relatively small but well-known auto manufacturer that specializes in the production of taxicabs, airport limousines, ambulances, and light commercial vehicles. It has also managed to sell several thousand passenger automobiles annually, despite the formidable competition of the Big Three and other auto makers.

In the small but enthusiastic market for Bristol cars, the company has a reputation for making a high-quality product.

Bristol buys a higher percentage of auto parts than its bigger, more integrated competitors. To stay competitive in respect both to quality and price, it has leaned heavily on suppliers for technical assistance and competitive prices. To attract vendors to the Bristol business, in turn, the company has standardized on many engine and chassis parts (and to a lesser degree on body parts because of the number of styles it produces). This enables it to combine requirements into sizable orders that will command a volume discount.

Bristol's purchasing department enjoys an excellent reputation among auto parts suppliers. Although purchasing alone selects vendors, their representatives are given every opportunity to visit and consult with engineering and production personnel. This policy works to the advantage of Bristol as well, because it is so dependent on suppliers for new ideas and technical advice. Suppliers, in fact, provide much of the engineering talent that Bristol, unlike its big competitors, simply cannot afford.

The director of purchases and his staff have always prided themselves on being fair with suppliers—respecting their right to make a "fair" profit; giving sales personnel explanations of why they didn't get, or lost, Bristol business; refusing to play one supplier against another by requesting vendors to quote a second time after competitive bids have been received.

Purchasing had relied largely on the competitive bid system in getting prices on standard parts for a number of years. Its buyers were veterans in the automotive industry and had a good basic knowledge of markets and a general idea of what other auto makers were paying for the same or similar parts. Both they and the director of purchases felt that if they were generally in the same price area as their large competitors they were doing well. In recent years, however, the purchasing group had cause to doubt the wisdom of relying so extensively on the competitive bid system.

"Even though the auto market is booming," the director of purchases, Steve Brown, told his buyers at a weekly meeting, "we're under tougher competitive fire than ever before. The big boys have held the price line, so we have to also. Yet our costs keep climbing and climbing. We can't be sure any more that we're getting the lowest possible prices through competitive quotations."

Vendors' bids were creeping higher and the number of requests for price increases on current contracts was growing, he pointed out. He added that this was the classic reaction to a rising market, particularly from vendors who had a good backlog of orders.

"We've got to learn to say 'no'," the director of purchases told his buyers, and he called for less reliance on competitive quotes and more on negotiation, coupled with cost analysis. His new policy was put to the test shortly thereafter, when Bristol's main supplier of camshafts came in with a request for a 5 percent increase, based on increased material and labor costs. The vendor, Global Parts Company, had obtained the business six months earlier on a low bid, winning out over two other suppliers.

The director of purchases and the buyer, Ned Dillon, agreed to resist the requested increase by calling for negotiation. They invited the local representative and the regional sales manager in for a discussion. Before the meeting took place, Dillon called on Bristol's cost estimating group for help in analyzing Global's costs and possible justification for a 5 percent increase. The cost estimators studied the raw material content of the camshaft Global supplied, the machining operations and amount of labor they required, the probable overhead, and general and administrative costs. The director of purchases and the buyer applied Bristol's usual "fair profit" formula and concluded that the supplier was entitled to no more than a 4 pecent increase, and possibly less.

In preparation for the negotiation, the buyer and the director of purchases agreed to ask a cost estimator to sit in on the session and briefed him on the overall strategy. "I think we can hold this guy to 2 or 3 percent," the director of purchases said, "although if we can send him away with nothing, so much the better. We might be able to get our requirements from the Crown Company at the current price, but you know the delivery problems we had with them a couple of years ago. Global has been doing a good job for us, and I think we need him as much as he needs us, so we've got to be flexible."

"Maybe so," replied Dillon, "but I have a hunch Global doesn't have all the business it would like to have in the shop right now. Even though it's trying to raise the price, I think it's a little hungry. Anyway, we ought to try to find out. We can do a little probing as we go along."

The negotiating team of Brown, Dillon, and the cost estimator went through a "dry run" an hour before the supplier's team arrived, concentrating on their estimates of the vendor's costs. Brown instructed Dillon to lead the discussion and call on him only when larger matters of policy came up. He urged both the buyer and the estimator to take every opportunity to put the supplier's representatives on the defensive.

After a detailed discussion on raw material, manufacturing and tooling costs, labor rates, overhead, and so forth, the supplier admitted that the price increase he was asking may have been "rounded out to about 5 percent." He agreed that any new price for the camshafts should include only added metal costs, added labor costs, and the profit related to these costs—but should not include additional profit on tooling, overhead, and administrative costs.

Global's regional sales manager said that he would be willing to go along with a 3 percent increase on the basis of the more precise costing carried out by Bristol's estimators. At that point, one of the estimators turned to Dillon and said, unexpectedly, "One of your other suppliers was ready to come in lower than that, wasn't he?" The buyer, aware that the statement was based more on conjecture than on fact, looked embarrassed, hesitated and then said, "Yes, but we've got to go over his costs again." He then returned to the discussion of Global's costs.

At this point, the supplier's representative asked for a recess. After consulting with the other members of his team, he opened the second session with a proposal that Global be relieved of responsibility for quality control. Under a plan developed a few years before, Global inspected Bristol's parts before they were shipped, then certified that they met quality standards. Its quality report showed the quantity of the lot shipped, date of inspection, size of sample, acceptable quality level, number of rejects, and related information. "If you can take this job off our shoulders," Global's sales manager said, "we can hold the increase to 2 percent."

The proposal obviously caught the Bristol group short, and the Global sales manager quickly followed up with the statement that he could give the group an accurate figure on inspection costs then and there. So there would be no reason, he added, to recess. "It's a good deal all around," he said, "inspection costs run a little less than 1 percent of the price of each unit. Shall we go ahead?"

QUESTIONS

1. Was the Bristol purchasing department's planning for this negotiation adequate? Why?
2. Was Brown acting correctly in having the buyer lead the negotiation session? Evaluate his instructions to the buyer and estimator on tactics to use. Do you think the instructions reflect Bristol's traditional attitudes toward vendors? Why?
3. Was the estimator being ethical when he made the remark about another supplier being "ready to come in" at a lower price? What do you think of Brown's handling of that part of the discussion?
4. What do you think Brown's next move should be? Give your reasons.

CHAPTER 13
THE CRAIG ENGINE COMPANY

In May 1984 sales were down, margins were tight and management was concerned at the Craig Engine Company, a major manufacturer of small jet engines. As a result, Jim Thomas, assistant manager of purchasing, was directed to negotiate substantial cost savings of at least $2 million with one of his key parts suppliers.

THE COMPANY

The Craig Engine Company was a large manufacturer of jet engines used in small military, commercial, and private aircraft. Sales of the Craig Company were in excess of $2 billion per year. Although Craig was known as an innovator in its field, customers viewed Craig's engines as of equal performance and quality with those manufactured by its competitors. As such, their primary criterion for making a purchase decision was price. This had resulted in very lean profit margins for Craig.

In addition to tight profit margins, in 1984 Craig was also experiencing a 35 percent cutback in the sales of its engines owing to a weakened economy. Instead of buying new airplanes, customers chose to refurbish their old ones in an attempt to save money. Although this had meant a substantial increase in the sales of spare parts for Craig, the revenue associated with this increase was small compared to the revenue lost from the decreased sales of new engines.

OFFSHORE PARTS PROCUREMENT

The Able Company, a German manufacturer of jet engines, was a primary supplier of high-precision sheet metal parts for the Craig Company. The Able Company was one of the few companies in the world capable of producing such parts. These parts were purchased in kits from the Able Company (one kit per engine) at an approximate rate of 150 per year. A kit consisted of several different parts that became part of an integrated assembly. The kits produced by Able consisted of several different sheet-metal parts and subassemblies. The contract between the two companies, which began in 1980, ran through the year 2000 and provided for renegotiation every three years. The contract was written in U.S. dollars, and in 1980, the exchange rate was one and a half German marks to one U.S. dollar. The exchange rate in 1984 was three German marks to one U.S. dollar.

Among other things, the contract guaranteed the Able Company 75 percent of Craig's business for these kits, while Craig reserved the right to produce the other 25 percent in-house, which it had done up to this point. The contract also specified the method by which the Able Company would determine its price. This was the combination of a base price, which the two companies jointly established in 1980, and the effect of a mutually-agreed-upon escalator clause, provided this total did not exceed Craig's in-house costs for fabricating the same parts. In addition, Able was entitled to all documented cost increases (resulting from more expensive materials and changes in processes) incurred in response to changes in Craig's specifications. The Able Company then added a 60 percent markup from which it recovered its overhead and profit.

The Able Company could recover any extraordinary expediting costs associated with accelerating Craig's delivery schedules. Able was also entitled to recover the costs of all materials and equipment that became obsolete as the result of Craig's specification changes. These obsolete material costs were to be reviewed on a quarterly basis and to be mutually agreed upon before becoming recoverable.

The current price of each parts kit to Craig was $160,000, which included the 60 percent markup. During the last year Able had spent an extra $18,000 per kit for more expensive materials in order to meet Craig's new and more stringent specifications. In addition, the change to the new specification had made $750,000 worth of equipment and materials obsolete. Furthermore, the Able Company had recently spent an extra $100,000 in overtime and expediting to meet Craig's accelerated delivery schedule earlier in the year. It was clear from Able's correspondence that it expected to be compensated for these incurred costs, but Craig had not yet paid any of these invoices.

THOMAS'S ASSIGNMENT

Because of his familiarity with the parts kits and with the Able Company, Thomas was given the assignment of negotiating a substantial reduction in the costs (at least $2 million) proposed by the Able Company. He was told that this project would be closely monitored by upper management because of the dollar amount involved. As he left his office to go to a staff meeting, Thomas pondered what action he should take.

QUESTIONS

1. Identify potential areas for cost reduction in dealing with Able.
2. Develop a strategy for Mr. Thomas to follow in reducing the cost of the engine kits from Able.
3. What special circumstances should Mr. Thomas be aware of as he begins his negotiations with Able.

This case was written by Ross Reck during the Case Writing in Purchasing Workshop held at Arizona State University. Copyright © 1984, The National Association of Purchasing Management. Reprinted by permission.

CHAPTER 13
THE CHANCELLOR COMPANY

The Chancellor Company, producer of metals and metal products, was reeling from the impact of rising costs, a declining market, and ruinous price cutting in its metals—particularly by foreign suppliers. The company had been slow to respond to changing conditions; it continued to build inventories and dragged its feet in meeting price competition.

Determined to fight back, the president flatly demanded at a meeting in late January that his department heads make firm commitments as to what savings they would make in their particular departments in the coming year. Bernard Bunsen, director of purchasing, went on record: His group would bring material costs down by at least 7 percent over the previous year, adjusted for volume. He called his headquarters staff together to discuss the cost-reduction program.

"To some extent," he said, "we've been lulled into a kind of complacency by the buyer's market we're in. But it's a two-edged sword. As purchasing people we like it when there is abundant supply at very attractive prices—but we have to realize that our company is taking a beating in that same market. We simply have to relight the competitive fires that are such an important part of the purchasing environment."

He then laid out the general outlines of the new program. "Instead of asking for—or demanding—a flat percentage price reduction from each supplier," he said, "we are going to set an average goal and go after it with some good old-fashioned purchasing." He spelled out some details of the plan in a blunt memorandum to all plant and regional purchasing managers:

- The 7 percent goal is an across-the-board commitment; all prices will have to come down, not just a few big ones. Reductions on individual buys may vary. The 7 percent is an average figure.
- Everyone in the purchasing organization must make a contribution—in headquarters and in the field, at big plants and small plants.
- As a general guideline, headquarters will not accept any negotiated price increases. No blanket orders or contracts are to be extended at an increased price without written approval from headquarters. Before approval is requested, contracts must have been put out for competitive bids and discussed and approved by the headquarters office or a regional purchasing manager.
- Purchasing managers or buyers who have accepted price increases since January 1 must ask that prices be rolled back to the prior level. Suppliers unwilling to comply with the request will be eliminated as sources and their contracts terminated as quickly as possible.
- Exceptions will be made in only two cases: (1) when there are absolutely no other sources for the item, and (2) when some other offsetting concession is made.

"We'll obviously get some resistance on this," Bunsen told his staff, "not only from suppliers but from some of our field purchasing people. I know of at least a couple whose comeback will be, 'We've already done as much as we can.' I know it's tough opening old contracts. But it has to be done." He closed by asking the plant purchasing representatives to submit—within a week to ten days—a report on what techniques and approaches each planned to use in negotiating, or renegotiating, contracts with suppliers.

Rick Shaw, purchasing agent at one of the company's smaller plants, was responsible for purchases amounting to slightly over $2 million a year. His biggest purchase was of bulk chemicals used in metal treating, followed in order of dollars expended by packaging materials such as pallets, strapping, plastic and paper packaging materials; maintenance, repair, and operating (MRO) materials such as lubricants, welding supplies, safety equipment, hand tools and hardware, paint, and electrical items; materials-handling equipment; office supplies and equipment; and transportation services.

QUESTIONS

1. Assume that you are Rick Shaw, and prepare your report to Bernard Bunsen. Wherever possible, indicate specific approaches to be taken to particular items.
2. Discuss the tactics you will use in presenting your proposals to suppliers.

CHAPTER 14
RUMFORD MACHINE COMPANY

After careful investigation of competing types of equipment, a committee that included representatives of purchasing, engineering, and production decided to buy a new multipurpose machine tool for the Rumford Machine Company. It was the latest model of a numerically controlled unit that could perform drilling, milling, and boring operations on a single piece in any sequence. The machine was manufactured by Bradley-Donald Machine Tool Company, a leader in the field and a supplier to Rumford on numerous occasions in the past.

During the negotiations for the equipment, in which all committee members participated, Rumford Company engineers had asked for several modifications on the machine to meet their particular problems. The supplier's technical representatives agreed that the changes could be made. The price finally agreed upon was $93,000, and the Bradley-Donald representatives were told they would receive a purchase order by mail.

The Rumford Company's purchasing manager asked his engineers to send him a detailed listing of the changes they wanted made on Bradley-Donald's standard model of the machine. From this he had a set of specifications transcribed to the purchase order; then he issued the order carrying the price of $93,000 agreed on previously.

Within a few days the Bradley-Donald Company acknowledged the order but not on the copy of the Rumford Company purchase order designated for this purpose. Instead of his own acknowledgment form, the purchasing manager received Bradley-Donald Company's contract form. He examined the form closely and reviewed the clauses carefully with the company's legal department. They agreed that there was nothing inimical to Rumford's interests in the "fine print" on the contract form. The purchasing manager, however, was not satisfied with the simple statement that the contract called for "one Brad-O-Matic, Model 64, installed . . . $93,000." No mention of changes previously agreed to appeared on the form. He called Bradley-Donald's district sales manager in to discuss the matter.

The supplier's representative pointed out that it was customary for the company to acknowledge orders on that form—and, in fact, it had done so previously on orders from the Rumford Company.

When the purchasing manager objected to the fact that his original specifications were not included in the contract, the sales representative replied that he did not have authority to change the contract. But, he added, he would insert the words "changes to come" beneath the model description and notify his home office that the order would be followed by a letter from the purchasing manager detailing the modifications to be made on the standard machine.

The purchasing manager agreed, and after the words had been inserted in the contract, both men initialed both copies. Before the day was out the purchasing manager had sent a letter to the Bradley-Donald Company's home office specifying the changes to be made on the machine and mentioning the contract he had initialed.

In the final stages of the installation of the machine, the Rumford Company received an invoice for $101,500, covering "one Brad-O-Matic, Model 64" at $93,000 and additional charges of $8,500 for "modifications as per your letter." Just before he planned to call Bradley-Donald's sales office, the purchasing manager received an urgent call from the shop. The test runs on the machine were not up to expectations, and it was obvious that it could not meet the performance standards that the Rumford Company's engineers expected of it. They could get no satisfaction from the supplier's technical representatives, who said that there must have been some misunderstanding as to the capabilities of the machine. They suggested that the matter be taken up with their district sales office and perhaps the company's home office.

The purchasing manager called the district office and protested to the manager. He asked for an immediate change in the invoice and adjustment of the machine to meet the Rumford Company's requirements. Following his call, he dictated a letter to the Bradley-Donald Company home office outlining the situation and making the demands.

The Bradley-Donald Company answered that the extra charge was justified because it covered instructions given after the contract had been signed for a standard machine. It claimed that the words "changes to come" merely indicated that such instructions would follow but were not a part of the contract and were not included in the contract price. As to the performance of the equipment, they would be glad to continue giving technical assistance and advice at no cost but would not be held to any warranties in the contract. The machine to which the warranties applied, they claimed, had been altered at the customer's instructions and to the customer's specification.

The Rumford Company refused to accept the machine, and the Bradley-Donald Company sued for the full amount of the invoice.

QUESTIONS

1. Who comes into court with the strongest case? Why?
2. Analyze the mistakes in the Rumford Company's conduct of negotiation and contract procedure, pointing out how the company could have protected itself by alternative approaches.

CHAPTER 15
LUND STAGELITE CORP.

Jan Dawson was the intelligent, ambitious, and highly articulate purchasing manager for Lund Stagelite Corp., manufacturer of theatrical lighting equipment for commercial and institutional use. Sales of the company's products, about two-thirds of which were made to order and about one-third produced for stock, averaged $18 million annually.

Approximately 55 percent of that figure was spent every year on purchased material and supplies.

Before coming into purchasing ten years ago, Jan had spent close to eight years in various positions in the manufacturing and production-control departments of the company. She was well known in the company, respected for the competence she displayed in every job she had held but was considered by many to be motivated solely by a desire for personal advancement. In the course of her career, she developed an immunity to what others thought of her and concentrated on certain goals that she believed were in her own and her company's interest.

One of these goals was the establishment of a materials-management system for the Stagelite Company. Jan had developed a strong and very efficient purchasing department in the company. But her own experience and her regular study of other industrial purchasing departments had convinced her that a broader type of organization was needed to handle the materials cycle in her company. She made no secret of her view that there should be a materials department with jurisdiction over all activities involved with the acquisition, handling, and storage of raw materials. The department would, of course, be headed by a materials manager.

"Put your proposals down on paper," her executive vice-president said one day following a conversation on the subject. "I'm interested, but I'd like something a little more concrete on which to base my judgment."

Jan immediately prepared a memorandum to Harry Silvis, executive vice-president. Following a general description of the materials management concept, she outlined the objectives of such a program, using a list adapted from a definitive article on materials management she had read in a trade magazine. The list of objectives was as follows:

1. To provide materials at the lowest possible overall cost
2. To keep investment in raw material inventories at the lowest level consistent with sales and production objectives
3. To maintain lowest storage and carrying costs and develop optimum turnover rates
4. To improve interdepartmental communication and thereby reduce administrative costs
5. To develop and maintain favorable relations with suppliers
6. To maintain continuity of supply
7. To keep down acquisition and possession costs and minimize obsolescence and deterioration of inventories
8. To improve techniques of purchasing and inventory control

Specifically, she suggested that these objectives could be achieved by the Stagelite Company if purchasing, inventory, and material-control, and traffic functions were combined into one department. The three groups would balance one another, she said: Purchasing would buy materials against a planned program; inventory control and material control would maintain stocks at desired inventory levels (against known production requirements) and establish proper turnover rates; traffic would certify receipt of materials and be responsible for storing and dispensing them to the production department. Buyers and material-control planners would act as teams in determining timing and amount of raw material purchases.

The purchasing department had four buyers, three clerks, and a purchasing manager. Inventory and material planning had eight planners and two clerical assistants, while the traffic department had a traffic manager and a clerk. Inventory turnover was three times per year. The buyers and planners argued constantly about due dates and lead times. Purchasing always insisted they didn't receive sufficient lead time to acquire material, while planners claimed the purchasing department was too slow in placing orders. Jan felt these problems could be resolved through more frequent and improved communication. Currently, each department reported to Sid Scofield, the production manager. Sid in turn reported to Harry.

Jan listed these advantages as accruing to the company under a materials-management organization:

> Responsibility for materials would be centralized and clearly defined.
> Fewer people would be needed than in individual departments. Duplication of files would be eliminated; fewer copies of purchase orders and receiving reports would be needed.
> Buyers could schedule deliveries from vendors on a much more rational basis when they had up-to-date knowledge of present inventory levels and anticipated production requirements. The time lag involved in getting this information would be eliminated. Therefore "peak-and-valley" ordering, frequent rescheduling of open orders, and short-lead-time ordering would be reduced and relations with vendors greatly improved. Close cooperation with vendors to match production requirements with their capabilities would help prevent emergencies.
> There would be less repackaging and material handling, because packaging would be specified to meet production requirements.
> More opportunities for advancement would be offered to personnel in all affected departments. The experience that inventory and material-control personnel would receive would make them natural candidates for promotion to buying positions.

The executive vice-president passed a copy of the purchasing manager's memorandum to Sid and asked for his comments. Part of his reply was as follows:

> The materials-management organization suggested is more to the advantage of the purchasing department than to that of the Stagelite Company. It would eliminate the material-control function and build up the purchasing function but without the benefits claimed. Material planners would be dominated by higher-paid buyers, who would buy when and as much as they pleased without reference to others.
> Responsibility is clearly defined now. Production control has responsibility for inventories. Purchasing has responsibility for getting material in on time. Material control has responsibility for maintaining stocks of raw materials at optimum levels. That's the way it should be.
> Inventory turnover would not be any better than it is now. Turnover depends on amounts purchased and amounts used. Sales, then schedules, determine usage, and variations in these two elements are great. A combined buyer-specifier team would not improve the situation.
> The alleged improvement in vendor relations is more of a device to improve purchasing's position. A buyer's success is measured by the relations that he or

she builds up with the vendors and the job that his or her vendor does. The more the buyer can claim "better vendor relations," the more the buyer inflates his or her own importance.

Promotion opportunities exist for everyone in the Stagelite Company through our regular merit system. The material planner would be dependent on the buyer for advancement—again strengthening the purchasing department at others' expense.

Harry studied the two memorandums and a week later prepared his own answer to Jan and Sid.

QUESTIONS

1. What factors move firms to consider the materials-management approach to organization?
2. Do you think the proposed materials-management system would work for Lund? Why or why not?
3. You are Harry Silvis, write a memorandum analyzing Jan Dawson's and Sid Scofield's positions. Make and explain in detail your decision as to whether Lund Stagelite Company will consider establishing a materials-management organization.

CHAPTER 16
GLASSWORKS, INC.

In August 1987 Thomas Barnes, president of Glassworks, Inc., was wondering how he could improve inventory management at his small but growing firm. Glassworks, Inc., is a small business located in a middle-size southwestern city. The company employs approximately ten people and its sales are in the hundreds of thousands of dollars. Major sales include glass and mirrors for automobiles, homes, and commercial jobs. Inventory control is the responsibility of the office manager, Joan Smith. Her approach to inventory management varies by the specific account. One large dollar account is automotive windshield glass, which is stocked on consignment. Auto Supplies, Inc., sells this glass to Glassworks, Inc., and makes daily deliveries based on the number of windshields replaced the previous day. An identifying clothespin is attached to each windshield in stock. This clothespin is dropped into a basket when the glass is removed from stock. The purchaser then reorders it, and delivery is made on the following day. Each clothespin has the type of auto glass and the size listed on it. On other glass items an index card is taped to the package. When the glass item is issued for use, the index card is detached and sent to the front office. Other items, which are stored in the shop, are controlled by a visual review of each item's stock level that is taken each Monday. Reorders are placed to bring stock up to the desired level. Office supplies are also checked weekly for replenishment purposes. On small-dollar items extra packages are kept under the shelf, and when one is opened, a replacement order is placed.

Glassworks, Inc., also receives commercial orders. Material for large jobs is special ordered for the job, and inventory records are kept by the job number. Once a year a physical inventory is taken of all the inventory in the shop. The company makes no attempt to calculate shrinkage/loss of its inventory.

One of the major issues facing the firm is determining the correct quantities of mirror and regular glass to purchase. Currently, regular sheet glass and mirrors are purchased in a quantity that allows the firm to receive a transportation saving over that realized on a lesser quantity. Glass is stored on the floor in vertical racks or cases. Breakage of large sheets is not a major problem. When a new job comes in, employees go to the rack and bring a sheet to the cutting table. After cutting, if the remainder is determined to be too small to be used, it is thrown away. Otherwise, it is placed in a location with other "scraps." Workers are to check scraps first on jobs that require smaller sizes of glass. Scraps are in various sizes and are not categorized. Therefore, the amount of time required to locate a scrap piece of a particular size is significant, especially when considering the delicate handling required on leftover glass. Mirrors that are custom cut also go into the scraps area. Once or twice a year scraps less than a certain size are thrown away.

Until recently, most inventory shelving was reachable by individual employees, but since the ceilings were thirty-foot-high, a new high-level storage rack was built to take advantage of the wasted space.

Receiving of material is handled by whoever is available when the carrier arrives with the material. This individual signs the bill of lading. Scheduling of jobs is done by the front office and broken into field orders (work in the field) and shop orders. The two front-office workers have a daily list of jobs, which they receive the previous night from Joan.

Pricing is done from job scheduling sheets and is usually based on a price per square foot of glass. Field orders have both a labor and material component. Occasional errors are made in figuring glass prices for off sizes. Joan indicated the firm had not increased prices charged to their customers for the past two years.

QUESTIONS

1. What recommendations would you make to Thomas Barnes to improve his inventory control?
2. Are records, receiving/stores, and disposition critical to this firm's profitability.

CHAPTER 17
TRIGSON & HOWELL

Trigson & Howell specializes in the production of processing equipment for the petroleum, food, and pharmaceutical industries. The company does most of its own work in the fabrication of equipment sections requiring piping and metal sheet or plate. Accessories, such as meters, controls, and other components, are purchased from outside suppliers. Units vary greatly in size, and short-run demand from the company's customers is unpredictable. Of twenty orders in the shop at one time, more than half may be for petroleum plants. When these are complete, there may be a period of six months or more in which no orders are received from that industry, and most of the company's production is scheduled for the food industry. As a result, there is unevenness in the use of raw materials, and management is particularly concerned that they have on hand a reasonable supply of all major items to meet the varying demands of customers.

The materials cycle on a given project begins when a bill of materials goes to the stores department, which is under purchasing jurisdiction. The storeskeeper checks off all items in stock and allocates the quantities necessary to the job, subtracting this amount from the balance-of-stock figures. The bill of material then goes to the purchasing manager, who places orders for the unchecked items. He also issues orders for special parts not ordinarily carried in stock. In ordering stock items—materials and components used regularly in most T&H products—the purchasing agent uses a table of economic ordering quantities based on annual usage. Orders are placed in these quantities or multiples thereof, and any excess over the amount of the immediate need is added to the reserve stock to be applied against the next requirement.

By this system, the supply of unallocated stock is constantly, though unevenly, replenished. Also, because the allocation is made on the records but physical stocks are not assigned until they are issued from stores against an order, there is a further cushion for immediate shop demands. The presumption is that materials on order, which cover the total needs for work in process, will be delivered in ample time to replace quantities that have been "borrowed" from preceding deliveries. On materials that are in current demand there may be from two to half a dozen purchase orders outstanding or in transit. Thus although orders are placed on what amounts to individual job requisitions, materials are actually received and put into production on a flow basis, with rapid turnover.

The purchasing manager does not see the bill of materials until engineering drawings and calculations have been completed. Manufacturing time ranges from three to four weeks on simpler jobs to four months on more complex units. Ordinarily, this provides enough lead time for procurement of purchased parts, such as meters. But there are times when the shop wishes to take advantage of open time and begin work on the assemblies that T&H fabricates itself. When this happens, as it has with increasing frequency, the pressure on purchasing mounts.

The company bid on a number of pieces of equipment for a large food concern in late August and received the orders during the first week of October. Requirements of one-half-inch stainless steel tubing for the orders totaled 1,200 feet, and the normal order quantity was 500 feet. As the work orders were received, three purchase orders for that quantity were issued. Normal delivery time per order is about two and a half weeks. Two shipments of 500 feet each were expected by the end of the month, and 500 feet by the November 10.

Two weeks after the orders were in the house, the production manager stopped the purchasing manager in a hall. "Look," he said, "I have people sitting around out there in the shop twiddling their thumbs. I want to get to work on these Consolidated Food orders right now, then hold the units for final assembly. But we're all held up because you haven't gotten us enough stainless tubing. What kind of a deal is this?" The purchasing manager answered that his figures indicated that there was enough reserve stock on hand. They checked the situation together.

They found that on the first of October there were 1,100 feet of tubing on hand, but all of it was allocated to other orders. In fact, total allocation amounted to 1,550 feet; but against this additional requirement, two orders of 500 feet each had been placed in September for early October delivery. Total supply on hand and on order was therefore 2,100 feet, or 550 feet more than was needed at that time. The average unit of demand, or quantity called for on a single work order, was 450 feet. On the basis of annual usage of 10,000 feet, usage during the lead time of two and a half weeks would amount to 500 feet. Looking at it either way, the purchasing manager said, there was ample safety stock on hand.

He pointed out that the orders for the October jobs would add another 300 feet to the reserve, making it 850 feet in all. This, he said, was almost equal to a full month's normal usage, 70 percent over average usage during a lead-time period, and almost two average unit demands.

The production manager wanted tubing, not explanations. The fact remained that there was not enough in stock for his immediate need, despite the theoretical reserve. He rejected the purchasing manager's reasoning that the safety factor had been appreciably increased by the three latest orders. A reserve equal to "almost two" unit demands still covers only one demand adequately, he argued, so the situation was really no better than before.

He held that stock policy must be set in the stores department and not as a corollary to purchasing policy; that it must be measured in terms of actual physical, unallocated stock, not in purchase commitments; and that the predetermined minimum stock quantity should have as much force in initiating a purchase for replenishment as a work order or a requisition for actual use.

"The trouble with your system," he said, "is that you really make no provision at all for safety stock. When these new deliveries come in, you will claim to show a reserve of 850 feet of tubing, but it will actually be working inventory, not reserve. Your stock clerk will allocate it against the next order. You won't know about it, and won't buy again until he has too little on hand to fill an order. In other words, there is no safety factor at all—only a succession of stockout failures, which you may or may not be lucky enough to cover up before they become production failures."

The purchasing manager defended his policy on the ground that the determination of best ordering quantities necessarily took inventory needs and costs into consideration; that minimum stock quantities would have to be calculated as a function of lead time and usage, which were inherent in the purchasing formula; and that any scientific method (that is, formula) must be based on averages, particularly average usage, and not on exceptional rates of usage like those experienced in the October orders.

The production manager disagreed on two basic points. In his opinion lead time was wholly irrelevant to the size of safety stock, being of concern only as a matter of procurement in the timing and size of purchase orders. Second, he said, average usage broken down to anything less than the full-year period was mathematically bound to be wrong as often as it was right; the only dependable criterion for safety in stock was maximum demand or usage within the shorter period.

QUESTIONS

1. Is the production manager justified in his emphasis on the importance of having inventory in advance of need?
2. What would be the effect of his proposals on the size and cost of inventory?
3. What could he do specifically to help purchasing provide better service on materials?
4. Does the purchasing manager give enough importance to a safety factor in inventory; and does the reserve stock that he cites actually constitute a safety stock, or is it working inventory, as the production manager charges?
5. Is it good policy to purchase stock items in quantities greater than the immediate need?
6. Because the purchasing manager is in charge of inventory and stores, what factors other than stockouts must he consider?
7. Does the purchasing manager place too much reliance on order quantity tables as a means of solving inventory problems; and is he making proper use of the order-quantity formula? What elements in the T&H operation tend to limit the effectiveness of this method?
8. Does purchasing lead time have any significance in respect to safety stocks? Can purchasing and inventory policies be separately determined? Is average usage an adequate guide to the amount of protective stock needed?

CHAPTER 17
WILLISTON MILLS

Williston Mills is a family-owned woodworking and specialty shop. The company normally employs about eighty workers. Avery Williston, the present principal owner and manager, came up through the mill. Long firsthand familiarity with materials and with every phase of plant operations has given him an intuitive knowledge of quantities and costs; he prides himself on his ability to estimate jobs quickly and accurately. The business has grown in volume and profits under his leadership. He is impatient with details and paperwork and has developed numerous rules of thumb to guide his decisions and action. "Practical results"—his only measure of performance—have been generally satisfactory. In addition to his general management and supervisory activities, he used to do most of the purchasing. With increasing shop demands on his time, however, he decided to break in an assistant to take over the buying.

His choice for this assignment was Edward Jarvis, a young man presently in charge of the stockroom, who had shown considerable aptitude and interest in the business. Jarvis was not altogether inexperienced in buying, for he had the responsibility of keeping the supply inventory replenished. The system was a very simple one. Arbitrary minimum stock limits had been placed on each item, based on experience as to average usage and on Williston's judgment. When the supply was down to this minimum quantity, restocking orders were placed in the quantity of the convenient commercial unit—nails by the keg, glue by the barrel, jigsaw blades by the gross, and so forth. Sometimes this system entailed reordering every week. On the rare occasions when an item came uncomfortably close to running out of stock, the minimum-quantity limit was revised upward to forestall a recurrence of this condition.

Williston was a firm believer in "learning by doing." Consequently, Jarvis was introduced to his new duties by being handed a copy of the latest job order. It called for 12,000 instrument carrying cases, twelve by six by six inches in size, to be made and delivered at the rate of 1,000 per month, with the option of continuing the contract for a longer period. There were eight items of purchased material: plywood for the body of the case, vinyl covering, cloth lining, locks, handles, name plates, brass corner reinforcements, and carrying straps. Nails and adhesive would be furnished from general supply stock. Williston estimated that the material bill would amount to about $25,000.

"I want you to buy the materials for this job and keep them coming in as we need them," he said. "On the plywood and yard goods, allow 10 percent for waste in cutting; the rest is all counted out for you. We figure on keeping two weeks ahead at all times; that's for insurance. Anything you can buy in carload lots, do so; that's the cheapest way. On everything else, find out how long it takes to get the stuff delivered, and how much we would be using in that length of time. Buying in those quantities will get the shipments coming in just about when the old shipment is used up. We don't want a lot of stock hanging around here waiting until we're ready to use it; that ties up money for no good purpose—we want to keep our money working, too. You can stretch an order a little to bring it to even quantities, but don't do it just to get a quantity discount; that's a sales trick to pad the order."

Jarvis calculated total requirements on the job, checked the files to see where Williston bought the various items, and phoned the suppliers to get prices and delivery time. He then made a preliminary analysis (Exhibit 1) to set up the buying schedule according to the manager's instruction.

Jarvis respected Williston's judgment and was generally in agreement with the policy of maintaining a flow of materials to correspond with the rate of use. However, he questioned the efficiency of a buying schedule that involved upwards of two hundred purchase orders a year on such relatively simple requirements. He noted that more than half these orders would be for amounts of less than $100, which seemed uneconomical in view of the total amount to be spent. Despite Williston's warning on quantity discounts, it disturbed him to see that except for the single instance of plywood, which could be purchased in carload quan-

EXHIBIT 1

	Annual Usage	Price	Annual Cost	Weekly Usage	Delivery Time	Order Quantity
Plywood	1,100 sheets 4 ft x 8 ft	15 cents sq ft, less 5% in carloads of 400 sheets	$5,026	22 sheets	1 wk	Carload (18-wk. supply)
Vinyl	4,000 yd 36 in. wide in 50-yd rolls	70 cents/yd, less 5% in lots of 25 rolls	2,800	80 yd	3 wk	5 rolls
Lining	3,000 yd 42 in. wide in 50-yd rolls	44 cents/yd, less 5% in lots of 25 rolls	1,320	60 yd	1 wk	2 rolls
Locks	12,000	60 cents each, less 5% in lots of 1,000; less 10% in lots of 5,000	7,200	240	3 wk	750
Name plates	12,000	12 cents each, less 3% in lots of 1,000	1,440	240	2 wk	500
Handles	12,000	14 cents each	1,680	240	2 wk	500
Straps	12,000	22 cents each	2,640	240	1 wk	240
Corner pieces	96,000	3 cents each, less 5% in lots of 10,000	2,880	1,920	2 wk	4,000
			$24,986			

tity, the discount privilege on five other items was sacrificed even though total requirements were large enough to come into the quantity discount brackets if ordering quantities were increased beyond the stipulated two weeks' supply. He felt there was a serious discrepancy in this policy, too, for his experience in storeskeeping made him aware of the fact that plywood, the one item to be purchased in quantity, was by far the bulkiest and most difficult to store, and the heaviest to handle in and out of stock.

Jarvis was anxious to make a good record on his first major purchasing assignment. At the same time he realized that his own conclusions, like Williston's buying policies, were only a matter of judgment and that he had no comparable background of experience to support his judgment. Before making an issue of the matter or making a recommendation to change the buying schedule, he needed more tangible reasons. He had done some reading on the principles of storeskeeping and had in his possession a copy of best-order-quantity table (see Table 1). Such procedures had not seemed particularly important in a relatively small stores operation like that at Williston Mills, but he decided to make a second calculation on that basis to see whether it would confirm his own thinking.

Using the figure of annual usage on the various items and assuming the lowest rate of inventory-carrying cost, he checked the indicated best order quantities and made a second tabulation (Exhibit 2).

Table 1 Best Order Quantity Multiplier

Annual Use $	Year's Supply to Order				Stock Carrying Rate	Annual Use $	Year's Supply to Order			
	.11 A	.25 B	.50 C	1.00 D			.11 A	.25 B	.50 C	1.00 D
1	8	5.3	3.75	2.65	Code	260	.495	.328	.232	.164
2	5.6	3.70	2.62	1.85		280	.477	.316	.224	.158
3	4.6	3.08	2.19	1.54		300	.460	.308	.219	.154
4	4.0	2.65	1.87	1.32		325	.444	.294	.208	.147
5	3.6	2.38	1.69	1.20		350	.427	.284	.199	.142
6	3.26	2.16	1.56	1.08		375	.412	.273	.193	.137
7	3.03	2.00	1.42	1.00		400	.400	.265	.187	.132
8	2.84	1.88	1.33	.935		425	.388	.257	.182	.128
9	2.68	1.77	1.25	.885		450	.377	.250	.177	.125
10	2.52	1.67	1.18	.836		475	.368	.244	.173	.122
12	2.30	1.53	1.08	.765		500	.360	.238	.169	.120
14	2.14	1.42	1.00	.710		550	.341	.226	.160	.113
16	2.00	1.32	.936	.663		600	.326	.216	.156	.108
18	1.90	1.25	.885	.626		650	.314	.208	.147	.104
20	1.79	1.19	.840	.593		700	.303	.200	.142	.100
25	1.60	1.06	.750	.530		750	.292	.194	.137	.097
30	1.45	.968	.682	.482		800	.284	.188	1.33	.0935
35	1.35	.900	.635	.448		850	.275	.182	.129	.0910
40	1.25	.838	.592	.419		900	.266	.177	.125	.0885
45	1.2	.790	.559	.395		950	.260	.172	.121	.086
50	1.13	.747	.530	.374		1000	.252	.167	.118	.0836
60	1.07	.682	.485	.342		1100	.242	.160	.114	.080
70	.960	.636	.450	.318		1200	.230	.153	.108	.0765
80	.896	.594	.420	.297		1400	.214	.142	.100	.0710
90	.840	.556	.394	.278		1600	.200	.132	.0936	.066
100	.800	.530	.375	.265		1800	.190	.125	.088	.063
110	.767	.508	.359	.254		2000	.179	.119	.084	.059
120	.730	.484	.342	.242		2500	.160	.106	.075	.053
130	.704	.468	.328	.232		3000	.145	.096	.068	
140	.675	.447	.317	.224		3500	.135	.090	.064	
150	.653	.433	.306	.216		4000	.125	.084	.059	
160	.632	.420	.296	.210		4500	.120	.079	.056	
170	.614	.407	.287	.203		5000	.113	.075		
180	.595	.395	.279	.198		6000	.107	.068		
190	.580	.384	.272	.192		7000	.096	.064		
200	.560	.370	.262	.185		8000	.089	.059		
220	.540	.357	.253	.178		9000	.084	.056		
240	.515	.342	.242	.171		10000	.080			

Application of the Table
(Using Stock Carrying Rate Code A)
If you use $10,000 per year, order 1 month's supply per order

1,000	3 months'
250	6 months'
65	1 year's
15	2 years'
5	4 years'
1	8 years'

Exhibit 2

| | | Weeks Supply to Order | | |
	Annual Usage	Williston Policy	Best Order Quantity	
Plywood	$5,026	18	5.6	125 sheets
Vinyl	2,800	3	7.2	12 rolls
Lining	1,320	1	11.1	14 rolls
Locks	7,200	3	4.8	1,200*
Name plates	1,440	2	10.6	2,500*
Handles	1,680	2	9.7	2,400
Straps	2,640	1	8.0	1,920
Corner pieces	2,880	2	7.2	14,000*

*On these three items, best order quanity automatically brings purchases into the quantity discount bracket and reduces annual cost by $360, $43, and $144, respectively.

The tables showed that the entire purchasing program could be carried out with only about one-fourth as many purchase orders, receiving operations, and invoice payments as under Williston's proposal. As to material cost, the quantity discount savings of $547 were offset nearly half by failure to take a $254 discount on the plywood by buying in smaller quantities. Before presenting any recommendation to Williston, he made a further calculation to appraise the real effect of this in relation to the purchase investment in plywood and the potential effect in respect to purchases of vinyl and lining cloth. He tabulated these figures in Exhibit 3.

From this standpoint, Williston's instructions to buy plywood in carload lots seemed well justified, for the best-order-quantity table did not take variable prices into consideration. The advantage was even more pronounced on the other two items. By the same reasoning, therefore, the indicated buying policy was to increase the order quantity on vinyl and lining cloth to twenty-five rolls of each, at

Exhibit 3

Plywood	
Net savings on 400 sheets bought in one lot	$96.00
Extra initial investment required	1,224.00
Return on extra investment—7.8% in 18 weeks	

Vinyl	
Net saving on 25 rolls bought in one lot	43.75
Extra initial investment required	411.25
Return on extra investment—10.6% in 15.6 weeks	

Lining Cloth	
Net saving on 25 rolls bought in one lot	27.50
Extra initial investment required	214.50
Return on extra investment—12.8% in 20.8 weeks	

the quantity discount price. Jarvis revised the order quantities noted in Exhibit 2 accordingly.

Williston examined Jarvis's figures with interest. He was skeptical of Exhibit 2 but could take no exception to Figure 3 even though it was in conflict with his theory of quantity discounts.

"We can afford to tie up $600 to save $70 twice a year," he said, "but remember, you're asking me to triple the investment, as you call it, on the rest of the materials as well. If we did that all along the line, I might have trouble meeting the payroll every Friday, or in keeping our suppliers happy so that they will continue to send along the smaller quantities we need to keep the plant running."

QUESTIONS

1. Avery Williston's quantity buying policies logically consider many important factors—lead time, rapid turnover, and minimum idle investment. The discrepancy between his conclusions and those of the scientifically derived table suggest that other factors have been overlooked. What are some of the hidden factors? What additional cost information must he have to calculate best order quantity more effectively?

2. Are the best order quantity tables applicable in a business like Williston Mills? To what extent should they be used?

3. Jarvis stresses the smaller number of orders to be written. Because these are routine and repetitive, just how important is this factor? Because suppliers' prices take quantity brackets into account, should Jarvis be concerned about quantity per order?

4. Williston links order quantity policy with problems of working capital. Would he do better to borrow for working capital, if necessary, to take advantage of the purchase savings and maintain his credit rating with suppliers? Is investment in materials actually idle, as he assumes?

5. Assuming that Jarvis takes over all purchasing for Williston Mills, what steps should he take toward formulating an order quantity policy? How would it affect the present system on supply items? What circumstances and what specific characteristics of materials should he recognize as limiting or modifying application of a general policy?

CHAPTER 18
JT INDUSTRIES

Alice Davies, purchasing manager for JT Industries (JTI) has been confronted with a new problem dealing with demurrage charges assessed by the Great Southern Railroad on inbound and outbound rail shipments from her plant.

JT Industries, a Florida-based company, primarily serves the southeastern agriculture industry by providing custom-mixed fertilizers. As a result of the large demand for fertilizers of all kinds, JTI receives large shipments of bulk liquid and granulated components for their mixing process.

Demurrage is the fee that railroads charge for the extended use of a freight car, basically a penalty payment for the railroad's inability to use the car for revenue purposes. The current updated average demurrage tariffs and provisions, applied to JTI were:

1. All time starts at 12:01 A.M. after placement at site.
2. All weekends and holidays count as demurrage days *except* Christmas Day, Thanksgiving Day, and New Year's Day.
3. Private cars on private tracks are not assessed charges regardless of whether they are loaded or empty.
4. Credits (two per loaded car and three per unloaded car) are subtracted from total demurrage days to yield chargeable days, which are rated at $30/day for the *first ten such* days and $60/day thereafter.

Liquid nitrogen is shipped in tank cars that are privately owned and leased on a trip-by-trip basis. Inbound phosphate, potash, lime, and other granulated materials can arrive in either private or railroad-owned equipment. Outbound mixed-fertilizer loads are usually shipped using railroad-owned cars, of one hundred-ton capacity each.

JTI uses a public rail spur for all their loading and unloading needs. It takes them approximately six hours to unload a tank car and ten hours to unload a hopper car. Loading times for fertilizer are generally two to three hours per car. JTI currently has enough track space to accomodate two tank cars and up to eight hopper cars per day.

JTI usually has no problem with demurrage except during the peak planting seasons of spring and fall when fertilizer is in greatest demand and Davies's concerns are whether their limited track space will cause increased charges under the updated tariffs. Ms. Davies was reviewing records of car unloadings during August. (Table 1)

QUESTIONS

1. Assume you are Alice Davies. What would you recommend to your company president in order to control these costs in both short and long term?
2. Calculate the demurrage costs for unloading the railroad cars during August.

This case was prepared by Joey Thompson under the guidance of Larry Giunipero.

Table 1 JTI Industries Demurrage Unloadings

CAR #	Actual Place Date Starting 12:01 am	Release Date	Days On Hand
001	Aug. 01	Aug. 06	5
002	Aug. 05	Aug. 08	3
003	Aug. 12	Aug. 14	2
004	Aug. 12	Aug. 19	7
005	Aug. 20	Aug. 24	4
	Demurrage Days	TOTAL	21

CHAPTER 18
CUSTOMCRAFT ASSOCIATES

Customcraft Associates, designers and manufacturers of expensive, custom-built office furniture—desks, chairs, tables, cabinets, and the like—has an annual volume of about $21 million, and sales are increasing an average of 10 percent yearly. The company's products are sold and bought strictly as luxury items, so that the question of cost is secondary to the skill and reputation of its internationally known designers. The furniture is sold throughout the United States and Canada, but it goes primarily to such large cities as San Francisco, New York, Denver, Chicago, Pittsburgh, Toronto, Montreal, and Atlanta.

The company is located in a small town about forty miles north of San Francisco, where Junius Dolp, founder, president, and major stockholder, first established himself as a cabinetmaker. Ambitious and acquisitive as well as artistic, Dolp started the business about a dozen years ago with the help of some private investors, who now own about one-third of the company's stock.

Buying for the company is under the general supervision of Chris McTiernan, manager of manufacturing and purchasing. Dolp, however, does most of the buying of the major raw material, hardwoods. He negotiates annual contracts with brokers for domestic birch and cherry, imported teak, and walnut and mahogany. Releases against these contracts are issued by McTiernan. Dolp also insists, almost obsessively, on getting involved in the purchase of packaging and protective materials used on outbound shipments of Customcraft furniture. McTiernan, who had had wide experience in general industry before joining Customcraft, respected Dolp's expertise in lumber purchasing but felt that he was unnecessarily extravagant in his selection of packaging materials. "Looking at some of that material, Junius," he once remarked, "people would think you were shipping the Mona Lisa back to the Louvre." "Well," Dolp replied, "at times I have been referred to as the da Vinci of furniture designers."

Requisitioning and buying of components was done somewhat informally. Requests for purchase were initiated by both McTiernan and the chief designer, Maurice Ratelle. Theoretically, all requisitions should have been approved by McTiernan, but he did not object to Ratelle's sending an occasional one directly to Barbara Todd, who was responsible for preparing and placing all purchase orders.

Todd, a young college graduate with a degree in business administration, was actually hired for a position in the accounting department but had picked up a grab bag of duties in her two years with Customcraft. In addition to her accounting tasks, she was responsible for processing purchase orders, as mentioned, and for handling all administrative details of Customcraft's shipments to customers. Because of her heavy work load, Todd's efforts in the last two areas were primarily clerical; she had little time to negotiate with suppliers, much less to analyze and evaluate freight rates and charges, transportation modes, or specific carriers.

McTiernan's instincts and experience led him to feel that purchasing—of both materials and transportation—could be put on a more businesslike basis. He decided to broach the subject to Dolp but to do so somewhat indirectly by focusing first on transportation rather than the more sensitive area of purchasing.

Outbound shipments were almost exclusively handled by the San Francisco office of a coast-to-coast trucking company, with occasional orders picked up by local carriers for transport to San Francisco for transshipment either by rail or air.

Customcraft placed a relatively large number of small purchase orders, mainly with specialty vendors in the Chicago area, for customized laminations, quality hardware, trim, fasteners, drawer slides, and so on. Because of rush orders from customers, numerous design changes during the manufacturing process, and the generally erratic demand for components of custom-built products, a steady stream of small shipments—sometimes two or three a week from individual suppliers—arrived at the Customcraft plant. Because shipping instructions were generally limited to "ship best way" or "ship as soon as possible" (sometimes a combination of the two was used), the shipments came in by a variety of ways: bus, truck, United Parcel Service, U.S. mail, and frequently air freight.

McTiernan approached Dolp with the idea that an assistant with purchasing and transportation responsibilities exclusively be assigned. "We could get a little bit more organization in our buying," he said, "but I think the big advantage would be to give us a better handle on transportation costs."

Dolp demurred. "You have good control over purchasing now, Chris," he said, "and I don't see any great problems staring us in the face. As for transportation, it seems to me that we can't do much better than we're doing now. As I understand it, our suppliers ship F.O.B. the buyer's headquarters. It's easier all around. Span-America Transit has been doing a good job for us for years, and I'm sure the price is right. Anyway, freight rates on the kind of luxury stuff we make are built right into prices. Our customers are not the kind that quibble over freight costs when they're spending a couple of thousand dollars on a desk. Why should we go to the trouble and expense of adding overhead when we are doing OK now?"

Dolp then reminded McTiernan that he and his wife were leaving on a long-planned around-the-world trip the following week. "Maybe I'll feel different about it after I see how much it costs to move the two of us around the world," he said with a smile. "Let's talk about it when I get back."

During Dolp's absence McTiernan discussed his ideas with Todd, carefully avoiding any implication that Todd might be given the job if Dolp agreed that he should have an assistant. Todd said that she shared McTiernan's conviction that more clearly defined policies and procedures on purchasing and transportation would be in the company's best interests. Privately, she speculated that the change might be in her best interests, inasmuch as she had been handling many of the purchasing and shipping procedures up to now.

QUESTIONS

1. Assume that you are McTiernan and describe and explain the strategy you would use in an effort to convince Dolp of the soundness of your suggestions.

2. Can inbound and outbound freight be combined for cost advantages?
3. Discuss the impact of packaging on freight costs.

CHAPTER 19
AUXILIARY COATING COMPANY

The Auxiliary Coating Company uses Solvosol, a flammable water-soluble commodity chemical, in several of its products. The primary use is in a trade specialty called Stripeeze, a paint, varnish, and lacquer remover.

There are five producers of Solvosol, but three of them share about 85 percent of the market. These three also share equally in Auxiliary Coating's annual requirement of 3.6 million pounds. The producers are the Finesse Company, Continental Reactants, Inc., and the Specialty Commodity Corporation. Finesse is located in Baton Rouge, Louisiana; Continental in Bayonne, New Jersey; and Specialty in Chicago, Illinois. Auxiliary Coating has three plant locations: Washington, D.C.; Cleveland, Ohio; and Pensacola, Florida. Solvosol is currently priced at fifteen cents per pound, freight allowed.

Expansion plans of the three dominant producers and an announced joint venture that will result in a new producer, Bi-Products Company, with a capability of producing 100 million pounds in two years, interested Auxiliary's purchasing manager, Colin Pearson.

"The current market in this stuff is balanced, with an overall demand of about 450 to 500 million pounds," he said to his senior buyer, Raymond Paul. "I think when this new facility comes on stream, we'll see the price coming down. That should be within the next two years."

Auxiliary Coating buys Solvolsol in 10,000-gallon tank cars and 5,000-gallon tank trucks. The Solvolsol weighed 8 lb/gallon. Auxiliary Coating presently purchases its requirement by plant location as follows:

	Washington, D.C.	Cleveland, Ohio	Pensacola, Florida
Finesse Co.	300,000	300,000	600,000
Continental	600,000	300,000	300,000
Specialty	300,000	600,000	300,000

"We've had no specific offer from Bi-Products," Pearson told Paul. "But they are talking about prices in the range of twelve cents a pound within eighteen to twenty-four months. We've been getting mixed reports about them, some good, some bad. Our technical department, for example, is on the pessimistic side—they have some real doubts about the feasibility of Bi-Products' new process for producing Solvosol."

Bi-Products Company was located in Pittsburgh and had shipping charges of .80/cwt to Washington, D.C., .50/cwt to Cleveland, and 2.00/cwt to Pensacola in 5,000-gallon tank trucks. Their freight terms were F.O.B. Pittsburgh Freight Collect. Pearson expected freight charges to a new plant in Texas to run 3.00–

3.50/cwt and to one in California at 4.00–4.50/cwt. Rail car shipment costs were expected to be 80 percent of truck rates.

"We're under a lot of pressure," he continued. "More competitors have entered the market with products like our Stripeeze, and our marketing department is thinking of lowering the price on it. I don't think it's such a good idea —after all, Stripeeze is still the leader and still the best product on the market.

"But we'll go along and try to get the raw-material costs down this year. I'd even be willing to switch as much as two-thirds of our requirements to one supplier if it could come up with a suitable incentive for us."

Auxiliary Coating's forecasts for the coming year indicate a usage of 4.0 million pounds of Solvosol; for the following year, 4.4 million pounds; the year after that, 5.0 million pounds; and the following year, 5.4 million pounds.

All three suppliers of the product have been fairly equal in product quality, service, and price. Auxiliary Coating has split its business at each location to accommodate the suppliers' wishes of the largest share closest to their producing point.

The company, which has been producing Stripeeze, among other products, at all three locations, has been considering building a fourth plant in the Southwest or Far West. The market in that area has been growing steadily and presently accounts for about 15 percent of Stripeeze production. Most of this is supplied from the Pensacola and Cleveland plants.

QUESTIONS

1. As senior buyer, Raymond Paul, you have the job of analyzing your company's requirements for Solvosol, current supply and price trends in the commodity, and the chances of negotiating more favorable contracts with one or more of your present suppliers.
2. Draw up a set of recommendations covering a purchase plan for Solvosol for the next three years, including the negotiating strategy you suggest be used with the suppliers.

CHAPTER 20
HALEY BROTHERS, INC.

After several years of pleasant but in many ways frustrating experience as purchasing manager for Haley Brothers, Dan Dinnock was getting restless. He had no complaints about his personal treatment from the company, an old, conservative manufacturer of construction scaffolding, metal tubing, and industrial wheelbarrows and wagons. But the management was strictly engineering oriented and gave other departments, including purchasing, very little chance to use initiative, to innovate, or to depart very far from established ways of doing things. Dan, who made it a point to stay abreast of the latest procurement techniques through reading in trade magazines and attending educational sessions of his local purchasing association, felt stifled every time one of his suggestions for improvement was politely rebuffed.

He took a new lease on life, however, when Haley Brothers bought out a nearby small firm called City Safety.

The firm made a line of traffic and safety devices for city and state municipalities and private firms. These included safety barricades and men-working and caution signs. His department was given a bigger buying job (the smaller firm's purchasing had been done by the two partners), and he gladly accepted the challenge of increased responsibility. The very fact that Haley Brothers was expanding, he reasoned, indicated that management might be more receptive to new ideas than they had been in the past.

One of the new concepts in purchasing that intrigued Dan was value analysis. Here, he thought, was a technique that could help make purchasing a scientific, profit-producing function. Still a little gun shy from previous resistance to his suggestions by management, he determined to build a strong case for value analysis—prove its worth beyond doubt—before proposing to his superiors the idea of a formal value analysis program.

Without mentioning it outside his department, he set up a small, informal value analysis program with his buyers. They met for two hours every Friday afternoon to review components they purchased for both divisions of the company. They submitted each of the parts selected for analysis to the "Ten Tests for Value" made famous by the General Electric Company. When a promising project appeared to be developing, one person was given the job of accumulating cost data on the part, estimating savings through substitution, capabilities of various vendors of the part, projected savings over a given period, and similar data. This extra activity was burdensome in terms of time and effort, but the entire group was enthusiastic about its possibilities.

After half a dozen inconclusive meetings, the group finally came up with a project that showed promise. Studying the function of four threaded rods used on a line of industrial wagons, they questioned the special design of the rod and the fact that the thread was cut on a screw machine. Buyer Jane Bolton, follow-up person on this project, ultimately came up with the following information:

> The holding function of the rod is not critical, could just as easily be performed if the thread were rolled (a much cheaper process than screw machining). The special bend in the rod was designed during the manufacture of an earlier-model wagon, is no longer necessary in the current streamlined design. A standard rod widely used in the automotive industry would do the job just as well. A specialty supplier, now making similar parts, could supply the rolled-thread, standard rods to Haley Brothers for approximately eighty cents each. The company is currently paying four dollars each for the specially designed part.

In his enthusiasm over coming up with a substantial potential saving, Dan lost some of his caution. He went directly to the president. "T. J.," he said, "just look at this. An 80 percent reduction in part cost on just this one item. And we use thousands of them. Our group came up with this almost in their spare time. Think what we could do with a real value analysis program—with a full-time value analyst." He went on to explain the basic principles of the technique.

The president listened attentively and complimented the purchasing manager on "an excellent cost-reduction suggestion." But he seemed unimpressed by Dan's proposal to establish a formal value analysis program. "Our engineers will get around to these things eventually," he said, apparently assuming that the products of the toy and game division were already so well engineered that value analysis of them was unnecessary. "You can be a good stimulus to them by this approach—which is really only good buying to begin with, isn't it? Go and talk to the engineers about what you're doing and the two of you can probably work out a good cost-reduction program."

A week later Joan Anderson, one of Dinnock's buyers was meeting with the marketing manager and engineers of City Safety. She had been called in because the previous purchasing manager had left the company. Bob Friend, the marketing manager was discussing with Michael Lind, the design engineer, the bad reports on the safety devices that fit around the manhole covers. "The city purchasing manager claims his workers can't store more than three of these on a pickup. They are heavy and bulky."

"However," Michael replied, "they serve a vital purpose—keeping pedestrians from falling into openings and making street traffic aware of worker activity. In addition, they protect the city workers."

"I feel they have to be rigid and sturdy—we have to overdesign them," Bob said. "What you're saying is true Mike, but I don't want to lose customers to a competitor who builds a design that allows easier storage at a lower cost—currently we do quite well in this market."

Joan immediately spoke up, "Remember, we saved costs on the industrial wagons by going from machine threaded to a rolled thread. Why couldn't we use our value analysis program to explore a better solution?"

Michael indicated this was an engineering project. "How can you guys in purchasing help?"

"First we can search out suppliers for ideas. They are experts at what they do. Second, we can provide all necessary cost and availability input," Joan said. "And I think we would go a lot further a great deal quicker if we did it as a team."

"You know they did save us money on that wagon," Bob pointed out.

"Okay," said Michael, "just remember, you guys don't write any specifications, and I want to be part of supplier meetings, and I hope you will keep us informed."

"Mike, our intent is to better City Safety's product line in this area so Bob can sell a product that is superior to our competitors and cost effective," Joan told him.

The following week, specifications for the manhole protection device (see Exhibit 1) were completed by engineering. Figures compiled by the committee were as follows:

Sales volume per year	$100,000
Average sales price/unit	$240
Cost of direct material/unit	$95
Cost of labor/unit—4 hrs. $15/hr.	

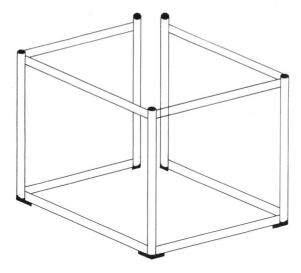

Exhibit 1 Design for Manhole Guard

Dan talked with Joan prior to the second meeting with Michael. "This is a key project. We need to put our best foot forward, because it could provide a real boost to our value analysis efforts." Dan quickly realized that obtaining support from upper management would greatly enhance chances for the success of a value analysis project. After appointing Joan to head the value analysis project, he returned to his office and listed several alternatives for pursuing value analysis on a continuing basis:

- Develop and document more than one value analysis project and present them as a "package" to the president, detailing in dollar figures the total savings to be achieved in one year.
- Present savings on a given project—the industrial wagon, for example—in cumulative form, and show, if possible, their effects on the profit margin on that product. Or if the product is a highly competitive one, show how value analysis savings would make more competitive pricing possible.
- Using the kind of figures developed above, make a formal presentation to the president, asking for an organized value analysis program in the plant. Show the potential "payoff" on value analysis as compared with the cost of setting up a value analysis organization.
- Alternatively, suggest that purchasing be allowed to "borrow" an engineer from design engineering for a few half-days a week to work on value analysis projects developed in conjunction with buyers and vendors.
- Go around management for the time being, and try to expand the informal program by bringing the production and engineering departments into it. Later, with concrete results obtained by this method, present a united front to management and ask for a formal value analysis program.

QUESTIONS

1. Put together a value analysis package on the manhole protector. It should include new ideas, your role in this project, and specific questions you want answered.

2. What are some alternative designs you could come up with for the new manhole protector design?
3. Which of the alternative approaches suggested for obtaining top-management approval would you support? Discuss.

The authors wish to acknowledge help from the Purchasing Management Association of St. Louis and the St. Louis Purchaser.

CHAPTER 21
ELECTROVAX, INC.

On October 1 Donald Frank, purchasing manager for Electrovax, had just got off the phone with Amanda King, manager of facilities engineering. Amanda had told him that an order for one hundred double-stacked trailers had to be placed with Trailrig, Inc., on Thursday. Donald had indicated he felt such action was not in line with proper purchasing practices and furthermore that the project should be competitively bid. Amanda had insisted that the double-stacked trailers must be completely installed within forty-five days, or Electrovax, Inc., could lose a billion-dollar government contract.

Electrovax was a growing firm located in suburban Philadelphia. It received almost 100 percent of its business from defense contracts. A large government contract that was to be awarded in the near future required that the successful company have adequate facilities. Owing to growth in other contract areas, Electrovax was short on space to support such a project. Marketing and facilities had met in late September to discuss the quickest method to alleviate this problem, and Amanda had suggested double-stacked trailers. Double-stacked trailers are similar to mobile homes, except that they are two stories high. Electrovax had used such facilities in the past to meet office and manufacturing space shortages. In this case the firm could perform light manufacturing in the trailers. A major benefit of double stacking was the reduction in land area, which made the cost per square foot lower than with the traditional one-story trailer.

Trailrig, Inc., had supplied the company with double-stacked trailers in the past and had performed very well. Trailrig's headquarters was located in Tampa, Florida, and manufacturing was performed in Harrisburg, Pennsylvania, and Tampa. The company had erected double-stacked trailers throughout the Northeast and was well-known for its quality. In addition, Amanda had got to know the personnel at Trailrig through initial plant visits and local contact with Tex Ruxpen, the company's sales representative for the Northeast. "I feel Trailrig meets five major criteria. They have performed well in the past; have double-stacked trailers all over the Northeast; have a fine reputation; will manufacture at a location only four hours from our plant; and have an excellent support staff," she stated at a meeting on the trailer project. However, when Donald asked her to provide a sole-source justification, she refused the request. "The price has been competitive, Don. We don't need to waste valuable time bidding this job!"

After she had finished, Donald said, "It is true that Trailrig is a good supplier; however, market conditions change, and both you and I know that there are other suppliers out there."

"To our knowledge, none has put up double-stacked trailers in the Northeast," she replied. "We need those trailers in forty-five days, or we could lose a billion-dollar job!"

Late Wednesday, Donald researched his sources for double-stacked trailers. On Thursday he received the requisition. He sent out six bids over the Thermofax (fax) machine, asking for replies by Friday. He had called all six after the "faxing" to ensure that they had received the information and understood the requirements.

On Friday he received three bids, while three other firms declined to bid. The prices, F.O.B. Philadelphia, Pennsylvania, were as follows:

		Delivery	Manufactured
Washco	$4.5 million	45-day delivery	Lincoln, Neb.
Trailrig	4.3 million	60-day delivery	Harrisburg, Pa.
Builtrite	3.9 million	45-day delivery	Salt Lake City, Utah

After receiving the bids, Donald asked Amanda to send facilities engineers to each location on Saturday to check the manufacturing capabilities of each plant. Meanwhile, he requested a Dun and Bradstreet report on all three suppliers. Monday morning the facilities engineers reported all three shops were technically capable of producing double-stacked trailers to Electrovax's specifications. It was found that Builtrite had only limited experience with double-stacked trailers, although its quality on single-stacked trailers was excellent.

Donald then asked the three companies to submit their best and final price and delivery. Final quotes were unchanged, except that Trailrig agreed to a forty-five day delivery. Based on these results, Donald's decision was to eliminate Washco and have the other two, Builtrite and Trailrig, fly in Tuesday for final negotiations. The Trailrig group met him cordially, and all were neatly dressed in their three-piece suits. They promised forty-five-day delivery and quality in line with their past standards. Matthew John, salesperson from Builtrite, came in Tuesday afternoon and was casually dressed in a sport coat, no tie, and deck shoes. While his dress caused initial concern, he was quite honest in his admission of having built very few double-stacked trailers. He did point out, however, that his shop had the full capabilities to do the work.

After meeting with both suppliers, Amanda continued to favor Trailrig. "Their experience is worth it," she said. Donald knew he would have to decide immediately. He knew that a billion-dollar order hinged on the right decision.

QUESTIONS

1. What are some additional factors that Donald should consider in the evaluation?
2. What financial information should he review?
3. From whom would you buy, and why?

This case was prepared with the assistance of Richard Straw.

CHAPTER 22
ALBREE MOTOR PARTS

The vice-president of Albree Motor Parts was much impressed by the conveyor system in a new plant erected by one of its customers. The installation, he learned, had cost $110,000. It had been specially designed for that plant and was an integral part of the operating plan. The customer was well pleased with it. He had no breakdown of operating costs specifically applicable to this equipment but considered it the key to overall plant efficiency.

Materials handling was a major expense in Albree's own operation, amounting to nearly 30 percent of total manufacturing cost, or about $3 million a year. This included the movement of raw materials in and out of stores to the machines and through several fabricating processes and delivery of fabricated parts to the production assembly line and then to finished stores. The plant was well laid out for sequence of operations and had been extensively mechanized; but because the handling equipment had been acquired piecemeal as the company expanded and new needs arose, it was not completely coordinated. Considerable rehandling was required at and between work stations. By means of power-lift trucks, manual handling was kept at a minimum. Total investment in materials-handling equipment was carried on the company's books at the depreciated value of $130,000. Replacement cost at current prices was estimated at $300,000. There was $90,000 available in the capital-equipment reserve account, accumulated on depreciation schedules.

The vice-president sent the chief engineer and the general superintendent to inspect the installation at the customer's plant. At the same time he asked Northeastern Equipment Company, makers of that equipment, to survey Albree's situation and make recommendations. Northeastern's proposal after this study was to retain about half the present equipment, with minor changes, replacing the rest with an overhead conveyor installation similar to the one that had appealed to the vice-president in the first place but tailored to Albree's special requirements. The cost was estimated at $140,000. It seemed probable that savings of double that amount would be effected in materials-handling costs each year. The superintendent felt that certain modifications and additions to this plan would be necessary to obtain maximum benefit. With these changes $8,500 was added to the bid.

A conference was called, including the president, treasurer, and director of purchases, to consider the proposal. The discussion centered largely on the extra charge. The president and treasurer held the view that Northeastern, a specialist in the field, was best qualified to tell what was needed; they felt that only the original proposal should be considered. The superintendent contended that the problem at this point was to find the best possible solution to the materials-handling needs and that those who were to use the equipment could make a practical contribution to that decision. It would still be possible to make any necessary compromise, for cost or any other reason, but it seemed more logical to him to have an optimum goal as the starting point. In the present instance the indicated saving was more than ample to provide the complete installation.

The engineer agreed that the suggested changes were desirable, if not absolutely necessary, but recommended that cost studies be made to see whether the added investment would be justified economically. As a matter of fact, he pointed out, their cost information on the whole project was not only meager but hypothetical. It seemed fairly certain that substantial savings could be made, but he felt that these should be verified and calculated more accurately before the money was invested.

The director of purchases had two suggestions. He proposed, first, that Newell Company, which had installed most of the present conveyor equipment, should be asked for advice and costs of modernizing the existing installation, if possible, to achieve the same result. Second, he believed that competition should be invited to bid on systems comparable to Northeastern's, so that results and costs could be better evaluated. The engineer supported this view. The vice-president was cool to both suggestions. As to the first, plant efficiency was already suffering from a patchwork policy on materials handling. As for alternative sources for new equipment, he had great confidence in Northeastern, having inspected the installation, and he felt under some obligation to that company on account of the survey they had made. The director of purchases felt no such obligation to Northeastern. He did feel a responsibility to his own company to explore the alternative possibilities. He could at least secure descriptive literature from a number of manufacturers without committing the company in any way; if any of these products seemed appropriate, the group could then decide which manufacturers, if any, should be invited to make a proposal.

The chief engineer mentioned that he was planning to attend the annual Materials Handling Show in Cleveland some weeks hence. He suggested that the others also attend this exhibit to see at first hand what types of equipment were being shown and to judge how they might fit Albree's needs. The vice-president, superintendent, and director of purchases also made the trip. They found several systems that were interesting, ranging all the way to full automation, and noted some new developments that could be incorporated to advantage in their own specification. By process of elimination, their preference was narrowed to two firms, Fitch Corporation and Merritt Conveyors, whose product was basically similar to Northeastern's. Bids were invited from each of these companies. When these quotations were received, Albree had four proposals to consider.

Newell Company offered supplementary equipment amounting to $22,000, which would expand the present installation to take care of increased volume without any significant change in present methods or flow.

Northeastern, as previously noted, proposed to replace half the present equipment with a new overhead system that was considerably faster and more efficient. The cost was $148,500. The director of purchases believed he would be able to dispose of the replaced equipment within a reasonable time for about $45,000, or 70 percent of its current book value.

Fitch's proposal was substantially the same as Northeastern's on a bid of $144,000.

Merritt bid on a completely new system, costing $275,000. Certain features of their equipment, they believed, were so far superior to the present installation that a fully integrated system would show much greater efficiency. In this case the disposal of old equipment would bring up to $75,000.

In tabulating these several proposals the director of purchases found it difficult to evaluate relative performance and efficiency, because there was no direct factor of productivity that could be measured and applied against cost as in the case of production machinery. In consultation with the manufacturing and cost accounting department, he listed three factors that might serve as useful indicators.

1. Direct maintenance charges of 5 percent annually on total cost of equipment.
2. Estimated savings in labor for materials-handling operations. With Newell's additional equipment, four of the present employees could be dispensed with or transferred to other duties. Northeastern's and Fitch's installations could be operated with nine fewer employees. Merritt's system, more completely mechanized and coordinated, would require fourteen fewer people than the present sytem.
3. To measure potential improvement in overall manufacturing efficiency and cost saving, a cost study was projected as accurately as possible for each of the proposed systems. Under present conditions materials handling represented 30 percent of total manufacturing cost. With the additional Newell equipment, this would be reduced to 28 percent. With the Northeastern or Fitch equipment, it would be further reduced to 25 percent. With the completely new Merritt sytem, it would be only 22 percent.

The cost department further applied standard and overhead and depreciation schedules for the new investment. These included a 10 year straight line depreciation schedule, no salvage value, a 50 percent tax rate, savings in labor of $7/hour, and 8 hour workday for 250 days/year.

Technically, the engineer believed that any one of the four proposed systems would be adequate. In order of excellence, he rated them (1) Merritt, (2) Northeastern, (3) Fitch, and (4) Newell. He stressed that this rating did not include any economic factors. It did give some weight to the newness of the equipment. This gave the edge to Merritt in the immediate evaluation, an advantage that might be modified if all bids contemplated a wholly new installation.

As a matter of personal preference, the vice-president and superintendent were still favorably disposed toward Northeastern, largely on the basis of the successful installation they had inspected.

QUESTIONS

1. Evaluate the four proposals on the basis of information gathered and judgments expressed. Which factors should prevail in the final decision—management's concern with capital expenditure, the superintendent's preference as user of the equipment, the engineer's technical appraisal, or the purchasing director's economic analysis?
2. How and by whom should the final decision be made?
3. Could the problem be solved more expeditiously and just as competently without the conference method?

4. Should the director of purchases have been called into conference at an earlier stage of the project, that is, before Northeastern's original proposal was invited and received?
5. The vice-president and superintendent retained their original preference for Northeastern's equipment in spite of the elaborate studies; what were the advantages, if any, in making this additional investigation?

CHAPTER 23
GUNTHER STOVE COMPANY

The executive committee of Gunther Stove Company had designated Franklin Associates, a management consulting firm, to make a thorough study of the company's organization and procedures and to recommend any changes that might be made to improve efficiency. This study was prompted not by any serious dissatisfaction with present performance but to get the benefit of an expert, objective evaluation. The study was made in great detail, covering every department, using checklists and standards that the Franklin organization had developed for the purpose. When the data had been assembled and analyzed, Gary Franklin presented his report to the committee. It was generally favorable, with a number of suggestions regarding each department designed to simplify or expedite the work. His recommendations concerning purchasing were to bring traffic control under the jurisdiction of this department; to add one buyer, preferably with engineering training; to set up a special fund that would permit the handling of small local orders on a petty cash basis, eliminating considerable paperwork on these dealings; and to transfer the checking of invoices to the accounting department, because he felt that no department should audit its own transactions.

"By the way," said Alex Gunther, the company president, "how is our purchasing department doing? I've been in the management of this company forty years, and I've never had a satisfactory answer to that question."

Franklin said that in his judgment the department was doing very well.

"How well?" Gunther persisted. "Would you rate it as 95 percent, 90 percent, 85 percent, or what?"

Mr. Franklin said that it was impossible to set objective standards of performance that would permit a rating of this sort. There were too many variables and intangibles involved. A rating depended, first, on what you expected and, second, on whether that expectation was reasonable.

"But you must have some basis for saying that our buyers are doing a good job, and that's what I'm trying to get at. After all, purchasing is a pretty tangible business. We spend X number of dollars, and we buy X tons or carloads of iron and nickel and bolts and coal and shipping cases. What I want to know is whether we're getting full value for our dollars and whether it's costing us more than it should to buy those materials. I'm not interested in how many purchase orders we issue or how much we deduct in cash discounts. I'm interested in the quality of our buying performance and in results. What I'd like to see is a simple report, maybe six or eight really significant figures, that would give me the picture."

"I think we can get the figures for you," said Franklin. "You'd have to make your own evaluation, as we do. At the start I doubt that you could rate them any closer than *excellent, good,* or *fair.* After the first few months, when you have a chance to make comparisons, you may be able to apply some sort of scale—if you still think it's worthwhile."

Franklin went back to the purchasing manager, and together they worked out a report to give Gunther the information he wanted. Their first step was to define the areas of purchasing activity to be considered in an evaluation; the second step was to select measurable factors in each of these areas that were known or available from existing records and that would indicate to a significant extent the quality of performance and results obtained. They decided on the following areas:

1. Effectiveness of procurement as a service of supply
2. Price performance in buying
3. Cost reductions, specific savings
4. Inventory performance
5. Administrative performance, efficiency, cost of purchasing
6. Miscellaneous intangibles

Under each of these headings they jotted down everything that came to mind pertinent to that area of activity and responsibility. Despite Gunther's aversion to statistical information, they found that much of the information was basically of this nature. However, the figures acquired more than statistical significance when they were related to other figures in the form of a ratio or as a proportion of the total; one of the problems was to find the appropriate standards of comparison and methods of presentation. Some of the factors were of a negative nature, inverse to the quality of purchasing performance; nevertheless, they were important in any complete evaluation. "We'll have to differentiate," said Franklin, "between those that are rated on a low score, as in golf, and those that are rated on a high score, as in bowling. If we get to the point of making a numerical rating, there are simple mathematical means to take care of this, but we'll run into the even tougher problem of assigning weights to the various factors."

The list of suggested possible indicators grew much longer than the half-dozen criteria that Gunther had requested, but it was a necessary preliminary to the process of selection. When they had finished, the following factors were noted on their worksheet:

1. Service of supply

   - Numbers of delinquent deliveries
   - Machine downtime due to lack of material
   - Schedule revisions necessary due to lack of material
   - Successful substitutions made by purchasing department to avoid downtime or schedule revisions
   - Number of rush orders handled (proportion of total orders; of dollar volume)
   - Number of change orders issued
   - Follow-up action (number of orders; cost of follow-up)

- Number and amount of premium transportation charges paid to get deliveries on time
- Numbers of deliveries rejected by inspection department
- Cost of reworking substandard materials
- Number of overdue orders in open-order file
- Commodities for which alternate supply sources have been established and used

2. Price performance
   - Number of price changes, up or down, from previous prices paid
   - Number of orders placed on competitive bidding
   - Number of orders placed by negotiation
   - Commodities covered by term contracts (how long a term?)
   - Actual prices paid compared with published market (market at time of purchase or at time of use; should this be shown for individual key commodities, as currently kept in chart form in purchasing office, or could it be put in the form of comparative price indices?)
   - Inventory valuation, actual cost versus replacement cost
   - Variances from standard costs
   - Direct material cost per unit of product
   - Average cost of selected commodities, year to date and projected to annual average on the basis of current price

3. Cost savings
   - Specific instances, savings projected on basis of annual usage, cumulative totals
   - Savings through change of source
   - Savings through change in method of buying
   - Savings by substitution
   - Savings by change in specification
   - Savings by standardization
   - Savings in transportation costs
   - Savings in manner of packaging

4. Inventory performance
   - Ratio of dollar inventory to sales volume
   - Inventory increase or decrease during month
   - Extent of forward coverage (weeks)
   - Inventory turnover (by commodity classifications)
   - Number of items under maximum-minimum stock control
   - Number of stockouts
   - Quantity discounts earned by revision of stock limits

5. Efficiency of operation
   - Total cost of purchasing related to dollar volume
   - Number of buyers
   - Number of nonbuying personnel (breakdown by functions)
   - Number of requisitions unprocessed within twenty-four hours
   - Number of small orders ($50 and under)
   - Cash discounts earned and forfeited
   - Average waiting time for salespeople

6. Miscellaneous
   - Sales of scrap and waste
   - Hours spent in staff training courses
   - Number of vendors' plants visited
   - Business and professional meetings attended

"I have evaluated your department on a number of other intangible factors," Franklin said, "such things as morale, public relations, organization, supervision, and the like, as well as on adequacy of records and procedures. You'll hear about these when the general manager discusses my report with you and other department heads. There's no doubt they have a distinct bearing on performance, and they are reflected in many of the items we have set down here. They are measurable, too, but not in the same sense as your specific activities. They are factors that you, as department head, should be evaluating for yourself and on which top management will evaluate you. I have recommended a simple plan for doing this systematically and confidentially throughout all departments of the company."

QUESTIONS

1. Consider, first, the general areas selected for evaluation. Are they all pertinent and necessary for this purpose?
2. What changes, if any, would you suggest in this approach, and should the various areas be weighted according to their relative importance?
3. Should an effort be made to include the intangibles that Gary Franklin has reserved for separate rating?
4. If his proposal for a general evaluation system is adopted, will it obviate the need for, or reduce the usefulness of, the detailed evaluation of performance, which was not included in his original recommendation?
5. Consider the measurements suggested under each heading. Which are most significant?
6. Prepare an outline for a monthly performance report based on the selected factors.
7. Is Mr. Gunther unreasonable or impractical in asking for a mathematical rating of purchasing performance?
8. What advantages, if any, would accrue to the purchasing department from systematic evaluation?

CHAPTERS 24, 25
HEIGHTS GENERAL HOSPITAL

Rose Silver was for several years purchasing manager for a medium-size electric-cooking-utensil company in New Jersey. In that position she was responsible for buying raw materials and components as well as maintenance, repair, and operating (MRO) supplies. She worked closely and harmoniously with engineering and production personnel and was respected for her competence and her ability to get along with people.

Although she did not make final decisions on prices and suppliers when machinery and equipment was being bought, Silver sat in on negotiations for such purposes. The negotiating teams in those instances usually comprised the manufacturing vice president (team leader), the engineering manager, the production manager, and herself. Although primarily an observer during the actual negotiations, she played a valuable role in the collection and coordination of data in the prenegotiation planning phase.

When her father died, Rose Silver felt compelled to return to her native Georgia to care for her mother. In her search for a position in the Atlanta area, she responded to an advertisement in the executive employment section of a local newspaper. Heights General Hospital, a six-hundred-bed institution, the ad read, had an opening for a purchasing director with broad experience, not necessarily in the health-care field, who had the potential to move up to the position of materials manager as the hospital implemented its plans for a major expansion of its facilities. The salary mentioned was in line with those offered for comparable industrial positions for which she had been interviewed. Sensing the interesting career opportunities in the growing health-care field and attracted by the idea of being able to participate in a form of social service while earning a living, she applied for the job.

Silver had interviews at several levels of the hospital organization, including one with the purchasing manager, who was retiring after having served for many years, first in the receiving department, then the stockroom, and finally the purchasing department. She had a particularly extensive discussion with Warrington Ranson, the hospital administrator, who seemed impressed by both her personal and professional qualifications. "We've got a lot of work ahead of us," he told her. "We need an aggressive yet cooperative purchasing executive who can bring a lot of expertise into this hospital. Our medical and technical people are tops in their professions. I want our administrative people to be equally good in their specialties."

One day, when she had been on the job for about six months, Rose Silver received an interoffice call from Dr. Earl Spiller, head of the radiology department. Dr. Spiller was a long-time member of the hospital's medical staff and had one of the highest incomes. In turn, his department generated substantial revenues for the hospital. The hospital, which owned the equipment he used, paid him a minimum salary and a third of the gross earnings of the department. "Rosie," he said cheerily, "come up here right away, will you? And bring your order pad with you, please." A bit stunned at first, Silver attended to a couple of details and then went to the doctor's office.

He got right to the point. "I want you to order a Model L-971 high-intensity X-ray processor from New Age Radiology, Inc.," he said, glancing at papers on his desk. "The price is $21,700. I dealt with Elmer Jarvis, the New Age regional manager on this, so if you have any questions, take them up with him, OK?"

"Well, it's not really quite OK yet, Doctor," Silver replied. "There are a number of things about this purchase that I'd like to discuss with you. It just isn't good business to buy an expensive piece of equipment of this size without . . ."

"Look, Rose," Spiller interrupted, "in this department we're dealing with people's health—their lives, even—and we can't afford to go shopping around for the lowest bid. It's my responsibility to get the best thing for the job, and I want that machine. New Age is the only company capable of supplying the kind of equipment I need."

"I'm not questioning your judgment or your authority, Doctor," she said. "At this point, I'm not questioning the price you mentioned or even suggesting that we put the requirement out to bid. All I'm saying is that there are a number of aspects about a purchase like that where I can be helpful—and protect the interests of the hospital. There's shipping, contract terms . . ."

Spiller broke in again: "Rosie, Mr. Jarvis assured me that all those details would be taken care of. Look, I've got to get out of here in a few minutes to catch the plane to the Bahamas. Be a good girl and get that order moving immediately, please." With that he left the room.

QUESTIONS

1. Is there any justification for Dr. Spiller's circumventing normal purchasing procedures, selecting the supplier, and approving the price of the L-971 machine?
2. What aspects of the purchase would come within Rose Silver's scope of responsibility in any case?
3. What other hospital departments would be of assistance to her in ensuring that there would be no problems in ordering, receiving, and installing the machine?
4. How should Silver proceed if she wants to meet the expecations of the administrator that she will bring "business expertise" to the job of buying for Heights General Hospital?

CHAPTER 26
THE METRO CONVENTION CENTER

In an effort to increase its share of the booming convention business, a large eastern city established the MetroCenter Development Corporation (MDC), a quasi-governmental body made up of business executives—all volunteers—and several public officials. The agency's major responsibility was to plan and supervise the development of a large convention center. This included contracting for engineering, architectural, and construction services. The corporation set up its own small staff of structural specialists and consultants to monitor the project.

Although the agency, by special legislation, was not subject to the rather stringent procurement regulations of the city, its choices of suppliers (engineering, architectural, and construction services) were generally based on the lowest "responsible" bids.

The architects and engineers who designed the superstructure for the new convention center called for 18,000 hollow steel balls, or nodes, about eight inches in diameter, to connect 77,000 steel rods and tubes supporting the space frame. Their specifications related primarily to the geometry of the frame. Technical details of the materials and methods, according to newspaper reports, were left up to the contractor. The MDC was to be responsible for testing the final product.

Some time after delivery began, hairline surface cracks and porous sections were found on many of the cast steel nodes. At first, it appears, a certain percentage of rejections was considered acceptable. But the percentage continued to grow, until ultimately nearly 12,000 nodes—a full year's production—were rejected before action was taken.

If the parts had been used in construction, they could have failed, causing sections of the frame to collapse. That potential disaster was avoided by discovery of the faulty castings. But another type of disaster, in this case a financial one, was not. Construction was delayed for at least six months and possibly up to two years, meaning that the city was deprived of many millions of dollars of income from conventions that were already scheduled for the new center and had to be moved to other cities.

It was not easy to get all the facts in the case, since lawsuits were anticipated and the contractor and foundry representatives were reluctant to discuss them publicly. This is what was known:

- The engineering firm that designed the node and tube arrangement said the rejected nodes were structurally sound. A strucural specialist and consultant to the development corporation said they were not.
- The geometry of the node makes it difficult to produce without flaws. Furthermore, the stresses it is subject to in a space frame are "complex and misunderstood," according to the consultant, who made the comment to a local newspaper reporter.
- The development corporation had done very little inspection at the supplier's foundry, a representative of the agency admitted. "Casting metal is something of a black art," he added, "and casters tend to be very protective of their processes."
- Some of the people involved, said one newspaper report, blamed the whole problem on the fact that the development corporation officials, the engineers, and the architects believed that detailed design decisions should be delegated.

The defective castings fiasco and the subsequent delay in building the convention center were politically embarrassing to the city's mayor. She had recently been reelected after a campaign in which she promised to help "make the city the convention capital of America." The mayor asked several business executives to serve on a committee to investigate various aspects of the botched project. Victor Kohlage, corporate director of purchases of a large manufacturing firm, was asked to analyze the entire convention center procurement action and report on what went wrong, why it did, and how such problems could be avoided in future programs of this kind.

QUESTIONS

1. Assume that you are Victor Kohlage. Analyze the facts given and prepare a summary report for submission to the city council and the local news media.
2. What actions, if any, legal or otherwise, would you take?

CHAPTER 26
STATE GOVERNMENT SITUATION

In a certain state the Department of General Services (DGS), Division of Purchasing, issued an invitation to bid (ITB) for general-convenience copiers. DGS is the central purchasing staff for the state and enters into purchase agreements made by many of the state agencies. Individual agencies have their own purchasing function for unique items. DGS intended to establish a twelve-month copier contract covering the fiscal year October 1 through September 30 of the next year. The ITB categorized copiers on the basis of group, type, class, and acquisition method. The following chart outlines this information.

GROUP
Group 1 - Plain bond copiers
Group 2 - Magazine-finish copiers

TYPE (FEATURES)
Type 1   - Copiers possess minimal features.
Type 2   - Copiers have two-sided copying capability.
Type 3   - Copiers have ability to reduce size of documents.

CLASS (MACHINE SPEED)
Class 1   - Low-speed copiers
Class 2   - Low-speed/low-volume copiers
Class 2A - Accelerated low-speed/low-volume copiers
Class 3   - Intermediate-speed copiers
Class 3A - Accelereated intermediate-speed copiers
Class 4   - High-speed copiers
Class 4A - Accelerated high-speed/high-volume copiers

ACQUISITION METHOD
Monthly rental
Annual rental
Two-year lease
Outright purchase

As can be seen from the chart, there are forty-two combinations on the bid package. For example, a group 1, type 1, class 1, is a plain-bond, low-speed copier with minimal features. In addition to the forty-two combinations, there are four main acquisition methods, from rental to purchase.

Bids were sent to twelve major copier suppliers. All twelve responded and were considered responsive potential contractors. DGS intended to establish this contract by issuing single awards to the lowest responsive bidder in each particular copier category.

Kory Kopier Company (Kory), a major participant and competitor in this field, filed a petition requesting a formal administrative hearing to challenge DGSB's policy decision to award the state's yearly copier contract via the single award method. Kory was seeking a recommended order that would require the DGS to procure the copiers in question utilizing the multiple award approach.

DGS filed a response to Kory's petition denying the validity of their arguments against the proposed competitive award process. In addition, the Gulf Coast Copier Corporation (Gulf Coast), the current market leader in general-convenience copiers, was allowed to intervene and subsequently filed a motion to dismiss Kory's petition. Gulf Coast was a very price-competitive supplier. The single award system would tend to help Gulf Coast obtain business. This was in contrast to Kory, which was a well-known name brand in the copier business and justified slightly higher commercial prices on the basis of its claim of superior copier quality.

CONTRACTING METHODS

Controversy in this case revolved around the type of acquisition method utilized by DGS—the single award system or the multiple award system. The single award system requires the development of product specifications or a product description that can be clearly understood. Once these parameters are established, a single award can be presented to the lowest responsive bidder in each product category. This technique is considered an effective means of procurement in government circles, since it allows any commercial vendor an equal opportunity to compete without favoring any particular name-brand product. This increased competition generally leads to better prices.

The multiple award type of acquisition system is normally used as an exception to single award contracting. This method is utilized in cases where it is difficult or impracticable to develop adequate product specifications or where users have many different requirements. After a government agency negotiates a multiple contract with contractors who offer similar (but not identical) products, user agencies order directly from any of the contractors on the approved list. User agencies are usually required to order the lowest-priced items listed on the multiple award schedule that meet their individual needs. However, special needs often justify ordering higher-priced products.

HISTORY OF COPIER PROCUREMENT AT DGS

Historically, copiers were sold to various state departments through multiple pricing agreements established by the DGS. However, three years ago the DGS had begun entertaining competitive bids for one year, single award contracts for general-purpose, walk-up convenience copiers. Currently, each ITB categorized the state's requirements for copiers according to the various options previously mentioned. As the DGS's policy stood now, if one or more responsive bid within a copier category were received, a contract was awarded to the lowest responsive bidder. If, however, the DGS failed to receive competitive bids in a category, multiple award contracts were issued to all qualified vendors for that particular category only.

Last year the DGS had solicited competitive bids for the term copier contract and awarded a contract to the single low responsive bidder in all categories in which it received at least one responsive bid. In categories where no responsive bids were received, the DGS chose to negotiate with the lowest-priced nonresponsive bidder in an attempt to eliminate the bidder's nonresponsive terms. If the vendor agreed to withdraw terms that varied from the specifications, the DGS made a single award in the category to that particular vendor. However, if all vendors in the category refused to withdraw nonresponsive conditions, no award was made. This process was successful, since no multiple awards were made on the current contract.

CONTRACT DISPUTE POSITIONS

DGS View

The DGS, Division of Purchasing, cited seven major issues to support its copier purchase decision through single award competitive bidding:

1. Single awards ensure fair competition and an equal advantage to all qualified vendors desiring to do business with the state.
2. Competitive bidding that leads to a single award is reasonable, since (a) the majority of agency needs can be satisfied by devising categories based upon machine speed, copy volumes, and features; and (b) using bid categories based upon machine speed and feature, competing vendors can subsequently offer functionally similar equipment.
3. The market demonstrates that competitive pricing is available on copiers. Therefore, by competitively bidding the copier term contract, the state is assured the benefit of lower, competitive pricing.
4. Single awards promote uniformity and standardization in the terms and conditions in state agency contracts for copiers. Multiple award contracts promote numerous and confusing conditions, since each vendor would use its standard contract.
5. Single award contracts ensure that the state has maximum compliance with its maintenance and service conditions. This avoids the multiplicity of maintenance and service provisions contained in individual vendor's catalogs.
6. A single award contract permits the user agency acquiring copiers to readily identify the lowest-priced copier with the features and speed required by the user agency.
7. State statutes and rules relating to this area support the DGS view.

Gulf Coast View

Gulf Coast Copier also stated its reasoning for dismissal of Kory's petition. Gulf Coast argued that according to its interpretation of state policy, DGS had no discretion to decide on a multiple award copier contract rather than a single award.

Gulf Coast claimed that public policy strongly favored single award contracts and that such contracts were required except (a) when competitive bids were solicited and none received, or (b) in the case of an emergency; or (c) if the item to be acquired was a single-source commodity.

Kory Copier View

Kory Kopier maintained that the proposed system of single awards for copiers did not best promote the efficiency and economy of the state and that instead the DGS should enter into a multiple award contract with each qualified vendor for all tested and approved copiers. Kory stated four major reasons supporting its position:

1. Copiers are not fungible. Differences among copiers make acquisition based solely on the direct costs of copiers unreasonable, uneconomical, and inefficient. Kory believes a single award system requires its copiers and the competition's to be compared as equals regardless of any dissimilarities or differences that may exist.
2. Copiers vary not only in terms of price but also in terms of quality of copies produced, dependability, service experience, and capabilities of vendors to provide necessary follow-up after acquisition. Kory claims these critical criteria are de-emphasized under a single award approach and can be properly evaluated and acted upon only through a multiple award system.
3. User agencies have a wide variety of circumstances and needs that affect their copier requirements. These needs are best known only to the user agencies, which have no significant say under the single award system.
4. The single award approach has superficial appeal because of apparent cost savings. However, when it is realized that copiers are not all alike, it is evident that the apparent savings are unrealistic, since no yardstick on cost savings can be established.

QUESTIONS

While both sides present a number of significant points in regard to the situation, several questions become apparent.

1. From the standpoint of a public policy official, what issues favor the single award process over the multiple award system?
2. What method would you favor as a user or as a buyer, and why?
3. Based on the information given in this situation, can reasonable and acceptable specifications and categories for copiers be devised?
4. Ruling on all petitions and motions in this case have been reserved until after a formal administrative hearing has been completed. As the hearing officer in charge, how would you rule?

This case is based on an actual situation. However, the names of the state and the individual manufacturers are kept anonymous. The case was prepared by Larry Giunipero with the assistance of Phil Croy.

Selected Bibliography

AMMER, DEAN S. *Materials Management and Purchasing,* 4th ed. Homewood, Ill.: Richard D. Irwin, Inc., 1980.

AMMER, DEAN S. *Purchasing and Materials Management for Health Care Institutions,* 2nd ed. Lexington, Mass.: D. C. Heath & Company, 1983.

BAILY, PETER and FARMER, DAVID. *Purchasing Principles and Techniques,* 3rd ed. London: Pitman Books Ltd., 1977.

BAILY, P. J. H. *Purchasing and Supply Management,* 2nd ed. London: Chapman & Hall, Ltd., 1969.

BAKER, R. J., et al. *Purchasing Factomatic.* Englewood Cliffs, N.J.: Prentice-Hall, Inc., 1977.

BARLOW, C. WAYNE and EISEN, GLENN P. *Purchasing Negotiations.* Boston: CBI Publishing Co., 1983.

BIERMAN, EDWARD J. *The C.P.M. Study Guide,* 5th ed. Oradell, N.J.: National Association of Purchasing Management, 1988.

BURT, DAVID N. *Proactive Procurement.* Englewood Cliffs, N.J.: Prentice-Hall, Inc., 1984.

BURT, D. N., NORQUIST, W. E., and ANKLESARIA, J. *Zero Based Pricing.* Chicago: Probus Publishing, 1990.

CASH, R. PATRICK. *The Buyer's Manual.* New York: National Retail Merchants Association, 1979.

COMBS, PAUL H. *Handbook of International Purchasing,* 2nd ed. Boston: Cahners Books, 1976.

COREY, E. R. *Procurement Management.* Boston: CBI Publishing Co., 1978.

DIAMOND, JAY and PINTEL, GERALD. *Retail Buying,* 3rd ed. Englewood Cliffs, New Jersey: Prentice-Hall, 1989.

DOBLER, DONALD W., BURT, DAVID N., and LEE, LAMAR, JR. *Purchasing and Materials Management,* 5th ed. New York: McGraw-Hill, 1990.

DOWST, SOMERBY R. *Basics for Buyers.* Boston: CBI Publishing Co., 1971.

DOWST, SOMERBY R. *More Basics for Buyers.* Boston: CBI Publishing Co., 1980.

FARRELL, PAUL V., ed. *Alijian's Purchasing Handbook,* 4th ed. New York: McGraw-Hill Book Company, 1982.

FISHER, ROGER and URY, WILLIAM. *Getting to Yes—Negotiating Agreement Without Giving In.* New York: Penguin Books, 1983.

HAKANSSON, HAKAN. *International Marketing and Purchasing of Industrial Goods.* New York: John Wiley & Sons, Inc., 1982.

HALL, R. W. *Zero Inventories.* Homewood, Ill.: Dow Jones-Irwin, 1983.

HOLMGREN, J. H. and WENTZ, W. J. *Material Management and Purchasing for the Health Care Facility.* Ann Arbor, Michigan: ALPHA Press, 1982.

HOUSLEY, CHARLES E. *Hospital Purchasing: Focus on Effectiveness.* Rockville, Md.: Aspen Publications, 1983.

International Federation of Purchasing and Materials Management. *Glossary of Purchasing and Supply Terms.* The Hague: IFPMM, 1972.

JOHNSTON, WESLEY J. *Patterns in Industrial Buying Behavior.* New York: Praeger Publishers, 1981.

KELLY, HUGH J. *Food Service Purchasing: Principles and Practices.* New York: Chain Store Publishing Corporation, 1976.

KUDRNA, D. A. *Purchasing Manager's Decision Handbook.* Boston: Cahners Books, 1975.

LEENDERS, M. R. and BLENKHORN, D. L. *Reverse Marketing.* New York: The Free Press, 1988.

LEENDERS, M. R., FEARON, HAROLD E., and ENGLAND, WILBUR B. *Purchasing and Materials Management,* 9th ed. Homewood, Ill.: Dow Jones-Irwin, 1989.

LEWISON, D. M. and DELOZIER. *Retailing.* 4th ed. Columbus, Ohio: Merrill, 1986.

Machinery and Allied Products Institute. *The Purchasing Function: From Strategy to Image.* Washington, D.C.: MAPI, 1982.

MILES, LAWRENCE D. *Techniques of Value Analysis and Engineering.* New York: McGraw-Hill Book Company, 1972.

MONCZKA, R., CARTER, P., and HOAGLAND, J. *Purchasing Performance Measurement.* East Lansing, Mich.: Michigan State University Business Services, 1979.

MONCZKA, R. M. and GIUNIPERO, L. C. *Purchasing Internationally: Concepts and Principles.* Chelsea, MI.: Bookcrafters, 1990.

MURRAY, JOHN E. *Murray on Contracts.* Pittsburgh, Pa.: Purchasing Management Association of Pittsburgh, 1978.

MURRAY, JOHN E. *Purchasing and the Law* (with periodic supplements). Pittsburgh, Pa.: Purchasing Management Association of Pittsburgh, 1975.

National Association of Purchasing Management. *Guide to Purchasing.* Oradell, N.J.: NAPM, 1965, 1967, 1973, 1975.

PAGE, HARRY ROBERT. *Public Purchasing and Materials Management.* Lexington, Mass.: D. C. Heath & Company, 1980.

POOLER, VICTOR H. *The Purchasing Man and His Job.* New York: American Management Association, 1964.

"Practical Purchasing Management," *Purchasing World.* Solon, Ohio: Huebner Publications, Inc., 1984.

RECK, ROSS R. and LONG, BRIAN G. *The Win Win Negotiator.* Escondido, Cal.: Blanchard Training and Development, Inc., 1985.

RITTERSKAMP, JAMES J., JR., ABBOTT, FORREST L., and AHRENS, BERT C. *Purchasing for Educational Institutions.* New York: Bureau of Publications, Teacher's College, Columbia University, 1961.

SCHONBERGER, R. J. *Japanese Manufacturing Techniques.* New York: The Free Press, 1982.

SHERMAN, STANLEY N. *Government Procurement Management,* 2nd ed. Gaithersburg, Maryland: Wordcrafters Publications, 1985.

State and Local Government Purchasing, 2nd ed. Lexington, Kentucky: The Council of State Governments/National Association of State Purchasing Officials, 1983.

ZENZ, GARY J. *Purchasing and the Management of Materials,* 6th ed. New York: Wiley, 1987.

Index